Women
Anthropologists

Women Anthropologists

A BIOGRAPHICAL DICTIONARY

Edited by Ute Gacs
          Aisha Khan
          Jerrie McIntyre
          Ruth Weinberg

Greenwood Press
New York • Westport, Connecticut • London

Library of Congress Cataloging-in-Publication Data

Women anthropologists.

Bibliography: p.
Includes index.
1. Anthropologists, Women—Biography—Dictionaries.
I. Gacs, Ute.
GN20.W63 1988   306′.092′2 [B]   87–11983
ISBN 0–313–24414–6 (lib. bdg. : alk. paper)

British Library Cataloguing in Publication Data is available.

Library of Congress Catalog Card Number: 87–11983
ISBN: 0–313–24414–6

First published in 1988

Greenwood Press, Inc.
88 Post Road West, Westport, Connecticut 06881

Printed in the United States of America

The paper used in this book complies with the
Permanent Paper Standard issued by the National
Information Standards Organization (Z39.48–1984).

10 9 8 7 6 5 4 3 2 1

Contents

Abbreviations

AMWS	*American Men and Women of Science: The Social and Behavioral Sciences*
ACAB	*Appleton's Cyclopedia of American Biography*
BDA	*Biographical Dictionary of America*
CA	*Contemporary Authors*
DAB	*Dictionary of American Biography*
IWW	*The International Who's Who*. 50th ed. London: Europa Publications.
NAW I	*Notable American Women: 1607–1950*, 3 vols. (Vol. I, A-F; Vol. II, G-O; Vol. III, P-Z). Edward T. James et al., eds. Cambridge: Belknap Press of Harvard University, 1971.
NAW II	*Notable American Women: The Modern Period*. Vol. IV. Barbara Sicherman et al., eds. Cambridge: Belknap Press of Harvard University, 1980.
NCAB	*The National Cyclopedia of American Biography*
WW	*Who's Who*. 138th annual ed. New York: St. Martin's Press.
WWW	*Who's Who in the World*. 7th ed. Chicago: Marquis Who's Who, Inc.

Acknowledgments

The editors gratefully acknowledge the following individuals who assisted us in developing our original idea, compiling our list of women for the dictionary, locating suitable contributors, and/or commenting on portions of the manuscript: Paul Bohannan, Johnetta Cole, May Ebihara, David Gamble, Sidney Mintz, Wayne Oler, Sydel Silverman, and Eric Wolf. Special thanks to Ara Wilson for a much-appreciated discussion of some of the issues raised in the introduction. We also wish to express our gratitude to our families and friends for their support; to the School of Behavioral and Social Sciences at San Francisco State University and to the Arthur and Elizabeth Schlesinger Library (Radcliffe) for access to the files of *Notable American Women* (1971); and to Judi Sayler, Patricia Case, Ann Sheldon, Marie Bolton, Fox Vernon, Janis Moore, and Michael Green for their proofreading, research, and computer expertise.

Introduction

This volume is a product of both our experiences as undergraduate students during the fluorescence of the women's movement in the 1970s and our interest in the representation of women anthropologists in courses on anthropological history and theory. Along with the great number of discussions generated over the past decade and a half on various forms of male bias in anthropology, we have observed that by and large, anthropology courses have tended to gloss over the participation and contributions of many of the female practitioners of our discipline. A few, such as Margaret Mead, Ruth Benedict, and Elsie Clews Parsons, are standard and familiar exceptions. However, most of the women who preceded or worked during the same periods—or were of the same "schools"—as many of the discipline's most prominent men, are often left unmentioned or mentioned briefly in an ancillary, special-interest manner. While there are individual book-length biographies and autobiographies, articles, and edited compilations that explore anthropology through the lives and work of particular anthropologists, this volume provides access to information on a greatly expanded number of women anthropologists, to afford a glimpse of their work and a sense of each as an individual. The lives of the women depicted here are intended to add to discussions about the history of anthropology, women's history, the history of science, and the relationship between ideas, career or life course, personal experience, and social context. We have directed this volume as a resource and reference work primarily toward undergraduate and graduate students in anthropology, women's studies, history, and sociology.

This work differs from other biographical dictionaries on women in both its concentration on one academic discipline over time and its assessment of anthropological contribution. Over the approximately five years during which this volume has evolved conceptually, we have found that filling the gaps is not a matter of simply deciding whom to include; compiling a list of women raised deeper issues of assessing achievement and value. The women represented here were chosen as examples of a range of accomplishments, from their readily recognizable efforts as pioneers in theory, methodology, subject of study, or geographic region; to those who persevered despite political blacklisting or other harassment; to those who deflected or transformed racial/ethnic, age, and/or class disadvantages; to those who combined in a novel way a variety of training, skills, and interests in their work. Thus, this volume is not intended merely as a compilation of Great Achievers in the traditional sense of success defined by a list of academic appointments, awards, and publications. It is also a recognition of and a response to the fact that definitions of achievement are often idiosyncratic and reflections of current ideology. Although the anthropologists included were indeed chosen for their contributions (many are widely known for their work), our choices were meant to involve the reader in rethinking the usual criteria for significance.

The fifty-eight anthropologists covered in this volume encompass a period of approximately one hundred years. For heuristic rather than analytical purposes we have divided them into two groups: the first generation, born before 1901; and the second generation, born between 1901 and 1934. The criterion of birth-date is arbitrary; it enables us to include some of our earliest predecessors, as well as some forebears still active today. Most first- and second-generation women were American or British by nationality, conducted their research in America, or were affiliated with American organizations and universities. There-fore, our sample is most representative of the United States. There are also, however, biographies on women from New Zealand, Latin America, South Africa, and the Soviet Union.

In addition to the usual biographical information, contributors were asked to give special consideration to the following topics:

1. Early and/or pioneering anthropological studies dealing with sex roles and the status of women in particular societies or with the status of women anthropologists

2. Circumstances surrounding fieldwork, such as access to both men and women in the culture(s) studied, financing and arranging fieldwork, and political constraints (if any) encountered

3. Career difficulties experienced, such as obstacles to entering graduate school, pub-lishing, or acquiring a paid position

4. The state of the discipline and the subject's particular school or department as well as the social environment of the time

5. Instances in which the subject was the first woman (or the first woman anthropologist) to receive an award, office, or special recognition

6. Marital status and how this affected the subject's career, especially with regard to conducting fieldwork, alone or with others

Selection of these anthropologists was not made on the basis of any particular sampling technique, nor was our coverage intended to be exhaustive. Rather, we chose them as representative of the issues we felt this volume as a whole should address. First, the biographies are intended to reveal something of the special nature of being female in the domains of fieldwork, research, formal higher education or training, and public life. Interestingly, gender does not emerge as the most salient issue for a number of these anthropologists, in terms of their research interests or perceptions of their life experiences. Nevertheless, it should become apparent to the reader that the professional lives of the majority of these anthropologists were, in varying ways, mediated by being female.

Second, the biographies reveal something about the anthropological endeavor as part of personality and life experience. The need to understand how the formulation and implementation of ideas are linked to personal life experiences has been recognized by a number of anthropologists. Silverman (1981:ix), for example, comments that the significant growth of anthropology over the past three decades, along with the need for standardization of information for teaching purposes, has produced a series of " 'isms,' concepts and names of notables divorced from the social and personal contexts out of which they emerged.'' In a similar vein, Leach (1984:22) has stated that what the anthropologist sees is in part a projection of personality, and that therefore the particular personal background of the anthropologist is crucial to understanding the significance of that person's work for anthropology's history. Indeed, a number of women in this volume were engaged in a variety of interests and occupations before their involvement in anthropological pursuits. These include work in the arts; women's rights, civil rights, and labor activism; social work; teaching in other academic disciplines; and writing (e.g., Benedict, Blackwood, Densmore, Dunham, Fletcher, Green, Hurston, Laird, O'Neale, Parsons, Powdermaker, Rubin, Shepardson, Smith, Steed, Underhill). From this perspective we can ascertain something about the role of serendipitous circumstance, private advocates (such as family members or friends), or life crises in embarking on an anthropological career, as well as in the formulation and development of theory and methodology. Not the least important item of note in this regard is that some of these anthropologists had no formal course of study, training, or academic degree in anthropology prior to their fieldwork, or ever (e.g., Bunzel, Densmore, Kroeber, Laird, Leakey, Smith, M. Stevenson, S. Stevenson).

Next, the biographies say something about the state of anthropology during the subject's formative and productive periods. Though there are similarities in the biographies, no simple or convenient conclusions about anthropology as a profession or as a body of knowledge can be drawn from these brief accounts, which cover roughly ten decades. Yet each woman's experience with mentors, colleagues, discrimination, bureaucratic barriers, informants, financial support, personal relationships, and theoretical and methodological trends is a piece of anthropological history. Synthesizing these pieces into a whole portrait of our discipline requires further and detailed study of the issues raised. What is evident from the biographies are suggestions of how anthropology as a discipline has shaped and been shaped by its sizable female membership.

Finally, the biographies are a lens through which to view the wider social climate of the subjects' time. Whether there is a complementarity between the diversity of individual experiences and the total picture that can be drawn from their collective significance remains to be seen. Since the biographies in this volume span a considerable period of time and represent a relatively small sample, the patterns reflected in the lives and experiences of these anthropologists must be considered as topics for further investigation. Nonetheless, these biographies demonstrate some of the ways in which person, discipline, and society articulate in particular ways at particular times, to create science and scholarship.

Though the biographies are not uniform in their emphases—partly due to the idiosyncrasies of each subject's life and to the biographers' interests—what emerge are certain intriguing commonalities shared by the women. The following is a brief highlighting of these commonalities, pointing to potential areas of further inquiry.

Among the most interesting of these commonalities is that relationships with others—collaborations, friendships, patronage—are significant to the work of many of these anthropologists, during their fieldwork and/or throughout their careers. Some (e.g., Deloria, Densmore, Reichard) worked with their sisters; some worked with other women anthropologists (e.g., Helm and Lurie, Mead and Metraux, de Laguna and McClellan). Many worked with spouses in husband-wife teams (e.g., Berndt, Fischer, Friedl, Gunther, Hanks, Helm, Hunt, Keur, Kroeber, Laird, Leakey, Leighton, Mead, Metraux, M. Stevenson, Wallis, Wilson). Some were aided in important ways by local women residents of their field sites (e.g., Kaberry); some were accompanied to the field by female friends (e.g., Fletcher, O'Neale). Some had female financial patrons (e.g., Densmore, Fletcher, Hurston), while others such as Parsons and Rubin funded research through Columbia University and the Research Institute for the Study of Man, respectively. In addition, many women had female mentors or were mentors to other women through the university and other settings.

Although these anthropologists also engaged in significant research and writing as individuals separate from associations with spouses and other colleagues, their relationships with others are important because they raise questions about the nature of anthropological research. To some degree anthropologists have had an image of being lone, intrepid individuals who make discoveries on their own and who are solely responsible for what is produced. Although individuals certainly do make discoveries in the common sense of the term (e.g., Leakey, Nuttall, Proskouriakoff), more prevalent are processes of cooperative association. Many of the biographies point to the need for exploring in detail the diversity of ways anthropological knowledge has in fact been developed. Recognizing the different styles and expressions of the social relationships that are entailed in doing research broadens our understanding of the distinct "voices"—individual and relational—affecting the form and content of data gathering and analysis (here I am drawing from Carol Gilligan [1982]). In practical terms, this recognition enables us to continue to elaborate alternative means and standards of research. Collaborative relationships point to other areas for further investigation.

As one important example, the associations among women in these biographies offer a promising addition to the current scholarship on female friendships, until recently a relatively unexplored topic in social history.

Comparing the institutionally based and supported research of the majority of women anthropologists with their own or others' independent, noninstitutionally based work adds another dimension to the history of anthropology. A number of women included here never enjoyed an official university position, a full-time appointment or tenure, and/or faced years of unemployment after receipt of their degree (e.g., Bunzel, Deloria, Gunther, Kelly, Landes, Leacock, Nuttall, Powdermaker, Steed, Weltfish). While the specific reasons for this vary from decade to decade, a more general issue can be raised. Though institutional discrimination bars women from job security and often formal recognition, the lack of secure ties with an institution may enable a degree of freedom from the constraints and expectations imposed by an institution and its foremost members. Although hardly compensation for unequal treatment, the ability to pursue one's own interests, in one's own fashion and at one's own pace, could provide a means of exploring the possibilities for experimentation with alternative ideas and methods, which in turn could generate different kinds of data or theory. This is not a gender-specific issue. Nevertheless, it is important to bear in mind that what constitutes the acceptable knowledge of any discipline and how it is gained and used is often guided by institutions or academic departments that have been created and controlled by particular men.

An intriguing number of women in the volume have been involved in writing fiction (e.g., Benedict, de Laguna, Garfield, Gillmor, Hurston, Kroeber, Kuper, Metraux, Reichard, Shepardson, Steed, Underhill, Wallis). The novels, poetry, mysteries, and plays were often but not solely concerned with anthropological settings or characters. Whether or not directly anthropological, writing served these women as a creative outlet or alternative voice for their feelings and observations. Discussion of the relationship between anthropology and literature has, among other things, been concerned with author/ethnographer distinctions and the relationship between ethnographic and fictional texts. A comparison of the fictional and ethnographic writing of these anthropologists is another point of departure in explorations of the articulation between aesthetic and scientific perspectives, between "subjective" and "objective" depictions of reality.

Finally, a significant number of anthropologists in this volume have been committed to applied research, public dissemination of information, and/or in-fluencing public policy (e.g., Densmore, Fletcher, Garfield, Green, Gunther, Hanks, Keur, Leacock, Leighton, Lurie, Mead, Metraux, Parsons, Powder-maker, Smith, M. Stevenson, S. Stevenson, Underhill, Wallis, Wedgwood, Weltfish, Wilson, Wormington). For some of these anthropologists, work with Native Americans or for the Bureau of Indian Affairs, for particular institutes, or for governmental offices during World War II made their contributions nec-essarily and by definition public and applied. For others, political motivations directed much of their research and writing to lay audiences and targeted groups such as minorities and women. Employing the discipline's knowledge toward other than ivory tower pursuits has been a familiar topic of contention among anthropologists. The assumption that the more esoteric the knowledge, the greater its merit has been challenged from a number of viewpoints. However, these biographies raise questions about women's role in the professionalization of the discipline. Popularizing has been considered (at least implicitly) as counter to establishing and maintaining professional status because it supposedly weakens intellectual content and is a less dignified endeavor than scholarship for the benefit of one's colleagues. Although the women indicated here produced a great deal of work with their colleagues in mind, they made additional efforts to disseminate information broadly and gather data on projects directed toward elucidating particular social problems or issues. Their work is a challenge to one-dimensional evaluations of significant, valuable, or legitimate research.

We also might ask whether, at least at certain periods, women could more easily engage in applied research and develop and share their work in public contexts, rather than in more restricted (and often male-dominated) academic settings. Perhaps related to this is that a number of "first generation" women either initiated or were prime movers in scientific clubs, which were often phi-lanthropic organizations and often involved the participation of men. The women active in these clubs were serious about their interests in furthering scientific research and in communicating discoveries and debates to the public, through sponsorship of lecture series, museum exhibits, and the like. What this suggests is that in being a forum for women's intellectual interests, these clubs, like other public forums, enabled women to participate in a variety of activities from which they might otherwise have been excluded.

We invite our readers to pursue these and other issues in further detail and to become familiar with the work of these anthropologists, using the biographies and bibliographies as a point of departure.

AISHA KHAN

Editors' Note

References to works written by other women in the volume appear in the bibliography of the cited woman rather than in the general references. For example, Ruth Benedict's *Patterns of Culture* (1934) is cited in the Margaret Mead biography. The complete reference is found in the Ruth Benedict bibliography. Cross references are indicated by an asterisk following a person's name.

Women
Anthropologists

Ruth Fulton Benedict

(1887–1948)

Ruth Fulton Benedict was an American cultural anthropologist known for her theory of culture-and-personality, for her studies of Pueblo culture and Japanese culture, and her concern with "enlightened change" in all societies.

She was born June 5, 1887, daughter of Frederick Fulton, who was just starting a medical career, and Bertrice Shattuck Fulton, who had graduated from Vassar College five years before. A year and a half later another daughter, Margery, was born. By then the family had moved to Norwich, New York, where the Fulton and Shattuck families lived. Exactly two months after Margery's birth, Frederick Fulton died. Her father's death profoundly affected Ruth Fulton, a trauma accentuated by the responses to death in her family. Relatives brought the two-year-old to see her father in his coffin, pale and dressed for death. Nearby, her mother wept uncontrollably, a display of grief repeated ritually year after year.

So Ruth Fulton remembered the scene: a contrast between her father's calm and tragic face and her mother's grief-distorted face. Vividly, evocatively, and deliberately, she redrew the scene throughout her life; the habit of contrasting distinct images was set, and over the years other contrasts emerged. Early, there was a contrast with Margery Fulton, the younger sister who seemed outgoing, cheerful, and talkative next to the somber and silent older sister. In 1895 the Norwich Public School discovered that Ruth Fulton was partially deaf: a factor that justified her "difference" from the rest of the family—at least in Ruth's eyes. Her mother was not so patient and paid Ruth a penny for every prompt answer.

Bertrice Fulton was an ambitious woman and in the 1890s took her daughters with her in search of a satisfactory job. She found one, at the Buffalo (New York) Public Library, and enrolled the two girls in the elite St. Margaret's Academy. During her adolescent years Ruth Fulton began to write stories, creating heroes and heroines in an attempt to define her own "female nature." In

1905 she and her sister entered Vassar College together, and there, in an "all female" environment, Ruth Fulton formed emotional ties that determined her subsequent intimacies and intellectual adventures. After graduation Margery Fulton married Robert Freeman, a minister, and Ruth Fulton traveled to Europe with three friends.

The return from Europe precipitated years of doubt and uncertainty. Ruth Fulton began a journal, and filled its pages with despairing remarks about her activities—social work in Buffalo, 1910–11, and teaching in Los Angeles (where she lived with the Freemans), 1911–14. She added, too, a newly explicit contrast between the "male" and the "female" in her temperament. But drawing vivid contrasts did not help her sort through a personal dilemma. Then in 1914 she married Stanley Rossiter Benedict, brother of a Vassar friend and a biochemist who admired Frederick Fulton's work. Love would be the answer, Ruth Benedict wrote, and "babies" might quiet her restlessness.

The early years of the Benedict marriage coincided with World War I. In an effort to make a worthwhile contribution, Ruth Benedict started three biographical studies of three feminists. She finished Mary Wollstonecraft, leaving Margaret Fuller and Olive Schreiner undone. In the Wollstonecraft essay, Benedict explored definitions of "being a woman," and in one sentence established an autobiographical theme: Wollstonecraft, she said, attained "her idea by the rich processes of living."

After the war, discouraged by lack of enthusiasm from publishers, Ruth Benedict put her feminist essays aside. Her marriage no longer seemed "the answer," and in the fall of 1919 Benedict enrolled at the New School for Social Research. She took two anthropology courses, probably partly (as she later said) to understand the recent "conflict among nations." Her two teachers, Alexander Goldenweiser and Elsie Clews Parsons,* themselves made a startling contrast, another version of the male-female dichotomy through which Benedict drew her own life. She did not describe Goldie, as he was known, and Parsons that way but during those years wrote several essays dealing with the "woman issue."

By 1921 Parsons decided that Benedict should become an anthropologist and took her uptown to meet Franz Boas at Columbia University. The encounter could not have been easy for the slightly deaf woman—Boas's mumble was legendary—but Benedict convinced the head of the department of her commitment and was accepted into the anthropology Ph.D. program. At Columbia she learned a discipline and found a new set of "figures" through whom to interpret her life: Boas himself, Edward Sapir, and Margaret Mead.*

Boas was important as mentor, teaching Benedict not only the content of a discipline but the importance of inserting personal concerns into the planning and presentation of research. Under his tutelage, Benedict channeled her preoccupations with individual choice into an innovative anthropological approach. Her dissertation, "The Concept of the Guardian Spirit in North America" (1923), demonstrates this in discussing the cultural implications of an individualized religious experience.

In 1923 Edward Sapir, then in Ottawa, wrote to Benedict about her dissertation, initiating a friendship that was significant anthropologically, poetically, and personally. Questioning her role as "Anne Singleton," the pseudonym Benedict took when she published sonnets (during the 1920s), Sapir eventually influenced his colleague to take her anthropology more seriously. She would learn to transfer the intensity and the arrangement of a poem into her descriptions of other cultures. Sapir also encouraged Benedict to pursue her interest in the interaction between individual creativity and cultural patterns.

Ruth Benedict's friendship with Margaret Mead was more complex, and had an immeasurable impact on both women's anthropology. What started as a teacher-student relationship (Benedict taught Mead that anthropology "mattered") quickly became a friendship of colleagues, and then a significant intimacy. To work out an understanding of love between women, Benedict and Mead used cross-cultural data on human relationships, on individual "difference," and on cultural constraints. For Ruth Benedict, conversations with Mead clarified her anthropological goals and approaches, a process completed by several field trips.

Her first field trip had been combined with a visit to the Freemans in Pasadena, when Benedict did a small study of the Serrano Indians (1922). Then, in 1924, Ruth Benedict went to the Southwest Zuni Pueblo for the first time—her formative fieldwork. On this and on subsequent trips (1925: Zuni and Cochiti Pueblos; 1927: Pima Indians), Benedict wrote to Mead and in letters developed her understanding of Pueblo culture specifically and of culture-personality isomorphism in general. "Culture is personality writ large," she wrote (1934a). Contrasts became Benedict's anthropological mode when she discovered the "unbelievable" difference in temperament and custom between the Pueblo and the neighboring Plains Indian tribes.

By 1930 Benedict's friendship with Sapir had waned, her marriage to Stanley Benedict was over, and intimacy with another woman had led her to acknowledge her "female nature." It was time to put her career in order, and Benedict decided to write a book. Published in 1934, *Patterns of Culture* brought together anthropological, poetic, and personal insights of the past ten years and became an American classic.

Benedict's three contrasting portraits of the Pueblos, the Dobuans, and the Kwakiutl Indians painted, by implication, a portrait of the United States. Her own field observations led to a characterization of the "placid and harmonious," cooperative Pueblo Indians; Reo Fortune (1932) provided data for the portrait of the mean-spirited, paranoiac Dobu Islanders; Boas's data gave her the portrait of the self-aggrandizing, megalomaniacal Kwakiutl. In a famous contrast, the Zuni Pueblo was "Apollonian" compared to the surrounding "Dionysian" Plains Indians, a contrast that referred both to the "tone" of the culture and to the personalities of individuals. The portraits of a near-socialistic, a jealously possessive, and highly competitive society told a powerful lesson to a 1930s America facing the Great Depression. And Ruth Benedict did not rest content with ethnographic parable: she argued a case for tolerance of nonconformity and for the power of human societies deliberately to change their existing arrangements.

Throughout the 1930s, while editing the *Journal of American Folklore* (1924–39) and teaching at Columbia (1923–31), Ruth Benedict made her lessons for America more explicit. The anthropologist argued that American society had gone awry, training individuals for roles they could not assume (1938b) and fostering personalities that either conformed or chafed into "neurosis." She turned, too, from scholarly journals to more popular periodicals, her audience the "common man" first introduced in *Patterns of Culture* (Benedict 1934a). Field observations (Benedict took students with her into the field, in 1931 to an Apache reservation and in 1939 to a Blackfoot reservation) and her own experiences as a "noncongenial" member of American culture underlined and politicized these 1930s arguments. Concern about the possible suppression of differences in her own society culminated in *Race: Science and Politics* (Benedict 1940).

In 1941 when America entered World War II, Ruth Benedict was ready to devote her anthropology to the cause of a "lasting peace." At the Office of War Information (Bureau of Overseas Intelligence), Benedict prepared anthropological reports on allied and enemy nations. Her "last assignment" was a study of Japanese culture. This, like her other wartime work, was to provide data that would help officials plan a wise postwar policy.

The anthropologist could not take a field trip, but in *The Chrysanthemum and the Sword* (Benedict 1946a), Benedict fully developed the concept that marks her contribution to anthropology. "Patterns" represented the culture itself, a method for studying cultures, and a political position. The pattern of Japanese culture, worked out through intricate notions of *ON* (debt and obligation) and of "taking one's proper station," molded the behavior and the personality of Japanese individuals. Symbolized by flower and sword, the pattern rooted in past tradition offered a plan for future, "engineered" change.

Experienced, though not necessarily articulated by the average Japanese, the pattern could be seen and explicated by an "outside" observer. From many pieces of data, Benedict redesigned for her American readers the design the Japanese had made for themselves over centuries. She provided her readers with insight into a "most alien" culture, and their own familiar culture. More to the point, in 1946 with MacArthur governing the "defeated nation," Benedict intended that her book provide ground rules for his governance.

The Chrysanthemum and the Sword, like *Patterns of Culture*, became a best-seller (though whether MacArthur used it is not known). And as in her earlier book, one of Benedict's main goals was to change the attitudes of her American readers. Her work as an anthropologist was pedagogical: she taught her audience the virtues of "seeing how other people arranged their lives," the necessity of tolerating individual differences if a society is to survive, the power of culture over nature. Human beings, she wrote, can change the terms of their existence and, with insight brought by anthropology, can make these changes wisely.

Ruth Benedict was not an optimist; she was a "liberal" in the classic sense. She had faith in human intelligence, and in the ability of individuals to take lessons from a situation clearly drawn for them. For her, ethnographic accounts prodded an individual into reseeing the terms of his or her own familiar context and making steps toward improvement. Harking back to her feminist studies, the faith was grounded in the idea of a "passionate experience of living." It was faith that produced a distinct anthropology, one not consistently appreciated.

After her death on September 17, 1948 (the anniversary of her father's birth), Benedict's work was criticized and often ignored by professional anthropologists. Critics claimed her fieldwork was weak and her characterizations of cultures impressionistic. In part this claim misunderstands the broader goals embedded in her word *pattern*. Pattern constituted a fieldwork method, a way of collecting data that recognized the integrity of a culture: pieces fit together. What critics called impressionism was Benedict's effort to show that cultures were whole units, in the way that individuals had consistent personalities, over and above the contradictory details. By presenting vivid portraits of contrasting cultures, Benedict intended to "open the eyes" of her readers and compel them to recognize that existing arrangements were not "god-given" (Benedict 1946a:14). For her argument she simplified but did not distort the societies she studied. Her descriptions of the Apollonian Zuni and of the "paradoxical" Japanese have been modified; their basic truths have not been denied.

Benedict's anthropology has been called cultural determinism. Again there is a mixture of accuracy and of misunderstanding in this comment. In an argument against "nature" and for the infinite capacity of human beings to change, Benedict did emphasize the power of "custom" and learning. But in her remarks on the individual in culture, she never implied either that inborn temperament was negligible or that the individual had no control over her surroundings. She knew the significance of temperamental differences—especially those that crossed cultural categories (e.g., based on gender)—and consequently preached tolerance. She knew the extent to which an individual could deliberately alter the conditions of her life and in doing so alter society (Benedict 1934a; 1935; 1946a). Benedict never outlined a program for change beyond increasing cultural tolerance and the "awareness" of individuals. Her anthropological data and theory constituted her "pioneer idea" and became a "force in shaping our modern world" (from "Mary Wollstonecraft," in Mead 1959:492).

Recently Ruth Benedict has come back into favor. For one, her life illustrates an important intersection of women's history and the history of a social science. For another, the strengths of her anthropological approach are appreciated by anthropologists concerned as she was with the impact on data of the researcher's position in her home society and with the impact on an audience of reported "facts." Benedict's reminder that anthropology is both, and inseparably, a personal and a political endeavor has new significance in the 1980s.

References and Works About Ruth Benedict

Barnouw, Victor
1957   The Amiable Side of "Patterns of Culture." *American Anthropologist* 59:532–
        36.
1980   Ruth Benedict. *American Scholar* 49:504–9.
Fleming, Donald
1971   Ruth Fulton Benedict. In *NAW II*. Barbara Sicherman et al., eds. Pp. 128–31.
        Cambridge: Belknap Press.
Mead, Margaret
1959   *An Anthropologist at Work*. Boston: Houghton Mifflin Co.
1968   Ruth Fulton Benedict. In *Encyclopedia of the Social Sciences* 2:48–53. New York:
        Macmillan Co.
1974   *Ruth Benedict*. New York: Columbia University.
Mintz, Sidney
1984   Ruth Benedict. *In Totems and Teachers*. Sydel Silverman, ed. New York: Co-
        lumbia University Press.
Modell, Judith
1983   *Ruth Benedict: Patterns of a Life*. Philadelphia: University of Pennsylvania.
Pandey, Triloki N.
1972   Anthropologists at Zuni. *Proceedings of the American Philosophical Society*
        116:321–27.

Selected Works by Ruth Benedict

1922   The Vision in Plains Culture. *American Anthropologist* 24:1–23.
1923   *The Concept of the Guardian Spirit in North America*. (Ph.D. diss., Columbia
        University.) *Memoirs of the American Anthropological Association* 29:1–97.
1930   Psychological Types in the Cultures of the Southwest. In *Proceedings of the
        Twenty-third International Congress of Americanists*, pp. 572–81.
1931   Tales of the Cochiti Indians. *Bureau of American Ethnology (BAE) Bulletin 98*.
        Washington, D.C.: Smithsonian Institution.
1932   Configurations of Culture in North America. *American Anthropologist* 34:1–27.
1933   Myth. In *Encyclopedia of the Social Sciences* 11:170–73.
1934a   *Patterns of Culture*. Boston: Houghton Mifflin Co.
1934b   Anthropology and the Abnormal. *Journal of General Psychology* 10:59–82.
1935   *Zuni Mythology*. 2 vols. Columbia University Contributions to Anthropology.
        New York: Columbia University Press.
1936   Marital Property Rights in Bilateral Society. *American Anthropologist* 38:368–
        73.
1938a   Religion. In *General Anthropology*. Franz Boas, ed. Boston: D.C. Heath.
1938b   Continuities and Discontinuities in Cultural Conditioning. *Psychiatry* 1:161–67.
1940   *Race: Science and Politics*. New York: Modern Age.
1943a   Franz Boas. *American Sociological Review* 8:223.
1943b   Franz Boas. *The Nation* 156:15–16.
1943c   Franz Boas. *Science* 97 (n.s.): 60–62.

1943d Franz Boas As an Ethnologist. *Memoirs of the American Anthropological Association* 61:26–34.

1943e Recognition of Cultural Diversities in the Postwar World. *Annals of the American Academy of Political and Social Sciences* 228:101–7.

1943f Two Patterns of Indian Acculturation. *American Anthropologist* 45:207–12.

1946a *The Chrysanthemum and the Sword: Patterns of Japanese Culture.* Boston: Houghton Mifflin Co.

1946b *The Study of Cultural Patterns in European Nations. Transactions of the New York Academy of Science* 8 (Series 11): 274–79.

1948 Anthropology and the Humanities. *American Anthropologist* 50:585–93.

1949 Child Rearing in Certain European Countries. *American Journal of Orthopsychiatry* 19:342–48.

1952 *Thai Culture and Behavior.* Data Paper No. 4, Southeast Asia Program. Ithaca, N.Y.: Cornell University.

1958 Fragments of a Journal. *American Scholar* 28:33–36.

1970 Synergy: Some Notes of Ruth Benedict. Selected by Abraham Maslow and John J. Honigmann. *American Anthropologist* 72:320–33.

JUDITH MODELL

Catherine Helen Webb Berndt

(1918–   )

Catherine Webb Berndt is an Australian social anthropologist known especially for her research in Aboriginal Australia and Papua New Guinea; the status of Aboriginal women; inequality in male-female relations in traditional societies; pioneer writings in the field of oral literature; and her work toward fostering changes in government policy concerning social conditions of Aboriginals.

She was born on May 8, 1918, in Auckland, New Zealand, at her great-aunt Catherine's home, Tower House. Her mother, informally adopted by Catherine's great-aunt, had grown up there, as did Catherine, the eldest of three children. After her parents separated, her father went to Australia, and her mother returned to Tower House with the children. Today Berndt hardly remembers her great-uncle James, except for his lowland Scots voice singing to her, the Tower House flagpole used for signaling to his trading ships returning from the Pacific, and the enticing smells of surgarcane, pineapples and oranges from those ships, conjuring up images of exotic places. Her mother had nine brothers and sisters, enough father surrogates and close mothers to compensate for the absence of a "real" father. Through one uncle, who was a friend of Reo Fortune's, she later came to know Margaret Mead.* This uncle, a law graduate who received his Ph.D. from London University, encouraged her to read more widely on anthropology and related subjects.[1]

Catherine Webb's mother's parents and their siblings (her great-aunt included) were born in Nova Scotia, where a fleet of ships had brought religious and economic exiles from the west of Scotland. In the 1850s they set off again, to settle in the north of New Zealand. According to the records, they did not try to take over land but negotiated with local Maori owners for cash payments (cf. McKenzie, 1935). Not all kept their own language, Gaelic. Webb's grandfather could not understand his Gaelic bible and gave it to her, but she found nobody to help her with it. And she was ashamed to learn that her mother's forebears had been on the "wrong side" at Culloden. All this had a powerful emotional effect on her as a child.

When she was about ten years old, her father returned and her mother joined him in Wellington with the two younger children. Under the care of her great-aunt, Webb was sent to St. Cuthbert's, a Presbyterian school, after previously attending a state coeducational primary school. She jumped from second to fourth year, straining her social relations with her classmates; but because her great-aunt was ill, she had to become a weekly boarder at the school. She had tried stubbornly to be allowed to take the matriculation examinations in three years instead of the customary four. At fourteen she chafed at the restraints of boarding school life, even though her sister came to Auckland to join her. When finally permitted to take her exams, she passed well; and after that the four-year school rule was changed.

After her great-aunt died, Webb went to Hutt Valley High School near Wellington. She sat for a University Bursary, and at 16 entered Victoria University College, now the Victoria University of Wellington. No anthropology courses were available, so she majored in Latin with French as a second subject. When a senior academic from another New Zealand university visited Wellington and Webb asked about opportunities for becoming an anthropologist, he told her she would need a private income: "Learn typing, and then if you prove good enough you might become a secretary to an anthropologist!"

After Catherine Webb completed her B.A. degree (she worked during that time in various libraries), her mother separated again from her father. She took her children (including another, small sister born after the reconciliation) to Dunedin so Webb could take a one-year undergraduate anthropology unit in preference to M.A. coursework in Latin. The outcome of that year was a Certificate of Proficiency in Anthropology. Her teacher was Dr. H. D. Skinner, director of the Otago Museum, best known for his work on the Moriori of the Chatham Islands. He had a broad vision of anthropology, which Webb found exciting and stimulating. He was unable to provide direct financial support for her further study but said that if she could manage her fare and a year or so in Sydney, he would write to Professor A. P. Elkin, whose Department of Anthropology was then the only one in Australasia.

Why anthropology? asked some of Webb's relatives. Her mother, however, expressed approval from the start: she herself had not been allowed to proceed to university studies, let alone a career, but she played second violin in a local orchestra and was an avid reader, preferring biographies to fiction. Moreover, Webb's father liked travel books and anthropology. Their household had an ever-changing array of library books. The Tower House bookshelves had been well stocked, too, especially on Scots history and folklore, and on missionary enterprises.

Missionaries were frequent visitors to Tower House and the Wellington household, talking about their experiences and encounters in foreign places. For Webb, they raised incipient questions about motives and intentions and cross-cultural relations generally, along with the more subtle issues of influence, persuasion, and "propaganda."

This strand of interest, as well as reading and her preoccupation with Scots versus Pakeha (New Zealander of European descent) and Scots versus English identity, symbolized in the fate of Scots Gaelic as a disappearing language, linked up with her university studies and experiences. Among her friends were students of Maori and part-Maori descent who talked freely about their problems in a country that then had a reputation for harmony in "race relations."

Webb's mother, before her death in 1940, had urged her to go on with her plans for anthropology. In Professor Elkin's room in Sydney a few weeks later, Webb met a student, Ronald M. Berndt, from Adelaide, whose interest was Australian Aborigines. The following year they married and spent six months doing fieldwork at Ooldea (western South Australia), where seminomadic people were coming south from the central ranges to the transcontinental railway line. This was Catherine Berndt's first encounter with traditional Aboriginal Australians who spoke no English—a good introduction to the task of learning a language from scratch with no written or other materials. She learned several dialects of the Western Desert Language, a useful basis for later fieldwork in desert regions farther north. Professor Elkin hoped she would concentrate on women, more completely than Phyllis Kaberry,* working alone, had been able to do. Her husband also hoped her work would complement his with men. She was enthusiastic but shy. However, the women were friendly and helpful and eager to teach her. Mostly she would talk with them in their camps or in her own windbreak during the day, or at evening ceremonies. Small groups would sometimes pause at the Berndts' tent among the sandhills, strategically placed beside the track down to the soak, the only freshwater source and the site of a small mission station.

Catherine Berndt did not come into anthropology as a militant feminist. She was brought up to believe in the basic overall equality of both sexes and also in the need for reform. However, she came to realize the importance of personality differences and socioeconomic factors as contributors to dominance and authority patterns. The prominent position of her great-aunt in the family was a clear example of this. She was a rather formidable figure, kind but used to having her own way and impatient of evasion or "soft talking."

Berndt found working with Aboriginal women increasingly congenial as she came to know them better—as individuals, and as members of their particular social groups. This was made easier and also, she says, more productive because she was accepted as part of a husband-wife team, a normal ingredient in Aboriginal society. She could identify more or less completely with women, without having to feel, as Phyllis Kaberry did, that she needed to study men's activities and perspectives, too. That meant coming into close contact also with young children.

Because she and her husband have been able to carry out all of their fieldwork in the same places at the same time, this pattern of being together-but-separate has continued. She likens it to what she argues is the theme of women's roles in Aboriginal Australia—"independence within a framework of interdependence." She rejects the view of Eleanor Leacock* (1981a) and Diane Bell (1983) that *autonomy* is a more appropriate word. To her, the term *autonomy* denies the fundamentally cooperative basis of traditional Aboriginal living. Since that early fieldwork at Ooldea, she has become increasingly convinced that all the evidence points to there being such a basis, in religious as well as in domestic affairs. According to Berndt, equality should not be defined in terms of similarities.

After Ooldea, the Berndts divided their time between attending courses in the Sydney department and field research in a number of widely different areas with grants from what was then the Australian National Research Council. Anthropological field-workers were few, and Aboriginal culture was changing rapidly. She continued to focus on women: among urban people of partly Aboriginal descent in Adelaide, on the lower River Murray, and at Menindee in western New South Wales; and among traditional people in northern South Australia (e.g., in the Oodnadatta area). In 1944, through a special arrangement with Professor Elkin and E. W. P. Chinnery, then director of Native Affairs in the Northern Territory, the Berndts were appointed as welfare officers and anthropologists to look into problems relating to some of Vestey's large pastoral holdings. Their research covered a great many stations, from Wave Hill and Birrundudu north to the Katherine area, the Army Aboriginal settlements, and the Daly River. In each place Catherine Berndt tried to learn the main language or dialect spoken there. In the Wave Hill region and then farther north, she learned more about women's secret and quasi-secret rituals that extended across immense areas, including the Western Desert. In those days women did not mind outsiders knowing about these, provided secrecy was maintained in their particular regions. With so much outside intrusion the situation is different now, and for reasons of privacy as well as secrecy, Berndt is considering not publishing any such material except in the most general terms. She sees this as a real dilemma.

From 1946 through 1951 the Berndts were engaged in fieldwork throughout North Australia. In 1951–52 they went to the eastern Highlands of Papua New Guinea, Catherine Berndt with an Ohio State Fellowship from the International Federation of University Women. They were in the territory of a small language group surrounded by three larger ones. For the first time she had to use a male interpreter from farther north to learn Kafei (Kamano), which many of the women spoke or understood, in order to learn their own language, Usurufa. She arranged for the interpreter's wife, also a Kafei speaker, to be present during all her group discussions. It was a difficult region, accessible only through bush tracks, where sporadic fighting and feuding continued. At first the local men did not want their womenfolk to be exposed to the dangers of contact with outsiders, whom they believed to be returning spirits of the dead. Eventually, however, Berndt collected myths and oral histories from about twenty women, with a larger range of contacts on other occasions. She became more deeply absorbed in the question of the effects of myth and dramatic performances on behavior, including the issues of sex and violence in regard to children's viewing and listening. This led to her later interest in the wider field of mass media.

Berndt had been a Junior Research Fellow (1947–51), then a Research Fellow (1951–53) in Elkin's Department, with a Diploma of Anthropology and an M.A. with First Class Honors in Anthropology. In 1953 the Berndts went for two years to the London School of Economics, Catherine with a British Council grant and (in 1954–55) a Winifred Cullis Award from the International Federation of University Women; her husband had (1953–54) a Nuffield Fellowship that included her fares and main living expenses. Her thesis was on myth in action in her New Guinea research area. After completing their Ph.D. work late in 1955, the Berndts left for the United States and Canada, where Ronald's Carnegie Award covered travel and living expenses for them both to make a survey of relations between anthropology and sociology. Also, the Bureau of Indian Affairs arranged for them to visit Navaho, Pueblo and Hopi communities and schools.

Back in Australia early in 1956, the Berndts moved to the University of Western Australia, in Perth, where Ronald was to build up teaching and research in anthropology. They decided between them that Catherine's role in this process would be on a part-time basis, even when other permanent full-time positions became available: this would allow her more flexibility in research and writing without being caught up in administration. Catherine Berndt does not regret that decision, although at times she found herself involved in teaching to an extent that was more consistent with full-time status. In 1983 the university conferred on her an Honorary D.Litt. in recognition of her services to anthropology. She is now an Honorary Research Fellow in Anthropology in the department.

In 1950 Catherine Berndt was awarded the Percy Smith Medal by the University of Otago (New Zealand), and she and her husband (one medal each) the Edgeworth David Medal for Anthropology. In 1965 they both made a survey for the Indian University Grants Commission, of anthropology in Indian universities and colleges and museums. In 1968 they both had travel grants from the Wenner-Gren Foundation to participate in the International Congress of Ethnological Sciences in Japan. In 1980 she received the New South Wales Premier's Special Children's Book Award, with medal, for *Land of the Rainbow Snake*, stories from western Arnhem Land that she had arranged and translated. Djoki Yunupingu, the Aboriginal illustrator, shared in the award. Berndt is one of the few Honorary Fellows of the Royal Anthropological Institute in London, and in 1982 was only the seventh woman to be elected a Fellow in the Academy of the Social Sciences in Australia. She and her husband jointly have an Australian Research Grants Scheme to fund a program of continuing to write up the vast amount of their Australian Aboriginal research materials. She is a foundation member of the Australian Institute of Aboriginal Studies and currently (since

1978) a member of its Advisory Committee on the Arts. Her Aboriginal research continues, with further visits to various places in the Western Desert (notably Balgo), the Kimberleys and Arnhem Land, and with a range of commitments among urban women of Aboriginal descent.

Looking back on her earlier field research, Berndt recalls that in making a survey of attitudes toward Aborigines in one town in South Australia, she (but not her husband) was often asked, "Why aren't you at home raising a family instead of worrying about such things?" (1950:3–8). Later on, she would have found fieldwork very difficult without the company of her husband in pastoral areas of north Australia, and in the then newly "controlled" eastern New Guinea Highlands—dissimilar in many respects, but both colonial-frontier regions where individual women without male support were noticeably disadvantaged. Such experiences convinced her of the need for more attention to women's side of the social spectrum and their special problems.

Like her husband, she considers that they owe it to future generations to provide legible and detailed records of the material they have recorded over such a long period of field research. Most of her work is still unpublished, including a volume on Aboriginal women in which she hopes to commemorate some outstanding Aboriginal women she has known. She argues that setting the record straight for women should not be at the expense of men. This, she says, exemplifies the wider challenge to anthropology that demands accuracy in recording, interpreting, and presenting empirical data as well as in theoretical and conceptual statements.

In 1950 the first monograph in the new series of *L'Homme* was Berndt's *Women's Changing Ceremonies in Northern Australia*. Lévi-Strauss in his Preface wrote that this work was an important contribution to Australian research. "This young ethnographer, already known for other and remarkable enquiries, brings here, by adopting an exclusively feminine perspective, a vision that until now has been very rare, of the life and recent evolution of an indigenous community" (translated from the French original). In her work, he says, she does not hesitate to study culture contact changes; thus it "seems to offer a perfect model to all those—administrators and missionaries—who would wish to ensure that their stay in faraway places is of benefit to science and to people" (Berndt 1950a:3–8). In regard to religion and magic, he sees it as an important contribution to the sociology of religion; and he praises its attention to individual people in their social contexts. Berndt says now that she would like to rewrite the monograph: "But isn't that how a person should always feel, looking back on earlier work?"

Note

1. All quotes unless otherwise cited are from personal interviews with Dr. Berndt.

References and Works About Catherine H. Berndt

Lévi-Strauss, Claude
1950 Preface (pp. 3–8). Women's Changing Ceremonies in Northern Australia, by Catherine Berndt. *L'Homme* 1:1–88.
Reay, Marie
1963 The Social Position of Women. In *Australian Aboriginal Studies*. H. Sheils, ed. Pp. 319–34. Melbourne: Oxford University Press.

Selected Works by Catherine H. Berndt

1950a Women's Changing Ceremonies in Northern Australia. *L'Homme* 1:1–88.
1950b Expressions of Grief Among Aboriginal Women. *Oceania* 20 (4):286–332.
1952 A Drama of North-eastern Arnhem Land. *Oceania* 22 (3): 216–39; (4): 275–89.
1953 Sociocultural Change in the East-Central Highlands of New Guinea. *Southwestern Journal of Anthropology* 9:112–38.
1954 Translation Problems in Three New Guinea Highland Languages. *Oceania* 24 (4):289–317.
1957 Social and Cultural Change in New Guinea: Communication, and Views About "Other People." *Sociology* 7:38–57.
1958 Anthropology and Mission Activity. *South Pacific* 10 (2):38–43.
1959 The Ascription of Meaning in a Ceremonial Context, in the Eastern Central Highlands of New Guinea. In *Anthropology in the South Seas*. J. D. Freeman and W. R. Geddes, eds. Pp. 161–83. New Plymouth, Australia: Avery.
1960a The Concept of Primitive. *Sociologus* 10:50–69. (Reprinted 1968 in Ashley Montagu, *The Concept of the Primitive*. Pp. 7–31. New York: The Free Press.)
1960b Assimilation versus Apartheid. *Proceedings of the 4th Pan-Indian Ocean Science Association Congress, Karachi*. Pp. 35–47.
1961 The Quest for Identity: The Case of the Australian Aborigines. *Oceania* 32 (1): 16–33.
1962 Mateship or Success: An Assimilation Dilemma. *Oceania* 33 (2): 71–89.
1963 Art and Aesthetic Expression. In *Australian Aboriginal Studies*. H. Sheils, ed. Pp. 256–80. Melbourne: Oxford University Press.
1964a The Role of Native Doctors in Aboriginal Australia. In *Magic, Faith, and Healing*. A. Kiev, ed. Pp. 264–82. New York: Free Press of Glencoe.
1964b Uses and Misuses of Anthropology. *Anthropological Forum* 1 (2):168–87.
1965 Women and the "Secret Life." In *Aboriginal Man in Australia*. R. M. Berndt and C. H. Berndt, eds. Pp. 238–82. Sydney: Angus and Robertson. (Reprinted 1984 in *Religion in Aboriginal Australia: An Anthology*. M. Charlesworth et al., eds. Pp. 315–34. St. Lucia, Australia: University of Queensland Press.)
1966 The Ghost Husband: Society and the Individual in New Guinea Myth. In *The Anthropologist Looks at Myth*. J. Greenway, ed., M. Jacobs, compiler. Pp. 244–77. Austin: The University of Texas Press.
1969 A Time of Rediscovery. In *Aboriginal Progress: A New Era?* D. E. Hutchison, ed. Pp. 16–34. Perth: University of Western Australia Press.
1970a Monsoon and Honey Wind. In *Echanges et communications: mélanges offerts à*

Claude Lévi-Strauss. J. Pouillon and P. Maranda, eds. Pp. 1306–26. Paris: Mouton.

1970b Digging Sticks and Spears, Or, the Two-Sex Model. In *Woman's Role in Aboriginal Society.* F. Gale, ed. Pp. 39–48. (1974 ed., pp. 64–84.) Canberra: Australian Institute of Aboriginal Studies.

1973 Oral Literature. In *The Australian Aboriginal Heritage.* R. M. Berndt and E. S. Phillips, eds. Pp. 72–90. Sydney: Ure Smith, for the Australian Society for Education Through the Arts.

1977a Out of the Frying Pan . . . ? Or, Back to Square One? In *Aborigines and Change: Australia in the '70s.* R. M. Berndt, ed. Pp. 402–11. Canberra: Australian Institute of Aboriginal Studies; Atlantic Highlands, N.J.: Humanities Press.

1977b The Language of Myth: An Eastern Highlands Perspective. In *New Guinea Area Languages and Language Study.* S. A. Wurm, ed. vol. 3, pp. 39–48. Canberra: Department of Linguistics, Research School of Pacific Studies, The Australian National University.

1978a Categorisation of, and in, Oral Literature. In *Australian Aboriginal Concepts.* L. R. Hiatt, ed. Pp. 56–67. Canberra: Australian Institute of Aboriginal Studies.

1978b In Aboriginal Australia. In *Learning Non-aggression.* Ashley Montagu, ed. Pp. 144–60. New York: Oxford University Press.

1979a The Rainbow Serpent Lives. In *Through Folklore to Literature.* M. Saxby, ed. Pp. 133–50. Sydney: Ibby Australia Publications.

1979b Aboriginal Women and the Notion of 'the Marginal Man.' In *Aborigines of the West: Their Past and Their Present.* R. M. Berndt and C. H. Berndt, eds. Pp. 28–38. Perth: University of Western Australia Press.

1980 Aboriginal Children's Literature. In *Children's Literature. More Than a Story.* Pp. 69–135. Deakin University Open Campus Programme. Geelong: Deakin University School of Education.

1981a Interpretations and 'Facts' in Aboriginal Australia. In *Woman the Gatherer.* Frances Dahlberg, ed. Pp. 153–203. New Haven and London: Yale University Press.

1981b Ageing in Aboriginal Society: Traditional and Contemporary Perspectives. In *Towards an Older Australia.* A. L. Howe, ed. Pp. 271–85. St. Lucia, Australia: University of Queensland Press.

1982a Australia. In *Legends of the World.* R. Cavendish, ed. Pp. 379–89, 391, 419–20. London: Orbis.

1982b Sickness and Health in Western Arnhem Land: A Traditional Perspective. In *Body, Land and Spirit.* Jan Reid, ed. Pp. 121–38. St. Lucia, Australia: University of Queensland Press.

1982c Aboriginal Women, Resources and Family Life. In *Aboriginal Sites, Rights and Resource Development.* R. M. Berndt, ed. Pp. 33–38, 39–52. Published for the Academy of the Social Sciences in Australia. Perth: University of Western Australia Press.

1983 Mythical Women, Past and Present. In *We Are Bosses Ourselves: The Status and Role of Aboriginal Women Today.* F. Gale, ed. Pp. 13–25. Canberra: Australian Institute of Aboriginal Studies.

1985a Mondalmi: One of the Saltwater People. In *Fighters and Singers: The Lives of Some Aboriginal Women.* I. White, D. Barwick, and B. Meehan, eds. Pp. 19–39. Sydney: George Allen and Unwin.

1985b Traditional Aboriginal Oral Literature. In *Aboriginal Writing Today*. Jack Davis and Bob Hodge, eds. Pp. 91–103. Canberra: Australian Institute of Aboriginal Studies.

Coauthored Works

Berndt, Catherine H. as primary author, with R. M. Berndt

1971 *The Barbarians: An Anthropological View*. London: Watts, New Thinker's Library. (1973 Pelican edition, Penguin books.)

1972 Aborigines. In *Socialisation in Australia*. F. J. Hunt, ed. Pp. 115–40. Sydney: Angus and Robertson. (2nd revised ed., 1978. Pp. 119–46. Melbourne: Australian International Press and Publications.)

1982 Aboriginal Australia: Literature in an Oral Tradition. In *Review of National Literatures, Volume 11, Australia*. L. A. C. Dobrez, ed. Pp. 39–63. New York: Griffon House.

1983 *The Aboriginal Australians: The First Pioneers*. Melbourne: Pitman. (First published 1978, as *Pioneers and Settlers. The Aboriginal Australians*. Melbourne: Pitman, pp. i–xvi, 1–150.)

Berndt, Catherine H., with R. M. Berndt as primary author

1964 *The World of the First Australians*. Sydney: Ure Smith. (Latest revised edition, 1985. Adelaide: Rigby.)

1970 *Man, Land and Myth in North Australia: The Gunwinggu People*. Sydney: Ure Smith.

1982 *Aboriginal Australian Art: A Visual Perspective*. Sydney: Methuen Australia.

1987 *End of an Era. Aboriginal Labour in the Northern Territory*. Canberra: Australian Institute of Aboriginal Studies. (Also with J. E. Stanton)

SUSAN KALDOR

Beatrice Mary Blackwood
(1889–1975)

British social anthropologist Beatrice Blackwood was known especially for her research in Melanesia among the Buka Islanders and northern Bougainvillians in the Solomon Islands, and among the Kukukuku in the Eastern Highlands of New Guinea.

Born on May 3, 1889, in London, she was the daughter of James Blackwood, a successful London publisher and direct descendant of William Blackwood, the founder of *Blackwood's Magazine* and publishing house in Edinburgh.[1] Blackwood never married and at the time of her death was survived only by her sister, Mary French. At a certain point in her life, Blackwood reputedly chose between marriage and a career, choosing the latter because she was "so plain."

As a child Blackwood recalled "her own strenuous efforts to resist the conventional education in suitable accomplishments for a young lady of the period" (Penniman 1976b:235). However, as was common for young English women of her social class at the time, she was sent to Germany for finishing school. She learned German thoroughly and studied Greek and Latin as well. In 1908 she successfully completed an examination that earned her a scholarship to Somerville College, one of two colleges for women at Oxford University. At Somerville she read English literature and studied the etymology of German and Scandinavian languages. Her interest in languages was paralleled by her facility in learning to speak them, a skill that served her well in her later career as an ethnographer.

Prior to 1920 women students at Oxford and Cambridge were not awarded actual university degrees; thus Blackwood was graduated in 1912, having successfully completed all the requisite coursework but without an official degree. When the policy regarding the granting of degrees to women at Oxford was changed, Blackwood received both her B.A. and M.A. (1920). Immediately after graduating, she joined the staff of the Anatomy Department at Oxford as an assistant to Arthur Thomson, a comparative anatomist and physical anthropologist. Having decided to pursue an academic career, she began to study for a B.Sc. in embryology, which she received in 1923. Between 1916 and 1918 she also read for a diploma in anthropology, which she received with distinction. While preparing for her diploma, she engaged in archaeological research in France, where she met Abbé Breuil, one of the foremost French prehistorians of the time. Breuil once commented on how fearless Blackwood was in leading the vanguard in the exploration of new caves, where her small build enabled her to crawl into extremely narrow, newly excavated passageways (Penniman 1976b:235). She also conducted archaeological research in England, especially in the immediate vicinity of Oxford, and collected antiquities from the late Iron Age and the Saxon and Roman periods for the Ashmolean Museum. Soon after receiving her diploma in anthropology, Blackwood was appointed demonstrator and lecturer in ethnology at Oxford, a position she held from 1923 to 1959.

During the early 1920s R. R. Marett, a scholar of comparative religion and a leading intellectual at Oxford, encouraged Blackwood to pursue her interest in the study of the relative intelligence of different races—a topic of much interest at that time within the fields of physical and social anthropology—by applying for a scholarship to conduct research on this topic in the United States. She received a grant from the Rockefeller Foundation and arrived in New York in September 1924. At the American Museum of Natural History, she first met Clark Wissler, with whom she was favorably impressed. Wissler, in conjunction with Robert Yerkes of the National Research Council, had just started a new psychological institute at Yale University. He suggested that Blackwood become affiliated with the institute and that he supervise her research. However, although officially affiliated with the Institute at Yale, Blackwood worked primarily with Brigham, a psychologist at Princeton University and an expert in the field of intelligence testing. At Princeton she was the only woman in the Psychology Department. Even though she conducted psychological tests to gather data on intelligence, Blackwood questioned the validity of testing intelligence apart from environment and remained wary of the problems of interpreting the tests.

In 1925 Blackwood left Princeton for Fisk University in Nashville, Tennessee, the first of numerous visits she made to colleges, universities, government institutions, Indian reservations, and communities across the United States and Canada. She traveled to Birmingham, Selma, Atlanta, Chattanooga, and New Orleans in the South and to Winnipeg and Alert Bay in Canada to gather genealogical data and conduct intelligence tests among blacks and North American Indians. Where possible, she obtained permission to do physical measurements of head size. She believed the genealogical data to be important in determining the effect of inheritance on intelligence. During the fall she spent time in Minnesota conducting tests among the Chippewa Indians and writing a research report while at the Mayo Clinic in Rochester. She conducted more research in the South during 1926 and 1927, and visited several Indian reservations in the Southwest, where she collected Hopi kachinas and Navajo blankets for the Pitt Rivers Museum. Her research in the United States resulted in two publications:

"A Study of Mental Testing in Relation to Anthropology" (1927) and "Racial Differences As Recorded by the Colour-top" (1930).

Returning to England, Blackwood prepared to carry out comparative field research in Melanesia, under the auspices of a grant from the Committee for Research on Problems of Sex, of the National Research Council in Washington, D.C. This committee was supervised by Wissler at Yale and administered by the Oxford Committee for Anthropology. Blackwood was one of a small number of female anthropologists—including Margaret Mead,* Hortense Powdermaker,* and Camilla Wedgwood*—who were the first women to conduct field research in Melanesia. She spent twelve months in the Solomon Islands studying two communities: Petats, off the coast of Buka, and Kurtatchi in northern Bougainville (1929–30). She published the results of this research in her book *Both Sides of Buka Passage* (Blackwood 1935a).

While in the field, Blackwood corresponded with Brenda and C. G. Seligman, then affiliated with the Department of Ethnology at Oxford. At the request of C. G. Seligman, who was interested in the relationship between psychology and anthropology, Blackwood collected dream material, some of which she published in her ethnography. Seligman's comments about these dreams are provocative. In 1932 he wrote to Blackwood, "Has it struck you that taken en masse those dreams, especially the dreams of women, betoken a society in which marriage seems generally unhappy, or at least one with a good deal of marital friction. Would you say that this is on the whole the case?" (Seligman to Blackwood 9 Oct. 1932). Blackwood's reply to Seligman's query unfortunately no longer exists. However, her book contains much detailed information about marriage in Buka and the fact that most first marriages, arranged during childhood, ended in divorce, whereas second marriages, based on choice, were more lasting. Her book, favorably received by anthropologists (Hogbin 1936), established her as a competent ethnographer and field-worker. It contained possibly the first published eyewitness description of childbirth in a Melanesian society, detailed accounts of technological processes, and records of indigenous foods and their vitamin content. Although never a strong theoretician, Blackwood was well respected for the thoroughness of her observations.

After Arthur Thomson's death in 1935, Blackwood transferred from the Anatomy Department to the Department of Ethnology at the Pitt Rivers Museum. As a member of the curatorial staff, she returned to Melanesia for further research—this time on mainland New Guinea (1936–37). On behalf of the museum, she was to observe traditional Stone Age manufacturing techniques and collect Neolithic tool specimens. Against the advice of the government anthropologist in New Guinea, she decided to contact the Kukukuku people in a remote region of the Eastern Highlands of New Guinea. This area had only recently been opened to whites and a patrol post established to aid gold prospectors working in the region. Undaunted by the isolation, the rugged terrain, and the reputed hostility of the Kukukuku, Blackwood arrived in the area with a kitten and a ball of wool. "It amused the Kukukuku greatly to see the kitten playing with

the wool, and brought a good many from long distances to trade with her''
(Penniman 1976b:236).

In addition to the artifacts and field material she collected, Blackwood also
produced a short documentary film entitled *A Stone Age People in New Guinea*
(1936). The three reels, unique for their time, include Blackwood's flight inland
to the Upper Watut River region and the reactions of people who were seeing
an airplane for the first time. Among other things, Blackwood filmed Kukukuku
male purification rites, techniques used to manufacture stone club heads, and
the use of stone tools and bows and arrows. She also recorded the practice of
head binding among the Arawe of New Britain and the tribal dances performed
at Salamua, New Guinea, to celebrate the coronation of King George VI (1937).
Blackwood's poor health and the murder of a Chinese storekeeper by the Kukukuku forced her to leave the region after only nine months. From there she
traveled to Madang Province, where she collected data and artifacts from the
Bosmun of the Lower Ramu River (1951) and then to the Arawe in New Britain.

The results of Blackwood's research among the Kukukuku were published by
the Pitt Rivers Museum as ''The Technology of a Modern Stone Age People in
New Guinea'' (Blackwood 1950); and additional material was recently edited
by C. R. Hallpike (Blackwood 1978). In recognition of her outstanding work
among the Kukukuku, she received the Rivers Memorial Medal from the Royal
Anthropological Institute in 1943.

After leaving New Guinea, Blackwood returned to her position as assistant
curator at the Pitt Rivers Museum, where she worked closely with the museum's
new curator of ethnology, T. K. Penniman. Founding editor of the museum
publication series, she also catalogued the museum's extensive ethnographic
collections and became a demonstrator in ethnology at Oxford University. She
published a monograph on the classification of artifacts in the museum (1970),
with a long introduction on the origin and development of the Pitt Rivers Museum. She was active in various scholarly organizations, including the Society
of Americanists, the Congress of Pacific Sciences, the Society of Antiquaries,
and served on the Council of the Folklore Society and of the Royal Anthropological Institute. Blackwood taught at Oxford for over thirty years and continued
to work at the Pitt Rivers Museum, which served as the forum for most of her
professional contributions—research, collection, and writing—until her death in
1975.

Note

1. I would like to thank Peter Gathercole and B. A. L. Cranstone for giving of their
time to discuss Beatrice Blackwood. Dr. Cranstone also made available to me the Blackwood Papers and Blackwood's film footage shot in New Guinea housed in the Archives
of the Pitt Rivers Museum at Oxford University.

References and Works About Beatrice Blackwood

Hallpike, C. R.
1978 Introduction. *The Kukukuku of the Upper Watut.* C. R. Hallpike, ed. Pitt Rivers Museum, Oxford University.
Hogbin, Ian
1936 Review of *Both Sides of Buka Passage. Oceania* 7 (1): 142–43.
Penniman, T. K.
1976a Obituary: Beatrice Mary Blackwood. *American Anthropologist* 78(76): 321–22.
1976b Obituary: Beatrice Mary Blackwood. *Oceania* 46 (3): 235–37.

Selected Works by Beatrice Blackwood

1927 A Study of Mental Testing in Relation to Anthropology. *Mental Measurement Monographs.* No. 3: Baltimore.
1930 Racial Differences As Recorded by the Colour-top. *Journal of the Royal Anthropological Institute.*
1931 Mountain People of the South Seas. *Natural History:* Journal of the American Museum of Natural History 31:424–33.
1931/32 Report on Fieldwork in Buka and Bougainville, *Oceania* 2:199–219.
1932 Folk Stories from the Northern Solomons. *Folklore* 43:61–96.
1935a *Both Sides of Buka Passage: An Ethnographic Study of Social, Sexual and Economic Questions in the North-Western Solomon Islands.* Oxford: Oxford University Press.
1935b Treatment of the Sick in the Solomon Islands. *Folklore* 46:148–61.
1936a *A Stone Age People in New Guinea.* Documentary film, 3 reels. Pitt Rivers Museum, Oxford University.
1936b Fieldwork in Bougainville: An Interlude. In *Custom Is King, Essays Presented to R. R. Marett.* Pp. 167–78. L. H. Dudley Buxton, ed. London: Hutchinson's Scientific and Technical Publications.
1939a Life of the Upper Watut, New Guinea. *Geographical Journal* 94(1): 11–28.
1939b Folk-Stories of a Stone Age People in New Guinea. *Folklore* 50(3): 209–42.
1939c Use of Plants Among the Kukukuku of Southeast-Central New Guinea. *Proceedings of the Sixth Pacific Science Congress* 4:111–26. Berkeley, California.
1939d Artificial Cranial Deformation in New Britain. *Congrès International des Sciences Anthropologiques et Ethnologiques.* Compte rendu de la Deuxième Session. Copenhagen 1938:293–94.
1940 Crafts of a Stone Age People in New Guinea. *Man* 40:11.
1950a The Technology of a Modern Stone Age People in New Guinea. *Occasional Papers on Technology* 3:3–59. Pitt Rivers Museum, Oxford University.
1950b Reserve Dyeing in New Guinea. *Man* 50:53–55.
1951 Some Arts and Industries of the Bosmun, Ramu River, New Guinea. In *Suedseestudien, Gedenkschrift zur Erinnerung an Felix Speiser,* Pp. 266–88. Basel: Museum für Völkerkunde.
1970 The Classification of Artifacts in the Pitt Rivers Museum, Oxford. *Occasional Papers on Technology* 11. Pp. 27–78. Pitt Rivers Museum, Oxford University.

1970   The Origin and Development of the Pitt Rivers Museum. *Occasional Papers on Technology* 11. Pp. 7–16. Pitt Rivers Museum, Oxford University.
1978   The Kukukuku of the Upper Watut. Edited with an introduction by C. R. Hallpike. *Monograph Series No. 2*, Pitt Rivers Museum, Oxford University.

Coauthored Works

Blackwood, Beatrice and Danby, P. M.
1955   A Study of Artificial Cranial Deformation in New Britain. *Journal of the Royal Anthropological Institute of Great Britain and Ireland* 85:173–91.

Unpublished Material

Miscellaneous letters, Diaries, Field Notes and Photographs. Pitt Rivers Museum Archives, Oxford University.

NANCY LUTKEHAUS

Alice Mossie Brues
(1913–   )

Alice Mossie Brues is an American physical anthropologist best known for her work on the population genetics of the ABO blood group system.

Brues was born October 9, 1913, in Boston, Massachusetts, the second child of Beirne Barrett and Charles Thomas Brues. Her mother was an amateur field botanist and avid collector of native American basketry. Her father was professor of entomology at Harvard University and coauthor of the first key to insect families published in North America. He, too, was a great collector; and Brues recalls being sent off as a young girl to collect insects from flowers. Her parents liked to travel, and family trips throughout the United States provided Brues with the opportunity to experience the ethnic and ecological diversity of the country. Brues's only sibling, Austin M. Brues, obtained a medical degree and pursued a career in cancer research.[1]

Brues attended primary and secondary schools in the Boston area. She won a scholarship to Bryn Mawr College, where she majored in philosophy and psychology. After receiving her B.A. from Bryn Mawr in 1933, she proceeded to Radcliffe College, where she began graduate study in anthropology. She was initially interested in comparative religions but came under the spell of Ernest Hooton, one of the founding fathers of physical anthropology; and her interests drifted back to the more biological. As a graduate student she was familiar with Hooton's bone laboratory, and later, his statistics laboratory with its 1930s state-of-the-art data-processing machines. For her dissertation she chose to do research in human genetics, concentrating her analysis on the inheritance of eye color, body build, and freckling in family groups. The results of this work were published in the *American Journal of Physical Anthropology* and the *American Journal of Human Genetics* (1946b, 1950).

Brues completed her Ph.D. in 1940. At the time, there were few women in physical anthropology; but Brues herself once commented that people were not so painfully conscious of those things as they are now. Coming from an academic family as she did, it seemed natural to Brues to get a Ph.D., and natural to get one in a field allied to biology.

Brues stayed at Harvard as a research associate at the Peabody Museum (1940–41) and worked with Hooton on the statistical analysis of anthropometric data from U.S. Air Force personnel. This was a project designed to provide information on body size and shape that could be used for uniform sizing and military equipment design, including design of oxygen masks for high altitude flights. Brues continued this research as assistant statistician at Wright Field (1942–44) until the end of the war. She then worked briefly at the Massachusetts Institute of Technology as a consultant on the size and fit of gas masks.

After the war Brues took a position as assistant professor of anatomy at the University of Oklahoma School of Medicine. Since few departments of anthropology at that time employed physical anthropologists, many worked in either museums or anatomy departments (Spencer 1981). While at Oklahoma, Brues described the skeletal material from a number of archaeological sites, did some work in forensics, and extended her work to the population genetics of the A-B-O blood group system. In 1959 she took the first computer programming course offered by the university. This course provided a foundation in the technical skills that she used in developing the simulation models of genetic change for which she is well known.

In 1965 Brues accepted a position as visiting professor of anthropology at the University of Colorado in Boulder. She moved there permanently in 1966 and chaired the department between 1968 and 1971. She retired from teaching and became emerita in 1984. During her career in anthropology Brues held a number of important professional positions. She was curator of physical anthropology at the Stovall Museum in Norman, Oklahoma (1956–65). She was a member of the Executive Board of the American Association of Physical Anthropologists (1963–66), as well as vice president (1966–68) and president (1971–73) of the association. Additionally, she was on the Executive Committee (1977–78), served as vice president (1976–77) of the Human Biology Council, was elected to membership of Sigma Xi and Phi Beta Kappa, and in 1986 was recognized by the American Academy of Forensic Sciences for her outstanding contributions to forensic science.

Brues is probably best known for her 1959 essay, ''The Spearman and the Archer.'' In this essay Brues explored the relationship between body build and weapon use in human evolution. She convincingly argues that a large muscular body build would be selectively advantageous if the primary weapon were a bludgeon, a linear body build advantageous for populations using spears, and a lateral body build with short limb segments for populations using the bow. This essay stands as one of the first attempts to define the selective effects of behavior on biological characteristics. Brues recognized the speculative nature of many of the points raised and encouraged her readers to pursue the topic further: ''All of the suggestions are speculative and should be critically questioned in principle, as well as with respect to those details which are found to have been misrepresented as a result of overgeneralization. It is hoped, however, that these ideas will illuminate the complex problem of selection in man'' (Brues 1959:468). The problem of human selection is one she has continued to work on throughout her life.

Brues's first published paper in population genetics, *Selection and Polymorphism in the A-B-O Blood Groups* (1954), is considered a classic in physical anthropology (Weiss and Chakraborty 1982:382). At the time it was written, the A-B-O blood groups were the major genetic polymorphisms known in human populations but generally considered not to have any selective value, and the very striking worldwide frequency distributions were attributed to genetic drift. Brues's approach to the problem was characteristically straightforward. She pointed out that although there was considerable variation in A-B-O frequencies among human populations, it was less than the total possible range of variation. Thus, for example, the frequency of A ranges from 0 to 54 percent but no higher, and the frequency of O is rarely less than 50 percent. Brues interpreted this as inconsistent with the effects found under random genetic drift. She then hypothesized, on the basis of a mathematical model simulating genetic change over time, that natural selection favoring the heterozygote could explain the observed frequency distribution.

Later, using a more sophisticated computerized simulation model, Brues (1963) was able to show that the worldwide distribution of A-B-O frequencies was consistent with the hypothesis that natural selection favored the heterozygote. She was one of the first to develop computer simulation models to test the possible combination of evolutionary forces that could account for the distribution of a trait, and her work represented a considerable methodological as well as theoretical advance.

Brues went on to use simulation modeling to examine a number of other problems of interest to anthropologists, such as the evolutionary forces affecting the A-O blood group frequencies of North American Indians, the importance of mutation in combination with selection in changing gene frequencies, and the interaction of gene flow and selection in changing gene frequencies and maintaining regional genetic differences. This work was particularly valuable for demonstrating the interaction of evolutionary forces.

Another important theoretical contribution was a solution to "Haldane's Dilemma." Calculations by Haldane showed that the replacement of one gene by another through natural selection results in numerous genetic deaths, and thus the "cost" of natural selection appears to be unreasonably high. In a thoughtful paper entitled "The Cost of Evolution vs. the Cost of Not Evolving," Brues (1964b:383) examined the problem and was able to show that "a species undergoing appropriate gene substitutions will always fare better in terms of the total number of deaths during the period of adjustment than will a population which is unable to make such substitutions." This paper stimulated a request from the editor of *Science* for a review article on genetic load, which was published in 1969.

Brues always maintained a strong interest in human geographical variation,

or what is sometimes referred to as "racial" variation. She approached the
subject as a natural historian, first describing the variation and then attempting
to understand its evolutionary significance. Brues considered the study of geographical variation in humans to be one of the scientific responsibilities of physical anthropology. She was well aware of the complex genetic basis of such
variation and never hesitated to work on problems that others considered difficult.
One such difficult problem was human pigmentation; and in a 1975 paper on
the subject, Brues challenged her colleagues to rethink the whole question:

The field of pigmentation may not even be a suitable one for the student who wants a
good quick dissertation project, or the faculty member who wants a publication in time
for the next swindle sheet he sends to the dean. Perhaps it is a study only for the tenured.
I guarantee you moments of madness when you try to decide how to classify medium
brown hair and various other ambiguous phenotypes which human flesh, at least human
keratinized epidermis, is heir to. (Brues 1975:391)

In her teaching at the University of Colorado, Brues broadened the scope of
departmental offerings. She initiated courses in human gross anatomy, quantitative methods, human osteology, human variation, primate neuroanatomy, nutritional anthropology, and human growth. Brues felt that teaching and research
were complementary activities. Research was concerned with addressing un-
answered questions of significance in the profession, and teaching pointed out
some of these questions. Brues once commented that it was always the innocent
undergraduates "who don't know there are questions you shouldn't ask" that
kept one from being complacent.

At the time of her retirement from teaching in 1984, one of Brues's favorite
courses was that on modern human variation, for which she wrote a textbook,
People and Races (Brues 1977). The book describes physical and genetic differences between populations as geographical phenomena, but does not propose
a rigid system of racial classification. For Brues, the number of races one dis-
tinguishes is a matter of choice, depending on how much detail is desired (Brues
1977:2). Although the subject of racial variation and classification is a very
controversial one, Brues notes in her introduction that geographical variation
can be observed in most widespread animal species, not just in humans. Her
position is clear:

I believe that in a period in which the word "race" has become politically and emotionally
charged, most people welcome an opportunity to discuss the perfectly simple physical
differences that distinguish populations of geographically different ancestry. The very air
of conspiracy with which some people avoid talking about racial differences is enough
to give the impression that these differences are in some way sinister. I do not feel this
way. Racial differences need not be thought of as something puzzling or uncomfortable
about strangers: they can also be something interesting about your friends." (Brues
1977:vii–viii)

As in all of her writing, the prose style is clear and uncluttered, with that refreshing charm and dash of pungent wit that is pure Brues. In retirement, Brues continues her work with computer simulation of genetic changes.

Note

1. I will always be indebted to Dr. Brues for sharing with me an account of her life and development as an anthropologist. She made researching this biographical sketch a most enjoyable experience.

References and Works About Alice M. Brues

Weiss, K. M., and Chakraborty, R.
1982 Genes, Populations, and Disease 1930–1980: A Problem-oriented Approach. In *A History of American Physical Anthropology*. F. Spencer, ed. Pp. 371–404. New York: Academic Press.

Selected Works by Alice M. Brues

1943a Body Measurements of Female Flying Personnel. Army Air Forces, Material Center, Memorandum Report #ENG–49–695–32-A.

1943b Body Measurements of AAF Flyers (Graphic). Army Air Forces, Material Center, Memorandum Report #ENG–49–695–32-L.

1945 Study of Anthropometric Data. Chemical Warfare Service Development Laboratory, M.I.T., Memorandum Report #166, 61 pp.

1946a Alkali Ridge Skeletal Materials. *Papers of the Peabody Museum of American Archaeology and Ethnology*. Vol. 11, pp. 463–82. Harvard University.

1946b A Genetic Analysis of Human Eye Color. *American Journal of Physical Anthropology* 4:1–36.

1946c The San Simon Branch. Excavations at Cave Creek and in the San Simon Valley. II. Skeletal Material. *Medallion Papers*, no. 25. 26 pp.

1950 Linkage of Body Build with Sex, Eye Color and Freckling. *American Journal of Human Genetics* 2:215–39.

1954 Selection and Polymorphism in the A-B-O Blood Groups. *American Journal of Physical Anthropology* 12:559–98.

1957 Skeletal Material from the Nagel Site. *Bulletin of the Oklahoma Anthropological Society* 5:101–5.

1958 Identification of Skeletal Remains. *Journal of Criminal Law, Criminology and Police Science* 48:551–63.

1959 The Spearman and the Archer—An Essay on Selection in Body Build. *American Anthropologist* 61:457–69.

1960 Computer Analysis of Blood Group Polymorphism. *Abstracts of 1960 Meeting of American Society of Human Genetics*, p. 21.

1962 Skeletal Material from the McLemore Site. *Bulletin of the Oklahoma Anthropological Society* 10:69–78.

1963 Stochastic Tests of Selection in the ABO Blood Groups. *American Journal of Physical Anthropology* 21:287–99.

1964a Genetic Drift in the Differentiation of the American Indigenes: Evidence from the Blood Groups. *Actas y memorias, XXV, Congreso Internacional de Americanistas*. Pp. 119–20.

1964b The Cost of Evolution vs. the Cost of Not Evolving. *Evolution* 18:379–83.

1965 Physical Anthropology. In *Biennial Review of Anthropology*. B.J. Siegel, Ed. Pp. 1–139. Stanford: Stanford University Press.

1966 Probable Mutation on Effect and the Evolution of Hominid Teeth and Jaws. *American Journal of Physical Anthropology* 25:169–70.

1968 Mutation and Selection—A Quantitative Evaluation. *American Journal of Physical Anthropology* 29:437–38.

1969 Genetic Load and Its Varieties. *Science* 164:1130–36.

1972 Models of Race and Cline. *American Journal of Physical Anthropology* 37:389–99.

1973 *The Maintenance of Genetic Diversity in Man*. Addison-Wesley Module Series in Anthropology.

1974 Models Applicable to Geographic Variation in Man. In *Computer Simulation in Human Population Studies*. B. Dyke and J. W. MacClauer, eds. Pp. 129–41. New York: Academic Press.

1975 Rethinking Human Pigmentation. *American Journal of Physical Anthropology* 43:387–91.

1977 *People and Races*. Macmillan Series in Physical Anthropology. New York: Macmillan.

1980 Comments on Krantz's Sapienization and Speech. *Current Anthropology* 21:779–80.

1981 Interaction of Gene Flow and Selection, Or Australia Revisited for the Nth Time. *UCLA Anthropology Series* 7:55–64.

Coauthored Works

Brues, Alice M. et al.

1944 The Importance of Human Sizing Standards in Aviation. *Journal of Aviation Medicine* (August): 3–8.

DARNA L. DUFOUR

Ruth Leah Bunzel

(1898–   )

Ruth Leah Bunzel is an American cultural anthropologist, known especially for her pioneering work among Zuni women potters, Pueblo ceremonialism, and culture-and-personality studies.

Bunzel was born in New York, the youngest of four children, to Jonas and Hattie Bernheim Bunzel. The family, of German and Czech heritage, lived on the upper east side of Manhattan. Ruth's father died of heart trouble when she was ten, and her mother alone raised Ruth and her older siblings, Bessie, Madeleine, and Sydney. Her mother inherited money from her family's Cuban tobacco–importing business and raised the children in a Jewish household that was largely acculturated to American ways. Although English was spoken at home, Ruth's mother encouraged Ruth to study the German language, which she did as an undergraduate at Barnard College, Columbia University. The political atmosphere surrounding World War I, however, caused her to change her major. She followed in her older sister's path and attended college with no particular career plans, ultimately receiving in 1918 a Bachelor's degree in European history.

Bunzel took a job as secretary to Franz Boas at Columbia, replacing Esther Goldfrank*, a friend of Bunzel's sister Madeleine, who had left this position to undertake graduate work in anthropology. When Boas interviewed Bunzel for the job, he remembered her (according to Bunzel) as a student who had taken a course with him at Barnard, and who had been inquisitive in the classroom. In the summer of 1924 Boas was traveling to Europe, and Bunzel, out of work, accompanied her older friend Ruth Benedict* to Zuni Pueblo, New Mexico. Bunzel recounts that Boas told her not to waste her time at Zuni with secretarial duties and encouraged her to undertake a project of her own while there. He told her to "do a study on the relation of an artist to her craft," and suggested pottery.[1] Boas interpreted this as how potters work and how they think about what they are doing. He suggested a few preliminary readings, and Bunzel was on her way. Bunzel, who had had no formal training in anthropology or art history, began to study Pueblo potters and their work by donning a blue smock and making pottery herself with the women. This project became her dissertation and ultimately resulted in a classic publication, *The Pueblo Potter* (1929).

Bunzel's career as an anthropologist was thus launched, as she notes with delight, by accident. Bunzel received the support she needed for her work from Boas. She remembers that he "always encouraged women," a marked contrast to attitudes in other departments where women were forced to sit in cloakrooms so as not to distract the men in the class. Bunzel describes Cora Du Bois* as experiencing this at Harvard in order to attend class. Boas recognized that women could contribute something unique to anthropology, since they were allowed access to areas that were closed to men.

Upon Bunzel's return from the field, Boas had lost another secretary to anthropology. Bunzel began graduate work with him and became part of a unique network of women anthropologists based at Columbia who were to have a profound and lasting impact on anthropology—notably Southwestern ethnology. Besides Margaret Mead,* Bunzel worked at Columbia with Esther Goldfrank, Ruth Benedict, Gladys Reichard,* and Elsie Clews Parsons,* all of whom shared an interest in the Southwest. Their experience at Columbia and in the field provided a lifelong network. Benedict led Bunzel into the field and served as a mentor (along with Mead) in later work on personality-and-culture. Elsie Clews Parsons personally funded Bunzel's second trip to Zuni to study ceremonialism, as well as funding other field trips and publications, of both Bunzel and other Columbia students. Although in retrospect this network appears very well defined early on, it actually seems to have been something that evolved over the years based on mutual research interests.

Another important network for Bunzel in the 1920s, however, was her Zuni family. Her first season was spent renting a house with Benedict from Flora Zuni, a teacher of sewing at the Day School, which was located about a quarter of a mile east of the pueblo toward Blackrock. In later seasons Bunzel lived with, and was ultimately formally adopted into, Flora Zuni's family. She participated with them in such ceremonial activities as corn grinding—a task she describes as needing great endurance—baking bread, and the presentation of ceremonial food. Her acceptance into the family included initiation into Flora's clan, the Badger clan, and the acquisition of a Zuni name: Maiatitsa, which meant "blue bird" and reflected the blue smock she wore. Bunzel received a second name—Tsatitsa—from Nick Dumaka, a former governor of the pueblo, and one of her prime informants. Bunzel reports that he gave her this name because he was jealous of the name bestowed upon her by Flora and her clan. As a member of a native household, Bunzel found that she suddenly had little free time or privacy as she worked alongside her Zuni hostesses. "I used to go around to the houses where they were grinding, and they would invite the girls to come and grind; and then the men would come and sing the grinding songs.

It was such a pleasant activity, but it also took much sweat from the brow. So I, too, would go and grind.''

Bunzel spent five consecutive summers (1924–29) at Zuni and several winter seasons as well, enabling her to see the entire seasonal round. Bunzel enjoyed the fieldwork but found it "hard and lonesome." Her first season was devoted to pottery, the second to ceremonialism, and the third to learning the language in detail. At the time of her fieldwork, most young people had been to school and spoke English. After the first season with Benedict, Bunzel worked alone in the field. Infrequent trips for supplies were made with her friend Clyde Kluckhohn, who drove from Navajo country to Zuni to pick up Bunzel, and then on to Gallup, New Mexico, for hot baths and the dentist.

In her first season Bunzel was directed toward pottery by Boas. The Zunis at that time made pots for storing and cooling water, choosing metal containers available from traders for cooking. Pottery was ceremonially used and traded as well. Many pots were sold to an Anglo trader in Zuni in exchange for credit toward food and supplies. The trader in turn took the pots, and later silver jewelry, to tourist markets, where they were sold. Bunzel found that the women talked easily but in a nonspecific way about their craft, and she learned about pottery making by observation and participation. "From no woman in any pueblo did I get any rule of proportions," she noted in 1924.

[T]he most general principles I could elicit were "It must be even all around, not larger on one side than another. . . . '' The pueblo potter is guided entirely by her tactile sense and her unconscious feeling for proportion in mixing clay. We must therefore believe the potter when she says[,] "I carry all the designs in my head and never get them mixed up." (1929:49–53)

She became skilled at fashioning the vessels herself, and at one point she could walk about with a pot on her head, and climb a ladder balancing a pot with her hand. *The Pueblo Potter*, the result of her Zuni fieldwork, reflects Bunzel's identification with the thoughts of the women as they performed their craft. It also provided the first channel for an expression of Bunzel's lifelong interest in psychology—studying the artist and her inner feelings (Bunzel 1938a, 1953).

Bunzel's next major effort, sponsored by Elsie Clews Parsons, was a study of Zuni ceremonialism, several parts of which were published, along with work on folklore, by the Bureau of American Ethnology (BAE) (Bunzel 1932a, b, c, d). Bunzel found the Zunis more resistant in this sensitive ceremonial area and notes that her home was watched at night to see who came and went. She selected her informants from among young people or the elderly, whom she paid on a daily basis. One young man was from an influential family and made drawings of kachinas for her, which she used for reference when interviewing other informants. Her best informant, and perhaps best friend, at Zuni was an older, well-known man, a former governor of the pueblo, "Zuni Nick" Tumaka. This was one of her closest relationships, and she later confessed he "wanted to marry her." Nick died after Bunzel had been at Zuni several seasons. After his death an elder came and informed her that her old friend had died because he had given away his religion and had nothing with which to defend himself. According to Bunzel, "her family" and many other Zuni blamed her for his death.

Bunzel, while thorough in her fieldwork, never violated Zuni tradition as other anthropologists, most notoriously the Stevensons, had done before her. She did not take photographs of sensitive dances and never attempted to have inappropriate access to any kiva ceremonies that were strictly off-limits to outsiders. Upon arriving at Zuni one year after the BAE volume on ceremonial topics had been published, she was approached by a Zuni priest who had a copy of the book. He asked her if she wrote it, and if she had noted prayers in the volume. She translated some from the text. The priest confirmed that they had been accurately transcribed, and to her surprise he left without objection. She notes that many elderly Zunis recognized that such a publication would serve to preserve prayers, as well as having the obvious negative impact of making them public.

Her work at Zuni ultimately led to the completion of her doctorate at Columbia in 1927, with a thesis on pueblo pottery. *The Pueblo Potter*, a seminal work in the field, was the first to combine both art and psychology in an anthropological work. The formal degree, according to standard Columbia practice, was not granted until publication of the thesis two years later in 1929. Bunzel reports that she enjoyed the intellectual environment at Columbia, but never engaged in the broader social community. Because there were no openings in the regular academic schedule, Bunzel earned a very modest living teaching evening courses in anthropology at Columbia. She did not obtain a Trustee's Appointment for full-time work because, she feels, she was a woman. She similarly never received tenure. Moreover, there was no major support for the program in general, since Boas, because of his outspoken nature, was not popular with the administration. He relied heavily on small grants from individuals such as Elsie Clews Parsons. Bunzel reports that although she did not mind teaching, she much preferred doing her own work. Throughout her career Bunzel found that getting books and articles published was quite easy, especially with private funding from those such as Parsons. She wrote prolifically on her work in the Southwest, not just about Zuni but in *The Pueblo Potter* about Hopi, Acoma, and San Ildefonso, and about San Felipe as well (Bunzel 1928a, 1928c).

In the early 1930s Bunzel made several field trips to Mexico and Guatemala. She had been interested in Mexico because of its cultural relationship with the Southwest. When interviewing for a Guggenheim Fellowship, however, the chairman encouraged her to consider Guatemala rather than Mexico, as no American anthropologist had yet done any significant work there. She was persuaded and went to Guatemala to gain a general knowledge of the country, rather than with a particular research problem in mind. She met an American and traveled through the highlands on his motorcycle, ultimately becoming charmed by the village of Santo Tomas Chichicastenango and choosing it as the center of her work because of its importance as a ceremonial and market center. Zuni and Chichicastenango were similar in that both were ceremonial centers with traditional cultures functioning at a vibrant level. She spoke some Spanish and learned some Quiché. She quickly met a German priest, who allowed her to live in his home. Although she had two field trips of rather long duration (more than six months) in Guatemala, she never became as integrated into the local culture as she felt she had been at Zuni. This may have been the result of a lack of a specific focus for her work there.

Bunzel was thus one of the first American anthropologists to work in and publish about Guatemala, an area dominated until that time by German scholars. Out of this experience came several works, including a monograph on Chichicastenango (1952) and articles (Bunzel 1940, 1976). These reflected her growing interest in culture-and-personality: a study of alcoholism in two cultures, represented by two villages in Guatemala and Mexico.

Bunzel observed that alcohol provided a social setting for nearly all interaction in both places. She reported that in the town of Chamula, in Chiapas, Mexico, alcoholism was pervasive. Drinking was always social and never done alone. People functioned even when drunk, and there was no moral judgment about drunkenness. In Chichicastenango, although every transaction started with a drink, negative attitudes toward drunkenness prevailed. Consumption in the Guatemalan town was confined to market days and special fiestas at which pervasive drunkenness usually resulted, releasing built-up anger and frustration. Bunzel concluded that psychological factors accounted for the difference in drinking behavior, noting more extreme conflicts of frustration and hostility, repression and guilt, in Chichicastenango. While these conflicts were apparently not evident in Chamula, Bunzel notes that there the energy consumed by drinking reduced efforts at more productive activities. A factor of the drinking in both cultures was the profit to be made in serving alcohol to the Indians. Bunzel also saw how haciendas kept Indians in debt and the role alcohol played in this subjugation. In her scholarly article (1940) she recommended reforming labor laws to give greater independence and security to young people.

In the late 1930s Bunzel went to Spain; she felt she should become familiar with the country that had such an historical impact on Native Americans. She went to summer school there and spent most of her time in the south, perfecting the Spanish she had learned from the Guatemalan Indians. She was in Spain at the outbreak of the Spanish Revolution and found herself in Europe during World War II. Based in England at that time, she worked for the Office of War Information. She translated broadcasts for Spain, and incoming broadcasts as well.

Following the war Bunzel returned to New York and Columbia University. The balance of power in the postwar world had changed, and the academic community was responding to a new interest in other cultures that had begun to take root. Exemplary of the flourishing attitude was the introduction of a unique research group aimed at studying contemporary cultures around the world. Bunzel learned of the project through Benedict, who one night after a party asked Bunzel how she would spend a $100,000 grant were it forthcoming. Shortly afterward funding came from the Office of Naval Research, and the Research in Contemporary Cultures project was born. It dealt with the nations thought to be most relevant to the rebuilding of the postwar world. A research group was formed around each selected national culture (which included Russia, China, France, England, and Germany), consisting of a scholar and nine or ten members of that nationality who lived locally but who had grown up in their native countries. They were interviewed and conclusions were drawn, based on this small group, about their national character. The emphasis of the work was on a theoretical level. That is, the goal was to define how individuals of a given nation would react to increased American involvement on a global scale. Specific application of the findings was left to governmental analysis. Bunzel, who had developed an interest in China, directed that group, while Benedict had overall responsibility for the entire project. Final reports were generated but never published publicly.

The Research in Contemporary Cultures project reflected the development and application of Bunzel's interest in psychology. The research method most used for the project was that of interviewing, although no systematic approach was taken. Bunzel had taken her interest in psychology (first developed at Zuni under the tutelage of Benedict, who was then working on *Patterns of Culture* [1934a]) into the realm of culture-and-personality. Bunzel knew Karen Horney, and her neo-Freudian influence is evident in Bunzel's study on alcoholism in Central America with that study's emphasis on frustration, repression, and variety of cultural expression. In 1936 Abram Kardiner organized a seminar on the psychological aspects of culture at the New York Psychoanalytic Institute with Bunzel, Benedict, and Edward Sapir. Kardiner ultimately brought the weekly seminar to Columbia in 1937, where Ralph Linton and Cora Du Bois joined it. (This seminar no doubt influenced the direction of the postwar national character project.)

Reaching retirement age in the mid–1960s, Bunzel became less actively involved in anthropology. She continued to teach at Columbia and maintained an office there, occasionally reworking old papers. Her teaching had never been a source of great pleasure for her; she remarked that "sometimes one had stimulating students, most times not." One senses that Bunzel was an extremely private person and preferred the company of a few close friends. She maintained several lifelong relationships, mostly with her female colleagues. She never married. Bunzel was not sentimental about her relationships in the field. After her return to New York from Zuni, she gradually allowed her contacts there to lapse, the frequency of cards and letters dropping off. With one exception in 1938 she never returned to Zuni after her fieldwork came to an end there in 1929. Her Zuni family wrote to her for a time, having adopted her into the fold, but she did not write back often. She felt that when she left Zuni, she stepped into another life and other relationships.

There is little in Bunzel's Greenwich Village home that reveals her past. Only a single Zuni olla, more than a hundred years old and beautifully made, sits on a kitchen shelf. At the age of eighty-six and still very much the pragmatist, she will not offer her thoughts on what other directions her life might have taken. When commenting on her life and work, her warmest memories are not of her colleagues or her Zuni friends but of the New Mexico sky. She remembers "sleeping on the pueblo roof on summer nights, far from New York, and being awestruck at the spaciousness and beauty and intricacy of nature."

Note

1. All quotes, unless otherwise cited, are from interviews conducted with Ruth Bunzel in 1985. The authors wish to thank her for her cooperation during the interviews.

References and Works About Ruth Leah Bunzel

Pandey, Triloki Nath
1972   Anthropologists at Zuni. *Proceedings of the American Philosophical Society* 116 (4): 321–37.

Selected Works by Ruth Leah Bunzel

1928a Notes on the Katcina Cult in San Felipe. *Journal of American Folklore* 41:290–92.
1928b The Operation of Social Forces As Illustrated in a Study of Zuni Households. *Twenty-third International Congress of Americanists Abstracts*, no. 14.
1928c Further Notes on San Felipe. *Journal of American Folk Lore* 41:592.
1929   *The Pueblo Potter: A Study of Creative Imagination in Primitive Art.* New York: Columbia University Press.
1932a The Nature of Katcinas. *Bureau of American Ethnology (BAE) Annual Report* 47:837–1006. (Reprinted 1958 in *Reader in Comparative Religion*, A. W. Lessa and Evon Vogt, eds. Pp. 401–4.)
1932b Introduction. Zuni Ceremonialism. *BAE Annual Report* 47:467–554.
1932c Zuni Origin Myths. *BAE Annual Report* 47:545–609.
1932d Zuni Ritual Poetry. *BAE Annual Report* 47:611–835.
1932e Zuni Beliefs Reviewed. *El Palacio* 33:139–40.
1933a *Zuni Texts.* New York: G.E. Stechert and Co.
1933b Zuni. In *Handbook of American Indian Languages*. Franz Boas, ed. Part 3, pp. 385–515. Washington, D.C.: Government Printing Office.
1938a Art. In *General Anthropology*. Franz Boas, ed. Pp. 535–88. Boston: D.C. Heath.
1938b The Economic Organization of Primitive Peoples. In *General Anthropology*. Franz Boas, ed. Pp. 327–408. Boston: D. C. Heath.
1938c The Emergence. *Journal of American Folklore* 41:288–90.
1940   The Role of Alcoholism in Two Central American Cultures. *Psychiatry* 3:361–87.
1952   *Chichicastenango, a Guatemalan Village.* Locust Valley, N.Y.: J. J. Augustin Publishers.

1953 Psychology of the Pueblo Potter. In *Primitive Heritage*. Margaret Mead and Nicolas Calas, eds. Pp. 266–75. New York: Random House.

1964a Report on Regional Conferences (Anthropology and World Affairs). *Current Anthropology* 5:430, 437–42.

1964b The Self-effacing Zuni of New Mexico. In *The Americas on the Eve of Discovery*. Harold Driver, ed. Pp. 80–92. Englewood Cliffs, N.J.: Prentice-Hall.

1976 Chamula and Chichicastenango: A Reexamination. In *Cross-Cultural Approaches to the Study of Alcohol*. Michael W. Everett, Jack O. Waddell, Dwight B. Heath, eds. Pp. 21–22. The Hague: Mouton.

Coauthored Works

Bunzel, Ruth, and Margaret Mead
1960 *The Golden Age of American Anthropology*. New York: George Braziller and Co.

DAVID M. FAWCETT AND TERI MCLUHAN

Frederica de Laguna

(1906–)

Frederica de Laguna is an American ethnologist and archaeologist especially known for her pioneering work in northwestern North America. Responsible for organizing the first Department of Anthropology at Bryn Mawr College.

Frederica Annis Lopez de Leo de Laguna was born on October 3, 1906, the first child of two distinguished philosophers, both of whom taught at Bryn Mawr College. Frederica and her younger brother, Wallace, who became a geologist, grew up in a vigorous intellectual atmosphere, and she "never imagined any other setting or career than academic".[1] She might have added "adventurous," for both intellectually and in the more traditional physical sense, she has been a notable pioneer in anthropology.

De Laguna early acquired a sensitivity to other cultures through her father's enthralling accounts of his adventures as a young man teaching English in the Philippines and of his travels in Japan.

Named for her father's favorite sister, Frederica, she became, as she puts it, "the apple of his eye." He looked after every aspect of her welfare, made up stories and songs for her, and helped her with her homework and later studies. During her early childhood she was quite sickly, but by her teens she had outgrown her maladies.

As a girl, she twice went with her family on sabbaticals. On their first leave (1914–15), the de Lagunas spent the winter at Cambridge and the spring at Oxford. There, eight-year-old de Laguna "discovered my nationality," when her British playmates tied her to a tree because they said America was selling arms to Germany.

On her family's return to Bryn Mawr, de Laguna attended the progressive Phoebe Anne Thorne School. Through private tutoring she learned French well enough to be enrolled as a boarder in the Lycée de Jeunes Filles at Versailles during her parents' second sabbatical (1921–22). This was a second deep cross-cultural immersion, especially since her best friend at school was from Martinique. Throughout her schooling, her father sharply watched her progress, providing her with primary documents for whatever event was being discussed.

She entered Bryn Mawr on a scholarship in 1923. De Laguna found much that she expected; what surprised her was the role-playing required by her dual status as both faculty daughter and student. Her academic career was brilliant, and she planned a double major in economics and psychology, until a bout of pleurisy forced her to drop the latter. During her senior year she became so entranced by Trevelyan's account of Garibaldi that her first published book, in 1930, was an adventure story for boys based on his Sicilian campaign.

At graduation she won the prestigious Bryn Mawr European Fellowship, but before going abroad she first took a year in anthropology at Columbia University. Her parents had been much impressed by a lecture given by Franz Boas, and they thought that anthropology might satisfy their daughter's efforts to find a unifying human discipline and also suit her love of the outdoors.

Before attending Columbia, her father gave her the second edition of Alfred Kroeber's *Anthropology*. She found it "supremely boring"—a verdict she reaffirmed in 1985, stating that in the twenties nobody knew enough to ask the really intriguing questions in anthropology. Still, she set off for Columbia full of confidence.

She soon discovered that anthropology could not yet bring together her many interests. At his weekly seminar Boas listened to her criticize the methodology of Huntington's *Civilization and Climate* but made no comment, a sign of approval. She enjoyed his "haphazard" linguistics course in which Ella Deloria* was the chief informant, and was not required to take statistics. Ruth Benedict's* course in folklore and Gladys Reichard's* in social organization both stimulated her. Boas had just published *Primitive Art* and, feeling nostalgic about the Eskimo, he suggested that for her dissertation she explore the possible relationship between Upper Paleolithic and Inuit (Eskimo) art. Several scholars were then suggesting that the Inuit were the direct descendants of Cro-Magnon man. De Laguna herself had been fascinated by the Eskimo since girlhood, when her father had given her Stefansson's *The Friendly Arctic* and *My Life as an Eskimo*. These and other books made her "crazy to go to the Arctic." At age thirteen she wrote to the explorer Donald MacMillan offering to chew his boots if he would let her go north with him.

Taking up her European fellowship in 1928, de Laguna first went to England for a brief introduction into British prehistory and then joined a field school in the Dordogne where, like most of the party, she fell ill. Nothing, however, could alter the excitement of the excavation or of meeting Abbé Breuil, who was sketching in the cave of Trois Frères. The Upper Paleolithic was "always alive" for de Laguna, who later passed this sense of it on to her students.

Moving next to Paris, she attended lectures by Breuil and learned from him how to draw with a camera obscura. She also met other French anthropologists before she returned to London for a seminar with Bronislaw Malinowski. Strongly anti-American at the time, he baited the young scholar unmercifully. She, in turn, was disillusioned by the seminar. Although she greatly admired his Trob-riand writings, when Malinowski greeted her some years later as his "spiritual child," she was unwilling to acknowledge the relationship. After some inde-pendent reading in Danish prehistory, she followed Boas's advice and went to Copenhagen to consult with the great Arctic archaeologist Therkel Mathiassen. This was a critical turning point in her life. He invited her to help him excavate in Greenland that summer, and the planned six weeks turned into six months.

Despite the rugged sea voyages and rigorous field conditions, the experience was so exciting and intellectually challenging that de Laguna knew nothing would stop her from becoming a professional anthropologist, a decision that later led her to break her engagement to an Englishman she had met at Columbia.

The dig was the first professional excavation in Greenland. Mathiassen and de Laguna unearthed the hitherto unknown Inugsuk culture dating back to Norse times, and came to have a profound respect for each other's abilities. To de Laguna it seemed as if her childhood dreams of Arctic adventuring had come true.

Upon her return to Columbia she wrote her dissertation (published in 1932 and 1933), concluding there was no certain proof or disproof of a historic connection between Upper Paleolithic and Eskimo art.

By the time she received her Ph.D. (1933), she had already done pioneering research in Alaska (1930, 1931, 1932, and in 1933 with Dr. Kaj Birket-Smith). She had located numerous archaeological sites in Prince William Sound and in Cook Inlet, excavating the most important of them, particularly Yukon Island with its Kachemak Bay culture. These years of work led to *The Archaeology of Cook Inlet, Alaska* (de Laguna 1934), a publication setting up the basic frame-work of south Alaskan archaeology so solidly that the Alaska Historical Society reissued it in 1975. The archaeology of Prince William Sound is described in *Chugach Prehistory* (de Laguna 1956) as a companion piece to Birket-Smith's ethnography *The Chugach Eskimo* (1953). Earlier she and Birket-Smith co-authored *The Eyak Indians of the Copper River Delta, Alaska* (1938).

In 1935 de Laguna launched another pioneering anthropological survey, this time going down the Tanana and Yukon rivers as far as Holy Cross in two skiffs that she and her male assistants built at Nenana. They did not find the hoped-for traces of early humans but located more recent archaeological sites throughout a vast area. De Laguna also collected Indian myths and a priceless collection of Ingalik masks, and she alerted other anthropologists to the valuable, but unpub-lished linguistic work of Father Jules Jette—work she saw at Nulato. This survey was the basis for her ambitious *The Prehistory of Northern North America as Seen from the Yukon* (de Laguna 1947).

De Laguna's next field research (1936) was on the Pima Indian Reservation in Arizona, where she spent six months surveying the social conditions for the U.S. Soil Conservation Service. She asserts that this was the only time in her long career that she felt her gender to be a drawback. Although officially des-ignated as chief of the party, she found that the men had secretly elected another male, without informing her. Since the project proved to be a boondoggle, she was glad that a National Research Council Fellowship enabled her to quit. Nevertheless, her Southwest experience engendered warm ties with other anthropologists interested in the area, especially with Dr. Harold Colton and his wife at the Museum of Northern Arizona. The fellowship allowed her more than a year to study in various museums and libraries in the United States and Canada.

In 1938 she went to Denmark to study the Alaskan collections she and Birket-Smith had assembled. The trip was largely financed by royalties from the second of two detective stories she had published in 1937 and 1938. She was also a delegate from the University of Pennsylvania Museum to the International Congress of Anthropological and Ethnological Sciences being held in Copenhagen.

During World War II de Laguna joined the first class of Waves in the U.S. Navy, leaving the service in 1945 as lieutenant commander. By 1947, however, she was back in the field with Douglas Leechman, of the National Museum of Canada, and a former Bryn Mawr student, Catharine McClellan, making an archaeological survey of the area to be flooded by the Saint Lawrence Seaway. In 1949 she resumed long-term anthropological investigation in Alaska. The first season was devoted to locating archaeological sites in southeastern Alaska and talking about them with elderly Tlingit. She lived in the Tlingit village of Angoon (1950) and at Yakutat (1952 and 1954). From there she embarked on four field seasons (1954, 1958, 1960, and 1968), with the Athapaskan Atna of the Copper River. The overall aim of this extensive research was to understand the specific cultural histories of a continuum of native societies in coastal and interior northwestern America.

On these trips de Laguna was assisted by graduate students from various institutions, including Bryn Mawr, and McClellan became a junior collaborator on three of them. The publications from the work reveal de Laguna's growing interest in a holistic approach to cultural patterning through time. Her earlier studies had been much influenced by Danish scholars who built their theories in various ways from circumpolar distributions of culture traits. These influences are apparent in *The Prehistory of Northern North America as Seen from the Yukon*, although in that work, de Laguna went beyond earlier formulations to introduce the concepts of a North Pacific Cultural Continuum and a later Circum-Pacific Cultural Drift. In *The Story of a Tlingit Community* (de Laguna 1960a), she drew together into a unified whole the archaeology, ethnohistory, and ethnography of Angoon. This was one of the first of such studies of a North American Indian society. Her Yakutat research resulted in a volume on archaeology (de Laguna, Riddell et al. 1964) and in her crowning three-volume *Under Mount Saint Elias* (de Laguna, 1972). This work has been hailed not only by professional anthropologists but by the Yakutat Tlingit themselves, who honored the author at a potlatch in 1986.

After the war, too, de Laguna had read the third edition of Kroeber's *Anthropology*, and this time found it to be doing what she "had wanted anthropology to be doing all along"—to tie together human behavior, values, patterns, and style, and to incorporate human history. When de Laguna was visiting professor at Berkeley in 1959, she and her mother enjoyed discussing with Kroeber his key ideas in this and other books.

De Laguna had held various low-paying jobs at the University of Pennsylvania Museum (1931–34), which also helped sponsor her early field trips. In 1938 she began teaching at Bryn Mawr. Anthropology had never been taught there and was very much on trial. At first she could give only one elective course, but she did so well that a fund raised in honor of the retiring president, Marion E. Park, enabled her to set up a field school in Arizona and add a course in American Archaeology. After the war she helped organize and became the first chair of the joint department of sociology and anthropology, and in 1967 of the Department of Anthropology in its own right. Building the department was a struggle, but it soon attracted many undergraduates and growing numbers of graduates. De Laguna recalls the last busy years of administration and teaching as a pleasant time. At her retirement in 1975 she won the Lindback award for teaching and was made a Kenan Professor, which carried with it money for research. The same year, she also was elected to the National Academy of Science, at the same time as Margaret Mead.*

College retirement did not mean professional retirement. In 1977 she published her autobiographical *Voyage to Greenland: A Personal Initiation into Anthropology*, and in 1979 she once again went to Greenland, recording texts at Upernavik, where she first worked with Matthiassen in 1929, and revisiting the tiny island of Tunungassoq where she first resolved to become an anthropologist. In 1978 and 1985 she was a guest at archaeological digs in Alaska—at her old site on Yukon Island, Cook Inlet, and at Karluk, Kodiak. Other travels were less directly tied to her past research but always had goals, for example learning about prehistoric and Viking sites in Scotland. On a visit to her former graduate student, Professor Hiroke Sue Hara in Japan, she lectured on various northern topics and the role of women's colleges in America. She also gave a course on the history of anthropology at the University of Pennsylvania and a seminar at Bryn Mawr on A. I. Hallowell's work.

De Laguna had come to know Hallowell when she was building up the Bryn Mawr department and sometimes invited staff from the University of Pennsylvania to give necessary courses. She in turn sometimes taught part-time at the university. Both she and her mother developed warm ties with Hallowell and Loren Eiseley and their wives, benefiting especially from Hallowell's concepts of the self and worldview.

So dynamic and productive a figure has, of course, held numerous offices in both local and national professional organizations. She was president-elect (1965–66) and president (1966–67) of the American Anthropological Association (AAA) in the stormy years when it was in a financial crisis and becoming politicized over issues relating to the Vietnam War. De Laguna maintained that if the constitution did not specify a political role, political expressions should then be a matter for individual, not AAA, action. She gave service of a different kind when as a council member of the AAA (1960), she edited and published *Selected Papers from the American Anthropologist: 1888–1920* (de Laguna 1960b). Begun in 1958 by de Laguna and her graduate students, this volume helped lay the groundwork for the now flourishing field of the history of anthropology. Royalties from the book go to the AAA, which republished it in 1976.

De Laguna considers some of her important contributions to anthropology to be her recognition of the true nature of prehistoric Eskimo burins (items that had been dismissed as ''boot-creasers'' by others) and her correct prediction in 1930 that a stone lamp with a human figure in the bowl belonged to Kachemak Bay III culture. That her opening up of south Alaskan archaeology has stood the test of time is attested to by the republication of her major monographs on the area. But she cites *Under Mount Saint Elias* (1972) as her best work, and surely it is unmatched by any other study of North American natives. Embodying an enormous amount of archaeological, ethnohistoric, and ethnographic data, it shows the patterning of Yakutat Tlingit culture through time and reveals the interplay of the Tlingit worldview and the individual. It well reflects the influences of her mentors Boas, Kroeber, and Hallowell.

She declares that she never ''felt prepared to do theory,'' but several of her papers, her comments in the volume of selected papers from the *American Anthropologist*, and above all, her presidential address of 1967 set out a consistent viewpoint revolving around questions of objectivity and subjectivity in fieldwork, values, the individual and culture, and the historic sweep of cultures. In her address she spoke out forcefully against overspecialization, for she sees anthropology as the ''only discipline that offers a conceptual schema for the whole content of human experience'' (1968).

Note

1. Unless otherwise cited, all quotes are from interviews with Frederica de Laguna in 1985.

Selected Works by Frederica de Laguna

1932–33   A Comparison of Eskimo and Paleolithic Art. *American Journal of Archaeology* 36 (4) and 38 (1): 77–107.

1934   *The Archaeology of Cook Inlet, Alaska*. Philadelphia: University of Pennsylvania Press for the University Museum. (Reprinted 1975 by the Alaska Historical Society with new foreword, preface, and plates.)

1935   Expedition to the Yukon. *The University Museum Bulletin* (December). Pp. 50–57.

1936a   Preliminary Report of an Archaeological and Geological Reconnaissance of the Middle and Lower Yukon Valley. *Miscellanea* 1 (2): 31–40. Philadelphia: American Philosophical Society.

1936b   Indian Masks from the Lower Yukon. *American Anthropologist* 38 (4): 569–85.

1937   A Preliminary Sketch of the Eyak Indians, Copper River Delta, Alaska. *Twenty-fifth Anniversary Studies*. Pp. 63–75. Philadelphia Anthropological Society.

1939   A Pottery Vessel from Kodiak Island, Alaska. *American Antiquity* 4 (4): 334–43.

1940a Lévy-Bruhl's Contributions to the Study of Primitive Mentality. *The Philosophical Review* (September): 552–56.

1940b Eskimo Lamps and Pots. *Journal of the Royal Anthropological Institute* 70 (1): 53–76.

1946   The Importance of the Eskimo in Northeastern Archaeology. In *Man in Northeastern North America*. Papers of the Robert S. Peabody Foundation. Frederick Johnson, ed. Vol. 3, pp. 106–42. Andover, Mass.

1947   *The Prehistory of Northern North America as Seen from the Yukon*. Society for American Archaeology, Memoir No. 3.

1952   Some Dynamic Forces in Tlingit Society. *Southwestern Journal of Anthropology* 8:1–12.

1953   *Some Problems in the Relationship Between Tlingit Archaeology and Ethnology*. Memoirs of the Society for American Archaeology 9:53–57.

1954   Tlingit Ideas About the Individual. *Southwestern Journal of Anthropology* 10:172–91.

1956   *Chugach Prehistory: The Archaeology of Prince William Sound, Alaska*. University of Washington, Publications in Anthropology 13. Seattle: University of Washington Press.

1957   Some Problems of Objectivity in Ethnology. *Man* 228:179–82.

1958   Geological Confirmation of Native Traditions. *Yakutat Alaska* 23 (4): 434.

1960a *The Story of a Tlingit Community: A Problem in the Relationship Between Archaeological, Ethnological and Historical Methods. BAE, Bulletin 172*. Washington, D.C.: GPO.

1960b *Selected Papers from the American Anthropologist, 1888–1920*. Evanston, Illinois: Row, Peterson, and Co. (As ed.) (Reprinted 1976 by the American Anthropological Association.)

1961a Salvage of Ethnological Data and Its Problems. *Symposium on Salvage Archaeology*. John M. Corbett, ed. Pp. 49–55. Washington, D.C.: National Park Service.

1961b An Anthropologist Examines the Campus. *The Nurture of Scientists in America*. Pp. 20–26. Columbia University School of Engineering.

1962   Intemperate Reflections on Arctic and Subarctic Archaeology. *Prehistoric Cultural Between the Arctic and Temperate Zones of North America*. Arctic Institute of North America Technical Paper No. 11. John M. Campbell, ed. Pp. 164–69. Toronto: Arctic Institute of North America.

1963   Yakutat Canoes. *Folk* ("Essays Presented to Kaj Birket-Smith on his Seventieth Birthday, January 20, 1963.") 5:219–29.

1965   Childhood Among the Yakutat Tlingit. *Context and Meaning in Cultural Anthropology, in Honor of A. Irving Hallowell*. Melford E. Spiro, ed. Pp. 3–23. New York: Free Press.

1968   Presidential Address—1967: On Anthropological Inquiry. *American Anthropologist* 70 (3): 469–76.

1970   The Atna of the Copper River, Alaska: The World of Men and Animals. *Folk* 11/12:17–26.

1972   *Under Mount Saint Elias: The History and Culture of the Yakutat Tlingit*. Smithsonian Contributions to Anthropology, no. 7 (in three parts). (Transcriptions of native music by David P. McAllester.)

1975 Matrilineal Kin Groups in Northwestern North America. In *Proceedings: Northern Athapaskan Conference*, 1971. Vol. 1, pp. 17–145. Canadian Ethnology Service, Paper No. 27. Ottawa: National Museum of Man Mercury Series.

1977 *Voyage to Greenland: A Personal Initiation into Anthropology* (autobiography). New York: W. W. Norton and Co.

1979 Therkel Mathiassen and the Beginnings of Eskimo Archaeology. In *Thule Eskimo Culture: An Anthropological Retrospect*. Archaeological Survey of Canada, Paper No. 88. Allen P. McCartney, ed. Pp. 10–53. Ottawa: National Museum of Man Mercury Series.

1981 The Role of Women's Colleges in the United States. *Bulletin of the Institute for Women's Studies*. Ochanomizu University, Tokyo. Pp. 1–2 (Japanese introduction); pp. 2–11 (text in English); and pp. 11–20 (translation into Japanese by Dr. Hiroko Hara).

1983 Aboriginal Tlingit Sociopolitical Organization. *The Development of Political Organization in Native North America*. Proceedings of the American Ethnological Society, 1979. Elizabeth Tooker, ed. Pp. 71–85.

Coauthored Works

de Laguna, Frederica, and Kaj Birket-Smith (senior author)
1938 *The Eyak Indians of the Copper River Delta, Alaska*. Det Kgl. Danske Videnskabernes Selskab. Copenhagen.

deLaguna, Frederica, Henry B. Collins (senior author), et al.
1972 *The Far North: 2000 Years of American Eskimo and Indian Art*. Washington, D.C.: National Gallery of Art.

deLaguna, Frederica, and Catharine McClellan
1981 Ahtna. *Handbook of North American Indians*. William C. Sturtevant, gen. ed. Vol. 6, *Subarctic*, pp. 641–63. June Helm, vol. ed. Washington, D.C.: Smithsonian Institution.

de Laguna, Frederica, Francis A. Riddell, et al.
1964 *Archaeology of the Yakutat Bay Area, Alaska. BAE, Bulletin 192*. Washington, D.C.: GPO.

CATHARINE MCCLELLAN

Ella Cara Deloria
(1888–1971)

Ella Cara Deloria was a Native American (Yankton Dakota) anthropologist and linguist known for her ethnographic fieldwork with three Siouan-speaking groups: the Dakota, Lakota, and Nakota.

Deloria, whose native name was Anpetu Waste Win (Beautiful Day Woman), was born during a snowstorm on January 30, 1888, on the Yankton Dakota Reservation at Lake Andes, South Dakota. She was the eldest of four children born to Philip Joseph (Tipi Sapa, or "Black Lodge") and Mary Sully Bordeau Deloria, the granddaughter of Irish artist Thomas Sully. Ella's native name was seldom used in her interaction with her people, and she later became known as Aunt Ella to native kin and younger anthropologists.[1]

Although she spent most of her formative years among the Hunkpapa and Sihasapa Lakota (Sioux) on Standing Rock Reservation, Ella Deloria, along with other native North Americans, became a student of her natal Siouan language and cultures. Deloria conducted much of her research on Standing Rock, Pine Ridge, and Rosebud reservations and used the general term *Dakota* to cover all the dialects spoken by these western Teton groups. Possibly because her father converted to Christianity and was the first Native American to become an Episcopal minister (founding St. Elizabeth's Mission and its school near Wakpala), Ella's involvement with the people at Standing Rock seems to have been largely confined to church-related and educational activities. Participation in indigenous rituals and ceremonies was largely lacking; it was part of the missionizing and educational milieu of the time to negate native lifestyles and strive for education in the context of the dominant society.

Undoubtedly, her father influenced her choice of a teaching career, and she is remembered by reservation residents for her contributions as an educator. Her training included schooling at St. Elizabeth's Mission and All Saints School (also Episcopalian) in Sioux Falls, South Dakota. She won a scholarship and attended Oberlin College, in Ohio, from 1911 to 1913, when she transferred to

Teachers' College, Columbia University, and finished with a B.S. in 1915. She returned to teach at All Saints and in 1923 took a job with Haskell Institute, a Bureau of Indian Affairs school in Kansas, where she taught physical education and dance in an experimental program. She was also secretary for American Indian work of the National Board of the YWCA in New York City, illustrating a pattern of professionalism followed by some native women.

Her career as an anthropological linguist began when Franz Boas invited her to teach the various Siouan dialects to the anthropology students at Columbia. Not only did she work with Boas, with whom she coauthored *Dakota Grammar* (1941), she also worked with Ruth Benedict.* Benedict's influence may be seen in her later work, for she became absorbed in producing a dictionary that probed the psychological implications of the Lakota language. This project, which occupied her from 1962 until her death, was initially supported by a National Science Foundation grant (1962–66) to the University of South Dakota's Institute of Indian Studies.

Her life as an educator was constantly interspersed with fieldwork, which began around 1927. She resigned her teaching position at Haskell to devote time to Dakota research and to publish scholarly works with Boas until his death in 1942. She also sent material on traditional Dakota culture to Ruth Benedict. Deloria traveled to most Sioux reservations to interview elders on Siouan language and cultural topics. She was amused that most Siouan speakers made remarks about her, believing that she could not understand or speak their language; and they were surprised and delighted when she responded in their native tongue. This extended fieldwork resulted in the above-mentioned *Dakota Grammar* and in *Dakota Texts* (Deloria 1932), a rich bilingual collection of folk tales, legends, and *Iktomi* (Trickster tales), told by storytellers from several reservations. *Dakota Texts* is valuable for its commentaries dealing with translation and semantic difficulties, the performance features of stories, and statements regarding the cultural context of the tales.

Deloria also translated, arranged, and annotated the works of other scholars. Particularly important are the George Bushotter manuscripts, a series of texts on Dakota life written in 1887 while Bushotter worked for the Bureau of American Ethnology (BAE) under James Owen Dorsey. Deloria's annotations and comments on these materials remain unpublished. In addition, she translated texts recorded by two missionaries: Gideon and Samuel Pond's collection of Santee Sioux tales and personal histories.

In 1937 Boas asked Deloria to verify and correct myths compiled by James R. Walker, a physician who lived on the Pine Ridge Reservation from 1896 to 1914 (see Jahner 1983). Deloria worked on both the linguistic/phonetic aspects and the content of Walker's materials. She spoke with one of Walker's narrators, Edgar Fire Thunder (age 78), in investigations of a secret holy men's society reported by George Sword. She also interviewed Ten Fingers, possibly the grandson of the holy man Finger whom Walker had interviewed, and talked to various people on the reservations. In letters to Boas she frankly discussed which stories people recognized (those of Left Heron and other informants) and which they felt were not really Dakota myths (e.g., George Sword's stories). Since Deloria found no variant tales of those that Sword had related to Walker, she concluded that these stories were examples of creative fiction rather than oral tradition. She recognized that gifted Lakota storytellers such as Sword had elaborated on traditional tales and even incorporated aspects of European folklore with Dakota elements in their stories (Jahner 1983).

Ella's letters to Boas reflected the conflict between her professional commitments and deeply felt kinship obligations. She took care of her father during a long illness and lived for much of her life with her sister, Mary Susan, whom she helped support. Mary Susan, an artist known as Mary Sully, did the artwork for *Speaking of Indians* (Deloria 1944b), Deloria's popular account of traditional Dakota culture. Deloria often spoke of taking care of her nephews (Vine Deloria, Jr., among them) and obviously derived pleasure in her role as aunt. Her attitude toward Siouan kinship displayed analytical and purposive direction, for she once told her great-nephew, "I am really your Grandmother in the Lakota way, but you can call me 'Aunt Ella,' too." Her perspective reflected typical Lakota incorporativeness regarding kinship, which she often conferred upon younger ethnographer-colleagues, for whom she acted as "aunt." This speaks to Lakota perceptions of proper behavior for women.

Ella and Mary Susan exemplify two early Siouan female professionals—one an anthropologist and the other an artist—who provided emotional support to one another during their sojourns in New York City. Though they did not express this culture conflict, the two sisters may be viewed as two professional native women who faced the dilemma of choosing between careers in both white and native worlds. Indeed, during Ella's lifetime this author noticed subtle changes in her attitudes toward Dakota identity. In the cultural context of the early twentieth century, Ella had remarked of her cousin, "Poor Anna, she married a full-blood." However, years later when one of her nephews married a full-blood, she seemed inexplicably pleased.

In many ways, Ella Deloria stood within and outside her own culture. Insiders are those persons who are socialized from an early age as participants in a particular culture, as Deloria was. Many native ethnographers of her era and earlier, such as Francis and Bright Eyes La Flesche of the Omaha, were primarily viewed as informants or assistants to ethnographers from outside the culture. These ethnographers may be professionally trained or amateur, usually male and Caucasian, who as "friends of Indians" believe themselves "experts" on Indians. They are sometimes inclined to think that they know more about Indians than the Indians themselves know. In developing her writing and analytical skills to interpret the insider's perspective—the "emic" voice (see Medicine 1980)—Deloria did not experience alienation from her Dakota identity as do some native people who become professional ethnographers through university training.

While *Dakota Grammar* is significant for researchers in Native American linguistics and bilingual education, *Dakota Texts* and *Speaking of Indians* are valuable to students of ethnic literature. *Dakota Texts*, a scholarly work, contains folktales recorded directly from storytellers. These are accompanied by free and literal translations, as well as commentaries on Dakota grammar and customs. Deloria's valuable footnotes to the stories have made literary analysis of old texts accessible to modern scholars (Medicine 1980).

Speaking of Indians, intended for a primarily white readership, examines both traditional and contemporary Indian life through Ella's devoutly Christian perspective; yet she retains her reverence for traditional Dakota spiritual concerns, such as the sun dance and the vision quest. The book is divided into three sections. The first part rejects stereotyped portrayals of Indians and discusses them as people with "a scheme of life that worked," after a line in Stephen Vincent Benet's poem *Western Star*. With the coming of European settlers, Deloria found that Indian tribal societies were forced to cope with rapid social change toward assimilation and were further damaged by a tendency to view all tribes as the same. The second part of the book delineates the importance of kinship obligations among the Sioux, especially the contrast between the white culture's emphasis on acquiring possessions and the Sioux culture's value of sharing as expressed through giveaways (Picotte and Pavich 1983). In this section Deloria also mentions the egalitarian nature of Sioux society: "Outsiders seeing women keep to themselves have frequently expressed a snap judgment that they were regarded as inferior to the noble male. The simple fact is that woman had her own place and man his; they were not the same and neither inferior nor superior" (1944:39). The third part of *Speaking of Indians* examines the obstacles facing the Sioux after they were relocated to reservations, following the decimation of the buffalo herds and the loss of the nomadic way of life. She asserts that based on their notions of kinship, "the Indians believed that the mighty leaders in Washington would indeed care for their Indian children" (Picotte and Pavich 1983:xvii). Although the tone of the book is sometimes viewed as "conciliatory," it concludes with a call for justice and basic human rights for American Indians (Picotte and Pavich 1983:xviii).

During her sixties and seventies Deloria continued her field research with brief interludes of full-time work: as the director of St. Elizabeth's School (1955–58) and briefly at the Sioux Indian Museum in Rapid City and the W. H. Over Museum at the University of South Dakota (Vermillion). She also supported herself through small research grants, lecturing, writing, and consulting work; but her limited income greatly handicapped her literary output. Columbia transferred her notes and manuscripts to the American Philosophical Society in Philadelphia, which also holds the Deloria-Boas correspondence; and she was never able to work with these materials again. Her later materials are stored at the University of South Dakota. Her last concentrated writing endeavor occurred while she was living in a motel in Vermillion. After suffering a stroke in 1970, she died the following year.

Deloria's body of work remains among the fullest accounts of Dakota culture in the native language. It is unique as a native woman's perspective, which had previously been lacking in writings on the Lakota/Dakota/Nakota peoples, and as an interpretation of Dakota reality to other peoples. Though acknowledged by her colleagues Margaret Mead,* Jeannette Mirsky, and Esther Goldfrank* for having collected this body of information, this author feels that many contemporary Siouan scholars recognize her influence as a full-fledged ethnographer. She produced a definitive dictionary and grammar, provided thorough descriptions of traditional social organization and religious life, edited and translated texts dictated by various storytellers, and composed commentaries and annotations to these texts. At the same time, she honored her family obligations as a Dakota woman and left a lasting legacy for scholars and for the culture that had sustained her.

Note

1. This writer and her family lived in Vermillion, South Dakota (1968–69), where Aunt Ella became a part of the household—coming almost every day for dinner and visiting. Much of my contribution is based upon this interaction.

References and Works About Ella Cara Deloria

Demallie, Raymond J.
1980   Ella Cara Deloria. In *NAW II*. Barbara Sicherman et al., eds. Pp. 183–85. Cambridge: Belknap Press of Harvard University.
Jahner, Elaine A., ed.
1983   Introduction. *Lakota Myth*, by James R. Walker. Lincoln: University of Nebraska Press.
Medicine, Bea
1980   Ella C. Deloria, The Emic Voice. *Melus* (Multi-Ethic Literature in the U.S.) 7(4):23–30.
Murray, Janette K.
1974   Ella Deloria: A Biographical Sketch and Literary Analysis. Unpublished Ph.D. Diss., University of North Dakota.
Picotte, Agnes, and Paul N. Pavich
1983   Introductory Notes. *Speaking of Indians*. Vermillion, S.D.: State Publishing Company.

Selected Works by Ella Cara Deloria

1929   The Sun Dance of the Oglala Sioux. *Journal of American Folklore* 42 (166): 354–413.
1932   *Dakota Texts*. New York: G. E. Stechert and Co.
1944a   Dakota Treatment of Murderers. *American Philosophical Society Proceedings* 88:368–71.
1944b   *Speaking of Indians*. New York: Friendship Press.
1954   Short Dakota Texts, Including Conversations. *International Journal of American Linguistics* 20 (1):17–22.
1962   Easter Day at a Yankton Dakota Church. *Museum News* 23:4–5. University of South Dakota.

1967   Some Notes on the Yanktons. *Museum News* 28:3–4, 5–6. University of South Dakota.

Coauthored Works

Deloria, Ella, and Franz Boas
1933   Notes on the Dakota, Teton Dialect. *International Journal of American Linguistics* 8:97–121.
1941   *Dakota Grammar*. Memoirs of the National Academy of Sciences 23, Second Memoir. Washington, D.C.: Government Printing Office.
Deloria, Ella, and Jay Brandon
1961   The Origin of the Courting Flute. *Museum News* 22:6–7. University of South Dakota.

Unpublished Manuscripts

Written by Ella Deloria and housed in the Institute of Indian Studies, University of South Dakota, include:

Courtship and Marriage.
Cultural Insights for Education of Indian Children.
Cultural Insights for Ministry to the Indian People.
Dakota Names with English Translations.
The Dakota Way of Life. 392 pp.
Lakota Dictionary.
Learning Dakota.
Major Groupings of the Dakota Sioux Peoples.
The Man Who Came to Teach and Die.
Map Showing the Locations of Indian Bands in Dakotas.
Medical Terms.
1963 Midwest Indian Youth Leadership Seminar. Eau Claire, Wisc. 6 pp.
Monosyllabic Terms. 16 pp.
100 Item Test List. 17 pp.
Origin Story of Peyote.
Preparations of the Bride.
Rites and Ceremonials of the Teton. 247 pp.
The Santee Sun Dance. 3 pp.
Societies are Predestined in the Animal World: A Legend to Explain Dakota Societies.
Stems in Dakota. 100 pp.
Story about Ella Deloria's Father in Cheyenne Country. 8 pp.
Story of Paha Wakan.
Ti' you spaye (Social Kinship).
Tranvestitism. 8 pp.
Yankton Monument.

BEATRICE MEDICINE

Frances Theresa Densmore

(1867–1957)

Frances Theresa Densmore was a pioneer American ethnomusicologist, known especially for her prolific recordings and publications on North American Indian music.

Born in Red Wing, Minnesota, on May 21, 1867, to Benjamin and Sarah Adalaide Greenland Densmore, Frances Densmore was the granddaughter of Judge Orrin Densmore and was raised with a younger sister, Margaret Louise; a brother, William York, died in infancy. Her father, a civil engineer, established and operated the Red Wing Iron Works with his brother Daniel from 1866 to 1912. Her mother "was greatly devoted to her family and her church" and was actively involved "in all things pertaining to the welfare and upbuilding of the community" (*Daily Republican Eagle* 1920). As Densmore explained, in her childhood she often heard Indian music coming from a Sioux encampment on Prairie Island in the Mississippi River, which was within view of the Densmore home. With her mother's encouragement she became fascinated with these "interesting people."

The Densmore family was musical, and Frances began to study piano and harmony at an early age. After attending public schools, she went to the Oberlin Conservatory of Music, where she studied piano, organ, and harmony from 1884 to 1886. Following several years of employment as a music teacher and church organist in St. Paul and Red Wing, she went to Boston to study piano with Carl Baermann and counterpoint with John K. Paine of Harvard. While there, she learned of the work Alice Cunningham Fletcher* had started with the Omaha Indians in 1880. With the urging of John Comfort Fillmore, she wrote to Fletcher about her own interest in American Indian music. Fletcher's reply, which was highly supportive, marked a turning point: "If she had been less gracious in her response, it is probable that I would not have taken up the study of Indian music" (Densmore 1942:528).

In 1893 Densmore began a ten-year preparatory period of study during which

Fletcher was a major teacher, mentor, and friend. Continuing to teach piano, to serve as choir director and organist, and to give public lectures on musicological subjects (including Wagnerian operas), Densmore heard more Indian singing at the 1893 Chicago World's Fair, where Fletcher was among participants in a special Congress of Anthropology (Lurie 1966). In 1895 Densmore added American Indian music to her lecture topics and with permission illustrated her lecture with some of Fletcher's materials, a practice she continued until 1900 (Hofmann 1968:24). The lectures took her to music clubs, schools, art institutes, scientific societies, and other settings in many cities. During 1898 she studied piano in Chicago with Leopold Godowsky, a renowned Polish-American pianist, teacher, and composer.

The year 1901 brought Densmore's first publication, her first visit to the Chippewa of Ontario, and her first transcription of a Sioux song. Accompanied by her sister, Margaret, she embarked on her first field trip in 1905, transcribing, by ear, songs of the Chippewa of Grand Portage and witnessing singing and dancing at the White Earth Reservation, Minnesota. In May 1907, using a borrowed phonograph, she recorded Indian songs for the first time at White Earth. When she submitted the results to William H. Holmes, then chief of the Bureau of American Ethnology (BAE) of the Smithsonian Institution, he responded with enthusiasm and allotted her $150 for recording Indian songs (Densmore 1942). After purchasing a small Edison home phonograph, Densmore returned to the Chippewa agency at Onigum. Later that year, with more funds, she continued her work at White Earth. In 1908 the BAE provided her with a Columbia graphophone, a machine designed to meet the demands of home recording. Later Densmore experimented with other recording devices as these were developed, however, this machine, with its galvanized iron recording horn, remained her favorite through 1940.

Holmes's 1907 response marked the onset of Densmore's fifty-year association with the BAE, one marked by various titles: Research Associate, Special Researcher in American Indian Music, and Collaborator. The work was supported by an annual government appropriation of $3,000. Densmore selected her projects and locations, discussing her plans for the next year during annual, two-day trips to Washington, D.C. While focused on the recording and preservation of American Indian music and the study of its relationship to the rest of culture, she also collected musical instruments (see Densmore 1927a), herbs, and other materials used in conjunction with songs; recorded a wealth of ethnographic data; and took numerous photographs. Since she was eager to avail herself of all opportunities, her work was done in a variety of settings, which ranged from reservations to world's fairs, pageants at Wisconsin Dells, her own home, and offices visited by Indian delegations to Washington, D.C. Densmore's travels (documented in *BAE Annual Reports* [under "Special Researches"], Hofmann [1968], and elsewhere) took her throughout the United States and into British Columbia. They resulted in studies of the music of the Cocopa, Makah, Winnebago, Sioux (Teton and others), Mandan and Hidatsa, Northern Ute, Nootka and Quileute, Ojibwa, Onondaga, Omaha, Apache and Navajo, Santo Domingo, Cheyenne and Arapaho, Maidu, Choctaw, Pawnee, Papago, Menominee, Chippewa, Yuma, Yaqui, Seminole, Acoma, Isleta, Cochiti, Zuni, Chitimacha, and Alibamu Indians. Many of these studies appeared as *BAE Bulletins*, as did her work with the Tule Indians of Panama.

In addition to Smithsonian-sponsored work, Densmore's research was sometimes funded by other sources. Besides grants (National Research Council and University of Michigan), the interest and support of Eleanor Hague, a trustee of the Southwest Museum, enabled Densmore to collect music among the Cheyenne, Arapaho, Maidu, and the Santo Domingo Pueblo Indians (1935–38). The Southwest Museum published these studies and honored Frances Densmore with an appointment as associate in ethnology in 1950. In 1954 she served as consultant in Indian music at the University of Florida and continued field research, making her fourth trip among the Seminoles at the age of eighty-seven.

One of the major results of Densmore's work is the Smithsonian-Densmore collection of sound recordings. Deposited as wax cylinders first at the BAE, the collection was accessioned to the National Archives in March 1940. In 1941, because of the generosity of Eleanor Steele Reese, $30,000 became available to support transfer of the collection to a permanent base and a more accessible medium. Appointed as consultant at the National Archives, Densmore (1940–42) prepared a handbook for the collection, which included 3,353 songs collected from seventy-six groups between 1907 and 1940 (Hofmann 1946:48–49). After a delay because of the war, the collection was transferred to the Archive of American Folksong at the Library of Congress in June 1943. In 1948 Densmore was appointed to a position in the Library's music department to choose selections and prepare commentaries for a series of ten LP albums proposed to make representative samplings available to the public. Seven of these albums were issued before her death.

In addition to her energetic collecting, transcription, analysis, and scholarly publications, Densmore maintained an active schedule of public lectures throughout her life. She also frequently wrote essays, summaries, and short articles for general audiences to increase public understanding of Indian music and culture. She readily shared materials with composers. Several used them in their own compositions and/or harmonized them for use in vocal, instrumental, orchestral, or operatic performances, finding a rich source of inspiration in Indian melodies. Densmore also encouraged others in their interest in American Indian music.

Densmore's career resulted in more than twenty books and over one hundred articles. Her contributions did not go unrecognized during her life. The Sioux honored her in song when Red Fox named her Two White Buffalo Woman and adopted her as a daughter in 1911 (see Hofmann 1968). Oberlin College conferred an honorary M.A. (1924). The National Association of American Composers and Conductors honored her with its Award of Merit for service to American music (1940). Macalester College bestowed the honorary D.Litt. (1950). She received a congressional tribute in 1952. The Minnesota Historical Society honored her with a distinguished service citation (1954). Her organizational affiliations were also numerous.

Densmore, like Alice Fletcher,* never married. Although she enjoyed her own circle of friends, "she had no interest . . . in social life" (Lurie 1966–70). Unlike her younger sister, Margaret, Frances Densmore was businesslike, pragmatic, unemotional; some found her manner to be brusque, affected, and imperious. Throughout her life she maintained an austere existence and, in the perception of some, was almost a stereotypic Victorian woman, except for her frequent travels and her habit of smoking cigarettes (Cronin 1976). It is clear that she was dependent on Margaret, a school teacher whose own knowledge of Indians could have supported a separate career. Margaret left teaching in 1912, after fourteen years in the profession, in order to care for their mother and to accompany Frances. After their mother's death in 1920, she was Densmore's constant companion until her own death in 1947. Frances appreciated her younger sister's good memory, sensitivity, adaptability, her "protection," cooking, and the fact that she knew how to drive (Hofmann 1968). She frequently acknowledged Margaret's major role in her own achievements, and as she said in 1949, "I don't know what I would have done without Margaret. She drove our car on all our expeditions for more than twenty years. She cooked for me . . . but most important of all, she had a wonderful way with the Indians. They would do anything for her."[1]

Trained in music, Densmore approached field research as a musician and a humanist. Although not formally trained in anthropology, she quickly became adept at observing human behavior, establishing rapport, developing linguistic competencies, and dealing with adverse field conditions. Characterized by her "nothing downs me" philosophy, she was adaptable and industrious. Following in the footsteps of Alice Fletcher and Erminnie Smith,* who had begun fieldwork in the late nineteenth century, Densmore rapidly established herself as a tireless scholar whose energies were directed toward her profession and the sharing of her knowledge and enthusiasm with others. Her deep respect for American Indians and their lifeways, her sympathetic understanding of their historical and continuing plights, her easy relationships with them, and her dedication to collecting their least-acculturated music before it disappeared resulted in the preservation of enormous amounts of ethnomusicological and ethnological information. Among her best works are *Chippewa Music* (Densmore 1910), *Chippewa Music—II* (Densmore 1913), and *Teton Sioux Music* (1918), classic in their rich detail.

While Densmore's approach to fieldwork and her experiences are documented in numerous studies, references to problems encountered because of her gender are rare. Densmore's pattern was to present herself and her credentials to appropriate government officials, missionaries, and traders on the various reservations and then, usually with the help of the agent (later, superintendent), to arrange living quarters. She next located an interpreter, preferring a graduate or former student of Hampton Normal and Industrial Institute or of the Carlisle

School, and sought a detached building near the agency or trading post (neither isolated nor too convenient) where she could record. Then she met with principal members of the Indian community, explaining her purpose and procedures. She sought to record a cross section of the group's musical culture and to understand how music related to other aspects of life. Densmore was most interested in recording the oldest songs from the most reliable singers, and in many cases worked with males who were sixty-five years of age or older because there were fewer knowledgeable female singers than male. Both were paid in cash either after each song or at the end of the day. Rates were constant from one tribe to the next, and special songs such as those used in treating the sick brought more pay. Interpreters were paid by the hour. Recording was done wherever feasible; detached buildings were the ideal, and Indian homes, agency issue rooms, the agent's parlor, school laundries and storerooms, empty jails, and so forth, the reality. All who helped her, Indian or non-Indian, were always identified and publicly thanked in the resulting publications.

Believing that there was "more to the preservation of Indian songs than winding the phonograph" (Hofmann 1968:v), Densmore, in addition to recording, devoted her field time to observing, taking photographs, and collecting information needed to interpret music in its cultural context. Thus her studies include ethnographic details on daily life, material culture, customs, and religion, as well as on musical instruments, the background of singers, and the functions of music. Of particular interest to her—perhaps because she, too, was a poet— was the poetry of Indian songs. She also had a deep interest in the close relationship between music and medicine among Indians. From her first encounter with songs of the Midéwiwin, or Grand Medicine Society, in 1907, she investigated the causes of illness, private and public ceremonial curing methods, and sources of healing powers of medicine men and women in many tribes. Musically, she found healing songs to be characterized by irregular accents, hypnotic rhythms, slow tempi, and the coincidence of voice and instrumental accompaniment (see Hofmann 1968; Densmore 1927c, 1948).

Transcriptions and analyses were done after leaving the field. Intent on making "the strange" intelligible to outsiders, Densmore employed a Western approach to transcription, indicating key signatures, meters, and the like, and showing the essential features of a melody rather than all its details. Similarly, her musical analyses focused on particular features of interest to Western musicians. The results were presented in chart/tabular form, and as her data base grew, Densmore began to compare statistics.

As a pioneer ethnomusicologist, Densmore remained one of the most important figures in twentieth-century American Indian music research until her death. Among early contemporaries with similar interests was Natalie Curtis (Burlin) (1875–1921), best known for *The Indians Book* (1907), which included musical transcriptions and native and English texts for 149 songs from eighteen tribes, with emphasis on the Southwest.

While Densmore was familiar with nineteenth-century studies of American

Indian music, including those of Franz Boas, and was initially supportive of John Comfort Fillmore's theoretical ideas about latent harmony in Indian music, she soon moved away from theoretical considerations, working in isolation and remaining relatively unaffected by contemporary European and American discussions about world musics. Some present-day ethnomusicologists reject her statistical summaries of Indian musical styles as superficial and find her transcriptions less reliable than those of some of her contemporaries. Her statistical approach is thus best seen as one type of description of musical style, and one that was to encourage others to move toward the development of more detailed, descriptive transcriptions.

Densmore supported the development of the Society for Ethnomusicology and in 1956 became one of its first officers, second vice president. Contemporary ethnomusicologists acknowledge Densmore as a pioneer whose attempts at comprehensive collecting spanned numerous developments in the recording industry, and whose preservationist goals, interest in the relationship between music and the rest of life, and prolific documentation in written, visual, and aural forms established a solid baseline for studies of stability and change in American Indian music. As Densmore herself noted, "[My] objective has been to record the structure of the Indian songs under observation, with my interpretation. Other students, scanning the material, may reach other conclusions. My work has been to preserve the past, record observations in the present, and open the way for the work of others in the future" (1942:550).

Note

1. Orville Olson, curator of Goodhue County Historical Society, Red Wing, Minn., personal communication, 1985.

References and Works About Frances T. Densmore

Angel, Madeline
1977   *Red Wing, Minnesota: Saga of a River Town*. Minneapolis: Dillon Press.
Archabal, Nina Marchetti
1977   Frances Densmore: Pioneer in the Study of American Indian Music. In *Women of Minnesota: Selected Biographical Sketches*. Barbara Stuhler and Gretchen Kreuter, eds. P. 95. St. Paul: Minnesota Historical Society.
Cronin, Jacqueline M.
1976   *Frances Densmore: A Profile*. Research report submitted in partial fulfillment of the requirements for the M.S., Depart. of Library and Audiovisual Education, School of Education, St. Cloud State University, St. Cloud, Minn.
Hofmann, Charles
1946   Frances Densmore and the Music of the American Indian. *Journal of American Folklore* 59:45–50.

Hofmann, Charles
1968   *Frances Densmore and American Indian Music. A Memorial Volume.* Contributions from the Museum of the American Indian, Heye Foundation, vol. 23. New York: Museum of the American Indian, Heye Foundation.
Kurath, Gertrude
1958   Memorial to Frances Densmore. *Ethnomusicology* 2 (2): 70–71.
Lurie, Nancy Oestreich
1966   Women in Early American Anthropology. In *Pioneers of American Anthropology.* June Helm, ed. Pp. 29–81. Seattle: University of Washington Press.
Daily Republican Eagle (Red Wing, Minnesota)
1920   Pay Tribute to Beloved Woman. [Concerns Sarah Adalaide (Greenland) Densmore.] January 22, p. 1.

Selected Works by Frances T. Densmore

1909   Scale Formation in Primitive Music. *American Anthropologist* 9:1–12.
1910   *Chippewa Music. Bureau of American Ethnology (BAE), Bulletin 45.* Washington, D.C.: GPO.
1913   *Chippewa Music—II. BAE, Bulletin 53.* Washington, D.C.: GPO.
1918   *Teton Sioux Music. BAE, Bulletin 61.* Washington, D.C.: GPO.
1922   *Northern Ute Music. BAE, Bulletin 75.* Washington, D.C.: GPO.
1923   *Mandan and Hidatsa Music. BAE, Bulletin 80.* Washington, D.C.: GPO.
1926   Music of the Tule Indians of Panama. In *Smithsonian Miscellaneous Collections* 77 (11). Washington, D.C.: Smithsonian Institution.
1927a *Handbook of the Collection of Musical Instruments in the United States National Museum.* Bulletin 136. Washington, D.C.: United States National Museum.
1927b The Study of Indian Music in the Nineteenth Century. *American Anthropologist* 29:77–86.
1927c The Use of Music in the Treatment of the Sick by American Indians. *Musical Quarterly* 13:555–65.
1928   The Melodic Formation of Indian Songs. *Journal of the Washington Academy of Science* 18 (Jan. 4): 16–24.
1929a *Chippewa Customs.* Washington, D.C.: BAE Bulletin 86.
1929b *Papago Music. BAE, Bulletin 90.* Washington, D.C.: GPO.
1929c *Pawnee Music. BAE, Bulletin 93.* Washington, D.C.: GPO.
1929d What Intervals Do Indians Sing? *American Anthropologist* 31:271–76.
1932a A Resemblance Between Yuman and Pueblo Songs. *American Anthropologist* 34:694–700.
1932b *Menominee Music. BAE, Bulletin 102.* Washington, D.C.: GPO.
1932c *Yuman and Yaqui Music. BAE, Bulletin 110.* Washington, D.C.: GPO.
1934   The Songs of Indian Soldiers During the World War (I). *Musical Quarterly* 20:419–25.
1936   *Cheyenne and Arapaho Music.* Southwest Museum Papers No. 10. Los Angeles: Southwest Museum.
1937   The Alabama Indians and Their Music. In *Publications of the Texas Folklore Society, No. 13 (Straight Texas).* J. Frank Dobie, ed. Pp. 270–93. Austin.
1938a *Music of Santo Domingo Pueblo, New Mexico.* Southwest Museum Papers No. 12. Los Angeles: Southwest Museum.

1938b The Influence of Hymns on the Form of Indian Songs. *American Anthropologist* 40:175–77.

1939a *Nootka and Quileute Music. BAE, Bulletin 124.* Washington, D.C.: GPO.

1939b The Poetry of Indian Songs. In *So Live the Works of Men, Seventieth Anniversary Volume Honoring Edgar Lee Hewett.* Donald D. Brand and Fred E. Harvey, eds. Pp. 121–30. Albuquerque: University of New Mexico Press.

1942   The Study of Indian Music. In *Annual Report of the Smithsonian Institution for the Year Ended June 30, 1941.* Pp. 527–50. Washington, D.C.: Smithsonian Institution.

1943a Choctaw Music. In *BAE, Bulletin 136.* Anthropological Papers No. 28. Pp. 101–88. Washington, D.C.: GPO.

1943b Music of the Indians of British Columbia. In *Bureau of American Ethnology, Bulletin 136,* Anthropological Papers No. 27. Pp. 1–99. Washington.

1943c The Use of Meaningless Syllables in Indian Songs. *American Anthropologist* 45: 160–62.

1944   Traces of Foreign Influences in the Music of the American Indians. *American Anthropologist* 46: 106–12.

1945   The Importance of Recordings of Indian Songs. *American Anthropologist* 47: 637–39.

1948   The Use of Music in the Treatment of the Sick by American Indians. In *Music and Medicine.* Dorothy M. Schullian and Max Schoen, eds. pp. 25–46. New York: Henry Schuman.

1950   The Words of Indian Songs as Unwritten Literature. *Journal of American Folklore* 63:450–58.

1956   *Seminole Music. BAE, Bulletin 161.* Washington, D.C.: GPO.

1957   *Music of Acoma, Isleta, Cochiti and Zuni Pueblos. BAE, Bulletin 165.* Washington, D.C.: GPO.

1958   *Music of the Maidu Indians of California.* Publications of the Frederick Webb Hodge Anniversary Publication Fund, Vol. 7. Los Angeles: Southwest Museum.

CHARLOTTE J. FRISBIE

Ellen Irene Diggs

(1906–   )

Black American anthropologist Ellen Irene Diggs is best known for her research on Afro-Latin American culture and society, and the history of the African diaspora.

Ellen Irene Diggs was born in Monmouth, Illinois, a small college town located in the state's agricultural belt near the Iowa border. She was raised in the supportive environment of an industrious working-class nuclear black family. Despite this relative comfort, very early in her childhood Irene Diggs became cognizant of and disturbed by incidences of poverty and inequitable wages. She recounted, "I just could not understand why and how people who did little or nothing had so much, while people who did the unpleasant, dirty work and worked so hard had so little."[1] In her household of orientation, the management of money was of primary concern. Her father taught all of the children how to handle money, calculate interest payments, and appreciate the value of saving.

In addition to her father's financial instructions, Irene Diggs learned, under her mother's tutelage, the handwork of needlepoint, crewel, and embroidery. Her mother also instilled in her an appreciation and knowledge of flowers, trees, pet animals, and a great deal of nature lore. Like most black families of the era, education was perceived as the most significant way to rise above one's working-class origins and lead a more affluent life-style.

During Irene Diggs's youth the town of Monmouth had a population of about 10,000, of which 200 to 300 were black. Although Monmouth was a college town, it was located in rural Illinois. Books, magazines, and newspapers stimulated Irene Diggs's interest in knowing the world outside that small town. From her voracious reading as a youth, Diggs became determined that she would "visit and see these far distant places and people with my own eyes and for my ownself." Moreover, education was seen to be of the utmost importance, and Irene was resolved to learn as much as she could.

A tuition scholarship, given yearly by the Monmouth Chamber of Commerce for the highest scholarship in the high school class, was awarded to Irene Diggs. For one year she attended nearby Monmouth College. Then Diggs transferred to the University of Minnesota, which had more extensive course offerings. There she majored in sociology and minored in psychology. She recalled that at Minnesota she "was completely lost in a student body of ten or twelve, maybe fourteen thousand students." There, too, she met with a kind of racism she had previously never encountered. So novel to her was this type of blatant racism that she did not interpret racist incidences as such. For example, a human-behavior professor warned her not to enroll in his class because it was "fast stepping." He assumed that Diggs, as a young black woman, would be intellectually incapable of keeping up with the course. Diggs, suggesting her youthful naïveté of the event, noted that she responded to the professor, "I am a fast stepper."

While she was an undergraduate, Diggs did not avail herself of academic advising. She selected courses on her own, including those in the fields of economics and anthropology. Satisfying requirements for graduation, Diggs received her B.A. in 1928.

Before Irene Diggs attended Minnesota, she had never seen a copy of a black magazine or a black newspaper. Her high school reading list had included only two books about blacks, one of them being *Up from Slavery* by Booker T. Washington. Diggs states that there was an absence of outstanding black leaders in the Monmouth community from whom she could gain inspiration. She felt herself searching for a role model, and a level of excellence to strive toward, from black people. When her sister married a Baptist minister from Georgia, she accompanied them down south by automobile. And there, in Atlanta, a new vista was opened to Diggs. In the city of Atlanta she toured colleges operated by blacks and with black faculties. A large black community included both intellectuals and leaders. She made the decision then to return to Atlanta and to attend a black university.

Diggs enrolled in Atlanta University and pursued a graduate degree in the fields of sociology and anthropology. During her second semester on campus, the distinguished and controversial W. E. B. DuBois returned to teach there. DuBois was a professor of economics, history, and sociology at Atlanta University. He had resumed his position with the university following an effective but argumentative career (1910–34) with the National Association for the Advancement of Colored People (NAACP) as editor of its publication, *The Crisis*. For all appearances, DuBois represented the intellectual and leader Irene Diggs had been seeking for guidance and inspiration.

Diggs registered for DuBois's courses. The title of one course reflects some of the concepts with which he was grappling—"Karl Marx and the Negro Problem." Apparently, DuBois appreciated Diggs's intellectual ability, which she demonstrated in her coursework, scholarship, and research; he asked her to become his research assistant for the summer. The summer project for which Diggs would assist DuBois was to be his seminal work, *Black Reconstruction*

(1935). Not only did she research material for the manuscript but Diggs also proofread and checked the footnotes. It was a unique opportunity to be closely associated with DuBois at this time, since he was articulating some of the most influential ground-breaking theoretical doctrines concerning race, class, and the African experience in the Americas. Under DuBois's tutelage, Diggs received the university's first master's degree in sociology in 1933.

For eleven years (1932–43) Diggs remained at Atlanta University serving as Dubois's research assistant. Over the course of these years, she helped research five of his books, including his social history, *Black Folk: Then and Now* (1939)—an updated version of his landmark piece *The Negro* (1915)—and the essay *Dusk of Dawn* (1940). And DuBois and Diggs cofounded the journal, *Phylon: A Review of Race and Culture*. A driving force throughout DuBois's work of that period, which would become discernible in Diggs's own work on Latin America and the African diaspora, was a conviction of the necessity of African historiography to fill an incredible void of information, and the need for serious study of peoples of African descent in the New World from historical and cultural perspectives.

In the early 1940s Diggs set off for an independent career of her own, following a summer holiday in Cuba. She spent the next summer at the University of Havana summer school studying the Spanish language. As a Roosevelt Fellow of the Institute of International Education at the University of Havana, Diggs continued her stay in Cuba, where she met Fernando Ortiz, the internationally known ethnographer. Again the opportunity to study under a distinguished scholar became available to her.

In Cuba Diggs was able to travel throughout the island analyzing and investigating the impact and continuities of African cultural elements in Cuban society. Collecting folklore, recording music, photographing festivals, and observing rituals and dance were some of the activities that engaged her in rural and urban areas. There Diggs gradually reached a full awareness of the degrees to which transgenerational behavioral patterns could affect a population. She also observed that certain elements of African cultures were functioning quite visibly among twentieth-century Afro-Cuban descendants of Yoruban and Dahomeyan peoples, as an aspect of their Cuban identity.

A critical concept formulated in those years in Havana (1943–45) was the functional differences in race relations operating in Latin America in comparison with those found in North America. Working within the historical framework emphasized by DuBois and Ortiz, Diggs began to analyze the various meanings of race in the Americas. She wrote, "Basically, the differences between the 'problem of race' in the United States and Latin America is their different definitions of who is white" (Diggs 1971:34:5:107). These social stratification systems were based on two different colonizing processes and the cultural history of the European countries involved.

Like a number of other scholars, such as Charles Wagley, Marvin Harris, and Harry Hoetink, Diggs analyzed the Latin American social systems as having developed largely on the basis of a combination of class and racial lines that were articulated in at least a triracial model (white, mulatto, black). In contrast, the two-tier system (white, black) found in the United States was based on the taint of ancestry (most U.S. blacks were descendants of slaves), and Diggs described this as "the primary factor in the Negro problem" (1971).

The Cuba of Diggs's student days was a highly stratified neocolonial society, heavily under the influence of the United States. Its only seat of higher education was the University of Havana. As might be expected, this institution was reserved for the elite, since only they could afford such a privilege. Hence, most university students were members of the upper classes, and were white or light-skinned Cubans. Because of the emphasis on class as a social category, Diggs was viewed from her upper class position, that is, as an American rather than as a "black," which would have implied lower social status. Cuba had not only provided a fieldwork experience for her as an anthropologist, but it had also given her an experience for international living. Those experiences afforded her the opportunity to synthesize ideas that laid the basis for future scholarship. When Irene Diggs finished her studies in Cuba, receiving her doctorate in 1944, she returned to the United States where the cold reality of a world at war awaited her.

Following the end of World War II, Irene Diggs journeyed to South America (1946–47). She traveled throughout a number of countries, but spent much of the year abroad in Montevideo, Uruguay, as an exchange scholar under the auspices of the U.S. Department of State, Division of International Exchange of Persons. In Montevideo she continued archival research and became a participant observer in the Afro-Uruguayan and Afro-Argentinian communities.

Another important aspect of Diggs's interest, that of acting as a patron of the arts, gained further momentum during her stay in Uruguay. Later on she would publish articles concerning fine art, painters and sculptors, and the theater in Uruguay.

At the invitation of the president of Morgan State College, Baltimore, Maryland, Irene Diggs joined its faculty in 1947. She was a member of the Department of Sociology and Anthropology for twenty-nine years, and retired in 1976. Her class load at Morgan was heavy by anyone's standards, though typical of that found in many black colleges and universities. She taught fifteen hours a week and prepared seven courses a year. Never did she have less than twelve hours of class, nor less than five preparations in any one of those many years spent on the Morgan State campus.

Because of classroom commitments it was difficult for Diggs to prepare book-length manuscripts. Instead, Diggs's work appeared in a wide variety of media. She wrote many articles for the *Journal of Negro History* and *Phylon* as well as for newspapers, and reviews for a variety of academic journals. She was also featured on television and radio programs.

Diggs's anthropological perspective reflects a time when the discipline was wrestling with the import of the school of functionalism and its application to the cultures and societies of peoples of African descent in the New World. Hence, there are two elements that have been central to her outlook on anthropology. The first incorporates the view that culture must be conceptualized as consisting of learned patterns of adaptive behavior that are altered through time by a process of orderly change. Second, this requires that the process of this evolutionary, adaptive behavior change must be documented by a historical analysis that incorporates social and economic events. Her work on the chronology of Afro-American history and African history illustrates her use of this perspective.

However, issues of feminism and woman-focused research as a particular facet of scholarly concern have never been a significant part of Irene Diggs's outlook or work. According to Diggs, her position at Morgan State was never handicapped because of sex discrimination, a factor of great importance to many faculty women today. And although black women and black families have been topics of research for Diggs, they do not represent any notable directions in her scholarly career. For the most part, her work on black women derives from her participation and service on civic and statewide fact-finding commissions on mental health, corrections, and family welfare.

Over the years Diggs has excelled in her role as the committed scholar active in community affairs. She was a founding member of the Women's Committee of the Baltimore Art Museum and was on the board of the Peabody Conservatory. Diggs participated only in those organizations that were of genuine interest to her, deliberately avoiding the role of being the token, repeatedly same black face—which as she noted, can erode the effectiveness of contribution and limit the inputs of other qualified persons.

In 1964 Irene Diggs received the Distinguished Alumni Award from Monmouth College. She had the opportunity to return to Havana in 1976 as a Special Visitor to the UN International Seminar on the Eradication of Apartheid and in Support of the Struggle for Liberation in Southern Africa. In 1978 the Association of Black Anthropologists honored Dr. Diggs for her five decades of valuable contributions to the study of peoples of African descent in the Americas.

Diggs spent nearly thirty years on the faculty of a black institution, Morgan State University. There she touched the lives of an enormous number of students in the classroom and was an outstanding member of the faculty. Diggs commented:

I do not agree with many of the theories and findings in anthropology which have to do with non-white people; . . . I believe that more studies should be made, using the same techniques, of Whites, especially poor Whites in the United States. But I sincerely believe that anthropology can be, if properly taught, one of the most beneficial subjects Blacks and Whites can study. (Bolles 1983:1–2)

Note

1. I would like to thank Dr. Irene Diggs for taking the time to be interviewed and for her continual assistance in my various projects.

References and Works About E. Irene Diggs

Bolles, A. Lynn

1981 *Irene Diggs: Coming of Age in Atlanta, Havana, and Baltimore.* Paper presented at the 80th Annual Meeting of the American Anthropological Association, Los Angeles.

1983 Irene Diggs: A Biographical Sketch. *Outreach, Morgan State University and the Middle Atlantic Writers Association* 5:1–2.

Selected Works by E. Irene Diggs

1951 The Negro in the Vice Royalty of Rio de la Plata. *Journal of Negro History* 25 (3): 281–301.

1965 Legacy. *Freedomways* W. E. B. DuBois Memorial Issue 5 (1): 18–19.

1971 Attitudes Toward Color in South America. *Negro History Bulletin* 34 (5): 107–8.

1976 Cuba Before and After Castro. *The News American*, July 15.

1978 Acceptance Address. American Anthropological Association Meetings, Association of Black Anthropologists, Los Angeles.

A. LYNN BOLLES

Mary Tew Douglas

(1921–)

British social anthropologist Mary Tew Douglas is known for her studies of religion and symbolism in tribal and contemporary society, pollution and moral order, and for grid and group analysis.

Mary Tew was born on March 25, 1921, to Gilbert Charles Tew and Phyllis Twomey Tew. The eldest of two daughters, she was educated at Sacred Heart Convent, Roehampton, England. Tew later attended the University of Oxford, where she studied philosophy, politics, and economics. She received her B.A. in 1943. Tew interrupted her education during World War II to volunteer for national service. She worked for the Social Service Department of the Colonial Office, serving as secretary of the Penal Reform Subcommittee.

In 1946 she returned to Oxford, pursuing a master's degree in anthropology (1947) as well as a B.Sc. (1948). At Oxford Tew studied under Meyer Fortes, Max Gluckman, and E. E. Evans-Pritchard. She was awarded her Ph.D. in 1951. Tew's dissertation was based on fieldwork in the southwest Belgian Congo (Zaire), conducted in 1949–50 and 1953. She was funded by a fellowship from the International African Institute, with additional support from the Institut de Recherche Scientifique dans l'Afrique Centrale. Like other women anthropologists of the time, in the field she worked primarily with women. "My material was African and access to it was gained through staying with the women as they cooked, divided food, talked about illness, babies and proper care of the body" (Douglas 1975:203). Her dissertation, published as *The Lele of the Kasai* (1963), explores the theme of social accountability, most particularly by examining how male elders manipulate raffia cloth debts in order to restrict the access of younger men to women (Rayner 1985:208).

In 1951 Tew married the economist James A. T. Douglas. They had two sons and one daughter. That same year she began her long association with the University of London and Professor Daryll Forde, upon whose guidance and counsel she relied (Douglas 1963:xiv).

Douglas has been called one of the "leaders of the new British 'structural-ism' " (Kuper 1973:206). In terms of theory her work is similar to that of Emile Durkheim. "When I first read Durkheim his sociological determinism affronted me. . . . But outrage or no outrage, Professor Evans-Pritchard in the chair of anthropology at Oxford made it very clear that our subject stood in direct line of descent from Durkheim" (Douglas 1975:212). Her research also clearly demonstrates the influence of Evans-Pritchard, whom she acknowledges as the person who first taught her anthropology. In her analysis of his contributions to anthropological theory, she states that he was one of the first anthropologists to attempt to relate moral philosophy and religion in a systematic manner with social behavior. Douglas has dubbed his method for doing so a "theory of social accountability" (Douglas 1980:2–4).

This theory rests on the assumption that human society consists of active, intelligent members who are endowed with will; and it traces belief in divine attributes to institutionalized moral values (Douglas 1982a:10). It encompasses a method for the systematic comparison of beliefs with and between cultures. Through field research an investigator attempts to place a people's beliefs within the social context of their daily lives by looking at confrontations. The researcher then examines how a society handles confrontations (e.g., by accusation or acceptance of responsibility) and invokes moral judgments to hold people accountable for their behavior; and how ideas of blame and compensation are worked into social institutions are examined. "By fastening on moral principles and their use in building systems of accountability, the sociologist has a way of giving value to individuals' free negotiating activities" (Douglas 1982a:9). Examination of social accountability is found throughout Douglas's works.

In the course of looking at accountability, Douglas investigates the nature of classification systems. She proposes that the rules of society that regulate behavior also divide reality into structures that constitute the basis of human thought. To Douglas, classifications used to name and transform things into "meaningful social reality" are imbued with moral significance—the result being that every activity, however mundane, carries ceremonial and ritual significance in that each involves bringing order; symbolic order reflects social order (Wuthnow 1984:84–87). It is not surprising, then, that activities of everyday life are the focus of interest for Douglas. Her research studies have included analysis of dirt, pollution, food, and consumption as she looks at the ritual dramatization of social patterns.

Her methodology includes a formula introduced by her for classifying social relations (Douglas 1970a). By tracing two independent variables—grid and group—she is able to explain changes in rite, symbol, and myth in a systematic and theoretical way. "All I am concerned with is a formula for classifying relations which can be applied equally to the smallest band of hunters and gatherers as to the most industrialised nations. All we need to know is the way in which these relations are structured according to two independently varying criteria which I have called grid and group. Group is ... the experience of a bounded social unit. Grid refers to rules which relate one person to others on an ego-centred basis'' (Douglas 1970a:viii). Comparative analysis of cultures and their underlying social organizations occurs by looking at the various combinations of grid and group.

Douglas is perhaps best known for her studies of pollution. In *Purity and Danger* (1966) she discusses the role of pollution in various aspects of daily life and explores how rituals of purity and impurity form part of an accountability system. Using the human body as a symbol, she hypothesizes that "primitive" ideas of pollution relate directly to concern with dangers arising from disorder, and that anxiety about bodily margins expresses anxiety about group survival. (See Spiro 1968:391–93 for a critique of this hypothesis.) Douglas (1966) also argues that modern notions of dirt express basically the same idea as "primitive" notions of pollution.

Where there is dirt there is a system. ... Shoes are not dirty in themselves, but it is dirty to place them on the dining-table. ... In short, our pollution behavior is the reaction which condemns any object or idea likely to confuse or contradict cherished classifications. ... (48)

Our practices are solidly based on hygiene; theirs are symbolic: we kill germs; they ward off spirits. (44)

Douglas sees food as one more system of social information to be decoded. She proposes that the choice of animals and plants to be eaten, how they are prepared, and how they are presented is socially structured and organized. Expanding upon the same theoretical base as her pollution studies, she suggests that concern with food taboos reflects a greater social concern with encroachment and danger, since food is reflective of overall social organization.

The most recent writings of Mary Douglas represent an application of her theoretical framework to issues in contemporary society. In *The World of Goods*, written in collaboration with Baron Isherwood (1979), she examines the social context of consumption and concludes that goods are social markers; that acts of consumption are one means of giving and getting information for attaining and keeping power; and that through acts of consumption, individuals ritually reaffirm their status. *Risk and Culture* (Douglas and Wildavsky 1982) looks at the growth of the environmental protection movement during the 1960s and 1970s and compares ideas about pollution in both tribal and industrial societies. Douglas and Wildavsky submit that beliefs surrounding pollution are culturally determined and have little to do with an object's relationship to dirt or danger. They point to the American political system as the direct cause of environmental movements, stating that it fosters sectarianism and promotes the efforts of the periphery to undermine the center. Although there are political overtones about toxic substance regulation in this book, the primary emphasis is not on issues but on analysis of pollution beliefs in contemporary American society. "The

Effects of Modernization on Religious Change'' (Douglas 1982b) addresses the premise that religion and science cannot coexist. Douglas disagrees with the suggestion that there will be a demise of religion. She sees religion originating in social relations and suggests that religion and ritual will continue to play an important role because social relations may change, but they do not disappear (Wuthnow 1984:128–31).

Douglas's academic career has been long and distinguished. She served as lecturer in anthropology at the University of Oxford in 1950 and at the University of London (1951), retiring with a full professorship in 1978. Douglas also served as the resident scholar and director of the culture program at the Russell Sage Foundation, New York (1977–81), and taught at Northwestern University (1981–85) as the Avalon Professor of the Humanities—a joint appointment with history and the literature of religion. She was the recipient of the Rivers Memorial Medal (1968), served as vice-chairperson for the Royal Anthropological Institute (1975–77), and cochaired the International Commission on the Anthropology of Food (1978). Douglas has delivered several eminent lectures, among them the Henry Myers lecture for the Royal Anthropological Institute and the Fraser Memorial Lecture (1976). She is currently teaching at Princeton University.

As a student Mary Douglas was advised that

the central task of anthropology was to explore the effects of the social dimension on behaviour. The task was grand, but the methods humble. . . . We had to stay with a remote tribe, patiently let events unfold and let people reveal the categories of their thought. Irresistibly the scrutiny would strip human thought of its claim to independence. . . . In these far-off fields we could see that the main structures of thought are generated in the hurly-burly of political life and draw their stability from the institutions they underwrite. (Douglas 1975:212)

From this early instruction, Mary Douglas has contributed to the body of anthropological knowledge for some thirty-seven years. In that time she has provided methodologic as well as theoretic enrichment for understanding the role of rite, symbol, myth, and social relations in tribal and contemporary society.

References and Works About Mary Douglas

Barnes, Barry, and Steven Shapin
1977 Where is the Edge of Objectivity? A Review of *Implicit Meanings: Essays in Anthropology. British Journal for the History of Science* (March) pp. 61–66.
Contemporary Authors
1981 Douglas, Mary (Tew). *CA*, Frances C. Locher, ed. Pp. 143–44. Detroit: Gale Research.
Kuper, Adam
1973 *Anthropologists and Anthropology: The British School 1922–1972*. London: Allen Lane.

Peacock, James L.
1975 *Consciousness and Change: Symbolic Anthropology in Evolutionary Perspective.* New York: John Wiley & Sons.
Rayner, Steve
1985 Douglas, Mary (1921). In *The Social Science Encyclopedia.* Adam Kuper and Jessica Kuper, eds. Pp. 208–9. London: Routledge and Kegan Paul.
Spiro, Melford E.
1968 Review of *Purity and Danger: An Analysis of Concepts of Pollution and Taboo.* *American Anthropologist* 70:391–93.
Welbourn, F. B.
1970 Mary Douglas and the Study of Religion. *Journal of Religion in Africa.* Vol. 46 (9):81–95.
Who's Who
1986 Douglas, Prof. Mary. *WW* 1986–1987. 138th annual Ed. P. 483. New York: St. Martin's Press.
Wuthnow, Robert et al., eds.
1984 *Cultural Analysis: The Work of Peter L. Berger, Mary Douglas, Michel Foucault, and Jurgen Habermas.* Boston: Routledge and Kegan Paul.

Selected Works by Mary Douglas

1950 *Peoples of the Lake Nyasa Region.* International African Institute (written as Mary Tew).
1951 A Form of Polyandry Among the Lele of the Kasai. *Africa* 21 (1): 1–12.
1954 The Lele of the Kasai. In *African Worlds: Studies in the Cosmological Ideas and Social Values of African Peoples.* Daryll Forde, ed. Pp. 1–26. London: Oxford University Press.
1958 Raffia Cloth Distribution in the Lele Economy. *Africa* 28 (2): 109–122.
1959 Age Status Among the Lele. *Zaire* 13 (4): 386–413.
1960 Blood Debts Among the Lele. *Journal of the Royal Anthropological Institute* 90 (1): 1–28.
1962 Lele Economy Compared with the Bushong. In *Markets in Africa.* Paul Bohannan and George Dalton, eds. Pp. 211–33. Evanston, Illinois: Northwestern University Press.
1963 *The Lele of the Kasai.* London: Oxford University Press.
1964 *Man in Society: Patterns of Human Organization.* The MacDonald Illustrated Library. (As ed.)
1966 *Purity and Danger: An Analysis of Concepts of Pollution and Taboo.* London: Routledge and Kegan Paul.
1967a Witch Beliefs in Central America. *Africa* 37 (1): 72–80.
1967b Primitive Rationing. *Themes in Economic Anthropology,* ASA 6. R. Firth, ed. Pp. 119–146.
1968a Pollution. In *International Encyclopedia of the Social Sciences.* Vol. 12, pp. 336–42. New York: Macmillan.
1968b The Relevance of Tribal Studies. *Journal of Psychosomatic Research* 1: 21–28.
1968c The Social Control of Cognition: Factors in Joke Perception. *Man* 3 (3): 361–67.

1969   Is Matriliny Doomed in Africa? In *Man in Africa*. Mary Douglas and Phyllis M. Kaberry, eds. Pp. 121–35. London: Tavistock Publications.

1970a *Natural Symbols, Explorations in Cosmology*. New York: Pantheon Books.

1970b *Witchcraft Accusations and Confessions*. London: Tavistock Publications. (As ed.)

1973   *Rules and Meanings: The Anthropology of Everyday Knowledge*. New York: Penguin.

1975   *Implicit Meanings, Essays in Anthropology*. London: Routledge and Kegan Paul.

1976   Relative Poverty—Relative Communication. In *Traditions of Social Policy: Essays in Honour of Violet Butler*. A. H. Halsey, ed. Pp. 197–215. Oxford: Basil Blackwell.

1978a *Cultural Bias*. Occasional Paper No. 35. Royal Anthropological Institute of Great Britain and Ireland. London: Routledge and Kegan Paul.

1978b Judgments on James Frazer. *Daedalus*: 151–64.

1978c *The Illustrated Golden Bough*. Sir James George Frazer. Abridged and Illustrated. Garden City, N.Y.: Doubleday.

1979a World Views and the Core. In *Philosophical Disputes in the Social Sciences*. Stuart Brown, ed. London: Harvester Press.

1979b Passive Voice Theories in Religious Sociology. The 1978 Paul Douglass Lecture. *Review of Religious Research* 21 (1): 51–61.

1980   *Edward Evans-Pritchard*. New York: The Viking Press.

1982a *In the Active Voice*. London: Routledge and Kegan Paul.

1982b The Effects of Modernization on Religious Change. *Daedalus. Religion* 3 (1): 1–19. Proceedings of the American Academy of Arts and Sciences.

1982c *Essays in the Sociology of Perception*. London: Routledge and Kegan Paul.

1983   An Appreciation of Meyer Fortes. *African Studies Newsletter* (February 11). Northwestern University.

Coauthored Works

Douglas, Mary, and Daryll Forde
1956   Primitive Economics. In *Man, Culture and Society*. Harry L. Shapiro, ed. Pp. 330–44. New York: Oxford University Press.

Douglas, Mary, and Jonathan Gross
1981   Food and Culture: Measuring the Intricacy of Rule Systems. *Social Science Information* 20 (1): 1–35.

Douglas, Mary, and Baron Isherwood
1979   *The World of Goods, An Anthropological Theory of Consumption*. New York: Basic Books.

Douglas, Mary, and Phyllis M. Kaberry, eds.
1969   *Man in Africa*. London: Tavistock Publications.

Douglas, Mary, and R. S. Khare
1980   International Commission on Anthropology of Food and Food Problems: Statement on Its History and Current Objectives. *Appetite* 1: 317–20.

Douglas, Mary, and Steven Tipton, eds.
1983   *Religion in America*. Boston: Beacon Press.
Douglas, Mary, and Aaron Wildavsky
1982   *Risk and Culture*. Berkeley: University of California Press.

RUTH WEINBERG

Cora Du Bois

(1903–   )

Cora Du Bois is an American cultural anthropologist, especially known for her studies in culture-and-personality, change in complex society, and her multidisciplinary approach to methodology.

Cora Du Bois was the younger of two children, born October 26, 1903, to Jean Jules and Mattie Schreiber Du Bois in Brooklyn, New York. While reared and educated primarily in the United States, Du Bois spent five years of her childhood and youth residing and traveling in Western Europe, where she visited relatives and learned to speak French and German. Du Bois' father, of an upper-middle-class French Swiss family, acquired American citizenship during World War I but retained close ties with his Swiss relatives until his death. Her mother belonged to a German middle-class group that emigrated in 1848 but retained its interest in Germany. Thus, Du Bois grew up with a keen sense of her European heritage but with a certain coolness toward members of her immediate family—in particular, her mother, whom she considered an overly dependent and vain woman. This relationship may have encouraged her "to feel something of a distant observer of human affairs."[1]

Du Bois attended high school in Perth Amboy, New Jersey, and in 1927 received her B.A. from Barnard, where she was also elected to Phi Beta Kappa. History was her undergraduate major and the field in which she received an M.A. from Columbia in 1928 in medieval thought and culture. However, she had been exposed to anthropology in an introductory course at Barnard (1927) given by Franz Boas and Ruth Benedict* and decided to pursue a Ph.D. in that field. As a student of history Du Bois had been stimulated by the broad thinking of Spengler regarding civilization and historical processes. In studying anthropology she sought to discipline that broad historical base with a field of study that dealt with specific facts about specific cultures in specific time periods.

Benedict, who knew that Du Bois did not want to remain at Columbia, where Boas wanted her to study the medieval contacts between western Europe and eastern African groups, suggested that she apply to the recently established Department of Anthropology at the University of California at Berkeley. Receiving cordial replies from both Alfred Kroeber and Robert Lowie, Du Bois in 1929 crossed the continent to study in Berkeley, "knowing nothing of the program or its two dominant figures."

Cora Du Bois' professional career can be divided into four periods, beginning with Berkeley where she received a Ph.D. in anthropology in 1932. Her dissertation was a "dull and tedious library job" assigned her by the anthropology department and entitled, "Girls' Adolescent Rites in the New World." However, in 1929 she undertook a series of fieldwork projects among Native American tribes of northern California, coastal Oregon, and the lower Columbia River, beginning with the Wintu at Kroeber's suggestion. A Social Science Research Council grant-in-aid helped support her fieldwork in 1932–35. During this period Du Bois was also a teaching fellow in the Berkeley Department of Anthropology (1930–32) and then a research associate (1932–35). Although Du Bois does not view this period as one of great intellectual stimulation for her, it was a time of disciplined thinking and gathering of data. Lowie served as her principal intellectual guide; Kroeber was busy building a department. "Both were rather casual advisors."

The second phase of Du Bois' career began in 1935–36, when she became a National Research Council Fellow in Boston and New York to investigate types of psychiatric training suitable for professional anthropology. "Anthropological field work among American Indians on the West Coast had shown me repeatedly the blind alleys encountered in investigating social process, if psychological orientations and techniques were not employed. Furthermore, the obvious differences between peoples of different cultures challenged explanation" (Du Bois 1944:viii). Thus, a year divided between the Harry A. Murray Psychological Clinic at Harvard and, at Abram Kardiner's invitation, at the New York Psychoanalytic Society's joint seminar provided Du Bois with the interdisciplinary collaboration she sought. This led to her two-year (1937–39) field study of Alor, Indonesia, where she investigated problems in culture-and-personality. In 1939 she returned to the United States and taught at Sarah Lawrence College while analyzing her data and writing her landmark study, *The People of Alor* (Du Bois 1944).

World War II interrupted this second phase of Du Bois' academic career. In 1942 she joined the war effort as chief of the Indonesia Section of the Research and Analysis Branch of the Office of Strategic Services. Following the war she stayed with the U.S. State Department until 1949, serving as chief of the South East Asian Branch of the Division of Research for the Far East in the Office of Intelligence. During this third phase of her career, Du Bois published widely on Southeast Asia, the World Health Organization for which she was a consultant in 1950–51, and on cross-cultural education. From 1951–54 she served as director of research for the Institute of International Education.

"During those 12 years I felt trapped in what some called applied anthropology and others called 'relevance.' I had by then learned that I had little aptitude for, or sympathy with, power, managerial administration, or so called applications" (Du Bois 1980:3). Du Bois put herself back in the academic marketplace and in 1954 was offered the Radcliffe Zemurray Professorship, a tenured post for a woman scholar's affiliation with relevant departments—in her case, the Harvard Department of Anthropology and the then still vigorous Department of Social Relations. She remained in this position, the only tenured woman in two departments, until her retirement in 1969. This fourth phase of Du Bois' career was a rich one, filled with honors, varied publications, extended research in India (1961–72), and teaching. It was climaxed by her election in 1968 to the presidency of the American Anthropological Association, a high honor, reflective of her considerable achievements in the profession.

Du Bois has characterized fieldwork as "the crucial educational experience and the determining polish of professionalism in anthropology" (Du Bois 1970a:233). Her fieldwork experiences spanned a forty-year period and ranged from descriptive and historical ethnography among Native Americans, to ethnological and psychological research in the small, remote society of Alor, to a long-term study of sociocultural change in the complex society of India.

As a Berkeley graduate student and research associate in the early 1930s, Du Bois was engaged in salvage ethnography among the Native Americans of California and Oregon whose cultures were rapidly disappearing. "There I was tied to a dilapidated car and stayed in roadside cabins on a minimal living and travel allowance. My task was largely salvage ethnography, and I never really left my own culture except by an act of imagination" (Du Bois 1970a:221). Training for ethnographic fieldwork at that time was minimal. When Du Bois inquired of Kroeber how to prepare for her first summer expedition among the Wintu, for example, she was told "to take pencil and paper."

By contrast, Du Bois' second phase of fieldwork was intensive and motivated by a set of specific theoretical issues. Her eighteen-month expedition in 1938–39 to the island of Alor in Indonesia was the direct outcome of her collaboration with psychiatrists, psychologists, and anthropologists interested in the relationship of cultural factors, institutionalized and informal, to personality formation. It was an effort to collect data that would allow better testing of the ideas that had emerged from the joint seminar with Kardiner and others. "It [the seminar] was a good exercise, but there was no opportunity to check our conclusions. Were individuals predominantly what we might suppose them to be from the institutions under which they lived, the childhood conditioning they received, the values they shared, the goals for which they strived?" (Du Bois 1944:viii). Thus, Du Bois headed off to a part of the world that had long fascinated her, where she hoped to find a society relatively untouched by Western influences and colonial administrations. Her stay in the interior mountainous village of Atimelong required learning Dutch, the administrative language of the then Netherlands East Indies; Malaya, the lingua franca of the area; and Abui, the previously unstudied and unwritten language of the Alorese.

The resulting publication, *The People of Alor*, was a landmark study. Methodologically, it was innovative in its use of a variety of techniques—ethnographic description of institutions and childhood; the collection of eight long autobiographies and of children's drawings; the use of word associations, the Porteous Maze test, and Rorschachs—to collect data pertinent to a specific research problem and in the collaborative analysis of those data. As one of the first efforts at psychocultural synthesis, it was also of great theoretical import. In her review of *The People of Alor*, Hortense Powdermaker* said:

We are only at the beginning of research on the cultural conditioning of personality and all studies of this type are necessarily of a pioneer character. This one is particularly important because of its thoroughness and because of its exploratory nature. Students in the field of personality and culture are deeply indebted to both Dr. Du Bois and her collaborators. (Powdermaker 1945:161)

Du Bois' years with the State Department intervened, and she did not again undertake anthropological fieldwork until 1961, this time in India. Nonetheless, she traveled extensively during this period, spending a total of nineteen months in South Asia, thirteen months in Europe, and shorter periods in other parts of the world. *Social Forces in Southeast Asia* (1949) was published during this period and represented a move away from the more psychological research undertaken in Alor to a broad interest in acculturation and the political historical forces producing it. She believed that the line of research taken in Alor could not be pushed much further; and meanwhile her experiences in the State Department during and after World War II had inevitably shifted her attention toward questions of social, political, and cultural change, since these were the focus of arguments over policy.

In 1961, while at Harvard, Du Bois initiated a long-term, interdisciplinary study (1961–72) of sociocultural change in Bhubaneswar, Orissa, India, a town that represented old and new forces in that society. It was a new state capital of administration that had been an ancient temple center. For more than a decade she and a series of American and Indian graduate students investigated different aspects of ongoing change there. As with her Alor study, this project in India was interdisciplinary and collaborative in nature, involving students from such disparate fields as anthropology, sociology, religion, and urban planning.

Working in a complex culture such as India was both an attraction and a challenge for Du Bois. She was attracted by its complexity and the sociocultural wealth of experience Indian friends and informants provided but was increasingly disenchanted with facile "social science" methods used to investigate such complexity.

The longer I live the greater is my pleasure in, and my perception of, complexity; by the same token the more acute has become my distrust of facile socio-cultural generalizations. I am indebted to my Indian friends and acquaintances for gratifying this bent. As I look back, I realize that inadvertently I have been directed to this personal and professional position by the sequence of my field experiences: the archival nature of ethnography in California, the vital but exotic primitive society of Alor, and finally this experience with the complex high culture of India. (Du Bois 1970a:236)

In the end, Du Bois was dissatisfied with the results of her own research in Bhubaneswar, a survey of changing values, and chose not to publish the material. However, she directed nine Ph.D. dissertations that investigated different facets of change there and continued to serve as consultant and mentor to her younger colleagues, most of whom have continued to do research in Bhubaneswar and other parts of India.

Du Bois' life and career has been long and varied, spanning much of the twentieth century. While she in no way identifies with feminism, in several respects her life exemplifies many of the goals and values of contemporary feminism. Du Bois pursued an academic career at a time when it was uncommon for women to do so, and without any special mentor relationships. She moved from one set of goals to another in a largely independent fashion, gaining recognition by right of her accomplishments, and finally becoming one of Harvard's few tenured women professors. She was a pioneer for subsequent generations of women anthropologists.

Du Bois' collaborative research, beginning with her very first publication with Dorothy Demetracopoulou (Lee) on the Wintu (1931) and concluding with her research in India, is illustrative of the cooperative values within women's studies today. Similarly, her orientation to interdisciplinary research is congruent with contemporary feminism. As a fieldworker Du Bois was sensitive to the need to examine women's as well as men's lives. In Alor, for example, she collected autobiographies from and tested both women and men. In addition, her theoretical orientation at that time necessitated that she carefully examine women's lives, particularly as mothers. In India, by contrast, Du Bois had limited contact with women because of linguistic barriers, her limited Oriya and their nonexistent English, but she encouraged her graduate students to learn Oriya and to work with women as well as with men. Finally, as an exacting but supportive teacher and mentor to numerous students, Du Bois epitomizes the ideal professional women who is assertive and accomplished but also cooperative and nurturing.

During her long career Du Bois has been awarded numerous honors. After World War II she received the U.S. Army Exceptional Civilian Award (1945) and the Order of the Crown of Thailand Peace Medal (1949). Harvard, Wilson, Mills, Mount Holyoke, and Wheaton colleges have all conferred honorary degrees upon her. Du Bois received the American Association of University Women Achievement Award for 1961 and was cited as Outstanding Woman in the Field of Education in *Who's Who of American Women* in 1967. She was a fellow at the Center for Advanced Study in the Behavioral Sciences at Stanford (1958–59) and the recipient of a National Science Foundation grant (1961–72). In addition, her two principal professional organizations awarded her their top honor by electing her president, first of the American Anthropological Association (1968–69) and then of the Association of Asian Studies (1969–70).

Finally, Du Bois' professional career can be viewed as bringing her full circle intellectually—from an early interest in broad historical processes, through a series of precise research projects in small-scale societies, to concerns with broad patterns of sociocultural change in contemporary complex societies. Her views of anthropology as a discipline have similarly shifted from a cautious acceptance of it as a social science (Du Bois 1970a:223) to the more recent conclusion that anthropology is a "philosophical humanism . . . not a pure or social science as the word 'science' is now used. It is rather a science in the earlier sense of the word, as it was used in the past century: an attempt to understand. [And] the goals of our discipline are to advance an understanding of the panhuman condition and its specific variations" (Du Bois 1980:9).

Note

1. All quotes not otherwise cited are from personal interviews with Cora Du Bois. I wish to express my appreciation to Cora Du Bois for sharing with me many personal memories of her life and career and for providing me with a detailed curriculum vitae and list of publications.

References and Works About Cora Du Bois

Powdermaker, Hortense
1945   Review of *The People of Alor. American Anthropologist* 47:155–61.

Selected Works by Cora Du Bois

1932a Tolowa Notes. *American Anthropologist* 34 (2): 248–62.

1932b Study of Wintu Mythology. *Journal of American Folklore* 45 (178): 375–500.

1935   Wintu Ethnography. *University of California Publications in American Archae-ology and Ethnography* 36 (1): 1–148.

1936   Wealth Concept As an Integrative Factor in Tolowa-Tututni Culture. In *Essays in Anthropology in Honor of Alfred Louis Kroeber.* Robert Lowie, ed. Pp. 49–65. Berkeley: University of California Press.

1937a Some Anthropological Perspectives on Psycho-analysis. *Psycho-analytic Review* 24 (3): 246–63.

1937b Some Psychological Objectives and Techniques in Ethnography. *Journal of Social Psychology* 3:285–301.

1938   Feather Cult of Middle Columbia. *General Series in Anthropology*, no. 7:1–47.

1939   The 1870 Ghost Dance. *Anthropological Records* 3 (1): 1–151.

1940   How They Pay Debts in Alor. *Asia* (September):483–86.

1941a Why People Quarrel in Alor. *Asia* (February):91–94.

1941b Attitudes Toward Food and Hunger in Alor. In *Language, Culture and Personality: Essays in Memory of Edward Sapir.* Leslie Spier, ed. Menasha, Wisc.: Memorial

Publication Fund. (Reprinted in *Personal Character and Cultural Milieu*. Douglas G. Haring, ed. Pp. 158–70. New York: Syracuse University Press, 1948.)

1944 *The People of Alor*, with analyses by Abram Kardiner and Emil Oberholzer. Minneapolis: University of Minnesota Press. (Reissued 1960 by Harvard University Press, with new chapter.)

1945 The Alorese. In *The Psychological Frontiers of Society*. Abram Kardiner, ed. Pp. 101–5. New York: Columbia University Press.

1949 *Social Forces in Southeast Asia*. Minneapolis: University of Minnesota Press. (Reprinted 1959, Cambridge: Harvard University Press.)

1950 Cultural Facets of South Asian Regionalism. In *South Asia in the World Today*. P. Talbot, ed. Pp. 27–44. Chicago: University of Chicago Press.

1951a Culture Shock. In *To Strengthen World Freedom*. Special Publication Series 1:22–24. Washington, D.C.: Institute of International Education.

1951b The Use of Social Science Concepts to Interpret Historical Materials: Comments on Two Preceding Articles. *Far Eastern Quarterly* 11 (1): 31–34.

1952 The World Health Organization in a World of Changing Value. *Institute of International Education News Bulletin* 28 (1): 5–9.

1953 Research in Cross-cultural Education. *Institute of International Education News Bulletin* 28 (9): 5–8.

1954a Motivation of Students Coming to the U.S. *Institute of International Education News Bulletin* 29 (9): 2–7.

1954b Educational Incentives to Citizenship and Public Morality. In *Yearbook of Education*. R. K. Hall, N. Haurs, and J. A. Lauwern, eds. Pp. 440–44. London: Evans Ltd.

1955a Some Notions on Learning Intercultural Understanding. In *Education and Anthropology*. George Spindler, ed. Pp. 89–105. Stanford, Calif: Stanford University Press.

1955b The Dominant Value Profile of American Culture. *American Anthropologist* 57 (6): 1232–39.

1956 *Foreign Students and Higher Education in the United States*. Washington, D.C.: American Council on Education.

1958 Robert H. Lowie: Anthropologist. (Obituary.) *Science* 127 (3291): 181–82.

1959a Cultural Interplay Between East and West. In *The East and West Must Meet: A Symposium*. Benjamin H. Brown, ed. Pp. 3–20. East Lansing: Michigan State University Press.

1959b The Public Health Worker As an Agent of Socio-Cultural Change. *Health Education Monographs* 5:3–19. (Reissued 1961 in *The Planning of Change: A Challenge to Social Practitioners and Behavioral Scientists*. W. G. Bemis et al., eds. New York: Rinehart and Winston.)

1960a The Form and Substance of Status: A Javanese-American Relationship. In *In the Company of Man: Twenty Portraits of Anthropologists*. Joseph B. Casagrande, ed. Pp. 211–32. New York: Harper and Row.

1960b Paul Radin: An Appreciation. In *Culture in History: Essays in Honor of Paul Radin*. Stanley Diamond, ed. Pp. ix–xvi. New York: Columbia University Press for Brandeis University.

1963a Curriculum in Cultural Anthropology. In *The Teaching of Anthropology*. David Mandelbaum et al., eds. American Anthropological Association Memoir 96: 27–38.

1963b Socio-cultural Aspects of Population Growth. In *Human Fertility and Population Problems*. Roy O. Greep, ed. Pp. 251–56. Cambridge: Schenkman Publishing Co.

1963c Present Interests of Anthropology in the United States. In *The Behavioral Sciences Today*. Bernard Berelson, ed. Pp. 26–37. New York: Basic Books.

1970a Studies in an Indian Town. In *Women in the Field: Anthropological Experiences*. Peggy Golde, ed. Pp. 221–36. Chicago: Aldine Press.

1970b The Association for Asian Studies in a Changing Society: A Structural-Functional Appraisal (Presidential Address). *Asian Professional Review* 1 (2): 1–11.

1973 Schooling, Youth and Modernization in India. In *Population, Politics and the Future of Southern Asia*. James F. Guyst and W. Howard Wriggins, eds. Pp. 296–317. New York: Columbia University Press.

1974 The Gratuitous Act: An Introduction to the Comparative Study of Friendship Patterns. In *The Compact: Selected Dimensions of Friendship*. Newfoundland Social and Economic Papers No. 3. Elliott Leyton, ed. Institute of Social and Economic Research, Memorial University of Newfoundland.

1980 Some Anthropological Hindsights. *Annual Review of Anthropology* 9:1–15.

1960b *Lowie's Selected Papers in Anthropology*. Berkeley: University of California Press. (As ed.)

Coauthored Works

Du Bois, Cora, and D. Demetracopoulou
1931 Wintu Myths. *University of California Publications in American Archaeology and Ethnography* 28 (5): 279–403.

Du Bois, Cora, and Emil Oberholzer
1942 Rorschach Tests and Native Personality in Alor, Dutch East Indies. *New York Academy of Sciences* (trans. series 2) 4 (5): 168–70.

SUSAN SEYMOUR

Katherine Dunham

(1912–   )

Afro-American dancer, choreographer, and anthropologist Katherine Dunham is best known for her research on the forms and functions of dance, particularly in Afro-American cultures of the Caribbean and Latin America, North America, and in Senegal, West Africa.

Katherine Dunham was born in 1912 in Glen Ellyn, a small suburb of Chicago. She spent her childhood and youth in Joliet, Illinois, except for a brief interlude after her mother's death, when she stayed with relatives in a Chicago black ghetto. In *A Touch of Innocence* (1959), an autobiographical account of her childhood, Dunham describes those who influenced her early life: her mother, an accomplished, educated woman of property with French-Canadian and Indian ancestry, whose influence extended beyond her early death; her father, who operated a small dry-cleaning establishment, ambitious and overbearing, of Malagasy and West African descent; her stepmother, also an educated woman and teacher; and her older brother, Albert, Jr., who was to become a brilliant philosopher, protégé of George Herbert Mead and Alfred N. Whitehead, and who preceded her to the University of Chicago and served as advisor and mentor. With his encouragement she passed the difficult entrance examination, joining the intellectual elite who were admitted to that institution, along with a number of other black students, notably anthropologist St. Clair Drake.

Signs of the three lifetime pursuits that Dunham developed while at the University of Chicago—dance, anthropology, and theater—were already apparent in her early life. Her mixed ancestry and association with culturally different relatives and neighbors attuned her to cultural variation (Dunham 1959). During a visit with relatives in Alton, Illinois, and St. Louis, she became acquainted with a southern variant of black expression and in her autobiography speaks of the beginning of her "possession by the blues" (1959:179). She learned the value and uses of the theater through observing the black theater—both in front and behind the scenes—which flourished during her childhood stay with her aunt in Chicago. As a young girl she was inspired to plan and direct a cabaret for a church social, for which she performed a Russian dance in costume. During high school she was active in athletics and in the Terpsichorean (dance) Club. She continued her interest and lessons in dance throughout junior college in Joliet, and by the time she moved to the University of Chicago, she was able to partly support her education by giving dance lessons. She also worked part-time as an assistant librarian (Beckford 1979).

While attending the University of Chicago, Dunham studied modern dance and ballet with Ludmilla Speranzeva; with Mark Turbyfill of the Chicago Civic Opera Company as ballet master, she formed a black dance group that performed at the Chicago Beaux Arts Ball in 1931. Madame Speranzeva assisted her in establishing the Chicago Negro School of Ballet, which stressed ballet, Spanish, and modern dance (Beckford 1979). She and her group performed in a number of settings in the following years. Because of her growing reputation and her interest in folklore and dance, Ruth Page, noted choreographer, invited her to appear as a solo lead with the Chicago Civic Opera Theater in La Guiablesse (1934), based on Martinique folklore. As part of the cultural movements that included—and some of which grew out of—the Harlem Renaissance, other artists of the time (such as poets Langston Hughes and Claude McKay, writer Zora Neale Hurston,* and dancers Asadata Dafora, Martha Graham, Agnes DeMille, Lester Horton, and many others) were using African and West Indian themes in their works. Katherine performed in one of the productions of the Cube Theater, founded by her brother and a colleague; there she met poet Langston Hughes, anthropologist St. Clair Drake, dramatists Ruth Attaway and Canada Lee, and W. C. Handy (Beckford 1979).

At the university Katherine pursued her interest in dance through the study of cultural anthropology. She was introduced to African dance traditions by Robert Redfield and was influenced by his ideas on folk societies, as exemplifying cohesive social organization and sacred outlook, in which art was an intrinsic part of social and ceremonial life (Aschenbrenner 1981). Faye-Cooper Cole engaged her in his interest in the use of percussive instruments for communication in nonliterate societies. He also impressed on his students the importance of detailed field observations. Melville Herskovits's work on Haitian and African cultures influenced the young student to choose Haiti as her primary field area. She was intrigued by Caribbean cultures because there the practices and beliefs of African cultures were stronger and far less influenced by European cultures than in the United States (Dunham 1941). A. R. Radcliffe-Brown, Bronislaw Malinowski, and Margaret Mead* "dropped in" at the Anthropology Department, conveying the excitement of a new field to this aspiring young student of culture, in the stimulating intellectual atmosphere of President Robert Hutchins's tenure at the university (Dunham 1969:66).

Eric Fromm and sociologist Charles Johnson were also interested in the young student's development, as a dynamic, brilliant, and personable individual who had escaped many of the restrictions put on her as a black person (Pratt).[1] With their influence she was invited to appear before the board of the Julius Rosenwald Foundation, which gave financial aid to young artists, to present a proposal for the study of dance and society in the West Indies. During her interview she demonstrated her thesis about the relationship between dance and culture by performing in the styles of ballet, modern dance, and African movement, revealing the intimate relationship between dance movement and the values and lifestyles of a society. Surprised and impressed, the board agreed to support her research (Dunham 1969).

In her research design, Dunham planned to compare the dance forms of Haiti, Jamaica, Martinique and Trinidad, before returning to Haiti for a longer, more intensive study. Herskovits advised her in her plan of study during a nine-month preparatory course at Northwestern University. She was instructed in the techniques of fieldwork, briefed on Caribbean cultural patterns and etiquette, and given practical advice on preparations for living in tropical and impoverished countries (Dunham). Arriving in Haiti in 1935, Dunham encountered the rigid caste system based on skin color, which she had to circumvent in order to pursue her research. She formed friendships with peasants and others lowest on the social scale, despite disapproval of elite and middle-class acquaintances. Herskovits had provided her with letters of introduction to political and intellectual leaders in Haiti and elsewhere. Some of these were helpful, in particular, anthropologist Dr. John Price-Mars, who had published considerable work in French on African survivals in Haitian religion. For the most part, her most fruitful contacts came through informal contacts and introductions. In particular, it was the peasant class—generally those of darkest skin—rather than the more socially exalted mulattoes, who followed the Vodun with its sacred dance. The latter, who identified with European, especially French, culture, rejected African cultural expressions.

Dunham encountered anti-American feeling among Haitians, since the U.S. Marines had only shortly before been withdrawn after a "protection action" to contain political unrest. Her black heritage, however, helped her gain access to the information she needed. In Haiti and among the Maroons in Accompong, Jamaica, the people regarded her as one of the lost people of Nan Guinée, or Africa, and they exhorted her to instruct her people in the ancestral secrets they revealed (Dunham 1969).

Dunham's preference for associating with the peasants of Haiti was reinforced by her appreciation of the strength, selflessness, and courage of the "authentic African woman" in the New World, who was given her "just due" rather than being in the background as in African cultures such as Senegal, in which Muslim traditions are strong. Dunham viewed the true African woman as highly independent and self-reliant. In some African cultures and among Haitian peasants, women own and maintain property and conduct business. Haitian women often do not marry because of patriarchal laws, but form long-term liaisons with men referred to as *placée* (Pratt; Dunham). In contrast, she notes that among the elite and middle class, wives and daughters were in the background, seldom entering into discussions and usually serving while their husbands and sons entertained (Dunham 1969:128).

In Accompong, in the mountains of Jamaica, Katherine Dunham first had her research skills put to the test. The Maroons were reluctant to perform, before a stranger, dances—such as the Koromantee, a war dance—that were sacred and politically sensitive for a people with a history of rebellion. Their desire to communicate their knowledge through her to the "lost peoples" overcame their caution, and shortly before she departed, she witnessed the dance, experiencing the value of patience and respect for the feelings and reticences of people in accomplishing research aims (Dunham 1947). Her concern for fieldwork ethics grew more pronounced as she became involved in the African-based Vodun religion. She felt a personal conflict between her role as initiate and that of observer and scientist. Educated in Western traditions, Katherine Dunham could not suppress her "never-ending quest for the novel" and concern for scientific research in order to embrace the beliefs of those she came to know and respect (Dunham 1969). When she would begin to experience the power of the religious ceremonies, the scientist would take over, noting clothing, language, and other traits, and she did not experience possession by the gods. She always found the "split in attitude" and the feeling of being "outsider within" difficult in investigating personal habits, such as marriage customs and religious beliefs (Dunham 1969:105).

Katherine Dunham gives credit to her friend Dumarsais Estimé, later president of Haiti (1946–50), for awakening her social conscience (Dunham 1969:42). She was introduced to him during her first trip to Haiti. Although Estimé's aspirations of economic and social progress for his fellow Haitians included no place for the Vodun—he placed his faith in education and economic development rather than in culture and art—she was nevertheless affected by his vision and his devotion to the cause of black people. She and her family had encountered discrimination: her father had to fight to settle in the white suburb of Glen Ellyn; her brother had not received due recognition, despite his brilliance and popularity, throughout his educational career; and she had an unpleasant exchange with a teacher as a child and also later at the library where she worked (Dunham 1959; Beckford 1979). As a result of her association with Estimé, she became more politically aware. However, she found in her art a means of expressing social convictions, through development of skills and creativity, self-esteem, and cultural freedom among her students; and promotion of understanding of and respect for African-based cultural expression by professionals and lay audiences. Further, she believes that participation in art and dance, in the broadest of "rhythmic movement and kinesthetic response" is a basic human need (Dunham personal communication, 1970).

Dunham saw herself and Estimé as in the "avant garde of negritude" (1969:145), referring to the concept later developed by her friend Leopold Senghor, president of Senegal. Yet she herself had problems with the term: "I do not admit to a spiritual or cultural poverty in Black people which would make it necessary to coin a word or system of thinking of oneself outside the human division'' (1969:5). This view was in concurrence with her need for artistic freedom and the liberty to choose cultural alternatives. Still, she recognizes the value and importance of the traditional African beliefs and values to all black people, to give them a sense of ''peoplehood'' and a history.

Dunham also experienced a duality between the drive merely to record, to authenticate by detail, and to reveal through dramatic form the meaning of the experience: ''I seemed always to live this sort of dual existence of having my intellect absorbed in searching out and annotating the real and authentic steps and movements and an eye trained to see all of this color and movement and drama translated into theater idiom'' (Pierre 1941:11). Here her interest in theater can be seen as integral to her anthropological mission, since in the broad sense, religious rituals are theater. Later she would use the conventions and techniques of theater, as Mead and Malinowski and others used literary devices, such as vivid descriptions and character depictions, to convey ethnographic insights and materials to lay audiences. She was able to communicate the spirit of social occasions and ceremonies through the nonverbal communication and physical setting of her dance performances.

After the ''Great Experience''—her fifteen-month odyssey, including nine months in Haiti—Dunham decided to pursue further her work at the University of Chicago, rather than at ''bourgeois'' Northwestern. This choice was her first step in breaking away from a purely academic career, although she was never to completely sever ties with academia. Shortly after her completion of requirements for her bachelor's degree, Redfield—who had seen some of her dance programs—remarked, ''What's wrong with being a dancer?'' (Dunham 1969:67). This had the effect of releasing her from further graduate studies and from her felt obligations to the Rosenwald and Guggenheim Foundations, both of which had supported her research, and to her anthropology teachers and to others who had helped her in her academic career. She turned to the dissemination and interpretation of her knowledge and insights through the medium of her choice, dance. Through her skill in communicating by kinesthetic response, combined with the visual effects of theater, she was able to lead her audiences to a profound comprehension of a different lifeway (Pratt).

Katherine Dunham's description of her research findings (1947) has been published in Spanish, French, and English, all of which she speaks. In addition, she can communicate in French Creole and Portuguese. Claude Lévi-Strauss (1947), who met her after seeing a performance, wrote a foreword to the French edition, commenting on the emotional richness and social cohesion in Vodun ceremonials, compared with restrictions on these expressions in European civilization. In the essay, Dunham categorizes types of Haitian dance, devoting most of the work to the Vodun, or sacred dance. She discusses its significance, socially and politically, and describes the sacred paraphernalia, instruments and musicians, and organization of dance groups. The last two chapters are devoted to her views concerning the functions of dance and the interrelationships between the forms of dance and their social and psychological functions. For all dance, release—the externalization of energy and emotions—serves a critical function (Dunham 1947). To the African, the release of energy is an important aspect of therapy, since "holding in" feelings can make one ill (Herskovits 1966). Dunham has applied this principle in her work with youth in East St. Louis, encouraging young men, in particular, to vent frustration in energetic, disciplined movements expressing aggression. Girls and young women experience positive feelings about developing sexuality through skilled movements of hip and abdomen, as well as feelings of personal competency in performance.

Dunham's functional approach, influenced by Herskovits, was reinforced throughout her dance career. She believes that much of her success, especially during the war years, lay in the social and psychological functions of dance: "I was living through my needs and the community's needs. By putting this process into theater we were creating a powerful experience with deep authenticity." Pearl Reynolds, a member of Dunham's company, described the response of a postwar British audience to *Shango*, a dance expressing the essence of the Caribbean god of thunder and war, as a scream of recognition of shared experiences and suffering (Reynolds). Psychiatrists recommended that patients attend Dunham performances and later asked them about their responses (Dunham).

The first professional Dunham company was formed in 1939, performing in Chicago and New York. Katherine Dunham supported these early beginnings through the federal writers' and theater projects, doing research on the Black Muslims as a cult; she produced and choreographed the ballet *L'Ag'Ya*, based on martial arts practiced in Martinique for the Federal Theater Project. There she met John Pratt, costume and set designer, whom she married in 1941. He designed her productions throughout her subsequent career. They adopted a daughter, Marie Christine, in 1951.

Dunham opened a School of Arts and Research for dance in New York in 1943, which included a Department of Cultural Studies and an Institute for Caribbean Research. With their home base in New York, Dunham and her dancers appeared in concert, musical comedy, and movies, and repeatedly toured the United States, Canada, Europe, Asia, and Latin America between 1940 and 1963, when the group disbanded. They received critical acclaim in the United States and abroad. Nevertheless, they encountered social discrimination in many cities with regard to public accommodations and audience segregation. Dunham frequently took stands against audience segregation and worked with the NAACP and Urban League to integrate audiences (Clark and Wilkerson 1978). She believes that the desegregation of dance performances and companies has been one of the company's most important achievements.

Throughout her career Dunham has collected materials and information from cultures around the world, using them in performances and housing them in the Katherine Dunham Museum, established in 1967. In addition, she has maintained a position in academia, lecturing on dance and anthropology at the University of Chicago, Yale, the Royal Anthropological Society of London, and the Anthropological Societies of Paris and Rio de Janeiro. She was visiting professor at Case Western Reserve, and she has been artist-in-residence at Southern Illinois University at Carbondale and at the University of California at Berkeley. She has received numerous honorary degrees and won many awards, including a Professional Achievement Award from the University of Chicago Alumni (1968), the Albert Schweitzer Music Award (1979), and the Kennedy Center Honors Award (1983), as well as medals and citations from the Government of Haiti.

In 1964 Katherine Dunham became artist-in-residence at Southern Illinois University at Carbondale, at the invitation of President DeLyte Morris, and choreographed the opera *Faust*. In the following years she traveled to Senegal, where she represented the United States at the Festival of Black Arts in Dakar and trained the National Ballet of Senegal (1965–66).

The greatest challenge of Katherine Dunham's career began in 1967, when she moved to East St. Louis to develop the Performing Arts Training Center of Southern Illinois University at Edwardsville. Working with gang members and other young street people and with children, Dunham applied her views on the role of dance in society to develop a group of self-aware, skilled, and knowledgeable young people, both in and outside of professional dance. She recalls:

There have been three stages of education in my life—the University of Chicago, the world, and East St. Louis . . . this city has been torn apart through the apathetic mentality induced by being on the dole . . . the inability for socialization and finally, the riots. . . . It is my aim here to socialize the young and old through "culturation," to make the individual aware of himself and his environment, to create a desire to be alive. (Mazer 1976)

Note

1. All references in parentheses that include surnames but no dates, as well as quotes not otherwise cited, are from personal communications with Katherine Dunham, John Pratt, and Pearl Reynolds. I would like to express my appreciation to Katherine Dunham and to John Pratt, posthumously, for their assistance in the preparation of this biography.

References and Works About Katherine Dunham

Aschenbrenner, Joyce
1978   Anthropology As a Lifeway: Katherine Dunham. In *KAISO: Katherine Dunham, An Anthology of Writings*. VéVé A. Clark and Margaret B. Wilkerson, eds. Berkeley: University of California.
1981   *Katherine Dunham: Reflections on the Social and Political Contexts of Afro-American Dance*. New York: Congress on Research in Dance.
1984   Public Ritual in an Urban Setting. *Anthropology and Humanism Quarterly* 9(2):8–14.
Aschenbrenner, Joyce, and Carolyn Hameedah Carr
1985   The Dance Technique of Katherine Dunham As a Community Rite de Passage, presented at American Popular Culture Association, Louisville, Ky.

Beckford, Ruth
1979   *Katherine Dunham, A Biography*. New York: Marcel Dekker.
Buckle, Richard
1948   *Katherine Dunham, Her Dancers, Singers, Musicians*. London: William Clowes and Sons.
Clark, VéVé, and Margaret B. Wilkerson, eds.
1978   *KAISO: Katherine Dunham, An Anthology of Writings*. Berkeley: University of California.
Harnan, Terry
1974   *African Rhythm, American Dance: A Biography of Katherine Dunham*. New York: Alfred A. Knopf.
Haskins, James
1982   *Katherine Dunham*. New York: Coward, McCann and Geoghegan.
Mazer, Gwen
1976   The Katherine Dunham Legend. *Living Together* Chicago Sun Times, November. (Katherine Dunham Collection. Southern Illinois University, Carbondale.)
Pierre, Dorathi Bock
1941   A Talk with Katherine Dunham. *Educational Dance*. The Dance Collection, Lincoln Center, New York (August–September).

Selected Works by Katherine Dunham

1938   The Future of the Negro in Dance. *Dance Herald* 3 (5). The Dance Collection, Lincoln Center, New York.
1941a The Negro Dance. In *The Negro Caravan*. Sterling A. Brown, Arthur P. Davis, and Ulysseus Lee, eds. New York: Dryden Press.
1941b Form and Function in Primitive Dance. *Educational Dance*. The Dance Collection, Lincoln Center, New York (October).
1946a Ethnic Dancing. *Dance Magazine*. The Dance Collection, Lincoln Center, New York. (September).
1946b *Journey to Accompong*. New York: Henry Holt and Co.
1947   Las Danzas de Haiti, *Acta Antropologica* 11 (4). Mexico (in Spanish and English). (Reprinted as Les Danses d'Haiti. Paris: Fasquel Press, 1957; and Dances of Haiti, Center for Afro-American Studies, University of California at Los Angeles, XXV, 78p. 1983.)
1959   *A Touch of Innocence*. New York: Harcourt, Brace and World.
1969   *Island Possessed*. Garden City: Doubleday and Co.
1974   *Kasamance*. New York: Third Press.

JOYCE ASCHENBRENNER

Ann Kindrick Fischer

(1919–1971)

Ann Kindrick Fischer was a social anthropologist known for her study of the concept of role and for her contributions to medical, psychological, and applied anthropology.

Fischer was born Anna Ruth Kindrick on May 22, 1919, in Kansas City, Kansas, eldest of the three daughters of Thomas W. Kindrick and Gertrude Anna Miller. Her parents' families were in some part frontier people—from Texas and Oklahoma on her father's side and Missouri on her mother's side. Her father was a small-scale contractor and something of a traveling man. Her relations with him were considerably strained, at least in later years. Her mother died at the age of thirty-four, when Ann was just twelve.

Her mother's death was undoubtedly a crucial formative and traumatic experience for her. Fischer's later phrasing of it was that she had been "orphaned." Her mother's sister, Mary Miller, a professional woman (bookkeeper), became her effective mother and was legally made her guardian. At least one of her two younger sisters (Wanda Jean and Betty Lou) was cared for by her other aunt, Opal Miller. Fischer was not on speaking terms with her father at the time of his death in 1962.

As a child Kindrick was schooled in Kansas City. In 1936 she entered Christian College at Columbia, Missouri. It is worth noting that she did not live at home again—a pattern more characteristic of men than of women in her generation. At Christian she completed an Adjunct in Arts degree (1938). She later transferred to Ottawa College in Kansas, and then in 1940 to the University of Kansas at Lawrence, where she received her Bachelor of Arts degree (1941). From 1941 to 1942 she did additional graduate work.

By the time she had reached her twenties, Kindrick had experienced the world in certain aspects that may be considered atypical and unusual. Being firstborn in what came to be an embattled family undoubtedly sensitized her to birth order (see Fischer 1962). Being "orphaned" gave her a sharp sense of the difference between the theory and practice of family life. It had the additional and specific effect of exposing her to the practical example of her diminutive but determined maiden Aunt Mary as a role model and as a constant source of stability when her family and father had seemingly failed her. A certain feminism would seem to be the logical derivative of these experiences. But they also led Kindrick to the recognition of the separability of biological and sociological motherhood. To be sure, it was some time before she was able to digest, analyze, and communicate these experiences. They appear, nonetheless, to be personal concerns transmuted by training and experience into anthropological insights, since they surface later in her professional work.

During World War II Kindrick lived in Washington, D.C., where she was briefly married to James Meredith. In Washington she served as registrar of the School of Advanced International Studies (1944–46).

She first became interested in anthropology after taking a course in physical anthropology given by Loren Eiseley at the University of Kansas (see Fischer 1970a). In 1946 she entered Radcliffe in the Department of Anthropology. This was the traditionalist wing of the discipline at Harvard at the time, and graduate students tended to be polarized by the separation of the anthropology program from the social anthropology program of the interdisciplinary Department of Social Relations. Somewhat exceptionally, she maintained academic and informal contact with both programs. Though the formal direction of her graduate work was in the hands of Ernest Albert Hooton, also particularly important influences on her scholarly development were Clyde Kluckhohn, David Aberle, and Gregory Bateson. Florence Kluckhohn was a strong if somewhat daunting role model.

At Cambridge Kindrick met and was courted by John Lyle Fischer, a graduate student in the Department of Social Relations. While doing fieldwork on Truk, they were married on Jack's birthday, July 9, 1949. It was an unusually happy marriage and a remarkable professional union as well. Their common interests and a certain complementarity of both talents and temperaments led to a smooth and effective professional collaboration. An important component of both their personal and professional relationship was the fact that they had both undergone psychoanalysis during the period of their graduate studies. This shared experience deepened the intimacy of their relation to each other, while also serving as a strong and enduring intellectual orientation in their professional work.

Fischer's research was nonetheless significantly autonomous and independent of her husband's. The fieldwork for her doctoral dissertation began with three months alone on the island of Romonum in Truk lagoon. It was a characteristically forthright combination of career and motherhood: she was pregnant at the time. The nature of this first field experience and the others that followed she described and analyzed in detail in particular relation to sex roles (Fischer 1970a). Her dissertation, ''The Role of the Trukese Mother and Its Effect on Child Training,'' was approved in 1957.

Fischer's daughters—Madeleine (Nikko) and Mary Ann—were born at Kolonia, Ponape, in 1950 and 1952. (Fischer often remarked matter-of-factly that her decision to have children had delayed her professional career by ten years.) During the family's prolonged stay on Truk and Ponape (1949–54), Trukese was the family language. Fischer also had a reading knowledge of French and German.

Fischer's undergraduate degree at the University of Kansas (1941) was in sociology. Her graduate work at University of Kansas (1941–42) and then at Radcliffe (1946–49) took her into social anthropology. To her credit, she never saw any real disjunction between the two fields, and while her subsequent professional work involved substantial exposure to alien cultures—Truk and Ponape, Houma Indian and Japanese—it also entailed intimate involvement in the study of her own society—a New England village, social work, medicine, and the southern black family. She moved easily among these worlds, not only because of personal gifts of perceptiveness and sensitivity but also because she was able to integrate a theoretical position that encompassed them and made them accessible to intelligent, disciplined, and skeptical exploration.

Central to this theoretical bent was her extraordinary use of the concept of role—extraordinary in both precision and flexibility. Fischer seems to have reached this insight early (see Fischer 1949), and it is expressed with elegant clarity in her doctoral dissertation:

The concept of role is a linking concept between the system which prescribes the behavior patterns, and the individual who must live them out. Such a link could never be rigid, nor could it ever be extremely flexible. In either case it would threaten both the integration of the system, and the integration of the individual. Thus, a role may have two facets, one as a system of ideal behavior patterns, and one as a range of behavior within which the individual may still be considered as playing out of his role. . . . Any individual in any role must perform his acts within a larger setting as he plays not one, but several roles at any given time. Thus a mother may be a wife, a sweetheart, a daughter, a grandmother, a sister, a wage earner, simultaneously. What she does as a mother is influenced by her other roles, by all that she has learned through the social system from her own life, by her own, and the idiosyncracies of others, which play upon the situation. These latter, the idiosyncracies, account for the range of possible behavior in a given role. (1957:103)

This common sense quality to Fischer's conceptualization endows the idea of role with a high order of explanatory power and a no-nonsense way of generating and testing both descriptions and explanations. It removes the concept of role from the context of a vague and abstract "dynamic principle" in some sort of dialectical relationship to status, and renders it immediately operational as a mode of apprehending the real actions of real people.

Fischer pursued the theme of role analysis throughout her subsequent research. In large part the common focus was on nuclear family roles: woman, mother, child, adolescent, the family, and socialization. In all of this work a prominent emphasis is placed on the contrast between the ideal and the actual. In life as well as in research, she looked beyond the normative to discern the revealing variation that lay beneath it.

A striking example of her insight is her application of role theory to the welfare system:

Since children are expensive, economics plays an important part in the role of the father. The state takes over this economic role in case of need. Not only are the economic aspects of the husband-father role in a fatherless family taken over by the state, but the state sometimes attempts to regulate the conduct of the reciprocal role, that of the wife-mother. If the state assumes the economic functions of her husband, a dependent mother, like a good wife, must conduct herself as though she were married to the impersonal state. The sexual rights to a woman in our society are assumed to be accompanied by the assumption of economic obligations to her. The burden of proof that the economic obligations are not accompanied by the sexual rights falls upon the woman who has a lover, so far as the state is concerned. (Fischer 1964:164)

The conception of the welfare state as a cuckolded husband is a uniquely penetrating idea, resonant with implications for the emotion generated by welfare politics. It is also vintage Ann Fischer.

Returning to Cambridge from Ponape, she became a research assistant on the Ford Foundation Six Cultures Project (1954–57), a comparative study of socialization under the direction of Beatrice B. Whiting at Harvard's Laboratory of Human Development. Ann Fischer's husband joined her in a study of children in a New England town (Fischer & Fischer 1963; Fischer, Minturn et al. 1964; Fischer, Whiting et al. 1966). This was followed by a postdoctoral year as research associate at the Children's Medical Center, studying the hospital (funded by the Russell Sage Foundation).

In 1958 Jack Fischer accepted an appointment in the Anthropology Department at Tulane. In 1959 Ann Fischer became the first anthropologist to hold a fellowship in biostatistics and epidemiology when she was appointed training assistant at the School of Public Health and Tropical Medicine (Halpern 1973:292). This additional postdoctorate year of training resulted in a number of medical papers discussing such conditions as allergy, kuru, and lupus.

Fischer's teaching spanned six of Tulane's eleven colleges. She was appointed assistant professor in the School of Social Work (1960) and was promoted to associate professor (1963). She retained her appointment in the School of Social Work until 1966, even though in 1964 she was also appointed to the Anthropology Department at Newcomb College. She became a full professor in 1968. She was a thoughtful and engaged as well as dedicated teacher.

In accordance with the complexity of her academic position, Fischer played many different academic roles. Her research interests followed several different paths—medicine, social work, feminism, and ethnology (see bibliography).

The Fischers spent 1961–62 at the University of Kyushu in Fukuoka, and 1963–64 at the Center for Advanced Study in the Behavioral Sciences at Stanford. At Tulane Ann Fischer was increasingly involved in the complex committee structure of the university and served in many of the most responsible positions on the campus, including the university senate and the President's Advisory Committee. She felt a particularly deep commitment to the Committee for Educationally Disadvantaged Students. Hers was a quiet but firm and effective voice in many matters of controversy, and especially those involving minority rights. Concerned about the plight of the Houma Indians (Fischer 1965a), she waged a largely invisible battle that eventually destroyed the tripartite segregation of the school system in their area and subsequently contributed to a real improvement in their general situation. Their fight for official recognition as Indians continues, but Fischer's personal achievements on their behalf have been a major turning point in their history.

Fischer's interest in the role of women is consistent throughout her career. In addition, her writings on the general position of women as anthropologists (Fischer and Golde 1968) and as field-workers (Fischer 1970a) are detailed and insightful. In *Field Work in Five Cultures*, she frankly discusses the problems of combining family and professional responsibilities, as well as the relative advantages and disadvantages of being a woman in the field.

A satisfying role in field work is often difficult for a woman to develop, partly because of the lack of professionalization of women in other parts of the world. . . . There is no one way that a woman will be accepted in all cultures. On the other hand, in every culture a woman is approached differently and has access to slightly different kinds of information than does a man. (1970a:288)

Although the Tulane Department of Anthropology of Fischer's time has been singled out as one of the least sexist in the nation (Sanjek 1978), this was not true throughout the university. In support of the rights of women, Fischer chaired a Committee of the Tulane Chapter of the American Association of University Professors studying discriminatory treatment of women. She authored a report (Fischer 1968) that was practical and effective in documenting the situation and monitoring changes in it.

The accomplishments of Ann Fischer's last years are even more remarkable in having been attained in the face of a cruel and debilitating illness known to be terminal. Her courage, stoicism, and acceptance of the inevitable were inspiring. Within the limitations of what she could not change, she continued to play her many roles with energy and dedication. Indeed, throughout her life much of her success in combining family and career responsibilities resulted from her clear perception of roles and how they work.

Fischer was an accomplished anthropologist. She was also a very feminine woman, a very maternal mother, and a very loyal and supportive wife. Her success in these roles seems inextricably interwoven with the keenly intelligent and fully professional analysis she makes of them in her published work.

References and Works About Ann Fischer

Halpern, Katherine Spencer
1973　Ann Fischer 1919–1971. *American Anthropologist* 75:292–94.

Selected Works by Ann Fischer

1948　People of Genadendal. *The Geographical Magazine* 21:248–49. London.

1949　Culture-in-personality. *Seminar Papers in Concepts in Social Anthropology* 1948/ 49. Tozzer Library, Harvard.

1950　Trukese Privacy Patterns. *Naval Research Reviews* (July):9–15.

1957　The Role of the Trukese Mother and Its Effect on Child Training. Unpublished Ph.D. dissertation, Radcliffe.

1962　Sibling Position As a Factor in the Choice of Pediatric Nursing As a Career. *Journal of Health and Human Behavior* 3:283–88.

1963　Reproduction on Truk. *Ethnology* 2:526–40.

1964　Culture, Communication, and Child Welfare. *Child Welfare* 43:161–69.

1965a History and Current Status of the Houma Indians. *Midcontinent American Studies Journal* (special issue: *The Indian Today*) 6:149–63. (Reprinted 1968 in *The American Indian Today*. Stuart Levine and Nancy Lurie, eds. Deland, Fla.: Everett, Edwards.)

1965b The Relevance of Culture to the Crisis Tasks of Adolescence. *Tulane Studies in Social Welfare* 8:43–52.

1966　Flexibility in an Expressive Institution: Sumo. *Southwestern Journal of Anthropology* 22:31–42.

1968　*Women at Tulane.* Report to the Tulane Chapter, American Association of University Professors (Mimeo).

1969　The Personality and Subculture of Anthropologists and Their Study of U.S. Negroes. In *Concepts and Assumptions in Contemporary Anthropology*. Stephen A. Tyler, ed. Pp. 12–17. Southern Anthropological Society Proceedings, No. 3. Athens: University of Georgia Press.

1970a Field Work in Five Cultures. In *Women in the Field*. Peggy Golde, ed. Pp. 267– 92. Chicago: Aldine.

Fischer, Ann, ed.
1970b Current Directions in Anthropology: A Special Issue. *Bulletins of the American Anthropological Association* 3 (3, pt. 2).

Coauthored Works

Fischer, Ann, Joseph D. Beasley, and Carl L. Harter
1966　Attitudes and Knowledge Relevant to Family Planning Among New Orleans Negro Women. *American Journal of Public Health* 56:1847–57.

1968　The Occurrence of the Extended Family at the Origin of the Family of Procreation: A Developmental Approach to Negro Family Structure. *Marriage and Family Living* 30:290–300.

Fischer, Ann, and Christine Derbes
1962   Delay in Seeking Medical Advice Among Tuberculosis Patients. *The British Journal of Diseases of the Chest* 56:30–38.
1966   Further Comments on Otterbein. *American Anthropologist* 68:497–99.

Fischer, Ann, Vincent J. Derbes, and John J. Stretch
1966   Lupus erythematosus and Sunshine: An Attempted Correlation. *Dermatologia Internationalis* 5:63–68.

Fischer, Ann, and John L. Fischer
1957   *The Eastern Carolines*. New Haven: The Pacific Science Board, National Academy of Sciences, National Research Council, in association with Human Relations Area Files.
1960   Aetiology of Kuru. *The Lancet* I (7139):1417.
1961   Culture and Epidemiology: A Theoretical Investigation of Kuru. *Journal of Health and Human Behavior* 2:16–25.
1963   The New Englanders of Orchard Town, U.S.A. In *Six Cultures—Studies of Child Rearing*. Beatrice Whiting, ed. Pp. 868–1010. New York: John Wiley & Sons.

Fischer, Ann, John L. Fischer, and Frank Mahony
1959   Totemism and Allergy. *International Journal of Social Psychiatry* 5:33–40.

Fischer, Ann, and Peggy Golde
1968   The Position of Women in Anthropology. *American Anthropologist* 70:339–43.

Fischer, Ann, Carl L. Harter, Virginia Ktsanes, and Joseph D. Beasley
1965   *Family Survey of Metropolitan New Orleans: Instruction Manual*. New Orleans: Tulane University, Population and Family Studies Unit (Mimeo).

Fischer, Ann, Dorothy K. Howerton, and Christine Derbes
1964   *Syllabus for Research Practicum*. Tulane University School of Social Work. Mimeograph.

Fischer, Ann, and Virginia Ktsanes
1969   *Family Structures in New Orleans Through Two Generations*: A Study of Family Structure, Family Composition and the Cycle of Family Life (mimeo).

Fischer, Ann, Leigh Minturn, William W. Lambert, John Fischer, et al.
1964   *Mothers of Six Cultures*. Sections on Orchard Town, New England, pp. 8–12, 189–99. New York: John Wiley & Sons.

Fischer, Ann, John W. M. Whiting, Irvin L. Child, William W. Lambert, et. al.
1966   *Field Guide for a Study of Socialization*. Six Cultures Series, vol. 1. New York: John Wiley & Sons.

Fischer, Ann, Gail R. Williams, John L. Fischer, and Leonard Kurland
1964   An Evaluation of the Kuru Genetic Hypothesis. *Journal de Génétique Humaine* 13:11–21.

MUNRO S. EDMONSON

Alice Cunningham Fletcher

(1838–1923)

American anthropologist Alice Cunningham Fletcher was especially known for her pioneering fieldwork among various Native American groups, including the Omaha, and for early writings on Indian music; advocate for Indian reform and Indian education.

Fletcher was born in Havana, Cuba, on March 15, 1838. Her mother, Lucia Adeline Jenks, was an educated socialite from Boston; her father, Thomas Gilman Fletcher, a graduate of Dartmouth (1824), was admitted to the bar in New York (1827). Thomas Fletcher had been in ill health for a number of years, and the family traveled to Havana hoping that the Cuban climate would restore his health. They returned to New York in the summer of 1838, where Thomas Fletcher died of consumption in November 1839. Alice Fletcher had an older half brother by her father's previous marriage. Her mother subsequently remarried a man named Gardner. Young Alice attended exclusive schools in New York.

As a young woman, Fletcher traveled in Europe and taught in several private schools; she also became a successful public lecturer for the temperance, anti-tobacco, and women's rights movements. In the early 1870s she joined Sorosis, a pioneer New York women's club. Fletcher helped found the Association for the Advancement of Women (1873) and served as its secretary for several years.

During that time, she first met Frederic W. Putnam, director of the Peabody Museum at Harvard, while preparing a series of eleven lectures, "Ancient America," sponsored by the Minnesota Academy of Sciences. In addition, she worked at shell mound excavations in Florida and Massachusetts beginning in 1878. Her lecture series discussed evidence of early man, the mound builders, and the value of anthropological study. Putnam encouraged her to become involved in anthropology, and he trained her informally in scientific approaches to archaeology. With his assistance she joined the Archaeological Institute of America and helped him raise money to preserve the Serpent Mound in Ohio in 1879. Although archaeology remained a lifelong interest, Fletcher, with the encouragement of

Lewis Henry Morgan and other friends, soon became interested in observing firsthand the cultures of living Native Americans.[1]

In 1879 Fletcher met Suzette (Bright Eyes) and Francis La Flesche, a sister and brother from the Omaha tribe, on a speaking tour of the United States. They described the conditions of reservation life and sought the support of politicians and other prominent citizens, hoping to prevent the removal of the Omaha from their tribal lands. The La Flesches represented Omaha tribal members who felt that individual legal title would guarantee the security of the Omaha and their land.

After Fletcher had gained the confidence of the La Flesches, she expressed her desire to observe the culture and conditions of contemporary Indians. At a time when anthropology solely depended on reports of native peoples from adventurers and missionaries, this forty-two-year-old Victorian woman eagerly packed up camping gear in a wooden wagon and returned with the La Flesches to the Omaha reservation in Nebraska. When the Omahas asked why she had come, she replied, ''I came to learn, if you will let me, some things about your tribal organization, social customs, tribal rites, traditions and songs. Also to see if I can help you in any way'' (Lurie 1966:48).

On her first trip to the Omaha reservation, she not only observed their culture but also became active in their struggle to gain individual title to tribal lands. She gathered signatures of forty-five Indians on a petition and personally presented the document to Congress. Returning East, Fletcher worked with members of the liberal Lake Mohonk Conference of the Friends of the Indians to exert political influence in Washington, D.C. She composed an initial draft of legislation that Congress enacted as the Omaha Act of 1882. The Omaha Act and the Dawes Severalty Act of 1887 gave each Indian legal title to a plot of land and also granted them citizenship.

The political climate of the times was reflected in the title of an article by Carl Schurz (1881): ''The Indian Dilemma—Civilization or Extinction.'' Many people, including Fletcher, subscribed to Lewis Henry Morgan's theory that Native Americans were the living representatives of his primary evolutionary stages of ''Savagery'' and ''Barbarism.'' Fletcher supported various methods of promoting Native American acculturation into the next stage: that of ''Civilization.'' For example, she promoted educational opportunities for Indians, raising money to send members of the Omaha tribe to be educated in the East. She was also appointed by the Women's Indian Association to administer a loan fund for Indians to be used for the purchase of land and building homes.

After passage of the Omaha Act of 1882, Congress appointed Fletcher special agent to oversee the allotment of the Omaha tribal lands, which she accomplished with the assistance of Francis La Flesche. In 1887, following passage of the Dawes Act, Fletcher received another congressional appointment to supervise the allotment of the Winnebago and Nez Percé tribal lands.

Fletcher spent the better part of three years in Idaho carrying out the task of Nez Percé allotment. She was accompanied to the Nez Percé reservation by E.

Jane Gay. They had attended the same boarding school together in New York, where Gay had befriended Fletcher but had lost touch until they met at a public lecture sometime during the 1880s. Gay then spent considerable time learning the relatively new art of photography so that she could accompany the Nez Percé expedition as official photographer. Instead she found herself going along as unofficial expedition cook in order to watch over her friend's poor health.

Because the tribe was divided on this issue, the land allotment turned into a bitter and lengthy process. The Christian Nez Percé, like the La Flesches, were eager to become full U.S. citizens and to own property. The traditional Nez Percé, who had followed Chief Joseph in a futile attempt to reach Canada, opposed the division of the tribal lands. The white settlers in Idaho saw the Dawes Act opening more land for white expansion. Fletcher, however, surveyed the tribal lands and insisted on placing the Indians on the choicest tracts. The settlers held an "indignation" meeting and sent a representative to Washington to request that Congress replace Fletcher as allotment agent, presumably with someone more in sympathy with the interests of the whites (Mark and Hoxie 1981:15). According to Gay, Fletcher viewed the cattlemen as "buzzards sitting on a fence, waiting for the old horse to die" (Mark and Hoxie 1981:66).

In 1885, at the request of the U.S. Senate, Fletcher produced a 700-page report on the state of Indian legislation, education, and acculturation. In 1886 she was sent by the secretary of the Interior to Alaska to observe the conditions of the Alaskan Indians and incorporate her findings into the report.

Although Fletcher spent twelve years of her life acting as a congressional special agent overseeing the allotment of the Omaha, Winnebago, and Nez Percé lands, she considered this work necessary but an impediment to her "real" work—the recording of Native American tribal music, language, and customs. In 1886 Putnam had appointed her an assistant of the Peabody Museum. In 1891 her friend the Pittsburgh socialite Mary Copley Shaw established a fellowship for her at Harvard. This economic security allowed her to cease government work, and the fellowship supported her until her death. Fletcher thus became the first woman with an official paid appointment at Harvard.

Alice Fletcher also pioneered in the study of Indian music, an interest that began on her first visit to the Omaha. When she became bedridden with inflammatory rheumatism, the Indians came and sang to her to pass the time. She and Francis La Flesche made faithful transcriptions of the songs and later recorded them. Their monograph on the subject was published in 1893. Fletcher, working variously with John C. Fillmore of the Milwaukee Music School and Edwin S. Tracy, her musical collaborator, eventually transcribed and preserved hundreds of songs of Plains Indians.

Based on five years of fieldwork with two Pawnee men, Fletcher and Francis La Flesche also made a transcription of a Pawnee ritual ceremony, published as "The Hako" (Fletcher and Murie 1904). After twenty-nine years Fletcher and La Flesche finally published their voluminous work *The Omaha Tribe* in 1911. This volume is considered a definitive work on the life and organization of the tribe. Probably only one other white nineteenth-century American, Frank Hamilton Cushing, had spent as much time living with an Indian group, the Zuni, as Fletcher had with the Omaha.

Fletcher lived with Jane Gay and Francis La Flesche (whom she informally adopted) in a house at 214 First Street, S.E., in Washington, D.C., which her benefactor, Mary Copley Shaw, had purchased for her in 1892. The drawing room became a gathering place for Washington society. Intellectuals such as Simon Newcomb, an economist and astronomer, and Ainsworth Spofford, President Lincoln's secretary and later librarian of Congress, came to tea with "Her Majesty," as Fletcher was nicknamed, probably as much for her own imperious bearing as for her resemblance to Queen Victoria. Fletcher and Gay often spent their summers traveling separately. In 1907 Gay moved to England and lived with British physician and midwife Dr. Caroline Sturge until her death at age eighty-nine in 1919. Alice Fletcher continued to live in the Washington house with Francis La Flesche until her death in 1923 (Mark and Hoxie 1981:xxxv).

Fletcher was not only an ethnographer and preserver of Indian culture but a theorist as well. Fletcher and Franz Boas, another student of Putnam's, independently and simultaneously developed a theory of totemism that argued that tribal peoples did not believe they were actually descended from the totem animal. When she discovered he was publishing articles dealing with the concept of Totemism (1896:439; 1897:336; 1898:48), she rushed to get her work "The Import of the Totem" (1898) into print.

Boas disagreed, however, with Fletcher's interpretation of the Ghost Dance phenomenon. Fletcher held that the Indians' belief that a messiah would deliver them had resulted from their removal from rich lands onto barren reservations and from rapid changes in their tribal structures. After she presented a paper entitled "The Indian Messiah" at the American Folklore Society in 1890, Boas commented that the "craze" should not be attributed to political causes but rather to "nervous diseases" (Mark 1980a:74).

Alice Fletcher was one of the first women to be professionally recognized for her work in anthropology. In 1882, when anthropology was officially recognized by the American Association for the Advancement of Science, Fletcher presented two papers based on her field observations of Plains Indians. Fletcher was a charter member and vice president of the Women's Anthropological Society (1885) and a founding and charter member of the American Anthropological Association (1902). She sat on the editorial board of the *American Anthropologist* from 1899 to 1916. She served as president of the American Folklore Society, president of the Women's Anthropological Society (in 1893, the year of the first joint meeting with the Anthropological Society of Washington, which led to the acceptance of women members in the ASW), and after the acceptance of women as members, served as president of that organization as well (1903).

Fletcher was in charge of Indian exhibits at the New Orleans Industrial Exposition (1884–85) and a member of the special Congress of Anthropology, Chicago World's Fair, 1893. She was a founding member of the School of

American Research (later known as the School of Social Research), serving on its board of regents from 1908 to 1912. In 1910 Fletcher traveled to England, where she was honored as one of America's leading anthropologists. She spoke at Cambridge and was elected vice president of the British Association for the Advancement of Science.

Even this accomplished and famous woman felt the restrictions of the times put on her sex, writing to Putnam in 1894, "I am aware that being a woman I am debarred from helping you as I otherwise could." However, Fletcher maintained a lifelong active interest in the women's rights and women's suffrage movements. Looking back, she saw the years between 1860 and 1870 as "a marked period in the history of American women" that resulted in a larger worldview for women, as evidenced by "the establishment and growth of Women's Clubs." Women were an integral part of human society and to create social change, she felt that "mutual respect, mutual regard, mutual help, both in thought and action" between women and men were necessary.

Fletcher has been criticized by contemporary anthropologists and Native American activists for her involvement in the allotment program. In fact, dividing up the tribal lands neither transformed the Indians into successful farmers nor gave them a secure political and economic base. By 1933 two-thirds of Indian lands that had been so allotted had been sold to whites to pay off debts. Even Fletcher herself observed, when visiting the Omaha in 1910, that "the Act has not been altogether evil nor has it been wholly good for the people" (Lurie 1966:49).

Alice Fletcher was a prominent, well-known anthropologist in her day. She educated the public and raised funds for anthropological works and projects in order to establish anthropology as a science rather than an avocation. The vast body of information collected through her extensive ethnographies and records of vanishing cultures, as well as her early contributions to the evolution of fieldwork and enduring contributions to the establishment of the School of American Research, are her lasting legacies. Alice Cunningham Fletcher's lifelong dedication to scientific research and the preservation of information concerning quickly changing and disappearing Native American cultures significantly shaped the development and future of American anthropology.

Living with my Indian friends, [she said,] I found I was a stranger in my native land. As time went on, the outward aspect of nature remained the same, but change was wrought in me. I learned to hear the echoes of a time when every living thing even the sky had a voice. The voice devoutly heard by the ancient people of America I desired to make audible to others. (Mark 1980a:88)

Note

1. All quoted material not otherwise cited comes from the Alice Fletcher Papers, Smithsonian Institution.

References and Works About Alice Cunningham Fletcher

Gay, E. Jane
1905   *Choup-Nit-Ki: Letters of Jane Gay from Idaho.* 2 vols. E. Jane Gay Papers, Schlesinger Library, Radcliffe College.
Hough, Walter
1923   Alice Cunningham Fletcher Obituary. *American Anthropologist* 25:254–57.
La Flesche, Francis
1923   Alice Cunningham Fletcher Obituary. *Science* 58:115.
Lurie, Nancy O.
1966   Women in Early American Anthropology. In *Pioneers of American Anthropology.* June Helm, ed. Pp. 29–83. Seattle: University of Washington Press.
Mark, Joan
1980a   *Four Anthropologists: An American Science in Its Early Years.* Pp. 62–95. New York: Science History Publications.
1980b   Vita: Alice Fletcher: Activist Anthropologist: 1838–1923. *Harvard Magazine* 35 (March–April).
Mark, Joan T., and Frederick Hoxie, eds.
1981   *With the Nez Percé: Alice Fletcher in the Field, 1889–92* by E. Jane Gay. Lincoln: University of Nebraska Press.
Wilkins, Thurman
1971   Alice Cunningham Fletcher. In *NAW I.* Edward T. James and Janet W. James, eds. Pp. 630–33. Cambridge: Belknap Press of Harvard University.
Wilson, Dorothy Clarke
1974   *Bright Eyes: The Story of Susette La Flesche, an Omaha Indian.* New York: McGraw Hill.

Selected Works by Alice Cunningham Fletcher

1883a Sun Dance of the Ogalalla Sioux. *Proceedings, American Association for the Advancement of Science* 21:580–84.
1883b Observations on the Laws and Privileges of the Gens in Indian Society. *Science* 2:367.
1883c Symbolic Earth Formations of the Winnebagoes. *Science* 2:367–68.
1883d On Indian Education and Self-Support. *Century Magazine* 4:312–15.
1884a The White Buffalo Festival of the Uncpapas. *16th Annual Report, Peabody Museum* 3:260–75.
1884b The Elk Mystery of Festival of the Ogalalla Sioux. *16th Annual Report, Peabody Museum* 3:276–88.
1884c The Religious Ceremony of the Four Winds as Observed by a Santee Sioux. *16th Annual Report, Peabody Museum* 3:289–95.
1884d The Shadow or Ghost Lodge: A Ceremony of the Ogalalla Sioux. *16th Annual Report, Peabody Museum* 3:296–307.
1884e The Wa-Wan, or Pipe Dance of the Omahas. *16th Annual Report, Peabody Museum* 3:308–33.
1885a Observations upon the Usage, Symbolism, and Influence of the Sacred Pipes of

Friendship Among the Omahas. *Proceedings, American Association for the Advancement of Science* 33:615–17.

1885b Land in Severalty to Indians; illustrated by experiences with the Omaha Tribe. *Proceedings, American Association for the Advancement of Science* 33:654–65.

1888a *Indian Education and Civilization.* Special Report, U.S. Bureau of Education, Department of the Interior, Washington, D.C.

1888b On the Preservation of Archaeologic Monuments. *Proceedings, American Association for the Advancement of Science* 36:317.

1889   Report of the Committee on the Preservation of Archaeologic Remains on the Public Lands. *Proceedings, American Association for the Advancement of Science* 37:35–37.

1890   Phonetic Alphabet of the Winnebago Indians. *Proceedings, American Association for the Advancement of Science* 38:354–57.

1891   Indian Messiah. *Journal of American Folklore* 4:57–60.

1894   Love Songs Among the Omaha Indians. *Memoirs, International Congress of Anthropologists.* C. S. Wake, ed. Pp. 153–57. Chicago: Schulte.

1896a Indian Songs and Music. *Proceedings, American Association for the Advancement of Science* 44:281–84.

1896b Sacred Pole of the Omaha Tribe. *Proceedings, American Association for the Advancement of Science* 44:270–80.

1898   The Import of the Totem. *Science* 7:296–304.

1899   A Pawnee Ritual Used When Changing a Man's Name. *American Anthropologist* 1:82–97.

1900   *Indian Story and Song from North America.* Boston: Small, Maynard and Co.

1903   The Significance of Dress. *American Journal of Archaeology* 7:84–85.

1915a *Indian Games and Dances with Native Songs Arranged from American Indian Ceremonials and Sports.* Boston: Small, Maynard and Company.

1915b The Study of Indian Music. *Proceedings of the National Academy of Sciences* 1:231–35.

1920   Prayers Voiced in Ancient America. *Art and Archaeology* 9:73–75.

Coauthored Works

Fletcher, Alice C., and Francis La Flesche

1911   The Omaha Tribe. *Twenty-seventh Report of the Bureau of American Ethnology.* Washington, D.C.: Government Printing Office.

Fletcher, Alice C., Francis La Flesche, and J. C. Fillmore

1893   A Study of Omaha Indian Music. *Archaeological and Ethnological Papers, Peabody Museum of American Archaeology and Ethnology* 1:237–87.

Fletcher, Alice C., and James Murie

1904   The Hako: A Pawnee Ceremony. *Twenty-second Report of the Bureau of American Ethnology.*

ANDREA S. TEMKIN

Ernestine Friedl

(1920–   )

Ernestine Friedl is an American cultural anthropologist, known for her studies of Greek village life, peasant society, urban migration studies, and the social and cultural variables of sex role variation.

Ernestine Friedl was born in Hungary in 1920. When she was two years old, she and her mother joined her father in the United States, settling in the West Bronx of New York City. Her classmates in elementary school were ethnically diverse and included Irish, German, and Jewish children. When she was in the eighth grade, she and her family moved to Washington Heights in Manhattan. The Depression hit her father's sales business, and they moved back to the Bronx a year later.

Friedl attended Walton High School for girls and continued her education at Hunter College. At the beginning of her college years, she thought she might be a psychologist, but "after the first psychology course, I learned it was not for me. I thought I might like to teach but I wasn't sure of the subject or what level."[1]

While at Hunter College, she participated in a faculty-student committee for planning undergraduate teas. These teas were expected to improve faculty-student relations outside the classroom. Remembering that committee, she says, "It seems to have affected my life pretty thoroughly." It was through this committee that she met Dorothy L. Keur,* an anthropologist whose example enticed her into anthropology, and Harry Levy, a classicist who later became her husband. It was her respect and admiration for Dorothy Keur that led Friedl to choose physical anthropology as the course to fulfill the science requirement at Hunter College.

Elsie Steedman, a dedicated and enthusiastic teacher, taught the course in physical anthropology. In this class Friedl discovered her fascination with anthropology and elected to take additional courses in cultural anthropology and linguistics, and concluded that anthropology was the subject she would like to teach.

Having determined her field, Friedl sought advice on how to pursue her goal. Harry Levy explained that if she wanted to teach at the college level (the only realistic setting for instruction in anthropology), she would have to get a Ph.D. She commented, "At the time I didn't even know what a Ph.D. was or how to go about getting one. When I asked Harry how long it would take, he said three years. Well, it took me nine, but I was working full time through most of it."

Friedl graduated from Hunter College in January 1941 with a B.A. in pre-social work and began graduate studies in cultural anthropology at Columbia University in February 1941. Harry Levy went into the army in 1943, returning in 1945. He spent a year at Harvard in the combined roles of visiting scholar and veteran student under the G.I. Bill. In the meantime Friedl was teaching at Wellesley College.

On becoming an anthropologist, Ernestine Friedl says she "evolved." Through graduate studies at Columbia and teaching in the Boston area, she began to assume the identity of "anthropologist." In her words, "My original interest was in teaching. I had no idea what it meant to be a research scholar."

At Columbia University, Ralph Linton and Ruth Benedict* were Friedl's most influential professors. Linton was a wonderful lecturer and provided her with an inspiring model for teaching. Recalling Linton's lectures, Friedl says, "He once remarked that the thing to do was to put all the important things that you wanted to get across into the digressions because people's attention is captured by the digression. I've since done it and it works." Linton's book *The Study of Man* had appeared in the late 1930s. It was an influential textbook for the next two decades; his conception of status and role became a classic in the social sciences. These concepts provided Friedl with foundations that she used in her work.

Intellectually, Ruth Benedict was the most important influence on Friedl, introducing her to Émile Durkheim and the French school. Benedict's broad philosophical training and poetic imagination generated intellectual curiosity and stimulated thought, not through organized lectures but rather, as Friedl remembers, by rambles through ideas with occasional flashes of brilliance.

Linton sent Friedl into the field to study the Chippewa of Wisconsin. She worked with them during the summers of 1942 and 1943. Although Linton was interested in issues of culture-and-personality at the time, she used her Chippewa experience as a foundation for a historical dissertation on leadership styles and their relation to political organization. Until Linton went off to Yale in 1947, he was her dissertation advisor. After his departure, Julian Steward took on the role, but Friedl says:

I wrote the dissertation mostly on my own. At Columbia in those days, you really got your degree by yourself. It was sink or swim. I had some advice from A. Irving Hallowell at the University of Pennsylvania who was a specialist on the Chippewa and a friend. Julian Steward read and approved my final draft, but we never discussed it.

Friedl's desire to teach was realized in the fall of 1942, when she began teaching evenings at Brooklyn College. Next term, in the spring of 1943, she was teaching full-time at Brooklyn College. While engaged in this full-time teaching, she finished her course work at Columbia.

Friedl began to work on her dissertation while teaching at Wellesley College. She went back to Brooklyn College to teach for a year before she took a job at Queens College, where she taught until 1973.

Hortense Powdermaker* was a colleague at Queens. She and Friedl were the only anthropologists in the joint anthropology/sociology department for several years. Powdermaker's dedication to research provided a collegial model for Friedl's development as an anthropologist.

Friedl received her Ph.D. in 1950 while she was teaching full-time at Queens College, with a teaching load of five classes a semester. Typically, a teaching load included three classes of introductory anthropology with thirty students and two other classes of the same size. As a result, she taught many different topics, including the peoples and cultures of Latin America and of Asia, American Indians, introductory sociology, and urban sociology. "It was a great way to learn a lot," she recalls.

After relatively limited fieldwork among the Chippewa, Friedl was eager to go into the field for an extended period. From her class preparation she had become interested in the changes that were going on in rural communities around the world. New technologies along with increased commercial farming were having significant consequences for culture and social structure, which were visible everywhere. She wanted to explore these changes. Originally, she wanted to study rural India, but it was also important to her to work where her husband could profit from accompanying her.

For a classicist, the logical choices for field sites were Greece or Italy. At the time (1954) there had been little European field work by American anthropologists; for example, no one had completed a study in Greece. Friedl knew that John Campbell had worked in a shepherd community in the mountains of Greece, but that was not the sort of setting that interested her. "I never did reach John until after we came back from the field. In any case, I wanted to study communities undergoing rapid change rather than those where the maintenance of old traditions and folklore would have had to be emphasized."

Friedl was awarded a Fulbright grant to study a Greek village and said, "It affected the rest of my life." The experience was intense:

Greek human relationships are difficult and emotionally trying. There is a constant verbal combat, and the continuing respect from others depends upon being able to hold your own in the contest. Harry was good at it, but the lack of privacy and the agonistic relationships took its toll on both of us in spite of our respect and admiration for the villagers.

Harry Levy was an active participant in the fieldwork and also gained new insights into ancient Greek history and culture. Friedl comments that he often said knowing the villagers had brought the ancient texts and statues to life. His skill and interest in the modern Greek language and his gift for verbal play were great assets in the field. Friedl relied on him to help record genealogies and to be present while she interviewed men, which would not have been possible had she been alone.

She has recorded the results of her field experiences in her book *Vasilika* (Friedl 1962). In her article, "Fieldwork in a Greek Village" (Friedl 1970), she describes her theoretical orientation. During the first field trip to Greece, she was engaged in a basic community study, which meant discovering cultural patterns and analyzing social structure. She sought Margaret Mead's* advice before she went into the field and followed it by choosing to work in a village with a population small enough to be able to know everyone in it.

Vasilika is a small farming village on the edge of the Boetian plain in the eastern shadow of Mount Parnassus. At the time of Friedl's fieldwork, Vasilika had a population of 216. The current population is significantly less than that.

Recalling the field experience, she notes:

It was an intense year; and when you have a year like that, you remember everything. We had a peculiar love-hate response to it. When we first came back from the field we talked so much about the problems: how difficult the relationships were with people, how you are always calculating where you stand in relation to someone else. You are constantly playing that kind of game; and it is not a game that Harry and I like to play, even to the extent that it is played in the States. But as the years went by, I lost all sense of the struggle and remembered only the warmth of the human associations and the satisfaction of learning so much from the villagers. As a result we kept going back to Greece.

In 1964–65 Friedl did fieldwork among the migrants in the area from Vasilika to Athens, and up through 1976 she and her husband spent summers in Greece, always including a day or two in the village. The year 1971–72 was spent in Athens working on the book *Women and Men* (Friedl 1975). By then Levy had retired from the vice chancellorship of the City University of New York and from his subsequent professorship at Fordham University.

Friedl's current interest in gender roles began in Greece.

I was impressed by how powerful the women were in Vasilika. They had a lot of influence in that community. When the Spindlers, who edited the series in which *Vasilika* appeared, wanted a book on the relationship between the community and the larger society, it didn't interest me. Instead, I told them I was wondering what anthropologists knew about the comparative position of women. I thought that anthropologists ought to have something to say about women's roles and I wanted to find out what it was.

Before 1970, when Friedl started her service on the Committee on the Status of Women in Anthropology in the American Anthropological Association, she did not think women anthropologists had any problems. That committee's work laid the basis for her education on women's issues.

We turned up evidence which showed that although most women anthropologists had received their Ph.D.s from institutions which had well-known and established departments of anthropology, women were not teaching in these institutions. Yet it couldn't be for lack of talent. No one assumed that their training or ability were different from those of the men who graduated from the same institutions, but the men were teaching there and the women were not.

Friedl says that she had been insulated from the problem because she had not felt it personally. New York City was and continues to be, according to her, remarkably good for women academics, although for several decades Columbia conformed to the pattern of not tenuring women.

Friedl thought that she might spend a summer putting together what anthropologists have to say about women for George and Louise Spindlers' series. They agreed to the idea and she began working on it. The result (although it took much longer than a summer) was her book *Women and Men*. In this book she explores the gender role definition among hunter and gatherer societies and horticultural societies.

I originally planned a fuller book. I was going to include plow agriculturalists and industrial societies. I wrote a draft of a section on Greece and Ireland[,] but the sets of conditions that had relevance for hunters and gatherers and horticulturalists were not entirely germane for state societies. I thought only the first half of the projected book was worth publishing. In my judgment, the main contribution is the hunters and gatherers section. The other was too densely written for easy comprehension. I am now rethinking the issues in the light of all the recent literature on the subject. I will have to reeducate myself.

Friedl's contributions to professional organizations derive from her lifelong interest in administration. She served as secretary and then president of the American Ethnological Society (1967) and president (1974–75) of the American Anthropological Association (AAA). At that time the AAA was rethinking the structure and function of its journal, the *American Anthropologist*. She feels that she helped to clarify that issue and to accomplish a reorganization of the way the executive board functioned. She kept her administrative side alive by chairing the Department of Anthropology at Duke University (1973–78). In 1985 she completed five years as dean of arts and sciences at Duke University.

She views the constant small and occasional large crises of administration as the process by which administrators contribute to change. Each issue is an object of passionate concern at the time it surfaces. Later the memory of why each issue was so vitally important fades; but without the devotion to solving problems, both small and large, no progress is possible. "Administration is completely engrossing."

Note

1. All direct quotations are taken from an interview with Ernestine Friedl in New York City on August 1, 1985.

References and Works by Ernestine Friedl

1944 A Note on Birch Bark Transparencies. *American Anthropologist* 46:149–50.

1956 Persistence in Chippewa Culture and Personality. *American Anthropologist* 58:814–25.

1958a Hospital Care in Provincial Greece. *Human Organization* 16:24–27.

1958b Chippewa (Ojibway) Rorschachs from 72 Women and 25 Men (with introduction). *Microcard Publications of Primary Records. Culture and Personality* 2 (7).

1959a The Role of Kinship in the Transmission of National Culture to Rural Villages in Mainland Greece. *American Anthropologist* 61:30–38.

1959b Dowry and Inheritance in Modern Greece. In *Transactions of the New York Academy of Sciences* 22:49–54. (Reprinted 1967 in *Peasant Society: A Reader.* J. Potter et. al., eds. Pp. 57–62. Boston: Little, Brown.)

1962 *Vasilika: A Village in Modern Greece.* New York: Holt, Rinehart and Winston. (Reprinted 1971 in *Kinship.* Penguin Modern Sociology Reading. Jack Goody, ed. Pp. 64–68.)

1963a Studies in Peasant Life. In *Biennial Review of Anthropology.* B. Siegel, ed. Pp. 276–306. Stanford, Calif.: Stanford University Press.

1963b Some Aspects of Dowry and Inheritance in Modern Greece. In *Mediterranean Countrymen.* J. Pitt-Rivers, ed. Pp. 113–35. Paris: Mouton.

1964a Lagging Emulation in Post-Peasant Society. *American Anthropologist* 66:569–86.

1967 The Position of Women: Appearance and Reality. *Anthropological Quarterly* 40:97–108.

1970 Fieldwork in a Greek Village. In *Women in the Field.* P. Golde, ed. Pp. 193–217. Chicago: Aldine.

1975 *Women and Men: An Anthropologist's View.* New York: Holt, Rinehart and Winston.

1976a Kin, Class and Selective Migration. In *Mediterranean Family Structures.* J. Peristany, ed. Pp. 363–87. Cambridge: Cambridge University Press.

1977 Folktales Collected Among the Chippewa Indians. In *Wisconsin Chippewa Myths and Tales.* Victor Barnouw, ed. Madison: The University of Wisconsin Press.

1978 Society and Sex Roles. *Human Nature* 1:8–75. (Reprinted 1979 in *Culture and Conflict.* J. Spradley and D. McCurdy, eds.)

1983 Bypassing Peer Review for Scientific Facilities. *Science* 222:1079.

Coauthored Works

Friedl, Ernestine, E. Bruner, and R. Flannery
1960 An Anthropological Concept of Culture. In *Reports of the Working Committees, Northeast Conference on the Teaching of Foreign Languages.* Pp. 19–27.

Freidl, Ernestine, and Muriel Dimen, eds.
1976   Regional Variation in Modern Greece and Cyprus: Toward a Perspective on the Ethnography of Greece. *The New York Academy of Sciences Annals* 268:444–65.
Friedl, Ernestine, and Viola E. Garfield, eds.
1964   *Symposium on Community Studies in Anthropology.* Proceedings of the 1963 Meetings of the American Ethnological Society. Seattle: University of Washington Press.

LYNNE M. HOLLINGSHEAD

Viola Edmundson Garfield

(1899–1983)

American cultural anthropologist Viola Edmundson Garfield was highly regarded for her definitive studies of the Tsimshian of British Columbia and Alaska, particularly their social organization, and for the crest (totemic) art of the north Pacific Coast.

At a time when anthropology had become an academic profession under the firm hand of Franz Boas and almost all of his graduates came from European and/or wealthy backgrounds, Viola Garfield was an exception. Her attraction to anthropology came from direct experience with another culture, rather than the stimulation of classwork with Boas at Columbia, although that came later. Her family was rural, rather than urban, with modest finances.

Viola Edmundson was the oldest of the six children of William Henry and Mary Louanna (née Dean) Edmundson. As each new arrival occupied her mother's time, Edmundson assumed an increasingly maternal and domestic role toward each of her younger siblings. Her mother was the more dynamic influence, urging all of her children to attend college. She kept a detailed diary on Edmundson's development and read enthusiastically until she went blind and died in her nineties. She was very much the role model of a strong and competent woman. She must have also been pragmatic and practical, since these traits were passed to her daughter.

A few years after her birth in Iowa, her family moved to Coupeville on Whidby Island to the north of Seattle, Washington, joining her father's younger brother, who had homesteaded there as a veteran of the Spanish American War. Her imagination was not stifled by her family, although it may not have been actively encouraged. She did very well at the local one-room school house, skipping the fourth grade. By sixteen she was earning her own living, working as a domestic. Of particular importance was her job as housekeeper for the family of the female superintendent of schools, providing access to a well-stocked library, which she was free to use, and earning her the money to start at the University of Washington in 1919.

In her second year, however, funds ran out. Along with another girl in the dorm whose sister was working as a teacher for the Bureau of Indian Affairs (BIA), she transferred to the Bellingham Normal School (now Western Washington University) and earned teaching certification. She often remarked that she had difficulty with the childlike treatment given to trainees there, so different from the university, where students were regarded as adults.

She and her friends were hired by the BIA but were sent to different schools. In this way, Edmundson came to teach fourth grade to Tsimshian children at New Metlakatla, on Annette Island, southeastern Alaska. Ever curious, she was often surprised at the way the Tsimshian behaved, but she was not critical or judgmental; if anything, she was fascinated. She noted that children did not compete with each other in public, nor try to excel above the group. At night an old man would come to the "teacherage" (school house) and tell traditional stories in English, even though the native language was very much in use. The policy of the American government at that time was to discourage and punish the use of native languages, particularly among students. Although teachers were instructed to enforce this directive, Edmundson humanely decided to ignore it.

Her fascination with another culture began at a wedding in the town, when it became apparent that descent was traced through the mothers. She used this experience in her first publication, a short story comparing the earlier marriage of a mother's brother with the modern one of his sister's son and heir (1933a).

She did not develop any lasting friendships in New Metlakatla, although there are still elderly Tsimshian who recall with some huff that they had to bring a midafternoon snack to her every day. While she may have been tolerant of their traditions, she was nonetheless something of a typical schoolmarm.

After a year filled with these and other enriching experiences, she decided to return to Seattle and continue her education. Yet she still lacked sufficient funds. Again, she worked as a housekeeper while earning a degree from a secretarial school. Then she went to work at the Seattle Chamber of Commerce. There she rose from the typing pool to become the secretary of Charles Garfield, an Alaskan sourdough, miner, customs inspector, and roustabout before moving to Seattle and becoming active in the fur exchange.

Almost a year after his wife of many years had died, Viola Edmundson and Charles Garfield were married in 1924. They eloped to Coupeville, where her family hosted the wedding. At the time, the marriage was something of a scandal, not because the full year of mourning had not been observed, but because Charles was two years older than Viola's own father. Since the couple had almost forty years of a happy life together, the gossips were proved wrong. As Viola Garfield was fond of saying, "I never met a man I liked better." His first marriage was childless; but Viola fully intended to raise a family, proud of her experience gained in dealing with her own siblings and other charges. To her regret, there were no children.

Eventually, with her husband's full encouragement, Garfield went back to the University of Washington in 1927. By now she was aware that her interests were those of an anthropologist, with a special interest in the Tsimshian. As yet, there was no anthropology department, however. The man who was to establish it was Dr. Melville Jacobs, trained by Boas at Columbia, but still attached to the sociology department. He introduced her to the monumental tome on Tsimshian mythology that Boas had published with the help of Henry Tate, a Tsimshian commoner from Port Simpson.

After earning her B.A. in 1931, Garfield entered graduate school, again in sociology by default, but did anthropological fieldwork back in New Metlakatla for her M.A. on Tsimshian marriage patterns by clan, class, and race. She then joined the new anthropology department as its perpetual junior member, a colleague who was treated as a former student. Whenever a new course was proposed or an unpleasant task was at hand, it was assigned to her. She was in many ways trapped at the University of Washington—both by her marriage to Charles, who was devoted to Seattle, and by her ties to family and locale—working under the urbane, senior scholars trained by Boas. They were often critical, demeaning, or arrogant with each other, but as their former student, she got along with all of them and provided a cohesion the department might have lacked otherwise. She was particularly devoted to Erna Gunther,* who was chair of the department and director of the museum for about twenty-five years. Her colleagues were too devoted to their own interests to share in a rotated position. Both women were criticized for maintaining good relations with the public and community groups. This was considered to be lacking in scholarly dignity for serious academics.

She taught during the academic year and spent the summers taking graduate work at Columbia under Boas and Ruth Benedict.* With funds provided through Boas, she also did fieldwork among the Tsimshian, initially studying the intricacies of wood carving and of Tsimshian social relations and rituals. Of enormous help to her endeavors was William Beynon, a Wolf chief at Port Simpson, who was supplying data for Boas and other scholars, especially Marius Barbeau of Ottawa. Later he worked closely with Amelia Susman (Schultz), sent out by Boas to study the language.

Her dissertation, "Tsimshian Clan and Society," was finished in 1935, but owing to the rule that only published dissertations conferred the degree, her Ph.D. dates from its publication in 1939.

Because she saw matrilineality used in context, she understood that the men held the positions of authority within the matrilines and crests, but as brothers and nephews more than as sons. She always recognized this sort of male privilege among the Tsimshian but was careful to note areas where women held their own. "Perhaps more than their neighbors the Tsimshian recognized the importance of women in the maintenance of class and rank" (Garfield and Wingert 1966:28). For all of her published research on the artistry of wood carving as done by men, in her classes and conversations she took pains to show its complementarity with the basketry done by women. When I asked her how she regarded Lévi-Strauss's use of her material for his famous study of the saga of Asdiwal, she replied that she had been so put off by the mechanistic treatment of women as items in his theory of marriage exchange that she had not gone on to read his other work. Yet it was this accolade from the French master of a unified an-thropology that did much to earn for her work increased respect. Her ethnography is meticulous and reliable but not exhaustive.

Garfield continued to teach anthropology at the University of Washington until she retired. Although she gained tenure, she never rose above the rank of associate professor. She had her own priorities, and they were not those of most of her later colleagues. Toward the end of her career, she bore the indignity of having one of them inform her with all seriousness that "it was no longer fashionable to study Indians."

Writing was a slow and arduous task for her, yet she kept up a steady list of slim but significant publications. Most of these have withstood the test of time to become recognized classics of North Pacific ethnography. Of particular note were her studies of the economics of slavery (Garfield 1945), of Angoon clans (Garfield 1947), on trans-Pacific moieties (Garfield 1953a), and her ever-popular works on totem poles and mythology (Garfield 1940, 1980).

She was passionately devoted to the teaching of undergraduates, recognizing in this the foundation for everything else. She was equally concerned with relations with the wider community. She undertook a speaking tour through Washington State to promote the university and anthropology. For several years she taught an extension class on a cruise ship traveling between Seattle and Alaska. With her husband, who knew Alaska well and spoke the regional trade language, Chinook jargon, Garfield visited every Tlingit village, although she published only on Angoon. She was justifiably proud of a small and choice art collection she had assembled. She was long an active member of the Pen Women, counting several of its members among her closest friends. It was decided that contributors to her festschrift (Miller and Eastman 1984) should write their articles for the broadest possible audience, as Garfield had always done.

Garfield had planned to travel a great deal after retiring, but a painful nephritis prevented that. She always encouraged the young to do as much as possible while they were able, warning that the future might not go as expected.

She was close to her family, particularly her younger "siblings and niblings." Her mother died only several years before her, an avid reader and listener until the end.

Her husband died decades before her, but she lived in their modest house until retirement. Then, for as long as possible, Garfield lived alone in a lake-view apartment, ever the willing hostess. Finally, she went to live with the family of her youngest sister.

She had started smoking in one of Ruth Benedict's classes and smoked her entire life. This aggravated medical conditions as they occurred in her later life. Finally, she required surgery to clear the arteries of her neck and lower limbs, but this was only partially successful. (Ever the scholar, she allowed the operation to be filmed and shown on local television.) Her legs had to be amputated; but even with that, she continued to rave about how wonderful it felt to have a fresh supply of oxygen to her brain. Undaunted, she moved into a rest home near her brother and in short order was elected president by its members. She began a new interest, devoting herself to issues concerned with the care of the elderly and disabled.

In 1983 she spent Thanksgiving with her family and returned to the nursing home. The next morning her pulse was barely discernible, and her brother stood at her bedside as she faded away. Without common knowledge, she had commissioned a ceramic urn for her ashes a few weeks before. Some have said that the measure of a life comes at death; in Garfield's case, the sensitive anticipation and gentleness of her exit conveys much about her worth as a human being.

All of her life, Garfield earned money by skillfully taking care of others, often in a subsidiary position. The mark of her stature is that she continued to learn useful and important things while doing this. Bolstered by her imagination, attentive care, and determination, she enriched the lives and minds of many.

References and Works About Viola Edmundson Garfield

Miller, Jay, and Carol M. Eastman, eds.
1984   Viola Edmundson Garfield. In The Tsimshian and Their Neighbors of the North Pacific Coast. Pp. 311–315. Seattle: University of Washington Press.

Selected Works by Viola Edmundson Garfield

1933   The Dog-Eaters. *Town Crier* (Seattle), December 16, pp. 28–29.

1939a   The Potlatch. *Seattle Grade Club Magazine* 15 (3):12.

1939b   Tsimshian Clan and Society. *University of Washington Publications in Anthropology* 7 (3): 167–340.

1940   *The Seattle Totem Pole.* Seattle: University of Washington Press.

1945   A Research Problem in Northwest Economics. *American Anthropologist* 47(4): 626–30.

1947   Historical Aspects of Tlingit Clans in Angoon, Alaska. *American Anthropologist* 49(3): 438–52.

1951a   Anthropological Research in Southeastern Alaska. *Proceedings of the Alaskan Science Conference of the National Academy of Science.* National Research Council Bulletin 122:44.

1951b   *Meet the Totem.* Sitka, Alaska: Sitka Printing Co.

1952   Survey of Southeastern Alaska Indian Research. *Selected Papers of the Alaskan Science Conference.* Pp. 20–37. Arctic Institute of North America; Quebec: Montreal.

1953a   Possibilities of Genetic Relationship in Northern Pacific Moiety Structures. *American Antiquity* 18(3): 58–61.

1953b   Contemporary Problems of Folklore Collecting and Study. *Anthropological Papers of the University of Alaska* 1(2): 25–37.

1955   Making a Bird or Chief's Rattle. *Davidson Journal of Anthropology* 1(11): 155–68.
1961   *Symposium: Patterns of Land Utilization and Other Papers*. American Ethnological Society Publication. (As ed.)
1967   Tsimshian. In *Encyclopædia Britannica*. Chicago: University of Chicago.
1980   *The Seattle Totem Pole*. Seattle and London: University of Washington Press. (Originally published in 1940.)

Coauthored Works

Garfield, Viola, Marius Barbeau, and Paul Wingert
1951   The Tsimshian and Their Neighbors. In *The Tsimshian: Their Arts and Music*. American Ethnological Society Publications 18 (1): 3–72. Seattle: University of Washington.
Garfield, Viola, and Wallace L. Chafe, eds.
1962   *Symposium on Language and Culture*. American Ethnological Society Publications. Seattle: University of Washington Press.
Garfield, Viola, and Wilson Duff
1952   Anthropological Research and Publications. *Anthropology in British Columbia* 3:5–9.
Garfield, Viola, and Linn Forest
1948   *The Wolf and the Raven*. Seattle: University of Washington Press.
Garfield, Viola, and Ernestine Friedl, eds.
1964   *Symposium on Community Studies in Anthropology*. Proceedings of the 1963 Meetings of the American Ethnological Society. Seattle: University of Washington Press.
Garfield, Viola, and Ruth Underhill
1944   Indian Arts and White Materials: III. Totem Poles. In *Indians at Work*. Washington, D.C.: Bureau of Indian Affairs, Government Documents Card Catalogue.
Garfield, Viola, and Paul S. Wingert
1966   *The Tsimshian and Their Arts*. Seattle: University of Washington Press.

JAY MILLER

Frances Gillmor

(1903–   )

Frances Gillmor is an American folklorist, Aztec scholar, and novelist who pioneered in the collection and study of oral traditions in the American Southwest and Mexico.

Though she established her home and career in the American Southwest, Frances Gillmor's roots lay in the Northeast. Born in Buffalo, New York, on May 21, 1903, Gillmor spent her early life in Scotch-Irish communities in St. George, New Brunswick, and Brockton, Massachusetts. Her parents, Abner Churchill Gillmor (a businessman) and Annie McVicar Gillmor, nurtured their only child's independence and encouraged her writing. Gillmor remembers a childhood fascination with Indians (the Passamaquoddy), an appreciation of the customs and traditions of the region, and a determination to become a writer.[1] Her first novel, *Thumbcap Weir* (1929) set on the coast of the Bay of Fundy incorporated experiences and stories from her youth.

In 1921, encouraged by her parents and awarded an academic scholarship, she enrolled at the University of Chicago. She interrupted her undergraduate education in 1923 and worked as a reporter for the *Palm Beach Times, Palm Beach Independent,* and *St. Augustine Record.* Her mother's ill health took the family to Arizona in 1926, where the culture of the Southwest captured Gillmor's imagination and inspired her career. She returned to her studies, enrolling in anthropology, geology, and philosophy. Gillmor earned a B.A. and M.A. in English from the University of Arizona (1928–31). Her master's thesis focused on John and Louisa Wetherill, the famous explorers and traders who lived at the Navajo reservation at Kayenta, Arizona. Gillmor's first field experience was spent living with the Wetherills among the Navajo. Louisa Wade Wetherill, or Asthon Sosi (Slim Woman) as she was known locally, enjoyed an enviable rapport with the Navajo. Consequently, Gillmor was provided an entrée into Navajo life rarely afforded non-natives, particularly women, at that time. In addition to customs, she observed numerous tribal rituals such as sand-painting ceremonies while a guest on the reservation. Her thesis was later published as *Traders to the Navajo* (1934), written in collaboration with Louisa Wade Wetherill. As a tribute to its sensitive and honest portrayal of Navajo culture, the book received an eloquent endorsement from the tribe. Gillmor's experiences also inspired her ethnographic novel *Windsinger* (1930), notable for its authentic description of Navajo customs and beliefs.

Gillmor's education and career were to dovetail for the next twenty-three years. Upon completion of her M.A., she worked for two years as an English instructor at the University of New Mexico. In 1934 she accepted a position in the English Department at the University of Arizona, where she continued to teach. During the next decade her interests turned from creative writing to scholarship, though not before publishing a third novel—*Fruit Out of Rock* (1940), set on an Arizona ranch—and several short stories. A desire to work among the Pueblo Indians took her to Mexico to study Spanish, and she consequently became interested in Aztec culture and ethnohistory. While laying the foundations for her scholarly work, she doubled as a free-lance journalist, covering the Trotsky trial in Mexico City in 1937 for the *Arizona Daily Star,* and conducting interviews with Diego Rivera, the renowned Mexican artist.

During the summer of 1938 she attended the Instituto de Filosofia y Letras in Mexico to study the Aztec codices, working under noted Mesoamerican archaeologist Alfonso Caso. She returned to Mexico the following summer to take courses in pre-Hispanic archaeology and Nahuatl at the Universidad Nacionál Autónoma de México. She then began the laborious research on her principal project, a biography of Nezahualcoyotl, poet-king of the Aztecs and ruler of Texcoco in the fifteenth century, published as *Flute of the Smoking Mirror* (Gillmor 1949). Working from the codices, she reconstructed not only his life but the political and cultural climate. She vividly portrayed details of life in fifteenth-century Mexico, with its religious rituals, fiestas, songs, and dances, foods, and customs. Her description is based on meticulously documented research involving the study of pictorial depictions in the codices and analysis of the annals, which accompany and explicate the texts. These represent a codification of the oral narrative that traditionally accompanied the codices. Thus, Gillmor produced a well-documented ethnohistory of the Valley of Mexico that is accessible to both laypersons and scholars. The *Flute of the Smoking Mirror* consciously reflects Nahuatl literary style and choice of metaphor, and represents a literary as well as a scholarly contribution.

Gillmor continued her formal education in Mexico, studying pre-Hispanic culture at the Escuela Nacionál de Antropología e Historía (1952). Already a full professor of English at the University of Arizona, having been promoted in recognition of her scholarly and professional contributions, she nonetheless pursued her doctorate. At age fifty-four she earned that degree from the Universidad Nacionál Autónoma de México (1957). Under the direction of codex scholar Rafael Garcia Granados, and later anthropologist and historian Pablo Martinez del Rio, her thesis dealt with the life of Aztec ruler Huehue Moteczuma Ilhuicamina, or Montezuma I. Undertaking research in the codices similar to that which produced *Flute of the Smoking Mirror,* she wrote a thesis so highly regarded by her committee that her degree was awarded with special distinction. Later published as *The King Danced in the Marketplace* (1964), it enjoyed the same acclaim as its predecessor and was subsequently translated into Polish and Spanish.

While her scholarly reputation in Aztec history and culture became established, Gillmor simultaneously earned distinction in the field of folklore. She had long been captivated by oral traditions—family stories, legends, and tales—avidly incorporating these into her fiction. Intrigued by the possibility of pursuing folklore as an academic discipline, she attended Indiana University's Folklore Institute in 1946, studying with eminent folklore scholar Stith Thompson. At that time the theoretical orientation in folklore was primarily comparative. Text rather than context was the central focus; studies involved the transmission, diffusion, or variation of works in oral tradition. Hence, collecting texts formed the basis of most fieldwork, while the texts themselves provided the primary materials for study. Gillmor brought to her folklore scholarship a genuine enthusiasm and affection for oral lore that incorporated but also transcended its systematic comparative study. For her, folklore was foremost a valuable component of a people's cultural heritage, to be ''received from them with affection, with gentleness, with respect'' (Gillmor 1960:56).

To preserve and study the oral cultural heritage of her beloved Southwest, Gillmor endeavored to collect a body of materials from which scholars might draw. This material included verbal arts—legends, tall tales, family stories, proverbs, and jokes—as well as examples of traditional wisdom, such as superstitions or remedies. She recognized that the Southwest possessed a rich vein of lore that, unlike that of the southern Appalachians, had yet to be tapped. To this end, she organized and chaired an interdepartmental University Folklore Committee to promote the collection and study of oral traditions in the Southwest. The committee (including anthropologist Edward Spicer) strove to incorporate the study of folklore and regional folkways into the curriculum, as well as train students as fieldworkers to assist in the collection of texts. To preserve the collected materials and make them available to scholars, Gillmor established the University of Arizona Folklore Archive. Now part of the Southwestern Folklore Center at the University, it serves as a repository for the collected narrative traditions of English- and Spanish-speaking peoples of the Southwest. (Native American materials were principally collected and preserved by the Anthropology Department.) Serving as a catalyst, Gillmor organized and inspired a dedicated corps of professionals, students, and laypersons to recognize and preserve the oral traditional culture of the region. Through her tireless efforts and infectious enthusiasm, she generated a climate of awareness and appreciation of regional folkways that was to become her legacy.

Her reputation soon extended beyond the Southwest. She was invited to participate in the Mid-Century International Folklore Conference held at Indiana

University (1950), and was active in the American Folklore Society (AFS). In 1953 Gillmor helped organize the AFS annual meeting in Tucson, held concurrently with the meeting of the American Anthropological Association. She served as vice president of the AFS (1958 and 1964). Her professional activities also included serving as regional editor of *Western Folklore,* associate editor of *Arizona Quarterly,* and member of the editorial board of *New Mexico Quarterly.* Gillmor's particular area of scholarly interest lay in the traditional dance dramas of Mexican villages, about which she published several monograph-length studies. In 1959 she was awarded a Guggenheim Fellowship to study folk drama at village fiestas in Spain, for comparison with those of Mexico. In recognition of her international stature in the discipline, she was named a Fellow by the American Folklore Society (1962).

While pursuing her career as a scholar, Gillmor remained a dedicated teacher. She notes with gratitude that the University of Arizona adjusted her teaching schedule to alternate semesters. During semesters on leave, she pursued her research, writing, or continuing education. She preferred not to devote her energies to both teaching and research simultaneously, fearing that students would not enjoy her full attention if research were competing for her time. She enjoyed a warm relationship with her students; and in recognition for her talents in the classroom, she was awarded the University of Arizona's Creative Teaching Award in 1970.

Throughout her long and distinguished career, Gillmor has enjoyed the encouragement and assistance of numerous individuals, from Louisa Wetherill to her professors and colleagues in anthropology and folklore. But she had no established network to rely upon—she essentially generated her own. This is particularly true in her pioneering work in Southwestern folklore. Armed with a tape recorder, typewriter, and bedroll, she set off into small villages, where she lived among the residents, observing their customs. Her warm and gracious manner endeared her to her informants, and she enjoyed their acceptance and trust. She writes, "I am constantly amazed at the trust people have in me, a perfect stranger, coming to their village and talking about their plays. They lend me their manuscript, often the only one in the village, and let me carry it off, keeping it for two or three days while I copy it" (*Arizona Daily Star,* May 18, 1973, p. 13). She never felt any disadvantages in being a woman, her independence and self-confidence overcoming the limiting stereotypes of women's roles in her day.

Frances Gillmor's work is her life. Married to her profession, her students and colleagues are her family. Though fiercely independent, she has always enjoyed a close rapport with people. With characteristic energy and enthusiasm, she has successfully combined creative writing and scholarly research, teaching, and continuing education. Frances Gillmor's contributions to Mesoamerican anthropology and history and to Southwestern folklore constitute her scholarly legacy. Her personal legacy rests with the hundreds of students whose lives she has touched.

Note

1. The author would like to thank Dr. Frances Gillmor for her support and cooperation during the preparation of this entry.

References and Works by Frances Gillmor

1934 *Traders to the Navajos: The Story of the Wetherills of Kayenta.* In collaboration with Louisa Wade Wetherill. Boston: Houghton Mifflin. Reprinted, Albuquerque: University of New Mexico Press, 1952.

1942 Spanish Texts of Three Dance Dramas from Mexican Villages. *University of Arizona Bulletin* 13 (4): 1–83.

1943 The Dance Dramas of Mexican Villages. *University of Arizona Bulletin* 14 (2): 1–28.

1945 Opportunities in Arizona Folklore. *University of Arizona Bulletin* 16 (1): 1–55. (As ed. and contrib. to special issue.)

1949 *Flute of the Smoking Mirror: A Portrait of Nezahualcoyotl, Poet-King of the Aztecs.* Albuquerque: University of New Mexico Press.

1953 Contributions to *Four Symposia on Folklore: Held at the Midcentury International Folklore Conference.* Indiana University Folklore Series No. 8. Stith Thompson, ed. Bloomington: Indiana University Press.

1954 Comentarios sobre Congresos de Folklore, *Universidad de México* 8:17–19.

1955 Estructuras en la Zona de Texcoco durante el Reino de Nezahualcoyotl según las Fuentes Históricas. *Revista Mexicana de Estudios Antropológicos* 14(1):363–71.

1956 From Report to Literature. *Arizona Quarterly* 12:344–51.

1959a The Tribulations and Triumphs of Collecting Arizoniana: A Folklorist's Point of View. *Arizona Librarian* 16:13–20.

1959b The University of Arizona Folklore Archive. *The Folklore and Folk Music Archivist* 2 (1): 2.

1960 Listening to the Little Grandfathers. *Papers and Proceedings of the Southwestern Library Association Eighteenth Biennial Conference.* Pp. 56–64. Tucson, Oct. 27–29, 1960.

1961a Folklore Study in Spain. *Journal of American Folklore* 74:383–90.

1961b Organization of Folklore Study in Mexico. *Journal of American Folklore* 74:383–90.

1964 *The King Danced in the Marketplace.* Tucson: University of Arizona Press.

1969a Mouros e Crisitaos no Mexico. *Revista Brasileira de Folclore* 8 (23): 17–23.

1969b University of Arizona Folklore Committee. *Journal of American Folklore* 82:8–11.

1970 Diferentes Conceitos de "Los Tastaones," um Drama Tradicional de Jalisco. *Revista Brasileira de Folclore* 10 (23): 215–23.

1975 Foreword. *At the Sign of Midnight: The Concheros Dance Cult of Mexico,* by Martha Stone. Pp. v-vi. Tucson: University of Arizona Press.

1983 Symbolic Representation in Mexican Combat Plays. In *The Power of Symbols: Masks and Masquerade in the Americas.* N. Ross Crumrine and Marjorie Halpin, eds. Pp. 102–10. Vancouver: University of British Columbia Press.

JO KIBBEE

Esther Schiff Goldfrank

(1896–   )

Esther Schiff Goldfrank is an American cultural anthropologist known for her work among the Blackfoot (Blood) and Pueblo Indians of North America and for her collection of native mythology and analyses of indigenous economies.

The daughter of Dr. Herman J. Schiff and Matilda Metzger Schiff, Esther grew up in a middle class home in New York City. Both parents and her only sibling, Jack, died before she was twenty. Schiff attended the Ethical Culture High School, then enrolled in Barnard, where she received an A.B. in economics in 1918. After graduating, she worked on Wall Street as a secretary for one year—not an unusual occupation for a female college graduate at that time. In 1919, on the recommendation of Annie E. B. Meyer, registrar of Barnard College, she applied for the position of secretary to Franz Boas, chair of the Columbia Anthropology Department, and was immediately hired.[1]

In October 1919 Schiff knew little about anthropology and had, by her own admission, no great academic ambitions. She was bright and curious, however; and when she learned that Boas was planning a trip to Laguna Pueblo during the summer of 1920, she asked to be taken along. Boas was surprised by her request and somewhat disconcerted at the idea of taking a young, untrained, and unmarried woman with him into the field. He also lacked funds to support her. Having planned to go west, Schiff had purchased her own rail ticket; and her insistent pleas to be taken along led Boas to seek the advice of Elsie Clews Parsons,* who often cooperated with him and helped with financial support. Parsons made it clear that the decision to take Schiff was his alone, but she agreed to pay additional field expenses. Thus, Schiff's entry into anthropology was accidental, but the support of Boas and Parsons played an important role in providing her the initial opportunity to do fieldwork. Schiff's family was scandalized at the idea of her living alone with a man—albeit a well-known professor—and they were fearful of the dangers she might confront in an isolated Indian village. She nevertheless insisted on going; and she spent parts of the summers of 1921 with Boas (and a few weeks with Elsie Clews Parsons) collecting ethnographic data in Laguna. In 1922 she returned to Laguna and then went with Boas to Cochiti, New Mexico.

In September she resigned as Boas's secretary in order to devote herself entirely to academic studies, but her plans were interrupted shortly thereafter by a whirlwind romance and her marriage in December to Walter S. Goldfrank, a New York businessman. He was a widower and the father of three young boys. Managing this large household understandably altered her study routines, and any plans for a career in anthropology were further interrupted in June 1924 with the birth of her daughter, Susan, and the family's subsequent move to White Plains, New York.

Goldfrank wrote her monograph *The Social and Ceremonial Organization of Cochiti* (1927) during her pregnancy. In it she noted the presence of factionalism and the lack of social harmony among the Cochiti, as well as a tendency toward centralization of authority induced by historical and economic conditions. Her description of Pueblo life in Cochiti differed notably from that presented seven years later in Ruth Benedict's *Patterns of Culture* (1934).

Then, in the fall of 1924, at the invitation and urging of Elsie Clews Parsons and with the encouragement and support of her husband, Goldfrank left her infant in the care of a nurse for one month to continue her anthropological investigations in Isleta Pueblo.

Her previous experiences in the field had been pleasant, often exhilarating and generally quite fruitful. She had made close friends among her informants and had maintained a warm relationship with the "mother" by whom she had been adopted in Cochiti.

Life in Isleta proved very different from these earlier experiences. This Pueblo was tightly controlled, the villagers secretive and aloof. In two previous attempts Parsons had worked with informants outside the village without much success. Goldfrank's relationship with the Isleta family with whom she boarded remained distant and unrewarding. The family neither cooperated nor introduced her to potential informants, and most of the villagers refused to communicate with her. Just when she was most dejected, the father of the family said he knew a good storyteller and told her where he lived. Goldfrank visited him in his room but was uneasy about walking home in the dark, so she asked that they meet in her room. At her informant's insistence, Goldfrank locked the door of her room and covered the windows with sheets to make it clear that she did not wish to be disturbed. On various pretexts the son and daughter of the household demanded entry into her room during the interview. When the son demanded his gun "to go deer hunting," Goldfrank became alarmed. Her informant agreed to further meetings in Albuquerque, where his fellow villagers would not find him.

Aware that Parsons, too, had encountered difficulties in Isleta, Goldfrank was pleased that she had been able to gather some valuable data, but she was also convinced that caring for a family of four children and continuing fieldwork were incompatible ventures for the foreseeable future. Goldfrank contrasted

Boas's belief that "marriage and a family come first in a woman's life" with Parsons's warm and continual encouragement to stay in the field. Whatever conflicts Goldfrank experienced, she concurred with Boas at the time and reports that she had no regrets about leaving. She agreed that being a mother was more important than being an anthropologist.

The sudden death of Walter Goldfrank in 1935 put an end to this part of her life. By then her stepsons were grown and living away from home. She no longer had need for the sizable suburban home that echoed with memories of happier days. She soon returned to New York with her eleven-year-old daughter but found that domesticity alone in the city was no more satisfying than it had been in Westchester.

After an absence of thirteen years, she returned to Columbia and to anthropology. Her daughter was away at school much of the day, and Goldfrank was confident that she could study and still manage a household. By her own account, reentry into the field was not easy. She was warmly welcomed at Columbia, but her status was ambiguous. Her contemporaries—Margaret Mead,* Ruth Benedict,* and Ruth Bunzel*—all had their doctorates and had achieved considerable fame. With no training other than her B.A., some fieldwork, and the publication of her work on the Cochiti, Goldfrank understandably found no professional niche in the department. But both Bunzel and Benedict were friendly, and Benedict suggested that her experience as a mother might qualify her for work on a study of adolescents sponsored by the General Education Board of the Rockefeller Foundation. Collaborating with Jeannette Mirsky, the staff anthropologist, Goldfrank analyzed data on adolescent adjustment in several high schools in various sections of the United States.

In the fall of 1937, after this study had been completed, Goldfrank increased her attendance at Columbia but did not work for a graduate degree. She wrote:

I was forty years old [the average age of the students was about twenty-five], I had been in the field four times. I had published, and I felt confident that if I had anything worth saying I would find a platform from which to say it. And I didn't want to teach. My overriding concern was to flesh out my early field and family experiences, and since I was not working for a degree, I could be selective. Indeed, to many of the students, I must have seemed little more than an aging dilettante. (Goldfrank 1978:111)

While attending courses of her own choosing, Goldfrank also participated in the sessions on culture-and-personality being conducted by Abram Kardiner and Ralph Linton. During this period she began arguing with Ruth Benedict about Pueblo society, relying on her data from her own observations in Laguna and Cochiti. Though never close friends—their political beliefs, life-styles and world-views were quite different—Goldfrank and Benedict treated each other with mutual respect. Goldfrank's experiences in the Pueblos, however, had led her to raise serious questions about the Appollonian view of these communities presented in Benedict's *Patterns of Culture*. Despite their differences, Benedict immediately agreed to include Goldfrank among a group of anthropologists studying the Blackfoot (Blood) Indians under her direction in the summer of 1939. That summer's research provided the raw material for two articles (Goldfrank 1943b, 1945a).

In March 1940 Goldfrank married Karl August Wittfogel. A world-famous historian and Sinologist, Wittfogel was director of the Chinese History Project at Columbia University and soon began discussing his theories on irrigation societies with Ralph Linton, then chair of the Columbia Anthropology Department, and with Julian Steward, Linton's successor. Because of her early interest and training in economics, Goldfrank found Wittfogel's theories on irrigation stimulating. He encouraged her to pursue a historical approach to answer a question raised by her study of the Blood Indians of Canada: Why did they differ significantly from the Teton Dakota and also from the closely related Blackfoot in the United States? Ethnographers had found the Dakota to be relatively egalitarian, whereas Goldfrank's data showed their society to be more tightly organized, more hierarchical and prone to violence. To find the origins of these differences, Goldfrank worked intensively with historical sources and ultimately concluded that the explanation for the divergence in Teton and Blood social character after 1850 could not be explained in terms of aboriginal differences in culture. Instead she proposed that they were a product of the nature of the relationship between the Dakota and the government of the United States, on one hand, and the Blood and the government of Canada, on the other.

Goldfrank (1978) discussed some of the issues that divided her and Benedict with regard to the Blood. They differed over kin terms and over the existence of "vested interests" in tribal societies. To outsiders the disputes appeared to be minor quibbles, of interest only to a specialist. In reality the disputes reflected a deep schism within anthropology itself during that period. The kinship argument arose when Goldfrank reported that while a man might call his younger brother's son "grandson," the younger brother's son often referred to that same man as "uncle" rather than "grandfather." Goldfrank saw this change in terminology as evidence of cultural change and the influence of external factors on the culture of the Plains Indians. Benedict's idealized and configurational perspective required symmetry in kinship terms, and she was thus skeptical of Goldfrank's field data. Benedict's idealism also pervaded her perspective on the economics of tribal societies. She objected to Goldfrank's suggestion that aboriginal differences in wealth—encouraged by policies of the Canadian government—could have created "vested interests." Benedict's concept of tribal societies precluded such interests (Goldfrank 1978).

Goldfrank's joint paper with Karl Wittfogel (1943), focused attention on the role of irrigation in the structure of society. It was, however, her 1945 article "Socialization, Personality, and the Structure of Pueblo Society" in which Goldfrank openly contradicted the image of the Pueblos presented by Benedict. This paper launched a debate over the validity of the configurational approach in anthropology. By 1953 many well-known anthropologists agreed with E. Adamson Hoebel that *Patterns of Culture,* despite its great influence in anthropology, "bears only a tangential relationship to the facts of Pueblo ethnography. The factual criticisms . . . only begin to indicate the extent of the artistic and poetic idealization of Pueblo culture that Benedict presented" (Hoebel 1954:724).

During the late fifties Goldfrank edited and gathered materials and paintings for Elsie Clews Parsons's manuscript "Isleta Paintings" (1962). Edward Dozier, himself part Pueblo Indian, called this beautiful volume, "the only pictorial ethnographic account of Pueblo ceremonial life executed entirely by a native artist." He considered it a unique contribution that might never be repeated because "Pueblos guard the religious aspect of their culture, and the strictures that befall the informer are so stringent that few have dared to reveal ceremonial secrets" (Dozier 1963:936).

The artist of "Isleta Paintings" had asked that his name remain secret during his lifetime to insure his protection from the wrath of his community. When Goldfrank learned that the painter had died in 1953, she felt it important to name him and present the known details of his life. The *Artist of "Isleta Paintings" in Pueblo Society* was published in 1967. In Goldfrank's words, it is "a sad story of a talented artist astride two cultures." Though still lacking significant details because of Pueblo secrecy, the volume was described by Alfonso Ortiz (1968:838) as "rich ethnographic fare."

Goldfrank was elected secretary-treasurer (1945–47), president (1948), and editor (1952–56) of the American Ethnological Society. During the forties and fifties Goldfrank continued writing about the Pueblo Indians and the Blood, always drawing on her field notes and linking ethnographic facts firmly to both specific historical events and ecological conditions. Her autobiography *Notes on an Undirected Life as One Anthropologist Tells It* was published in 1978 by Queens College.

She never taught, and all told, she spent only six months in the field. Her career was constrained, in part, by her own vision of her role as a mother and wife and at least for a short period, by the very real demands of a large suburban household. These perspectives and roles were very much a part of the world into which she was born and raised. Despite these constraints, her fieldwork yielded valuable data, which she utilized in her writings to develop a perspective on anthropology that focused attention on history, political relationships, and ecology. Her marriage to Wittfogel and their interlocking interests strengthened her own convictions about the contingent nature of history and politics and pitted her against many proponents of culture-and-personality theory during the late thirties and forties. As much as her advanced age permits, Goldfrank continues her participation in anthropology. Today she and her husband live in New York and maintain contact with a wide network of anthropologists.

Note

1. The author extends her gratitude to Esther Goldfrank for her support and cooperation during the preparation of this draft.

References and Works About Esther S. Goldfrank

Dozier, Edward P.
1963 Review of Elsie Clews Parsons' *Isleta Paintings*. *American Anthropologist* 65 (4): 936ff.
Ortiz, Alfonso
1968 Review of Esther S. Goldfrank's *The Artist of "Isleta Paintings" in Pueblo Society*. *American Anthropologist* 70:838.

Selected Works by Esther S. Goldfrank

1923 Notes on Two Pueblo Feasts. *American Anthropologist* 25 (2): 188–96.
1926 Isleta Variants: A Study in Flexibility. *Journal of American Folklore* 39:71–78.
1927 The Social and Ceremonial Organization of Cochiti. *American Anthropological Association Memoir*, No. 33:5–129.
1937 Culture Takes a Holiday. (Profile of Ellery Sedgwick.) Unpublished.
1943a Historic Change and Social Character: A Study of the Teton Dakota. *American Anthropologist* 45 (1): 67–83.
1943b Administrative Programs and Changes in Blood Society in the Reserve Period. *Applied Anthropology* 2 (2): 18–24.
1945a *Changing Configurations in the Social Organization of a Blackfoot Tribe During the Reserve Period*. American Ethnological Society, Monograph 8. New York: J. J. Augustin.
1945b Historic Change and Social Character: A Study of the Teton Dakota. *American Anthropologist* 45:67–83.
1945c Socialization, Personality, and the Structure of Pueblo Society. *American Anthropologist* 47 (4): 516–37.
1945d Irrigation Agriculture and Navaho Community Leadership: Case Material on Environment and Culture. *American Anthropologist* 47 (2): 262–77.
1945e Two Anthropologists, the Same Informant: Some Differences in Their Recorded Data. *Journal of the Anthropological Society of Oxford* (May 1945) 16 (1): 42–52.
1946a More About Irrigation Agriculture and Navaho Community Leadership. *American Anthropologist* 48 (3): 473–82.
1946b Linguistic Note to Zuni Ethnology. *Word* 2 (3): 191–96.
1948 The Impact of Situation and Personality on Four Hopi Emergence Myths. *Southwestern Journal of Anthropology* 4 (3): 241–62.
1949 Presidential Report at Annual Meeting of the American Ethnological Society, December 30, 1948. *American Anthropologist* 51 (2): 371ff.
1951a Observations on Sexuality Among the Blood Indians of Alberta, Canada. In *Psychoanalysis and the Social Sciences, III*. Geza Roheim, ed. Pp. 71–98. New York: International Universities Press.
1951b "Old Man" and the Father Image in Blood (Blackfoot) Society. In *Psychoanalysis and Culture*. George B. Wilbur and Warner Muensterberger, eds. Pp. 132–41. New York: International Universities Press.
1952 The Different Patterns of Blackfoot and Pueblo Adaptation to White Authority.

In *Acculturation in the Americas*. Twenty-ninth International Congress of Americanists. Sol Tax, ed. Pp. 74–79. Chicago: University of Chicago Press.

1954a Discussant of Ruth Underhill's Paper "Intercultural Relations in the Greater Southwest." *American Anthropologist* 56 (3): 658–62.

1954b Notes on Deer-Hunting Practices at Laguna Pueblo, New Mexico. *Texas Journal of Science* 6 (4): 407–21.

1955 Native Paintings of Isleta Pueblo, New Mexico. *Transactions of the New York Academy of Sciences* (series 2) 18 (2): 178–80.

1962 Isleta Paintings. *BAE Bulletin 181*. Washington, D.C.: Government Printing Office.

1967 *The Artist of "Isleta Paintings" in Pueblo Society*. Smithsonian Contributions to Anthropology, No. 5. Washington, D.C.: Smithsonian Institution.

1974 Introduction. "Adoption Practices of the Blood Indians of Alberta, Canada," by Marjorie Lismer. *Plains Anthropologist* 1 (2): 19–63.

1976 Socialization, Personality and the Structure of Pueblo Society (with particular reference to Hopi and Zuni). *Selected Papers from the American Anthropologist 1921–1945*. George W. Stocking, Jr., ed. Washington, D.C.: American Anthropological Association.

1978 *Notes on an Undirected Life as One Anthropologist Tells It*. Queens College Publications in Anthropology, no. 3. Flushing, New York.

1983 Another View: Margaret and Me. *Ethnohistory* 30 (1): 1–14.

Coauthored Works

Goldfrank, Esther, and Karl Wittfogel
1943 Some Aspects of Pueblo Mythology and Society. *Journal of American Folklore* 56 (219): 17–30.

GLORIA LEVITAS

Vera Mae Green

(1928–1982)

Afro-American social/applied anthropologist Vera Mae Green was known best for her study of family and ethnic relations in the Dutch Antilles and the United States, and for her efforts to foster the growth and development of a methodology for the study of Afro-American anthropology.

Green was born in Chicago, Illinois, on September 6, 1928. She was the only child of a hard-working but poor black family who lived in a part of the black community that she has referred to as the "rented-room poor" (Green 1972:102). She never married or had any children of her own.

Because she grew up among the urban poor, Green was able to articulate and understand that among so-called poor people there was diversity and variation. This was the hallmark of one of her major contributions to anthropology as she explored the diversity of black families and culture in the United States and the Caribbean throughout her career. As St. Clair Drake (1980:24) points out, "Well into the 1960s she was the only Afro-American anthropologist who was a Caribbeanist. . . . When she chose the Caribbean she was breaking new ground; when she chose the Dutch Caribbean it put her into the category of the unusual."

Green's interest in the field of anthropology came at a young age, because she was an avid reader. She told stories of being a youthful Saturday movie matinee critic of Hollywood's portrayal of Native Americans. She said her friends did not want to sit next to her because she spoiled the show by telling them that some aspect of material culture or symbolic expression was out of place.

Green attended local public schools in Chicago. She won a college scholarship and spent some time at William Penn College, where she completed her undergraduate studies in sociology and psychology. At Roosevelt she studied under the eminent black anthropologist St. Clair Drake and sociologist Horace Cayton, authors of *Black Metropolis*. Drake encouraged Green to seek graduate study in the social sciences, but her lack of finances eliminated that possibility. Therefore, like many young, black professionals of that period, Vera took a divergent path to get to anthropology. During the early 1950s she worked at various social welfare jobs in Chicago, such as group worker, social welfare aide, and child welfare worker. In addition, she was a community tenant-relations aide and social worker for the Chicago Housing Authority (Cole 1982:633). She felt that she was doing something for people, rather than studying about their problems. However, the quest for further education remained with Green, particularly as she felt subsumed by the bureaucracy of Chicago social welfare agencies.

In the mid–1950s Green moved to New York City where she formally began her study of anthropology at Columbia University. Under the direction of Charles Wagley and Eleanor Padilla, she studied the relationships among social stress, health, and disease in New York's East Harlem (Cole 1982).

During her days at Columbia, Green came under the tutelage of Gene Weltfish,* noted scholar of Native Americans. Green was a member of the student support group for Weltfish, when her tenured position at Columbia was eliminated during the McCarthy era purge. Although blacklisted for over ten years, Weltfish and her former student remained good friends. Their relationship continued until Weltfish died in 1980.

In 1955 Green received her master's degree in anthropology from Columbia University. Sensing a need to apply her anthropology rather than to just study it, Green left Columbia to enter the field of international community development with the United Nations. In 1956 she trained in Mexico, where she worked in a mestizo community and earned the UNESCO title of fundamental educator. She also did community development work in India.

In 1963 Green continued her work on the diversity of poverty when she served as one of Oscar Lewis's research assistants in his study of a poor urban area in Puerto Rico and in New York. Green was an ideal research assistant because East Harlem, the site of the U.S. mainland portion of the Lewis study, was where she had previously conducted fieldwork. In addition, Green brought a tremendous firsthand understanding of the study of the poor to her research, because it had been a part of both her personal and previous professional experiences.

Following the fieldwork in Puerto Rico and New York, Vera Green returned to Illinois, this time to the University of Illinois, where Oscar Lewis was professor of anthropology. Lewis encouraged Vera to complete her doctorate. However, it was Edward Spicer who provided Green with the way to enter the doctorate program at the University of Arizona in Tucson, where she received her Ph.D. in 1969. Her doctoral fieldwork was carried out on the Dutch Caribbean island of Aruba. Her dissertation, "Aspects of Interethnic Integration in Aruba, Netherlands Antilles," was done under the direction of E. H. Spicer, with H. T. Getty, and E. P. Dozier as members of her committee. She was one of the first Afro-American anthropologists to study interethnic relations in the Caribbean and the first to look at the Dutch Caribbean as a culture area. Gifted in languages, Green's fluency in Spanish, French, Urdu, Tamil, Dutch, German, and Papimento is indicative of her wealth and variety of fieldwork experiences.

Vera Green taught at the University of Iowa (1969) and the University of Houston (1969–72) before she joined the faculty at Rutgers University in 1972. During her tenure at Rutgers she served as graduate advisor and chair of the Department of Anthropology, as well as chair of the undergraduate division of the department at Livingston College. From 1976 until her death in 1982, she served as director of the Latin American Institute of Rutgers. The institute offered interdisciplinary graduate and undergraduate certificates in Latin American Studies and sponsored lectures and programs concerning affairs of the region. Because of her extensive network of friends, acquaintances, and contacts, numerous eminent Caribbean and South American scholars and politicians came to Rutgers under the auspices of the Latin American Institute. Green was deeply concerned with the issue of international human rights. Her actions on behalf of human rights bespoke a scholar committed to the betterment of the human condition, and a person who was a member of the Society of Friends, the Quakers.

Vera Green made significant contributions to Caribbean studies, interethnic studies, black family studies, and the study of poverty and the poor. What she contributed was not only the rich ethnographic data from her fieldwork, she also introduced sophisticated methodological frameworks to the discipline that had not been used before when studying ethnic relations or diversity among the poor.

In her dissertation, later published as *Migrants in Aruba* (1974), Green showed that contrary to data reported for the Windward Islands or other areas of the West Indies, in Aruba there was a high degree of integration between natives and non-natives at all levels. She also showed how studying voluntary associations that cut across class and ethnic boundaries gave a more accurate and dynamic picture of what was happening on the island than did the more traditional methods of community and family studies.

During the 1970s Green continued to point out the methodological pitfalls of making simplistic observations of complex issues surrounding black family life in the United States and the Caribbean. Most anthropological (and other social science) studies had failed to recognize the diversity of black populations in the United States. In her article "Confrontation of Diversity Within the Black Community," she eloquently shows how well-meaning people who have a lack of understanding of the history of blacks, often do disservice to the understanding of black culture. She states that

the lack of understanding of the history of Blacks in the United States, including the variation of slave utilization, coupled with the narrow theoretical orientation of some of the more recent social science studies has stimulated the development of a limited conception of the Black experience, past and present; this in turn paves the way for internal conflict (among Blacks). (Green 1970:271)

In her article "The Black Extended Family in the United States," Green (1978) focused her criticism on black family studies that had ignored the ecological differences among blacks. She developed a model that accounted for the depth in richness of the black experience. She showed that black culture experience was more diversified than the traditionally studied "folk" blacks in the rural areas of the South and in the slums of the urban ghettos (Green 1978). For Green, black cultural experiences are not singular or two-dimensional urban/rural phenomena, but plural situations. This is expressed in the variety of symbolic forms of material culture, social organization, and adaptation to diverse environments. Green proposed a nine-part model in which she encouraged research of black history and culture in seven additional geographical areas, including the southern Tidewater-Piedmont area, the coastal Southeast, the areas of French tradition, the areas of American Indian influence and triracial influence, old eastern colonial areas, and the midwestern and far western areas (Green 1978). At the time of her death, she was working on a manuscript in which she was refining this model. She planned to present it as a baseline to help social-change agents (social workers, community developers, and others) understand the diversity of American black culture.

In her classroom Green stressed the perspective of understanding the range of variation found among not only blacks but all peoples, and in particular the poor. It appeared to her that poor populations fell victim to streamlining by scholars, so that diversity was eliminated in order to fit their model. A number of graduate students who studied under Green in the mid–1970s incorporated the concept of range of variation in their dissertations and professional publications.

Green was also interested in the area of migration, especially as it pertained to fostering the abolition and/or the maintenance of ethnic or racial identity. Her research in three areas of the New World showed that while race and color are factors that help to define the status of persons of African descent, socioeconomic status and cultural behaviors are also mitigating forces that should be considered (Green 1975). That is, whatever attribute categorized an individual in a particular group in one setting may not be useful to imply that those criteria are operational in another setting. Again, she cautioned researchers to search out all forms of black cultural variations before making generalizations about any of them. While she did not disregard the importance of ethnicity as set forth by Frederick Barth (1969), she did conclude that "the data from the Netherland Antilles and the United States indicate that ethnicity is not universally imperative—it can be 'disregarded and temporarily set aside by other definitions of the situation' " (Green 1975:95).

Her concern with the human condition led her to apply her professional skills in anthropology and her firsthand knowledge of international issues to question the sincerity of the commitment of countries like the United States to human rights protection. In the introduction of the book she coedited with Jack L. Nelson, *International Human Rights* (1980), she looked at the paradoxes in the human rights arena between the lofty principles advocated and what political leaders actually did about the problem of human rights violations. Using the United States as a case in point, Green says that while this country advocates the rhetoric of international human rights, it has shown reluctance in actually signing documents that would have global impact.

As one solution to this problem, she advocated a worldwide agreement on the definitions, characteristics, and examples of human rights that would lead to appropriate development, monitoring, and enforcement. She notes that while some issues such as physical slavery achieve international scrutiny on moral and legal grounds, many other human rights issues are not exposed because of the vested interests of nations and the lack of an international consensus with moral and legal force (Green and Nelson 1980).

Green was a member of numerous professional associations. She served on the executive board of the American Anthropological Association, on the executive committee of the Mid-Atlantic Council for Latin American Studies, as convener of the Quaker Anthropologists and as president of the Association of Black Anthropologists (ABA) (1977–79). During that time she was responsible for providing support and inspiration for many young black anthropologists. She was given a service award by the ABA in 1980 for her outstanding contributions to the field of anthropology and for her commitment to people of color.

At the time of her death from cancer, Vera Mae Green was a Fellow at the Institute for Advanced Studies at Princeton, where she was in the process of working on two manuscripts, one dealing with community studies among the poor and the other a reorganization of her fieldwork done in Chicago and in Houston. The contents of her will illustrate how she continues to influence who and what she considered to be valuable and most cherished. All of her possessions, including a notable collection of Caribbean paintings, were auctioned to support two scholarship programs for black or Puerto Rican students in need at Rutgers and William Penn College, and to support the Zora Neale Hurston* collection of southern black culture at the University of Florida at Gainesville. Her vast library and all her papers were given to the Tuskegee Institute, a long-standing black university in Alabama.

Vera Green was a committed scholar, an advocate for the poor and a black woman who believed in doing things. An only child, she never married. Diminutive in stature, her seemingly inexhaustible energies touched many in a direct and indirect fashion. In conversation on any given day, when asked how she was doing, Vera Green usually replied, "Honey, I'm just trying to make it." And then, in a second breath—"You know, in your work, why don't you try looking at. . . . "

References and Works About Vera Mae Green

Cole, Johnetta B.
1982   Obituary on Vera Mae Green. *American Anthropologist* 84:633–35.

Selected Works by Vera Mae Green

1970   The Confrontation of Diversity Within the Black Community. *Human Organization* 29 (4): 267–72.

1972 Comments on Charles Valentine, Racism and Recent Anthropological Study of U.S. Blacks. *Human Organization* 31 (1): 102.

1973 Methodological Problems Involved in the Study of the Aruban Family. In *Proceedings of the 2nd Conference on the Family in the Caribbean*. S. Gerber, ed. Pp. 17–29. Puerto Rico: Institute for Caribbean Studies.

1974 *Migrants in Aruba*. Assen, Netherlands: Van Gorcum.

1975 Racial vs. Ethnic Factors in Afro-American and Afro-Caribbean Migration. In *Migration, Change and Development: Implications for Ethnic Diversity and Political Conflict*. Helen Safa and Brian duTroit, eds. Pp. 83–96. The Hague: Mouton.

1978 The Black Extended Family in the United States: Some Research Suggestions. In *The Extended Family in Black Societies*. D. B. Shimkin, E. M. Shimkin, and D. A. Frate, eds. Pp. 379–87. The Hague: Mouton.

1981 U.S. Blacks: The Creation of an Enduring People? In *Persistent Peoples: Cultural Enclaves in Perspective*. G. Kushner and C. P. Castile, eds. Pp. 69–77. Tucson: University of Arizona Press.

1982 Dominica. In *Political Parties of the Americas*. Robert J. Alexander, ed. Pp. 345–51. Westport, Conn.: Greenwood Press.

Coauthored Works

Green, Vera Mae, and Jack Nelson, eds.
1980 *International Human Rights: Contemporary Perspectives*. New York: Earl M. Coleman Enterprises.

A. LYNN BOLLES AND YOLANDA T. MOSES

Erna Gunther

(1896–1982)

American cultural anthropologist Erna Gunther was known for her ethnography, ethnobiology, and ethnohistory of Native Americans of the Northwest Coast. Gunther also played a major role in building public appreciation for the art of Northwest Coast Indians.

Gunther was born on November 9, 1896, the only child of a middle class family in Brooklyn, New York. Her father, Casper Gunther, was a jeweler and diamond buyer who had emigrated from Germany. From him Erna learned her fluent German, and she learned French from her maternal grandmother, who spoke little English. Erna's mother, Susannah Ehren, had been a tutor and governess before her marriage. Her maternal grandfather had been professor of physics at Heidelberg University. In this household Erna absorbed a lifelong dedication to teaching and public service.

Gunther's first love was the humanities; but by 1919, when she graduated from Barnard College with a degree in English, she had already been converted to the study of anthropology by Franz Boas, from whom she had taken courses as an undergraduate and who became her first mentor. Boas undoubtedly shaped Gunther's fundamental orientation to her discipline. She remained a good Boasian: faithful to the ethnographic facts and loath to speculate beyond them, determined to let the natives speak for themselves and dedicated to establishing the cultural context for arts and customs.

But it was Leslie Spier, also a student of Boas, whose approach to anthropology most powerfully influenced Gunther's early scholarship. In 1921 she and Spier married and moved to Seattle, where Spier was teaching at the University of Washington. The couple's two children, Robert and Christopher, were born in Seattle. Gunther and Spier had been fellow students at Columbia University, but Spier was older than Gunther and had already established a formidable reputation. Although she herself chose the First Salmon ceremony as her dissertation topic, the way she defined the problem shows the influence of Spier's concern with the processes of diffusion. Gunther earned an M.A. from Columbia in 1920 and completed her doctorate in 1928, when her dissertation, *A Further Analysis of the First Salmon Ceremony,* was published.

Gunther had made her first field trip in 1921, when she and Spier, newly married, spent two months with the Havasupai, but her longest and most intensive research was devoted to the Puget Sound Salish (1922–23), the Klallam (1924–25), and the Nootkan-speaking Makah of western Washington (1930–35). In the late 1950s she began another kind of fieldwork, visiting museums in North America, Europe, and the Soviet Union, tracking down the collections of the earliest European explorers to visit the Northwest Coast.

During the early years of her career, Gunther was interested in explaining the diffusion of cultural traits. Her two works on the First Salmon ceremony analyzed the diffusion of the practice of honoring the first salmon and determined that it served an important function in the cultural systems in which it occurred. Although Gunther's interest in the connections between culture and ecology later found expression in her pioneering ethnobiological publications, she abandoned the comparative work represented by her studies of the salmon ceremony.

The Puget Sound Salish first engaged Gunther's interest, since Boas had given her the late Hermann Haeberlin's Puget Salish research notes to edit for publication (Gunther and Haeberlin 1924; Gunther as ed. 1925b). Her work with the Klallam was cast in the same mold, and like the Puget Salish ethnography, remains a primary source for the region (Gunther 1925a, 1927).

Gunther's interest in folklore was kindled when she collected Havasupai stories for Leslie Spier. She went on to edit Haeberlin's collection of Puget Sound Salish folktales (Gunther 1925b). She recorded a sizable number of Klallam stories (1925d), which she proudly characterized at the time as "the first scientific collection of Puget Sound folklore" (Shephard Collection).[1]

Despite her determination to pursue a professional career while raising her family, and her considerable scholarly achievement, Gunther was not able to obtain full-time academic employment until she was appointed at the University of Washington, after she and Spier separated (1930). During the years she was married to Spier, Gunther had occupied the anomalous position of a professional woman connected to a powerful man. Although she could not compete directly for job openings at the universities where her husband was employed, her qualifications brought her to the attention of the administration, which was willing to find peripheral positions for her. (For example, Washington made her "associate" faculty in anthropology in 1926.) Ironically, her divorce, coming when it did, conferred a professional advantage. First, Spier negotiated a bona fide position for her when he resigned from the university (Spier 1930, Regents Files). Second, as a divorced woman, Gunther escaped the early 1930s' purge of married women from Washington's faculty, undertaken by an administration desperate to reduce expenses.

After Gunther and Spier divorced in 1931, she was very much on her own. She and Melville Jacobs were the only anthropologists left on the faculty at the

University of Washington, but a widening personal and professional antipathy blocked any frank scholarly discussions. Although other faculty joined the department, Erna remained intellectually somewhat aloof from them. She enjoyed close friendships with Robert Lowie and Alfred Kroeber at the University of California at Berkeley, but her work does not show direct influence from either.

For most of her thirty-six years at the University of Washington, Gunther was chair of Anthropology and director of the Washington State Museum on campus. After Spier's departure, Gunther was the more senior of the two remaining anthropologists (Jacobs did not receive his degree until later), which made her the logical choice for department chair and museum director—jobs formerly held by Spier.

Faced with mandatory retirement, Gunther resigned from Washington in 1966 to accept the chair of anthropology at the University of Alaska in Fairbanks but stayed in Alaska only three years. In 1969 she returned to Seattle, where she carried out an active program of research, writing, and museum consulting until a few years before her death.

On the occasion of her resignation from Washington, Kenneth Read, then chair at Washington, wrote to her:

The department is now one of the largest in the country, and this is due in no small measure to your foresight during the years when you were chairman [sic]. All that we have done since then is built upon what you yourself constructed . . . a very sound foundation. . . . I know that it is almost fully due to you that this University has such an outstanding collection of regional artifacts. (Erna Gunther Collection)

From the mid–1930s to the mid–1950s, Gunther's responsibilities as department chair and museum director absorbed most of her energies. Perceiving herself to be as vulnerable as in the lean Depression years, Gunther hoped to protect herself and her department by cultivating public support.

Later, from the late 1950s to the late 1970s, much of her time and energy was consumed by her continuing campaign to arouse public support for anthropology and for the arts and crafts of Northwest native peoples. She offered a series of very popular telecourses (1953). In the 1950s she served for several years on the accreditation committee of the American Association of University Women, visiting colleges and counseling administrators.

Above all, she was sincerely committed to building appreciation not only for Northwest Coast art but also for the Indian people who produced it. During her long professional life and her very active retirement, Gunther consistently supported Indian causes. She opposed the federal policy of terminating Indian treaty status; she supported the National Congress of American Indians; and she helped local Indian women start the Seattle Indian Women's League with its shop for native artists to sell their work.

Although the strategy of building public support succeeded in preserving both museum and department, and Gunther herself as director and chair, respectively, it alienated her from professionally oriented colleagues such as the linguist Melville Jacobs (who complained to Boas in 1936 that Gunther valued publications for their contribution to public relations rather than for their scholarly merit (Jacobs Collection).

In an effort to create an intellectual community, Gunther organized a group of University of Washington women faculty who met regularly to read papers on their research. During all the years Gunther was at Washington, she and Viola Garfield* were the only tenured women on the anthropology faculty. For personal reasons Garfield was not active in the group, so however valuable the group may have been, it did not provide Gunther with professional peers.

As a woman who was professor, chair, and museum director, Gunther had in fact few peers in the entire community of American anthropologists, and none in the Northwest. She missed the intellectual give-and-take that should have directed her professional development along the mainstream of the discipline.

Others might argue that Gunther's anomalous status also contributed to her two major professional losses at Washington: her positions as chair of anthropology in 1955 and as director of the museum in 1962. Despite acknowledging that women in general were at a disadvantage (a marginal note in one of her Barnard notebooks complains of "distinct discrimination everywhere against *woman*" [Gunther Collection, 1919]), Gunther never attributed her own professional defeats to her gender (Gunther personal communication, 1975).

Although the volume of publications never again matched what she had produced in the 1920s, in the late 1930s Gunther's scholarship began to break new ground. "Ethnobotany of Western Washington" (Gunther 1945a), her most popular work, was an innovation, since at the time there had been no ethnobiological investigation of the Northwest culture. She had earlier analyzed the zoological knowledge of the Makah (Gunther 1936) and continued to encourage her students to collect information on native names and uses for birds and animals as well as plants.

Gunther's 1949 study of the Indian Shaker Church, combining ethnographic and historical sources, marked another shift—from the classic ethnographic method of her earlier work to the syncretic approach that was to characterize her later research.

Gunther is probably best known as an authority on Northwest Indian art. Her conversion from ethnography to more specialized "art ethnohistory" can be credited to her experience directing the Washington State Museum and cataloging and preparing exhibits of Northwest Coast art at other museums. The inadequacy of most documentation spurred her to search journals and diaries of the explorers who collected the pieces. She made a series of pilgrimages to the European museums where pieces from early collections might be found. Concern over the inaccessibility of primary sources led her to translate Aurel Krause's description of the Tlingit (1956b) and Jacobson's journal of explorations (1977).

Paradoxically, as Gunther matured and developed a broader perspective on the anthropological enterprise, the focus of her own interest narrowed from the theoretical and comparative to the regional and culturally specific. She chose to present a clear picture of one group of people through the lens of their beautiful artifacts rather than pursuing questionable generalizations. Describing the goals of her work, she said:

[T]his material establishes the continuity and depth of the principles of Northwest Coast Indian life and the areal extent of certain cultural similarities. It brings personalities to these painted, singing people who approached the ships in their handsome canoes. This was the living Northwest Coast, and the cultural traits of these people, partly forgotten, still have enough of the spark of life to make one hope that this great culture may inspire and guide their descendants who are facing a modern world. (Gunther 1972:xiv)

Note

1. The author has consulted the following sources: Erna Gunther, Melville Jacobs, and Esther Shepard collections as well as the records of the University Regents, University of Washington Archives, Seattle.

References and Works About Erna Gunther

Amoss, Pamela, and Viola Garfield (senior author)
1984   Erna Gunther (1896–1982). *American Anthropologist* 86 (2): 394–99.

Selected Works by Erna Gunther

1925a Klallam Folktales. *University of Washington Publications in Anthropology* 1:113–69.

1925b Mythology of Puget Sound by Hermann Haeberlin. *Journal of American Folklore* 37:371–438. (As ed.)

1926   Analysis of the First Salmon Ceremony. *American Anthropologist* 28:605–17.

1927   Klallam Ethnography. *University of Washington Publications in Anthropology* 1:171–314.

1928   A Further Analysis of the First Salmon Ceremony. *University of Washington Publications in Anthropology* 2:129–73.

1930a Accretion in American Indian Folktales. *Folklore*: 300–18.

1936   A Preliminary Report of the Zoological Knowledge of the Makah. In *Essays in Anthropology Presented to A. L. Kroeber*. Robert Lowie, ed. Pp. 105–18. Berkeley: University of California Press.

1941   Introduction. *Moveable Masks and Figures of the North Pacific Coast Indians*, by Robert Bruce Inverarity. Bloomfield Hills, Mich.: Cranbrook Institute of Science.

1942   Reminiscences of a Whaler's Wife. *Pacific Northwest Quarterly* 33 (1): 65–69.

1944   Cultural Backgrounds. In *The Indian in American Life*, by Gustavus E. E. Lindquist. Pp. 22–45. New York: Friendship Press. (Reprinted 1976 by New York: AMS Press.)

1945a Ethnobotany of Western Washington. *University of Washington Publications in Anthropology* 10:1–62.

1945b Catalog. *Indian Art of the Pacific Northwest*. Mills College Art Gallery, Oakland, Calif.

1947 Early Man in the Pacific Northwest. In *Biogeography*. Pp. 39–43. 8th Annual Biology Colloquium Proceedings. Oregon State Chapter of Phi Kappa Phi. Oregon State College: Corvallis, OR.

1948 The Education of American Indians. *Pi Lambda Theta Journal* 26:195–200.

1949 The Shaker Religion of the Northwest. In *Indians of the Urban Northwest*. Marian Smith, ed. Pp. 37–76. New York: Columbia University Press.

1950a The Westward Movement of Some Plains Traits. *American Anthropologist* 52:174–80.

1950b The Indian Background of Washington History. *Pacific Northwest Quarterly* 41:189–202.

1952 Catalog. *Indians of the Northwest Coast*. Taylor Museum, Colorado Springs Fine Arts Center.

1953 Viewer's Guide to Northwest Indian Life. Seattle: University of Washington Press.

1956a The Social Disorganization of the Haida As Reflected in Their Slate Carving. *Davidson Journal* 2:149–53.

1956b Translation. *The Tlingit Indians,* by Aurel Krause. Seattle: American Ethnological Society and the University of Washington Press.

1956c Material Culture, The Museum of Primitive Art. *College Art Journal* 9:290–95.

1956d Catalog. *Exhibition of the Indian Baskets of Western America*. Seattle Art Museum.

1960 A Re-evaluation of the Cultural Position of the Nootka. In *Men and Cultures: Selected Papers of the Fifth International Congress of Anthropological and Ethnological Sciences, Philadelphia, 1956*. Anthony F. C. Wallace, ed. Pp. 270–76. Philadelphia: University of Pennsylvania Press.

1961 Indian Craft Enterprises in the Northwest. *Human Organization* 20:216–18.

1962a Seattle Fair—Indian Art. *Art in America* no. 2.

1962b Makah Marriage Patterns and Population Stability. *Proceedings of the 34th International Congress of Americanists*. Pp. 538–45. Vienna: Verlag Ferdinand Berger.

1963 The Sculptural Art of the Northwest Coast. *The Beaver, Outfit* 293:4–13.

1964 Sitka's Museum. *Museum News* (May): 21–28.

1965a Indian Woodcarvers of the Pacific Northwest. *The Delphian Quarterly* 48 (1): 1–6.

1965b Indian Weavers of the Pacific Northwest. *The Delphian Quarterly* 48 (2): 22–27.

1966 Catalog. *Art in the Life of the Northwest Coast Indians*. The Rasmussen Collection of Northwest Indian Art at the Portland Art Museum. Portland Art Museum, Portland, Ore.

1968 Art in the Life of Primitive Peoples. In *Introduction to Cultural Anthropology*. James A. Clifton, ed. Pp. 77–114. Boston: Houghton-Mifflin.

1971 Northwest Coast Indian Art. In *Anthropology and Art: Readings in Cross-Cultural Aesthetics*. Charlotte M. Otten, ed. Pp. 318–40. Garden City, N.Y.: Natural History Press, for the American Museum of Natural History.

1972 *Indian Life on the Northwest Coast of North America as Seen by the Early Explorers and Fur Traders During the Last Decades of the Eighteenth Century*. Chicago: University of Chicago Press.

1977 Translation. *Alaskan Voyage, 1881–1883: An Expedition to the Northwest Coast of America,* by Johan Adrian Jacobson. Chicago: University of Chicago Press.

Coauthored Works

Gunther, Erna, and Hermann Haeberlin
1924 Ethnographische Notizen über die Indianerstämme des Pudget-Sundes. *Zeitschrift für Ethnologie* 51:1–74. (Reprint 1930 The Indians of Puget Sound, University of Washington Publications in Anthropology, Vol. 4 [1].)

PAMELA T. AMOSS

Jane Richardson Hanks

(1908–   )

American anthropologist Jane Richardson Hanks is known for her contributions to the ethnology of both North American Indians and Southeast Asia, especially for her pioneering studies of rural Thai villagers and upland tribal peoples.

Jane Richardson was born August 2, 1908, in Berkeley, California. Her father, Leon Josiah Richardson, was professor of Latin in the Classics Department at the University of California at Berkeley (UCB), and her maternal grandfather, Warren Wilkinson, had founded the Institute for the Deaf and Blind in Berkeley. She grew up near the UCB campus in a familial and social setting that was cultivated and well-bred, with her early schooling focused on literature, languages, music, and art. She also developed appreciation for different cultural traditions by experiencing the ethnic diversity of San Francisco, seeing an international exposition, and living for a year abroad studying in France and traveling extensively. She received an A.B. in 1930 and embarked on another trip to Europe, during which she was particularly intrigued by the mixture of Western and Middle Eastern cultures in Greece.

Upon her return to Berkeley, fortuitous events turned her toward anthropology, a discipline with which she had no prior familiarity. Herbert Bolton, a professor of Mexican history, hired Hanks to translate Italian sources on Father Chino, an early missionary in the American Southwest. After some discussion with Bolton about her fascination with Mexican history and also Greece as a cultural crossroads, he advised her to speak to Alfred Kroeber. Kroeber, upon discovering that she had no previous anthropological training, promptly enrolled her in three undergraduate ethnology courses, given by Robert Lowie and Ronald Olson. After completing these courses and two language examinations, she was admitted to graduate studies in anthropology at UCB in 1933. She was also unexpectedly asked to serve as one of several teaching assistants (T.A.s) for Olson's undergraduate introductory anthropology courses. By dint of hard study and help from

Olson and fellow T.A.s, she managed to acquire the basics of four-field anthropology.

From 1933 to 1936 Richardson taught introductory anthropology as a T.A., took graduate courses, and enjoyed the intellectual and social company of fellow students. In an effort to stimulate more informal contacts between faculty, students, and visiting scholars, Richardson, true to her upbringing, also organized daily four o'clock teas in the department, a practice that continued long after her departure. In addition to associations with faculty such as Kroeber, Lowie, and Olson, students also congregated frequently at the home of Paul Radin, who lived in Berkeley for some years after a brief teaching position at UCB. For her, this was a time of "intense exuberance in having found the discipline that integrated my diverse interests and experiences."[1]

During the UCB years a critical mentor for Richardson was Kroeber, who, she believes, was receptive to "mavericks" and "people who walked in from odd parts of life . . . [because] there might well be something in them." Jane Richardson was one of these; and Kroeber, recognizing her intelligence and potential, helped to further her graduate training in several important ways. When Kroeber wanted to expand his 1919 article on culture change as exemplified in women's dress styles, in the summer of 1934 he hired her as a research assistant to collect additional materials, realizing that her somewhat Edwardian upbringing and acquaintance with European art history were well suited to the task. The new information she collected from libraries and dress collections increased the time span of the study, and she introduced a mode of calculating "moving averages" to the quantitative analysis of changes. The resulting work, Richardson and Kroeber's famous "Three Centuries of Women's Dress Fashions" (1940), charted cyclical changes in various features of dress styles over time. (It is noteworthy that Jane Richardson, the research assistant, was graciously listed by Kroeber as the senior author.)

Kroeber, having seen evidence of her research ability, now felt that she needed field experience. He arranged for her to participate in a program sponsored by the Laboratory of Anthropology at Santa Fe (funded by the National Research Council) to provide graduate students selected from various schools with the opportunity to learn field methods under the guidance of an experienced anthropologist. Thus, in the summer of 1935, Richardson went to study Kiowa Indians in Oklahoma in the company of Bernard Mishkin (Columbia), William Bascom (Northwestern), Weston LaBarre (Yale), and Donald Collier (Chicago), with Alexander Lesser (Columbia) as field director. Focusing on "salvage" ethnography, oral histories, and the recording of Kiowa music, she found her first field trip to be "an extremely important solidifying of a number of things that one had been thinking about academically. We had studied the American Indians, and now here they were in the Kiowa. The processes of culture change and such became reality to us." Of great importance to her was the tutelage of Lesser, for whom she developed abiding respect and admiration.

After she returned from the Kiowa, Kroeber's faith in her potential was manifest once again. Seeing that she needed to expand her horizons beyond Berkeley, Kroeber obtained a UCB traveling fellowship for Richardson to pursue graduate studies wherever she wished. She selected Columbia because Ruth Benedict,* Lesser, and George Herzog (in ethnomusicology) were on the faculty, and because she loved New York City. In the fall of 1936 Richardson went to New York for two years of further course work and to write a dissertation (the second year supported by a scholarship from Columbia). Here, she found new associations and experiences. With Boas's retirement in 1936, Benedict became acting chair, and for Richardson, a compassionate, thoughtful, and supportive mentor. In addition to Benedict and Lesser, Richardson also received encouragement and intellectual stimulation from fellow students, such as Charles Wagley, Natalie Joffe, Bernard Mishkin, Jack Harris, and Irving Goldman. For the first time in her life, she also became involved in political activism as students raised funds for the Spanish Republicans or accompanied Boas when he made anti-Fascist speeches to the public.

Richardson had originally planned to write a dissertation on ethnomusicology, based on her recordings of Kiowa music, but found that she could not handle musical transcriptions at the level Herzog demanded. So she turned instead to an analysis of legal cases that had been collected by the Kiowa research team. Her dissertation on Kiowa law, supervised by Benedict and Columbia's eminent law professor Karl Llewelyn, was completed in 1938 and published by the American Ethnological Society (Richardson 1940). Her Ph.D. was officially conferred in 1943, when she learned, very belatedly, that copies of the dissertation had to be deposited in the Columbia library in order to receive the doctorate.

By this point several other important events had occurred in her life. After Richardson passed her dissertation defense in 1938, Benedict got funds for her to work in Mexico. At this same time, the psychologist Abraham Maslow, who was also interested in anthropology, received a Social Science Research Council (SSRC) grant to study the outlook of young Blackfoot Indians. Needing a research assistant, he conferred with Benedict, who recommended Richardson because of her experience with Plains Indians. And she decided to postpone her trip to Mexico to help Maslow. Maslow also invited Lucien M. Hanks, Jr., a psychologist friend who shared his interests in anthropology, to join the research team. The three set off for a summer's fieldwork on the Blackfoot Reserve in Alberta, Canada. For Richardson, the fruits of this venture were not only the beginnings of research among the Blackfoot but marriage several months later to Lucien and the start of their long, productive collaboration. Although Lucien's doctorate from Columbia was in social psychology, he subsequently became increasingly committed to anthropology owing, at least in part, to Jane's influence.

After a brief period in Urbana, where Lucien Hanks had a position at the University of Illinois, the couple moved in 1942 to Bennington College, where he taught both psychology and anthropology. The birth of three sons (1940,

1943, 1947) did not curtail Jane Hanks's anthropological activities. During World War II she participated in Margaret Mead's* study of food habits of national minorities by administering questionnaires to ethnic groups in Urbana. She also interviewed Dutch nationals in Vermont for Benedict's "cultures at a distance" project for the Office of Naval Intelligence, as well as taught Lucien's anthropology courses at Bennington while he was in Burma with the Office of Strategic Services in 1944–45.

Lucien Hanks's experience in Burma kindled a deep and lasting interest in Southeast Asia that Jane Hanks came to share. In 1951 Lauriston Sharp of Cornell invited them to join a research project focused on the rural Thai village of Bang Chan. The Bang Chan project became famous in Southeast Asian ethnology as a pioneering community study in this region, and one that was unusually extensive in its long-term, broad-scale scope, involving researchers from many disciplines. The Hanks family spent two years in Thailand (the first year supported by Sharp's research grant, and the second by a Fulbright). Jane Richardson Hanks, recognized as an experienced anthropologist in her own right, was appointed a research associate at the Cornell Research Center in Bangkok and conducted field investigations of many aspects of Thai culture and history.

After the Hanks' return to Bennington in 1954, Jane maintained diverse kinds of anthropological activity. She wrote, both individually and collaboratively, a number of works on the Thai material, as well as book reviews. With her strong commitment to community service, Jane Hanks also conducted what was in a sense a personal anthropological "outreach" program. She was frequently called upon to deliver lectures and seminars on a variety of anthropological topics to diverse audiences, ranging from talks on American Indians at grade schools to a memorial lecture on Kroeber at the State University of New York at Binghamton. She also served as research associate in the Cornell Southeast Asia Program (1955), anthropological consultant for the 1958 conference of the International Institute of Home Economics Education at Cornell, and as a source of advice and help for numerous community and church groups in Vermont.

In the 1960s Jane and Lucien Hanks extended their Southeast Asia research from lowland Thai villagers to upland tribal peoples, organizing the Bennington-Cornell Survey of Hill Tribes of North Thailand, with Jane as associate director. Beginning in 1963–64 with a National Science Foundation grant, the Hankses began an extensive survey of the Akha, Yao (Mien), Lahu, Lisu, Karen, Meo (Hmong), Shan, and Khon Myang Thai in Chiengrai province, trekking to all villages in the area because this was a regional rather than community study. The research continued for a total of thirty-four months. The project had immense scope in its coverage of demography, ecology, economics, ethnicity, intergroup relations, history, and social change. It was also significant in expanding the purview of Thai studies beyond the central plains and in examining the relationships between lowland and upland peoples.

During the 1960s and more recent years, Jane Hanks also acted as a Peace Corps consultant on Thailand (1964, 1966), taught as Visiting Lecturer in Anthropology at Williams College (1968) and Visiting Professor in Anthropology at the State University of New York at Albany (1969–73, 1975–76), and co-chaired a SEADAG conference in Thailand on low-wage-earning Thai women (1975). She has also organized or participated in symposia, exhibitions, conferences, and workshops on Southeast Asia, China, Asian women, and American Indians. The recognition and respect she has achieved among Southeast Asianists were clearly demonstrated by her election in 1982 to the board of directors and the Southeast Asia Council of the Association for Asian Studies (AAS). In 1985 she was also elected chair of the Thailand/Laos/Cambodia Studies Group of the AAS.

Jane Richardson Hanks's career has spanned some fifty years of anthropology and reflects various facets of being both an anthropologist and a woman during this time. Both UCB and Columbia produced a large number of female Ph.D.s in anthropology; but it is also true that full-time teaching positions in anthropology were relatively scarce in the 1930s, and it is probable that men were more likely than women to get them. Pertinent here is a letter of recommendation that Kroeber wrote for her (unbeknownst to her) in 1935 regarding a possible job with the WPA Federal Writers' Project. He characterized her as "highly intelligent" and "very able." But he added, the "only reason I'd let you tempt her . . . is that she's a woman and therefore a regular anthro. [sic] career is uncertain for her" (Kroeber 1935).

In fact, she did establish an anthropological career; but it differed from that of most men, and probably single women, in its particular combination of commitments to family, profession, and community. Her work did not focus around an academic professorship, but she persisted in maintaining a foothold in anthropology through research, writing, lecturing, and attending Wenner-Gren, American Anthropological Association, AAS, and other professional meetings. The trajectory of her career is also interesting—and perhaps not unusual for other married women with children—because it seems to show two major peaks of professional activity: the first as a graduate student and newlywed Ph.D., then a renaissance of research and writing in later life as her children became grown, with a diversified mix of personal and professional activities between the two. Indeed, her output and reputation increased through her 50s and afterward, at ages when many other professionals begin fading into retirement.

Although women of Jane Hanks's generation may have faced various problems in academic careers, she herself "never felt disadvantaged" as a female doing fieldwork. Recognizing that both men and women must learn certain rules of native "gender etiquette" in order to gain acceptance into another culture, she did not feel that adherence to such customs (e.g., male precedence on entering a Blackfoot tipi) was onerous. Indeed, she believes that in some instances it was advantageous to be female because people were particularly courteous and solicitous. Furthermore, she found that being a mother was useful in creating rapport with other women, and that having one's children in the field brought benefits ("their contacts and activities feed into data collection") that perhaps "rub off somewhat more on the mother than the father." In the case of northern Thailand, however, she found that she was not expected to behave exactly as did native women because gender was overridden by the fact that she was a "foreigner" and "older person." She notes: "Best of all, there, is to be an old, vigorous foreigner. You can do practically anything you want then. But you must . . . act your age."

Nonetheless, Hanks believes that in general, "women have to adjust more artfully than men when entering a new culture" because they must "balance" three things: their professional activities, behavior congruent with native expectations of female roles in order not to "lose face" or rapport, and our own cultural norms about gender behavior and interaction. She concludes:

In sum, being female in the fieldwork situation is no different than being female in our own culture. . . . Our roles as women, wives, mothers, and daughters may conflict with the demands of a professional career, but we just pile one on top of the other. Adapting as best we can to the expected female behavior of the new culture we're in, we still adhere to the extent possible and convenient to the traditional female roles of our culture, but in the professional part we are more sensitive than the men to the necessity of balancing these demands. . . . This behavior is not limited to a husband-wife team in the field. A single woman alone in the field would experience much of the same pressures. The trick is to make it work for you.

Jane R. Hanks's contributions to anthropology are twofold. First, there are her substantial ethnographic contributions to the ethnological literature on North American Indians and Southeast Asia. She believes that the most satisfying aspect of being an anthropologist is the "tremendous thrill" of fieldwork. She notes: "I am person-oriented . . . not a theoretical person. I . . . keep everything close to the ethnographic levels where I feel comfortable." Such an orientation is consistent with her graduate training at UCB and Columbia during a period that stressed collection of ethnographic information, following a Boasian dictum that Hanks paraphrases as: "Be sure to recover this history before it's gone—this is the primary task of your generation—and fit in your theory later. But get this data!" Close attention to solid ethnographic detail is characteristic of her work, but she is not simply particularistic, because she learned from Benedict to view traits within a larger cultural whole, "a much bigger and more important dynamic, living thing." Moreover, the intelligence and sensitivity of her insights have led many Thailand specialists to regard various of her works (e.g., Hanks 1960, 1963; Hanks and Hanks 1963) as seminal stimuli to subsequent studies by others. Finally, it is important to note that although a good deal of her work has involved collaboration with Lucien, Jane Hanks is regarded as very much a scholar in her own right.

Hanks's second contribution is her role as a model and mentor for others. Through her written work and personal generosity, she has given not only insights into the lives of people in other cultures but also something of her own life to anthropology.

Note

1. All quotes not otherwise cited are from interviews and personal communications with Jane R. Hanks (to whom I express deepest appreciation for her gracious and magnanimous help in preparing this biography).

References and Works About Jane Richardson Hanks

Kroeber, A. L.
1935   Letter of Recommendation for Jane Richardson to Henry Alsberg, Director of WPA Federal Writer's Project, Washington, D.C., December 7, 1935. Courtesy of J. R. Hanks, files of the author.

Selected Works by Jane Richardson Hanks

1940   *Law and Status Among the Kiowa Indians*. (Under the name Jane Richardson.) Monographs of the American Ethnological Society, no. 1. New York: J. J. Augustin.
1960   Reflections on the Ontogeny of Rice. In *Culture in History: Essays in Honor of Paul Radin*. Stanley Diamond, ed. Pp. 298–301. New York: Columbia University Press.
1963   *Maternity and Its Rituals in Bang Chan*. Data Paper No. 51, Southeast Asia Program. Ithaca, N.Y.: Cornell University.
1965a   A Yao Wedding. In *Ethnographic Notes on Northern Thailand*. L. M. Hanks, J. R. Hanks, and L. Sharp, eds. Pp. 47–66. Data Paper No. 58, Southeast Asia Program. Ithaca: Cornell University.
1965b   A Rural Thai Village's View of Human Character. In *Essays in Honor of Prince Dhani Nivat Bidyalab*. Vol. 1, pp. 77–84. Bangkok: Felicitation Volumes of Southeast Asian Studies, the Siam Society.
1968   Rite and Cosmos, An Akha Diary. Unpublished Manuscript.
1974   Recitation of Patrilineages Among the Akha. In *Social Organization and the Applications of Anthropology: Essays in Honor of Lauriston Sharp*. Robert J. Smith, ed. Pp. 114–27. Ithaca, N.Y.: Cornell University Press.
1981   Hill and Valley Peoples of Thailand's Province of Chiengrai: A Changing Relationship. *Proceedings of the Third International Symposium on Asian Studies*. Pp. 541–49. Hong Kong: Asian Research Service.
1985   Letter to the author, May 8, 1985.

Coauthored Works

Hanks, Jane R., and L. M. Hanks
1945   *Observations on Northern Blackfoot Kinship*. Monographs of the American Ethnological Society, no. 9. New York: J. J. Augustin.
1949   *Tribe Under Trust*. Toronto: University of Toronto Press.
1955   Diphtheria Immunization in a Thai Community. In *Health, Culture and Community*. Benjamin Paul and Walter Miller, eds. Pp. 155–85. New York: Russell Sage Foundation.

1963 Thailand: Equality Between the Sexes. In *Women in the New Asia*. Barbara Ward, ed. Pp. 424–51. Paris: UNESCO.

1964 Siamese Tai. In *Ethnic Groups of Mainland Southeast Asia*. Frank LeBar, Gerald Hickey, and John Musgrave, eds. Pp. 197–205. New Haven: Human Relations Area Files Press.

Hanks, Jane R. et al.

1964 *A Report on Tribal Peoples in Chiengrai Province North of the Mae Kok River*. Data Paper No. 1. Bangkok: The Siam Society.

Hanks, Jane R., L. M. Hanks, and Lauriston Sharp, eds.

1965 *Ethnographic Notes on Northern Thailand*. Data Paper No. 58, Southeast Asia Program. Ithaca, N.Y.: Cornell University.

Hanks, Jane R., Hazel Hauck, and Saovanee Sudsaneh

1958 *Food Habits and Nutrient Intakes in a Siamese Rice Village: Studies in Bang Chan*. Data Paper No. 29, Southeast Asia Program. Ithaca, N.Y.: Cornell University.

Richardson, Jane, and A. L. Kroeber

1940 Three Centuries of Women's Dress Fashions: A Quantitative Analysis. *University of California Anthropological Records* 5 (2): 111–54.

MAY EBIHARA

June Helm

(1924–   )

American sociocultural anthropologist June Helm is known for her enthnographic accounts of the Dene Indians, hunting and gathering peoples of Canada's Northwest Territories, with special attention to socioterritorial groups, ethnohistory, political leadership and sociocultural change.

June Helm describes herself as a typical midwesterner, and for most of her life, her home has been the American Midwest.[1] Born in Twin Falls, Idaho, in September 1924, she was the only child of Julia Frances (née Dixon) and William Jennings Helm. As a young child Helm suffered from several severe illnesses. Her mother, a bright woman who was unable to attend college, lavished attention on the sickly child. When Helm was six the family moved to Kansas City, where she received much of her education.

For Helm and her mother there was no question that she should continue her education, but the family had little money for June to attend college. She was awarded a scholarship to Monticello, a private two-year girls' school in Illinois. In 1941, at the age of seventeen, she matriculated at Monticello but returned home three days later, having discovered that there was compulsory chapel. In an attempt to attend college without further delay and at a cost the family could afford, she enrolled at the University of Kansas City that semester and spent her first year there. During this year her father's machinery business prospered, as the country entered World War II. Because the family could now afford it, her father was persuaded that she should attend the University of Chicago.

Helm knew from an early age that she was interested in fossil evidence and anthropology. As she herself said, "I really think that it's your childhood and family background that determines your course." She was a shy, anxious child who empathized with the downtrodden of society. Yet because of her mother's drive and attention, Helm never felt anything was off-limits because she was a woman.

In 1942, with housing and finances resolved, Helm was able to matriculate in the Ph.B. program at Chicago.[2] There she was able to take her first anthropology course, Faye-Cooper Cole's Introduction to Anthropology. Upon completion of the degree, she moved into the master's program, focusing on sociocultural anthropology.

Helm completed her course work at Chicago at a time when the department was disrupted by the war and there was a high proportion of female students as a result. In the department she met the archaeologist Richard "Scotty" MacNeish, and they were married in 1945 so that Helm could go with MacNeish to Mexico for his dissertation fieldwork. "In those days you didn't feel that you could go without getting married." In Mexico she collected the field data that was the basis of her A.M. thesis, "A Re-Examination of the Concept of Ethos in Light of Two Mexican Communities," awarded in 1950.

The late 1940s was a period of professional confusion and questioning for Helm. During one period at the University of Chicago, she found herself incapable of writing papers about strictly theoretical issues. At one point she tried therapy as a way to come to terms with her professional block. In 1949 she accompanied MacNeish to his job at the National Museum of Canada. As part of his Mackenzie River Survey, MacNeish in 1950 visited a small village of Slave Indians (a division of the Dene/Athapaskan peoples) who wanted an English teacher for their children. In the summer of 1951 June Helm MacNeish went to the Slavey village, the experience she needed to break through her professional block. Teaching the children was a frustrating experience, but it was a service to the community that gave her lodging and entrée as an ethnologist. She was accompanied by Teresa Carterette, then a graduate student in anthropology, and thus began a lifelong pattern of working with other professionals, usually women, in the field (see Helm 1979).

The chance for participant observation among the Slave opened up a world of study for June MacNeish, who has focused on the Dene Indians of Canada's Northwest Territories for most of her professional life. Returning to her home in Ottawa after the initial experience, she was able to focus her reading on the history and ethnography of the area, of which there was little. She noticed that kin terminology she had recorded differed from that gathered from nonethnographer's accounts and assigned to the Slave by Leslie Spier. The socioterritorial organization in this small bush community did not match Julian Steward's "composite hunting band," to which he assigned the Northern Dene tribes, and her experiences raised questions about Northern Athapaskan leadership styles (Helm 1956b).

June MacNeish returned to the Lynx Point Slave community in 1952 to pursue the questions regarding kin terminology. In 1954 and 1955 she made two more trips to interview Slave and Chippewyan informants. Her research among the Slave was the basis of her Ph.D. dissertation, "The Lynx Point People: The Dynamics of a Northern Athapaskan Band," which was expanded and published as *The Lynx Point People* (1961).

In 1957 she collected kin terminology from the Hare at Good Hope, and these data opened questions about the effects of white acculturation on traditional marriage systems. The kin terminology data indicated that different processes of acculturation might have occurred among the various tribes in the Northwest Territories. In the Hare study, Helm found Iroquois cousin terms, terminological equivalence of *father's sister* and *mother's brother* with *mother-in-law* and *father-in-law,* and the apparent fact that terms for cross-cousins of opposite sex derived from husband and wife terms. This suggested that cross-cousin marriage had been practiced in the past (MacNeish 1960).

In 1958 June Helm MacNeish received her Ph.D. from Chicago. In general, she had been left on her own in her work. No teacher guided her or set her course. She was not part of any Chicago group or project studying North American Indians, and in fact, Robert Redfield, who died two months later, took time to guide her through her orals and usher her into her professional career. The other person who encouraged her in her early years was George Peter Murdock.

Also in that year Helm and MacNeish were divorced. She followed the suggestion of John Honigmann and applied for a job at the University of Iowa. In 1960 she became assistant professor of Anthropology at Iowa. She became full professor in 1966 and continues to teach there today. In 1968 she married architect Pierce E. King.

In 1959 Helm began her long association with the Athapaskan Dogrib Indians of the northwestern Canadian subarctic. In that year and in 1962 and 1967, she was accompanied to the field by her longtime friend, anthropologist Nancy O. Lurie.* It was in 1962 that Helm began to study the Dogrib at Rae, and this experience resulted in some of her richest and most characteristic writings. Helm has described the traditional society of the Dogrib hunters and gatherers and their relations with other Dene and whites during the last 200 years. Her data on socioterritorial groups have generated the most interest for cross-cultural and regional comparison and reveal Helm's early use of historical documents. Using documentation on regional bands going back seventy years, Helm described three types of socioterritorial groups and a flexible kinship system operating by what she called the "bilateral primary linkage principle" (Helm 1968a) which allowed multiple residence alternatives for the conjugal pair. Although there was a traditional understanding that a young husband should work for (and thereby reside with) his father-in-law until the birth of the first child, Helm argued there were no fixed rules other than the primary relative relationship (Helm 1968a). This, along with comparable data on other hunter-gatherer groups suggested that the patrilocal band was "not the universal form of hunter group structure that Service thought it was" (Lee and DeVore 1968:8).

While the Athapaskan data offered new insights on hunter group structure, the regional debate has focused on band organization in the aboriginal and postcontact states. From data on the Kutchin, Shepard Krech concludes that in this Northern Athapascan group epidemic diseases led to an estimated 80 percent reduction in the population and a postcontact shift from matrilocality to bilocality (Krech 1978, 1980). Helm finds no evidence of dramatic changes in social organization because of disease. In fact, during the period covered by censuses, from 1829 to the mid-twentieth century, the population remained static (Helm 1980:272). Helm concludes that the elimination of female infanticide after 1860, perhaps due to the influence of missionaries and traders, served "as a demographic counterbalance to mortality from exogenous diseases" (Helm 1980:274).

Helm has described domestic groups, child care, bride service, restrictions on women's activities, and female infanticide among the Dene but readily admits that her work, reflecting the dominant approaches of anthropology at the time, focuses on the public, not the private, domain. In her accounts women's roles are an integral part of the annual cycle but not the focus of attention. The young women Helm encountered in the early years of her fieldwork were burdened with childbearing and household duties. In Helm's experience, the aging of the young women she knew coincided with dramatic changes in economy, life-style, and women's activities, and she has seen their roles altered by a settled life, cash economy, and welfare payments.

Helm's work, which spans twenty-five years, offers a continuous and detailed picture of a particular region. Moreover, she has consistently made use of historical documents since the beginning of her research. "Census data of such quality on a set of hunting peoples—beginning a generation after contact, spanning 150 years, and covering several thousand persons—is perhaps unparalleled in the ethnographic-historical record" (Helm 1980:262). As Helm says, "Ethnohistory didn't exist as a term when I began," but she has consistently gathered data back to the early contact period.

By her own account, her years of fieldwork are over, with her concentration now on professional duties and projects. As she acknowledges, new theories and methodological approaches will encourage others to reanalyze her work among the Dene. In her active and productive career, Helm has held a number of important leadership positions. These include the following: editor of the American Ethnological Society publications (1964–68); witness and advisor to Indian Brotherhood of Northwest Territories (1973–74); chair of Section H (Anthropology), American Association for the Advancement of Science (1978); and president, American Anthropological Association (1985–87).

The anthropologist who returns to a region for professional reasons also becomes attached to specific people and shares an understanding and fondness for the culture. Helm has written that she is "temperamentally compatible" with the Dogrib (Helm 1979:161), a culture in which she perceives generosity and egalitarian values. "Perhaps it is simplest to say that the principle of generosity underlies all aspects of Dogrib ethos ideal—in the sense of magnanimity of spirit in all human dealings, in which openhandedness with material things is only one part" (Helm 1972:80).

Notes

1. The personal information, unless referenced otherwise, comes from an interview with June Helm on December 9, 1985. I would like to thank June Helm for her willingness to be interviewed and for her patient attention to detail in the draft stages.

2. The Chicago Ph.B. program aimed to create well-rounded persons in two years unless they intended to become intellectual specialists, in which case they would enter the A.M. program after two years.

Selected Works by June Helm

(Under the name June Helm MacNeish)

1954   Contemporary Folk Beliefs of a Slave Indian Band. *Journal of American Folklore* 67:185–98.

1956a   Problems of Acculturation and Livelihood in a Northern Indian Band. *Contributions à l'étude des sciences de l'homme* 3: 169–81.

1956b   Leadership Among the Northeastern Athapascans. *Anthropologica* 2:131–63.

1960   Kin Terms of the Arctic Drainage Dene: Hare, Slavey, Chipewyan. *American Anthropologist* 62: 279–95.

(Under the name June Helm)

1961   *The Lynx Point People: The Dynamics of a Northern Athapaskan Band.* National Museum of Canada Bulletin 176:ii–193.

1965   Patterns of Allocation Among the Arctic Drainage Dene. In *Essays in Economic Anthropology.* June Helm, ed. Pp. 33–45. Annual Proceedings of the American Ethnological Society. Seattle: University of Washington Press.

1966   Changes in Indian Communities. In *People of Light and Dark.* M. Van Steensel, ed. Pp. 106–9. Ottawa: Queen's Printer.

1968a   The Nature of Dogrib Socio-Territorial Groups. In *Man the Hunter.* Irven DeVore and Richard B. Lee, eds. Pp. 118–25. Chicago: Aldine Press.

1968b   The Statistics of Kin Marriage: A Non-Australian Example. In *Man the Hunter.* Irven DeVore and Richard B. Lee, eds. Pp. 216–17. Chicago: Aldine Press.

1969a   The Methodology of Band Composition Analysis. In *Contributions to Anthropology: Band Societies.* David Damas, ed. Pp. 212–17. National Museum of Canada Bulletin 228.

1969b   A Method of Statistical Analysis of Primary Relative Bonds in Community Composition. In *Contributions to Anthropology: Band Societies.* David Damas, ed. Pp. 218–39. National Museum of Canada Bulletin 228.

1969c   Relationship Between Settlement Pattern and Community Pattern. In *Contributions to Anthropology: Ecological Essays.* David Damas, ed. Pp. 151–52. National Museum of Canada Bulletin 230.

1972   The Dogrib Indians. In *Hunters and Gatherers Today.* Marco Bicchieri, ed. Pp. 51–89. New York: Holt, Rinehart, and Winston.

1973   *Subarctic Athapaskan Bibliography.* Iowa City: Department of Anthropology, University of Iowa.

1976   *Indians of the Subarctic: A Critical Bibliography.* Center for the History of the American Indian, Newberry Library. Bloomington: Indiana University Press.

1978a   Indian Dependency and Indian Self-Determination: Problems and Paradoxes in Canada's Northwest Territories. In *Political Organization of North American Indians.* E. Schusky, ed. Pp. 215–42. Washington, D.C.: University of America Press.

1978b   On Responsible Scholarship on Culture Contact in the Mackenzie Basin. *Current Anthropology* 19 (1): 160–62.

1979   Long Term Research Among the Dogrib and Other Dene. In *Long Term Field*

Research in Social Anthropology. G. Foster et al., eds. Pp. 145–63. New York: Academic Press.

1980   Female Infanticide, European Diseases, and Population Levels Among the Mackenzie Dene. *American Ethnologist* 7 (2): 259–85.

1981a   Dogrib Folk History and the Photographs of John Alden Mason: Indian Occupation and Status in the Fur Trade, 1900–1925. *Arctic Anthropology* 18 (2): 39–53.

1981b   Dogrib. In *Handbook of North American Indians*. Vol. 6, *Subarctic*, pp. 291–309. June Helm, vol. ed. Washington, D.C.: Smithsonian Institution.

Coauthored Works

Helm, June, T. Alliband et al.

1976   The Contact History of the Subarctic Athapaskans: An Overview. In *Proceedings of the Athapaskan Conference*. Vol. I. A. M. Clark, ed. Pp. 302–49. Canadian Ethnology Service Paper No. 27. National Museum of Man Mercury Series. Ottawa.

Helm, June, and David Damas

1963   The Contact-Traditional All-Native Community of the Canadian North: The Upper Mackenzie "Bush" Athapaskans and the Igluligmiut. *Anthropologica* (new series) 5:5–22.

Helm, June, and Beryl Gillespie

1981   Dogrib Oral Tradition as History: War and Peace in the 1820's. *Journal of Anthropological Research* 37 (1): 8–27.

Helm, June, and Royce Kurtz

1984   *Subarctic Athapaskan Bibliography, 1984*. Iowa City: University of Iowa Department of Publications.

Helm, June, and Eleanor B. Leacock

1971   The Hunting Tribes of Subarctic Canada. In *North American Indians in Historical Perspective*. Eleanor B. Leacock and Nancy O. Lurie, eds. Pp. 343–74. New York: Random House.

Helm, June, and Nancy Oestreich Lurie

1961   *The Subsistence Economy of the Dogrib Indians of Lac La Martre in the Mackenzie District of the Northwest Territories*. Northern Coordination and Research Centre, Department of Northern Affairs and National Resources, Canada.

1966   The Dogrib Hand Game. National Museum of Canada Bulletin 205: viii–101.

Helm, June, E. S. Rogers, and J. G. E. Smith

1981   Intercultural Relations and Culture Change in the Shield and Mackenzie Borderlands. In *Handbook of North American Indians*. Vol. 6, *Subarctic*, pp. 146–57. June Helm, vol. ed. Washington, D.C.: Smithsonian Institution.

Helm, June, and Vital Thomas

1966   Tales from the Dogribs. *The Beaver, Part I* (Autumn 1966). Pp. 16–20; *Part II* (Winter 1966). Pp. 52–54.

KAREN V. ARMSTRONG

Eva Verbitsky Hunt
(1934–1980)

Eva Verbitsky Hunt was a cultural anthropologist, known especially for her theoretical work in symbolic anthropology, kinship studies, ethnohistory, and regional research.

Eva Verbitsky was born April 12, 1934, in Buenos Aires, into a Jewish intellectual family.[1] Whereas her parents, Alejandro Verbitsky and Josefa Plotkin, were born in Argentina as well, both sets of grandparents came originally from Russia. They arrived in South America as young adults, soon after the 1905 Revolution. In Eva Verbitsky's family, women led active, professional lives. Her maternal grandmother was a physician, and her mother a specialist in childhood education. It was therefore only natural that Verbitsky, too, would prepare for a career. Coming from a line of strong women, she gained at home the confidence she needed to face the obstacles she met in later life.

While Eva Verbitsky enjoyed recognition for her contributions to the discipline of anthropology, she firmly believed that women in her generation still had more trouble than men in establishing themselves as anthropologists. She tended to be critical of those who glossed over the problem and was disappointed, for example, in Margaret Mead* for not having described in her autobiography (1972) the difficulties she had had—famous though she might have been—in gaining acceptance by colleagues in the field. All the same, she did not join the feminist movement that swept across university campuses in the 1970s. She remained a loner and worked to improve the status of women on an individual basis—encouraging promising female students and offering herself as a positive role model.

Verbitsky and her younger brother Pablo spent their childhood years in Buenos Aires. When she was seventeen, her father decided to leave Argentina and move the family to Mexico City; he was having political difficulties with the Perón government. Originally a journalist, he had become a screenwriter, and he continued his activities in Mexico until the 1960s, when he followed his son to

Cuba. Pablo had gone there soon after the Revolution and found work in Havana in radio and television and as a translator.

When the family left Argentina in the early 1950s, Eva Verbitsky had already demonstrated considerable talent for painting, and she continued to develop her skills in the exciting artistic community in Mexico. The family had many friends there who inspired her—among them, the great postrevolutionary muralist Diego Rivera. Although she devoted herself professionally to anthropology, she never stopped painting and produced some very good work (Bohannan 1981).

In 1953 Verbitsky received her bachelor's degree from the Universidad Feminina in Mexico City and entered la Escuela Nacionál de Antropología as a graduate student. There, she became a research assistant for the anthropologist Roberto Weitlaner, who, like her, was not native to Mexico. A gifted teacher, Weitlaner taught Verbitsky a great deal about doing fieldwork and took her on one of his expeditions to Oaxaca to study the Cuicatec Indians, a group to which she returned with Robert Hunt in the 1960s.

Verbitsky's second field experience took place in the mid–1950s. She went to Juxtlahuaca, in the Mixtec area of Oaxaca, to work as a research assistant for Kimball Romney. At that time Romney was a graduate student at Harvard University and had assumed the directorship of the Mexican aspect of John Whiting's Socialization in Six Cultures Project. She conducted most of the interviews with the mothers and many of the standardized observations of children.

Encouraged by Romney, Verbitsky left Mexico in 1957 to continue her graduate work at the University of Chicago, in a department noted for its focus on Mexican anthropology. This was a bold decision on her part, for she spoke no English and read it poorly. Members of the faculty, however, arranged for her to do her exams and papers in Spanish until such time as she had learned enough English. During her student days at Chicago, she studied with and was influenced by a number of people—most importantly, Robert McCormick Adams, Fred Eggan, and Eric Wolf. For her Ph.D. research she joined Sol Tax's Chiapas Project and wrote a dissertation entitled "The Dynamics of the Domestic Group in Two Tzeltal Villages." She received her doctorate in 1962.

In 1960 Verbitsky married Robert Hunt, who in that year entered the anthropology program at Northwestern University. A year later Eva Hunt became a research associate for Paul Bohannan in the same department. She taught a course there on kinship; Bohannan felt that she could do structural analyses of kinship with unequaled insight and accuracy (1981:892).

From the spring of 1963 to October 1964, Hunt returned to Mexico on National Science Foundation grant to do archival research and then, together with her husband, lived with the Cuicatec for ten months. She came back to the United States pregnant and gave birth to a daughter, Melissa, in March 1965. By September of that same year, Eva Hunt began teaching in the college at the University of Chicago.

In the mid–1960s there were no women faculty in the Graduate Department of Anthropology at the University of Chicago. Her appointment was strictly to the college, making it difficult for graduate students to work with her, particularly for those specializing in Mesoamerica. Fortunately, Hunt had teaching assistants for her undergraduate course on Mexico. Others met her in seminars—most importantly, Victor Turner and Terrence Turner's course Myth and Ritual, which met on Thursday evening and continued into the early hours of the morning.

The two Turners (not related) came to the University of Chicago together from Cornell in 1968. In the vanguard of the debates going on at the time about French structuralism and symbolic anthropology, they provided an exciting forum for faculty and students to give theoretical papers. Hunt gave a brilliant talk in the spring of 1969 on a female Cuicatec healer performing a curing ritual. Although she never published the piece on its own, it did become a chapter in her unfinished book-length manuscript, "The Buried Bell: Variation and Orthodoxy in a Mexican Indian Religion." Over the years Victor Turner influenced Eva Hunt's work a great deal, and he published her book *The Transformation of the Hummingbird* (1977a).

In 1969 Robert Hunt received an offer from Brandeis University, and Eva Hunt from Boston University. She remained at Boston until she died of cancer in 1980, after having courageously fought the disease for five years. She achieved the rank of associate professor and developed a devoted student following. None of her students specialized in Latin America, but many have applied Hunt's theoretical and methodological concerns to their own ethnographic areas.

In the 1960's Eva and Robert Hunt took the lead among anthropologists working in Mexico, by conducting regional research. The Hunts chose to study an entire district in the state of Oaxaca, not just one small village. Influenced by Eric Wolf, who insisted on the importance of looking at regions, they challenged the community study approach, so much in fashion since the 1930s, and returned to the tradition of Manuel Gamio, the Mexican anthropologist who had initiated regional investigations in Central Mexico in the 1920s.

"We are concerned with symbiotic relations between communities within a politically and socio-culturally defined region," they explained (Hunt and Hunt 1969:109). The Hunts focused on what they called "the interlocking of units in the local-regional system, and on the ties of the region as a whole with the larger socio-political units of the state" (1969:109–10). Interested in the conflicts that arose in an ethnically and socially mixed area, they studied the ways institutions such as the courts, the schools and the market have served different groups and created structures whereby individuals of varying cultures and classes could meet to resolve problems and exchange information and goods. They were also concerned with how irrigation systems affected social and political choices.

Eva Hunt's interest in the study of kinship systems led to a number of important articles, such as the one she wrote with June Nash (1967) and her piece entitled "Kinship and Territorial Fission in the Cuicatec Highlands" (Hunt 1976). Developing further some of the points made with June Nash, Hunt went on in the latter article to question Eric Wolf's assumption that in Mesoamerica the community is based on territorial, not kinship, factors. She argued that anthropologists working in Mesoamerica had missed the centrality of kinship ties because they were looking for unilineal segmentary social groups, which did not exist. They should have recognized that kinship in Mesoamerica is organized in "shallow, ambilateral descent groups or corporate bilateral groups" (1976:99). What is more, the kinship system is very much tied to the land, and kinship groups tend to split up over conflicts that emerge for control of the land. Hunt felt that the role played by other institutions, such as the national government, in these kinship splits had also been overlooked.

Hunt's work was path-breaking, both methodologically and theoretically. In a period when most anthropologists conducted community studies, she and Robert focused on regional analysis. When many in the field dismissed history, she actively sought ways to combine archaeology and ethnohistory with ethnography, identifying continuities from pre-Hispanic and colonial times and analyzing their transformations in the present. Finally, when Lévi-Strauss's structuralism and Victor Turner's symbolic anthropology divided people into fierce camps, she developed an approach to bring the two perspectives together.

Eva Hunt is best known for *The Transformation of the Hummingbird*. Drawing on the ideas of Freud, Malinowski, Durkheim, Cassirer, Lévi-Strauss, and Victor Turner, together with the interpretations of ethnohistorians who have worked in Mesoamerica, she argued:

As the psychoanalyst becomes the archaeologist of his patient's mind, the anthropologist can become the archaeologist of his society's culture. But for the cultural anthropologist, unlike the real archaeologist, few materials remain that can be dug from the ground. The stratigraphic layers are in the culture itself, in media which are sometimes ephemeral. . . . This archaeology of symbols is productive of coherent meaning and . . . the hummingbird treated in its historical context, can be decoded. (1977a:32)

Hunt used Lévi-Strauss's ideas about transformations and codes as well as Victor Turner's concepts of the multivocality of ritual symbols. Like Turner, she contextualized myth and ritual, which in Chiapas meant that she relied on ethnography, ethnohistory, and archaeology.

The hummingbird poem is of general interest to Mesoamerican culture history because it is one of the manifestations of the Aztec god Huitzilopochtli. Drawing on ancient Nahuatl and Mayan symbolism, decoding the pre-Hispanic transformational system, and explaining the cosmos and mathematical orders, Hunt finally demonstrated that the historical and cultural roots of this poem, centuries old, are still very much a part of the lives of the Indians in present-day Zinacantan.

Nearly five years after Hunt's death, a session at the 1984 American Anthropological Association meeting was organized in her memory. Summing up the session, symposium commentator James Fernandez suggested that in a period like the mid–1980s, when there is "much arbitrariness" and "transitivity in anthropological theory," it is particularly important to look at an approach like

Eva Hunt's, which analyzes the original "grand scheme" from pre-Hispanic times and the subsequent transformations. (James Fernandez, personal communication, 1984.)

Note

1. Robert Hunt kindly met with me in November 1984 to discuss the life and work of his deceased wife. Much of the material presented here is the result of that interview.

References and Works About Eva Verbitsky Hunt

Bohannan, Paul
1981   Obituary: Eva Verbitsky Hunt, 1934–1980. *American Anthropologist* 83 (4): 892–94.
Edmundson, Munro
1978   Review of *The Transformation of the Hummingbird. Hispanic American Historical Review* 58 (May): 307–8.
Luchtung, Wolfgang A.
1979   Review of *The Transformation of the Hummingbird. World Literature Today* 53 (Winter): 167–68.
Riviere, Peter
1978   Review of *The Transformation of the Hummingbird. Times Literary Supplement,* April 7, p. 394.

Selected Works by Eva Verbitsky Hunt

1961a Analysis comparativos de Cinco Comunidades en los Altos de Chiapas. In *Los Mayas del Sur y sus Relaciones con los Nahuas Meridionales.* Pp. 289–301. Mexico: Sociedad de Antropología.
1961b Review of Keur and Rubin (eds.), *Social and Cultural Pluralism in the Caribbean. Interamerican Journal of Social Sciences* 1:215–17.
1961c Review of Othon de Mendizabal et al., Las Clases Sociales en Mexico. *Interamerican Journal of Social Sciences* 1:215–17.
1969   The Meaning of Kinship in San Juan: Genealogical and Social Models. *Ethnology* 8:37–54.
1972   Irrigation and the Socio-Political Organization of the Cuicatec Cacicazgos. In *The Prehistory of the Tehuacan Valley.* Vol. 4. Richard MacNeish and Fred Johnson, eds. Pp. 162–257. Austin: University of Texas Press.
1974   Discussion and Commentary to C. Morris: Reconstructing Patterns of Non-Agricultural Production . . . Archaeology and Documents in Institutional Analysis. In *Reconstructing Complex Societies,* no. 20. C. Moore, ed. Pp. 60–65. American School of Oriental Research, Cambridge, Mass.
1975a Ceremonies of Confrontation and Submission: The Symbolic Dimension of Indian Mexican Political Interaction. In *Symbol and Politics in Communal Ideology: Cases and Questions.* S. F. Moore and B. Myerhoff, eds. Pp. 124–47. Ithaca, N.Y.: Cornell University Press.

1975b Review of *Conflict, Violence and Morality in a Mexican Village,* by Lola Ro-
manucci-Ross. *American Anthropologist* 77:946–49.
1976   Kinship and Territorial Fission in the Cuicatec Highlands. In *Kinship in Mesoamerica.* H. Nutini, P. Carrasco, and J. Taggart, eds. Pp. 97–137. Pittsburgh:
University of Pittsburgh Press.
1977a *The Transformation of the Hummingbird: Cultural Roots of a Zinacantecan Mythical Poem.* Ithaca, N.Y.: Cornell University Press.
1977b A Mexican Feast for Easter. In *The Anthropologist's Cookbook.* J. Kuper, ed.
Pp. 131–133. New York: Universe Books.
1978a The Provenience and Contents of the Porfirio Diaz and Fernando Lea Codices.
American Antiquity 43:673–90.
1978b The Buried Bell: Variation and Orthodoxy in a Mexican Indian Religion. Unpublished Manuscript. Boston University.

Coauthored Works

Hunt, Eva, and Robert Hunt
1967   Education As an Interface Institution in Rural Mexico and the American Inner
City. *Midway Magazine* 8 (2): 99–109.
1969   The Role of the Local Courts in Rural Mexico. In *Peasants in the Modern World.*
P. K. Bock, ed. Pp. 109–39. Albuquerque: University of New Mexico Press.
1974   Irrigation, Conflict and Politics: A Mexican Case. In *Irrigation's Impact on Society.* M. Gibson and T. Downing, eds. Pp. 129–57. Tucson: University of Arizona
Press.
1976   Canal Irrigation and Local Social Organization. *Current Anthropology* 17 (3):
389–411.
Hunt, Eva, Robert Hunt, and Roberto Weitlaner
1968   From Parallel-nominal to Patrinominal: Changing Cuicatec Personal Names.
INAH, Anales 19:191–223.
Hunt, Eva, and R. Montagu
1962   Nombre, Autoridad y el Sistema de Creencias en los Altos de Chiapas. *Seminario
de Cultura Maya* 1:141–47.
Hunt, Eva, and June Nash
1967   Local and Territorial Units. In *Social Anthropology: Handbook of Middle American Indians.* Vol. 6. M. Nash, ed. Pp. 253–83. Austin: University of Texas
Press.

JUDITH FRIEDLANDER

Zora Neale Hurston

(1903–1960)

Black American cultural anthropologist and writer Zora Neale Hurston was a collector of folklore and folk music in U.S. black, rural, and southern communities, and researcher on religion and voodoo, ritual, and women in the Caribbean.

There was little that was ordinary in either the childhood experiences of Zora Neale Hurston or in her varied career as anthropologist, folklorist, writer, and dramatist. Even her birth date has been debated, since there are several different dates given in her verbal and written accounts. Zora was the seventh of eight children, but her individuality set her apart and caused her mother to encourage her to "jump at the sun." That same individuality cost her the displeasure of her father, the Reverend John Hurston, who was a respected preacher, mayor, and carpenter in the small town of Eatonville, Florida, where Hurston was born on January 7, 1903. Hurston's family led a comfortable life until the death of her mother, when Hurston was nine. Despite the remarriage of her father, Hurston moved around among various relatives until she left in 1917 to work as a maid for a member of the Gilbert and Sullivan repertory troupe. Although she left the troupe in Baltimore, that move was formative because there she found a new employer who offered her assistance in entering Morgan Academy. Hurston graduated from Morgan in 1918.

Her determination to obtain an education resulted in her enrollment in Howard University's Preparatory Academy in 1918, and she received an associate of arts degree from Howard (1920). In Washington, D.C., she worked as a manicurist while earning money to pay her way through school. The Washington experience also proved significant because here she observed the intricacies of black stratification and was influenced by Black Renaissance scholars and acquaintances like Alain Locke, Sterling Brown, and Mae Miller. Hurston's intellectual ties with Alain Locke were strong, and he encouraged her anthropological interests; however, her formal anthropological training came later. As a member of the

Zeta Phi Beta sorority at Howard, Hurston is remembered by sorority sister, black sociologist, and social worker Ophelia Egypt: "She was majoring in anthropology. And of course we thought that was strange. . . . [S]he was sort of a loner. But she was brilliant, and she was writing even then."[1] Hurston's concern with women's roles in culture was implicit rather than explicit in her short stories but would become more obvious as she began her anthropological research.

Hurston's desire to combine writing and anthropology took her to New York in 1925, where some of her short stories were published by Charles Johnson of *Opportunity Magazine*. In 1925 she also entered Barnard College with the assistance of her employer, writer Fannie Hurst. At Barnard Hurston came under the influence of the dynamic, eclectic, and antievolutionist anthropology department at Columbia, founded by Franz Boas. With Boas's confidence and direction she collected and analyzed folklore in south Florida as part of her B.A. research. Despite her passion for folk literature, which grew out of her southern and Howard University experiences, she said that "I had to have the spyglass of anthropology to look through at that." Nevertheless, her correspondence with Alain Locke and black writer and dramatist Langston Hughes shows that she was incorporating some of her earlier views on the authenticity of black culture into her research approaches. Her "vacuum-cleaner" approach to the absorption of black description was a blend of the empiricism encouraged at Columbia and the respect for emic interpretation that was intuitive for Hurston. She earned her B.A. from Barnard in 1928, becoming one of the first black women to do so. Her graduate research was underwritten by a private grant from Mrs. R. Osgood Mason and a Rosenwald fellowship until 1932. Yet financial worries and restrictions that Mason placed on use of Hurston's research interfered with her advancement in anthropology.

Between 1928 and 1935 Hurston intensively collected southern folklore and published two books. Boas wrote the introduction for her folklore collection *Mules and Men* (Hurston 1935), and Hurston had asked Ruth Benedict* to comment on the manuscript. With Langston Hughes, Hurston experimented with theater and drama derived from her collections of black folklore and music. Some of her work was published in the *Journal of American Folklore* (Hurston 1930, 1931), on whose board Benedict served. And at Boas's suggestion Hurston provided guidance to Otto Klineberg's research team that was investigating musical ability in black communities of New Orleans. Nevertheless, her final attempt at Ph.D. work was frustrated by the failure of the Rosenwald Foundation to see the relevance of her proposed study of voodoo in Haiti; her application for fellowship and research support was rejected in 1935. Despite this, some of her anthropological research found its way into the plays she wrote or collaborated on in the 1930s and 1940s. During the Depression Hurston resorted to a job as dramatic coach with the WPA's Federal Theatre Project in New York City.

Hurston provides an interesting contrast between the emphases of the black and the white intellectual communities in the 1920s and 1930s. The tenor of the times was greatly marked by the massive migrations of southern blacks to northern cities and a preoccupation with understanding the themes in black culture. Whereas the Howard University and New York black intellectuals were concerned with overcoming the race issue and revealing the inherent dignity and originality in Afro-American culture, the white American intellectual community was searching for useful models for the representation of reality, and for ways in which fieldwork techniques might enhance an understanding of nonwhite cultures. Correspondence between Hurston and Locke during this period reveals that these black scholars were skeptical that whites were really open to the symbolic and ritual content of black folklore. Nevertheless, the work of Margaret Mead* and Ruth Benedict* was becoming popular with lay audiences, and Hurston may have been influenced by psychological approaches that were so prevalent at Columbia during the 1930s.

Although Hurston provided ground for the merger of the concerns of these two communities in her collaboration with Columbia scholars, her work was alternately criticized by both black and white communities. Her attempts at what would later be called emic ethnography were not well received by intellectuals of the period. Many of the black elite considered her folk approach demeaning; and it was only posthumously that her innovative techniques were fully appreciated by blacks and whites alike. Her ideas did not fit neatly into one mold, and her personality was more brash and assertive than people expected of female elites and intellectuals of the period. She eschewed the role of "lady," preferring to make a commitment to a career in unveiling hidden aspects of black culture. Consequently, her two short-lived marriages, to Herbert Sheen (1927) and to Albert Price III (1939), both resulted in divorce, and Hurston's life was devoted to her work.

A new phase of her career was marked by her research in Jamaica and Haiti in 1936. With support from a Guggenheim fellowship, she went to study voodoo cultures and their impact on the lives of the Haitian poor. Characteristically, Hurston was inducted into the cults, and she investigated and photographed voodoo rituals as well as "zombie" practices. However, her Haitian fieldwork was cut short by a serious illness. Her book *Tell My Horse* (Hurston 1938) documented her explorations of folk rituals and sex roles in Jamaica and Haiti; and while it was quite popular with the public, the book was badly received by scholars, who questioned her objectivity, research techniques, and ethnographic style. The direct participant's approach bothered many, often punctuated as it was by personal commentary. However, Melville Herskovits's response to Hurston's Haitian work was enthusiastic, although he called for additional research to elucidate many of her findings.

In this book Hurston's feminist perspectives emerge most clearly with respect to Jamaica, and are implicit in her analysis of Haitian ritual. Also explicit is Hurston's understanding of the links between folk culture and history. John Henry Clark, one of her scholarly contemporaries, described her work as provocative because "she was going from folklore into folk culture, and people didn't know what she was doing. . . . [T]hey were bothered by the whole thing.

People also reacted to women doing field research, and they thought only men were supposed to do that.''[2]

Much of Hurston's later work displayed her concern with women as culture bearers, but in the Caribbean work she also noted the exploitation of black women, referring to them as "the mules of the Caribbean." In addition, she speculated about the African roots of black women's roles in Haitian voodoo as well as American hoodoo. Hurston portrays black women as determined characters who, despite racism, mishaps, and violence, use spiritualism and voodoo to remain afloat and to hang on to their menfolk.

Following Hurston's rejection by the scholarly community in 1939, she retreated into a career as a lecturer at black colleges, a novelist, folklorist, and dramatist. However, financial and social pressures appear to have altered the nature of her writing. She authored several books, including her autobiography *Dust Tracks on a Road* (1942); she wrote scores of articles and contributed columns to local newspapers on race, politics, education, and culture. She was awarded several honorary degrees from Morgan College and Howard University, among others. Despite discrimination and segregation, she taught and held drama positions at North Carolina College for Negroes, at the University of North Carolina, and at Florida Normal College (1941–43).

In 1947 Hurston made a last attempt to get back to anthropology by proposing research in Honduras to find the ruins of a lost Mayan city, but the attempt was frustrated by the absence of research funding. Instead she wrote the last of her four novels in Honduras, *Seraph on the Swanee* (1948), which focused on dilemmas facing southern white women. Although Scribner and Sons published the novel, the reviews of the work were negative, and she encountered heightened professional difficulty after this. Nevertheless, Hurston continued to get enthusiastic responses from lay audiences, and the volume of her folklore gave her stature as a contributor to the understanding of black folk literature. She was criticized for her increasingly conservative political view, professional instability, and for "fictive" interpretations in her autobiography. Notably, her controversial and sometimes contradictory public stands against what she interpreted as uncritical support for black colleges and "indiscriminate desegregation," earned her considerable black intellectual opposition. Adverse public opinion related to an unfounded 1948 morals charge virtually destroyed her career and self-image, and in 1949 Hurston again retreated to the South, spending her last years in Eau Gallie, Florida.

Her best work was done before 1940. The rejection of several book manuscripts by Scribner and Sons between 1951 and 1953 was the prelude to illness, isolation, and financial problems, which sapped her professional energy. Unable to earn money, and mentally and physically weakened as a result of a stroke, Zora Neale Hurston entered a welfare home in St. Lucie County, Florida, in 1959, where she died in 1960. Chapters of her earlier autobiography, which had not been released until 1984, have suggested that Hurston may have been ten years older than her reputed age, and this may help explain her untimely death.

The profound talent yet personal tragedy of Zora Hurston's career sheds light on the difficulty that creative women in general and black women in particular had in academia and the professions during the 1920s and 1930s. Her work was innovative and pioneering in that few had documented the social context within which black folklore, voodoo, and ritual had existed; and even fewer had used the "Negro way of saying" things as their medium of expression. Hurston has sometimes been described as a major competitor with Richard Wright, Ralph Ellison, and Sterling Brown in presenting fictional models for the representation of black life. However, the intellectual attitude toward this kind of fieldwork and literature, reflecting the black poor in rural work camps and shanty towns, was negative. Hurston paid the price through her damaged scholarly reputation and her increased dependence on patrons and employers for support.

Her fluctuations between literature and anthropology caused some to consider her an anthropological dilettante. The fluctuations may have reflected, not choice, but a movement in the changing directions of that which was necessary to earn a living at a time when few intellectuals could survive on proceeds from written work, and when assertive black female thinkers and intellectuals were a rarity. In retrospect Hurston has been recognized as a creative giant, who took guidance from the early black female writer Frances E. W. Harper, as well as from her Howard University and Columbia University colleagues and mentors. Excerpts from her poem *Contentment* could well have served as her epitaph:

> When I consider how my life is spent, I am content
> That I have not reached the goal of my ambition does not grieve me
> Have I not laughed and wept? Loved and hated?
> In short, I have been altogether human
> For great love, soul strengthening tears, and the touch of God's creations
> Make up the sum of life.

Notes

1. This quote is from Elinor Des Verney Stinnette's "Excerpts regarding Hurston," in *An Oral Memoir of Mrs. Ophelia Settle Egypt*, 1981–82, pp. 48–50, from the Manuscripts Division of the Moorland-Springarn Research Center at Howard University, Washington, D.C. In addition, the author has consulted the Alain Locke Papers and the Hurston Correspondence at the Moorland-Springarn Research Center at Howard University.

2. This quote is from the author's interview with John Henry Clark, one of Hurston's contemporaries (interview manuscript on file at the Manuscripts Division of the Moorland-Springarn Research Center at Howard University, Washington, D.C.).

References and Works About Zora Neale Hurston

Asterlund, B.
1939   Zora Neale Hurston: A Biographical Sketch. *Wilson Bulletin for Libraries* 13 (May): 586.

Blake, Emma L.
1966   Zora Neale Hurston: Anthropologist and Folklorist. *Negro History Bulletin* 29
       (April): 149–50.
Byrd, James W.
1955   Zora Neale Hurston: A Novel Folklorist. *Tennessee Folklore Society Bulletin*
       21:37–41.
Gates, Henry Louis, Jr.
1985   A Negro Way of Saying. In *The New York Times,* "Book Review," April 21,
       pp. 1, 43, 45.
Helmick, Evelyn Thomas
1970   Zora Neale Hurston. *The Carrell* 2:1–19.
Hemenway, Robert E.
1977   *Zora Neale Hurston: A Literary Biography*. Urbana: University of Illinois Press.
Hughes, Langston
1940a *The Big Sea*. New York: Alfred A. Knopf.
1940b Harlem Litterati in the Twenties. *Saturday Review of Literature* 22 (June 22): 13–
       14.
Hurst, Fannie
1961   Zora Hurston: A Personality Sketch. *Yale University Library Gazette* 35:17–21.
Mikell, Gwendolyn
1982   When Horses Talk: Reflections on Zora Neale Hurston's Haitian Ethnography.
       PHYLON (Sept. 1982): 218–30.
1983   The Anthropological Imagination of Zora Neale Hurston. *Western Journal of Black
       Studies* 7 (1): 27–35.
Taylor, Robert L.
1943   The Doctor, the Lady, and Columbia University. *The New Yorker* (October 23):
       27–32.
Turner, Darwin
1971   Chapter on Zora Neale Hurston. In *In a Minor Chord: Three Afro-American
       Writers and Their Search for Identity*. Carbondale: Southern Illinois University
       Press.
Walker, Alice
1975   In Search of Zora Neale Hurston. *Ms*. 3 (March): 74–79.
1979   *I Love Myself When I Am Laughing: A Zora Neale Hurston Reader*. New York:
       Feminist Press. (As ed.)
Young, James O.
1973   *Black Writers of the Thirties*. Baton Rouge: Louisiana State University Press.

Selected Works by Zora Neale Hurston

1924   Drenched in Light. *Opportunity* 2 (December): 371–74.
1925   Spunk. *Opportunity* 3 (June): 171–73. (Reprinted 1925 in *The New Negro*. Alain
       Locke, ed. Pp. 105–11. New York: Albert & Charles Boni.)
1925   The Hue and Cry About Howard University. *Messenger* 7 (September): 315–19,
       338.
1927a Cudjo's Own Story of the Last African Slaver. *Journal of Negro History* 12
       (October): 648–63.

1927b Communication [regarding Negro settlement in early Florida]. *Journal of Negro History* 12 (October): 664–67.

1930   Dance Songs and Folk Tales from the Bahamas. *Journal of American Folklore* 43 (July-September): 294–312.

1931   Hoodoo in America. *Journal of American Folklore* 44 (October-December): 317–18.

1934a Characteristics of Negro Expression. In *Negro: An Anthology*. Nancy Cunard, ed. Pp. 39–46. London: Wishart.

1934b Conversions and Visions. In *Negro: An Anthology*. Nancy Cunard, ed. Pp. 47–49. London: Wishart.

1934c Shouting. In *Negro: An Anthology*. Nancy Cunard, ed. Pp. 49–50. London: Wishart.

1934d The Sermon. In *Negro: An Anthology*. Nancy Cunard, ed. Pp. 50–54. London: Wishart.

1934e Mother Catharine. In *Negro: An Anthology*. Nancy Cunard, ed. Pp. 54–57. London: Wishart.

1934f Uncle Monday. In *Negro: An Anthology*. Nancy Cunard, ed. Pp. 57–61. London: Wishart.

1934g Spirituals and Neo-Spiritualism. In *Negro: An Anthology*. Nancy Cunard, ed. Pp. 359–61. London: Wishart.

1934h *Jonah's Gourd Vine*. Philadelphia: J. B. Lippincott. (Reprinted 1971 with introduction by Larry Neal. Lippincott.)

1935   *Mules and Men*. Philadelphia: J. B. Lippincott. (Reprinted 1970 with introduction by Darwin Turner. New York: Harper and Row.)

1937   *Their Eyes Were Watching God*. Philadelphia: J. B. Lippincott. (Reprinted 1978. Urbana: University of Illinois Press.)

1938   *Tell My Horse*. Philadelphia: J. B. Lippincott. (Reprinted 1982. Berkeley, Calif.: Turtle Island Foundation.)

1939   *Moses, Man of the Mountain*. Philadelphia: J. B. Lippincott. (Reprinted 1984 with introduction by Blyden Jackson. Urbana: University of Illinois Press.)

1942   *Dust Tracks on a Road*. Philadelphia: J. B. Lippincott. (Reprinted 1971 with introduction by Larry Neal. Lippincott; 1984 with introduction by R. Hemenway. Urbana: University of Illinois Press.)

1945   The Rise of the Begging Joints. *American Mercury* 60 (March): 288–94. (Condensed in *Negro Digest* 4 [Dec.]: 45–48.)

1948   *Seraph on the Swanee*. New York: Scribner and Sons. (Reprinted 1974. New York: AMS Press.)

1951   Mourner's Bench, Communist Line: Why the Negro Won't Buy Communism. *American Legion Magazine* 50 (June): 14–15, 55–60.

1958–59 Hoodoo and Black Magic. (Newspaper column.) *Fort Pierce Chronicle*, July 11, 1958–August 7, 1959.

GWENDOLYN MIKELL

Phyllis Mary Kaberry

(1910–1977)

British social anthropologist Phyllis Mary Kaberry was especially notable for
her pioneering work on the study of women in Aboriginal Australia, Papua New
Guinea, and Africa.

Phyllis Kaberry identified herself as "mere English of the Australian variety."
Her parents were English, she was born in California, but she grew up in Sydney
when her father, an architect, moved his family (wife, two sons, one daughter)
there. Later she made London her home base. She never married.

When she left school in the early 1930s, Sydney had one university, the only
place in Australia offering a full course in anthropology. She studied with Raymond Firth, Ian Hogbin, and A. P. Elkin, graduating with a B.A. degree in
1933 and an M.A. (First Class Honors) in 1935. It was Elkin who influenced
her choice of a research area and topic. With a grant from the Australian National
Research Council, Kaberry embarked in June 1934 on her first fieldwork in the
Kimberley region of northwest Australia, at that time relatively unknown anthropologically. Her aim was to study the position of Aboriginal women. Apart
from a short interval in Sydney, she spent a year and a half there.

By 1936 Kaberry was at the London School of Economics in the University
of London working as a research assistant, mainly with Audrey Richards,* and
preparing her Ph.D. thesis under the supervision of Bronislaw Malinowski. The
thesis, revised for publication, appeared as *Aboriginal Woman: Sacred and
Profane* (1939), the year that she was awarded the degree. The subtitle points
to Kaberry's criticism of Durkheim's contention that in Aboriginal society men
were "sacred," women "profane."

In January 1939 Kaberry visited her family in Sydney; but in April, with an
Australian National Research Council Fellowship, she began twelve months'
fieldwork in New Guinea among the Abelam of the Sepik River. They had been
brought under Australian administrative control only two years earlier. On her
return to Sydney University, she wrote up partial results of her research (Kaberry

1941, 1941–42) and was Honorary Assistant Lecturer in the Department of Anthropology. With a Stirling International Fellowship (1941), she went to Yale, continued lecturing and writing, and in 1942 received a Yale University Carnegie Fellowship for culture contact research. Malinowski had died that year; and Kaberry was entrusted with collating, editing, and writing an introduction to his unpublished papers, compiled as *The Dynamics of Culture Change* (1945b). But instead of field research in Mexico and Central America, she chose "war duties" on the European side of the Atlantic. So in 1943 she was back in London, working at Chatham House at the Royal Institute of International Affairs, among other things, compiling a report on colonial problems of Southeast Asia, especially Malaya.

In 1944 Kaberry was persuaded to enter a new field when the government of Nigeria approached the International African Institute about organizing research among the Bamenda peoples in the Cameroons, then under British mandate. The study was to focus on the position of women (1945–46, 1947–48). She traveled widely through the region before concentrating on Nso (Nsaw) women in the southeast. In the 1948–49 teaching session, Kaberry joined the Department of Anthropology at the University College London as a lecturer under Professor Daryll Forde. She was preparing some of her African material for publication and by 1950 had completed *Women of the Grassfields* (1952). In this Colonial Research Publication she demonstrated that within the domestic setting, women as wives exercised real control over land by virtue of their rights as producers over the crops they grew.

Promoted to a readership (1951), Kaberry assumed a heavy load of teaching and administration (Chilver 1978). In 1957 she was awarded the Rivers Memorial Medal for outstanding fieldwork and, jointly with Sally (Mrs. E. M.) Chilver, an historian, the Wellcome Medal for Applied Anthropology (1960). With a Leverhulme Fellowship (1958) she spent another seven months in Nso and adjoining areas. Helped by Wenner-Gren and Hayter travel grants (1960 and 1963), she returned to the Bamenda, collaborating during part of this period with Sally Chilver. One of their tasks was a comparative study of political systems for a proposed symposium involving historians and anthropologists.

With one of her former students, Mary Douglas,* Kaberry coedited and contributed to a volume of essays in honor of Daryll Forde (*Man in Africa*, 1969). She reaffirmed her continuing interest in New Guinea with a chapter on Northern Abelam political organization (Kaberry 1971). Made an Honorary Research Fellow in 1977 after her official retirement from University College London, she continued to be active and busy, until her sudden death the same year.

In appreciating the tremendous difficulties of carrying out field research in "outback" Australia in the mid–1930s (a fact not necessarily appreciated these days even by anthropologists), the importance of the Durack family in her professional and personal life cannot be emphasized too strongly.[1] That influence was formative, because the Duracks at that time controlled a number of large pastoral holdings in the Western Australian Kimberleys when she first went there.

Mary Durack and her sister Elizabeth facilitated Kaberry's travels and contacts with Aboriginal people throughout the region, as well as with station owners and managers who were unenthusiastic or even hostile about research. Kaberry was fortunate that the Durack girls were more sympathetic to Aboriginal interests than many station people at that time, and her own enthusiasm made them more so. Also, their personal support gave her the emotional confidence she needed.[2]

In the year preceding her death, Kaberry was impatient to get on with what she thought still lay ahead. Writing projects she could not finish included a study of the Abelam yam cult in New Guinea, a monograph on the Nso Kingdom, a textbook on "pre-industrial" societies, and an entry on New Guinea ethnography for the *Encyclopædia Brittanica*.

Kaberry's writing and work over the years show increasing experience and maturity. Many themes developed more fully in later publications were present in her earlier Australian work—not the least of which was her insistence that people, including women, should be seen in their social contexts. In her Australian research she wanted to present Aboriginal woman "as she really is—a complex social personality, having her own prerogatives, duties, problems, beliefs, rituals, and point of view; making the adjustments that the social, local and totemic organization require of her, and at the same time exercising a certain freedom of choice in matters affecting her own interests and desires." But she tried to see women in perspective (Kaberry 1939:ix, xii-xiii). One dilemma she faced in her Aboriginal fieldwork was the traditional religious division of labor between men and women. Kaberry was permitted to see and hear "men-only" rituals and discussions, a procedure that apparently caused no problems at the time. Other anthropologists too have been invited to cross gender barriers in this respect, in certain circumstances.

A pioneer in studying systematically the roles of women in society for Aboriginal Australia, Kaberry was the first female anthropologist to devote her whole attention to that subject. It was also an abiding and consistent emphasis in her later research. Her *Aboriginal Woman* remains a classic in this respect, and not only as a valuable record of a survey. That topic had been entirely neglected as being unworthy of serious study (Reay 1963). It is not easy now to convey the tremendous impact of her work that launched a complete reassessment of Aboriginal women's place in traditional life (Berndt and Berndt 1977:249). However, one major difficulty was the reluctance of some anthropologists to accept the view that Aboriginal women were significant and pivotal participants in traditional religious affairs. Kaberry, in effect, reinstated Aboriginal women in the sacred sphere, a position denied them in the anthropological literature prior to the mid–1940s.

The argument was that if Aboriginal women appeared to have a place, this must be due to "contaminating" outside influences (the religion must have been

"broken down"), and that Kaberry must have confused magic with religion
(Murtagh 1940). Elkin, too, though he encouraged and sponsored Kaberry's
research and was willing to concede that Aboriginal women had a higher status
than some writers accorded them, did not agree with her about their religious
status. He insisted stubbornly on "the sacred character of the men." To him,
"women may be independent, powerful, and spiritual, and yet be profane, or
outside of that sphere of sacred belief and ritual, admission to which is by
religious initiation" (1939:xxx). To William Stanner (1941) also, men were
superior to women in religious matters. Kaberry contended that "until a systematic study of women's circumstances and attitudes has been made, we have no
grounds for assuming on the data now available, that the men represent the
sacred element in the community and the women the profane element" (Kaberry
1939:xii). That was the essence of her argument. Stanner called for more
"theory," not more ethnographic "facts." For Kaberry, more realistically, theory and facts had to go together. What was required, she wrote, was a "field-
worker who can spend a year or longer with one tribe and learn the language.
Until this has been done, it is impossible to take up the wider theoretical issues
as to why, for instance, the ceremonial life of the men is more complex and
richer artistically than that of the women" (Kaberry 1939:xii).

It is true that in England she gradually became "Africa-minded" (Elkin
1978:302), but she certainly did not desert the Australian field entirely as Reay
(1963) suggests. Her Australian links were still strong, through her friends,
family and colleagues, and she kept up with published and unpublished materials
on Aboriginal topics. Although her publications after *Aboriginal Woman* are
important and are anthropologically more sophisticated, her initial work probably
had the greatest single impact, both in Australia and internationally.

In 1939, after her London experience, she wrote to ask Mary Durack about
the possibilities of returning to the Kimberleys, adding that she would want to
move about more widely in the region "and to make a study of the language."
But an opportunity to work in New Guinea brought a change of plan: "I feel
the need of a new type of anthropological experience before returning to the
Aborigines" (M. Durack, 1/27/39, 2/14/39). This interest in New Guinea resulted
from Elkin's 1933 postgraduate seminar in which Kaberry met Gregory Bateson,
Margaret Mead,* and Reo Fortune, fresh from research in the Sepik area. Among
the Abelam in New Guinea, Kaberry worked with men until she learned enough
of the language to speak directly with women; but her reports show the same
concern with context and detail as did her Kimberley studies.

In her African research the continuities in her approach appear on a wider
canvas and in greater depth. She had learned that there were no easy short cuts
in the study of women: before generalizing about women's roles and statuses,
one had to ensure that all the relevant factors were taken into account. Otherwise,
any attempt "to decide whether the position of women in general is high or low,
or good or bad is, in my opinion, likely to prove profitless" (Kaberry 1952:viii).

In her foreword to *Aboriginal Woman*, Kaberry acknowledged her professional debt to Malinowski and to Firth. Dedicating the book to Malinowski, she noted that she admired him as an anthropologist because he approached the study of culture and civilization with the imagination and sensitivity of an artist, without sacrificing scientific objectivity and integrity of fact.

African anthropology gradually became Kaberry's dominant interest. *Women of the Grassfields* showed what an experienced anthropologist could do when invited to undertake a specific task designed to change the direction of administrative policies and attitudes on rural development (Read 1953). *Man in Africa* provided a much broader spectrum of the African scene (Beattie 1970). According to Sally Chilver, Kaberry's 1945–48 fieldwork and her conversations with administrative officers led to the appointment in the South Cameroons of a provincial (then principal) adult education officer, who implemented and executed some of the practical suggestions Kaberry had made.

By 1958 Grassfields women in a number of areas faced new problems. Because coffee was popular as a cash crop, under male control as all tree crops were, it occupied land near the homesteads, and women had to go farther afield to farm subsistence crops. Also, there was overstocking by immigrant cattlemen (Bororo or Cattle Fulani). Much of Kaberry's time was spent, contrary to her own and Sally Chilver's plans, in following up cattle-damage cases and persuading the departing British and incoming Cameroonian administrators to take a more serious view of such matters. A report she wrote (Kaberry 1959b) had some temporary results; but the problem of unequal development persisted, and women's work remained undervalued. Kaberry wrote a number of papers based on particular groups, but she favored a regional approach.

In a memorial service for Kaberry in February 1978 at the University Church of Christ the King in London, the provost of University College London read the lesson and professor Sir Raymond Firth gave the address. The choir sang "An Anthem from the Funeral Music for Queen Mary" by Purcell, commemorating an episode in her career: in Bamenda she had been "made a Queen Mother by the Fon of Nso" (Firth 1978:296).

The Nso memorial service for her, in Bamenda, was in keeping with that stature. All the palace masks were brought out in her honor as for a royal personage. It was well attended, with many chiefs and women trekking for miles. As usual in such a mortuary ritual, it concluded with the appearance of a fearsome mask called Kibaranko, appropriately worn on this occasion by a lecturer in history at Yaounde University. The affair was an even greater honor than her title, since it involved a summoning of her spirit. Conferred upon her years earlier, her title was Yaa Woo Kov, Lady of the Forest—the old forest capital where kings were buried in the past. At that time an elderly prince told her that henceforward she must not raise her voice in anger lest a wild wind arise and take off the rooftops. In short, she was held to be endowed with royal *sëm*, power to achieve things by psychic emanations (Chilver, personal communication 1985).

To Kaberry, women were important equally with men; but above all, she affirmed the importance of people, whatever their gender, rank, authority, or power. "Nomad of the spirit," her own title for a selection of her poems inspired by her Kimberley experiences (letter to Mary Durack, 20/12/42, from New Haven), captures the essence of Kaberry herself. She ventured eagerly into unfamiliar situations, geographically and theoretically, and made herself at home. And in fieldwork, as elsewhere, her unobtrusive friendliness brought friendliness in return. In Firth's words, "She led, not by waving a personal banner, but in her own modest way, by putting forward a range of interesting ideas, taking them up by very solid field research, and encouraging other people to develop them along their own lines" (Firth 1978:296–97).

Notes

1. I wish to express my thanks to Mrs. Sally Chilver and to Dame Mary Durack for their generosity in making available to me a great deal of material about Kaberry: Sally Chilver, in relation especially to her African work (correspondence with me dated 1985), and Dame Mary, for the Aboriginal side (letters from Kaberry to Dame Mary date from the mid–1930s till her death). I have had further discussions with Dame Mary and conversations with Dr. John Howard about their personal recollections.

2. Unpublished resource materials utilized in preparing this biography include the personal correspondence from Phyllis Kaberry to Dame Mary Durack (Miller) dated 1935–76, from within Australia (Kimberleys, Sydney), and from England, Papua New Guinea, the United States, and Africa. Dame Mary plans to house this collection in the Battye Library, Perth, Western Australia. Dr. Kaberry left her African field notes to the British Library of Economics and Political Science, London; her Australian Aboriginal field notes of 1934–36, including sketch maps and pictorial material, are housed in the Australian Institute of Aboriginal Studies, Canberra. At the time of the preparation of this biography, the whereabouts of her New Guinea material was unknown.

References and Works About Phyllis M. Kaberry

Beattie, J.
1970 Review of *Man in Africa*. (M. Douglas and P. Kaberry, eds.) *Africa* 40 (2): 172–75.
Berndt, R. M., and C. H. Berndt
1977 Obituary: Phyllis M. Kaberry, 1910–1977. *Anthropological Forum* 4 (2): 249.
Burnham, P., M. Rowlands, and E. M. Chilver
1977 Obituary of Phyllis M. Kaberry, *The Times* (London), November 18.
Chilver, E. M.
1978 Phyllis Kaberry. *Royal Anthropological Institute Newsletter* (RAIN) 24:11–12.
Elkin, A. P.
1978 Obituary: Phyllis M. Kaberry. *Oceania* 48 (4): 301–2.
Firth, R.
1978 Phyllis Kaberry 1910–1977. *Africa* 48 (3): 296–97.
Murtagh, J. G.
1940 [Review of] *Aboriginal Woman. The Advocate,* December 19. (The review is signed "J.G.M.''; but the copy given to R. M. and C. H. Berndt by Father

Anthony Peile notes that the "critic" [critique] was given to J. G. Murtagh by Father E. Worms. The page of handwritten comments bearing Father Worms's name, dated 11/22/40 [also from Fr. Peile], seems to bear this out.)

Read, M.
1953   Review of *Women of the Grassfields*. *Africa* 23 (2): 161–62.
Stanner, W. E. H.
1941   Review of *Aboriginal Woman*. *Oceania* 11 (3): 311–12.

Selected Works by Phyllis M. Kaberry

1935a The Forrest River and Lyne River Tribes of North-West Australia. *Oceania* 5 (4): 403–36.

1935b Death and Deferred Mourning Ceremonies in the Forrest River Tribes, North-West Australia. *Oceania* 6 (1):33–47.

1936   Spirit-Children and Spirit Centres of the North Kimberley Division, West Australia. *Oceania* 6 (4): 392–400.

1937a Subsections in the East and South Kimberley Tribes of North-West Australia. *Oceania* 7 (4): 436–58.

1937b Notes on the Languages of East Kimberley, North-West Australia. *Oceania* 8 (1): 90–103.

1938   Totemism in East and South Kimberley, North-West Australia. *Oceania* 8 (3): 265–88.

1939   *Aboriginal Woman: Sacred and Profane*. London: Routledge.

1941   The Abelam Tribe, Sepik District, New Guinea: A Preliminary Report. *Oceania* 11 (3): 233–58; (4) 331–63.

1941–42 Law and Political Organization in the Abelam Tribe, New Guinea. *Oceania* 12 (1): 79–95; (3) 209–25; (4) 331–63.

1945a British Colonial Policy in South-East Asia; and, The Development of Self-Government in Malaya. *United Kingdom Memorandum* No. 3, Royal Institute of International Affairs for the Institute of Pacific Relations.

1945b *The Dynamics of Culture Change: An Inquiry into Race Relations in Africa*. By B. Malinowski. New Haven: Yale University Press. (As ed.)

1950   Land Tenure Among the Nsaw of the British Cameroons. *Africa* 20 (4): 307–23.

1952   *Women of the Grassfields. Study of the Economic Position of Women in Bamenda, British Cameroons*. Colonial Research Publications No. 14. London: Her Majesty's Stationery Office. (Reprinted 1969. Kentfield, Calif.: Gregg International.)

1957a Myth and Ritual: Some Recent Theories. *Bulletin Institute Classical Studies* (University of London) 4:42–54.

1957b Primitive States. *British Journal of Sociology* 8:224–34.

1957c Malinowski's Contribution to Field-work Methods and the Writing of Ethnography. In *Man and Culture: An Evaluation of the Work of Bronislaw Malinowski*. R. Firth, ed. Pp. 71–91. London: Routledge and Kegan Paul.

1959a Nsaw Political Conceptions. *Man* 59:206.

1959b Report on Farmer-Grazier Relations and the Changing Pattern of Agriculture in Nsaw. Mimeographed.

1959c Traditional Politics in Nsaw. *Africa* 29 (4): 366–83.

1960   Some Problems of Land Tenure in Nsaw. *Journal of African Administration*, no. 10.

1962 Retainers and Royal Households in the Cameroon Highlands. *Cahiers d'études africaines,* no. 10.

1971 Political Organization Among the Northern Abelam. In *Politics in New Guinea.* R. M. Berndt and P. Lawrence, eds. Pp. 35–73. Perth: University of Western Australia Press.

Coauthored Works

Kaberry, Phyllis, and E. M. (Sally) Chilver

1960 From Tribute to Tax in a Tikar Chiefdom. *Africa* 30 (1): 1–19.

1961a The History and Customs of Ntem—As Provided by Chief John Nfowanko. New Delhi, India: Oxonian Press. (As eds.)

1961b An Outline of the Traditional Political System of Bali-Nyonga. *Africa* 31 (4): 355–71.

1965 Sources of the Nineteenth-Century Slave Trade: The Cameroon Highlands. *Journal of African History* 6 (1).

1967 The Kingdom of Kom in West Cameroon. In *West African Kingdoms in the Nineteenth Century.* Phyllis Kaberry and Daryll Forde, eds. London: Oxford University Press for the International African Institute (I.A.I.).

1968 Traditional Bamenda. Buea, Cameroon: Government Printer.

1970a Chronology of the Bamenda Grassfields. *Journal of African History* 11 (2).

1970b The Tikar Problem, a Non-Problem. *Journal of African Languages* 10 (2): 13–14.

Kaberry, Phyllis, and Daryll Forde, eds.

1967 *West African Kingdoms in the Nineteenth Century.* London: Oxford University Press for I.A.I.

CATHERINE H. BERNDT

Isabel Truesdell Kelly

(1906–1983)

American archaeologist who specialized in West Mexican prehistory, Isabel Truesdell Kelly was also known for her work on Southwestern archaeology, Plains Indian ethnography, international public health, and Mexican social anthropology.

Isabel Kelly was born January 4, 1906, in Santa Cruz, California, the first child of Thomas William Kelly and Alice Gardner Kelly. Her father was managing head of the West Coast office of Pictorial Review Dress Patterns. Kelly's aunt Louise Gardner, a strong-willed New England spinster who lived to be 100 years old, often traveled abroad with her nieces, Isabel and Evelyn.[1] On one of these trips, Kelly visited Bolivia when she was nineteen years old.

Kelly excelled in both academic subjects and sports at Santa Cruz High School. After graduating second in her class, she had planned to attend the University of California at Berkeley as a physical education major. Due to a case of mistaken identity, her request for enrollment in Berkeley's Physical Education Program was denied. Then, just prior to fall registration, she contracted a severe case of poison oak and had to register late. By that time fewer desirable courses were open; and to complete her general course requirements, she enrolled in an anthropology class. By the end of the semester, Kelly had decided to pursue a career in anthropology. At that time the Berkeley faculty included Robert H. Lowie, Alfred Kroeber, and Edward Gifford. Carl Sauer, an acclaimed geographer, discovered and fostered Kelly's energy, intelligence, and talent. She received her B.A. in anthropology at the age of twenty and completed her M.A. the following year. In 1932 she was awarded the Anthropology Department's twelfth Ph.D., graduating with Cora Du Bois* (eleventh), and Charles Vogelin (thirteenth).

With several publications completed, Kelly began her postdoctoral work with ethnogeographic research. As a National Research Fellow in the Biological Sciences (1932–34), she investigated the Southern Paiute Indians and their tribal boundaries (Kelly 1932, 1934, 1964). In 1935 Kelly went to Mexico for the first time as a research associate in anthropology to direct archaeological investigations at Culiacan, Sinaloa. The project was sponsored by the Institute of Social Sciences at the University of California at Berkeley, under the direction of Carl Sauer and Alfred Kroeber. In January 1936 she returned to a teaching assistantship in the Geography Department that was offered to her by Carl Sauer.

The following year she returned to the Southwest as a temporary research associate in archaeology. She arrived at the Gila Pueblo Archaeological Foundation in Globe, Arizona, on September 5, 1937. Her excavations and report writing on Hodges Ruin, a Hohokam site, continued to the end of the 1938 field season. With no further financial support, her unfinished field report was not published until forty years later (Kelly 1978b).

Publications of the two field reports mentioned above were also delayed because of Kelly's renewed commitment to Mexican anthropology. With only scant department funding but Carl Sauer's strong encouragement, she returned to west Mexico in 1939 and carried out archaeological reconnaissance. This endeavor included a ten-day mule trip from Nayarit to Puerto Vallarta, a twenty-day horseback trip from Autlán to Tuxcacuesco, and a monoplane ride to Guadalajara. In 1940 she gained Mexican residency, living in Tlaquepaque (1941–47) until she moved to her permanent home at Tepepan. She continued her field projects in Mexican archaeology at Colima, Apatzingán, Guadalajara, Autlán, Tenamaxtlan, Jalisco, and Sayula regions. For many of these areas, no archaeological investigation had ever been accomplished before or since her lifetime.

During the war years, university funds for projects and associate researchers had grown scarce. Kelly was determined to keep her research active with grants from the Guggenheim Foundation, Carnegie Institute, and the American Philosophical Society. Just as these funding sources ended in 1945, the U.S. Information Service offered Kelly a position as librarian at the Benjamin Franklin Library in Mexico City.

In 1946, with the strong recommendation of George Foster, who had previously held the same appointment, Kelly became Ethnologist-in-Charge of the Smithsonian's Institute of Social Anthropology (ISA) office in Mexico City. At the ISA she taught at the Escuela Nacionál de Antropología during part of the year and devoted the remaining time to research with students among the Totonac of Veracruz. Then, in 1951, when the ISA's concerns shifted to international public health, she began health care research in El Salvador and Mexico. After the closure of the ISA in 1952, she transferred to the Institute of Inter-American Affairs, the precursor of the Agency for International Development (AID), where she remained employed until 1960. Working for the Health Division of the Institute of Inter-American Affairs, Kelly studied newly created health centers in Mexico. The Institute also sent her to Oruro, Bolivia, to report on a proposed relocation of unemployed miners to the lower, warmer Yungas region. Following this study, she was assigned to an eighteen-month project in Pakistan, where she learned to speak Urdu.

In 1960 Kelly again turned to foundation-sponsored research in Mexico. She did this partly to protect her Mexican residency, which she would have forfeited had she remained out of the country longer. While living in Mexico, she became a research consultant in archaeology and ethnography for the Arizona State Museum. Grants from the Rockefeller Foundation, Wenner-Gren Foundation, and National Geographic Society enabled her to return to the Colima investigations (Kelly 1978a, 1980) and to publish data gathered during the Totonac research (e.g., Kelly and Harvey 1969).

Although Kelly never criticized archaeology as a male-dominated profession, she commented that nonsupport of women anthropologists was nearly universal. Others, such as Carl Sauer and Alfred Kidder, expressed frustration that she never received the professional appointment she deserved. In a letter to Sauer, Kidder acknowledged that Kelly should have had a permanent post.[2] "She is one of the most effective workers I know and thoroughly sound." There is some evidence that Kelly had chosen to stay in Mexico rather than accept employment elsewhere that might have interfered with her research. She also preferred working alone and had little patience for all but the most dedicated students.

Kelly received little professional support from the Anthropology Department at Berkeley, chaired at that time by Alfred Kroeber. Her extensive correspondence with Carl Sauer during the 1930s and 1940s documents her rather low opinion and distrust of Kroeber, who apparently had given little encouragement to women students. By the late 1940s Kelly's letters to Kroeber indicate a more tolerant attitude toward him. Perhaps her mounting achievements finally convinced her that Kroeber's opinions could no longer discourage her or interfere with her work. Her mentor, Carl Sauer, was her connection with the academic world that would have otherwise abandoned her in Mexico. Sauer treated her as a colleague; and she reciprocated his support by sending him colonial archival references, maps, and botanical samples.

Kelly possessed a wit and determination that all her friends warmly remember. Her letters are treasures of humorous daily encounters, insights, and descriptions of scientific discoveries. To Sauer she once bemoaned that her Mexican driver's license application requested everything, including "mother's maiden name; father's ditto; grandmother's favorite movie actress, and so on." In a 1955 letter to Kroeber, Kelly listed ten uncompleted projects that she felt would never be finished even if she lived to be 150, "for I write very slowly and painfully." At the time of her death in December 1983, she had not only finished most of these projects but had also initiated and completed reports on many more.

Kelly's work reflects her rigorous training in the use of descriptive data and her cautious theorizing. From uncovering the preclassic, monochrome Capacha culture complex in Colima to reporting on health services, Kelly "was very precise, very scientific, very demanding of high scholarship and principles in presenting data. A recommendation from Kelly was highly regarded" (Muriel Porter Weaver, letter to author, 8/8/84). At Apatzingán Kelly (1947) identified a sequence of cultural remains chronologically extending from Classic to Conquest times. "Now, more than twenty-five years after the publication of the Apatzingán report, there is little archaeological knowledge that can be added, a fact that emphasizes the need for intensive field work in western Mexico" (Weaver 1972:274). Kelly endured many rugged seasons of fieldwork to produce vital contributions to Mexican archaeology and anthropology. Isabel Kelly might appropriately be considered the mother of west Mexican archaeology.

Notes

1. The author wishes to thank Evelyn Kelly Brown, Elizabeth Sauer Fitzsimmons, George Foster, Irmgard Johnson, Robert Kemper, John Leighly, James J. Parsons, Marion Sterling Pugh, and Muriel Porter Weaver for their cooperation in providing information for this biography.

2. The author acknowledges the Bancroft Library, University of California at Berkeley, which provided access to archival correspondence between Carl Sauer and Isabel Kelly, Carl Sauer and Alfred Kidder, and Alfred Kroeber and Isabel Kelly.

References and Works About Isabel T. Kelly

Mallory, Lester
1985   Isabel Kelly. *Pantoc* 5 (Mexico).

Selected Works by Isabel T. Kelly

1930a The Carver's Art of the Indians of Northwestern California. *California University Publications in American Archaeology and Ethnology.* Vol. 24, pp. 103–19.

1930b Peruvian Cumbrous Bowls. *California University Publications in American Archaeology and Ethnology.* Vol. 24, pp. 325–41.

1930c Yuki Basketry. *California University Publications in American Archaeology and Ethnology.* Vol. 24, pp. 421–44.

1932   Ethnography of the Surprise Valley Paiute. *California University Publications in American Archaeology and Ethnology.* Vol. 31, pp. 67–210.

1934   Southern Paiute Bands. *American Anthropologist* 36:548–60.

1936   Chemehuevi Shamanism. In *Essays in Anthropology Presented to A. L. Kroeber.* R. H. Lowie, ed. Pp. 129–42. Berkeley: University of California Press.

1938a Excavations at Chametla, Sinaloa. *Ibero Americana.* Vol. 14. Berkeley: University of California Press.

1938b Northern Paiute Tales. *The Journal of American Folklore* 51:363–438.

1938c Band Organization of the Southern Paiute. In Tribal Distribution in the Great Basin. Willard Z. Park et al., eds. *American Anthropologist* 40:633–34.

1939a Southern Paiute Shamanism. *Anthropological Records.* Vol. 2, pp. 151–67.

1939b Chapter on Ethnology. In *Man in Nature: America Before the Days of the White Men.* Carl Sauer, ed. New York: Charles Scribner's Sons.

1941a The Relationship Between Tula and Sinaloa. *Revista Mexicana de Estudios Antropológicos.* Vol. 5, 199–207.

1941b Notes on a West Coast Survival of the Ancient Mexican Ballgame. *Notes on*

Middle American Archaeology and Ethnology. Pp. 163–75. Carnegie Institution of Washington, Division of Historical Research. No. 561, Vol. 1. Cambridge, Mass.

1941c El Problema de Tula. *Boletín,* no. 3. Pp. 1–6. Primera Mesa Redonda, Revista Mexicana de Estudios Antropológicos.

1943 West Mexico and the Hohokam. In *El Norte de Mexico y el Sur de Estados Unidos.* Pp. 206–22. Tercera Reunión de Mesa Redonda sobre Problemas Antropológicos de México y Centro América. México: Sociedad Mexicana de Antropología.

1944a Ixtle Weaving at Chiquilistlan, Jalisco. *Notes on Middle American Archaeology and Ethnology.* Pp. 106–12. Carnegie Institution of Washington, Division of Historical Research. No. 561, Vol. 2. Cambridge, Mass.

1944b Worked Gourds from Jalisco. *Notes on Middle American Archaeology and Ethnology* 2 (561):113–26. Carnegie Institution of Washington, Division of Historical Research.

1945 Excavations at Culiacan, Sinaloa. *Ibero Americana.* Vol. 25. Berkeley: University of California Press.

1947a *Excavations at Apatzingán Michoacán.* Viking Fund Publications in Anthropology, no. 7. New York.

1947b An Archaeological Reconnaissance of the West Coast: Nayarit to Michoacán. *International Congress of Americanists, 27th.* Vol. 2, pp. 74–77. Mexico City.

1948 Ceramic Provinces of Northwest Mexico. In *Cuarta Reunion de Mesa Redonda sobre Problemas Antropológicos de México y Centro America.* Pp. 55–71. México: Sociedad Mexicana de Antropología.

1951 The Bottle Gourd and Old World Contacts. In *Homenaje al Doctor Alfonso Caso.* Pp. 207–14. Mexico City: Imprinta Nuevo Mundo.

1952a *Public Opinion and the Xochimilco Health Center.* Washington, D.C.: Institute of Social Anthropology, Smithsonian Institution.

1952b *Public Opinion and the "Beatriz Velasco Aleman" Health Center.* Washington, D.C.: Institute of Social Anthropology, Smithsonian Institution.

1953 The Modern Totonac: Huastecos y Totonacos. *Revista Mexicana de Estudios Antropológicos.* Vol. 13 (2–3), 175–86.

1957 Some Aspects of Anthropological Collaboration in the Field of Public Health. Paper presented to the Department of Health, Education and Welfare, Washington, D.C.

1959a Some Observations with Respect to Agricultural Extension in Bolivia. U.S. Operations Mission to Bolivia, April. Mimeograph. 37 pp.

1959b La Antropología, La Cultura, y La Salud Publica. La Paz, Bolivia. U.S. Operations Mission to Bolivia. Mimeograph. 37 pp.

1960a An Approach to the Improvement of Diet. Conference on Malnutrition and Food Habits. Cuernavaca, Mexico.

1960b Handicrafts for Village Women in West Pakistan. Vol. 1960 (1). Published by the chief V-AID advisor, American Embassy, Karachi. Mimeograph. 7 pp.

1961 Mexican Spiritualism. *Kroeber Anthropological Society Papers,* no. 25. Pp. 191–206.

1964 Southern Paiute Ethnography. Glen Canyon Series 21, *University of Utah Anthropological Papers,* no. 69, Salt Lake City.

1965 Folk Practices in North Mexico: Birth Customs, Folk Medicine, and Spiritualism in the Laguna Zone. *University of Texas, Institute of Latin-American Studies Monographs*, no. 2.

1966   World View of a Highland-Totonac Pueblo. In *Summa Antropológica en Homenaje a Roberto J. Weitlaner*. Pp. 395–411. Mexico City: Instituto Nacional de Antropología e Historia.

1972   Vasijas de Colima con Boca de Estribo. *Instituto Nacional de Antropología e Historia Boletín*, no. 42. Pp. 26–31.

1974   Stirrup Pots from Colima: Some Implications. In *The Archaeology of West Mexico*. Betty Bell, ed. Pp. 206–11. Aijic, Jalisco: West Mexican Society for Advanced Study.

1978a   Seven Colima Tombs: An Interpretation of Ceramic Content. Studies in Mesoamerica III. *Contributions of the University of California Research Facility*, no. 36. Pp. 1–26.

1978b   Hodges Ruin: A Hohokam Community in the Tucson Basin. *Anthropological Papers of the University of Arizona*, no. 30.

1980   Ceramic Sequence in Colima. *Anthropological Papers of the University of Arizona*, no. 37.

Coauthored Works

Kelly, Isabel T., and H. R. Harvey
1969   The Totonac. In *Handbook of Middle American Indians*. Evon A. Vogt, ed. Vol. 8, pp. 638–81.

PATRICIA J. KNOBLOCH

Dorothy Louise Strouse Keur

(1904–   )

American cultural anthropologist Dorothy Louise Strouse Keur is known especially for Navajo archaeology, ecological studies in the Netherlands and Windward Islands, and her efforts to develop undergraduate anthropology at Hunter College.

An only child, Dorothy Strouse was born February 13, 1904, on West 110th Street, New York City. In her early childhood the family moved north to the Bronx, living first in the Morris Park section and later in the Riverdale section, where she still maintains an apartment. Neither of her parents had received a higher education, nor at that time was higher education for young women a popular idea. Her father worked first as a cutter and later as a buyer of necktie silks, a position from which he was often laid off for a week or two at a time without compensation. In contrast, her mother was a homemaker and a strong fundamentalist Protestant who hoped her only daughter would become a missionary.

Dorothy Strouse's motivation for a college education came not from her home but from her teachers at Morris High School. Not only did the teachers encourage her but several wrote to her parents strongly advising them to send Strouse to Hunter College. Fortunately, Hunter was tuition free and a five-cent subway ride from her home. As a result of her teachers' efforts, Strouse entered Hunter College in 1921.

At that time Professor Edward Sanford Burgess, a professor of botany, had developed an interest in anthropology and offered a few courses. According to Dorothy Strouse Keur, the lectures and course work "were rather disorganized and consisted of a patchwork of fact and theory, but they took hold of and stimulated me tremendously. . . . The idea of man as his own guinea pig, the ideal of greater objectivity, the concept of the relativity of values . . . held me enthralled."[1] The only course titles she remembers are the American Indian, Ancient Stone Tools, and Ceramics. As Professor Burgess's prize student, she was delegated to carry a bowl of soup each noon from the lunchroom to his office.

Upon graduation from Hunter in 1925 (summa cum laude and Phi Beta Kappa), Burgess, "in consideration for her kindness," offered Strouse the position of laboratory assistant, which she accepted. The salary was $150 a month, and Burgess made her promise to return half of that each month so that he could purchase Indian artifacts for the college.

Initially Strouse's duties were somewhat menial in nature, including such tasks as cleaning herbarium sheets. In time her duties expanded to conducting daily trips to the American Museum of Natural History to illustrate aspects of American Indian cultures or primate evolution. On one of her trips to the museum, Henry Fairfield Osborn, then president of the museum, listened as she explained the exhibits to the students. He was so impressed with what he heard that he urged her to continue her studies. Furthermore, Osborn also wrote to the president of Hunter College praising the caliber of Strouse's work.

Encouraged by Osborn's suggestion, Strouse enrolled for an A.M. degree at Columbia University, first attending summer classes, where she had the good fortune of studying under Leslie Spier and Edward Sapir. Later she matriculated as a part-time student during the academic year and studied under Franz Boas. Since she had chosen the origin of maize as the subject of her dissertation, she also took courses in botany with Carlton Curtis (one of Boas's few Columbia supporters in his World War I pacifist stance). During this project she was supported by Boas and Curtis and received her M.A. degree in 1928. Within a year new archaeological data disproved her thesis.

During this period Burgess suffered a stroke and was forced to retire, and his assistant, Elsie V. Steedman, took over the anthropology courses. Steedman became Strouse's mentor and trained her in the politics of advancing the status and scope of anthropology at Hunter. After Burgess's retirement, tenured anthropology faculty remained 100 percent female throughout World War II. In addition, Steedman strongly backed Strouse for promotion to the rank of instructor, which she received in 1928.

That same year Dorothy Strouse married John Y. Keur, "the boy around the corner," whose family had recently moved from Holland, where they were bulb growers. John Keur was a forestry student at Yale and later received a Ph.D. in biology from Columbia University. Like Dorothy, he entered the academic field teaching, first at Long Island University and later at Brooklyn College. Their two careers paralleled each other but were never in competition. John went into the field with Dorothy, serving as manager of field-workers on the Navajo archaeological excavations, and as collaborator and partner in their ecological studies in the Netherlands and the Netherlands' Windward Islands. Because of their strong partnership, Dorothy Keur's field situation was somewhat different from that experienced by many women.

The arrival of Duncan Strong at Columbia University motivated Keur to return there and study for a Ph.D. degree. She was already deeply interested in archaeology and had taken summer field courses with the School of American Research, under the aegis of Edgar Lee Hewett. For a course in North American archaeology given by Strong, Keur wrote a paper on Navajo origins. "A good paper," said Strong, "but it has not an iota of archaeology in it." "But I don't think there is any," Keur responded. "Then go out and do some," he replied, which she did on Big Bead Mesa, northeast of Santa Fe, with the aid of her husband and several Navajo workmen. The site is now preserved by the Bureau of Land Management. In April 1986, Keur received a New Mexico Governor's Award of Honor for Historic Preservation. The research formed the basis of her Ph.D. in 1941. Keur also did fieldwork in the Gobernador area, a site earlier than Big Bead Mesa where Navajos and Pueblos had lived in close proximity. For her early work in the Southwest, Keur was honored as one of the "Daughters of the Desert" at the Conference on Women Anthropologists of the Native American Southwest, in Tucson, in March 1986.

Along with her academic achievements, Keur was promoted to assistant professor in 1940, associate professor in 1947, and full professor in 1957. Except for a one-year sabbatical to complete her dissertation, Keur continued teaching fifteen to eighteen hours a semester at Hunter College. In addition, she was assigned a wide variety of courses to teach: Introduction to Cultural Anthropology, Religion of Non-Literate Peoples, Social Organization, Ethnology of Oceania, Ethnology of the Southwest, American Archaeology, Human Evolution, and Introduction to Physical Anthropology. Keur claims that she never intended to become a generalist, but demands of an expanding department forced her into this role.

Although Keur never relinquished her interest in archaeology or paleoanthropology, in the 1950s the ecological studies of Julian Steward and the community studies of Conrad Arensberg caught her interest. At the same time, through her marriage to John and visits to the Netherlands, Keur had developed an increasing knowledge of the Dutch language and culture.

This interest saw fruition in a Fulbright grant to both Dorothy and John Keur to study a rather isolated, small agrarian village with Saxon roots in the northern part of the Netherlands. The village of Anderen still adhered to old Saxon patterns of land divisions and usage, house forms and arrangements, and other social customs. The Keurs were fortunate in having the eminent Dutch sociologist Pieter Bouman of the University of Groningen as an advisor. The fieldwork took place during 1951–52 and resulted in the publication of *The Deeply Rooted* (Keur and Keur 1955), which was widely read in the Netherlands and used at one time as a supplementary text in sociology at the University of Nymegen.

As a result of disastrous flooding in the Netherlands in 1953, the Committee on Disaster Research of the National Research Council sent Dorothy Keur and Bradford Hudson, a social psychologist at the Rice Institute, to investigate both the sociological and psychological reactions of the people. The Committee on Disaster Research was interested in the behavior and reactions of the populace in the face of a major unexpected disaster. Based on visits and interviews in three communities differing in degree of flooding and disruption, Keur and Hudson developed a study plan that Dutch sociologists implemented.

During the 1950s, as anthropologists grew interested in the historical impact of colonial governments on developing nations, the Caribbean became a focal point for a number of studies. To this end, the Research Institute for the Study of Man invited the Keurs in 1956 to study the Dutch Windward Islands of St. Maarten, Saba, and St. Eustatius. The Keurs' principal objectives were to show the impact of Dutch colonialism on the life and culture of the people over time, and the variations found among the three small islands. The research results were published in *Windward Children* (Keur and Keur 1960).

Keur also published a number of more general pieces. No single theoretical theme runs through her writings, a reflection of her early training by Boas as well as her deep interest in the ever-expanding foci of the discipline.

Along with teaching and research, Keur was active in the professional associations of the discipline. She was secretary-treasurer of the American Ethnological Society (1947–49) and president (1955); a Fellow of the New York Academy of Sciences and chair of its anthropology division (1959, 1960).

From the inception of the Bronx campus of Hunter College, Keur served as the administrator for the Department of Anthropology on that campus, an office devoid of any clerical or laboratory assistance. When anthropology became an independent department under Ethel Aginsky, Keur's title was changed to sub-chairman. Despite many handicaps, Keur and Steedman developed such a fine collection of primate and human skeletal material and instruments that Sherwood Washburn called Hunter the best equipped undergraduate laboratory of physical anthropology in the United States. Keur also worked with the dean of students, advising students with special problems, particularly European refugees. Through generous grants from the Wenner-Gren Foundation, Keur administered a lecture series in anthropology at Hunter.

Keur was fully committed to the growth of anthropology at Hunter, which, along with Barnard, was for many years a pioneer in offering undergraduate courses in anthropology in New York City. Growth of anthropology at Hunter was not a problem of student enrollment; more significantly, the administration and many of the faculty did not recognize the academic validity of undergraduate anthropology courses.

Keur gave her energies largely to the development of undergraduate courses in anthropology, which she saw as vital in dispelling the rampant racism of her times. In both physical and cultural courses, she stressed the biological unity of Homo sapiens and the role of culture in human behavior, an area in which she had been well trained by Boas. In addition, she lectured on these topics to student clubs and community organizations. At the same time she was deeply interested in the careers of women anthropologists, many of whom lived and worked in the greater New York area, as well as others elsewhere who shared her research interests. Among those who were important as role models and/or support people were Ruth Benedict,* Ruth Bunzel,* Frederica de Laguna,* Erna Gunther,*

Margaret Mead,* Elsie Clews Parsons.* Gladys Reichard,* Elsie Steedman, and Gene Weltfish.*

Dorothy Keur retired from Hunter College in 1965, and John retired a year later from Brooklyn College. Apart from interesting interludes of travel, the Keurs now divide their time between their log cabin in Montana and their apartment in Riverdale. Keur still lectures, occasionally teaches a few courses, and attends professional meetings. She coauthored an oral history project with a Montana friend and published *Jerkline to Jeep: A Brief History of the Upper Boulder* (Keur and Staunton 1975).

In evaluating the role of anthropology in her life, Keur says, "It seems to me, at this vantage point of age and experience, that being an anthropologist gives one a special point of view, carrying a certain responsibility, but withal is a boon and a joy."

Note

1. It is to Dorothy L. Keur that I offer my deepest thanks for her untiring help and interest throughout the development of this chapter. She is a most generous and understanding woman and one worthy of the title Anthropologist. Unless otherwise noted, all quotes are from personal interviews with Dorothy Keur.

Works by Dorothy Louise Keur

1939   The Indians of Manhattan. *School Nature League Bulletin*, no. 5, series 9.

1940   New Light on Navajo Origins. *Transactions of the New York Academy of Sciences*. Pp. 182–87. New York: New York Academy of Science.

1941   *Big Bead Mesa: An Archaeological Study of Navaho Acculturation 1745–1812*. Society for American Archaeology, Memoir No. 1.

1944   A Chapter in Navaho-Pueblo Relations. *American Antiquity* 10 (1): 75–86.

1946–50   Articles. In *The Yearbook of the World Scope Encylopedia*. Archaeology, 1946, 1947. Anthropology and Archaeology, 1948, 1949, and 1950.

1960   Metropolitan Influences in the Caribbean; The Netherlands Antilles. *Annals of the New York Academy of Sciences* 83: Article 5.

1964a   The Nature of Recent Change in the Dutch Windward Islands. *International Journal of Comparative Sociology* (March). Vol. 5:40–48. Karnatak University, India.

1964b   Settlement Patterns on Land Newly Reclaimed from the Sea, in the Netherlands. In *Proceedings of the Seventh International Congress of Anthropological and Ethnological Sciences*. Moscow.

1969a   Windward Islands. In *Encyclopedia Nederlandse Antillen*, The Netherlands.

1969b   Social Stratification and Mobility. In *Encyclopedia Nederlandse Antillen*, The Netherlands.

1969c   Marriage and the Family. In *Encyclopedia Nederlandse Antillen*, The Netherlands.

1969d   Ethnic and Cultural Diversity. In *Encyclopedia Nederlandse Antillen*, The Netherlands.

Coauthored Works

Keur, Dorothy, and John Y. Keur

1955   *The Deeply Rooted: A Study of a Drents Community in the Netherlands*. American Ethnological Society, Monograph No. 25. Also, Assen, The Netherlands: Van Gorcum.

1960   *Windward Children: A Study in Human Ecology of the Three Dutch Windward Islands in the Caribbean*. Assen, The Netherlands: Van Gorcum.

Keur, Dorothy, and Russel La Due

1978   Univaria. In *Cultures of the Future*. Magorah Maruyama and Arthur M. Harkins, eds. Pp. 593–612. The Hague: Mouton.

Keur, Dorothy, and Ruth Staunton

1975   *Jerkline to Jeep: A Brief History of the Upper Boulder*. Harlowton, Montana: The Times Clarion.

ALICE JAMES

Theodora Kracaw Kroeber

(1897–1979)

Anthropologist and writer Theodora Kracaw Kroeber was best known for her interpretations of California Indian life and folklore.

Theodora Kracaw was born on March 24, 1897, in Denver and grew up in the gold and silver mining town of Telluride, in southwestern Colorado. She was the third child of parents who were proprietors of a general store, wholesalers to the mines and retailers to the citizenry. Life in Telluride was shaped "by its remoteness, its self-dependence; by the cosmopolitanism and the old-worldness of many of its people and customs"; and by its relative lack of age-gradedness (Kroeber 1970:128).

According to family lore, Theodora Kracaw's paternal ancestors were Protestants from Krakow, Poland, who emigrated to Germany in the eighteenth century and sojourned in England before settling in Baltimore, Maryland. Her mother, Phebe Johnston Kracaw, had grown up on a ranch in Wyoming. Her parents' marriage, Theodora Kroeber wrote later, "was a mating of congenial opposites: Phebe was outgoing and robust, Charles introverted and somewhat fragile" (Kroeber 1970:124).

All three of the Kracaw children were educated in the small but excellent Telluride schools, from which Kracaw's brothers, five and ten years older than she, went on to become physicians. She later regarded her childhood as a happy and protected one in a family in which she was the only young female.

In 1915, the year Kracaw graduated from high school, she and her parents moved to Orland, California, in the Sacramento Valley, because the lower elevation was thought to be better for her father's health. There, faced with business reverses and threatened with tuberculosis and blindness, he took his own life in 1917.

Theodora Kracaw had, meanwhile, enrolled at the University of California at Berkeley in 1915. At first she planned to major in English literature, then turned to economics, but finally decided on psychology in her senior year because her friend Jean Macfarlane was absorbed in it. Macfarlane, who was to become a professor of psychology at Berkeley, also became a lifelong friend, as did several other women Kracaw met during her undergraduate years. Later she maintained that although she liked individual women, she had "never taken to women en masse. . . . I imagine that my early situation had a lot to do with that. I have always been shy; I have always been introverted" (Kroeber 1982:21).

As an undergraduate, Theodora Kracaw took a beginning course in anthropology, not with A. L. Kroeber, who was head of the department at Berkeley, but with his ebullient assistant, Thomas T. Waterman. Graduating cum laude in 1919, she continued with graduate study in psychology at Berkeley. Her master's thesis in 1920 was on ten San Francisco families, each of them clients of the juvenile court. Working as a volunteer probation officer responsible for visiting and reporting on these families, she found it difficult to write objectively about them (Kroeber 1982).

The same year she received her M.A. degree, she married Clifton Spencer Brown, a graduate student of law at Berkeley. Clifton was in poor health in the aftermath of pneumonia contracted in France in World War I. The young couple nevertheless had two children, Clifton, Jr., and Theodore, before Clifton died in Santa Fe, New Mexico, in October 1923. Returning to Berkeley with her small sons, the young widow moved into the home of her widowed mother-in-law, who urged her to return to graduate work at the university, as she did in 1924.

The months she and Clifton had spent in the milieu of Santa Fe, and especially her purchase of a small string of turquoise beads, aroused her interest in American Indians and in art; she had received her "first directing breath" toward her new world (Kroeber 1982:198). Deciding to pursue anthropology at Berkeley, she had a conference on her course of study with Kroeber, who was about to leave on an archaeological expedition to Peru. On his return, she took seminars with him.

One of her fellow students, Julian Steward, later recalled Kracaw or Krakie, as an "attractive widow." "In Kroeber's seminar during the spring of 1926 she and I were assigned jointly the problem of working out element distributions on North American Indian hockey and other field games. I was never quite sure what became of our intellectual endeavors, for Kroeber continued this seminar for many years to train students in organizing data. The semester, however, terminated in the marriage of Kroeber and Krakie, to the delight of everyone. This marriage was one of the happiest I have ever seen" (Steward 1961:1047). Steward also noted that Theodora Kroeber was the "perfect anthropologist's wife."

In June, leaving her two young sons with her mother, Theodora and Alfred Kroeber embarked on an eight-month field trip to Peru, a new experience for Theodora Kroeber, who had never been on shipboard, had never camped out, and had never been on a dig. They and their hired crews dug principally at sites in the Nazca Valley, which proved to be as crucial to an understanding of the

Peruvian archaeological record as Kroeber had expected (Kroeber 1970). Theodora Kroeber's contribution was "style recognition and cataloging of sherds and specimens *in situ*," according to a vita she compiled in the late 1950s.

Alfred Kroeber, like Theodora, had had a brief, earlier marriage, to Henriette Rothschild of Oakland, California, who died of tuberculosis in 1913. Twenty-one years Theodora's senior, Kroeber was already established in his profession, known particularly for his surveys of California Indian cultures and languages and for his detailed studies of the Yurok of the northern coast and the Mohave of the southeastern desert. He encouraged her to continue work on her doctorate, but she felt she could not manage more responsibilities. Besides her two sons by her first marriage, whom Alfred Kroeber adopted, the Kroebers had two children of their own, Karl and Ursula. All three sons became academics, and their daughter became Ursula K. Le Guin, the noted fiction writer. Theodora Kroeber had no regrets about having left the doctoral program, commenting that she did not have ambition "in a public sense of ambition" (Kroeber 1982:101). As for Kroeber, she said, marriage and fatherhood helped "untie" a man who had been "diffident" and "difficult" in his earlier years and of whom many people had been afraid (Kroeber 1982:150, 159).

The Kroebers spent relaxed summers in an old farmhouse they bought in the hills above the Napa Valley, north of Berkeley. There, besides their anthropologist friends, they frequently had Indian visitors, especially Juan Dolores, a longtime Papago friend of Kroeber's, and Robert Spott, a young Yurok. During one of Spott's visits, he recounted to Theodora Kroeber the previously unrecorded Yurok legend that was to become the leading narrative in her first book, *The Inland Whale* (Kroeber 1959). She came to know other Yurok when, in the early years of her marriage to Kroeber, she accompanied him on field trips to the Klamath River. Later, in the 1950s, she went with him to visit the Mohave. She was to draw on her firsthand knowledge of these two tribes in coauthoring *Almost Ancestors* (Kroeber and Heizer 1968) and in writing her foreword to Kroeber's *Yurok Myths* (1976b).

Theodora Kroeber did not begin to write seriously until her children were grown and Kroeber had retired. In 1955–56, when the couple spent a year at the Center for Advanced Study in the Behavioral Sciences at Stanford, she wrote a full-length novel about Telluride, which has never been published but which established in her the habit of writing a passage, long or short, every day. She and her daughter, Ursula, in fact began writing about the same time (Kroeber 1982).

Alfred and Theodora Kroeber collaborated on only two papers, both of them stylistic analyses of English poetry (Kroeber and Kroeber 1961, 1970). Each was a superb stylist—Alfred Kroeber having a bent toward the classical and restrained, she toward the personal and intense. It was these qualities that made her anthropological writings attractive to general readers.

In *The Inland Whale* she retold a number of California Indian folktales in her own idiom, having selected, not the best-known tales, but those with a heroine and those bearing the stamp of one individual's originality. In her literary and psychological analysis of these selections, she wrote, "My tentative guess is that the budding, creating element in oral literature may well lie within the unique tale, invented by a single person, and tangential to the great, conventionalized, and channeled main stream of a people's literary *corpus* and tradition" (Kroeber 1959:157). Walter Goldschmidt, in reviewing the book, said that Theodora Kroeber had "rendered her stories amenable to the literate Westerner without knowledge of ethnology by cutting detail, eliminating endless repetition, sharpening the sense of plot and denouement, and above all by translating freely in her own sensitive, almost lyrical style" (Goldschmidt 1959:1153).

Theodora Kroeber spent the next two years immersed in the anthropological literature on Ishi, the sole survivor of the Yahi group, who in 1911 had been found starving in the Sacramento Valley town of Oroville. This last "wild Indian" of California had been, at A. L. Kroeber's request, brought to San Francisco by T. T. Waterman and housed in the University of California's Museum of Anthropology, where the two anthropologists befriended him but were not able to guard him from tuberculosis, which killed him in 1916. Realizing that Kroeber could not bring himself to write a full account of Ishi, Theodora shouldered the responsibility in *Ishi in Two Worlds* (Kroeber 1961). In this work she narrated the destruction of the Yahi by white settlers and Ishi's essentially solitary but courageous later years, first in the Mt. Lassen foothills and then in the urban museum. Writing this account was so painful a task that Theodora Kroeber was "very late coming to any real pleasure in it" (Kroeber 1982:308). Nevertheless, it was this book that established her reputation; it was an immediate best-seller in the United States and was translated into eight European languages and Japanese. It has become a modern classic. Her readers found, as had her publisher, August Frugé, that she had the gift of "making us part of a life we never took part in, of allowing our presence where we never were, of raising up a gone world" (Kroeber 1982:iii). The children's version of *Ishi* (Kroeber 1964) was even more difficult for Theodora Kroeber to write because of the challenge of presenting the subject of death to American children, who are shielded from it (Kroeber 1982).

Between the writing of two versions of *Ishi*, A. L. Kroeber had died. Confronted with his loss, Theodora Kroeber wrote her last major work, *Alfred Kroeber: A Personal Configuration* (1970), a sensitive biography with her inimitable phraseology and setting of mood, though not entirely reliable as to dates.

During this period she collaborated with Robert F. Heizer, a younger Berkeley anthropologist and friend, on two pictorial histories of California Indians. The first, *Almost Ancestors* (1968), consisted of over one hundred early photographic portraits with Kroeber's accompanying text. The second, *Drawn from Life* (1976), also with her text, reproduced Europeans' and white Americans' drawings and paintings of Indians from the period before 1880. In *Almost Ancestors* Kroeber described the three major physical types found among the 500 Californian tribes, gave a brief overview of their cultures, and told how they had been nearly extinguished. In her preface she remarked on the poor quality of the original plates and prints reproduced in the volume and went on to answer her own question: "Why offer so flawed and partial a record? It is all the record there is. . . . We believe you will see through the pictures, imperfect as they are, to the living human beings who sat for them" (1968:11).

In 1969 Theodora Kroeber married John H. Quinn (1940–   ), an artist and art psychotherapist; and in 1976 she wrote a frank article for a West Coast quarterly on the differing reactions of men and women to, first, the young wife of an older husband and, second, the old wife of a younger husband. In an interview for her oral history, she commented, "The age of a person is the least important thing to me" (Kroeber 1982:204).

Kroeber regarded herself as an "old thirties liberal." She voted Democratic all her life (Kroeber 1982:218) and participated in peace marches in her later years. In 1977 she was appointed a regent of the University of California to fill an unexpired term of nearly a year. Her last act in office was to present a memorandum to her fellow regents protesting the university's involvement in nuclear weapons research (reproduced in Kroeber 1982).

Among her last writings were her forewords (1976b and 1980) to two previously unpublished manuscripts of Yurok and Karok myths, which Alfred Kroeber had collected in northern California in the first decade of the twentieth century. In these she briefly described the almost identical cultures of the two tribes, discussed Kroeber's recording methods and the organization of the collections, and (in the second foreword) paid generous tribute to Edward W. Gifford, a later collector of myths and formulas among the Karok. She told of Yurok and Karok she had personally known, especially the old women, "soul-warming and impressive" (Kroeber 1980:xxvi).

Theodora Kroeber's great strength was as an interpreter of one culture to another. She showed the general reader, who might never read an academic work in anthropology, that California Indian history was inexorably "part of our own history. We have absorbed their lands into our holdings. Just so must we be the responsible custodians of their tragedy, absorbing it into our tradition and morality" (Kroeber 1961:i).

References and Works About Theodora Kroeber

Elsasser, Albert B.
1980   Theodora Kroeber-Quinn, 1897–1979. *American Anthropologist* 82:114–15.
Frugé, August
1982   Introduction. *Theodora Kroeber-Quinn: Timeless Woman, Writer, and Interpreter of the California Indian World.* Anne Brower, interviewer. Pp. i–iii. Berkeley: Regional Oral History Office, Bancroft Library, University of California.
Goldschmidt, Walter
1959   Review of *The Inland Whale* by Theodora Kroeber. *American Anthropologist* 61:1153–54.

Mandelbaum, David G.
1979–80   Memorial to Theodora Kroeber Quinn. *Journal of California and Great Basin Anthropology* 1–2:237–39.
Steward, Julian
1961   Alfred Louis Kroeber, 1876–1960. *American Anthropologist* 63:1038–60.

Selected Works by Theodora Kroeber

1920   A Case Study of Ten Juvenile Court Families with Particular Emphasis on the Psychological Interpretation of the Problems Presented. Unpublished M.A. thesis. Department of Psychology, University of California, Berkeley.

1959   *The Inland Whale*. Bloomington: Indiana University Press. (Second printing, 1963, University of California Press.)

1961   *Ishi in Two Worlds: A Biography of the Last Wild Indian in North America*. Berkeley: University of California Press.

1962   The Hunter, Ishi. *American Scholar* 31:408–18.

1963   About History. *Pacific Historical Review* 32:1–6.

1964   *Ishi: The Last of His Tribe*. Berkeley: Parnassus Press.

1967   *A Green Christmas*. Berkeley: Parnassus Press.

1970   *Alfred Kroeber: A Personal Configuration*. Berkeley: University of California Press.

1972   Literature of the First Americans. In *Look to the Mountain Top*. Charles Jones, ed. Pp. 13–18. San Jose, Calif.: Gousha Publishing.

1976a   Cross-Generation Marriage. *Co-Evolution Quarterly*, no. 11, pp. 102–6.

1976b   Foreword. *Yurok Myths* by A. L. Kroeber. Pp. xiii–xvii. Grace Buzaljko, ed. Berkeley: University of California Press.

1977   *Carrousel*. New York: Atheneum Press.

1978   *The Two Elizabeths*. Privately printed. Typescript reproduced in *Theodora Kroeber-Quinn* (1982).

1979   *Theodora* (self-obituary). Privately printed, Berkeley. Reproduced in *Theodora Kroeber-Quinn* (1982).

1980   Foreword. *Karok Myths* by A. L. Kroeber and E. W. Gifford. Pp. xv–xxx. Grace Buzaljko, ed. Berkeley: University of California Press.

1982   *Theodora Kroeber-Quinn: Timeless Woman, Writer, and Interpreter of the California Indian World*. Transcript of oral history conducted 1976–78 by Anne Brower. Regional Oral History Office, Bancroft Library, University of California at Berkeley.

Coauthored Works

Kroeber, Theodora, Forrest E. Clements, and Sarah M. Schenck
1926   A New Objective Method for Showing Special Relationships. *American Anthropologist* 28:585–604.
Kroeber, Theodora, Albert B. Elsasser, and Robert F. Heizer
1976   *Drawn from Life: California Indians in Pen and Brush*. Socorro, New Mex.: Ballena Press.
Kroeber, Theodora, and Robert F. Heizer
1968   *Almost Ancestors: The First Californians*. San Francisco: Sierra Club.

Kroeber, Theodora, and Robert F. Heizer
1979   *Ishi, the Last Yahi: A Documentary History*. Berkeley: University of California Press. (As eds.)
Kroeber, Theodora, and A. L. Kroeber
1961   Shropshire Revisited. *Kroeber Anthropological Society Papers*, no. 25. Pp. 1–17.
Kroeber, Theodora, Karl Kroeber, and A. L. Kroeber
1970   Life Against Death in English Poetry: A Method of Stylistic Definition. *Transactions of the Wisconsin Academy of Sciences, Arts and Letters* 57:29–40.

GRACE WILSON BUZALJKO

Hilda Beemer Kuper

(1911–   )

Social anthropologist trained in South Africa and England, Hilda Beemer Kuper
is known especially for her studies on the Swazi, as well as the urban African
population in Johannesburg and the East Indians in Natal.

Born on August 23, 1911, in Bulawayo, a trading town in the British colony
of Rhodesia, Africa, Hilda Beemer was the youngest of five children. Her parents,
Joseph Beemer from Lithuania and Antoinette Renner Beemer from Vienna,
immigrated to the developing colony in the period of British imperial expansion.
Hilda Beemer's interest in diverse peoples and issues was fostered early in her
childhood and youth in Africa, against the background of her immigrant heritage
and stories told to her of the Shona, Ndebele, and other native peoples of the
area.

When Hilda Beemer had just started school at age six, her father died. Her
mother subsequently moved the family to Johannesburg, a city she never came
to like. She completed her schooling in Johannesburg, developing an interest in
writing, which she thought she might be able to use in a career in the theater
or in law. Her interest in law arose from an increasing awareness of discrimination
and the plight of innocent victims: servants living in the backyard, the brutal
treatment of blacks by whites, and her own Jewish heritage. In Bulawayo, where
the family had many non-Jewish friends, she was not aware of anti-Semitism;
but it became apparent to her in Johannesburg as she realized that nearly all of
the family friends were Jewish.

In her family, as in many others, the dividing interests of ethnic and nation-
alistic identity arose during the First World War. Members of her mother's
family had been conscripted and died on the German side, while her father's
side had identified with colonial pioneers for the British and celebrated their
victory. This experience painfully taught her at an early age the difficulties of
group identification and helped to shape her later interests within anthropology.

South Africa has produced many important anthropologists with whom Hilda

Beemer Kuper is identified. At school in Johannesburg she first met Max Gluck-man when she was fifteen. They shared an interest in law and went on to attend Witwatersrand University at the same time. On the casual advice of a friend, she and Gluckman took an anthropology class from Winifred Tucker Hoernle, which had a profound effect on Hilda Beemer.[1] Through it, she came to view cruelty, injustice, and inequality "from an intellectual as well as emotional perspective, and . . . began to understand how, why, and where it could hap-pen."[2]

Hoernle's introductory class covered major approaches in anthropology at the time: evolutionism, diffusionism, Radcliffe-Brown's perspective on social or-ganization derived from Durkheim, along with ethnographies by Franz Boas, Robert Lowie, and Henri Junod. Hilda Beemer studied Durkheim's works very thoroughly in their original French, which she found considerably more stimu-lating than the English translations.

While still an undergraduate, Beemer undertook field research among the Indian population in Johannesburg; and later, working at the Institute of Race Relations, she researched the effect of racially restrictive liquor laws on women. In exploring the economic aspect of the women's liquor-brewing activities, she found they were vague about their money—it seemed to flow in constant exchange of support networks through borrowing and membership in voluntary associa-tions. She joined one of the associations herself (Kuper and Kaplan 1944b). All of this early work was "applied" in the sense that it addressed current problems and social issues.

In Hilda Beemer's third year, Isaac Schapera replaced Hoernle for a year and took a group of students—including Gluckman, Ellen Hellman, Camilla Wedg-wood,* and Hilda Beemer—on a field trip to Mochudi in Bechuanaland (now Botswana). They observed Schapera intensively interviewing informants, a field-work style that contrasted with Malinowski's participant observation methods about which they had studied. Despite their contrasting styles, Schapera was largely influential in sending Kuper to study with Malinowski.

Having finished her baccalaureate with honors in anthropology and French, Hilda Beemer set off for the London School of Economics (LSE) at the age of twenty-one to pursue a doctorate. Malinowski was the undisputed master in British anthropology during her period of study at LSE (1932–34). His seminars, in which he expounded on his brand of functionalism, attracted scholars from all parts of the world. He was sometimes challenged by Meyer Fortes, S. F. Nadel, and S. S. Hofstra, who openly disagreed with his approach, arguing that it was tautological. Malinowski provocatively dubbed this group the "Man-darins," after the scholarly class in China. The young student found that the occasionally sharp interchanges with the Mandarins and the constant exchange of ideas heightened her critical awareness. She initially agreed wholeheartedly with Malinowski's views but later accepted the Mandarins' critiques. She dis-agreed openly with Malinowski on the importance of history. Malinowski, like Radcliffe-Brown, rejected the value of speculative history of "primitive" peoples, whereas Hilda Beemer, once she began fieldwork among the Swazi, realized that their history was part of current reality. Despite Malinowski's insistence on loyalty from his students, "he took it well." Indeed, she had worked very closely with him as his research assistant on *Coral Gardens and Their Magic*, and felt fortunate that he was able to accompany her on her first field trip to the Swazi.

At the time she began her fieldwork, Swaziland was a British High Commission Territory. The Swazi population was an amalgamation of Bantu-speaking peoples resulting from migration and conquest in the sixteenth century by the royal clan, the Nkosi Dlamini. She first met the young Swazi king, Sobhuza II, at a conference on education in Johannesburg. Having an interest in anthropology, he agreed to her study. Thus began a lifelong friendship and respect between the two, which culminated in his appointing her as his official biographer. He authorized her work in the field; she states that she could never have succeeded without his support. He introduced her to family and Swazi notables, gave public instruction to cooperate with her, and assigned one of his own followers to be her assistant. Nevertheless, "In spite of Sobhuza's friendship—in some cases even because of it—the general attitude towards me, particularly in the early months, was one of suspicion and even fear. . . . To most Swazi I was *umlungu*, a white, who had to prove herself before she could be received as *umuntu*, a person" (Kuper 1963:5). Her efforts in learning the language greatly increased her "personhood" in Swazi eyes.

When Hilda Beemer Kuper went to the field, she intended to produce a general ethnography (Kuper 1947a:5) or a study of the changing role of the magician (Kuper 1984:200), but she decided to concentrate on rank and power and black-white relationships in her major publications. In *An African Aristocracy* (Kuper 1947a) and *The Uniform of Colour* (Kuper 1947b), the break with Malinowski in approaching her analysis of Swazi society within a historical framework can be clearly seen.

Owing in part to illness, she spent ten years writing up the material. Originally intended as one study, the works were published separately because of the shortage of paper following World War II. *An African Aristocracy* deals with the effects of the historical conquest by the Dlamini clan, and the formation of the Swazi state. She argued that the clan system, and its system of ranking, was the "dominant orientation" of the society. Birth rank determined access to office and power, and it ordered all members of the society in their productive and ritual lives. *The Uniform of Colour* focuses on the historical period of European domination. In this work she shows how skin color, as the manifestation of changed political and economic reality, was imposed over the indigenous system of clan ranking and power relationships, which had persisted symbolically, if not effectively, through a policy of accommodation by the Swazi king during nineteenth-century European colonialism. In this work, actors in a racially and culturally diverse state are analyzed from the point of view that they are operating within a single social system. Again departing from Malinowski, she did not make a concerted effort to provide a functional explanation of major elements of Swazi culture. She did, however, work at establishing how rank operated through all aspects of social life, arguing that rank itself was a dynamic relationship, changing with time and circumstances.

Kuper (1984) wrote that she had developed an interest in Marxism in her student days, although she turned away from the tendency among some Marxists toward economic determinism to concentrate on power relationships. However, the importance she places on the material conditions of life can be seen in her discussions of labor and the problems of the land-poor peasantry (Kuper 1947b). Her approach in *An African Aristocracy* was also influenced by the early American work in psychological anthropology. However, she criticized the Americans' approach as an oversimplification, reducing an entire culture to terms of individual personality. She tried to change the focus of this approach to social institutions—the ranking system—indicating variations in behavior and thought associated with them.

Reviewers have praised her work for its ethnographic detail and for her theoretical insights. Gluckman (1948) points out the importance of her illumination of the cogent role of women, and particularly of the Queen Mother, within a complex African state. For example, Kuper states that although the Swazi have a strictly patrilineal society, "power is inherited from men, and acquired by them; but it is transmitted through women, whose rank, more than any other single factor, determines the choice of successor" (Kuper 1947a:91).

In another major work, *Indian People in Natal* (1960), Kuper again provides significant ethnographic description of and analytical insight into a population with a very different history from the Swazi. While exploring initial problems in health patterns of the Indian population that differed significantly from Africans and Coloreds in similar socioeconomic circumstances, Kuper focused on the changing kinship system and family patterns within the context of an altered caste system. She found that, given patterns of migration as indentured servants (for the most part) and the lack of political enfranchisement within the South African policies of apartheid (instituted in 1950), Indians developed numerous voluntary associations to promote their interests. This book remains an important source on overseas Indian populations for researchers concerned with migration, politics, and adaptation patterns, as well as for those whose focus is on South Asian social institutions.

From the ethnographic insights of her many publications, the humanistic emphasis in her approach is perhaps most evident in her fiction writing. In her novel, *Bite of Hunger* (1965b); her play, *A Witch in My Heart* (1970); and her short stories set among the Swazi, the tensions and conflicts that are addressed in academic publications come to life through fictional characters.

Although Kuper does not consider herself a feminist—she is concerned for all human rights, not just on the basis of gender or color—her fictional works allowed her to write about women and the problems that faced them in a changing society. Perhaps one incident sums up the effectiveness of her writing in this genre. After a play she had written about East Indians ("The Decision," unpublished) had been produced by some students in Natal, three Indian couples, husband and wife, approached her and said that they were going to sue her. "Why?" she asked. "Because you had no right to write about our families," they said. "But I don't know you," she replied.

Family life and career were intertwined with her continuing professional involvement in Swaziland. She married Leo Kuper in 1935, during her first fieldwork experience. She had met him while at Witwatersrand University. He was practicing law at the time of their marriage, later taking his doctorate in sociology. Their marriage caused some consternation at the International African Institute, which was sponsoring her fieldwork. The institute had a policy that married women refund any money they had received, on the assumption that they would end their fieldwork and careers. When the institute inquired about this, she responded that she had no intention of ending her career.

Kuper has held academic appointments at Witwatersrand University (Senior Lecturer 1940–45), University of North Carolina (Visiting Lecturer 1947–49), University of Natal, Durban (Senior Lecturer 1959–62), and the University of California at Los Angeles (Professor 1963–78, Professor Emeritus 1978–present). She has also received a variety of awards: Rivers Memorial Medal, Simon Senior Research Fellowship at Manchester University (1958–59), Guggenheim Fellowship 1969–70, Center for Advanced Studies in the Behavioral Sciences Fellowship (Palo Alto, California, 1976–77), and the Medal of the Royal Order of Sobhuza II, Counsellor (1982), among others. Sobhuza granted her Swaziland citizenship following independence in 1970, after she had been denied by the British because she did not "fit" into any of the eligibility categories.

While working in South Africa in the 1950s, both she and Leo were involved in the passive resistance movement and the consequent development of the Liberal party. Leo was head of the Sociology Department at the university, where the atmosphere was tense and spies were present in the classrooms. Hilda Kuper, working as a Senior Research Fellow for the National Council of Social and Industrial Research and deeply involved in her research on the Indian population, participated in a massive women's protest when the apartheid pass laws were extended to women.

Kuper had come to feel "rooted" in Swaziland; however, her daughters Jenny (born in 1948 in North Carolina) and Mary (born in 1949 in South Africa) did not grow up there and did not meet Sobhuza until they were teenagers. Kuper feels that the uprooted existence of the anthropologist, particularly with a lifelong involvement in another place and culture, might have been difficult for her children while they were growing up.

Her strong commitment to Swaziland can further be seen in her work on Sobhuza's official biography. There were many difficulties on this project: working under the direction of a committee, the loss of voluminous notes "accidentally" shipped through South Africa, and dealing with politically sensitive material. Despite these obstacles, the biography was successfully completed. In speaking of Sobhuza, Kuper does not regret her full support of his personal leadership of the Swazi. She felt, and still feels, that he was a fine leader in the effort to free his people from the subjugation of colonial powers. At the same time, the traditional system of strong councilors checking absolute power had dissolved by the time of his death, and the power and intrigues of members of the royal clan have led to a complex situation in the modern state (see the 1986 edition of *The Swazi*).

While working at the Institute of Race Relations, upon finishing her baccalaureate, the director remarked to Kuper that she faced two disadvantages: first, that she is a woman, and second, that she is Jewish. She replied, "Well, that might be to my advantage." Her awareness of inequality and interest in its eradication, for both women and men, for all ethnic groups, might be said to stem from her lifelong determination to overcome these "disadvantages."

Notes

1. Winifred Tucker Hoernle was one of the first trained female social anthropologists to do fieldwork, beginning in 1912 among Khoi-Khoi peoples, specifically with Nama Hottentots. For further information, see Carstens 1985.

2. All quotes not otherwise cited are from Hilda Kuper, personal communication. I would like to thank Professor Kuper for her generosity and patience in working with me on this biography. I would also like to thank Professor Nancy E. Levine, Thom Ward, and the editors of this volume, particularly Aisha Khan, for their support.

References and Works About Hilda B. Kuper

1969   Kuper, Hilda Beemer. In *CA* (1st revision). Ethridge, J. M., and B. Kopala, eds. Vol. 1–4, p. 557. Detroit: Gale Research Co.
Gluckman, Max
1948   Review of *An African Aristocracy* by Hilda Kuper. *Africa* 18 (1): 63–64.
Langness, L., and G. Frank
1981   *Lives: An Anthropological Approach to Biography.* (Brief biographical sketch and an interview with H. Kuper, pp. 139–54.) Novato, Calif.: Chandler & Sharp.

Selected Works by Hilda B. Kuper

(Under the name Hilda Beemer)
1935   The Swazi Rainmaking Ceremony. *Bantu Studies* 9:273–80.
1937   The Development of the Military Organization in Swaziland. *Africa* 10 (2): 55–74; (3): 176–205.
(Under the name Hilda Beemer Kuper)
1941   The Development of a Primitive Nation. *Bantu Studies* 15: 341–68.
1945   Social Anthropology As a Study of Culture Contact. *South African Journal of Science* 41:88–101.
1946   The Swazi Reaction to Missions. *African Studies* 5 (3): 177–88.
1947a   *An African Aristocracy: Rank Among the Swazi.* London: Oxford University Press for the International African Institute (I.A.I.).

1947b *The Uniform of Colour*. Johannesburg: Witwatersrand University Press.

1950 Kinship Among the Swazi. In *African Systems of Kinship and Marriage*. A. R. Radcliffe-Brown and D. Forde, eds. Pp. 86–110. London: Oxford University Press for I.A.I.

1952 *The Swazi*. Ethnographic Survey of Africa, South Africa, Part 1. D. Forde, ed. London: I.A.I.

1955a The Shona. In *The Shona and Ndebele of Southern Rhodesia*. Pp. 9–40. Ethnographic Survey of South Africa. D. Forde, ed. London: I.A.I.

1955b Changes in Caste of South African Indians. *Race Relations Journal* 22 (4): 18–26.

1957a An Interpretation of Hindu Marriage Rituals in Durban. *African Studies* 16 (3): 221–35.

1957b The Amazement of Namahasha. *Africa South* 2 (1): 102–7.

1959 An Ethnographic Description of Kavady. *African Studies* 18 (3): 118–32.

1960 *Indian People in Natal*. Natal, S. Afr.: University Press.

1963 *The Swazi: A South African Kingdom*. New York: Holt, Rinehart and Winston. (Reprinted 1986, 2nd ed.)

1964 The Colonial Situation in Modern Africa. *Journal of Modern African Studies* 2 (2): 149–64.

1965a *Urbanization and Migration in Africa*. Edited and with an introduction. Berkeley: University of California Press.

1965b *Bite of Hunger, A Novel of Africa*. New York: Harcourt, Brace & World, Inc.

1967 Changes in Caste of the South African Indian. In *Caste in Overseas Indian Communities*. Barton M. Schwartz, ed. Pp. 237–65. San Francisco: Chandler Publishing Co.

1968a Celebration of Growth and Kingship: Incwala in Swaziland. *African Arts* 1 (3): 56–62, 90.

1969 Strangers in Plural Societies: Asians in South Africa and Uganda. In *Pluralism in Africa*. L. Kuper and M. G. Smith, eds. Pp. 247–82. Berkeley and Los Angeles: University of California Press.

1970 *A Witch in My Heart*. (Play with anthropological introduction.) London: Oxford University Press for I.A.I.

1971 Color Categories and Colonialism: The Swazi Case. In *Colonialism in Africa 1870–1960*. Victor Turner, ed. Vol. 3, pp. 286–309. Cambridge: Cambridge University Press.

1972a The Language of Sites in the Politics of Space. *American Anthropologist* 74 (3): 411–25.

1972b Royal Ritual in a Changing Political Context. *Cahiers d'études africaines* 12 (4): 593–615. `

1973a Clothing and Identity. *Comparative Studies of Social History* 16:348–67.

1973b Costume and Cosmology: The Animal Symbolism of the Ncwala. *Man* 8 (4): 613–30.

1976 Bird of the Storm. In *Essays on African Social Structure*. M. Fortes and S. Patterson, eds. Pp. 221–27. London and New York: Academic Press.

1978a The Monarchy and the Military. In *Social System and Tradition in Southern Africa*. J. Argyle and E. P. Whyte, eds. Pp. 222–39. Oxford: Oxford University Press.

1978b *Sobhuza II, Ngwenyama and King of Swaziland*. London: Duckworth. (Africana Publishing Company, U.S.A.)

1978c The Diviner and the Detective. In *Rite, Drama, Festival, Spectacle: Rehearsals Toward a Theory of Cultural Performance*. J. MacAloon, ed. Pp. 129–45. Philadelphia: ISHI.

1979   Schapera, Isaac. In *Biographical Supplement, International Encyclopaedia of the Social Sciences*. Vol. 18, pp. 694–97. New York: The Free Press.

1981a *Biography As Interpretation*. (Presented as the 11th annual Hans Wolf Memorial Lecture, 1980.) Bloomington: African Studies Program, Indiana University.

1981b Foreword. *Baba of Karo: A Woman of the Muslim Hausa* by Mary F. Smith. Pp. 7–10. New Haven: Yale University Press.

1984   Function, History, Biography: Reflections on Fifty Years in the British Anthropological Tradition. In *Functionalism Historicized: Essays on British Social Anthropology*. G. W. Stocking, Jr., ed. Vol. 2, *History of Anthropology*, pp. 192–213. Madison: University of Wisconsin Press.

Coauthored Works

Kuper, Hilda, and Selma Kaplan
1944b Voluntary Associations in an Urban Township. *African Studies* 3 (4): 178–86.
Kuper, L., and H. Kuper
1966   *Adaptation and Development of African Law*. Berkeley: University of California Press. (As eds.)

KATY MORAN

Carobeth Tucker Laird

(1895–1983)

Carobeth Tucker Laird was an American ethnographer and linguist, known especially for her efforts to preserve Chemehuevi language and mythology.

Laird, who received late recognition for her important contributions to anthropology and literature, began her career in 1919, when she accompanied the well-known linguist John Peabody Harrington on field trips through California and the Southwest. Even though she had collected a vast amount of ethnographic data on Chemehuevi culture and mythology for over twenty-three years, she did not publish until 1974.[1] The release of *The Chemehuevis* (1976) by Malki Museum Press established her reputation as a leading authority on the history and culture of the Chemehuevi people and facilitated the tribe's claims to aboriginal lands.[2]

Born on July 20, 1895, in Coleman, Texas, Carobeth Tucker was the only daughter of Methodist parents. Emma Cora Chaddock, her mother, and James Tucker, her father, had been married for twenty years before Carobeth was born. Tucker was an editor who operated a printing shop in Coleman, where he published a local democratic weekly, *The Voice*. An expert printer, he conceived the ambitious plan of publishing the Bible in Spanish to be distributed among Roman Catholics in Mexico (Laird, in press).

Laird has described her childhood in Texas as "introspective and overprotected" (Laird 1975a:ix). Although she read fluently at the age of five, her parents did not let her enter school until she was nine. She recalled being interested in writing at an early age. "When I was three years old, I didn't know my alphabet. I would sit down at my desk and cover pages and pages with scrawl, the same time repeating what I thought I was writing. Then I would give it all to my father and ask him to take it down to his newspaper office and print it into a book" (Cook 1978:34).

During the summer of 1909 Carobeth Tucker traveled with her parents to Mexico, where she discovered that she had a tremendous facility for languages. "It was in Mexico," she wrote, "that I first heard English spoken without a

Southern accent or flat Texas drawl, and it was then that I began my long love affair with the spoken as well as the written language" (*Contemporary Authors* 1983:557).

In Mexico City she fell in love with an older man whom the family had met on their trip. This brief romance ended without marriage and left Tucker with a child to support. After her first daughter Elisabeth was born, she moved with her family to San Diego in 1913. Faced with the responsibility of raising an infant, Tucker could not graduate from high school. While in San Diego, she spent many hours at the public library, bringing home "outdated books" on evolution and science. "I had come to believe that there were those who spent their lives in pursuit of the absolute truth, and I wanted above everything to belong to that elite band" (Laird 1975a:2).

After seeking the advice of the dean at the San Diego Normal School, she enrolled in their summer school program in Balboa Park to make up course deficiencies in mathematics and the social sciences. Of all the subjects she studied at the summer school in 1915, Tucker was most fascinated by a linguistics course taught by John Peabody Harrington, an eccentric linguist who was obsessed with recording the languages of Native Americans of the western United States. Harrington quickly noted Tucker's perfect ear for vowels, consonants, and dipthongs and trained her in the methodologies he employed. In 1916, soon after Harrington had joined the Bureau of American Ethnology (which employed him for forty years), they were married; and she joined him on his first field trips through California and the Southwest. For seven years (1916–23) she was more of an indentured servant than a wife to Harrington. Acting as his chauffeur and field assistant, she traveled with him from camp to camp and helped compile the vast amount of ethnographic notes he left behind.

Her autobiographical account of her life with Harrington, *Encounter with an Angry God* (1975a), is a wonderful testimony to the harsh realities of fieldwork during the formative years of American anthropology. Yet Harrington's passion for collecting as much information as possible from remaining Native American groups, at the expense of everyone who lived and worked with him, eventually contributed to the breakup of their marriage. While she lived with Harrington, she often longed for those things Harrington termed "artificial," such as regular baths or clean sheets. After becoming pregnant with her second child, she suggested that they might consider moving into a home with a yard. To Harrington this idea was outrageous; "children were scarcely people" and should be raised in dirt, he said. However, the possibility of "bringing up a child without ever talking to it or allowing it to hear human speech" appealed to him so that he could see what kind of language would evolve. After their daughter Awona was born, Harrington insisted that she wean the baby and leave the task of rearing her to her parents, who were already raising her first daughter, Elisabeth, in San Diego.

During the summer of 1919 Harrington sent his young wife alone to Parker, Arizona, where she met George Laird, a Chemehuevi Indian twenty years her senior. Laird (Wikontotsi), the son of Thompson Porter Laird (of Cherokee and Scottish descent) and Cloud Flower, a Chemehuevi woman, lived on the Colorado River Indian Reservation. Instructed by one of the elders in the use of pure southern Chemehuevi, Laird had participated in and witnessed old tribal ceremonies. Also fluent in Spanish, Mojave, and English, he became the principal consultant for her first book, *The Chemehuevis* and her later work *Mirror and Pattern* (1984).

After working with him for nearly four years, she divorced Harrington and married Laird. During twenty years of marriage they had five children and lived on a small ranch in Poway, near San Diego. George Laird worked as a miner and jack-of-all-trades, and they raised crops on their land. Laird, who had instructed his wife in the use of the Chemehuevi language, continued to dictate Chemehuevi texts depicting their myths and tribal history. Their daughter Georgia Laird Culp, a Chemehuevi leader, remembers seeing her parents recording late into the night, with her mother typing on a vintage Underwood and her father holding a kerosene lamp. This unusual consultant-ethnographer relationship, wrote Laird (1976), afforded her a more intimate, in-depth view of the culture than a scholarly work could offer. At the time of George Laird's death in 1940, Carobeth Laird had amassed the most complete collection of Chemehuevi myths ever recorded.

George Laird's sudden death left Carobeth Laird emotionally and financially destitute. While still pursuing her interests in Chemehuevi lore and culture, she supported herself and her family by working as a practitioner for the Christian Science Church until 1960. When Laird attempted to publish her manuscript on the Chemehuevis, she was discouraged by an anthropology professor at the University of California, Los Angeles, who described her ethnographic account as old-fashioned anthropology (Folkart 1983:22).

A series of medical disorders forced her to enter a nursing home in 1974. Although crippled by arthritis and a severe gastric disorder, she wrote a memoir of her dehumanizing experiences. *Limbo* (Laird 1979) is a frank account by a nursing home patient who, despite the staff's cruel and insensitive treatment, manages to keep her sanity and resourcefulness. This book also reminds the reader that the United States must find "a way to deal with its elderly population in a manner befitting its wealth and claim to civilization" (Laird 1979:2).

After her rescue from the nursing home by friends and relatives, Laird continued to write and lecture frequently at professional meetings in San Francisco, Sacramento, and Los Angeles. Confined to a wheelchair with a broken hip joint, she traveled to the University of Arizona in 1983 to receive an honorary doctorate in Humane Letters. At the time of her death, she was working on her third autobiography *Pilgrim and Stranger* (in press).

Carobeth Laird died on August 5, 1983, at her home in Poway. A memorial service conducted at Rancho Bernardo ended with a fitting quote from *The Chemehuevis*:

Modern Man has destroyed or outgrown the beliefs which he once accepted as verities, only to find, like Coyote, that life is scarcely worth living without the mystery and the magic, the dignity and the authority of Something beyond himself. Now, he runs on, blindly pursuing he knows not what, never reassured by the traditions and imprints of the past. (1976:235)

Carobeth Laird's contributions to the field of anthropology successfully combined ethnography and mythology. Thus, she believed that the principal culture carriers among the Chemehuevi were the songs and myths through which tribal memories as well as social mores were transmitted (Laird 1976). In Chemehuevi mythology the Coyote is the prototype of humankind; and as creator, he and his descendants Bat, Rattlesnake, Wolf, and Cottontail Rabbit set the pattern of social conduct. She theorized that myth originated when humans passed through their hunting and gathering stage. At that time the human mind was still open to consciousness, and there was no differentiation between the conscious and the unconscious mind. Everything that happened then, she explained, was perceived as real by the primal mind (Laird 1982).

In her assessment of the status of women among the Chemehuevi, Laird noted that women from early times never occupied a position of inferiority, that their voices were heard equally at gatherings, and that female shamans commanded the same respect as their male counterparts. She wrote that "during the early prehistory of the tribe when men could only produce small game, women were the main suppliers of food and their magic was in every way superior" (Laird 1976:235). Laird's last work, *Mirror and Pattern*, is a linguistic and structural analysis of Chemehuevi myths and language. The annotated text traces etymologies of words, discusses speech peculiarities, and illuminates the thought processes of those who spoke classical Chemehuevi.

The Carobeth Laird Collection of her field notes, tapes, and other memorabilia has been established at the University of California, Riverside, and a museum dedicated to Chemehuevi studies has been proposed.

Notes

1. After the discovery of Laird's manuscript on the Chemehuevis, Lowell Bean from California State University—Hayward arranged for its publication with Malki Museum.

2. The author wishes to thank Harry Lawton, Georgia Laird Culp, Jonathan Sharp, and Cliff Wurfel from Special Collections at the University of California, Riverside, for their cooperation during the preparation of this entry.

References and Works About Carobeth Laird

Bean, Lowell J.
1985   Memorial to Carobeth Laird (1895–1983). *Journal of California and Great Basin Anthropology* 7 (1): 3–6.

Contemporary Authors
1983   Laird, Carobeth. In *CA*. J. M. Ethridge and B. Kopala, eds. Vol. 1–4, p. 557. Detroit: Gale Research.
Cook, Arlene
1978   Carobeth Laird: Twilight Triumph. *Westways* (June):33–38.
Ellsberg, Helen
1976   Review of *Encounter with an Angry God. The Journal of San Diego History.* Pp. 63–64. San Diego: Serra Museum.
Folkart, Burt A.
1983   Writer, Discovered at 80, Dies at 87. *Los Angeles Times*, Aug. 10, p. 22.
Fowler, Catherine
1978   Review of *The Chemehuevis. The Journal of California Anthropology* 5:303–5.
James, Carollyn
1984   A Field Linguist Who Lived His Life for His Subjects. *Smithsonian* 15 (1): 153–74.
Swanson, Wayne
1983   Acclaim Tardy for Author-Anthropologist. *Los Angeles Times, San Diego County.* Part 5, August 23.

Selected Works by Carobeth Laird

1970   Medicine Dance (A Poem). *Chemehuevi Newsletter*, July, p. 7.
1974a The Buffalo in Chemehuevi Folklore. *The Journal of California Anthropology* 1 (2): 220–24.
1974b Chemehuevi Religious Beliefs and Practices. *The Journal of California Anthropology* 1 (1): 19–25.
1975a *Encounter with an Angry God: Recollections of My Life with John Peabody Harrington.* Banning, Calif.: Malki Museum Press.
1975b Two Chemehuevi Teaching Myths. *The Journal of California Anthropology* 2 (1): 18–24.
1976   *The Chemehuevis.* Banning, Calif.: Malki Museum Press.
1977a Intimation of Unity. *The Journal of California Anthropology* 4 (1): 50–54.
1977b Chemehuevi Myth as Social Commentary. *The Journal of California Anthropology* 4 (1): 191–95.
1977c Behavioral Patterns in Chemehuevi Myth. In *Flowers of the Wind: Papers on Ritual, Myth, and Symbolism in California and the Southwest.* Anthropological Papers No. 8. Thomas C. Blackburn, ed. Pp. 97–104. Socorro, New Mex.: Ballena Press.
1978a The Androgynous Nature of Coyote. *The Journal of California Anthropology* 5 (1):67–72.
1978b Origin of the Horse. *The Journal of California Anthropology* 5 (2): 251–55.
1979   *Limbo: A Memoir About Life in a Nursing Home by a Survivor.* Novato, Calif.: Chandler & Sharp.
1979–80   Chemehuevi Shamanism, Sorcery and Charms. *Journal of California and Great Basin Anthropology* 2 (1): 80–87.
1982   *Myths.* Audiotape recorded by Lynn Laredo at Southwest. Anthropological Assoc. (SWAA) Meetings, Sacramento, April 2. Special Collections, University of California, Riverside.

1984   *Mirror and Pattern: George Laird's World of Chemehuevi Mythology*. Banning, Calif.: Malki Museum Press.

In press   *Pilgrim and Stranger*. Novato, Calif.: Chandler and Sharp.

UTE GACS

Ruth Schlossberg Landes

(1908–   )

American social/cultural anthropologist Ruth Schlossberg Landes is known for her works on the social and religious life of Native North Americans (Ojibwa, Potawatomi, Sioux), studies of racial and ethnic groups, and pioneering work in the anthropology of education.

Daughter of an urbane New York labor leader, Ruth Schlossberg pursued her career in anthropology at the cost of a youthful marriage, yet with the full support of her parents. Her father, Joseph Schlossberg, was a self-educated immigrant who had grown to adolescence in Russia. He earned a graduate fellowship at Columbia University and lost it owing to leftist loyalties, was cofounder of the Amalgamated Clothing Workers of America, and devoted a long career as general secretary-treasurer of that union to writing on U.S. and international labor relations. Anna Grossman Schlossberg was born in the Ukraine, privately educated in Berlin, and migrated to New York City as a young adult. Ruth Schlossberg was the first child of a secularized Jewish household, and under its sponsorship she completed a B.S. degree (New York University) before she was twenty, and a masters of social work the following year. Her younger brother trained at Harvard and practiced law. Not content with a nascent career in social work, she embarked on research of her own—a new and unusual Negro-Jewish cult movement in Harlem—thereby meeting Franz Boas (by then, aged seventy-four) and Ruth Benedict* at Columbia. At their suggestion, she turned to anthropology. A crucial link was her father's longtime acquaintance with Alexander Goldenweiser, a fellow socialist, who recognized the anthropologist in her before she knew the academic discipline existed, and proposed she meet Boas.

The marriage from which Ruth Landes takes her professional surname began in 1929 but shortly foundered when she chose a career that her husband, a medical student, opposed. Today she writes:

I wept but could not change my mind. My parents did not try to dissuade me, though they tried to influence my husband. I did not marry for another 20 years and this too disintegrated over my scholarly way of life. I retained my first married name because divorce was then held severely or punitively against women.[1]

As it would turn out, personal independence (of the sort absolutely entailed in doing ethnographic work) under any name could be held against women, and this even within anthropology. But Landes's initial experience of the profession at Columbia disposed her rather to expect and eventually to insist on greater enlightenment.

Sympathetic to that interest in the condition of black Americans that had drawn Landes into anthropology, Boas and Benedict extended her circle of acquaintances among black intellectuals and gave her personal university research backing. Thus, her professional career began with the Harlem project, a study of the Garvey Movement as it led to establishment of a black Jewry (1929–32). The story was published as "Negro Jews in Harlem" (1967), but the original manuscript was lost amid early book-burnings in Nazi Germany. Boas had sent it in 1934 to his friend Richard Thurnwald, Africanist and editor of *Sociologus*. Much later, her further study of race relations would bring more crushing conflict with established interests, but her next turn was to a classic area of anthropology. She chose to do fieldwork among reservation Indians in Canada and the United States, and her informative reports from this period established her name among anthropologists of the next generation.

Landes's first fieldwork as an anthropologist in 1933 was among the Ojibwa of Ontario, where she hoped to "profit from a totally new experience." It was one she approached with trepidation. "In fact, through the next several years of fieldwork among three tribes of American Indians, I was in a constant state of tension but would not give up. My teachers never asked how I felt, though I was a very young innocent student; no one questioned the advisability of my living alone." By her twenty-eighth year she had completed the fieldwork, on which five published monographs were eventually based. *Ojibwa Sociology* (1937a) appeared the following year, *The Ojibwa Woman* (1938a) the next.

Thus, by age thirty Landes was a notably accomplished anthropologist. She had earned the Ph.D. from Columbia (1935) and developed her distinctive style in ethnography, a style as humanistic as that of Boas or Benedict, but one reflecting a distinctly pragmatic assessment of the social scientist's scope. For Landes, culture history and social structure are present in the acts, minds, and personalities she can observe, or they go lost. Accordingly, she returned to study relations of blacks and whites in urban centers rather than pursue, as another would have done, the field of Algonquian ethnohistory. It was therefore consistent, if hardly predictable, that her next vital move would bring her directly into contact with Robert E. Park, a pioneer in the study of race relations and advocate of direct observation as the method of sociology. Park was founder of the Chicago School, with which Landes had intuitively found herself in sympathy. She made contact with him through a personal friend. Park was in fact to be, briefly but effectively, her last mentor, and she perhaps the last notable student to have sought him out in his retirement. The fieldwork for which she wanted to prepare was a study of blacks in Brazil.

Because he liked her work, Park had invited Landes to Fisk University in Tennessee (where he had gone after the University of Chicago), where he was already examining the loosely structured context of race relations in Brazil with his student Donald Pierson. Landes taught at Fisk (1937–38), learning firsthand about the color bar in the southern United States and preparing at a distance to study the position of blacks in a very different American context. But the resulting monograph was not easy to produce. To the now-familiar stress of managing alone in the field, new dimensions were added, which Landes has chronicled in an extended account (Landes 1970a). Whereas an American male field-worker, Donald Pierson, had worked without hindrance in Bahia during 1935–37—penetrating the Afro-Brazilian candomble cults so successfully as to be taken on as *ogan* (a sort of all-purpose acolyte) by one of the male-cult-leaders, Landes found that gender rules affecting her in Bahia made a corresponding penetration of cults led by women quite impossible. As a female of the upper class, in Bahia, she was required to be escorted by an appropriate male of the same class. What made fieldwork possible at all was her great good fortune in forming a team with a Brazilian scholar-journalist who had for some years been defending the candomble sects, determined to establish them with constitutional rights. Edison Carneiro was of the right gender and class. As a mulatto, an esteemed folklorist, and engagé journalist, he moved easily into the world of cult leaders and their followers. Beyond his talents as master informant and as a tactical adviser for coping with Bahia's proto-Nazi secret police, Carneiro had the character and civility of a peerless co-worker. In ten months a great deal of work was accomplished.

The field study became notorious in provincial, conservative circles and began to earn the two anthropologists open verbal abuse from the local military establishment. Landes found herself labeled "communist" (by reason of ties with Columbia University), and at last the project succumbed to police espionage and provocative intervention. The team found refuge in Rio de Janeiro and with the advantage of influential friends there, broadened their work with a study of the macumba cults in this rather different region of Brazil. Then Boas and Benedict called Landes home for a research job with Gunnar Myrdal.

World War II delayed work on the book about Brazil, but at least one article, "A Cult Matriarchate and Male Homosexuality" (Landes 1940a) drew international attention. The predictable next step, after the war's end, should have been a university post. Instead Landes found she was blacklisted in important sectors of the academic establishment.

The case is surely without parallel in the annals of anthropology. The profession then was small and its inner circle smaller still. That the voices of women were few and rarely granted a serious hearing meant that the atmosphere of a men's club could prevail. However, the culpability in the case of a somehow unbalanced and bitterly vindictive Brazilian scholar was revealed by a generous and balanced one who knew the facts (Carneiro 1964). Landes charges that the censorius scholar was the psychological anthropologist (later UNESCO official) Artur Ramos, and that he continued a program of character assassination internationally until his death. Most of the harm within the United States was done informally, but Landes documents conspiracy to slander in one instance (Landes 1970a:128–33). The powerfully placed Melville Herskovits and Ramos are alleged to have jointly written a forty-odd-page letter in 1939 to Myrdal to the effect that his staff person had done research in Brazil by selling her sexual services to black informants. Since Herskovits had no direct knowledge of the person or the case, it must be assumed that his initial intervention was based on incomplete information, not malice. The part played by Ramos was less decisive only because of his marginal standing in anthropology. He remained unambiguously vindictive. Landes's colleagues in Rio de Janeiro and São Paulo advised her to attribute this damaging gossip to professional rivalry (Ruth Landes, personal communication, 1985). It must be supposed that in the mind of Ramos, a brash young North American woman had preempted the study he had staked out for his own, though quite unprepared himself to undertake "demeaning" field observation.

The result of the unsolicited letter, had the jointly signed document been received as intended, would have been that "no Landes person or profession existed." Landes recalls that Myrdal showed her the letter in wonderment: These were ridiculous people, yet "they must take you seriously." For ten years afterward she had no academic post, and for another decade no regular position. During the war Landes worked for President Roosevelt's Fair Employment Practices Commission (FEPC) in Washington. She writes now that she, true to her character, confronted Herskovits in 1949 on finding him at an anthropology meeting in New York City. It could not have escaped him that *The City of Women* (Landes 1947) fully vindicated her professional claims as a major student of Afro-American cultures. She had only to speak her name to see Herskovits flee (Ruth Landes, personal communication, 1985).

And Boas, Benedict, and Park were dead. The job market in anthropology was still controlled by senior patrons and still a better place for men than women, and for scholars in their twenties than for scholars facing their forties. Landes recalls, "The first and only permanent job in my scholarly right was offered in 1965 by McMaster University. Until then, without my parents' support financially and morally, I cannot imagine what I would have been." The special vulnerability of women in a world of powerful professionals is obvious.

Landes was fifty-six when she returned to Ontario. On the record, she had remained an unusually productive scholar throughout her long ordeal, and an unusually consistent one in face of the great variety of intellectual tasks she came to address in making her career as hand-to-mouth researcher.

Five books were published in the five years from 1965. A major comparative research project was undertaken, as always single-handedly, in her sixties and completed for publication (still pending) in 1975. The subject was bilingualism and biculturalism in Spain, Switzerland, South Africa, the United States, and Canada. These are five quite different polities, wherein ethnic relations have come to be mediated, in some measure, by official language policies. At a point when many anthropologists were wondering where their field would be in the future; and others, how sociolinguistic studies could be brought back into the social sciences, Landes was still doing research in the timeless manner of the first professional generation of anthropologists.

"I have written two books that are said to focus on women preeminently," she writes. "For me, the separate treatments of women were the accident of special materials about them that were previously neglected in the literature, and still are." She might have said the same of her other subjects: cult and conflict, disprivileged minority groups, family and personal values. In each case her analytical focus grew from the field materials. No such subject could be treated in isolation from the fullest context of culture and social structure, or divorced from the dramatic values of everyday experience that gave meaning to events in the present, in expectation, and in retrospect.

Perhaps the anthropologists who have best represented her holistic kind of humanism have not many followers in the rather specialized university departments of today. But true to her early models, the work she produced was always solidly in the tradition that defined direct observation and face-to-face encounter as the starting point for useful social inquiry. *The Ojibwa Woman* (Landes 1938a) focuses on personal motivation and illustrates the justice of her notion that women in that nomadic community were less constrained by custom and nagging rivalries than were the men. To make her case, she does not simply set out to look at the culture through women's eyes but considers gender roles and is brought to her conclusion empirically.

In *The City of Women* she comes to terms with the optimistic judgment of Pierson (1942) that race in Bahia was not a major determinant of social standing. She found

that they were oppressed by political and economic tyrannies, although not by racial ones. In that sense, the Negroes were free, and at liberty to cultivate their African heritage. But they were sick, undernourished, illiterate, and uninformed, just like other poor people among them of different racial origins. It was their complete poverty that cut them off from modern thought and obliged them to make up their own secure universe. (1947:248)

Poverty was just not one of Pierson's categories.

It may have been no surprise to her that the strength of the cult centers she studied often resided in unusually forceful women; she had expected this from library work on the Yoruba and Ibo peoples, whence much of Bahia's Afro-American culture derived, and with which some cult leaders had maintained personal and professional links. She could also look into herself, since her own response to adversity, though it had not been by way of calling upon possessing spirits, had always been to push on through. If her work has in some measure redressed the imbalance introduced by the preponderance of males in the field of ethnography, it has not done so by putting a reverse spin into her own writing but by showing a wider sensitivity to those moral trials and strategies of women that but rarely occupy center stage in a subject culture's public sphere. She has been willing to see excess in certain manifestations of masculinity; "boorish flirting privileges" between Sioux cross-cousins and "merciless teasing that charged encounters with hostility" did not strike her (1969:98) as the kind of stylized joking her male counterparts had reported. Dangerous conflict could be chronic, all dysfunction was not the artifact of reservation conditions, the strong could everywhere be expected to use the rules against the weak.

Though much of her work, particularly in the journal articles, consists in systematic comparison, she has kept to the model of her teachers. Her basic reference point on the way to understanding is not the system but the people. "You need understanding of the system as a means not as the end of your work." This seems to have been an informing characteristic of her anthropology from the start. If her method has meant that she does not usually pull theory away from incident, for separate elaboration, there are some who would argue that in this she does no less than set a properly Boasian benchmark for the profession.

Note

1. This and further quotations not otherwise acknowledged are from the pen of Ruth Landes and are cited from personal correspondence (1985). The authors have had the benefit of her gracious and detailed assistance in developing their manuscript.

Selected Works by Ruth Landes

1937a *Ojibwa Sociology*. New York: Columbia University Press.

1937b The Personality of the Ojibwa. *Culture and Personality* 6:51–60.

1937c The Ojibwa in Canada. In *Cooperation and Competition Among Primitive Peoples*. Margaret Mead, ed. Pp. 87–127. New York: McGraw-Hill.

1938a *The Ojibwa Woman*. New York: Columbia University Press.

1938b The Abnormal Among the Ojibwa. *Journal of Abnormal and Social Psychology* 33:14–33.

1940a A Cult Matriarchate and Male Homosexuality. *Journal of Abnormal and Social Psychology* 35:386–97.

1940b Negro Fetish Worship in Brazil. *Journal of American Folklore* 53:261–70.

1940c Ethos of the Negro in the New World. Microfilm. Schomberg Collection of New York City Library.

1945a A Northerner Views the South. *Social Forces* 23:275–79.

1945b What About This Bureaucracy? *The Nation* 161:365–66.

1947 *The City of Women*. New York: MacMillan. (Portuguese trans., Brazil, 1967).

1952a Preliminary Statement on Race Relationships. *Man* (September), no. 184.

1952b Race and Recognition. *The Listener* 6.

1953a Negro Slavery and Female Status. *Journal of African Affairs* (January).

1953b Relationships of Color. *West Africa* (April 25, May 2).

1955   Biracialism in American Society: A Comparative View. *American Anthropologist* 57 (6): 1253–64.
1958   Family Patterns of the Future. *Child Welfare* (November): 19–28.
1959   Minority Groups and School Social Work. *Social Work* 4 (3): 91–97.
1963a   Cultural Factors in Counseling. *Journal of General Education* (April) 15:55–67.
1963b   An Anthropologist Looks at School Counseling. *Journal of Counselling Psychology* 10:1.
1963c   Newcomers and Culture. Social Work Papers. University of Southern California, Los Angeles.
1963d   Culture and Education. In *Foundations of Education*. George F. Kneller, ed. Pp. 320–52. New York: John Wiley & Sons.
1964   Potawatomi Medicine. *Transactions of the Kansas Academy of Science* 66:4.
1965a   *Culture in American Education*. New York: John Wiley & Sons.
1965b   *The Latin-Americans of the Southwest*. St. Louis: McGraw-Hill.
1965c   The Potawatomi. *Encyclopædia Britannica*. Chicago: Encyclopædia Britannica, Inc.
1967   Negro Jews in Harlem. *Jewish Journal of Sociology* 9 (2): 175–89.
1968   *Ojibwa Religion and the Midewiwin*. Madison: University of Wisconsin Press.
1969   *The Mystic Lake Sioux*. Madison: University of Wisconsin Press.
1970a   A Woman Anthropologist in Brazil. In *Women in the Field*. Peggy Golde, ed. Pp. 119–42. Chicago: Aldine.
1970b   *The Prairie Potawatomi*. Madison: University of Wisconsin Press.

Coauthored Works

Landes, Ruth, and M. Zborowski, eds.
1950   Hypotheses Concerning the Eastern European Jewish Family. *Psychiatry* 13:447–64.

GEORGE PARK AND ALICE PARK

Eleanor Burke Leacock

(1922–1987)

Prominent American cultural anthropologist Eleanor Burke Leacock was known for her ethnohistorical studies of changing Montagnais-Naskapi (Innu) social and gender relations, her reevaluations of the work of Lewis Henry Morgan and Frederick Engels, her contributions to feminist theory, and her analyses of racism in American education.

Eleanor Burke was born on July 2, 1922, and grew up during the Depression in Greenwich Village, New York. Her mother, Lily Mary Batterham, had obtained a master's degree in mathematics and had taught secondary school. Her father, Kenneth Burke, was a renowned literary critic and social philosopher, despite his having dropped out of college before obtaining a degree. While she was a child, her parents bought a small farm in New Jersey, where her family spent summers. Her father did a lot of his work at home; and on the farm her mother and father both worked at outdoor tasks. Leacock remembered no overt criticism of sexism, but the structure of her parents' lives did not reinforce gender stereotypes. Her parents' social circle included artists, political radicals, and writers who lived in the neighborhood. In that milieu she learned to eschew materialism and to oppose racism and economic injustice; farm life taught her to respect the natural world.[1]

Both parents encouraged her and her two sisters to pursue their intellectual and artistic interests. It was assumed that they were intelligent and would work. She remembered wanting to make model villages like those in the American Museum of Natural History, and she liked painting but realized later that art would not provide a living for a woman. She attended public schools initially, but for high school she transferred to the Dalton School, where she had received a scholarship.

She was also to win a scholarship to Radcliffe in 1939. There, she became active in a circle of student radicals who excelled in studies, but who were considered undesirable (socialist, unaffluent, or Jewish) by more traditional students. In her second anthropology course, Alfred Tozzer told the women students that if they wanted to be anthropologists, they had better have independent means, because they would never get a job in anthropology. She recalled thinking, smugly rather than angrily, "I'll show you!" At the time, she believed that to be accepted in what was a man's world, she simply had to demonstrate her intellectual merit.

While at Radcliffe, she met Richard Leacock, a Harvard student interested in filmmaking, whose family lived in New York. After she and Richard were married, Eleanor Leacock transferred to Barnard in 1942. They waited for him to be drafted, and he was.

At Barnard she pursued her growing interest in anthropology. At that time she experienced her first personal case of sex discrimination. Although she had received the highest grade in a drafting course given at Columbia's Engineering School, she was denied the drafting assistantship she wanted, explicitly because she was female. The experience led her to confront the social injustice of sex discrimination more sharply than before.

After graduation in 1944, and like many other anthropologists opposed to fascism, she sought work in Washington, D.C., at the Office of War Information. Ruth Benedict* and Rhoda Metraux* approved her for employment. The FBI denied her clearance, however; the questions they asked about her, Eleanor Leacock was told by friends, included, "Did she wear Russian blouses? Did she have Jewish friends?"

She returned to New York, to enroll in graduate school at Columbia. Alongside her studies, she worked as an assistant at an experimental nursery school and immersed herself in antiracist community work. At Columbia her major influences were William Duncan Strong (for his ethnohistorical work) and Gene Weltfish* (for her blend of political engagement and ethnology). Her first advisor was Marian Smith, who took her as one member of a student field trip to British Columbia in the summer of 1945; Leacock observed Harrison Indian children. Smith included Leacock's study of household composition on the reservation, "The Seabird Community," in a book (1949) she was editing. Leacock went on to pass the masters' exams in 1946. In the Ph.D. oral exams, as in her classwork generally, Leacock avoided issues that would reveal her Marxist interests. After the Ph.D. oral exams, Leacock was informed that she had "no point of view," and therefore, no one in the department would serve as her thesis advisor. Instead of being upset, she was relieved that she would not have to work in a historical particularist framework. She assumed that when she had chosen a dissertation topic, she would find an advisor at Columbia.

With her husband's return at the end of the war, Leacock became pregnant with their first child, Elspeth. Her husband was offered the chance to shoot a series of films on human geography during 1948–49 in Europe. Ruth Benedict provided her with a small grant to purchase camera equipment of her own, to do short films on comparative child socialization in German Switzerland and Italy. In addition to shooting her films, Leacock began archival research in Paris on changes in the social organization of an Indian people in Labrador, the Montagnais-Naskapi (Innu), following the introduction of the fur trade, work that would become the basis of her doctoral thesis. As part of the research, she noted all passages in the *Jesuit Relations* (Thwaites 1906) that referred to women: years later this spadework would facilitate her research on the impact of conversion efforts and commodity production on women's status.

On their return, because Benedict died in the interim, Leacock showed the films to Margaret Mead,* who invited her to compare her work with Mead's Bali material. Leacock declined, having decided to pursue the thesis examining changes in an egalitarian society with the development of commodities. She showed Duncan Strong her detailed summary of the archival materials and asked him for money to do summer fieldwork in Labrador. He arranged for a $1,000 departmental grant. She left Elspeth with her father and stepmother (Richard was in Latin America for a summer film trip) and took year-old Robert "on her hip" to Labrador. She knew French but not Innu; her entrée to the field consisted of knowing there was a boat that went down the St. Lawrence and that she should go as far as it did, then ask people.

That summer, 1951, Leacock developed a field technique that later has been called "anthropology on the ground." Through several English-speaking informants, she ascertained where band members actually hunted, with whom and when. She then mapped local camp composition and hunting-trapping patterns at different times. In that way, she avoided the informants' characterization of events, or possible overgeneralization. Her path-breaking work exploded the prevailing antievolutionary and explicitly anti-Marxist theses (promoted by Frank Speck) that "communism in living" had never existed and that private property existed even in gatherer-hunter societies. She found that subsistence resources were not privately owned, even after centuries of commodity production: although the rights to trap in given places were privatized, the rights to gather, fish, hunt for food, and so on were still communal. She also found great flexibility in postmarital residence patterns, and especially matrilocality in the past, which called into question Julian Steward's thesis that hunting and trapping as men's activities predisposed foraging societies to be patrilocal. Further, her work revealed arenas of egalitarianism still evident in Innu life, including relations between women and men.

The next summer, she decided to return to Labrador with her family. She received a small grant from the Wenner-Gren Foundation to cross-check her findings with another band and to allow her husband to make a film. She went with Richard and the children to camp with Innu in another area of Labrador. Having learned phonetic transcription from Weltfish, Leacock recorded stories. She typed the stories in transcription and gave the Innu carbon copies. The Innu had taught themselves a script, but this was the first time they read their own stories. Previously, only Bible texts had been transcribed.

Her second son, David, was born shortly before she completed her dissertation. Although she received her doctorate in 1952, her committee pronounced the thesis on the impact of the fur trade on Montagnais-Naskapi (Innu) property and labor relations "unpublishable." She was not told why. Only after Marshall Sahlins heard her report on the research, and told Morton Fried and Elman Service (who were recent additions to the Columbia faculty) about it, was she invited to give a presentation at Columbia. Service then encouraged her to publish the thesis. It appeared as the *American Anthropological Association Memoir* 78 (1954).

For a variety of reasons, Leacock received no help from Columbia in job hunting. The important early support for women anthropologists shown by Columbia's department under the aegis of Boas was not continued in later years. In addition to being female, Leacock was married, she was a mother, and she was a politically engaged radical. The chair, Charles Wagley, told her to register at the employment service, where she was offered a part-time typing job in a physics lab. It would be eleven years until she would have her first full-time job teaching anthropology. In the interim, she worked at research and education jobs not considered then to be related to anthropology. Nevertheless, she continued to write, publish, and speak as an anthropologist, regardless of her employment situation. Her first position was on the interdisciplinary project on mental illness known as the Yorkville Project.

In 1955, when her second daughter, Claudia, was a baby, Leacock left the Yorkville Project to teach part-time at Queens College for a year. This was followed by a temporary, part-time position at City College. In 1958 she joined the Bank Street College of Education Schools and Mental Health project, aimed at improving teaching practice. The serious, progressive environment, being integrated in a project run by virtually all women, where being a mother was viewed as an asset, provided support for her during difficult personal times. During those years her first marriage ended, and she became involved with Jim Haughton, the Afro-American labor organizer and community activist who would become her second husband.

To keep her hand in the academy while working at Bank Street, she taught adjunct courses at New York University and, later, one course at night at Brooklyn Polytechnic Institute. In 1963, the new chair of the History and Economics Department, Helmut Gruber, hired her for a full-time anthropology slot. With greater job security, her writing and research burgeoned: the work on Lewis Henry Morgan concerning egalitarian societies and cultural evolution, the critique of the culture of poverty as class-based and racially biased, numerous articles on anthropology and education, and her book on class and culture in urban schools established her reputation as a scholar and critic reaching audiences both within and outside of anthropology. In particular, her anthropology and education articles revolved around a central concern with cultural influences on classroom learning, a rejection of "culture and personality" theory in educational practice, a call for attention in public education to ways that class and racial oppression were reproduced in the classroom. For comparison with U.S. urban elementary schools, she investigated decolonization efforts in primary school education in Zambia. She conducted the research at a time (1970) when many anthropoplogists were refused field entry because of perceived colonialist attitudes.

When the anthropology department at City College was overhauled in 1972, Leacock was brought in as chair, to rebuild the program. Her highly influential work on Engels was published the same year. She remained at City College until her death, having served on the Executive Committee on Anthropology at the City University of New York Graduate Center from 1976–79. Among the many honors Leacock received in the past decade, she was the first woman to be given the New York Academy of Sciences Award for the Behavioral Sciences (1983).

Sensitized by her own struggles to be taken seriously as an anthropologist regardless of motherhood and limited employment, Leacock was extremely supportive of junior colleagues, especially those who were marginally employed. Leacock's publication record is immense (over eighty articles and reviews, and ten books), broad in scope and keen in intellectual acuity. There can be no doubt that her work is of lasting significance in anthropology and far beyond the discipline. After all, she made truth of her smug rejection of Alfred Tozzer's advice. Her own engagement in fostering younger scholars and her work with others to oppose race, sex, and class stratification helped make such advice obsolete.

Leacock's research embodied her intellectual and political commitments. Her long-term feminism was melded always with an opposition to racial and class injustices, at home and abroad, as a unified whole. In keeping with her view of anthropology as having importance for general social concerns, in the early 1970s she brought the Engels thesis to the attention of the resurgent women's movement.

Since then she contributed additional research tracing the simultaneous emergence of class and gender oppression, as processes linked to commodity production, the formation of state institutions, or colonialism, and related models of development. Her impressive energy and analytical skills always focused on contemporary intellectual currents with political agendas. Her critiques of the "culture of poverty" thesis, male bias in anthropology in general, structuralism and sociobiology in particular, and racism and class bias in education influenced national and international constituencies far beyond anthropologists and the academy. Her writing was aimed at a broad audience, explaining complex issues in accessible language, consciously rejecting the convoluted academic prose she perceived as elitist. The ongoing purpose of her research and writing was human emancipation. In an article on women and development agendas, she wrote:

As women continue to seek collective forms of organization against oppression, anthropologists who study cultural evolution . . . have a choice: either to document the autonomous roles women played in egalitarian societies, for the perspectives they lend to organizational strategies and socialist goals; or to spin out ever more elegant rationales for exploitation. (Leacock 1981a:316)

Note

1. Most of the information for this biographical note comes from two sources: an interview with Eleanor Burke Leacock on January 26, 1986, and an as-yet unpublished autobiographical sketch by Leacock, titled "Being an Anthropologist."

Editors' Note: Eleanor Burke Leacock died unexpectedly in Honolulu on April 2, 1987, after suffering a stroke in Western Samoa where she was conducting fieldwork. We wish to express our gratitude for her consistent support for this volume.

Selected Works by Eleanor Burke Leacock

Being an Anthropologist. (Unpublished)

1949 The Seabird Community. In *Indians of the Urban Northwest*. Marian Smith, ed. Pp. 185–95. New York: Columbia University Press.

1954 The Montagnais "Hunting Territory" and the Fur Trade. *American Anthropologist Memoir 78*.

1958 Social Stratification and Evolutionary Theory. *Ethnohistory* 5(3):193–209.

1963 Introduction. *Lewis Henry Morgan, Ancient Society*. E. B. Leacock, ed. Pp. i–xx. New York: Meridian Books.

1967 Distortions of Working Class Reality in American Social Science. *Science and Society* 31 (1):1–21.

1968 Personality and Culture Theory in the Field of Education. *Proceedings, 8th International Congress of Anthropological and Ethnological Sciences*. Vol. 2. Tokyo: Science Council of Japan.

1969 *Teaching and Learning in City Schools*. New York: Basic Books.

1971a *Culture of Poverty: A Critique*. New York: Simon and Schuster.

1971b At Play in African Villages. *Natural History* (December) pp. 60–65.

1972 Introduction. *The Origin of the Family, Private Property, and the State* by Frederick Engels. Pp. 7–67. New York: International.

1976 Education in Africa: Myths of Modernization. In *The Anthropological Study of Education*. Craig J. Calhoun and Francis A. J. Ianni, eds. Pp. 239–50. The Hague: Mouton.

1977a Women in Egalitarian Society. In *Becoming Visible: Women in European History*. R. Bridenthal and C. Koonz, eds. Pp. 11–35. Boston: Houghton Mifflin.

1977b The Changing Family and Lévi-Strauss, or What Ever Happened to Fathers? *Social Research* 44(2):235–59.

1977c Women's Status in Egalitarian Society: Implications for Social Evolution. *Current Anthropology* 19(2):247–75.

1977d Race and the We–They Dichotomy in Culture and Classroom. *Anthropology and Education Quarterly* 8(2).

1981a *Myths of Male Dominance*. New York: Monthly Review.

1981b History, Development and the Division of Labor by Sex: Implications for Organization. *Signs* 7(2):474–91.

1982 Marxism and Anthropology. In *The Left Academy*. Bertell Ollman and Edward Vernoff, eds. Pp. 244–77. New York: McGraw-Hill.

1983 Interpreting the Origins of Gender Inequality: Conceptual and Historical Problems. *Dialectical Anthropology* 7:263–84.

Coauthored Works

Leacock, Eleanor, L. Menashe et al.

1969 *Social Science Theory and Method: An Integrated Historical Introduction.* Vols. 1–8. New York: Polytechnic Institute of Brooklyn.

Leacock, Eleanor, and June Nash

1977 Ideologies of Sex: Archetypes and Stereotypes. *New York Academy of Sciences Annals* 285.

Leacock, Eleanor, Helen Safa, et al.

1986 *Women's Work: Development and the Division of Labor by Gender.* S. Hadley, Mass.: Bergin and Garvey.

Leacock, Eleanor, and Mona Etienne, eds.

1980 *Women and Colonization.* New York: Bergin and Garvey/Praeger.

Leacock, Eleanor, and Richard Lee, eds.

1982 *Politics and History in Band Societies.* New York: Cambridge University Press.

Leacock, Eleanor, and Nancy Lurie, eds.

1971 *North American Indians in Historical Perspective.* New York: Random House.

CHRISTINE WARD GAILEY

Mary Douglas Nicol Leakey

(1913–   )

Mary Douglas Nicol Leakey is an East African prehistorian and archaeologist whose discoveries of fossil hominids and their material culture in Kenya and Tanzania aroused widespread interest in African prehistory and provided hominid paleontologists with challenging evidence of entirely new animal and hominid species.

Mary Douglas Nicol was born in London on February 6, 1913, to Erskine Nicol, a landscape artist of Scottish descent, and Cecilia Frere, whose family came from East Anglia. Young Mary Nicol, an only child, beloved by her three Frere maiden aunts, traveled to Italy, Switzerland, and France with her parents during the winter and spring while her father painted. The family returned to London every summer for Erskine Nicol to exhibit and sell his artwork. Though Mary Nicol had little regular schooling, her father spent time with her, teaching her to read and sharing his passion for Paleolithic archaeology. For a time she attended elementary school in France and viewed many of the legendary cave paintings of the Dordogne region. There, the Nicols befriended French prehistorian M. Elie Peyrony and collected cast-off Paleolithic tools, at that time not considered collectible enough for the local museum at Les Eyzies. In Cabrerets they became close friends of the Abbé Lemozi, the parish priest and an amateur prehistorian, who showed them the cave art of Pêch Merle. In 1926, when Mary Nicol was only thirteen years old, her father died suddenly at the age of fifty-eight.

After returning to England, her mother unsuccessfully attempted to continue Nicol's formal education. Mary Nicol drove away the private tutors her mother hired and was expelled from two convent schools. Since she "had never passed a single school exam, and clearly never would," Mary Nicol was not eligible to enter any unversity (M. Leakey 1984:34). Nevertheless, she educated herself by reading and attending geology lectures at University College, a part of London

University, and archaeology lectures at the London Museum, particularly those of Sir Mortimer (R. E. M.) Wheeler. In the summer of 1930 Nicol had her first opportunity to gain prolonged field experience, at the Hembury Dig in Devon. This excavation of an early Neolithic site in South Britain continued through the summers of 1930–32 and the spring of 1934. Mary Nicol's earliest published drawings of the Hembury finds brought her to Gertrude Caton-Thompson's attention in 1932–33, and Caton-Thompson invited Nicol to illustrate the book on her excavations in Egypt, *The Desert Fayoum*.

It was through Caton-Thompson that Mary Nicol met Louis Seymour Bazett Leakey, then a Research Fellow at St. John's College (Cambridge) and veteran of three research expeditions to East Africa. Nicol agreed to do the illustrations for Leakey's forthcoming book, *Adam's Ancestors*. L. S. B. Leakey, already an established and experienced archaeologist, shared Nicol's attraction to "wild places, working in the field, and being alone among wild animals" (M. Leakey 1984:42). Although he was ten years her senior, she states that Leakey treated her as an equal and a colleague.

By late 1933 what had begun as an intellectual partnership had expanded into romance; but Louis Leakey was already married to Frida Leakey, who was expecting their second child. Sir Thomas Kendrick of the British Museum warned Nicol, "Genius is akin to madness, Mary: you must be careful" (M. Leakey 1984:43). After Louis Leakey confessed the situation to his wife in early 1934 and announced his intent to divorce her, the scandal shocked the Cambridge community. Many people urged Mary Nicol to abandon her relationship with Leakey, which eventually cost him the support of Cambridge. Had it not been for this opposition, L. S. B. Leakey and Mary Nicol might never have settled in Kenya to pursue their search for human origins.

Nicol continued her fieldwork in Britain during 1934, at Hembury, Swanscombe, where a famous hominid skull was discovered the following year, and at Jaywick near Clacton. The work at Jaywick, Nicol's first chance to direct her own dig, resulted in her first publication (jointly with Kenneth Oakley) in the *Proceedings of the Prehistoric Society* for 1937. Leakey left England for his fourth East African expedition in October of 1934; Mary Nicol and her mother sailed to South Africa in January 1935, proceeding by train to Southern Rhodesia (now Zimbabwe). In April Mrs. Nicol returned to England, while her daughter, still refusing to be dissuaded, flew to Tanganyika (Tanzania) to join Louis Leakey.

When they returned to England in September 1935, they found that the continuing reaction to their affair had ended the possibility of Leakey's further association with St. John's College. In mid–1936 the Rhodes Trust offered Leakey a salary and expenses to undertake a two-year study of the Kikuyu in Kenya, for later publication. Louis Leakey's background as a white African raised by missionary parents in Kenya, with his knowledge of the Kikuyu language and culture, gave him unique credentials for such a venture. After his divorce from Frida became final, Mary Nicol and Louis S. B. Leakey were married in a simple civil ceremony on December 24, 1936, and departed for Kenya in January 1937.

While they resided at Nakuru, 100 miles north of Nairobi, Louis Leakey worked with his Kikuyu informants; and Mary Leakey conducted excavations at Hyrax Hill, uncovering a Neolithic settlement and nineteen mound burials. Nellie Grant, who ran a 1,000-acre farm at Njoro immortalized in her daughter Elspeth Huxley's books, also invited the Leakeys to excavate the Njoro River Cave in a forested section of her land. Dating to approximately the twelfth century B.C., the cave site yielded early Elmenteitan period artifacts: double-edged obsidian blades, bowl-shaped vessels, and stone beads in large quantities. Njoro River Cave also provided evidence of the ritual of cremation, with each burial accompanied by a stone bowl, mortar, and pestle (Leakey and Leakey 1950).

After World War II began, Louis Leakey did some work for British intelligence and smuggled guns to local anti-Italian guerrillas on the Ethiopian border. In 1940 he became curator of the Coryndon Museum in Nairobi, later to become the National Museum of Kenya; and the Leakeys moved into a bungalow next door.

From 1940 to 1944 Mary Leakey conducted fieldwork at Olorgesailie and Ngorongoro, Rusinga Island in Lake Victoria, Lewa (on the north side of Mount Kenya), and the Kavirondo area. The Olorgesailie site produced a profusion of Acheulean cleavers and hand axes, associated with large mammal bones such as hippopotamus and remains of over fifty giant baboons, possibly a troop cornered by *Homo erectus*. Rusinga Island contained rich deposits of Miocene fossils, and there Mary Leakey later discovered the 20-million-year-old partial skull of *Proconsul africanus*.

On November 4, 1940, the Leakeys' son Jonathan was born. He accompanied Mary Leakey on much of her wartime fieldwork. Richard E. Leakey, now a renowned paleoanthropologist, was born December 19, 1944; and Philip Leakey joined the family on June 21, 1949. Around this time the family moved to Karen, a suburb of Nairobi named after the writer Karen Blixen (Isak Dinesen). Mary Leakey hired *ayahs*, African nannies, to look after the boys while she continued her work. Theirs was no ordinary family life; and as the Leakey boys grew older, they accompanied their parents on fossil-hunting expeditions and occasionally made exciting discoveries of their own. In 1952 the Leakeys moved to a house they had designed, located on a five-acre plot of land, in the Nairobi suburb of Langata. Mary Leakey's lifelong attraction to animals, wild and domesticated, led her to form a pony club for children and a kennel club as well.

In 1947 Louis and Mary Leakey hosted the first Pan-African Congress of Prehistory and Paleontology, which was attended by leading prehistorians and included excursions to the Leakeys' favorite sites. As a result of the conference, the Royal Society in London agreed to finance the British-Kenya Miocene Expedition in 1947–48, work that the Leakeys continued long after this funding expired.

In 1948 on Rusinga Island in Lake Victoria, Mary Leakey found the first truly important fossil of her career. She discovered a *Proconsul africanus* specimen: half of the skull, upper and lower jaws, and all of the teeth. At the time, many believed that this find might be the "missing link" between the great apes and humans, though even now *Proconsul*'s evolutionary relationship to the first upright African apes (which appeared about 4 million years ago) remains uncertain (R. Leakey 1983). Mary Leakey carefully reconstructed the separate skull pieces and took it to Wilfred Le Gros Clark, a leading authority on primate evolution, to analyze in his laboratory at Oxford. Although *Proconsul* did not prove to be a direct human ancestor, the international press coverage surrounding her discovery was enough to persuade the government of Kenya and a private donor to continue their support of the British-Kenya Miocene Expedition. The Leakeys placed the skull on long-term loan with the British Museum of Natural History in Kensington, stipulating that it could be recalled at any time. Richard Leakey requested its return in 1970, but the fossil skull had been registered as British Museum property. When the Leakeys located copies of the 1948 correspondence with the British authorities, the British Museum finally relented and returned *Proconsul*, the first fossil of major importance discovered in Kenya, to the National Museum of Kenya in Nairobi.

In 1950 the entire family returned to England on leave. The Leakeys and son Jonathan joined their benefactor, Charles Boise, for a tour of the prehistoric painted caves in France and northern Spain, including the recently discovered Lascaux site. While they were visiting England, Oxford University awarded Louis Leakey an honorary degree; and they met Alex Wenner-Gren, founder of the Wenner-Gren Foundation for Athropological Research in New York.

One result of this chance contact was a Wenner-Gren Foundation grant awarded to Mary Leakey the following year. The grant enabled her to record selected Tanzanian rock paintings from the Kondoa area in central Tanzania, which she and Louis had originally begun to copy in 1935. The paintings are generally monochromes (commonly reds), showing animals with exaggerated features and humans bathing, hunting, playing music, or dancing but rarely performing everyday tasks. Leakey believes that the 1,500-year-old rock paintings may represent an artistic tradition dating back to the Paleolithic of 30,000 years ago, and that the artists may have been the precursors of the Hadza or Sandawe peoples. Out of 186 sites, 43 were determined to have paintings worth copying. The book was expensive to produce, and it was many years before *Africa's Vanishing Art* (M. Leakey 1983) finally appeared. Leakey states that the three months she spent on this fieldwork in 1951 represent one of the high points of her East African work (M. Leakey 1984:105–9).

During the years 1951–58 the Leakeys concentrated on Bed II of Olduvai Gorge in northern Tanzania, the second oldest layer composing the gorge's stratigraphy. At last they had sufficient funds to conduct regular excavations at Olduvai; and after several seasons Mary Leakey found another landmark fossil, a major turning point in her life. Early in 1959 they had decided to examine Bed I to see if stone tools of the Oldowan tradition could be found at the oldest level. As Mary scanned the surface accompanied by her pet Dalmatians on July 17, 1959, she saw a bone projecting from the surface—part of an upper jaw. Her discovery of the hominid skull known as "Zinj" or "Nutcracker Man" captured the limelight and led to substantial monetary support from the National Geographic Society in the United States. Louis Leakey labeled the skull that Mary Leakey had painstakingly reconstructed from fragments *Zinjanthropus*, derived from an Arabic word for East Africa, to denote a new genus within the hominid family. He chose the species name *boisei* to honor the Leakeys' long-standing benefactor, Charles Boise.

Mary Leakey's find created a worldwide sensation, for scientists had previously speculated that humans had evolved in Asia only a few hundred thousand years ago. The skull, at first believed to be 600,000 years old, was later revealed to be 1.75 million years old and from a side branch of the human evolutionary tree.

Other paleoanthropologists, notably Phillip Tobias, disputed Louis Leakey's newly invented classification. The most widely accepted classification of early hominids divides them into two genera: *Australopithecus*, the earliest hominid genus, and *Homo* (the genus that also includes modern humans), which probably evolved from a gracile australopithecine. Tobias asserted that "Zinj" represented a more heavily built, or robust, form known as *Australopithecus robustus* in South Africa, and renamed the fossil *Australopithecus boisei*. The robust australopithecines had apparently become extinct between 1.2 and 1.4 million years ago, while advanced gracile australopithecines had evolved into *Homo erectus* by about 1.1 million years ago (Tanner 1981:254).

Within the sequence from upper Bed I to lower Bed II to Olduvai, the Leakeys also came across other gracile but large-brained hominid fossils that were contemporary with *Australopithecus boisei*. Both types of remains have been found in association with stone tools and animal bones on living floors. Hunting, scavenging, and meat eating were common; and Bed I contains the foundation of an early dwelling. Until these discoveries, few anthropologists believed that two hominid groups—an early *Homo* species and a robust australopithecine—could occupy the same territory at the same time. Both Louis and Mary Leakey attributed the toolmaking ability they had formerly credited to *A. boisei* to the larger-brained, more gracile, upright hominids capable of a "precision grip" (see M. Leakey 1980). The toolmaker was christened *Homo habilis* by Louis Leakey, Phillip Tobias, and John Napier (1964); but some authorities still regard fossils from this group as gracile or "advanced gracile" australopithecines (see Tanner 1981). According to some archaeologists, *Homo habilis* gave rise to *Homo erectus*, the precursor of modern humans. There is still no general agreement on how these early hominids should be classified; and the taxonomic debates are more complex than this brief account reveals.

Though her gift for finding fossil hominids brought her more attention, Mary Leakey should also receive credit for her archaeological finds, particularly the Olduvai stone tool assemblages ranging from 2 million years to .7 or .8 million years ago. She has documented an overlap between the Oldowan stone tool industry and the Acheulian industry in Bed II at Olduvai and postulates that the change in tool traditions indicates the replacement of one hominid species (*A. boisei*) by another (*H. habilis*) (M. Leakey 1980). However, she notes that other investigators interpret overlapping sets of tools as different tool kits employed for particular purposes (M. Leakey 1984:153).

Mary and Louis Leakey grew estranged from one another during the last four years of Louis's life. Analyzing and publicizing their discoveries had indeed changed both their lives, as had their son Richard E. F. Leakey's professional maturation. Louis Leakey had always actively enjoyed traveling and public appearances; but now, according to Mary Leakey, he had become infatuated with his own status as a legendary figure. She describes losing respect for his work as his conclusions became more sensational and their disagreements more volatile (M. Leakey 1984:140–44). In 1972 Louis Leakey died of a heart attack while on a trip to England.

One of Mary Leakey's greatest accomplishments is her work at Laetoli, begun in 1974. Thirty miles from Olduvai Gorge, the Laetolil Beds consist of volcanic ash deposited by the volcano Sadiman, twenty miles to the east. Leakey had visited the site repeatedly without finding anything significant until her neighbor found fossils in a load of sand delivered for construction work. In those volcanic beds, or "tuffs," Leakey and her team discovered remarkably preserved hominid and animal footprints. The now-famous Footprint Tuff discovered in 1976 has well-established potassium-argon dates giving evidence that early hominids walked upright between 3.5 and 3.8 million years ago. By 1979, with eighty feet of the trail excavated, the researchers speculated that three hominids had been present (M. Leakey 1984). In addition, Leakey and her associates found remains of twenty-five early hominids (but no tools) and an unusual array of animal fossils representing fifteen new species, possibly a record for a single site (M. Leakey 1984:144).

The hominid remains from Laetoli have generated another taxonomic debate. Leakey and her associates had originally assigned these fossils to the genus *Homo* (Leakey et al. 1976); but Donald Johansen and Tim White maintain that the Laetoli specimens represent the same hominid species as the earliest known australopithecine fossil "Lucy" from Hadar in Ethiopia—namely, *Australopithecus afarensis*. Despite growing acceptance of this interpretation (Tanner 1981:178–87), Leakey has rejected it (M. Leakey 1984:180–84).

Mary Leakey has acquired several honorary degrees: D.Sc. from the University of Witwatersrand (1968)[1] and Western Michigan University (1980), D.Soc.Sc.

from Yale University (1976), and the D.Litt. from Oxford University (1981). Her awards include the Gold Medal of the Society of Women Geographers (1975),[2] the Linnaeus Gold Medal of the Royal Swedish Academy (1978), the Elizabeth Blackwell Award (1980), the Bradford Washburn Award (1980), and honorary membership in the American Association for the Advancement of Science. Jointly with L. S. B. Leakey, she has been the recipient of the Prestwich Medal, Geological Society of London (1969) and the Hubbard Medal of the National Geographic Society (1962).

Freed from the conventions of the university, Mary Leakey acquired her anthropological training as she and her husband explored and dug for artifacts for over thirty-five years. Her work at Olduvai Gorge, both independently and with her husband and sons, has resulted in extremely thorough and complete archaeological, geological, and fossil analyses covering abundant artifact and fossil assemblages over most of the last 1.8 million years. As a consequence, her efforts have given us a sustained look back at the oldest humans known.

Notes

1. Originally the Leakeys were slated to receive joint honorary degrees from the University of Witwatersrand in South Africa. Louis Leakey declined this honor as a gesture against apartheid and expected Mary Leakey to follow his example (M. Leakey 1984). Instead, she reasoned that their colleague, Phillip Tobias, would be deeply offended by their refusal, and noted that the University had strongly protested discriminatory admissions policies dictated by the government. Over her husband's protests, Leakey accepted her first honorary degree in 1968.

2. Leakey recounts an "undercurrent of Women's Lib among some of the . . . women [geographers] present, and Women's Lib is something for which I carry no banner, though quite often people seem to expect me to do so. What I have done in my life I have done because I wanted to do it and because it interested me. I just happen to be a woman, and I don't believe it has made much difference" (M. Leakey 1984:193).

References and Works About Mary D. Leakey

Hutchinson, Victoria France
1981   Leakey, Mary Douglas Nicol. In *CA*. Frances Locher, ed. Vols. 97–100, pp. 310–11. Detroit: Gale Research.
The International Who's Who
1986–87   Leakey, Mary Douglas. In *IWW*. 50th ed. P. 910. London: Europa Publications.
Leakey, Louis Seymour Bazett
1934   *Adam's Ancestors: The Evolution of Man and His Culture*. New York: Harper and Row.
Leakey, Louis Seymour Bazett
1974   *By the Evidence: Memoirs, 1932–1951*. New York and London: Harcourt Brace Jovanovich.

Leakey, Louis Seymour Bazett, P. V. Tobias, and J. R. Napier
1964 A New Species of the Genus *Homo* from Olduvai Gorge. *Nature* 202 (4927): 7–9.
Leakey, Richard E.
1983 *One Life: An Autobiography*. London: Michael Joseph.
Phillipson, David W.
1985 *African Archaeology*. Cambridge: Cambridge University Press.
Tanner, Nancy Makepeace
1981 *On Becoming Human*. Cambridge: Cambridge University Press.
Who's Who in the World
1984–85 Leakey, Mary Douglas. In *WWW*. 7th ed. P. 603. Chicago: Marquis Who's Who, Inc.

Selected Works by Mary D. Leakey

1943 *Notes on the Ground and Polished Stone Axes of East Africa* (Booklet). (First published 1943 in *Journal of East Africa and Uganda Natural History Society*.)
1945 Report on the Excavations at Hyrax Hill, Nakuru, Kenya Colony. *Transactions of the Royal Society, South Africa* 30:271–409.
1949 *Some String Figures from North East Angola* (Booklet). Lisboa, Portugal.
1965 Descriptive list of the named localities in Olduvai Gorge. App. 2 in L. S. B. Leakey, *Olduvai Gorge 1951–1961*. Vol. 1, pp. 101–7. London: Cambridge University Press.
1966a A Review of the Oldowan Culture from Olduvai Gorge, Tanzania. *Nature* 210 (5035): 462–66.
1966b Primitive Artefacts from the Kanapoi Valley. *Nature* 212 (5062): 579–81.
1967 Preliminary Survey of the Cultural Material from Beds I and II, Olduvai Gorge, Tanzania. In *Background to Evolution in Africa*. W. W. Bishop and J.D. Clark, eds. Pp. 417–46. Chicago: Chicago University Press.
1969 Recent Discoveries of Hominid Remains at Olduvai Gorge, Tanzania. *Nature* 223 (5207): 756.
1970a Stone Artefacts from Swartkrans. *Nature* 225 (5239): 1222–25.
1970b Early Artefacts from the Koobi Fora Area. *Nature* 226 (5242): 228–30.
1971a *Olduvai Gorge. Vol. 3* of *Excavations in Beds I and II, 1960–63*. Cambridge: Cambridge University Press.
1971b Discovery of Postcranial Remains of *Homo erectus* and Associated Artefacts in Bed IV at Olduvai Gorge, Tanzania. *Nature* 232 (5310):380–83.
1975 Cultural Patterns in the Olduvai Sequence. In *After the Australopithecines*. K. W. Butzer and G. L. Isaac, eds. Pp. 477–94. The Hague: Mouton.
1976 A Summary and Discussion of the Archaeological Evidence from Bed I and Bed II, Olduvai Gorge, Tanzania. In *Human Origins: Louis Leakey and the East African Evidence*. G. L. Isaac and E. R. McCown, eds. Pp. 431–59. Menlo Park, Calif.: Benjamin.
1978a Olduvai Fossil Hominids: Their Stratigraphic Positions and Associations. In *Early Hominids of Africa*. Clifford J. Jolly, ed. Pp. 3–16. London: Duckworth.
1978b Pliocene Footprints at Laetoli, Northern Tanzania. *Antiquity* 52 (205): 133.
1979a 3–6 Million Years Old—Footprints in the Ashes of Time. *National Geographic* 155 (4): 446–57.

1979b *Olduvai Gorge: My Search for Early Man*. London: Collins.
1980   Early Man, Environment, and Tools. In *Current Argument on Early Man: Proceedings of a Nobel Symposium Organized by the Royal Swedish Academy of Sciences*. Lars-König Königsson, ed. Pp. 114–33. New York: Pergamon Press.
1981   Tracks and Tools. *Philosophical Transactions of the Royal Society of London* (Ser. B) 292:95–102.
1983   *Africa's Vanishing Art: The Rock Paintings of Tanzania*. London: Hamish Hamilton/Rainbird.
1984   *Disclosing the Past*. Garden City, N.Y.: Doubleday.

Coauthored Works

Leakey, L. S. B., and M. D. Leakey
1950   *Excavations at Njoro River Cave*. Oxford: Clarendon Press.
1964   Recent Discoveries of Fossil Hominids in Tanganyika: At Olduvai and Near Lake Natron. *Nature* 202 (4927): 5–7.
Leakey, M. D. et al.
1948   *Dimple-based Pottery from Central Kavirondo, Kenya Colony*. Nairobi: Coryndon Memorial Museum.
Leakey, M. D., and R. L. Hay
1979   Pliocene Footprints in the Laetolil Beds at Laetoli, Northern Tanzania. *Nature* 278 (5701): 317–23.
Leakey, M. D., R. L. Hay, G. H. Curtis et al.
1976   Fossil Hominids from the Laetolil Beds. *Nature* 262 (5568): 460–66.
Leakey, M. D., R. L. Hay, D. L. Thurber et al.
1972   Stratigraphy, Archaeology, and Age of the Ndutu and Naisiusiu Beds, Olduvai Gorge, Tanzania. *World Archaeology* 3 (3): 328–41.

JERRIE MCINTYRE

Dorothea Cross Leighton

(1908–   )

Early medical anthropologist Dorothea Cross Leighton is known for several books on the Navajo and for contributions to understanding individuals in their socio-cultural environment.

Dorothea Cross was born September 2, 1908, in Lunenburg, Massachusetts, where her father, Frederick Cushing Cross, a graduate of M.I.T., was treasurer of the family wholesale grocery. Several members of the family were women she characterized as particularly "strong-minded."[1] One, a red-headed aunt, managed her Episcopalian minister husband's affairs. Another was her mother, Dorothea Farquhar Cross, a graduate of Bryn Mawr (1900), having "enjoyed college just immensely."

Though Dorothea Cross in her teens had considered entering the nursing profession, her mother encouraged her to attend Bryn Mawr. She majored in both chemistry and biology and graduated in 1930. She began work as a chemistry technician at Johns Hopkins Hospital in Baltimore but found herself too distanced from people and decided to become a physician. She felt she would be happier as a general practitioner in a small New England town.

Cross was immediately accepted into Johns Hopkins School of Medicine, where she earned her M.D. degree in 1936. Among the medical institutions at that time, Johns Hopkins was the only one to admit women to its program on an equal basis with male applicants. This admissions policy had been stipulated by a wealthy donor who had been influenced by M. Carey Thomas. Thomas, president of Bryn Mawr for years, had found it necessary to enroll in a European university to earn her Ph.D. Not surprisingly, Cross's experiences at both Bryn Mawr and Johns Hopkins upheld her conviction that women could do anything they wanted.

Consequently, she was shocked when three or four leading U.S. hospitals immediately rejected her application for a residency in medicine. She recalls that their refusals said bluntly, "Sorry, you're a woman," or words to that effect. Thus, she remained at the Hopkins-connected Baltimore City Hospital and at the end of her initial postgraduate training year (her internship), married classmate Alexander H. Leighton, who had chosen to specialize in psychiatry. She set aside her plan to become a general practitioner to join her husband as a resident in psychiatry at the Hopkins-associated Phipps Clinic in Baltimore.

At the Phipps Clinic the chief of psychiatry, Dr. Adolf Meyer, urged his students to obtain the patients' life histories to understand their illnesses. He also strongly suggested that budding psychiatrists write their own life histories, because self-knowledge increased their understanding of patients. Since the European-born Dr. Meyer encouraged knowledge of other cultures as well, the Leightons attended a monthly seminar in New York City conducted by anthropologist Ralph Linton and psychiatrist Abram Kardiner. This seminar was an experiment to see what a psychiatrist could deduce about the personalities to be found in a particular group from descriptions of the group's culture. The seminars stimulated the Leightons to plan research on psychiatric problems found in American Indian cultures, but they knew nothing of anthropology. They began their research year (1939–40) by auditing anthropology courses at Columbia University for three months to gain some understanding of the wide range of cultural details. During the remaining nine months, they conducted fieldwork in two cultures.

An earlier introduction to Clyde Kluckhohn, Navajo scholar and longtime member of the Department of Anthropology at Harvard University, led the Leightons to start their fieldwork among the Navajo near Ramah, New Mexico. In January 1940, they moved into a small hogan (traditional Navajo house) next to the large family hogan of an excellent Navajo interpreter and began interviewing Navajo residents. In May they traveled to Alaska and spent the summer with the St. Lawrence Island Inuit (Eskimo), who afforded a striking cultural contrast to the Navajo. To gain insight into conditions that promoted or inhibited human health, the Leightons collected life stories in both areas, as Dr. Meyer had trained them to do. They also observed Navajo and Inuit behavior patterns under many different circumstances and occasionally treated the sick.

When they returned to Johns Hopkins to resume their formal psychiatric training, Alexander Leighton received an appointment and Dorothea Leighton did not. Though each of the two psychiatric residents at Phipps customarily worked every day and alternated night duty (on call), staff officials had decided, without consulting the Leightons, that this usual arrangement would be unduly stressful to their marriage and awarded the appointment to Alexander Leighton alone.

That fall the Bureau of Indian Affairs (BIA) invited the Leightons to Washington to discuss ways to improve the health care services provided to Indian groups. The Leightons began by stressing the near-total ignorance of most white agency-employees concerning Navajo culture and Navajo ways of dealing with illness, and the deleterious effect such ignorance had on white physicians' treatment of Navajo patients. They recommended that the BIA commission a series of volumes, one for each Indian tribe, designed to help non-Indian BIA employees understand the culture and the people with whom they worked, with special emphasis on each tribe's concepts of illness and treatment. Agency officials requested that the Leightons write such a book on the Navajo. The task fell largely to Dorothea Leighton, because her husband's time was taken up with his psychiatric residency and because he was called into the navy when the United States entered World War II.

Leighton found that BIA employees without exception were enthusiastic regarding the proposed book, for the existing scholarly literature on the Navajo had been of limited use to the average person. Written for a lay audience, the Leightons' book *The Navaho Door* (1944) described something of the history, environment, ordinary family routines, religion, the Indian Service, white and Indian ideas of illness and treatment, and contained several short life-histories. Although Leighton has said the book was "very superficial in many respects," she also commented that "it was just splendid that we didn't know very much about anthropology because we didn't get lost in the intricacies of everything."

In 1942 Leighton accepted the position of Special Physician, Research, with the U.S. Office of Indian Affairs. Thus she became part of a research group, many of them women, applying psychological tests of personality development to samples of children from five Indian tribes. Gathering data in Arizona, New Mexico, and South Dakota, and then analyzing it in Chicago, the home base of the project, Dorothea was for the first time

doing something entirely on my own that Alec didn't even know very much about. . . . That was a very good experience for me, indeed, and I felt good about myself and about the work we were doing. . . . I think that I felt as if whatever I knew from any source had some relevance to what I was doing there.

Her work as research physician also led to her major publications, *The Navaho* (Leighton and Kluckhohn 1946), *Children of the People* (Leighton and Kluckhohn 1948), and *People of the Middle Place* (Leighton and Adair 1966). These and other publications that reported research findings on Papago, Hopi, and Sioux children provided a description of each culture aimed at enlightening average readers. Of these works, she is best known for *The Navaho*, which is required reading in many introductory anthropology classes.

For a short time after World War II, the Leightons lived in Washington, D.C. There, Dorothea finished work with the Zuni material (Leighton and Adair 1966), and their first child, Doreen, was born. In 1947 they moved to a small town outside of Ithaca, New York, to work at Cornell University; and their son, Frederick A., was born. After three years in a part-time job at Cornell, she joined the group headed by her husband that was launching the multiyear Stirling County (Nova Scotia) study. A ground-breaking project in psychiatric epidemiology, the study was an effort to discover the prevalence and character of psychiatric disorders in an apparently normal rural population in Nova Scotia.

Leighton developed a systematic approach to coding the interview results and coauthored the final report on the research, *The Character of Danger* (Leighton et al. 1963c). The Leightons acknowledge the shortcomings of the Stirling County study: particularly, the time that elapsed between the gathering of the data in 1952 and its eventual publication in 1963; the search for adequate methodology, which was responsible for much of the delay; and the lack of computers to handle the enormous mass of data until almost the end of the project.

In addition to the Stirling County Study, the Leightons became involved in similar studies overseas. The Leightons compared the results of one study conducted in Sweden by Swedish scholars with their own findings from Nova Scotia. They collaborated with Dr. T. A. Lambo, the first Nigerian to be trained in Western psychiatry, on another epidemiological study in Nigeria. Both the Swedish and the Nigerian studies were important in assessing the prevalence of psychiatric disorders in different cultures.

Leighton's participation in all the studies required considerable travel in addition to her other responsibilities. There was a significant amount of socializing with the local people and with the staff of approximately forty people in the first of the three Stirling County studies. The summer student assistants required some supervision and a good deal of entertaining as well. During this time of participation in her husband's research projects, Dorothea cared for her own two children as well as a young cousin. The Leighton family moved every spring and fall between Cornell and Nova Scotia for about seventeen years, except for one summer when they visited Europe and the British Isles. The end of the first round of the Stirling County study nearly coincided with the end of the Leightons' marriage; they were divorced in 1965.

That fall Leighton accepted a position in the School of Public Health at the University of North Carolina. Convinced that individuals going into public health should also be familiar with social science, she was involved for three years in a required interdisciplinary course that covered biology, the environment, and mental health. She was also asked by the Department of Anthropology to teach a course in medical anthropology, a newly named and recognized subfield of anthropology.

Some have said that *The Navaho Door* was the first publication in medical anthropology, although the Leightons had not thought of the book in that light. Because of the Leightons' medical training and psychiatric background, they naturally found it logical to pay attention to the health status and common medical problems of people with whom they worked, even if studying the people's health was not the principal objective of research. When their help was requested, they found that treatment to alleviate symptoms made it easier for them to get acquainted with both Navajo and Inuit people.

By 1965, when she began teaching at the University of North Carolina, several anthropologists sought to form a society for medical anthropology in order to increase the development of this new subfield. Leighton agreed to carry the matter forward and sent a questionnaire to those interested in forming the society.

She was subsequently elected president by mail, an office she held for the society's first two years. She also served as chair of her department for the two years before she retired from North Carolina in 1974.

Leighton has twice returned to teaching. In 1977 she was lecturer in the Department of Epidemiology and International Health at the University of California at San Francisco, and in 1981–82 she served as Visiting Professor in Anthropology at the University of California, Berkeley.

Her return to California—first to Berkeley and then Fresno—had very much to do with her sense of family history and of her existence as one of a line of women in that history. When she was growing up, she had very happy memories of both her grandmothers, especially her maternal grandmother, the one "on the strong-minded side" of the family. By the time she retired from teaching, her daughter had moved to Berkeley, had borne two daughters, been divorced, and was applying for admission to medical school. Joining her daughter in Berkeley would both help her daughter with the multiple responsibilities and at the same time enable Dorothea to act, in her turn, as grandmother.

Leighton frequently emerges from a very active retirement. For example, she participated in a panel on Navajo women at the American Athropological Association (AAA) meeting in 1981 and contributed an article to the resulting special journal issue. At the 1982 AAA meeting, she participted in a panel entitled "Women Emeritae Reflect on Anthropology." In her presentation she described herself as a physician who became an anthropologist by accident: "I don't know whether you knew I was a medical anthropologist or not; I didn't think of myself that way at that time. I was just . . . something or other . . . a mixture of things, operating as seemed appropriate."

Note

1. The author interviewed Dorothea Cross Leighton in Berkeley in April 1982; all quotes not otherwise cited are from that interview. I am most appreciative of not only her cooperation at that and subsequent times but also for her hospitality and for her friendship.

Selected Works by Dorothea Leighton

1956 The Distribution of Psychiatric Symptoms in a Small Town. *American Journal of Psychiatry* 112:716–23.

1957a Rorschachs of 87 Zuni Children. In *Primary Records in Culture and Personality*. Bert Kaplan, ed. Pp. 1–274. Madison, Wisc.: Microcard Foundation.

1957b Rorschachs of 107 Navaho Children. In *Primary Records in Culture and Personality*. Bert Kaplan, ed. Pp. 1–255. Madison, Wisc.: Microcard Foundation.

1968 A Contribution of Population Studies: Ameliorative Measures for the Disadvantaged. In *Commemorative Volume for Professor Eric Essen-Moller*. Eberhard Nyman, ed. *Acta Psychiatrica Scandinavica* 46 (Suppl. 219): 103–8. Lund, Sweden.

1969 *Memorandum: Recent Visit to the Navaho Reservation and Environs*. Manuscript. Alexander H. Leighton and Dorothea C. Leighton Collection, Special Collections Library, Northern Arizona University, Flagstaff.

1971 The Empirical Status of the Integration-Disintegration Hypothesis. In *Psychiatric Disorder and the Urban Environment*. Berton H. Kaplan, ed. Pp. 68–78. New York: Behavioral Publications.

1972a Cultural Determinants of Behavior: A Neglected Area. *American Journal of Psychiatry* 128:1003–4.

1972b Measuring Stress Levels in School Children As a Program Monitoring Device. *American Journal of Public Health* 62:799–806.

1974 Mental Health Problems. In *Community Medicine*. Abdel R. Omran, ed. Pp. 175–296. New York: The Springer Publishing Co.

1977 Behavioral Science, Mental Health and Mental Illness. In *The Behavioral Sciences and Preventive Medicine: Opportunities and Dilemmas*. Robert L. Kane, M.D., ed. Pp. 37–51. Washington, D.C.: Department of Health, Education and Welfare Publication No. 76–878 (National Institute of Health).

1978 Sociocultural Factors in Physical and Mental Breakdown. *Man-Environment Systems* 8:33–37.

1979 Community Integration and Mental Health: The Use of Longitudinal Data in Documenting Changes. In *Social and Psychological Research in Community Settings*. Ricardo F. Munoz et al., eds. Pp. 175–294. New York: Jossey-Bass.

1982a Anthropologist by Accident. Paper presented at the Annual Meeting of the American Anthropological Association, Washington, D.C. Mimeographed copy, Alexander H. Leighton and Dorothea C. Leighton Collection, Special Collections Library, Northern Arizona University, Flagstaff.

1982b As I knew Them: Navajo Women in 1940. *American Indian Quarterly* 6:43–51.

1984 *Eskimo Recollections of Their Life Experiences*. Northwestern Anthropological Research Notes. Moscow: University of Idaho.

Coauthored Works

Leighton, Dorothea, and John Adair
1966 *People of the Middle Place: A Study of the Zuni Indians*. Behavioral Science Monographs. New Haven: Human Relations Area Files, Inc.

Leighton, Dorothea et al.
1963a Psychiatric Findings of the Stirling County Study. *American Journal of Psychiatry* 119:1021–26.

1963b *Psychiatric Disorder Among the Yoruba*. Ithaca, N.Y.: Cornell University Press.

1963c *The Character of Danger: Psychiatric Symptoms in Selected Communities*. New York: Basic Books.

1971 Psychiatric Disorder in a Swedish and a Canadian Community: An Exploratory Study. *Social Science and Medicine* 5:189–209.

Leighton, Dorothea, and N. F. Cline
1968 The Public Health Nurse as a Mental Health Resource. In *Essays on Medical Anthropology*. Thomas Weaver, ed. Pp. 36–54. Athens: University of Georgia Press.

1972 Use of a Stress Scale with Mental Hospital Patients. *North Carolina Journal of Mental Health* 6:27–48.

Leighton, Dorothea, J. Jacobs, and G.M. Davis

1972 Measuring Stress Levels of School Children As a Program Monitoring Device: Three Years Experience in a Single School System. *Research Previews* 10:10–17.

Leighton, Dorothea, and Clyde Kluckhohn

1946 *The Navaho*. Cambridge: Harvard University Press.

1948 *Children of the People: The Navaho Individual and His Development*. Cambridge: Harvard University Press.

Leighton, Dorothea, and Alexander H. Leighton

1941 Elements of Psychotherapy in Navaho Religion. *Psychiatry* 4:505–24.

1942 Some Types of Uneasiness and Fear in a Navaho Indian Community. *American Anthropologist* 44: 194–209.

1944 *The Navaho Door: An Introduction to Navaho Life*. Cambridge: Harvard University Press.

1949 *Gregorio, the Hand-Trembler*. Papers of the Peabody Museum of American Archaeology and Ethnology. Vol. 40. Harvard University.

Leighton, Dorothea, Alexander H. Leighton, and I. T. Stone

1966 Poverty and the Individual. In *Poverty Amid Affluence*. Leo Fishman, ed. Pp. 72–96. New Haven: Yale University Press.

Leighton, Dorothea, Eric Mood, and Morris Shiffman

1969 Environmental Health. In *Mental Health Considerations in Public Health*. Washington, D.C.: U.S. Department of Health, Education and Welfare (National Institute of Mental Health).

Leighton, Dorothea, and I. T. Stone

1974 Community Development As a Therapeutic Force: A Case Study with Measurements. In *Sociological Perspectives on Community Mental Health*. Paul Roman and Harrison Trice, eds. Pp. 209–32. Philadelphia: F. A. Davis Co.

JOYCE GRIFFEN

Nancy Oestreich Lurie

(1924–   )

Nancy Oestreich Lurie is an American sociocultural anthropologist, known for her studies of North American Indians, especially the Winnebago, and her work in applied and action anthropology.

Born in Milwaukee, Wisconsin, on January 29, 1924, Nancy Oestreich was an only child raised in a four-generation household. Besides herself and her parents, Carl Ralph and Rayline Danielson Oestreich, there were her maternal grandparents and until she was twelve, a great-grandfather. She credits her upbringing among elders with allowing her to be at ease among American Indian families as an ethnographer years later. Nancy Oestreich knew when she was six years old that she would become an anthropologist. Her family believes that her great-grandfather's boyhood recollections of Indian settlements around Milwaukee were the determining influence that led her to choose an anthropological career.[1]

During her early years Oestreich's father, a professor of engineering at the University of Wisconsin, Milwaukee Extension Division (now the University of Wisconsin–Milwaukee [UWM]), stimulated her interests. He introduced her to the word *anthropology* as encompassing her interest in Indians; and when she was eight years old, he introduced her to Samuel A. Barrett, the director, and Will C. McKern, anthropology curator, of the Milwaukee Public Museum (MPM). At the time they were the only two anthropologists in Milwaukee. Nancy Oestreich's father knew them through his volunteer work on the museum's stamp collection; and they, along with the Oestreich family, encouraged her ambitions.

From the time of her first behind-the-scenes visit at the MPM, Nancy Oestreich knew that one day she would be a curator there. As soon as she was old enough to ride public transportation alone, she spent as much time as she could at the museum, sketching their world-famous ethnological dioramas and visiting the anthropology department to perform volunteer tasks.

Oestreich attended college, majoring in anthropology and sociology, at the University of Wisconsin (Madison). She received her B.A. in 1945. Before she had graduated, her first published article, "Butterflies and the American Indian," appeared in the *Wisconsin Archaeologist* (Lurie 1943:1–6). It dealt with a short survey of butterfly motifs and their significance in American Indian art, mythology, and children's games.

She conducted her first fieldwork during the summer between her junior and senior years under the guidance of her major professor, J. Sydney Slotkin. Slotkin suggested that she start learning field techniques by working among the Wisconsin Winnebago; they were nearby (World War II limited civilian travel), and according to George Peter Murdock's *Ethnographic Bibliography of North America*, "they had been scarcely noticed by scholars since Paul Radin's classic studies made years before" (Lurie 1972c:152).

Courses or texts on field methods "were not yet a regular part of the anthropological curriculum—certainly not for undergraduates" (Lurie 1972c:152). Slotkin simply impressed upon the young student the seriousness of her work and sent her into the field to learn to observe and record accurately, and to publish what she had learned (Lurie 1972c:152). While she was in the field, the Winnebago people added another dimension to the significance of her work—that "there was much for white society to learn from Indians which ought to be recorded accurately to bring about greater respect and fairness in Indian-white relationships" (Lurie 1972c:159). Oestreich's second publication, "Culture Change Among the Wisconsin Winnebago," resulted from this fieldwork (Oestreich 1944).

The following fall, one of the Winnebago she had met during the summer, Mitchell Redcloud, Sr., was hospitalized with cancer in Madison. Oestrich visited him regularly and recorded ethnographic data at his bedside. Fearing that he would not survive his scheduled surgery, Redcloud adopted her as his daughter. By doing so, he gave her "a Winnebago name, clan affiliation, and a host of relatives on whom I was to rely to continue the task which Redcloud and I had begun" (Lurie 1961c:xii). Indeed, Redcloud's family would figure importantly in Lurie's future ethnographic work.

After graduating from the University of Wisconsin, she continued her formal education in anthropology at the University of Chicago. She arrived at the university just after Sol Tax was brought in to help organize its postwar program in anthropology. Her thesis, "Trends of Change in Patterns of Childcare and Training Among the Wisconsin Winnebago," was carried out under Tax's and Fred Eggan's guidance. It dealt with the extent and manner in which "changes in child care and training kept pace with changes in Winnebago society as a whole" (Oestreich 1948:43). She chose this subject because money was available to complete a long checklist for a comparative study conducted by John Whiting; though it was not of abiding interest to her, it allowed her to get back into the field. Although Tax and his formulation of action anthropology would influence her later work, she graduated from the university before the famous "Fox Project'' and Tax's seminars on action research. The Fox Project was the summer field-training program on the Fox reservation in Iowa that initially led to the development of action anthropology, an open-ended process in which, if the people wish it, anthropological research is combined with helping to identify and solve community problems (see Lurie 1973:5–15).

In 1947 Nancy Oestreich began her professional career. She accepted the newly created position as instructor in anthropology in the Sociology Department at the University of Wisconsin, Milwaukee Extension Division, where she taught intermittently (1947–53). In 1948 she returned to graduate studies to pursue her Ph.D. at Northwestern University, ''attracted by Melville J. Herskovits' concern for observable cultural processes and emphasis on cultural relativism in acculturation studies.'' Her dissertation, which combined field and ethnohistorical research, compared cultural change in the Nebraska and Wisconsin enclaves of the Winnebago. While she was still at Northwestern, she met and married Edward Lurie, a graduate student in history. Their marriage ended amicably in 1963. They had no children.

In 1954 Lurie began work as an expert witness for Indian petitioners before the U.S. Indian Claims Commission, a quasi court created in 1946 for the hearing and determination of claims against the United States arising prior to August 13, 1946. Most of the claims involved land questions; and both the Justice Department, representing the federal government, and Indians' attorneys required ethnohistorical research and testimony concerning tribal identities, boundaries, and land use and occupancy. By the time the claims commission was terminated in 1978, Lurie had served as an expert witness on seven cases: Lower Kutenai; Lower Kalispel; Quinaielt-Quileute; Sac and Fox, et al.; Winnebago; Turtle Mountain Chippewa; and Eastern Potawatomi.

Lurie became a lecturer in anthropology at the University of Michigan in 1957, first in the Rackham School of Graduate Studies—the extension branch of the university (1957–59)—and then in the School of Public Health (1959–61). Her husband's position in the history department and the school's policy against nepotism precluded Lurie from seeking a regular appointment. In 1961, when her husband left the faculty, Lurie was able to obtain a tenure track appointment teaching applied anthropology at the University of Michigan School of Public Health.

During these years at Michigan, Lurie recorded, edited, annotated, and published the autobiography of *Mountain Wolf Woman* (Lurie 1961c). Lurie had first met Mountain Wolf Woman while doing fieldwork in 1945. She was inspired to document this woman's life by Paul Radin's *Crashing Thunder* (1928), the first full-length autobiography of an American Indian edited and published by an anthropologist. Mountain Wolf Woman, whom Lurie found remarkable in her own right, was Crashing Thunder's sister as well as contemporary; documenting her story provided a unique, comparative view of a Winnebago woman's life. Mountain Wolf Woman, the classifactory sister of Mitchell Redcloud, Sr., genuinely acknowledged Lurie as her niece and agreed to let Lurie publish her autobiography because "the request was made in terms of our aunt-niece relationship" (Lurie 1961c:93).

Several years after *Mountain Wolf Woman* appeared, Lurie wrote an article addressing the lack of attention, or otherwise stereotyped treatment, American Indian women had often received in historical studies. "Indian women have been virtually ignored by white historians [who] . . . have side-stepped that long period between Pocahontas and Buffy Sainte-Marie, Maria Tallchief, Maria Martinez and other modern women" (Lurie 1972a:1, 32).

While Lurie was still at Michigan, she renewed her acquaintance with June Helm,* a fellow graduate student from her University of Chicago days; Helm had concentrated on the Northern Athapaskan and was looking for a partner to work with the Dogrib in the Canadian Northwest Territories. They spent nearly five months in 1959 in an isolated village and returned to work in other Dogrib settlements in 1962 and 1967 (see Lurie 1961a, 1966).

In late 1960, familiar with Lurie's work and her understanding of American Indians, Sol Tax asked Lurie to serve as assistant coordinator for the American Indian Chicago Conference (AICC). Conceived and organized by Tax, the AICC was a test of action anthropology on a large scale in response to Indian dissatisfaction with the federal policies of the 1950s (see Lurie 1961d:478–500). Its purpose was to provide Indian people with the opportunity to define what they perceived as the major problems plaguing them and to make recommendations for policy improvement. Prior to the conference, Lurie and Tax "assisted the Indian steering committee in arranging regional meetings and disseminating the results of local discussions" in preparation for the conference. Four hundred sixty-seven American Indian people representing ninety tribes and bands came to the conference; and together they wrote the Declaration of Indian Purpose, which was subsequently presented to President John F. Kennedy. Convinced that "the *Declaration of Indian Purpose* clearly indicates that the conference of June 13–20, 1961 was successful in carrying out its objectives, justifying the Indians' efforts and Tax's faith in the methods of Action Anthropology" (Lurie 1961d:498), Lurie left the AICC with a commitment to action anthropology— and with a national image.

While at the University of Michigan and then after joining the anthropology faculty at UWM in 1963, Lurie worked on several action anthropology projects. The first involved her in a Wisconsin Winnebago self-survey project, a direct outgrowth of the AICC to be used as a basis for community planning; and the second involved her in a similar effort with the Indian community in Milwaukee. Then from 1969 to 1974 she worked with the Menominee "in their ultimately successful drive to repeal the 1954 legislation which had terminated their reservation and federal Indian status."

Lurie became a full professor of anthropology in 1966 while at UWM and served as department chair from 1967 to 1970. As chair she was deeply involved in establishing the univerity's Ph.D. program in anthropology and thus declined the position of chief ethnologist offered her by the National Museum of Man in

Ottawa. On leave during the school year 1965–66, Lurie taught at the University of Aarhus, Denmark, as a Fulbright-Hays Lecturer in Anthropology.

Then in 1972 Lurie "changed course and went into a new phase of intellectual growth." She left academia and accepted a full-time position as curator and head of the anthropology section of the Milwaukee Public Museum. Lurie was the first woman to head one of the museum's scientific sections. She had, of course, been greatly influenced by the MPM to become an anthropologist and had also maintained a strong interest in museology throughout her career. But she had also become more and more concerned about increasing general understanding of anthropology, believing that "museums offer scarcely realized opportunities to reach an enormous and varied public with anthropological data and concepts to enable people to reach more informed opinions" (Lurie 1981:184).

Lurie's dedication to the pursuit and application of anthropological knowledge has earned her numerous awards and honors. In 1982 she received one of the highest honors of her profession; she was elected to the presidency of the American Anthropological Association (AAA) and served the association's first two-year term under its newly revised bylaws. Lurie and president-elect June Helm worked together in seeing the AAA through the stresses of organizational transition. As Lurie observed, "Any two people who had done field work sharing a one room cabin in the Sub-Arctic in the winter and still were friends were equal to any task." Lurie had already served on the AAA Ethics Committee (as chair from 1971–72) and on the Executive Board (1977–80). She had also served as Section H (anthropology) representative to the General Council of the American Association for the Advancement of Science (1969–73), and had served as secretary-treasurer (1953), vice president (1964), and president (1967) of the Central States Anthropological Society.

Throughout her career, while teaching, curating, writing, and involving herself in the scholarly and organizational affairs of her discipline, Lurie has remained an active field ethnologist who considers fieldwork "an essential anthropological commitment." At the time of this writing, Lurie is engaged in "an ethnohistorical project relating documentary data on the Winnebago's role in the Black Hawk War of 1832 to newly collected field data, augmenting and clarifying historical records in regard to genealogical information and translations of place and personal names." Summer fieldwork conducted during 1982–84 involved Lurie's working with Winnebago traditionalists, transcribing the lyrics of sacred Winnebago songs recorded on wax cylinders by Frances Densmore* in the 1920s and 1930s. The lyrics of these songs have provided Lurie with access to esoteric data that earlier in her career she accepted as inappropriate for a young woman to pursue.

Reflecting her lifelong commitment to the social as well as scientific needs to which anthropology responds, Lurie has "always preferred the term consultant to informant" and respected her Indian associates' control over information concerning them. She has always been conscious of the political nature of anthropological work—and its consequences. Her writings have helped inform nonspecialists as well as specialists about the desires of American Indian peoples to live within their value systems, at the same time "respecting the rights of individuals who wish to assimilate into the larger society if that is their considered choice." Lurie's work has done much to dispel stereotypical notions about American Indians, although she "sees much more to be done, particularly by the increasing numbers of Indian scholars themselves, in educating mainstream American society."

Certainly the study of culture change, so pervasive in American anthropology when Lurie was a graduate student, had a decisive effect on Lurie's theoretical and methodological orientations. The works of Herskovits, Ralph Linton, and later, Edward Spicer, helped shape Lurie's theoretical pragmatism. The establishment of applied anthropology as a new field in 1941 and the growing interest in action anthropology provided Lurie with ways to assist in community development while maintaining her role as a social scientist. Lurie's views on difficulties or successes she may have encountered as a result of being a woman are expressed in her account of the lives of six early women in American anthropology: "the fact of being a woman has been and continues to be one of many personal variables, any one of which may figure most importantly in affecting the course of field work at different times and in various places" (Lurie 1966:81). Lurie's recognition of both the individual—the individual anthropologist and the individual in American Indian societies—and her recognition of the historical sense of events in their lives has made her work as relevant to the contemporary American Indian political scene as it is to contemporary anthropological discourse.

Note

1. All quotes not otherwise cited are from personal communications with Nancy O. Lurie in 1985 and 1986.

Selected Works by Nancy Oestreich Lurie

(Under the name Nancy Oestreich)

1943 Butterflies and the American Indian. *Wisconsin Archaeologist* 24 (1): 1–6.

1944 Cultural Change Among the Winnebago. *Wisconsin Archaeologist* 25 (4): 119–25.

1948 Trends of Change in Patterns of Child Care and Training Among the Wisconsin Winnebago. *Wisconsin Archaeologist* 29 (3–4): 40–140.

1950 Winnebago Folklore. *Badger Folklore* 2 (3): 3–61.

(Under the name Nancy Lurie)

1953 Winnebago Berdache. American Anthropologist 55 (1):708–12.

1955 Problems, Opportunities, and Recommendations. *Ethnohistory* 2 (4): 357–75.

1957 The Indian Claims Commission Act. *The Annals of the American Academy of Political and Social Sciences* 311 (May): 56–70.

1959 Indian Adjustment to European Civilization. In *Seventeenth Century America.*

James Morton Smith, ed. Pp. 35–60. Chapel Hill: University of North Carolina Press. (Reprinted in over ten history text anthologies.)

1960 Winnebago Protohistory. In *Culture in History, Essays in Honor of Paul Radin*. Stanley Diamond, ed. Pp. 790–880. New York: Columbia University Press.

1961a Dogrib Indians of Canada. *Lore* 11 (2): 60–65.

1961b Ethnohistory: An Ethnological Point of View. *Ethnohistory* 8 (1): 79–82.

1961c *Mountain Wolf Woman, Sister of Crashing Thunder*. Ann Arbor: University of Michigan Press. (As ed., trans., and annotator.)

1961d The Voice of the American Indian: A Report on the American Indian Chicago Conference. *Current Anthropology* 2 (5): 478–500.

1965 An American Indian Renascence. *Midcontinent American Studies Journal* 6 (2): 25–50. (Special issue, on topic of the American Indian today.) Lawrence: University of Kansas. (Also, as ed.)

1966 Women in Early American Anthropology. In *Pioneers of American Anthropology: The Uses of Biography*. June Helm, ed. Pp. 29–83. Seattle: University of Washington Press.

1968 Culture Change. In *Introduction to Cultural Anthropology*. James A. Clifton, ed. Pp. 274–303. Boston: Houghton Mifflin.

1969 Wisconsin: A Natural Laboratory for North American Indians Studies. *Wisconsin Magazine of History* 53 (1): 2–20.

1971a As Others See Us. *New University Thought* 7 (Spring): 2–7. (Reprinted 1973 in *Explorations in Anthropology*. Morton H. Fried, ed. Pp. 443–48. New York: Thomas Y. Crowell Co., Inc.)

1971b Menominee Termination. *The Indian Historian* 4 (4): 32–45.

1971c The World's Longest On-Going Protest Demonstration: North American Indian Drinking Patterns. *Pacific Historical Review* 40 (3): 311–32. (Reprinted 1974 in *The American Indian*. Norris Hundley, ed. Pp. 55–76. Santa Barbara, Calif.: Clio Press, 1974.)

1972a Indian Women: A Legacy of Freedom. In *Look to the Mountain Top*. Charles Jones, ed. Pp. 29–36. San Jose, Calif.: H. M. Gousha Co. (Appeared originally in *American Way*, April 1972, Pp. 28–35.)

1972b Menominee Termination: From Reservation to Colony. *Human Organization* 31 (3): 257–70.

1972c Two Dollars. In *Crossing Cultural Boundaries*. Solon Kimball and James Watson, eds. Pp. 151–63. San Francisco: Chandler Publishing Co.

1973 Action Anthropology and the American Indian. In *Anthropology and the American Indian*. James Officer, ed. Pp. 5–15. San Francisco: Indian Historian Press.

1974 Forked Tongue in Cheek or Life Among the Noble Civilages. *The Indian Historian* 28: 40, 52, 54.

1976a American Indians and Museums: A Love Hate Relationship. *The Old Northwest* 2 (3): 235–51.

1976b Not Built in a Day. *Lore* 26 (3): 3–20, 25–37. (Reprinted in *Milwaukee Public Museum Publications in Museology*, no. 6.)

1976c The Will-O'-Wisp of Indian Unity. *The Indian Historian* 9 (3): 19–24. (Reprinted 1979 in *Currents in Anthropology, Essays in Honor of Sol Tax*. Robert Hinshaw, ed. Pp. 325–35. The Hague: Mouton.)

1978a The Indian Claims Commission. *Annals of the American Academy of Political and Social Science* 436 (March): 97–110.

1978b Winnebago Indians. In *Handbook of North American Indians*. Vol. 15, *Northeast*, pp. 690–707. Bruce G. Trigger, vol. ed. Washington, D.C.: Smithsonian Institution.

1980 *Wisconsin Indians*. Madison, Wisc.: State Historical Society.

1981 Museum Land Revisited. *Human Organization* 40 (2): 180–87.

1982 To Save the Menominee People and Forests. *Proceedings*, Thirteenth Annual Conference of the Archaeological Association of the University of Calgary. Pp. 243–252. Calgary, Alta., Can.

1985 *American Indian Lives*. Milwaukee: Milwaukee Public Museum.

Coauthored Works

Lurie, Nancy O., and June Helm

1961 *The Subsistence Economy of the Dogrib Indians of Lac La Martre in the Mackenzie District of the NWT*. Ottawa, Canada: Northern Coordination and Research Centre.

1966 The Dogrib Handgame. *Anthropological Series 71, National Museum of Canada Bulletin*, no. 205. (With Gertrude P. Kurath's analysis of music and choreography). Ottawa.

Lurie, Nancy O., and Eleanor Burke Leacock, eds.

1971 *The North American Indian in Historical Perspective*. Also contributed chapter, The Contemporary American Indian Scene, pp. 418–80. New York: Random House.

Lurie, Nancy O., and Stuart Levine, eds.

1968 *The American Indian Today*. Also contributed chapter, Historical Background, pp. 49–81, and appendix, An American Indian Renascence, pp. 295–328. Deland, Fla.: Everett/Edwards, Inc. (Reprinted 1970 by Penguin Books, Baltimore.)

Lurie, Nancy O., and Vernan F. Ray

1954 The Contributions of Lewis and Clark to Ethnography. *Journal of the Washington Academy of Sciences* 44 (11): 358–70.

Lurie, Nancy O., and Phillip Sidoff

1975 Mexican Kickapoo Collection. *Lore* 25 (3): 24–29.

CECILE R. GANTEAUME

Catharine McClellan

(1921–   )

Catharine McClellan is an American cultural anthropologist who has documented the culture history of the peoples of Alaska and the Yukon Territory.

McClellan characterizes her own work as ethnohistoric, combining a "natural history" approach to data collection with a humanistic sense of the anthropological enterprise. Her attention to the oral literature and life histories of Arctic and subarctic peoples for more than thirty-five years is the clearest evidence of that commitment. "People used stories to instruct me," she has observed, and she in turn has used them as a key source of cultural knowledge.[1]

Students and colleagues who have known her in various fieldwork and academic contexts identify a specific personal and intellectual energy marking her engagement with her work. They emphasize her strong sense of ethics and propriety, her continued adherence to a holistic anthropology based on both archaeological and ethnographic data collection, and her passion for the field.

Born in York, Pennsylvania, on March 1, 1921, in the heart of Pennsylvania Dutch country, McClellan was one of four children in a family that valued, and had the means to provide, a privileged education for its three daughters and son. Her father, William Smith McClellan, the vice president of a lumber mill, and her mother, Josephine Niles McClellan, a woman active in civic affairs, encouraged Catharine McClellan's interest in botany and her general curiosity about the natural world. Educated at a private school stressing the classics, she then went to Bryn Mawr College (as did her mother and older sister). There, she majored in classical archaeology and took a newly instituted course taught by Frederica de Laguna* in American archaeology. She graduated magna cum laude with distinction in her major in 1942.

She first went into the field as an undergraduate with de Laguna, who came to be her mentor and field companion, as well as sharing her research interest in Arctic peoples. Many of the features that mark McClellan's anthropological "style" were shaped by her early training with de Laguna, a scholar equally committed to "a holistic concept of culture." De Laguna wrote that anthropologists should have "a sense of the past to explain the present," and she defined the anthropologist's task as the closest possible recording of the native's point of view (1957:179–81).

In the years just preceding World War II, McClellan and several other Bryn Mawr students and faculty received training from the U.S. Navy. When the war broke out, she worked for the navy in communications intelligence as an ensign and ended her service with the rank of lieutenant in the Naval Reserve. Returning to school for her Ph.D. under the G.I. Bill in 1946, McClellan chose the University of California (UC) at Berkeley, primarily to study with Robert Lowie and A. L. Kroeber. Unaware that one had to be admitted to join a graduate program, she departed for California without introduction. Though she never studied with Kroeber (who retired that year), his focus on cultural patterns drew her into anthropology and remained central to her work. His attention to the concept of culture attracted her far more than the approach of connoisseurs and collectors, which she thought characterized much of classical archaeology. Meeting Kroeber in later years, she said they got along because both were convinced that anthropology was, and should remain, distinct from sociology.

McClellan developed her interest in the historical dimensions of culture at Berkeley (1946–50). In 1948 and 1949 she and Dorothy Ranier, a fellow graduate student, made an ethnographic survey of the natives of the Yukon Territory for the National Museum of Canada. McClellan became the first American researcher to use the Hudson Bay Company's newly opened archives in London. Receiving her Ph.D. from UC Berkeley in 1950, she spent that summer as de Laguna's assistant, conducting archaeological and ethnological investigations of the Tlingit Indians in Angoon, Alaska; the following year she spent doing ethnographic work in the Yukon Territory, Canada.

If any central theme characterizes McClellan's anthropological being, it is her focus on fieldwork combined with what she calls "a Boasian core." Thus, her commitment to the urgency of recording and reconstructing Yukon Indian culture has been coupled with the type of research methodology practiced by Franz Boas, in which all ethnographic details have potential scientific value. With these priorities, McClellan has managed to combine her teaching with a rigorous research schedule. As an assistant professor at the University of Washington in Seattle (1952–56), she and de Laguna studied the Yakutat Tlingit and the Atna Athapaskans of the Copper River, Alaska, and made an archaeological survey of the Taku River in British Columbia. Before starting a job at Barnard College in 1956, she spent six months with the Alaskan Inuit (Eskimo) for the U.S. Public Health Service, a venture that provided good comparative data for circumpolar natives and that also convinced her that she had neither the inclination nor temperament to be an "applied anthropologist." During her tenure at Barnard College (1956–61), she continued work with the Atna (1958–60). While at the University of Wisconsin (1961–83), she worked more intensively at recording, documenting, and analyzing the oral traditions and cultural history of Northern

Athapaskans, including the Inland Tlingit, the Atna, the Tutchone, and the Tagish, returning frequently with graduate students to Yukon Territory.

Unlike other scholars of McClellan's generation, she does not believe that being a woman significantly restricted her career options or limited the nature of her anthropological work. Although she served on various committees in the 1970s that addressed women's rights—including one to initiate a women's studies program at the University of Wisconsin—she never engaged in the organized feminist movement. She neither construed her professional situation in terms of sex roles nor identified with an activist stance on the basis of gender. For example, she remembers Bryn Mawr fondly, not as a haven for women, but simply as an intellectually stimulating institution that did not admit men.

Concerning fieldwork, she comments that being a woman was in many ways an advantage. During the 1940s and 1950s white males in the Yukon were highly suspect; they were game wardens or some other variant agent of the government. Women, on the other hand, were usually missionaries or schoolteachers. McClellan was put in the latter category. Although this freed her from suspicion, she had to play the role that Indian men and women considered acceptable and decent for a respectable white woman. This sometimes meant maintaining a reserve about sexual and excretory topics, and also set up obligations to entertain the local white elite (Frederica de Laguna, personal communication).

McClellan's anthropology is marked by time-intensive fieldwork, exhaustive data collection, and a decided caution toward theoretical models that might dissuade the field-worker from, as she puts it, "following the ethnographic facts." De Laguna has suggested that McClellan's most evident strength as a scholar has been this ability to remain open to the serendipitous occasion—seizing ever more vantage points from which to see Indian culture in Indian terms. McClellan's criteria for good fieldwork always required multiple visits, corroborative evidence, meticulous detail, and repeated participant observation in cultural events. Remaining single for the first twenty-five years of her career allowed her a freedom of movement that permitted trips to the North nearly every year. Her marriage in 1974 to the anthropologist John Hitchcock, an expert on Nepal and India, has not broken that tradition.

McClellan has done extensive research on culture contact, both to study change and to see how Athapaskans have expressed their cultural traditions. For her, first encounters with whites are another element in the traditional environment, and the Indian stories about them provide the ethnographer with an additional context within which to record how Yukon Indians perceived their world. She has explored the conceptions of power that underlie the worldview of these hunting-and-gathering populations and has explained, for example, why access to major sources of power among the southern Yukon Indians differed for women and men. Her attention to ethnographic detail has contributed not only to our appreciation of the technology and oral literature of subarctic Indians but to the particular ways in which anthropologists now group and classify them.

McClellan's students recount that when she taught theory, she would fill a shopping cart with Boas's books and wheel it into the classroom just to impress them with the sheer volume of his work. Kroeber, Lowie, and de Laguna were also *de rigueur* readings for her graduate students. Many students recall the lively, unstructured lectures in which she presented a multisensory picture of peoples from the North by bringing Indian tools, clothes, and weapons for students to examine while she told stories of her most recent visits to the Inland Tlingit or Athapaskan friends.

McClellan also impressed her students with their ethical responsibilities and stressed anthropologists' ultimate responsibility to the groups they study. For example, she published very little on witchcraft, fearing that it might cause her informants harm. She has also made herself available as a resource to Indian organizations in legal negotiations with the Canadian government and has written a book with two of her graduate students on Yukon Indian culture history to be used in public schools.

Reflecting back on her own training and that of young anthropologists today, McClellan sees some crucial differences. In the 1940s with anthropology still committed to a holistic approach, it was assumed that one would know physical anthropology, archaeology and cultural theory at least at an elementary level, and world ethnography cold—which is rarely true today. The unstructured nature of graduate training in the late 1940s at Berkeley was characterized by a sink-or-swim approach, singling out those with initiative. McClellan's students maintain that she is still committed to that sort of program; she guides them in the ethics of investigation rather than in what to look at and in what to record of what people know. This focus on the field, on accurate accounts, on basic ethnography melds with her breadth of interest and knowledge to shape McClellan's continuing contributions to the archives of northern Indian culture history.

Note

1. This sketch is based on interviews with Catharine McClellan, Frederica de Laguna, Janice Sheppard, and a number of colleagues and students at the University of Wisconsin (Madison) who have known her over the last twenty-four years.

Selected Works by Catharine McClellan

1953a The Island Tlingit. *Asia and North America*, Memoir No. 9. Society for American Archaeology. Pp. 47–52.

1953b Wappo and Patwin Ethnography. In *The Archaeology of the Napa Region*. F. Heizer, ed. *Anthropological Records* 12 (6): 233–43. Berkeley: University of California Press.

1954 The Interrelations of Social Structure with Northern Tlingit Ceremonialism. *Southwestern Journal of Anthropology* 10 (1): 75–96.

1956 Shamanistic Syncretism in Southern Yukon Territory. *Transactions of the New York Academy of Sciences* (Series 11) 19 (2): 130–37.

1960   Tlingit (Revision of article). In *Encyclopædia Britannica*. 15th ed. Chicago: En-
       cyclopædia Britannica, Inc.
1961   Avoidance Between Siblings of the Same Sex in Northwestern North America.
       Southwestern Journal of Anthropology 17:102–23.
1963   Wealth, Women and Frogs Among the Tagish. *Anthropos* 58 (1–2): 121–28.
1964   Culture Contacts in the Early Historic Period in Northwestern North America.
       Arctic Anthropology 2 (2): 3–15.
1969   Comments in *Contributions to Anthropology: Band Societies*. National Museum
       of Canada Bulletin 228. Pp. 115. Ottawa.
1970a Indian Stories About the First Whites in Northwestern America. *Ethnohistory in
       Southwestern Alaska and Southern Yukon*. Margaret Lantis, ed. Pp. 102–33. Lex-
       ington: University of Kentucky Press.
1970b Introduction to *Athapascan Studies. The Western Canadian Journal of Anthro-
       pology* 2 (1): vi–xix.
1971   *The Girl Who Married the Bear*. Publications in Ethnology No. 2. Ottawa: National
       Museum of Canada.
1975a Feuding and Warfare Among Northern Athapaskans. In *Proceedings of the North-
       ern Athapaskan Conference, 1971*.
1975b *My Old People Say: An Ethnographic Survey of Southern Yukon Territory*. Pub-
       lications in Ethnology No. 6. Ottawa: National Museum of Man.
1981a History of Research in the Cordillera. In *The Handbook of North American Indians*.
       Vol. 6, *Subarctic*, pp. 35–42. June Helm, vol. ed. Washington, D.C.: Smithsonian
       Institution.
1981b The Inland Tlingit. In *The Handbook of North American Indians*. Vol. 6, *Sub-
       arctic*, pp. 469–80. June Helm, vol. ed. Washington, D.C.: Smithsonian Insti-
       tution.
1981c Intercultural Relations and Cultural Change in the Cordillera. In *The Handbook
       of North American Indians*. Vol. 6, *Subarctic*, pp. 387–401. June Helm, vol. ed.
       Washington, D.C.: Smithsonian Institution.
1981d The Tagish. In *The Handbook of North American Indians*. Vol. 6, *Subarctic*,
       pp. 481–92. June Helm, vol. ed. Washington, D.C.: Smithsonian Institution.
1981e The Tutchone. In *The Handbook of North American Indians*. Vol. 6, *Subarctic*,
       pp. 493–505. June Helm, vol. ed. Washington, D.C.: Smithsonian Institution.

Coauthored Works

McClellan, Catharine, and Julie Cruikshank
1976   Preliminary Investigation of the Social Impact of the Alaska Highway on Yukon
       Indians: Probable Parallels to the Impact of Pipeline Construction. *Berger Com-
       mission Records*. Ottawa.
McClellan, Catharine, and Frederica de Laguna
1981   The Atna. In *The Handbook of North American Indians*. Vol. 6, *Subarctic*,
       pp. 372–86. June Helm, vol. ed. Washington, D.C.: Smithsonian Institution.
McClellan, Catharine, and Glenda Denniston
1981   Environment and Culture in the Cordillera. In *The Handbook of North American
       Indians*. Vol. 6, *Subarctic*, pp. 372–86. June Helm, vol. ed. Washington, D.C.:
       Smithsonian Institution.

McClellan, Catharine, and Dorothy Rainier
1950   Ethnological Survey of Southern Yukon Territory, 1948. National Museum of
       Canada Bulletin 118. Pp. 50–53. Ottawa.

ANN STOLER

Margaret Mead

(1901–1978)

Margaret Mead was an American cultural anthropologist whose primary theoretical interests included child development; individual character formation, including culturally assigned gender roles; national character studies; cultural change; evolution; and such applied interests as nutrition, education, law, mental health, and ekistics.

During her long career (1928–78), Mead was a research, applied, and museum anthropologist, a teacher, and an interpreter of her discipline to the public. Instead of making what she perceived as the male world of academia her focus, Mead made a conscious decision to center her professional life at New York City's American Museum of Natural History, where she remained for almost fifty years, as assistant curator (1926–42), associate curator (1942–64), curator (1964–69), and emerita.

Mead conducted twenty-four field trips with major expeditions among six South Pacific peoples: on the island of T'au in American Samoa (1925–26); on Manus, Admiralty Islands (Papua, New Guinea, 1928–29, 1953, 1965, 1975); and among the Arapesh (December 1931–August 1932), Mundugumor (autumn 1932 for three weeks), Tchambuli or Chambri (first few weeks of 1933), and the Iatmul of New Guinea (several weeks, 1938–39). She also conducted fieldwork in Bali (1936–39) and among the Omaha (1930). With the exception of the Omaha, she developed a working knowledge of the native languages of each of these cultures and also used pidgin or Neo-Melanesian. She reported the results of her field studies in many scholarly publications, interpreted them in works intended for general audiences, and used them as the basis of her recommendations for "responsible social intervention."

During and after World War II, she focused her attention on problems of culture change, "transnational" and "cross ideological" cultural communications, and cybernetics (Mead 1963). Mead considered her *Continuities in Cultural Evolution* (1964b), an analysis of leadership roles and historical and evolutionary change, one of her most important theoretical works. As a research anthropologist, she is best remembered for her field research on gender and sex roles. She was the first anthropologist to study child rearing and women in cross-cultural perspective; she was also one of the first to develop the strategies and the methods of visual and psychological anthropology.

Mead readily absorbed the academic, progressive, and professional values of the old American family into which she, the eldest of four surviving children, was born (on December 16, 1901, in Philadelphia). Her father, Edward Sherwood Mead, a University of Pennsylvania economist, believed that intellect was a feminine attribute, and reinforced his daughter's confidence in the practical value of scientific knowledge. But Mead modeled herself after the adult women in her household, who managed to combine career, marriage, and child rearing. Her mother, Emily Fogg Mead, a political activist, feminist, and suffragist, took young Margaret along to study the Italian immigrants of Hammonton, New Jersey, the subjects of her doctoral dissertation in sociology, and so formally introduced Margaret to fieldwork. Mead's maternal grandmother, a former school teacher, supervised most of her early education at home, training her charge to observe both natural phenomena and human behavior. From an early age, then, Mead was encouraged to observe and record her observations, to respect scientific knowledge, cultural differences, and human equality. In Mead's own words, this background made her a woman "two generations ahead" of her time; it also set the groundwork for a career in anthropology (Mead 1972:2).

Mead earned her B.A. in psychology from Barnard College (1923) and her M.A. in psychology (1924) and Ph.D. in anthropology (1929) from Columbia University. From 1923–28 she was married to Luther Cressman, also a native of Pennsylvania, who began his relationship with Mead as a student for the ministry and ended it as a social scientist. Two additional marriages and divorces followed—to Reo Fortune, a New Zealand psychologist turned anthropologist (1928–35), and to Gregory Bateson (1936–50), a British anthropologist whose strong natural-science training would influence Mead's work. Mary Catherine Bateson Kassarjian (1939–   ), Mead's only child, is a linguist and anthropologist, specializing in Middle Eastern culture. (Mead had one grandchild, Sevanne Margaret [1970–   ]).

Margaret Mead consciously combined family and work relationships and turned her gender to her professional advantage; she collaborated with both Fortune and Bateson on fieldwork expeditions to New Guinea and Bali in the 1920s and 1930s, partnerships which made it possible for a woman to work in remote areas, and for a team of anthropologists to study "whole cultures in the field" including women and children, whom she, as a female anthropologist, found accessible. Recognizing the advantages of collaborative research, she continued, after her divorce from Bateson, to conduct field research with others, including, for example, return trips to Manus with Theodore and Leonora (Shargo) Schwartz and Barbara Honeyman Heath Roll (Mead 1970b:321f.).

Mead's apprenticeship under Franz Boas provided a compatible intellectual and social environment. Her mentor's humanistic anthropology was consistent with her family's progressive values; and Boas trained almost as many women for the profession as men. (Elsie Clews Parsons,* Gene Weltfish,* Ruth Underhill,* Ruth Bunzel,* Gladys Reichard,* Erna Gunther,* and Frederica de Laguna* were all trained at Columbia.) Mead first met Ruth Benedict* (1887–1948), who became an intimate friend and an important intellectual influence on her at Columbia, when the older woman acted as Boas's teaching assistant.

According to Mead, Boas had nothing to say "about hypotheses or paradigms" (Mead 1972:209). By the time Mead arrived on the scene, however, Boas had altered his research agenda, moving away from historical reconstruction and diffusion toward the study of the "inner development" of culture and the "relation of the individual to society" (Stocking 1976:15). Boas's students would continue to explore the related biological and cultural determinants of individual behavior; they also began exploration of the determining cultural patterns themselves, of their formation and interaction. The work of a number of Boas's students reflected the shift in his agenda: Benedict's Dionysian and Apollonian types in *Patterns of Culture* (1934) dramatically presented her case that cultures select, from the "great arc" of potential human behaviors, clusters of values that become the standard for individual behavior (Modell 1983). Mead's later work on culture-and-personality and sex and temperament directly descended from Boas's new agenda and from Benedict's configurationalist approach.

Mead's work also showed the influence of British anthropology, specifically its affiliation with the natural sciences. A. R. Radcliffe-Brown, for example, who had a direct influence on Mead, rejected the idea of "pattern" as an adequate explanation for cultural integration and looked instead to "system," an analogy drawn from natural sciences. Considering the idea of "culture" outside the realm of scientific inquiry, the British anthropologist focused instead on the concrete study of kinship; his intention was to develop a comparative anatomy of social systems. Two of Mead's early ethnographies, *Coming of Age in Samoa* (1928a) and *Growing Up in New Guinea* (1930a), heavily emphasized problems of individual development among female adolescents in Samoa and children in New Guinea; and in her treatise on Samoa, *Social Organization of Manu'a* (1930b), she first used the configurationalist approach, a legacy from lengthy conversations with Benedict (Mead 1972:195–96). But after her second marriage (to Reo Fortune, a disciple of British anthropologist W. H. R. Rivers), and after a brief study of kinship with Radcliffe-Brown that brought her into closer relationship to British anthropology, she undertook a technical study of *Kinship in the Admiralty Islands* (Mead 1934). Her decision to undertake fieldwork in a number of different cultures, instead of working among American Indians, was also a hallmark of what was to become a shared Anglo-American tradition. By the time Mead met Gregory Bateson, during a return field expedition to New Guinea, she had already bridged the two national traditions.

When Bateson met Mead and Fortune on the Sepik River in New Guinea in 1932, their intense conversations, influenced by Benedict's *Patterns of Culture* and Mead's recollection of Jungian pyschological types, informed their tentative assumption that cultures selectively emphasized and assigned different temperamental characteristics among men and women. Before their eventual marriage in 1936, Mead and Bateson's discussions of culture, gender, and personality found formal expression in her comparative study, *Sex and Temperament in Three Primitive Societies* (1935), a work based on field research among New Guinea's Arapesh, Mundugumor, and Tchambuli. Bateson, in the meantime, completed *Naven* (1936), in which he substituted a more dynamic, circular, interactional scheme for static theories of adaptation or harmonic integration offered by British social anthropology; "schismogenesis," later defined as "positive feedback," was a kind of protocybernetic theory or explanation for circular causal systems—later designated "steady states." Impressed with Bateson's training in the natural sciences and by his epistemological concerns, Mead was lastingly influenced by Bateson's circular feedback notion. She used it, for example, in her study of mother-child interactions in Bali and elsewhere.

Mead and Bateson's joint field trip to Bali (1936–39) offered the initial opportunity to combine their two perspectives, to test their theories, and to answer some of the criticisms of their work. Their studies of trance, dance, ritual, and child rearing allowed Mead a focus for her continuing work on character formation, while Bateson struggled with his theory of the dynamics of social interaction. The intent was to connect child development and character formation and to demonstrate the congruence between infant experience and broad culture patterns (M.C. Bateson 1984:19–20). While trying to understand the cultural organization of human behavior, the two also struggled to develop greater observational rigor and an understanding of the process of observation itself. In answer to criticisms of Mead's "impressionistic" field work and Bateson's "philosophical" ethnography, they attempted ambitious new photographic and notational methods. With thousands of spontaneously annotated stills and films, physical recordings of sequential moments, the couple hoped to document for others the relationships that connected the unfolding actions (Bateson and Mead 1942:12). The Balinese effort bore other bounties: for Mead, Bali had provided the missing temperament needed to complete the four-fold tale of "culturally defined temperamental expectations for men and women," that scheme originally conceived in *Sex and Temperament*. Her Balinese research was to serve as confirmation of the possibility for a wide human variation of cultural expressions of "maleness" and "femaleness," later documented in *Male and Female* (Mead 1949; 1972:218).

World War II brought a temporary halt to fieldwork and initiated Mead's brief experience as an anthropologist in government service. All of her wartime anthropology, whether it had to do with morale, food research, or the study of culture at a distance, related to her work on culture-and-personality, now invested with a new dynamism by Bateson's notions of interaction, circularity, and learning theory. In *And Keep Your Powder Dry* (Mead 1942), an analysis of the American character structure, Mead attempted to uplift the morale of Americans who would soon have to go to war, and to prepare them by offering a positive notion of their own national identity. Soon after Pearl Harbor Mead went to Washington to serve as the executive secretary of the Committee on Food Habits (1942–45), an off-shoot of the National Research Council's Division of Anthropology and Psychology. She used her position as a base from which to "coordinate various kinds of anthropological input into federal programs" (Mead 1979:150). She understood her mission to advise on coping with food rationing and shortages with the context of the "total complex of behavior" (Mead 1943:21). During the war, without access to direct field contact, Mead and her colleagues Ruth Benedict and Geoffrey Gorer developed the idea of "culture at a distance studies," research almost completely based upon émigré informants, documentary evidence, literature, and interviews. Mead, Benedict, Rhoda Metraux*—Mead's longtime collaborator—and others further applied this method after the war at the Columbia University Institute for Contemporary Cultures. Mead directed the institute from 1948–52. Many anthropologists have questioned "culture at a distance" techniques, for they were not based on direct field observation.

The political context of the war and prewar years strongly influenced Mead's notion of research and proper scientific activity. During the war Mead along with Bateson, Benedict, and several of their colleagues were indeed willing to apply their science to problems of morale and propaganda. And during the war Mead accepted the occasional necessity to control public exposure of scientific ideas and information. As a liberal Democrat, she hoped to preserve the Democratic "pattern," and she referred particular decisions to reveal or suppress information to this prior goal. After Hitler's defeat, however, she disdained covert, interventionist "black practices"; these compromises and the use of the atomic bomb led her to withdraw from government service and to attempt to influence public policy from lecterns, magazine columns, and television and radio appearances instead of from a Washington office.

Mead's sensitivity to timing and context is also dramatically apparent in the contrast between two of her major works: *Sex and Temperament*, written in 1935, implies almost complete cultural determination of sex roles, whereas her postwar book *Male and Female* acknowledges a dialectic of biology and culture. Those who criticize Mead for changing her stance on the biology-culture equation underestimate the role that political context played in determining the timing of her research agenda (Friedan 1963: Chap. 6). In the face of Fascist racism, Mead thought it dangerous to explore the biological basis for sex-typed behavior and so continued to emphasize culture. After Hitler's defeat she felt at liberty to explore the biological constraints and determinants of male and female behavior, a position entirely consistent with her holistic view of human behavior.

Convinced that the war had stimulated "pervasive cultural change on a global scale," in the 1950s Mead set about revisiting Manus and other Oceanic cultures to restudy the peoples who, she believed, were exchanging "new lives for old" at an unprecedented pace (Fox 1979:11). In *Culture and Commitment* (Mead

1970a), she explained that in this rapidly changing postwar world, the younger, not the older, generation would initiate change. Mead's continuing concern with cybernetics theory, reinforced by her participation after the war in the Macy Foundation conferences, was evident in her theories of learning, enculturation, and the maternal-infant bond (Fox 1979:10).

The pattern of Mead's career was unusual. Academic recognition came long after her professional status was well established. Mead became adjunct professor at Columbia University in 1954 in her early fifties, followed by chair of the Department of Social Sciences and professor of anthropology at Fordham University (1968–70). She held several visiting lectureships; beginning in 1957, for example, she acted as Visiting Professor at the University of Cincinnati, Department of Psychiatry, and in 1959 as Sloan Professor at the Menninger Foundation. She served as president of the Society for Applied Anthropology (1940), the World Federation of Mental Health (1956–57), the World Society for Ekistics (1969–71), the American Anthropological Association (1960), and the Scientists' Institute for Public Information (1972). She was the second woman—and the first anthropologist since Franz Boas—to become president of the American Association for the Advancement of Science (1975). In 1975 the National Academy of Sciences elected her to membership. Her numerous research grants ranged from National Research Council Fellow (1925–26) to Fogarty Scholar in residence at the National Institute for Mental Health (1973). She received twenty-eight honorary degrees in law, humanities, and science and more than forty distinguished awards for science and citizenship, including the Kalinga prize for the popularization of science, the Viking Medal in general anthropology, and posthumously, the Presidential Medal of Freedom. Mead made her generous personal, intellectual, and psychological support for developing social scientists a major principle. She founded the Institute for Intercultural Studies in 1944, a private, nonprofit agency dedicated to the support of research; she contributed much of her income to it.

Mead's fieldwork itself has been criticized by some as "impressionistic" and "mentalist" (Harris 1968:299, 393). Other critics question Mead's good fortune in finding three New Guinea tribes that strikingly illustrated the point she wished to make in Sex and Temperament about the cultural determination of sex roles. Soon after Mead's death Australian anthropologist Derek Freeman criticized her earliest Samoan fieldwork—executed in the late 1920s, when American anthropological training was in its infancy—from the perspective and standards of a modern discipline (Freeman 1983). Seeking to discredit Mead and the Boasians, Freeman claimed that they neglected the biological boundaries of human behavior. Mead in fact insisted on the interconnectedness of all phenomena, cultural and biological. Freeman grounds his criticism of Mead's 1920s work in American Samoa on the basis of his own work in Western Samoa; however, several critics have questioned the validity of this comparative basis. In short, the Freeman-Mead controversy—and the broader debate implied within it—is not resolved.

In retrospect, many of the criticisms leveled against Mead are not mindful of the historical context in which she worked. Because psychological anthropology, a field in which Mead pioneered, is no longer in vogue, contemporary anthropologists unsurprisingly distance themselves from Mead's culture-and-personality studies. Perhaps it is most useful to understand Mead as a major second-generation link between Franz Boas, founder of American anthropology, and today's third and fourth generations of American cultural anthropologists. Mead carried out Boas's agenda and developed it further. She, like Boas, promulgated a view of humanity within its physical, cultural, and biological contexts; and like Boas, she attempted to develop scientific methods for the human science anthropology. She is credited as one of the first American anthropologists to rely more upon the participant observer method than upon interviews, with introducing the methods of visual anthropology, and with pioneering in nutrition studies. Some find very early traces of symbolic anthropology in her Balinese fieldwork, a connection that links her directly to the contemporary scene. Finally, after Franz Boas established the boundaries, methods, and agenda for American anthropology, Mead brought the anthropological perspective to those outside the discipline—scholars and laypeople alike.

References and Works About Margaret Mead

Bateson, Mary Catherine
1984   *With a Daughter's Eye: A Memoir of Margaret Mead and Gregory Bateson*. New York: William Morrow.
Fox, R.
1979   Margaret Mead. *International Encyclopedia of the Social Sciences* 18. David L. Sills, ed. Pp. 513–28. New York: The Free Press.
Freeman, Derek
1983   *Margaret Mead and Samoa: The Making and Unmaking of an Anthropological Myth*. Cambridge, Mass.: Harvard University Press.
Goodman, R. A.
1983   *Mead's Coming of Age in Samoa: A Dissenting View*. Oakland, Calif.: Pepperine Press.
Gordan, Joan
1976   *Margaret Mead: The Complete Bibliography, 1925–75*. The Hague: Mouton. (As ed.)
Holmes, Lowell
1986   *Quest for the Real Samoa: The Mead-Freeman Controversy and Beyond*. South Hadley, Mass.: Bergin and Garvey.
Lipset, D.
1980   *Gregory Bateson: The Legacy of a Scientist*. Englewood Cliffs, N.J.: Prentice-Hall.
Modell, Judith S.
1983   *Ruth Benedict: Patterns of a Life*. Philadelphia: University of Pennsylvania Press.
Rice, E.
1979   *Margaret Mead: A Portrait*. New York: Harper and Row.

Webb, M. C.
1968 The Culture Concept and Culture Change in the Work of Margaret Mead. *Proceedings of the Louisiana Academy of Sciences* 31 (December): 148–65.
Yans-McLaughlin, Virginia
1987 Science, Democracy and Ethics: Mobilizing Culture and Personality for World War II. *History of Anthropology* 4:184–217.

Selected Works by Margaret Mead

1928a *Coming of Age in Samoa: A Psychological Study of Primitive Youth for Western Civilization.* New York: William Morrow.
1928b *An Inquiry into the Cultural Stability in Polynesia.* Columbia University Contributions to Anthropology. Vol. 9. New York: Columbia University Press.
1930a *Growing Up in New Guinea: A Comparative Study of Primitive Education.* New York: William Morrow.
1930b *Social Organization of Manu'a.* Bulletin 76 of the Bernice P. Bishop Museum. Honolulu: Bishop Museum.
1932 *The Changing Culture of an Indian Tribe.* New York: Columbia University Press.
1934 Kinship in the Admiralty Islands. *Anthropological Papers of the American Museum of Natural History* 34: 183–358.
1935 *Sex and Temperament in Three Primitive Societies.* New York: William Morrow.
1937 *Cooperation and Competition Among Primitive Peoples.* New York: McGraw-Hill.
1939 *From the South Seas: Studies of Adolescence and Sex in Primitive Societies.* New York: William Morrow.
1942 *And Keep Your Power Dry: An Anthropologist Looks at America.* New York: William Morrow.
1943 *Problem of Changing Food Habits.* Bulletin of the National Research Council 168:20–31.
1949 *Male and Female: A Study of the Sexes in a Changing World.* New York: William Morrow.
1951 *The School in American Culture.* Cambridge, Mass.: Harvard University Press.
1953 *Cultural Patterns and Technical Change; A Manual Prepared by the World Federation for Mental Health.* Paris: UNESCO.
1956 *New Lives for Old: Cultural Transformation—Manus.* New York: William Morrow.
1959 *An Anthropologist at Work: Writings of Ruth Benedict.* Boston: Houghton Mifflin.
1963 Curriculum Vitae. Margaret Mead Archives. Library of Congress, American Museum of Natural History, Office File K.
1964a *Anthropology: A Human Science: Selected Papers, 1939–1960.* Princeton, N.J.: Van Nostrand.
1964b *Continuities in Cultural Evolution.* New Haven: Yale University Press.
1965 *Anthropologists and What They Do.* New York: Watts.
1970a *Culture and Commitment: A Study of the Generation Gap.* Garden City, N.Y.: Natural History Press/Doubleday.
1970b Fieldwork in the Pacific Islands, 1925–67. In *Women in the Field.* Peggy Golde, ed. Pp. 292–331. Chicago: Aldine.
1972 *Blackberry Winter: My Earlier Years.* New York: William Morrow.

1973   *Twentieth Century Faith: Hope and Survival*. New York: Harper and Row.
1974   *Ruth Benedict*. New York: Columbia University Press.
1978   *Letters From the Field, 1925–1975*. New York: Harper and Row.
1979   The Use of Anthropology in World War II and After. In *The Use of Anthropology*. W. Goldschmidt, ed. Pp. 145–57. Washington, D.C.: American Anthropological Association.

Coauthored Works

Mead, Margaret, and James Baldwin
1971   *A Rap on Race*. Philadelphia: Lippincott.
Mead, Margaret, and Gregory Bateson
1942   *Balinese Character: A Photographic Analysis*. Vol. II. W. G. Valentine, ed. New York: The New York Academy of Sciences.
Mead, Margaret, and Muriel Brown
1966   *The Wagon and the Star: A Study of American Community Initiative*. Chicago: Rand McNally.
Mead, Margaret, and Ruth L. Bunzel
1960   *The Golden Age of American Anthropology*. New York: Braziller.
Mead, Margaret, and Paul Byers
1968   *The Small Conference: An Innovation in Communication*. Paris: Mouton.
Mead, Margaret, E. Carothers, et al.
1972   *To Love or Perish: The Technological Crisis and the Churches*. New York: Friendship Press.
Mead, Margaret, T. Dobzhansky et al.
1968   *Science and the Concept of Race*. New York: Columbia University Press.
Mead, Margaret, and Ken Heyman
1965   *Family*. New York: Macmillan.
1975   *World Enough: Rethinking the Future*. Boston: Little, Brown.
Mead, Margaret, and Frances B. Kaplan
1965   *American Women: The Report of the President's Commission on the Status of Women and Other Publications of the Commission*. New York: Scribner.
Mead, Margaret, and Frances Cook MacGregor
1951   *Growth and Culture: A Photographic Study of Balinese Childhood*. New York: Putnam.
Mead, Margaret, and Rhoda Metraux
1954   *Themes in French Culture: A Preface to a Study of French Community*. Stanford, Calif.: Stanford University Press.
1974   *A Way of Seeing*. New York: William Morrow.
1980   *Aspects of the Present*. New York: William Morrow.
Mead, Margaret, and Rhoda Metraux, eds.
1953   *The Study of Culture at a Distance*. Chicago: University of Chicago Press.
Mead, Margaret, and Martha Wolfenstein
1955   *Childhood in Contemporary Cultures*. Chicago: University of Chicago Press.

VIRGINIA YANS-MCLAUGHLIN

Rhoda Bubendey Metraux

(1914–   )

American cultural anthropologist specializing in culture-and-personality, Rhoda Bubendey Metraux is especially known for her studies of culture at a distance.

Prospect Park South was a new and prosperous Brooklyn community when Rhoda Bubendey was born on October 18, 1914, the second child and only daughter of Frederick Bubendey, a banker, and Anna Marie Kappelmann. Her father died when she was two, and Rhoda Bubendey was raised in her grandfather's home. Her grandfather had come to America in the 1870s as part of his apprenticeship in international banking. English and German were spoken in the home; and Bubendey and her brother were subjected to Saturday morning German lessons from a tutor they thoroughly disliked. Although Bubendey had a good relationship with her mother, she was closer to her brother and grandfather. The latter fulfilled the paternal role for the children, reading bedtime stories and generally spending a good deal of time with them.

Bubendey's early years were marked by a series of childhood illnesses, culminating in a serious case of whooping cough, which delayed her formal schooling. However, with a convalescing friend and a governess, who took charge of the children for the year, they visited museums, went to the movies, and generally explored the city. The children, in effect, devised their own curriculum. Bubendey recalls that year as her most valuable educational experience prior to college.

Bubendey advanced rapidly through school, graduating from high school at fifteen. Too young for residential college, she continued at the Packer Collegiate Institute in Brooklyn Heights for the two collegiate years, and pursued a growing interest in the theater. At Packer she found teachers who introduced her to the demands and excitement of the scholarly world. At seventeen she entered Vassar, the first junior college transfer accepted with junior year standing.

A summer trip to Germany in 1932 alerted Bubendey to the Nazi danger. She wrote a student play about German political conflict at the family level. "What

I was trying to get at in the theater was living people, so that when I finally met Malinowski and heard about anthropology, I was converted in one afternoon.''[1]

Bubendey graduated with a major in English literature in 1934, and married Arthur B. Proctor III, a West Point graduate. She accompanied her husband to a field artillery post in Maryland and prepared to be an officer's wife. After the sudden death of her husband, less than two years after their marriage, the young widow returned to New York. There, she enrolled in a secretarial school that promised to teach shorthand in three months, a skill that proved useful many years later when she did fieldwork.

She obtained a job at Oxford University Press and an apartment in Greenwich Village. Setting aside her playwriting aspirations, she turned to shorter literary forms while she learned about publishing and became an active member of a union.[2] Nothing in her family background prepared her for the fact that the desirable editorial positions were not then open to women. "It didn't occur to me that you couldn't decide what you wanted to be and get there."

Despite the gender barrier in publishing, she did not perceive all women as subjects of categorical discrimination; those women who did attain distinguished careers were evidence that one could achieve in some fields if not in others. She observed that patterns of religious and racial discrimination common in the 1930s produced groups of men as well as women who were unjustly treated in the job market.

In the fall of 1939 she met Bronislaw Malinowski at a Yale cocktail party. She had already decided to leave publishing and by the end of the afternoon, was a convert to anthropology and enrolled in a course on social structure he was teaching at the New School for Social Research. She recalls that Malinowski reduced the class to an acceptable size by using insults to discourage students. Long talks with Malinowski confirmed her belief that anthropology was a possible career. "I thought that a discipline that took into account the world outside, the world around one, as a reality, as well as the world of people's internal thoughts and emotions, the principles they lived by and so forth—I thought this was for me."

World War II had begun in Europe when she entered the graduate program at Yale in 1940. "The war and the discovery of anthropology are one and the same to me, the horror at one being supported by the wonderful possibilities of the other." She found her fellow graduate students to be exceedingly uninformed about the world in which they lived. The lack of financial aid for women was a personal problem and a moral issue that further contributed to her ambivalence about Yale. The few fellowships and the paid work assembling the Human Relations Area files went to male students; the three female students paid their way. However, the courses were rewarding. She recalls Malinowski's seminar and George Peter Murdock's introductory course with particular pleasure. Meeting Alfred Metraux was the most important personal event of the year; they were married in March 1941. At the end of the academic year, Murdock, then chair, said, "Isn't it wonderful? All the women students in my department have found husbands."

During the summer of 1941 the Metrauxs went to Haiti on a combined honeymoon and exploratory fieldwork trip. They were interested in the Caribbean because its complex and locally divergent colonial experiences offered rich comparative possibilities. Rhoda Metraux's first fieldwork experience went rather badly until finally her primary woman informant, together with several friends, took charge. They sat her down by the kitchen, determined to teach her some Creole so she could communicate with them. This experience set a pattern for all of Metraux's subsequent fieldwork.

I can set myself up in a field. I hope to have at least as few good contacts with people, but I leave a great deal of initiative to the people there, which is a very slow way of learning a culture. . . . [I]t's not the way Alfred ever worked, but it made us a good team. I sat and people came and told me what they were thinking about, and Alfred got people talking about things.

The Metrauxs went to Washington in September 1941. Alfred had accepted a position at the Smithsonian Institution to work with Julian Steward on the *Handbook of South American Indians*. The United States entered the war in December, and the government began recruiting people for wartime work. Margaret Mead* came to Washington as executive secretary of the National Research Council's Committee on Food Habits. Metraux applied for a position as Mead's research assistant. The interview was memorable; She was given one week to analyze radio soap operas, popular magazines, and a set of short essays by Vassar women on food habits to learn how Americans and the media were adjusting to the war effort and then report her findings to Mead.

Metraux's main task was to devise methods of working with public opinion. With Mead, she developed a system mainly of volunteers (primarily students) from anthropology departments who conducted open-ended interviews around the country. Mead and Metraux formulated current questions from the material previously collected and analyzed. This technique kept their opinion sampling well ahead of other opinion polls.

Metraux believes this work made a significant contribution to the war effort. It influenced the way rationing was handlled and the way material was given to newspapers. "We found right from the beginning that every time some agency of government would tell people to be good, you'd have an explosion. And every time you fed some factual material to the newspapers . . . and people could catch on to what was involved, the response was excellent." Mead and Metraux worked out a division of labor in which Rhoda did the data analysis and Mead, more experienced in American culture, placed it in a larger framework.

The partnership was interrupted when Alfred Metraux accepted a one-term teaching appointment in Mexico. When they returned to Washington, Rhoda

Metraux found herself assigned to the Office of Strategic Services, where she analyzed the effects both of individual personal experiences and public events on German civilian morale. This material is still classified.

When the war ended, the Metrauxs moved to Great Neck, New York. Alfred Metraux had been appointed to the Department of Social Affairs in the United Nations, and Rhoda Metraux enrolled at Columbia University to complete her Ph.D. Their wartime experiences had convinced a number of other anthropologists (among them Ruth Benedict,* Ruth Bunzel,* Geoffrey Gorer, Gregory Bateson, and Margaret Mead) that anthropology could make a distinctive and important contribution to international understanding. All had worked in interdisciplinary settings and were concerned about recovering, refining, and disseminating new research techniques that had been developed to handle problems addressed during the war. When Ruth Benedict received a substantial grant from the Office of Naval Research in 1947, Columbia University Research in Contemporary Cultures (RCC) was formed.

The Study of Culture at a Distance (Mead and Metraux 1953) is perhaps the most important document from RCC and its successor projects. Designed as a manual demonstrating both method and process, it provides a comprehensive survey of what was learned during the war about interdisciplinary research, intensive work with a limited number of informants, and analysis of secondary materials. Metraux's contributions, which deal with group processes and informant-interviewer dynamics, anticipate some of the later work in interpretive ethnography. Her article in the manual entitled ''Resonance in Imagery'' is a meticulous exploration of cultural patterning.

UNESCO had become interested in developing mass literacy programs for Third World nations. One participating nation, Haiti, requested that Alfred Metraux direct its literacy project. The Metraux family, now joined by an infant son, Daniel, went to Haiti. Rhoda Metraux was confined to Port-au-Prince by near-famine conditions and lack of medical facilities in the Marbial Valley, the study area. Her work focused on cultural patterning emphasizing regularities in the handling of authority in different settings, such as family, kinship, police, and temple.

I think I looked at patterning because I was well trained in poetics . . . and during the war the whole method of analyzing public opinion was based on concepts of patterning. What I was trying to do with public opinion was to see how pieces of a pattern fit together. I think anyone who writes verse is essentially interested in pattern.

Although her fieldwork was cut short by Daniel's illness, it did provide the material for her dissertation, ''Kith and Kin'' (1951).

In 1953 Metraux, accompanied by her young son and his Haitian nurse, undertook her first solo fieldwork in Montserrat, in the Caribbean. By this time firmly committed to collaborative work, she enlisted the help of Theodora Abel, a clinical psychologist, and Jane Belo, a pioneer in anthropological photography.

These colleagues planned to make working visits when Metraux was established and somewhat comfortable in the culture. Although illness ultimately prevented Belo from traveling, Metraux sent copies of all her field notes to Abel and Belo each week, permitting them to share in the process of the research. Abel visited Montserrat for a month, as planned, and administered a set of projective tests. Metraux spent the years from 1954 to 1967 in New York, raising Daniel and working on several projects. She was not interested in a permanent teaching position. Alfred Metraux was located at UNESCO's permanent headquarters in Paris, and theirs became a transatlantic marriage. When Mead's marriage to Gregory Bateson ended, Metraux and Mead established a cooperative household that endured until Mead's death in 1978.

In 1962 *Redbook* Magazine invited Mead to write a column. Although Mead and Metraux conceived the task as a joint undertaking, *Redbook* insisted that the column appear under Mead's name only. By this time Metraux and Mead were experienced collaborators and freely exchanged the work of drafting and revising. A circular relationship developed between the *Redbook* columns and Mead's lectures that enabled them to track some common concerns of Americans. In the late 1960s Mead obtained a National Science Foundation grant to investigate cultural imagery. She and Metraux viewed the analysis of imagery as one way of revealing the perceptual system shared by members of a society. Metraux went to Tambunam, a Iatmul village on the Sepik river, in the East Sepik Province, Papua New Guinea, which had been studied by Bateson and Mead in 1938. "I wondered whether it would be possible to describe a culture as a whole in terms of its own imagery, and make this intelligible to readers on the outside." Metraux made three field trips of six to eight months each between 1967 and 1972. The focus of this fieldwork was altered by the Tambunams themselves, who wanted to have their music recorded for future generations. Metraux, impressed by their desire to preserve a comprehensive record of their musical ceremonial heritage, devoted a good deal of time and effort to this project. Taking advantage of the time depth provided by Mead and Bateson's earlier work, Metraux also made an effort to visit all the Sepik communities where Bateson had worked. She is currently working on data from these trips.

Reflecting on her own experiences and those of women colleagues, Metraux believes that it is more difficult for women to obtain financial support in the initial stages of an anthropological career. However, she suggests that it is easier for a single woman to do basic ethnographic fieldwork than it is for a single man. She believes that in most field settings, a woman can more easily obtain a wider picture of the society because she can enlist male support and confidence more readily than a man can gain access to the women.

Metraux describes herself as a "third-generation Boas student." There is a somewhat painful irony in this; as a child she had known Boas, who was a member of the same intellectual circle as her grandparents. She regrets never having consulted him when considering a career in anthropology, especially since Boas welcomed women students and encouraged their fieldwork at a time when most departments only tolerated them. His influence is seen in Metraux's commitment to a holistic perspective and her way of working slowly into a culture. Metraux also acknowledges an intellectual debt to Malinowski, from whom she obtained a sense of fieldwork and institutional structure.

Notes

1. Unless otherwise noted, all quotes come from tape-recorded interviews with Rhoda Metraux conducted on October 7, 8, and 9, 1984. I am very grateful to her for so generously giving her time to this project.

2. The union was the Book and Magazine Guild, which became an early CIO affiliate, i.e., part of the Office and Professional Workers Union.

References and Works About Rhoda Bubendey Metraux

1973   Rhoda Metraux. *AMWS*. 12th ed. Vol. 2, p. 1693. New York: R. R. Bowker Co.

Selected Works by Rhoda Bubendey Metraux

1943   Qualitative Analysis: A Technique for the Study of Verbal Behavior. *National Research Council Bulletin 108*. Report of the Committee on Food Habits, 1941–43. Pp. 86–94. Washington, D.C.: National Academy of the Sciences.

1952a Affiliations Through Work in Marbial, Haiti. *Primitive Man* 25:1–22.

1952b Some Aspects of Hierarchical Structure in Haiti. In *Acculturation in the Americas*. Sol Tax, ed. Pp. 185–94. Chicago: University of Chicago Press.

1955a The Caine Mutiny. *Explorations* 5:36–44.

1955b The Consequences of Wrongdoing: An Analysis of Story Completions by German Children. In *Childhood in Contemporary Cultures*. Margaret Mead and Martha Wolfenstein, eds. Pp. 306–23. Chicago: University of Chicago Press.

1955c Parents and Children: An Analysis of Contemporary German Childcare and Youth Guidance Literature. In *Childhood in Contemporary Cultures*. Margaret Mead and Martha Wolfenstein, eds. Pp. 204–28. Chicago: University of Chicago Press.

1955d A Portrait of the Family in German Juvenile Fiction. In *Childhood in Contemporary Cultures*. Margaret Mead and Martha Wolfenstein, eds. Pp. 253–76. Chicago: University of Chicago Press.

1955e Implicit and Explicit Values in Education and Teaching as Related to Growth and Development. *Merrill-Palmer Quarterly* 2:27–34.

1955f Life Stress and Health in a Changing Culture. In *Family Mental Health and the State*. Pp. 113–26. London: World Federation for Mental Health.

1956   Effects of Cultural Anticipation and Attitudes Toward Aging. *The Neurologic and Psychiatric Aspects of the Disorders of Aging*. Pp. 248–51. Baltimore: Williams and Wilkins.

1957   Montserrat, B.W.I.: Some Implications of Suspended Culture Change. *Transactions of the New York Academy of Sciences* (Series 2) 20:205–11.

1959   Anthropology and Learning. In *Learning More About Learning*. Alexander Frazier, ed. Pp. 21–37. Washington, D.C.: Association for Supervision and Curriculum Development.

1960 Toward a New Age of Man. *Child Welfare* 39 (4): 5–10.

1961 Children's Drawings: Satellites and Space. *Journal of Social Issues* 17 (2): 36–42.

1962 The Image of the Scientist. In *Science and the Public*. Shirley M. Lind, ed. Pp. 17–21. Evanston, Ill.: Northwestern University.

1963a Gaining Freedom of Value Choice. In *New Insights and the Curriculum: Yearbook 1963*. Alexander Frazier, ed. Pp. 190–220. Washington, D.C.: Association for Supervision and Curriculum Development.

1963b International Communication of Science Information. *Journalism Quarterly* 40 (3): 332–38.

1965 Planning for a True Urban Culture. In *The Planner in Emerging Urban Society—A Confrontation*. David L. Sills, ed. Pp. 26–30. Washington, D.C.: American Institute of Planners.

1968 Malinowski, Bronislaw. In *International Encyclopedia of the Social Sciences*. David L. Sills, ed. Vol. 9, pp. 541–49. New York: Macmillan and Free Press.

1971 A World Transformed: An Exploration of Process. *International Mental Health Research Newsletter* 13 (2): 13–14.

1975a Cherishing and Preserving: Sex Differences and the Life of the World. *The Quarterly Journal of the Library of Congress* 32 (4): 270–73.

1975b Eidos and Change: Continuity in Process, Discontinuity in Product. *Ethos* 3 (2): 293–308.

1978 Introduction and Aristocracy and Meritocracy: Leadership among the Eastern Iatmul. *Anthropological Quarterly* 51 (1): 1–2, 47–59.

1979 *Margaret Mead: Some Personal Views*. New York: Walker. (As ed.) (Based on question and answer columns in *Redbook Magazine*, 1964–78.)

1980a Margaret Mead: A Biographical Sketch. *American Anthropologist* 82 (2): 262–69.

1980b The Study of Culture at a Distance. *American Anthropologist* 82 (2): 362–72.

Coauthored Works

Metraux, Rhoda, and Theodora M. Abel

1957 Normal and Deviant Behavior in a Peasant Community: Montserrat, B.W.I. *American Journal of Orthopsychiatry* 27 (1): 167–84.

1959 Sex Differences in a Negro Peasant Community, Montserrat, B.W.I. *Journal of Projective Techniques* 23 (2): 127–33.

1974 *Culture and Psychotherapy*. New Haven: College and University Press.

Metraux, Rhoda, with Theodora M. Abel and Samuel Roll

1987 *Psychotherapy and Culture*. Albuquerque: University of New Mexico Press.

Metraux, Rhoda, Lawrence Hinkle, Jr., John W. Gittinger, et al.

1957 Studies in Human Ecology: Factors Governing the Adaptation of Chinese Unable to Return to China. In *Experimental Psychopathology*. Paul H. Hoch and Joseph Zubin. Pp. 170–86. New York: Grune and Stratton.

Metraux, Rhoda, Lawrence Hinkle, Jr., Norman Plummer, et. al.

1957 Studies in Human Ecology: Factors Relevant to the Occurrence of Bodily Illness and Disturbances in Mood, Thought and Behavior in Three Homogeneous Population Groups. *American Journal of Psychiatry* 114 (3): 212–20.

Metraux, Rhoda, and Margaret Mead

1953	*The Study of Culture at a Distance.* Chicago: University of Chicago Press.

1954	*Themes in French Culture: A Preface to a Study of French Community.* Stanford, Calif.: Stanford University Press.

1957a	*Themes de "culture" de la France.* Trans. Yvonne-Delphée Miroglio. (With critical comments. Le Havre, Fr.: Collection de l'Institut Havrais de Sociologie Économique et de Psychologie des Peuples.)

1957b	Image of the Scientist Among High School Students. A Pilot Study. *Science* 126 (3270): 384–90.

1963	The Human Sciences: Their Contribution. In *A Guide to Science Reading.* Hilary J. Deason, ed. Pp. 28–49. New York: New American Library.

1965a	The Anthropology of Human Conflict. In *The Nature of Human Conflict.* Elton B. MacNeil, ed. Pp. 116–38. Englewood Cliffs, N.J.: Prentice-Hall.

1965b	Town and Gown: A General Statement. In *Urban Research and Education in the New York Metro Region.* Harvey S. Perloff and Henry Cohen. Pp. 1–42. New York: Regional Plan Association.

1970	*A Way of Seeing.* New York: McCall. (Reprinted 1975, New York: William Morrow). (Based on columns published in *Redbook Magazine,* 1962–69.)

1980	*Aspects of the Present.* New York: William Morrow. (Based on columns in *Redbook Magazine,* 1970–78.)

NINA SWIDLER

Zelia Maria Magdalena Nuttall

(1857–1933)

American archaeologist-ethnohistorian Zelia Maria Magdalena Nuttall was known especially for her investigations of pre-Columbian culture and her studies of Mexican peoples and native Mexican flora.

Nuttall was a brilliant archival researcher and self-trained archaeologist who very early carved a career for herself by pursuing independent research and publishing in scholarly journals. Before age 30 she was elected to several highly prestigious scientific societies on the basis of her work, and she was the winner of three medals for excellence for the exhibits of the results of her archival work and archaeology, which she presented in Europe and the United States. Nuttall was never a part of a university teaching faculty, and indeed there is no indication that she would have accepted such a position had it been offered. Early in her career she was appointed Honorary Assistant in Mexican Archaeology at the Peabody Museum of Harvard University in recognition of her research on Mexico, a post she held for forty-seven years.

Zelia Nuttall was a woman with enough wealth to make possible her chosen career. Her most enduring contribution to the field of anthropology was her discovery and introduction to the scientific community of two Mexican codices: The Codex Magliabecchiano in 1890 and the Codex Nuttall in 1902. She was the first to recognize the codices as historical documents after centuries of scholars had considered them only curiosities without historical significance. Her major contributions to Mexican archaeology were (1) her paper "Island of Sacrificios" (1910), in which she demonstrates the meticulous care she took in reporting on a small excavation there (an exception in that early day), and (2) her theory, later amply proved, of a general Archaic culture underlying the later high cultures in Mexico's prehistory.

Born on September 6, 1857, in San Francisco, California, Zelia Nuttall was the second of six children of Dr. Robert Kennedy Nuttall and Magdalena Parrott. Nuttall acquired her interest in Mexico at an early age from her mother, the

Mexico-born daughter of a San Francisco banker. Her father, a native of Ireland, arrived in San Francisco from Australia in 1850, to open his medical practice. In 1865, when she was eight years old, her father's health precipitated the family's move to Europe, where they remained for eleven years. By the time they returned to San Francisco in 1876, Nuttall was a young woman of nineteen with an excellent continental education acquired in France, Germany, Italy, and England. She had acquired fluency and literacy in four, possibly five, languages, to which she later added a self-taught literacy in the Aztec language in order to read and translate some of the early post-Conquest documents. For nearly fifty years she presented papers and published regularly in French, German, Spanish, and English.

At age twenty-three Nuttall married a Frenchman, Alphonse Louis Pinart, who as a young scholar had recently participated in an anthropological expedition to the Pacific. For an extended honeymoon the young couple traveled to France, Spain, the West Indies, and Mexico—Nuttall returning to San Francisco in late 1881. Their only child, Nadine, was born the following year. The marriage failed, and the couple divorced in 1888, at which time she received the court's permission to resume her maiden name and to change her daughter's name to Nuttall as well. Thereafter, she was known as Mrs. or Madame Nuttall.

Nuttall made her second visit to Mexico in the company of members of her family in 1884. She stayed five months, long enough to become enamored of Mexican culture and to begin the archaeological investigations that were to initiate her lifelong scholarly career. The small terra-cotta heads she collected from Teotihuacan were the subject of her first publication (1886b). During this first Mexican visit, she also undertook research in the Mexican National Museum, marking the beginning of her lifelong devotion to archival research into Mexican pre-Columbian and early colonial culture.

From 1887 to 1899 Nuttall and her daughter lived in Dresden, Germany, a location that allowed her to visit the great cities of Europe, where she studied archival materials in museums and libraries.

But it was in 1886 that Nuttall had her first taste of professional success when she presented a paper at the meeting of the Association for the Advancement of Science in Buffalo, New York. The same year, her paper on the terra-cotta heads of Teotihuacan was published, bringing her to the attention of Frederic Ward Putnam, curator of the Peabody Museum of Harvard. He was so impressed with the work that he named her Special Assistant in Mexican Archaeology to the museum and aided her acceptance into the prestigious Archaeological Institute of America. A few years later she was elected into the no-less-prestigious American Philosophical Society as well.

Because of her social position and background, Nuttall had many friends and acquaintances of wealth and position in Europe, the United States, and Mexico. Her archaeological and ethnohistorical papers and publications brought her into contact with the world of professional anthropology, and she was often able to bring these two groups together to further anthropological projects in the days when most research was supported by private donations. She herself was awarded small subsidies to aid her research from time to time, once for archival research in Russia, again for hiring a professional artist to copy the Codex Nuttall (1902a). Later the Mexican government offered her a small sum to carry out a field research project on the Isla de Sacrificios, help she ultimately did not accept, owing to unilateral changes in the terms under which she was to do the research.

The Isla de Sacrificios research was her only attempt at a thorough field archaeological project. In 1909, after a brief preliminary survey, she petitioned the Mexican government to allow her to excavate the island more thoroughly. Permission was at first granted along with a promise of $240 to help defray her expenses of camping on the island with an excavation crew. However, she did not carry out the project, because of behind-the-scenes maneuvering by the inspector of monuments. He managed to have her subsidy reduced to $100 and to have himself appointed as her supervisor. The inspector was known not only for his shoddy methods but also for his willingness to plunder sites for his own financial gain. Nuttall, justifiably insulted, resigned from the several important posts she held in Mexican archaeological circles, including her title as Honorary Professor of the National Museum. Not long after this, the inspector of monuments announced to the world his discovery of the ruins on the island Nuttall had discovered and reported orally to Mexican officials months earlier.

In 1902 Nuttall purchased an old colonial mansion in Coyoacán on the outskirts of Mexico City, as her principal residence. The house was purported to have been built by Pedro Alvarado of the Spanish conquest, and for this reason she named it Casa Alvarado. It was to be her home for the remainder of her life, a place where she entertained the famous of the world. Several of her archaeological finds were recovered from the garden of Casa Alvarado, while others came from nearby environs. It was at Casa Alvarado that the first complete study of Aztec pottery in a single site was carried out with Mañuel Gamio, her former protégé, directing the project.

Nuttall often generously invited young scholars into her home for extended periods to help them with studies of Mexican archaeology and colonial history. It was she who was primarily responsible for Gamio being able to study under Boas at Columbia University. George Vaillant was another of her several later-renowned protégés.

Her best-known archival discovery was the folding screen, pictorial Mixtec book, named Codex Nuttall in her honor. Over several years she was able to trace this ancient document from the Monastery of San Marcos, Florence, Italy, to its last owner, Lord Zouche of Haynworth in England. In her introduction to the codex, she relates how the book had been regarded as of little consequence, perhaps a children's book, in the centuries after the conquest. Nuttall proved the historical significance of the document and in so doing, established the significance of other codices known to exist and others yet to be discovered.

Another of her remarkable discoveries was that of the Drake manuscripts in the National Archives of Mexico. Her eagerness to pursue clues and leads uncovered in the old manuscripts led her, at the age of fifty-eight, to take a freighter to Alaska so that she could examine firsthand Neah Bay, Washington, which she was convinced was the place Sir Francis Drake described in the "Bay of New Albion."

Among her other accomplishments was her part in setting up an International School of American Archaeology and Ethnology in Mexico City. For twenty-five years she was Honorary Professor of Archaeology at the National Museum of Mexico, a post she resigned, in anger, after the Island of Sacrificios affair. She was also a longtime member of the Advisory Council of the Department of Anthropology, University of California at Berkeley. (Along with her friend Phoebe Apperson Hearst, she was one of the few persons active in organizing the department.) She was field director of the Crocker Archaeological Field Research Project at Berkeley for several years. She served on the International Jury of Awards at the Chicago Exposition in 1893 and at the Louisiana Purchase Exposition in 1904. She herself won exhibit medals at the Madrid Historical Exposition of 1892, the Chicago Exposition of 1893, and the Buffalo Exposition of 1901. In addition to maintaining membership in all the major anthropological and historical societies in the United States and Mexico, she was counted as a corresponding member of societies in London, Paris, Rome, Geneva, Stockholm, and Lima.

Since her personal correspondence has not been preserved, there is no direct evidence that Zelia Nuttall considered herself a feminist or that she sympathized with the cause of women's suffrage. Both have high probability, however, because she was a friend of suffragist Mary Adelaide Nutting at Columbia University and was acquainted with Jane Addams of Hull House, whom Nuttall once invited to Casa Alvarado (Ross Parmenter, personal communication, 1985). She was also a member of the Women's Anthropological Society of America founded by Matilda Coxe Stevenson.*

Nuttall was an assertive woman, holding strong convictions as to the worth of her theories concerning anthropology and prehistory and was never one to back away from a controversy when challenged. She quite justifiably possessed a superb confidence in her own scholarship and erudition and courageously presented her ideas to the world. In her knowledge of Mexican archaeology and colonial history, she was often so far ahead of other scholars working in the same fields that her theories were not infrequently challenged. She seemed to enjoy the heated disagreements with colleagues and more than once proved them wrong.

In her later years Nuttall made plans to establish Casa Alvarado as a center for the promotion of Mexican science, where her library and pre-Columbian artifact collection would be available for the use of scholars from around the world. But she died suddenly in 1933 before such plans could be completed.

During her lifetime she felt that colleagues did not appreciate the value of her work, and it was her hope that time would authenticate her theories. To some degree that hope has been realized, as her works continue to be cited in scholarly publications in the United States and abroad. However, a number of her theories were premature and have since been proved wrong. Nonetheless, Nuttall deserves much credit for pursuing and publicizing pre-Columbian and colonial Mexican research when little was known about it and when there were few Mexican scholars with the education and time to do the research.

To paraphrase D. H. Lawrence, who purportedly based his Mrs. Norris in "Tea Party in Tlacolula" on Nuttall, the world is filled with myriad people and a few individuals. Zelia Nuttall was an individual—strong, independent, assertive, keen of mind, and determined in her chosen career, in a day when such women were not valued.

References and Works About Zelia M. M. Nuttall

El Palacio
1933   Death of Zelia Nuttall. *El Palacio* 34:25–26.
Gomez de Orozco, Federico
1933   Dona Zelia Nuttall, nota bio-bibliografica. *Boletín del Museo Nacional de Mexico* 5: 61, 115–24.
Lurie, Nancy O.
1966   Women in Early Anthropology. In *Pioneers of American Anthropology*. June Helm, ed. Pp. 29–83. Seattle: University of Washington Press.
Means, Philip Ainsworth
1933   Zelia Nuttall: An Appreciation. *The Hispanic-American Historical Society Review* 13:487–89.
Parmenter, Ross
1966   Glimpses of a Friendship: Zelia Nuttall and Franz Boas. (Based on their Correspondence in the Library of the American Philosophical Society of Philadelphia.) In *Pioneers of American Anthropology*. June Helm, ed. Pp. 88–147. Seattle: University of Washington Press.
1971   Zelia M. Nuttall. In *NAW I*. Cambridge: Belknap Press.
1985   Zelia Nuttall Biography. Unpublished.
Tozzer, Alfred M.
1933   Zelia Nuttall. *American Anthropologist* 25:475–82.
Vaillant, George C.
1933   Madame Zelia Nuttall. *Natural History* 33:454.

Selected Works by Zelia M. M. Nuttall

1886a Preliminary Note of an Analysis of the Mexican Codices and Grave Inscriptions. *Science* 8:393–95.
1886b The Terra-Cotta Heads of Teotihuacan. *American Journal of Archaeology* 2:157–78, 318–30.
1888   Standard or Head Dress? *Peabody Museum*. Paper 1–1. Pp. 1–52. Cambridge.
1891   The Atlatl or Spear-thrower of the Ancient Mexicans. *Peabody Museum*. Paper 1–3. Pp. 169–99. Cambridge.
1897   Ancient Mexican Superstitions. *Journal of American Folklore* 10:275–81.
1900   The Meaning of the Ancient Mexican Calendar Stone. *American Association for the Advancement of Science Proceedings* 49:320.
1901a Chalchihuitl in Ancient Mexico. *American Anthropologist* 3:227–38.

1901b The Fundamental Principles of Old and New World Civilizations. *Peabody Museum. Paper 2*. Cambridge.

1902a Introduction to Codex Nuttall. (Facsimile of an Ancient Mexican Codex Belonging to Lord Zouche of Haynworth.) *Peabody Museum of American Archaeology and Ethnology*. Vol. I.

1902b Sorcery, Medicine and Surgery in Ancient Mexico. *Johns Hopkins Hospital Bulletin* 13:86–91.

1903a Introduction, Translation and Commentary on *The Book of the Life of the Ancient Mexicans*. Berkeley: Codex Fejervary-Mayer.

1903b *Codex Magliabecchiano, The Book of the Life of Ancient Mexicans*. (An anonymous Hispano-Mexican manuscript preserved at the Biblioteca Nazionale Centrale, Florence, Italy.) (As ed. and trans.)

1904a The Periodical Adjustments of the Ancient Mexican Calendar. *American Anthropologist* 6:486–500.

1904b A Penitential Rite of the Ancient Mexicans. *Peabody Museum*. Paper 1–7. Pp. 437–62. Cambridge.

1906a The Astronomical Methods of the Ancient Mexicans. *Boas Anniversary Volume*. Pp. 290–98. New York.

1906b The Earliest Historical Relations Between Mexico and Japan. *Publications in American Archaeology and Ethnology* 4:1–47. University of California.

1909   A Curious Survival in Mexico of the Use of the Purpura Shell. *Putnam Anniversary Volume*. Pp. 368–84. New York: G. E. Stechert & Co.

1910   The Island of Sacrificios. *American Anthropologist* 12:257–97.

1914   New Light on Drake. *Hakluyt Society*. (Series 2), Vol. 34.

1921   Francisco Cervantes de Salazar. Biographical Note. *Journal of the Societé des Americanistes* 13:59–90.

1922   Datos Históricos Relativos a la Llamada "Casa de Cortes" o Casa Municipal de Coyoacan. *Boletín de la sociedad cientifica "Antonio Alzate"* 40:387–421.

1926a The Aztecs and Their Predecessors in the Valley of Mexico. *Proceedings of the American Philosophical Society* 65:245–55.

1926b Official Reports on the Towns of Tequizistlan, Tepechpan, Acolman and San Juan Teotihuacan. 1580. (Translated and edited with an introduction and notes.) *Peabody Museum*. Paper 11. P. 2. Cambridge.

1927   Origin of the Maya Calendar. *Science* 45, supplements 12 and 14.

1928a The New Year of Tropical American Indigenes. *Boletín de la Union Pan-Americana* 62:67–73.

1928b The Strange Story of a Sixteenth Century English Piece of Ordinance and the Inquisition of Mexico. *Hispanic American Historical Review* 8:240–42.

1930   Documentary Evidence Concerning Wild Maize in Mexico. *Journal of Heredity* 31:217–20. (Republished 1931 in *El Palacio* 30:105–10.)

1932   Some Comparisons Between Etowan, Mexican and Mayan Designs. In *Exploration of the Etowah Site in Georgia*. W. K. Moorehead, ed. Pp. 137–44. New Haven: New Haven Publications for Phillips Academy, Yale University Press.

1933   Documentos Referentes a la Destruccíon de Templo e Idolos, Violacíon de Sepulcros y las Remociones de Indios e Idolos en Nueva España durante el Siglo XVI. *Sociedad Mexicana de Geografía y Estadistica*. Primer Centenario, Vol. 2:291–312.

BEVERLY NEWBOLD CHIÑAS

Lila Morris O'Neale

(1886–1948)

American anthropologist Lila Morris O'Neale was known for her ethnographic and archaeological studies of textiles of native peoples of the Indian Americas.

O'Neale was born on November 2, 1886, in the farm community of Buxton, North Dakota, where her parents had only recently settled. Her mother, Carrie Margery Higgins O'Neale, traced her family tree with great pride from 1662 to her English ancestors who were early settlers of New York State. A staunch Christian Scientist and a member of the Women's Temperance League, Carrie had completed Normal School and was an English teacher when she met George Lester O'Neale. George was fourteen years older than Carrie, and had emigrated from Ireland via Liverpool to the United States. They married in 1882 and moved to Buxton, where two children, Lila and Lester, were born when Carrie was over thirty.[1]

The lure of the western frontier resulted in the family relocating in San Jose, California, in 1898. Settling into a large family house, Carrie rented rooms to female students at the nearby State Normal School. The late nineteenth and early twentieth centuries were a period of rapid expansion for colleges in the United States with a marked increase in female enrollment. Because appropriate housing was a problem, Carrie's rooms were always full. A strong and opinionated woman, Carrie had considerable influence on her daughter, initiating Lila's lifelong interest in textiles as well as a love and respect for the English language.

Encouraged by her mother, O'Neale entered Leland Stanford Junior University in Palo Alto, California, at the age of nineteen. After completing a two-year course, concentrating on English literature, she entered the Secondary Diploma program in household arts at the State Normal School in San Jose. Household Arts encompassed a wide range of subject areas designed for elementary and secondary public school teachers and homemakers. The curriculum included cookery, nutrition, nursing, sewing, textiles, social economics, and course development. In 1909 O'Neale received her Secondary Diploma, and she completed her A.B. in English at Stanford University (1910).

Although prepared as an English teacher, a socially acceptable female occupation, she utilized her household arts training by accepting a position as a manual training teacher in the Oakland Public Schools (1910–13). A two-year period followed as an instructor in household arts at the State Normal School, San Jose. In addition to costume design, millinery, and household chemistry, O'Neale was responsible for an in-depth textile course. History and development of textiles, study of fibers, processes of manufacture, identification of fabrics, and dye analysis were taught in lecture and laboratory session. This course remained a favorite of O'Neale's, one she would repeat throughout her thirty-eight years of teaching.

In 1915 O'Neale enrolled at Teacher's College, Columbia University, eventually receiving a Bachelor of Science in household arts. Periods of teaching provided funds for further education. It is possible that her year at Columbia brought her into contact with Franz Boas and the burgeoning group of female students who, pursuing graduate studies in cultural anthropology, revolved around him. She held a position in household arts at the Stout Institute, Menominee, Wisconsin (1916–19), and then at Oregon Agricultural College, Corvallis (1918–26). O'Neale became an associate professor of household arts during this period and published her first article. Entitled "You and Your Clothes" (1921), it demonstrates her succinct writing style. Subsequent summer teaching stints took her to the University of Southern California and the University of California at Berkeley and Los Angeles.

In 1926, at the age of forty, she became dissatisfied with the limited academic approach taken by the home economist to textile studies and gave up her secure teaching position in Oregon. O'Neale then enrolled at the University of California (Berkeley) as a graduate student in household arts, financially aided by her brother, Lester. She intended to write her thesis on lace, but Alfred L. Kroeber had just returned from fieldwork in Peru with textiles excavated for the Field Museum in Chicago. O'Neale had the required expertise derived from her years of teaching textile analysis, and her first collaboration with Kroeber took place. She changed her research topic and wrote her thesis on fifty-six Nazca textile specimens in the University Museum of Anthropology. It is entitled "Structural and Decorative Design, with Color Distribution Characteristic of Ancient Peruvian Fabrics" (1927). Using a statistical approach based on categories she had defined for analysis, her research was informed by articles of M. D. C. Crawford, textile researcher at the American Museum of Natural History—on the loom in the New World and on design and color in ancient fabrics. After receiving her A.M. in 1927, O'Neale settled into three years of anthropological study and took her Ph.D. in this field in 1930 at age of forty-four.

O'Neale's relationship with A. L Kroeber was fundamental to her career as an anthropologist. Eventually, Kroeber came to accept her as a trusted and valued colleague whom he called Pat, as she was known to her friends, family, and colleagues. However, Kroeber had not encouraged O'Neale when she first decided to pursue doctoral studies. Perhaps it was her age or lack of anthropological background. She had no field experience, and Kroeber insisted on field research as the basis for the dissertation. Also, she was intimidating to other graduate students because of her age and stylish dress.

After several years of collaboration, Kroeber recognized the quality of O'Neale's scholarship and professionalism and suggested in 1929 that she study the material culture of the Hupa, Yurok, and Karok peoples of northern California, an area in which he had ongoing research projects. O'Neale decided to work with basket makers, being familiar with those baskets collected by Kroeber from this area for the Museum of Anthropology. She set off for the Klamath River with her lifelong friend Martha Thomas and gathered her data in only six weeks. Utilizing what has come to be called an ethnoaesthetic approach to fieldwork, O'Neale interviewed all the basket makers she could find—forty-seven females—in order to determine native aesthetics and categories for excellence in basket making. She wanted to "investigate the weaver's subjective attitude, to determine individual reactions to craft aspects" (O'Neale 1932:5).

This new approach to fieldwork was derived from Franz Boas's introductory remarks to *Coiled Basketry in British Columbia and Surrounding Region* (1928). Boas stated: "The problem I set myself was an investigation into the attitude of the individual artist toward his work. Much has been written on the origin and history of design without any attempt to study the artist himself" (Boas 1928:131).

O'Neale acknowledged freely adapting this methodology to her work on the Klamath River, and she added a new dimension by bringing to the field photographs of Yurok-Karok baskets from the collections of the Museum of Anthropology and Academy of Science, purchased by Kroeber and Pliny Earle Goddard. Each weaver was shown all the prints. Since the baskets were known to them, having been woven by their relatives or friends, memories and enthusiasm accompanied the presentation of each print. All aspects of basket making were discussed with O'Neale, with whom the weavers felt at ease. O'Neale learned that men, who also participated in the photograph sessions, were knowledgeable about the process of basket making, since income was earned in this manner. Some men collected materials for their wives, others prepared materials for the weavers, and great pride was taken in their wives' accomplishments.

As Boas and Kroeber had previously noted, O'Neale's conclusions also confirmed that excellence and formal diversity of a given art style hinged on perfection of technique. Her dissertation, *Yurok-Karok Basket Weavers*, was published in 1932. Kroeber, writing to Margaret Harrison of the Carnegie Institution in Washington, stated that O'Neale's basket report was "one of the most important and liveliest ever made in the field" (Kroeber 1948).

Further ethnographic and archaeological fieldwork and research were made possible by a Guggenheim Fellowship to Peru (1931–32). Archaeological textiles from Paracas as well as contemporary pottery-making in Ayacucho and Huancayo were subjects for articles. Four and one-half months of fieldwork in Guatemala (1936) resulted in *Textiles of Highland Guatemala* (O'Neale 1945). O'Neale's enthusiasm for textiles aided her in documenting this complex textile tradition of the Maya. Another purpose for this expedition was to look for pre-Columbian survivals in textile technology, materials, and iconography. Lucretia Nelson provided fine drawings, and photographs of Guatemalan textiles from three collections were included. O'Neale presented male, female, and children's costumes from 104 highland villages. This study presents an overview of Guatemalan textiles from 1880 to 1936 and is known as "the bible" to researchers who use textiles as an index for studying cultural change among the Maya.

A final ethnographic effort resulted in an article on Papago color designation in collaboration with Papago Juan Dolores, a senior museum preparator at the Museum of Anthropology, Berkeley. Conclusions reached by Dolores and O'Neale found that color designations appear to be in the native speaker's mind and relate to the context of the objects described.

At Berkeley, O'Neale had joined the faculty of household arts as lecturer— later associate professor—teaching historic textiles, history of costume, textile design, and research in textile analysis. The Household Arts Department had been located in the School of Agriculture with the faculty and students being predominantly female. By 1938, after considerable negotiation with President Campbell, and with O'Neale as prime mover, the name was changed to Decorative Art Department and relocated in the College of Letters and Science. An expanded curriculum was developed, interdisciplinary in nature, integrating art, anthropology, and architecture courses. O'Neale was named chair of the department. In addition, she filled in for Edward Gifford while he was on leave and became the first woman to teach anthropology at Berkeley (1931). She also served as acting curator for the Museum of Anthropology and became assistant curator with special responsibilities for textiles (1935). In 1940 she was the second woman to become a full professor in anthropology and household arts. She died in 1949 at the age of 62, the result of a forty-eight hour bout with pneumonia.

O'Neale is an admired and often quoted figure in archaeological textile studies, a pioneer in every sense of the word. She was the first to consider pre-Columbian Peruvian textiles from the perspectives of chronology and provenience. The fact that her large body of work was accomplished in only the last two decades of her life remind one that she didn't discover the appropriate direction for her talents until she was forty. Her research on pre-Columbian textiles from Peru, begun with Kroeber in the 1930 publication, *Textile Periods in Ancient Peru: I*, represents her major interest and passion. In her lifetime she was acknowledged as the foremost expert on prehistoric textiles of the Indian Americas. Any textile that came into the museum fell under O'Neale's scrutiny. "She always worked with awareness of the age and provenience of the pieces she was analyzing and tried to summarize and generalize about style and techniques in the various cultural units of which she was aware" (A. P. Rowe personal communication

1986). A limited chronology based on only three time divisions was all she had to work with, so it is her technical analyses and descriptions that are still used by contemporary textile researchers.

Honors received, in addition to the Guggenheim Fellowship, included Councillor of the American Anthropological Association, from 1932 on, and delegate of the University of California to the International Congress of Anthropological and Ethnological Sciences at London (1934). O'Neale was a member of Sigma Xi, the scientific honor society.

O'Neale chose not to marry or have children. An advocate of women's independence, her self-image was one of professionalism in an academic world dominated by men, but where women were making advances. Moreover, she successfully interacted with the male faculty of the anthropology department and museum, as evinced by her negotiations to relocate the Decorative Art Department with the collaboration of Kroeber and others.

Informed and inspired fieldwork, excellent analyses of ethnographic and archaeological textiles, and an incisive facility with words provided her with the skills and information to apply the perspectives of science, technology, and art to her research. O'Neale's enthusiasm and passion for textile research is expressed in these words:

My archaeological writings are done under a sort of compulsion I don't feel at all when I know the surface reactions, at least, of live informants. The dead mystify me and I am always conscious of the immense advantage they hold in any investigation dealing with methods and procedures. One cannot know sequences of movements or reasons for them. When you attempt surmises, you become more than ever serious. (Harrison 1948:659)

Note

1. The author wishes to thank Jean Atthowe, Ralph L. Beals, Bruce Bernstein, Adelle Brière, Bonnie Jean Clark Campen, Richard Conn, Lawrence E. Dawson, Margaret Estep, David Mandelbaum, Lucretia Nelson, and Ann P. Rowe for their assistance during the preparation of this biography.

References and Works About Lila M. O'Neale

Harrison, Margaret
1948 Lila M. O'Neale: 1886–1948. *American Anthropologist* 50:657–65.
Kroeber, A. L., et al.
1948 *The Faculty Bulletin*. Berkeley: University of California.

Selected Works by Lila M. O'Neale

1921 You and Your Clothes. Oregon Agricultural College, *Extension Bulletin 333.* Corvallis.
1927 "Design, *Structural and Decorative, with Color Distribution Characteristic of*

Ancient Peruvian Fabrics. Unpublished thesis submitted in partial fulfillment for the degree of Master of Arts, Department of Household Art, University of California, Berkeley.

1932 *Yurok-Karok Basket Weavers. Publications in American Archaeology and Ethnology*. Berkeley: University of California Press.

1933 A Peruvian Multicolored Patchwork. *American Anthropologist* 35:87–94.

1934a Peruvian "Needleknitting." *American Anthropologist* 36:405–30.

1934b The Paracas Mantle: Its Technical Features. *International Congress of Anthropological and Ethnological Sciences, Compterendu*. P. 262. London.

1935 Pequeñas Prendas Ceremoniales de Paracas. *Revista del Museo Nacional* 4 (1): 245–66. Lima.

1936a A Survey of the Woolen Textiles in the Sir Aurel Stein Collections. *American Anthropologist* 38:414–32.

1936b Guatemala Textile Investigation. In *Textiles of Highland Guatemala, No. 35*. Pp. 136–38. Washington, D.C.: Carnegie Institution of Washington.

1936c Wide Loom Fabrics of the Early Nazca Period. In *Essays in Anthropology in Honor of Alfred Louis Kroeber*. Pp. 215–28. Berkeley: University of California Press.

1937a Textiles of the Early Nazca Period. In *Archaeological Explorations in Peru, Part III*. Anthropology Memoirs 2:117–218. Chicago: Field Museum of Natural History.

1937b Middle Cañete Textiles. In *Archaeological Explorations in Peru, Part IV*. Anthropology Memoirs 2:268–73. Chicago: Field Museum of Natural History.

1942a Textile Periods in Ancient Peru: II, Paracas Caverns and the Grand Necropolis. *University of California Publications in American Archaeology and Ethnology* 39:143–202.

1942b Early Textiles from Chiapas, Mexico. *Middle American Research Records* 1:1–6. New Orleans: Middle American Research Institute, Tulane University.

1945 *Textiles of Highland Guatemala*. Publication 567. Washington, D.C.: Carnegie Institution of Washington.

1946a Mochica (Early Chimu) and Other Peruvian Twill Fabrics. *American Antiquity* 12:239–45.

1946b A Note on Apocynum Fabric. *American Antiquity* 13:179–80.

1948 *Textiles of Pre-Columbian Chihuahua*. Publication 574. Washington, D.C.: Carnegie Institution of Washington.

1949 Basketry. Weaving. In *Handbook of South American Indians*. Vol. 5, Pp. 69–138. Julian H. Steward, vol. ed. Washington, D.C.: U.S. Government Printing Office.

1976 Notes on Pottery Making in Highland Peru. In *Ñawpa Pacha*, no. 14. John H. Rowe and Patricia J. Lyon, eds. Pp. 41–60. Berkeley: Institute of Andean Studies.

Coauthored Works

O'Neale, Lila et al.
1949 Chincha Plain-Weave Cloths. Berkeley: University of California Anthropological Records.

O'Neale, Lila, and B. J. Clark
1948 Textile Periods in Ancient Peru: III, The Gauze Weaves. *University of California Publications in American Archaeology and Ethnology* 40:143–222.
O'Neale, Lila, and Juan Dolores
1943 Notes on Papago Color Designations. *American Anthropologist* 45:387–97.
O'Neale, Lila, and D. F. Durrell
1945 An Analysis of the Central Asian Silks Excavated by Sir Aurel Stein. *Southwestern Journal of Anthropology* 1:392–446.
O'Neale, Lila, and A. L. Kroeber
1930 Textile Periods in Ancient Peru: I. *University of California Publications in American Archaeology and Anthropology* 28:23–56.
O'Neale, Lila, and T. W. Whitaker
1946 Embroideries of the Early Nazca Period and Crop Plants Depicted on Them. *Southwestern Journal of Anthropology* 3:294–321.
O'Neale, Lila, G. R. Willey, and J. M. Corbett
1954 An Analysis of the Textile Material from Ancon and Puerto de Supe. In *Early Ancon and Supe: Formative Stage Sites of the Central Peruvian Coast, Part III*. New York: Columbia Studies in Archaeology and Ethnology, Columbia University.

MARGOT BLUM SCHEVILL

Elsie Clews Parsons

(1874–1941)

American sociologist, cultural anthropologist, and folklorist, Elsie Claws Parsons
was known best for her detailed ethnographies in the Franz Boas tradition, and
for her comprehensive collections of folklore.

Parsons was one of the founding mothers of American anthropology and
folklore. She was also an outspoken feminist, pacifist, and social critic. Presently
remembered for her ethnographic monographs on the Pueblos and Zapotecs and
for her collections of black folklore, in her day Elsie Clews Parsons rose to
fame—some might say infamy—for her controversial sociological texts. During
the early years of her career, she wrote several massive volumes attacking the
family and other institutions for restricting the freedom of individuals, particularly women. She made her arguments with the use of cross-cultural material,
challenging American society with unflattering comparisons to ''primitive'' cultures. Elsie Clews Parsons also demonstrated how society imposed on all people
the moral injustices of violence and war. Writing for the general public and for
specialized scholars, she used journalism, comparative sociology, and then cultural anthropology to challenge social conventions.

In a recent biography of his great aunt, the philosopher Peter Hare summarized
the work of Elsie Clews Parsons in the following way:

Though she was a prolific writer who published books and articles on a wide range of
topics, everything Elsie did from her first publication at the age of twenty-four in 1898
to her death in 1941 at the age of sixty-seven stemmed from her concern for the ways
in which the expression of an individual's personality is affected by the conventions of
society. (1985:19)

Elsie Worthington Clews was born on November 27, 1874, into a socially
prominent family. While at times restrictive, her privileged background provided
her with the status and financial means to live the life she chose to lead. She

used her social position cleverly to gain individual freedom, but in order to do so, she had to fight the rules of her class.

Her father, Henry Clews, had come to the United States to seek his fortune. By the time the Civil War broke out, he had become a successful financier on Wall Street.

Her mother, Lucy Madison Worthington, was a distant relative of President James Madison. Her family came from Kentucky, but she grew up in Iowa, where her father served as colonel of the Fifth Iowa Volunteers. When they lost all their money in the 1873 Crash, the Worthingtons quickly accepted the proposal for marriage that Henry Clews made to their daughter in 1874. The combination of the Worthingtons' name and Henry Clews' wealth promised the couple a secure place in society.

Elsie Clews was born in their first year of marriage and gave her mother trouble from the very beginning. While her mother placed a great deal of importance on behaving by the rules of their social class, Elsie Clews resisted. Graced with an independent spirit, she refused to accept the restrictions imposed on her because she was a girl. When she grew up, she tried to explain her obstinance in political terms, characterizing her youthful rebellion as feminism. In response to her mother's question, "What is feminism?" she proclaimed:

When I would play with little boys in Bryant Park although you said it was rough and unladylike, that was feminism. When I took off my veil or gloves whenever your back was turned or when I stayed in my room two days rather than put on stays, that was feminism. When I got out of paying calls to go riding or sailing, that was feminism. When I kept to regular hours of work in spite of all your protests that I was selfish, that was feminism. When I had a baby when I wanted one . . . that was feminism. (Cited in Hare 1985:90)

The Clews family lived in New York City, where Elsie Clews received her primary and secondary education through tutors and in Miss Ruel's School. Then, in 1892, Clews entered the newly founded Barnard College, against her mother's wishes, and only after having wrung permission out of her father. Twenty-three women graduated in Clews' class four years later.

As an undergraduate, Clews was influenced most by Nicholas Murray Butler, chair of the Department of Philosophy. She received a master's degree in sociology from Columbia (1897). Her thesis analyzed relief programs for the poor in New York City. She received her Ph.D., also in sociology, writing a dissertation entitled "The Educational Legislation and Administration of the Colonies" (1899).

Clews impressed Franklin Giddings, chair of Barnard's Sociology Department and an important theoretician in the evolutionist tradition. Once she received her Ph.D., he appointed her to teach at Barnard as a Hartley House Fellow (1899–1902) and then later as Lecturer (1902–05). With the exception of her participation in the opening session of the New School for Social Research

(1919), which she helped found, Clews did no formal teaching after 1905. However, she influenced a large number of younger anthropologists, subsidizing their field expeditions, doing fieldwork with them, and corresponding with them while they were writing up their ethnographic data.

But in these early years she made her greatest contribution as a teacher, through a series of course lectures she gave on the family. She later collected these talks into a book, *The Family* (Parsons 1906). This volume caused quite a scandal, for it recommended that couples should first live together in trial marriages before they made lifelong commitments and had children. Far too progressive for its time, *The Family* was considered so outrageous that it threatened the political career of her husband, Herbert Parsons, whom she had married in 1900.

Herbert Parsons, like Elsie Clews, came from a prominent family. His father was John Edward Parsons, a wealthy lawyer, and his mother was Mary Dumesnil McIlvaine. Young Herbert, a Republican, associated with the reformers of the party. He served in the elected position of board member of the Aldermen of New York City (1899–1903); and from there he went to Congress for three terms (1905–11). His most important political position, however, was chair of the Republican Party Committee in New York City (1905–10). Looking for social reformers to support him, Theodore Roosevelt was instrumental in getting Herbert elected.

The Parsons were very devoted to each other. During the twenty-five years they had together before Herbert's sudden death in 1925, they raised four children: Elsie (Lissa, b. 1901), John Edward (b. 1903), Herbert (b. 1905), and Henry McIlvaine (b. 1911). Two others died in infancy. Theirs was a marriage based on mutual respect. They led very independent lives, enjoyed different interests and friends. Still, there were tensions. Although her husband usually accepted his wife's distaste for conventions—"institutional" was her favorite epithet—at times he found her behavior embarrassing for his public career (Hare 1985:44).

One sensitive issue was Elsie Parsons's pacifism during World War I. She became close friends with the famous pacifist Randolph Bourne and wrote against war occasionally for Max Eastman's *Masses* and more frequently for Walter Lippmann's *New Republic*, which she helped found. Although he was not a "hawk," Herbert Parsons believed that the United States had a responsibility to participate in this war; and he served as a member of General Pershing's intelligence staff in France. However, when it came to feminism, the couple had fewer disagreements, for he supported the principle of equal rights for women.

Parsons' feminism was not as militant as her pacifism, but it was strongly and boldly present in her writings and personal behavior. While she did not march with the suffragists, she supported the vote for women, though with some reticence, because she believed that women, more than men, gained strength through maintaining ceremonialism and conventions. She feared they would use the ballot box to meddle in the private affairs of individuals. "When women are given the vote,'' Parsons predicted, ''they will tend in their politics to exercise their skill in manipulating the private habits (drinking, dressing, lovemaking, etc.) of their fellow citizens'' (Hare 1985:102). She used the Prohibition movement as an example of women's tendencies in that direction.

According to Parsons, women had been socialized to maintain the traditions of the collectivity, particularly those that protected the home and domesticity. They were wary of people who made individualistic choices. Women were not to blame for having such limited views, she continued. Their lack of vision reflected their inadequate educational and work experiences. In Parsons' view, therefore, if American society gave women the vote but did not improve the material and spiritual conditions of their lives, it would give them a voice without having prepared them to participate as equals in a truly progressive democracy, one that ideally respected the freedom of individuals.

Parsons' feminism was perhaps best represented in her scholarly works: *The Family* (1906); *Religious Chastity* (1913), published under the pen name John Main; *The Old-Fashioned Woman* (1913); and *Fear and Conventionality* (1914). In *The Family*, she argued that if women were to be capable wives and mothers, they needed to have the same opportunities as men. Using cross-cultural material culled from the literature available to researchers in the early 1900s, and using Giddings's evolutionary perspective, she suggested that the subordinate position of women in modern society was a carryover from ''primitive'' cultures: the civilized world was still awed and frightened by the female's reproductive functions.

Provocative as that idea might sound, as we have already seen, it was Parsons's proposal for trial marriage, discussed in her final chapter, that outraged the public:

As a matter of fact, truly monogamous relations seem to be those most conducive to emotional or intellectual development and to health so that quite apart from the question of prostitution, promiscuity is not desirable or even tolerable. It would therefore seem well from this point of view to encourage early *trial* marriage, the relation to be entered into with a view to permanency, but with the privilege of breaking it if it proved unsuccessful and in the *absence of offspring* without suffering any degree of public condemnation. (1906:348–49)

If trial marriage caused an outcry in 1906, the observations that followed her proposal would do the same today. Parsons went on to criticize the practice of what she called ''the voluntarily childless marriage'' or those arrangements that ''restricted the number of children to one or two,'' adding:

Unfortunately it seems to affect the classes who, for the sake of the cultural progress of the race would do well to have . . . more numerous offspring. The classes, on the other hand, who from economic and cultural points of view can least afford child-bearing are those who are most prone to it. (1906:351–52)

Fortunately, social Darwinism soon disappeared from her writing as Parsons drew away from Giddings and his use of Herbert Spencer. In the process, she became an advocate of the largely middle-class birth control movement. Margaret Sanger (1938:189), the pioneer of the movement, wrote how Parsons courageously supported her just before Sanger's trial in 1916. Parsons's break with evolutionism also led her to question whether America was really so different from "primitive" societies, particularly in its treatment of women.

In *The Old-Fashioned Woman* (1913), Parsons argued that women everywhere were subject to restrictive taboos. No longer tied to the idea that women's subordination in modern society could be dismissed as a primitive vestige, she drew on a wide variety of ethnographic examples and on her own observations of American high society to show that deep affinities existed among all peoples. Women in all cultures have been confined by social conventions, kept out of public sphere, and trained to prefer to work for men rather than to have men work for them. Still, she believed in the possibility of change and had no qualms about using a scholarly work to celebrate the signs of political unrest.

Parsons characterized her work before 1915 as "propaganda by the ethnographic method." Comparing customs in modern society and those in "primitive" cultures, she wanted people to question the value of holding on to certain traditions in our own culture. She believed that a society committed to progress should be more tolerant of individual self-expression and do away with practices that made everybody conform.

By 1915 she decided that empirical anthropology provided the best methods for studying the ways social forces within society checked self-expression. For a time she combined her generalizing sociological approach with empirical anthropology; then she devoted herself entirely to producing very detailed, specialized works. During this transition, she consulted Pliny Goddard at the American Museum of Natural History, Alfred Kroeber, and Robert Lowie. But Franz Boas was the anthropologist whose methodology and theoretical perspective influenced her the most.

Parsons was the first woman Franz Boas interested in anthropology (Rosenberg 1982:166). While they corresponded as early as 1907, their association became important only after 1915, when Parsons, now entering her forties, began to do intensive fieldwork and apply Boas's ideas about culture and cultural diffusion. Although Margaret Mead* suggested that Parsons's relationship with Boas always remained "a little formal" (Mead 1959:346), after a period of initial remoteness, they seem to have developed a reasonably close friendship (see Goldfrank 1978 and Hare 1985).

By May 1919 Parsons and Boas were doing fieldwork together at the Laguna Pueblo. She had already had several years of experience in the Southwest by this time, but Boas had not personally done research in the area. Over the next two years they went to the field two more times. When Boas subsequently published *Keresan Texts* (1928), he dedicated the monograph to her.

Over the twenty-five years Parsons spent doing fieldwork in the Southwest, she lived in Zuni, Laguna, Acoma, Jemez, Isleta, and among the Hopi. Given her family responsibilities, she usually made very brief trips, remaining for about a month at a time. Under these conditions it is amazing that she gathered as much material as she did, especially since the Pueblo peoples were extremely unreceptive to outsiders and vehemently opposed to talking about their sacred traditions. Accounts of her experiences there tell of innumerable obstacles and sneak visits with individuals who were willing to disobey the rules of their culture and divulge secrets to the anthropologist. Perhaps the most spectacular coup involved the Isleta painter Joe B. Lente, who made more than 140 paintings for Parsons, depicting such activities as birth, curing, death, and the ceremonial cycle. This collection is the only pictorial enthographic account of Pueblo rituals ever done entirely by a native artist (Goldfrank 1978).

Parsons usually enjoyed good relations with the people she studied. In 1920, for example, she was formally adopted into a Hopi family. While this honor did not earn her greater access to certain ceremonial activities, she was extremely proud of the recognition.

Soon after her first visits to the Southwest, Parsons, influenced by Boas's approach, decided to write a comparative and historical account of the Pueblos. She argued that the social organization of each Pueblo differed and that the entire group offered an excellent laboratory for studying the distribution of traits within a single culture area. Her extensive research over the years provided "the first modern survey of Pueblo social organization" (Eggan 1950:309).

The culmination of Parsons's massive research and many publications on the Southwest was her two-volume work *Pueblo Indian Religion* (Parsons 1939), also described as the first synthesis of material on Pueblo religious traditions (Ortiz 1972:xivi).

One of Parsons's major concerns was the relationship between Indian and Spanish cultures, which her contemporaries had recognized but not yet studied (Spier 1943). She also compared Aztec and Pueblo traditions (Parsons 1933), but her main subject remained the influence of Spanish culture on New World indigenous societies. To investigate how other Indian groups had accepted or rejected Spanish traditions, she chose a people in Oaxaca, Mexico, to compare with the Pueblos.

Parsons went on to explain that such a study could not be done by lifting culture traits here and there, but only by means of careful, in-depth ethnographies of individual places. She chose Mitla, in part because this indigenous community, steeped in its pre-Hispanic heritage, stood beside the old Mitla ruins and very near the fabulous site of Monte Alban.

Much of her historical work on the relationship between Indian and Spanish cultures in the New World was criticized in her day, particularly by Robert Redfield and the University of Chicago School. Despite differences of opinion (Hare 1985:156), Redfield had the University of Chicago Press publish Parsons's book *Mitla: Town of the Souls* (1936b). In the last years of her life, she continued her comparative work in Ecuador, but her book *Peguche: A Study of Andean Indians* (Parsons 1945) came out posthumously.

The other major area of Parsons's work was in folklore. In 1915 Boas, editor of the *Journal of American Folklore*, was looking for anthropologists to collect black folklore. She agreed to do so.

Melville Herskovits later described the important role Parsons played in developing the study of black folklore:

The contributions of Elsie Clews Parsons to the study of Negro folklore are so extensive as to comprise, in themselves, the bulk of the available materials in this field; they are so important that no significant work can be done in the future without using them as a base. The volumes of folktales published over her signature . . . are the more notable since they represent one of the first applications of modern field methods to the study of Negro folklore. (1943:28)

She gathered material from Cape Verde Islanders living in New England and from American blacks from Virginia to Florida, most importantly from those on the Sea Islands of South Carolina. She also worked in Haiti, the Dominican Republic, the Bahamas, Bermuda, and Barbados. Of her many publications, the most significant work was her three-volume *Folk-Lore of the Antilles, French and English* (1943). Parsons also subsidized the research expeditions of others who made similar collections of black folktales from all over the New World— from Nova Scotia, to Guiana, to Brazil (Spier 1943).

Parsons held many professional offices: president of the American Folklore Society (1919–20), associate editor of the *Journal of American Folklore* (1918–41), and treasurer (1916–22) and president (1923–25) of the American Ethnological Society. In 1940 she became the first woman elected president of the American Anthropological Association (AAA).

Parsons was also a major benefactor, and contributed over $30,000 to the *Journal of American Folklore*. Furthermore, through the Southwest Society, a luncheon club associated with the American Museum of Natural History and Columbia University, she gave thousands of dollars to support fieldwork and publication costs (see Goldfrank 1978).

Elsie Clews Parsons fell ill in December 1941, just before she was to preside as president at the AAA meetings. She died from complications that developed after an appendectomy. Daughter Lissa saw to it that her mother's final wishes were respected. Before she died, she had written explicit instructions, in keeping with her distaste for social conventions: "If convenient, cremation (ashes left at crematory); otherwise, if not convenient, burial, but not in a cemetery and without gravestone. No funeral, and no religious services whatsoever" (Hare 1985:167).

References and Works About Elsie Clews Parsons

Boyer, Paul
1971   Elsie Clews Parsons. In *NAW I*. Edward T. James et al., eds. Pp. 20–23. Cambridge, Mass.: Belnap Press of Harvard University.
Goldfrank, Esther
1978   *Notes on an Undirected Life: As One Anthropologist Tells It*. Flushing N.Y.: Queens College Publications in Anthropology No. 3. Pp. 21–34.
Hare, Peter
1985   *A Woman's Quest for Science: Portrait of Anthropologist Elsie Clews Parsons*. New York: Prometheus Books.
Herskovits, Melville
1943   Some Next Steps in the Study of Negro Folklore. *Journal of American Folklore* 56:28.
Kroeber, Alfred
1943   *American Anthropologist* 45:252–55.
Parsons, Henry McIlvaine
1941   *New York Herald Tribune*, December 20, 1941.
Reichard, Gladys
1943   *Journal of American Folklore* 56:45–56 (including bibliography).
Rosenberg, Rosalind
1982   *Beyond Separate Spheres: Intellectual Roots of Modern Feminism*. New Haven: Yale University Press.
Spier, Leslie
1943   Elsie Clews Parsons. (Obituary) *American Anthropologist* 45:244–51.

Selected Works by Elsie Clews Parsons

1900   Field Work in Teaching Sociology. *Educational Review* 20:159–69.
1906   *The Family*. New York: G. P. Putnam's Sons.
1909   Higher Education of Women and the Family. *American Journal of Sociology* 14:758–63.
1913a   *The Old-Fashioned Woman: Primitive Fancies About the Sex*. New York: G. P. Putnam's Sons.
1913b   *Religious Chastity*: An Ethnological Study. New York: Macaulay Co. (Reprinted 1975. Under the name John Main. New York: AMS Press.)
1914   *Fear and Conventionality*. New York: G. P. Putnam's Sons.
1915a   *Interpreting Ceremonialism*. *American Anthropologist* 17:600–603.
1915b   *Social Freedom*. New York: G. P. Putnam's Sons.
1916a   Feminism and Sex Ethics. *International Journal of Ethics* 26:462–65.
1916b   *Social Rule*. New York: G. P. Putnam's Sons.
1917a   Patterns for Peace or War. *Scientific Monthly* 5:229–38.
1917b   Provenience of Certain Negro Folk-Tales, I, Playing Dead Twice in the Road. *Folk-Lore* 28:408–14.
1917c   Provenience of Certain Negro Folk-Tales, II, The Pass Word. *Folk-Lore* 29:206–18.

1918   Pueblo-Indian Folk-Tales, Probably of Spanish Provenience. *Journal of American Folklore* 31:216–55.

1920   Notes on Ceremonialism at Laguna. *Anthropological Papers, American Museum of Natural History* 19:85–132.

1922   Winter and Summer Dance Series in Zuni in 1918. *University of California Publications in American Archaeology and Ethnology* 17:171–216.

1924a   Tewa Kin, Clan and Moiety. *American Anthropologist* 26:333–39.

1924b   Tewa Mothers and Children. *Man* 24:148–51.

1925   A Pueblo Indian Journal 1920–1921. *Memoirs, American Anthropological Association* 32.

1926   Ceremonial Calendar at Tewa. *American Anthropologist* 28:209–29.

1927   Witchcraft Among the Pueblos, Indian or Spanish? *Man* 27:106–12, 125–28.

1928   Spirituals and Other Folk-Lore from the Bahamas. *Journal of American Folklore* 41:453–524.

1929   Ritual Parallels in Pueblo and Plains Culture. *American Anthropologist* 51:642–54.

1932   Isleta, New Mexico. *Bureau of American Ethnology, Forty-seventh Annual Report.* Pp. 192–466.

1933   Some Aztec and Pueblo Parallels. *American Anthropologist* 35:611–31.

1936a   *Taos Pueblo.* General Series in Anthropology 2. Menasha, Wisc.: George Banta Publishing Co.

1936b   *Mitla: Town of the Souls.* Chicago: University of Chicago Publications in Anthropology.

1939   *Pueblo Indian Religion.* 2 Vols. Chicago: University of Chicago Publications in Anthropology.

1940   Relations Between Ethnology and Archaeology in the Southwest. *American Antiquity* 5:214–20.

1942   Anthropology and Prediction. *American Anthropologist* 44:337–44. (Posthumous)

1943   *Folk-Lore of the Antilles, French and English,* Memoirs of the American Folklore Society 26:3. (Posthumous)

1945   Peguche, Canton of Otavalo, Province of Imbabura, Ecuador: A Study of Andean Indians. Chicago: University of Chicago Press.

Coauthored Works

Parsons, Elsie C., and Ralph L. Beals

1934   The Sacred Clowns of the Pueblo and Mayo-Yaqui Indians. *American Anthropologist* 36:491–514.

JUDITH FRIEDLANDER

Hortense Powdermaker

(1896–1970)

British-trained American anthropologist Hortense Powdermaker was best known for her wide-ranging field studies, two of them ground-breaking areas for anthropological research. As one of the persons who guided American anthropology to professional maturity during the interwar period, she brought together psychological and cultural perspectives, and examined the heretofore mystified process of anthropological fieldwork.

Powdermaker was born in Philadelphia on December 24, 1896, to a German-Jewish family of business people. She was one of four children; one sister, Florence, later became a prominent psychoanalyst. When she was five, the family moved to Reading, Pennsylvania, and when she was twelve, they settled in Baltimore. As she describes her adolescence in retrospect, Powdermaker felt detached from and critical of what she considered the family's materialistic values and sterile culture. She attended Goucher College, where she took two courses in sociology that she found unsatisfying, and then concentrated on history and the humanities. During college she "discovered" the Baltimore slums and the labor movement, and following her graduation she moved to New York, where she found a job with the Amalgamated Clothing Workers of America. Unhappy with her desk-job assignment, she asked to be allowed to organize workers. Her two years as a union organizer in Cleveland and Rochester were, in a sense, an introduction to fieldwork, and evidently she was good at it. Eventually, however, she found the work limiting, and dreading the prospect of a lifetime career as a labor organizer, she resigned her job. Seeking a change of scene, she set off for England.

Having decided to stay for while in London, as a diversion Powdermaker registered for some courses at the London School of Economics (L.S.E.). One of them was social anthropology with Bronislaw Malinowski, and immediately she found that "anthropology was what I had been looking for without knowing it." It was the fall of 1925, and she joined the two other graduate students working under Malinowski, E. E. Evans-Pritchard and Raymond Firth. The small band soon expanded to include Isaac Schapera, Audrey Richards,* and a few others. (Powdermaker has described the relationship among them and with Malinowski as "a sort of family with the usual ambivalences" [Powdermaker 1966:42–43].) She took courses with others on the L.S.E. faculty, but the only one other than Malinowski who influenced her was Radcliffe-Brown. Although she still had no ambitions for an academic career, at Malinowski's insistence she registered for the degree and subsequently wrote a library thesis on leadership in "primitive" society. She was awarded the Ph.D. in 1928.

Malinowski's intellectual and personal influence on Powdermaker was powerful. A charismatic and generous teacher, Malinowski was not, however, a mentor in the sense of sponsoring her career. Like many of her contemporaries, Powdermaker spent ten years after receiving her degree devising research projects on her own and seeking support wherever she could find it. Malinowski's introductions opened doors that sometimes led to limited research funds, but the possibility of a professional position for her was apparently never considered.

As a student at the L.S.E., Powdermaker longed to have "a people" of her own, and she was eager to study at firsthand an "untouched primitive" society. In April 1929, with a small grant from the Australian National Research Council arranged by Malinowski, she went to New Ireland for ten months of fieldwork in the village of Lesu. This was a general ethnographic study guided by a functionalist orientation and covering the full range of cultural topics. Her relations with the people were evidently easy, and the fieldwork went smoothly. Although she suffered loneliness, she found it an advantage to work as a woman alone; it forced her into closer contact with the natives, and she had access to both women and men.

At the end of the Lesu fieldwork, Powdermaker returned to the United States. Through a chain of introductions initiated by Malinowski and Radcliffe-Brown, she obtained both a fellowship from the National Research Council to write up her material and an affiliation with the Institute of Human Relations at Yale. There, she met Edward Sapir, whose friendship was important to her; she credits Sapir with nurturing her interests in psychology. After *Life in Lesu* (Powdermaker 1933) was completed, Powdermaker hit upon the idea of trying to study a segment of her own society with the methods developed for fieldwork among nonindustrial societies. With a long-standing interest in American blacks and with the model of the Lynds' *Middletown* before her, she decided on a community study in the Deep South. Sapir supported the plan and helped her obtain a fellowship from the Social Science Research Council. In 1932–33 and the summer of 1934, she conducted fieldwork in Indianola, Mississippi—probably the first study of a modern American community by an anthropologist.

Powdermaker felt it was necessary to include both the white and black sectors in Indianola and to function as a participant observer in both. Her success in doing so under dangerous circumstances (which she felt was possible only because she was a woman and therefore nonthreatening), and her analysis of black-white interaction, are landmark achievements for the time. *After Freedom* (Powdermaker 1939) emphasizes black society but covers, in the functionalist tradition, all aspects of community life. While she made explicit use of acculturation theory, the most influential contribution of the study was her treatment of the psychological adaptation of both blacks and whites to the interracial situation. (Powdermaker 1943b).

In 1938 Powdermaker joined the faculty of the newly established Queens College in New York City, becoming the founder of its Department of Anthropology and Sociology. During World War II she also taught at Yale in an army training program focusing on the Pacific; and in this period she wrote extensively on racial problems, including a book for high school students on prejudice (1944a). With the end of the war, she decided to indulge her interest in movies (both an avocation and a topic that had proved significant in the Mississippi study) with a research project that was thoroughly novel for anthropology. Initially she planned to do a content analysis of movies, but at the suggestion of Paul Fejos of the Viking Fund, who offered her support, she incorporated fieldwork in Hollywood into the study. The work was carried out in 1946–47, during which time she also served as a part-time visiting professor at the University of California, Los Angeles.

The hypothesis underlying the Hollywood study was that the social system in which movies are made significantly influences their content and meaning. In carrying out the study, Powdermaker focused on the process through which a film is made and the social interactions entailed in each step of the process. She worked primarily through interviews, supplemented by material from the files of the Screen Writers Guild and the Producers' Association. Later she was extremely critical of the study and felt it was limited by her own psychological inability to remain detached, as well as the difficulty of gaining access to the "front office" studio powers. Despite her limited success in penetrating the seats of power in Hollywood, Powdermaker was ahead of her time in recognizing the need to consider all sectors of the movie industry and to "study up." *Hollywood, the Dream Factory* (1950) remains the only serious anthropological study of this key American institution, and it is the book for which Powdermaker is best known to nonanthropologists.

After Hollywood Powdermaker continued her concern with the mass media in her teaching and writing (Powdermaker 1953) and with a sabbatical ahead of her in 1953–54, decided to carry these interests forward in sub-Saharan Africa, where she had long wanted to do fieldwork. Her plan was to look at choices of leisure activities as an index to changing values and needs. Receiving a Guggenheim fellowship, she made arrangements to work in Uganda, where her friend and L.S.E. classmate Audrey Richards* was based. Shortly before she left for the field, Richards advised against going to Uganda and suggested Northern Rhodesia instead. Although she had neither special background in this area nor knowledge of the Bemba language, Powdermaker's eagerness to work in Africa and what she has described as her "natural optimism" made her determined to go.

While seeking a fieldwork locale in Northern Rhodesia, Powdermaker met A. L. Epstein, who was studying the mining town of Luanshya in the Copperbelt and who invited her to base herself there and share his house. Finding work through an interpreter unsatisfactory, she followed the practice of other anthropologists in the area and hired native assistants; one young man in particular became a kind of alter ego, and she relied on him heavily. Of necessity the study was based primarily on indirect sources of information—surveys and interviews conducted by assistants, essays by students, conversations recorded by her main informant, and the like. As in the Hollywood study, she encountered circumstantial and personal limits on participant observation, but she felt these were unrelated to her status as a woman. In general, she considered the age and psychological involvement of the anthropologist to be more important factors in fieldwork than gender.

Powdermaker found the *Copper Town* book (Powdermaker 1962) difficult to write. Eventually she drew her theoretical inspiration from the book of Erik Erikson and developed an approach that joined anthropological theories of cultural change with psychological theories of individual change. Powdermaker's continuing concern with self-awareness (which earlier had led her to psychoanalysis) and her interest in field methods came together in her final major work *Stranger and Friend*, (Powdermaker 1966), in which she compared and evaluated her four very different fieldwork experiences. This book is the prime source for her own views of her life and work. She retired from Queens College in 1968 and moved to Berkeley, where—as always, vitally interested in the life surrounding her—she began a study of youth culture. She remained actively engaged in work and in her relationships with friends until her sudden death of a heart attack at seventy-three.

Powdermaker accumulated many honors, among them the presidency of the American Ethnological Society and an honorary doctorate from Goucher College. The honor she valued most was the Distinguished Teacher Award from the Alumni Association of Queens College. At the same time, she felt that she did not enjoy the eminence that her achievements might have brought her had she been a man—a judgment in which the author of her obituary concurs (Wolf 1971).

Hortense Powdermaker was a sociable, deeply humane person, with a wide circle of friends outside of anthropology as well as within the field, both generous and demanding in personal relationships. While she had close women friends, her relations with male colleagues and students were easier than with females. Although she never married, she had a number of romantic involvements with men. She regretted not having experienced motherhood, for which she compensated in part by becoming foster mother to Won Mo Kim, a young Korean violinist.

Powdermaker's anthropology covers an unusually wide range of interests, and the assessments of it range widely as well. The Lesu study is now a standard source on Melanesia, although generally considered to be theoretically unremarkable. Her pioneering work in Mississippi has stood the test of time well and has achieved the status of a classic. One of the first efforts to extend anthropology to American society and the first to encompass an interracial situation, it describes social processes that came to national attention twenty years later with the civil rights movement. Her most criticized book, the Hollywood study, evoked harsh response perhaps precisely because of its accuracy and daring. In a retrospective assessment, her student Eric Wolf evaluates it much more positively than she herself did (see Wolf 1971). *Copper Town* received mixed reviews, with negative responses particularly from social anthropologists skeptical of her use of psychological concepts; and the book betrays the problems of field research undertaken with inadequate areal and linguistic preparation. *Stranger and Friend*, on the other hand, was hailed for its candor and insight into the anthropological enterprise. Beyond dispute, however, is that courage, conviction, and an unquenchable zest for new horizons marked the work and the life of Hortense Powdermaker.

References and Works About Hortense Powdermaker

Traeger, George L.
1971   Hortense Powdermaker: A Tribute. *American Anthropologist* 73:786–87.
Wolf, Eric
1971   Hortense Powdermaker, 1900–1970. *American Anthropologist* 73:783–86.

Selected Works by Hortense Powdermaker

1928   Leadership Among the Aborigines of Central and Southern Australia. *Economica* 223:168–90.
1931a Preliminary Report on Research in New Ireland. *Oceania* 3:1–12.
1931b Vital Statistics of New Ireland as Revealed in Genealogies. *Human Biology* 3:351–75.
1931c Mortuary Rites in New Ireland. *Oceania* 2:26–43.
1932   Feasts in New Ireland. *American Anthropologist* 34:236–47.
1933   *Life in Lesu: The Study of a Melanesian Society in New Ireland*. New York: W. W. Norton; London: Williams and Norgate.
1934   At Home on the Equator. *The Atlantic Monthly* 153:195–204.
1939   *After Freedom: A Cultural Study in the Deep South*. New York: Viking. (Reprinted 1968, New York: Atheneum Press.)
1943a Commemoration of Professor Malinowski. *Quarterly Bulletin of the Polish Institute of Arts and Sciences in America* 1:203–7.
1943b The Channeling of Negro Aggression by the Cultural Process. *American Journal of Sociology* 48:122–30. (Reprinted 1953 in *Personality in Nature, Society and Culture*. Clyde Kluckhohn and Henry A. Murray, eds. Pp. 597–608. New York: Alfred A. Knopf.)

1944a *Probing Our Prejudices.* New York: Harper and Brothers.

1944b The Anthropological Approach to the Problem of Modifying Race Attitudes. *Journal of Negro Education* 13:295–303.

1945 An Anthropologist Looks at the Race Problem. *Social Action* 11:5–13.

1950 *Hollywood, the Dream Factory: An Anthropologist Studies the Movie Makers.* Boston: Little, Brown and Company.

1951 Reply to R. Bierstedt's Review of Hollywood, the Dream Factory. *American Sociological Review* 16:382–83.

1953 *Mass Communications Seminar.* (Proceedings of an interdisciplinary seminar held under the auspices of the Wenner-Gren Foundation for Anthropological Research, May 11–13, 1951.) New York: Wenner-Gren Foundation. (As ed.)

1955 Communication and Social Change, Based on a Field Study in Northern Rhodesia. *Transactions of the New York Academy of Sciences* (Series 2) 17:430–40.

1956 Social Change Through Imagery and Values of Teen-Age Africans in Northern Rhodesia. *American Anthropologist* 58:783–813.

1960 An Anthropological Approach to the Problem of Obesity. *Bulletin, New York Academy of Medicine* 36:5–14.

1962 *Copper Town: Changing Africa, the Human Situation on the Rhodesian Copper-belt.* New York: Harper and Row.

1965a Comment on C. Frantz' Review of Copper Town. *American Anthropologist* 67:1284–85.

1965b Cultural Factors Affecting American Food Habits. *Proceedings: Nutritional Status, A Critical Evaluation.* Pp. 47–54. Ithaca: New York State College of Home Economics, Cornell University.

1966 *Stranger and Friend: The Way of an Anthropologist.* New York: W. W. Norton and Co.

1968 Field Work. In *International Encyclopedia of the Social Sciences.* David L. Sills, ed. Vol. 5, Pp. 418–24. New York: Macmillan and Free Press.

Coauthored Works

Powdermaker, Hortense, and Joseph Semper

1938 Education and Occupation Among New Haven Negroes. *Journal of Negro History* 23:200–215.

SYDEL SILVERMAN

Tatiana Proskouriakoff

(1909–1985)

Russian-born American archaeologist and epigrapher Tatiana Proskouriakoff, was known especially for her pioneering work with Maya hieroglyphic writing and for her perspective drawings and architectural reconstructions of ancient Maya cities.

Proskouriakoff was born on January 23, 1909, to Avenir Proskouriakoff, a chemist, and Alla Nekrassova, a physician, in Tomsk, Siberia. She and her older sister, Ksenia, were brought to the United States in the summer of 1916 when their father was commissioned by the tsar to inspect the munitions the United States was selling to Russia.

Proskouriakoff and her sister entered grade school in Philadelphia, where they said the most difficult adjustment initially was the acquisition of a new language. Prior to sailing to the New World they both had had scarlet fever, diphtheria, and measles; and as a result most of their hair fell out. Although they wore bonnets to cover up their almost bare heads, the other children at school teased them and made them quite uncomfortable until their hair grew back. Their mother insisted that both girls learn to play the piano and paint. They were also exposed to a very intellectual group of expatriate White Russians that had settled in Philadelphia.

Later Tatiana Proskouriakoff attended Pennsylvania State University and obtained a B.S. degree in 1930 in architecture. During the Depression very few new buildings were being constructed, and Proskouriakoff said she found it impossible to find a job that would allow her to design new structures. She knew she had to find some other line of work during those difficult economic times. On one of the bulletin boards at Pennsylvania State University, she saw a notice advertising a job opening for an architecture student. Linton Satterthwaite, Jr., of the Museum at the University of Pennsylvania was looking for someone to draw architectural reconstructions of buildings uncovered in archaeological excavations participants in his project had conducted at the Classic Maya ruin of

Piedras Negras in northwestern Guatemala. Proskouriakoff accepted the job opportunity "because it was the only thing available." Given that initial exposure to Maya architecture and archaeology, she was to pursue a very different career from the one she had envisioned.

Under Satterthwaite's direction from 1934 through 1938, Proskouriakoff produced an architectural restoration of Structure P-7 at Piedras Negras, and a perspective drawing of the acropolis at the same site. Satterthwaite placed at her disposal all of the unpublished maps and field notes that the various expeditions of the University Museum had obtained during the excavation seasons he directed (1933–40). The Museum at the University of Pennsylvania had been excavating at Piedras Negras since 1931, with Eldridge R. Johnson directing the work before Satterthwaite, his field assistant, took over in 1933.

The project of producing a series of perspective drawings of archaeological reconstructions to show the layperson what these ancient Maya cities would have looked like when they were occupied was originally conceived by one of Proskouriakoff's colleagues, Sylvanus Griswold Morley at the Carnegie Institution of Washington. In fact, it was Morley who personally undertook the task of raising money to finance Proskouriakoff's trip to Copán, Honduras, in 1939 and to Chichén Itzá, Uxmal, Kabah, Labná, Xpuhil, and Sayil in Yucatán, Mexico in 1940. At these sites she was able to take her own building measurements and complete the first series of in-the-field sketches. This ambitious undertaking allowed her to study and observe the diversity of environmental settings, city plans, and architectural styles in Guatemala, Mexico, and Honduras. Her justly famous perspective drawings were first published in *An Album of Maya Architecture* (Proskouriakoff 1946).

Her monograph *A Study of Classic Maya Sculpture* (1950) remains the definitive treatment in the field. From approximately 400 stelae (freestanding, carved stone monuments), Proskouriakoff developed an ingenious method of "styledating" that permitted all monuments with or without decipherable dates (in the Initial Series or Long Count calendrical or dating system) to be placed in time. She successfully charted changes in art styles depicted on Maya stone monuments during a 600-year time span.

Following her research on the style and content of Classic Maya sculpture, Proskouriakoff, by then a member of the Carnegie Institution of Washington, became involved in the Mayapán Project. That project attempted to deal with the demise of a major Postclassic (A.D. 1250–1450) Maya city in northern Yucatán, Mexico. The Mayapán Project was a good example of an integrated approach to ethnohistoric and archaeological data.

Proskouriakoff continued to work with other archaeologists affiliated with the Carnegie Institution of Washington. With Karl Ruppert and J. Eric S. Thompson, she began to study the murals of Bonampak in eastern Chiapas, Mexico; and with Edwin M. Shook she analyzed settlement patterns in the Guatemala highlands.

When the Carnegie Institution stopped funding archaeology projects in 1958,

Proskouriakoff joined the Peabody Museum at Harvard University. In 1977 she officially retired from her position as Honorary Curator of Maya Art, but continued to work actively on a book (reconstructing the political histories of Classic Maya cities) for the last decade. This book will be published by the University of Texas Press.

Proskouriakoff has called the late 1950s her "most exciting and fun-filled time." Since the late 1930s she had continued to work with the Piedras Negras stelae, focusing special attention on the style and artistic conventions employed. Late in the 1950s she concentrated on the integrated study of the artistic scene (or portrayal) and the hieroglyphic text. In organizing the Piedras Negras stelae, she first divided all the securely dated monuments into seven groups. Each of these groups began with a monument that displayed a particular scene—called the ascension motif—in which a Maya ruler is shown seated cross-legged upon a throne set within a temple doorway, with a ladder and footprints leading up to the throne. Proskouriakoff had noted that the earliest date recorded in each series was associated with the same hieroglyph—the "upended frog." This earliest or "initial date" occurred some twelve to thirty-one years before what she assumed must be the "inaugural" or "accession to the throne" date, since it occurred in the five-year period prior to the carving of the stelae depicting the "ascension motif." Therefore, Proskouriakoff concluded that the "upended frog" glyph might refer to the "naming" or initiation of the ruler, or perhaps to his birth date. Using these "initial dates" or "birthdates," she was able to compute the ages of seven Piedras Negras rulers. Using "inaugural dates," she could also state when they apparently took office. By articulating all the series of monuments, Proskouriakoff was able to establish for the first time a true dynastic sequence of political reigns. This path-breaking work entitled "Historical Implications of a Pattern of Dates at Piedras Negras, Guatemala" was published in 1960. If we were to single out one publication for which she will always be remembered and praised, certainly it is this one.

Prior to Proskouriakoff's 1960 publication, most prominent Mayanists had argued that the ancient Maya were "obsessed with time" and that the inscriptions consisted entirely of astronomical and calendrical information. Indeed, these were the only sections of the texts that had been translated. It is now known that the figures portrayed on the monuments, once thought to be gods or perhaps priests, were actual men and women. Many of the men were the rulers who administered the ancient Maya cities, and many of the women were their mothers, wives, or sisters. Proskouriakoff also demonstrated that the texts recorded the major feats and significant rites of passage in the lives of these rulers. Thus, Proskouriakoff can be credited with opening the "historic door" to the ancient Maya civilization, a door that all Maya scholars have passed through since her pioneering breakthrough in 1960.

For her brilliant discovery that the ancient Maya were recording their own dynamic political and dynastic histories, Proskouriakoff was awarded the fifth Alfred V. Kidder Medal in 1962 by a special committee of the American Anthropological Association. Ironically, in 1950 she had designed that very medal commemorating the two important culture areas to which Kidder had contributed so much during his archaeological career. One side of the medal depicts a ruin in the Southwest, and the other side shows a site in Mesoamerica.

Proskouriakoff then turned enthusiastically to the inscriptions of other sites, most notably Yaxchilán during the early 1960s and Uaxactún, Tikal, and Palenque in the 1970s. Her specific goal was working out the sequences of rulers and the nature of historical events recorded by those cities. In the process, she also continued to discover the meaning of a series of hieroglyphs that we now know referred to such things as (1) the names and titles of rulers, (2) the names of their royal wives or mothers, (3) special rituals dedicated to the memory of deceased ancestors, (4) the taking of captives, and (5) the rite of autosacrifice or bloodletting.

In addition to the Kidder Medal, Proskouriakoff was awarded honorary degrees from Tulane University and Pennsylvania State University in the early 1970s. Most recently (1984) she was the recipient of the prestigious Order of the Quetzal, the highest honor awarded to a foreigner by Guatemala, the country whose monuments provided the basis for many of her important discoveries.

Selected Works by Tatiana Proskouriakoff

1944   An Inscription on a Jade Probably Carved at Piedras Negras. *Carnegie Institution of Washington, Division of Historical Research, Notes on Middle American Archaeology and Ethnology* 2 (47): 142–47. Washington, D.C.

1946   An Album of Maya Architecture. *Carnegie Institution of Washington.* Publication 558. Washington, D.C.

1950   A Study of Classic Maya Sculpure. *Carnegie Institution of Washington.* Publication 593. Washington, D.C.

1951   Some Non-Classic Traits in the Sculpture of Yucatan. In *The Civilizations of Ancient America: Selected Papers of the 29th International Congress of Americanists.* Sol Tax, ed. Vol. 1, pp. 108–18. Chicago: Aldine.

1952a   The Survival of the Maya Tun Count in Colonial Times. *Carnegie Institution of Washington, Notes on Middle American Archaeology and Ethnology* 4 (112): 211–19.

1952b   Sculpture and Artifacts of Mayapán. *Carnegie Institution of Washington.* Year Book 51. Pp. 256–59.

1953   Scroll Pattern (Entrelaces) of Veracruz. Huastecos, Totonacos y sus Vecinos. Ignacio Bernal and Eusebio Dávalos Hurtado, eds. *Revista Mexicana de Estudios Antropológicos* 13 (2–3): 389–401.

1954a   Mayapán, Last Stronghold of a Civilization. *Archaeology* 7 (2): 96–103.

1954b   Varieties of Classic Central Veracruz Sculpture. *Carnegie Institution of Washington.* Publication 606, Contribution 58. Pp. 61–94. Washington, D.C.

1955   The Death of a Civilization. *Scientific American* 192 (5): 82–88.

1958   Studies on Middle American Art. In *Middle American Anthropology.* Pan American Union Social Science Monograph No. 5. Gordon R. Willey, Evon Z. Vogt, and Ángel Palerm, eds. Pp. 29–35. Washington, D.C.

1959 Definitions of Maya Art and Culture. *The Art Quarterly* (Summer):110–125.

1960a Historical Implications of a Pattern of Dates at Piedras Negras, Guatemala. *American Antiquity* 25 (4): 454–75.

1960b Varieties of Classic Central Veracruz Sculpture. *Carnegie Institution of Washington*. Publication 606. Pp. 61–94. Washington, D.C.

1961a The Lords of the Maya Realm. *Expedition* 4 (1): 14–21. Philadelphia: University Museum, University of Pennsylvania. (Reprinted 1966 in *Ancient Mesoamerica: Selected Readings*. John A. Graham, ed. Pp. 168–75. Palo Alto, Calif.: Peek Publishers.)

1961b Portraits of Women in Maya Art. In *Essays in Pre-Columbian Art and Archaeology*. Samuel K. Lothrop et al. eds. Pp. 81–99. Cambridge: Harvard University Press.

1962a Los Señores del Estado Maya. *Antropología e Historia de Guatemala* 14 (1): 11–17. (Originally published under the title "The Lords of the Maya Realm." Ernesto Chinchilla Aguilar, trans.).

1962b The Artifacts of Mayapán. In *Mayapán, Yucatán, México*, by Harry Evelyn Dorr Pollock et al. Carnegie Institution of Washington. Publication 619. Pp. 321–442. Washington, D.C.

1962c Civic and Religious Structures of Mayapán. In *Mayapán, Yucatán, México*, by Harry Evelyn Dorr Pollock et al. Carnegie Institution of Washington. Publication 619. Pp. 87–163. Washington, D.C.

1963 Historical Data in the Inscriptions of Yaxchilan, Part I. *Estudios de Cultura Maya*. Vol. 3, pp. 149–67. Mexico City: Universidad Nacional Autónoma de México.

1964a El Arte Maya y el Modelo genético de Cultura. In *Desarrollo cultural de los Mayas*. Evon Z. Vogt and Alberto Ruz Lhuillier, eds. Pp. 179–93. México: Universidad Nacional Autónoma de México.

1964b Historical Data in the Inscriptions of Yaxchilan, Part II. *Estudios de Cultura Maya*. Vol. 4, pp. 177–201. Mexico City: Universidad Nacional Autónoma de México.

1965 Sculpture and Major Arts of the Maya Lowlands. In *Handbook of Middle American Indians*. Gordon R. Willey, ed. Vol. 2, pp. 469–97. Austin: University of Texas Press.

1968a Olmec and Maya Art: Problems of Their Stylistic Relation. In *Dumbarton Oaks Conference on the Olmec*. Elizabeth P. Benson, ed. Pp. 119–34. Washington, D.C.: Dumbarton Oaks.

1968b The Jog and Jaguar Signs in Maya Writing. *American Antiquity* 33 (2): 247–51.

1968c Graphic Designs on Mesoamerican Pottery. Washington, D.C.: Carnegie Institution of Washington.

1969 *Álbum de Arquitectura Maya*. México City: Fondo de Cultura Económica.

1970 On Two Inscriptions at Chichén Itzá. In *Papers of the Peabody Museum of Archaeology and Ethnology* 61:457–67. Cambridge: Harvard University.

1971a Classic Art of Central Veracruz. In *Handbook of Middle American Indians*. Gordon F. Ekholm and Ignacio Bernal, eds. Vol. 11, pp. 558–72. Austin: University of Texas Press.

1971b Early Architecture and Sculpture in Mesoamerica. *University of California Archaeological Research Facility*, Contribution 11. Pp. 141–56. Berkeley: University of California Press.

1973 The Hand-grasping-Fish and Associated Glyphs on Classic Maya Monuments. In

Mesoamerican Writing Systems: A Conference at Dumbarton Oaks. Elizabeth P. Benson, ed. Pp. 165–78. Washington, D.C.: Dumbarton Oaks.

1974   Jades from the Cenote of Sacrifice, Chichén Itzá, Yucatán, México. *Peabody Museum of Archaeology and Ethnology Memoirs* 10 (1). Cambridge: Harvard University.

Coauthored Works

Knorozov, Yuri V., with Tatiana Proskouriakoff (as collaborating ed.)

1967   Selected chapters. *The Writing of the Maya Indians*, by Yuri Knorozov. Sophie Coe, trans. Peabody Museum of Archaeology and Ethnology, Russian Translation Series. Vol. 4.

Lothrop, Samuel K., W. C. Root, and Tatiana Proskouriakoff

1952   Metals from the Cenote of Sacrifice, Chichén Itzá, Yucatán. *Memoirs of the Peabody Museum of Archaeology and Ethnology* 10 (2). Cambridge: Harvard University Press.

Pollock, Harry E. D., Ralph L. Roys, Tatiana Proskouriakoff, and Augustus Ledyard Smith.

1962   Mayapán, Yucatán, México. *Carnegie Institution of Washington*, Publication 619. Washington, D.C.

Proskouriakoff, Tatiana, and John Eric Sidney Thompson

1947   Maya Calendar Round Dates Such as 9 Ahau 17 Mol. *Carnegie Institution of Washington, Division of Historical Research, Notes on Middle American Archaeology and Ethnology* 3 (79): 143–50. Washington, D.C.

Proskouriakoff, Tatiana, and Charles R. Temple

1955   A Residential Quadrangle—Structures R–85 to R–90. *Carnegie Institution of Washington, Department of Archaeology, Current Reports* 1 (29): 289–361. Washington, D.C.

Ruppert, Karl, J. Eric S. Thompson, and Tatiana Proskouriakoff

1955   Bonampak, Chiapas, Mexico. *Carnegie Institution of Washington*. Publication 602. Washington, D.C.

Shook, Edwin M., and Tatiana Proskouriakoff

1956   Settlement Patterns in Mesoamerica and the Sequence in the Guatemalan Highlands. In *Prehistoric Settlement Patterns in the New World*. Wenner-Gren Foundation for Anthropological Research, Publications in Anthropology, no. 23. Gordon R. Willey, ed. Pp. 93–100.

JOYCE MARCUS

Gladys Amanda Reichard

(1893–1955)

Gladys Amanda Reichard was a cultural and linguistic anthropologist, known for her work on the social life and language of the Navajo of the American Southwest, especially for her symbolic analysis of Navajo religion, and structural analysis of Navajo prayer.

It is fitting to begin this biography with the words of Marian Smith, a former student of Reichard and for many years a colleague at Columbia University:

Reichard's love of the Southwest was so great that there is some measure of comfort in the knowledge that her death on July 25, 1955, came after only a brief illness in Flagstaff, Arizona. Ever since her sabbatical among the Coeur d'Alene in 1938 she had spent her leaves and most of her vacations in the Southwest, and she had planned to retire there. The Museum of Northern Arizona furnished a congenial atmosphere, several of her closest friends were near at hand as Southwestern distances are reckoned, and the Navajo, who had been the center of so much of her fieldwork, were not far off. This combination of mental stimulation and personal warmth gave her the background in which she was most content. A similar combination of intellectual awareness and personal insight was reflected in all her published work and was present throughout her life. (Smith 1956:913)

Not only did Gladys Reichard integrate the personal and intellectual in her anthropology, anthropology itself was the major integrating force in her life. She became close personal friends with the anthropologists with whom she had studied or worked: Boas, Lowie, and especially Pliny Earle Goddard, who had introduced her to the Navajo. She was much concerned with the teaching of anthropology as well as with her own research and writing, and gave great thought to it. She did not marry and take on family commitments; instead she engaged her sister in collaborative work helping to take and to print the striking photographs with which some of her works on the Navajo are illustrated. And she established deep and long-standing friendships with some of the Navajo people with whom she worked over a period of many years.

Gladys Amanda Reichard was born on July 17, 1893, in Bangor, Pennsylvania. Her father, Noah W. Reichard, a doctor, and her mother, Minerva Ann Jordan, were Quakers; she was reared in an intellectually oriented household. She taught elementary school for six years before going to college. She majored in classics at Swarthmore but during her senior year learned of anthropology. Graduating Phi Beta Kappa at the age of twenty-six, Reichard pursued graduate work in anthropology at Columbia University with the benefit of the special Swarthmore Lucretia Mott Fellowship. She received her M.A. in 1920 and her Ph.D. in 1925. With the assistance of a Research Fellowship at the University of California, she conducted fieldwork among the Wiyot of Northeastern California in 1922–23 and wrote her dissertation on Wiyot grammar (1925).

In 1921 Reichard became an assistant in anthropology at Barnard College. When she returned from California, she was chosen by Boas for a full-time instructor's post in what for many years was the only undergraduate anthropology department in a woman's college. She taught at Barnard until her death in 1955. Full professorships back then did not come about as early as they do today. Prior to the postwar expansion of colleges, people with Ph.Ds had to work their way up through instructor and lecturer levels even to assistant professorship; and full professorship was a higher honor than it has become. Reichard was made full professor in 1951.

Reichard received recognition for her work, and it was supported with fellowships and grants. However, it should be noted that much of her Navajo research was made possible by the generosity of Elsie Clews Parsons,* who helped support the fieldwork of many of Boas's students. In 1926–27 Reichard received a John Simon Guggenheim Memorial Fellowship to study the Melanesian art collection in Hamburg, Germany. She analyzed the units of design and principles of composition on carved wooden bowls, shell ornaments, and decorated gourds in order to define specific styles of different localities, their relations to the area as a whole, and the extent to which "individuality may be expected" on the artist's part. In 1932 *Melanesian Design* (Reichard 1932) received the New York Academy of Sciences A. Cressy Morrison Prize in Natural Sciences.

Reichard's research spanned the gamut of sociocultural life, material culture, and daily activities, through social and economic organization, to religion and ritual, art and literature, and language and symbolism. Like her mentor Boas (whom she always referred to in class as "Papa Franz"), she maintained a lifelong interest in linguistics. She concentrated on the Navajo but did not limit her work to them. She was planning a study of Salish linguistics at the time of her death.

Like the other anthropologists of her generation, working in a period when a basic corpus of ethnographic materials was first being amassed, Reichard was of necessity developing new methods of data collection and analysis. It was her style, however, to present these simply and directly, with little elaboration. In her introduction to *Social Life of the Navajo Indians*, Reichard (1928a) stated merely that the census method for social organizational analysis had serious limitations in contrast with the genealogical method, because of the former's lack of historical depth. Therefore, in order "to answer the questions of interest, namely, clan as an institution, family, marriage, naming, property rights, etc.," Reichard collected genealogies that included some 3,500 individuals, or about 10 percent of the Navajo people. Instead of building her interpretation of Navajo society primarily on interview material, she built it on the analysis of actual relationships among people that spanned three or four, and up to nine, generations, a method some latter-day anthropologists think of as recent. With respect to the nature of historical change, Reichard (1939a:vi) wrote in her preface to *Dezba, Woman of the Desert*: "The Navajo with their difficult problems and varied contacts demonstrate for a single locality a conclusion valid for all cultures, namely that, regardless of major tendencies or drifts, apparently insignificant factors enter in and function so as to cause stupendous and unpredictable results."

The method Reichard adopted in her study of Navajo religion and symbolism, the last major work completed before her death, was to build her analysis on the *totality* of symbolic interconnections made by the Navajo she was talking with, interviewing, and observing (Reichard 1950a). She makes this totality available to her readers in the second volume of this work, *Navajo Religion*, which is an encyclopedic compilation of all symbolic associations she found in Navajo ritual and cosmology. Perhaps her work would be dismissed by contemporary structuralists as mere empiricism, but it is admired by some historically minded anthropologists as an unusually complete presentation of a people's symbol system seen in its own terms in all its complexities. Reichard was skeptical of analyses that she felt tried to fit—or squeeze—everything too neatly into a single pattern (Reichard 1942). Her generalizations about Navajo philosophy and modes of thought are at a more appropriate level of analysis than prematurely imposed "keys" to Navajo symbolic structure. For example, she discusses the principle now known for many non-Western cultures, that in contrast with the Western good-evil dichotomy, good *is* bad and bad good; the critical distinction is the presence or absence of the control achieved through ritual knowledge.

In her study *Prayer: The Compulsive Word*, Reichard stresses the unity that can be found behind the enormous diversity, when sought in terms of Navajo categories (Reichard 1944:1). At one level Navajo prayers have a basic structure, including invocation, petition, and benediction; at another level they are reducible to a few patterns, demonstrating Navajo "control of a literary medium" (1944:3); and beyond that, as demonstrated by the structural analysis of twenty-five prayers offered, there is great flexibility. Marian Smith wrote of Reichard's study that it had opened up a whole new field in religious analysis (Smith 1956).

Another characteristic of Reichard's work that is of interest to contemporary anthropology is the depth of her personal involvement in her field research and the way she used it in her books. She established herself with a Navajo family as a learner—as an apprentice in the art of weaving. Summer after summer she conscientiously worked at and mastered this task as she collected data on Navajo social organization and ritual life. In a disarmingly straightforward and lively style, Reichard interwove into analyses of Navajo society her own experiences with the daily pleasures, problems and practicalities of family events, the occasional emergencies, and the excursions, rituals, and festivities that punctuated the Navajo yearly cycle. *Spider Woman: A Story of Navajo Weavers and Chanters* details her experiences as a novice weaver (Reichard 1934). *Navajo Shepherd and Weaver* describes the entire weaving process, the symbolic and artistic attributes of designs, and Navajo attitudes toward skill and virtuosity (Reichard 1936a). With a view to correcting outsiders' stereotypes of the Navajo, Reichard put together actual incidents and individuals known from her fieldwork to create a fictionalized family in *Dezba, Woman of the Desert.* To outsiders, the Navajo may seem "so reserved as to be stolid, so patient as to be shiftless, so mobile as to be irresponsible," Reichard wrote. From the inside, however, they are "talkative and jolly," and "toward members of their own tribe to whom obligations are well defined, they are faithful, tolerant, dependable and generous" (Reichard 1939a:v).

Gladys Reichard had a well-formulated approach to pedagogy and was a popular teacher in her large introductory classes. In a 1950 interview for the *Barnard College Alumnae Monthly*, she explained that all courses in the department:

lay greater stress upon thought than upon memory. However, it is always borne in mind that without facts, accurately selected and applied, logical and convincing thought is impossible. Facts are therefore presented as a means to an end, not as an end in themselves. Emphasis is laid on the ability to find facts rather than on tabulation and memorizing. (1950)

Reichard incorporated her interest in the teaching/learning process into her fieldwork and analysis as well as into her own method of instruction. It was probably not mere happenstance that she chose to be taught a complicated and creative craft as her entrée into Navajo society. In *Spider Woman* she described how the teaching task was approached by people whose word for "to teach" was "to show" (Reichard 1934:21). When writing of Coeur d'Alene imagery, Reichard pointed out that although these people included obedience or pliability in their definition of ideal behavior, they definitely did not "encourage obedience or blind following to the exclusion of one's own thought." Instead the word for "stupid" meant "obedient in the sense of submissive" and also "dependent upon regimentation." The word "is applied to a horse which cannot exist, and shows no sense when out of sight of the other horses. It is . . . used of a person who cannot depart in any particular from group thought or behavior, and of a child which always does exactly what it is told, never takes the initiative or asks a question" (Reichard 1934:102).

In both her teaching and writing, Reichard evinced her commitment to contradicting stereotypic views of women's dependence, and her commitment to advancing their professional lives. As a characteristic example, when referring to a Navajo man fixing a leaky hogan roof in one of her books, she interjected after the pronoun "he" a parenthetical "or she, the women know how to do all a man does" (Reichard 1936a:198). And when she wrote a book on the Navajo for a popular audience, she made the stature and authority of Navajo women a central theme. In the first chapter, entitled "Matron," she introduced her main character, Dezba, with the opening sentence, "Dezba was the head of a large Navajo household." In the second paragraph, Reichard made clear that this did not mean Dezba's responsibilities were therefore limited to the familial in the Western sense, but that instead Dezba was the manager of the large herd of sheep owned by individual members of her family. In the ensuing episode, Dezba organized the men in her family for the government-supervised sheep "dipping"; mused on her good choice of the additional men her family would work with, all of whom knew balky sheep had to be handled carefully when plunged into the mange-preventing wash; and noted the problems of another woman who often managed badly (Reichard 1939a: 3, 9). As the book unfolds, Reichard indirectly but systematically puts across the point she had bluntly stated in *Social Life of the Navajo Indians*: "Economically, socially, religiously and politically women are on a par with men" (Reichard 1928a:54).

Reichard participated actively in professional organizations. During many of her early professional years, she was secretary of the American Folk-Lore Society (1924–35), and she also served a term as secretary of the American Ethnological Society (1924–26). Later she took on the responsible posts of editor for the American Folk-Lore Society (1940) and Secretary (meaning program director) of Section H, Anthropology, of the American Association for the Advancement of Science (1945). In 1945–47 she was made secretary-treasurer of the Linguistic Circle of New York. She also instituted a major in linguistics at Barnard but had to give up the program, since sufficient administrative support was apparently not forthcoming, and she was trying to chair two departments at once. Though she did not speak out formally on women's issues, it was characteristic of Reichard that when she cut back on her professional involvements in order to devote more time to her research and writing, the one activity she did not drop was her membership on the International Federation of University Women Committee for the Award of Fellowships.

References and Works About Gladys A. Reichard

Barnard College Memorial Booklet
1955   Gladys A. Reichard—A Tribute.
Lamphere, Louise
1986   Gladys Reichard Among the Navajo. In *Daughters of the Desert: Women Anthropologists in the Southwest, 1880–1980*. (Pamphlet) B. Babcock and N. Parezo, eds. Tucson: Arizona State Museum.

Mark, Joan T.
1980   Gladys Reichard. In *NAW II*. Barbara Sicherman et al., eds. Pp. 572–74. Cambridge: Belknap Press of Harvard University.
Smith, Marian
1956   Gladys Armanda (*sic*) Reichard. *American Anthropologist* 58 (5): 913–16.

Selected Works by Gladys A. Reichard

1921   Literary Types and Dissemination of Myths. *Journal of American Folklore* 34:269–307.

1922   The Complexity of Rhythm in Decorative Art. *American Anthropologist* 24:183–208.

1925   Wiyot Grammar and Texts. *University of California Publications in American Archaeology and Ethnology* 22:1–215.

1926a Wiyot: An Indian Language of California. *American Speech* 1:654–58.

1926b A Few Instances of Cultural Resistance in Southwest North America. *XXII International Congress of Americanists* 2:289–96. Rome.

1928a *Social Life of the Navajo Indians*. New York: Columbia University Press.

1928b Form and Interpretation in American Art. *XXIII International Congress of Americanists* 3:459–62. New York.

1930   The Style of Coeur d'Alene Mythology. *XXIV International Congress of Americanists* 4:243–53. Hamburg.

1932   *Melanesian Design*. 2 vols. New York: Columbia University Press.

1934   *Spider Woman: A Story of Navajo Weavers and Chanters*. New York: Macmillan.

1936a *Navajo Shepherd and Weaver*. New York: J. J. Augustin.

1936b Art Education Among Primitive Peoples. *Art Education Today*. New York: Teachers College Bureau of Publication.

1936c Color in Navajo Weaving. *Arizona Historical Review* 7:19–30.

1936d Attitudes Towards Violence: A Suggestion. *Essays in Anthropology Presented to A. L. Kroeber*. Berkeley: University of California Press.

1938a Grammar of the Coeur d'Alene Language. In *Handbook of American Indian Languages*, Vol. 3. Franz Boas, ed. Pp. 517–707. New York: J. J. Augustin.

1938b Social Life. In *General Anthropology*. F. Boas et al., eds. Pp. 409–86. New York: D. C. Heath and Co.

1939a *Dezba, Woman of the Desert*. New York: J. J. Augustin.

1939b *Navajo Medicine Man, Sandpaintings and Legends of Miguelito*. New York: J. J. Augustin.

1939c Stem-list of the Coeur d'Alene Language. *International Journal of American Linguistics* 10:92–108.

1940a *Agentive and Causative Elements in Navajo*. New York: J. J. Augustin.

1942   The Translation of Two Navajo Chant Words. *American Anthropologist* 44:421–24.

1943a Human Nature As Conceived by the Navajo Indians. *The Review of Religion* 7:353–60.

1943b Imagery in an Indian Vocabulary. *American Speech* 18:96–102.

1943c Individualism and Mythological Style. *Journal of American Folklore* 57:16–25.

1943d Franz Boas and Folklore. *American Anthropological Association Memoir* 61:52–57.

1944 Prayer: The Compulsive Word. *American Ethnological Society Monograph*, no. 7.

1945a Composition and Symbolism of Coeur d'Alene Verb Stems. *International Journal of American Linguistics* 11:47–63.

1945b Linguistic Diversity Among the Navajo Indians. *International Journal of American Linguistics* 11:156–68.

1945c Distinctive Features of Navajo Religion. *Southwestern Journal of Anthropology* 1:199–220.

1947 An Analysis of Coeur d'Alene Mythology. *American Folklore Society Memoir* 41.

1948 Significance of Aspiration in Navaho. *International Journal of American Linguistics* 14:15–19.

1949a The Navaho and Christianity. *American Anthropologist* 51:66–71.

1949b The Character of the Navaho Verb Stem. *Word* 5:55–76.

1949c Language and Synthesis. *Word* 5:224–33.

1949d 'Alk'id a 'inda k'ad (Then and Now). *Adahooniligli* (The Navaho Language Monthly) 4:8. Window Rock, Ariz.

1950a *Navaho Religion: A Study in Symbolism*. 2 vols. Bollingen Series 18. New York: Pantheon. (Reprinted 1983 by the University of Arizona Press.)

1950b Language and Cultural Pattern. *American Anthropologist* 52:194–204.

1955 Anthropological View of a Primitive Religion. *International Record of Medicine* 168:168–73.

Coauthored Work

Reichard, Gladys, and Franc J. Newcomb
1937 *Sandpaintings of the Navajo Shooting Chant*. New York: J. J. Augustin.

ELEANOR LEACOCK

Audrey Isabel Richards

(1899–1984)

British anthropologist Audrey Isabel Richards was especially known for her research among the Southern Bantu and the Bemba of Africa, as well as for her theoretical contributions to the understanding of hierarchic authoritarian societies in South and East Africa.

Audrey Isabel Richards was born in London on July 8, 1899, to Henry Erle and Isabel Butler Richards. Her mother came from a powerful lineage of bureaucrats and academics, and her family had numerous social contacts. While she was quite young, her father, a lawyer, served as a legel member of the Viceroy's Council in India and later became a professor of law at Oxford University.

After leaving India Richards completed her education in England. She attended Newnham College for women at Cambridge and received her undergraduate degree in natural science in 1921. After obtaining her M.A. from Newnham in 1928, she remained actively involved with the college for the rest of her life. The London School of Economics awarded Audrey Richards the Ph.D. in anthropology in 1929.

Her mentor, Bronislaw Malinowski, influenced the theoretical direction of her dissertation but not its subject. She chose to study food habits, looking at them through the functionalist orientation Malinowski had given her and adding other theoretical perspectives, such as the impact of geography on food organization. In her work she began to move closer to a modern-systems view and away from Radcliffe-Brown's ahistorical structural-functionalist perspective.

As one of Malinowski's first students at the London School of Economics (along with E. E. Evans-Pritchard, Raymond Firth, Isaac Schapera, and Hortense Powdermaker*), Richards also became a close friend of his family. In fact, it was she who informed the Malinowski children of their mother's death. At Malinowski's request she became the guardian of his children and fulfilled this role with love and responsibility. Helena Malinowski, his daughter, writes of

Richards with great affection and seems disappointed that the subsequent romance between her father and Richards did not culminate in marriage (La Fontaine 1985:14).

Audrey Richards began her fieldwork by doing research among the Bemba in Northern Rhodesia (now Zambia). Her fieldwork research strictly adhered to Malinowski's functionalist methods. As his student she stressed "primary social wants" and the satisfaction of biologically based "cultural needs" (Werbner 1983:658–60). This particular research was followed by repeated visits to the Bemba (1933–34 and 1957). She also studied the Tswana of the Northern Trans- vaal from 1939 to 1940 but had to discontinue her research because of World War II. She also undertook part-time fieldwork in Uganda from 1950 to 1955. It seems that from the initiation of her research endeavors, she encountered few problems. She returned to England to work in the Colonial Office at a time when "colonial governments made little use of anthropologists, viewed them with some suspicion and starved them of finance" (Richards 1977:32–53).

Richards culminated her career in England, where she joined Edmund Leach and other Cambridge scholars in 1962 for an ethnohistorical research project of the village community of Elmdon. Even in her retirement, she actively pursued fieldwork by immersing herself in village life for several years.

Richards's most prolific area of study was in the political organization of East African ethnic groups. Indeed, her recognition of the impact of the British Empire on the political structure and power of indigenous groups made her a major force in British scholarship. Her theories concerning the myriad relationships and integration with the colonial government are evident in most of her works (see bibliography). Her interests in political culture included descriptions of East African political systems, interrelational networks and coordinates of colonial and indigenous political systems, recruitment of chiefs, relationships between political and kin structures, constitutional problems, authority patterns and de- cision-making, and traditional loyalty and values. Her interest was continually renourished by her need to aid smooth integration of traditional African ethnic and colonial political organization. Without direct reference to systems theory, she painted a clear picture of real social order, including discussions of interaction with the British. This was unusual amid the British preoccupation with descrip- tions of African ethnic groups in a "pristine" state.

Richards viewed British interests as providing welfare in educational, health, agricultural, and other avenues. She considered it important for academics to research colonial and tribal encounters to facilitate realistic solutions. This effort was played out by Richards as the director of the East African Institute for Social Research and in her own writings. The British Empire recognized her efforts by awarding her the C.B.E. (Commander of the Order of the British Empire), an honor seldom awarded to a woman. Richards's influential position as the founder of the African Studies Centre in England also gave her a podium from which to spearhead her interest in social change.

Richards's work on food culture, nutrition, agriculture, and land use was a pioneer effort in the field of anthropology. Following a functionalist paradigm, her studies in Africa (Richards 1932a&b, 1939b, 1940, and 1956) integrated agricultural activities together with all the related aspects of culture. It represented the first anthropological study of reciprocal food-sharing and underproduction in an economy affected by rapid change, and it increased labor migration from rural into urban areas (Werbner 1983:658). Her Ph.D. dissertation, later published under the title *Hunger and Work in a Savage Tribe* (1932b), discussed theories of food use drawn from such disciplines as psychology and geography. Given today's food crisis, this study may be used as a model for continued research. Her publications on the Bemba (Richards 1939b, 1940) and the Chisungu (Richards 1956) concentrated on marriage, fertility, and female initiation ritual. Her view of tribal life was presented as an integrated whole, and major changes as well as integration were presented as being introduced from the outside. Additionally, Richards analyzed matrilineal kinship structures among the Southern Bantu in terms of food, as well as political and economic organization.

While "impatient with high-flown theory" (Ruel 1985:45), Richards concentrated throughout her career on gathering data. Her work exemplifies insightful, theoretical elaboration. For example, she repeatedly questioned conventional definitions of symbolism and suggested that there was a rational basis for specific symbols that have many meanings. Thus, she had anticipated Victor Turner's concept of multivocal symbols by at least a decade, as well as the study of the use of symbols for explanation and exaggeration.

Richards's intellectual history moved in two basic directions, forming a braided pattern of consistency. On the one hand, she was the teacher-writer, performing the role of academician; on the other hand, she was the creative administrator, dispenser, and organizer of new and practical ideas for research and learning.

Her teaching positions were as assistant lecturer in social anthropology at Bedford College (1928–30); lecturer in social anthropology at the London School of Economics (1931–32 and 1935–37); senior lecturer at Witwatersrand University, South Africa (1937–40); lecturer and reader in anthropology, London University (1945–49); and Smuts Reader at Cambridge University (1961–66). She also taught at Northwestern University and McGill University in Canada. Administratively, she was chair of the department at Witwatersrand; vice-principal at Newnham College (1958–60); director of studies in archaeology and anthropology at Newnham (1957); founder and director of the East African Institute for Social Research at Makere College, Uganda (1949–56) and the African Studies Centre at Cambridge University (1965–66).

Richards was honored in many ways. In 1955, at the age of fifty-six she was awarded a C.B.E. At the age of sixty-eight she became one of the few women awarded an F.B.A. (Fellow of the British Academy), given for distinguished achievement in scholarship. Richards became the second woman president of the African Studies Association (1963–66) and the first woman president of the Royal Anthropological Institute (1959–61).

Richards also held positions of public service. She was a member of the Colonial Social Science Research Council (1945–50 and 1956–62); Wellcome Gold medalist and Rivers medalist for fieldwork; director of the Anglia Television Company (1958–63); and a trustee of the Esperanza Fund.

Richards contributed much to the advancement of women in her profession, by example, advice, and often practical help. Over thirty years ago she was fighting to ensure that women who were awarded fellowships by the East African Institute had the same right to claim travel costs and subsistence allowance for a dependent spouse as that of men. (Bohannan, personal communication, 1985.) Raymond Firth (1985:343) wrote that "important as a pioneer in women's studies, she was a sensitive interpreter of female interests and attitudes, but she assumed rather than strove for equality with men."

Richards contributed significantly to the study of colonial alignment with indigenous political organization, to the ethnography of East Africa, to research on women, and to anthropological theory. She added to the field of traditional literature on kinship systems and became a regional specialist in the study of the culture of food and nutrition and agriculture in Africa. She also contributed to the expanding field of symbolism and the study of ritual. With her many friends and colleagues, she maintained a lively correspondence characterized by much thought and care and a warm display of affection.

References and Works About Audrey I. Richards

Firth, Raymond
1985   Obituary of Audrey Richards. *Man* 20 (2): 341–43.
Gulliver, P. H.
1972   Bibliography of the Principal Writings of Audrey Richards. In *The Interpretation of Ritual*, J. S. LaFontaine, ed. Pp. 285–89. London: Tavistock.
La Fontaine, J. S. et al.
1985   Audrey Richards: In Memoriam. *Cambridge Anthropology* 10 (1): 1–97.
Robertson, A. F.
1985   Audrey Richards, 1899–1984: An Appreciation. *African Affairs* 84 (334): 136–38.
Werbner, Richard
1983   Audrey Richards. In the *International Encyclopedia of Social Science*. Pp. 658–60.

Selected Works by Audrey I. Richards

1932a Anthropological Problems in Northeastern Rhodesia. *Africa* 5:123–44.
1932b *Hunger and Work in a Savage Tribe: A Functional Study of Nutrition Among the Southern Bantu*. London: Routledge. (Republished 1948, Glencoe, Ill.: Free Press; and 1964, Cleveland: The World Publishing Co.)
1934   Mother Right Among the Central Bantu. In *Essays Presented to C. G. Seligman*. E. E. Evans-Pritchard et al., eds. Pp. 267–79. London: Kegan Paul.

1935a A Modern Movement of Witchfinders. *Africa* 8:448–61.

1935b *Tribal Government in Transition: The Babemba of North-east Rhodesia.* London: Macmillan.

1936 The Life of Bwembya, a Native of Northern Rhodesia. In *Ten Africans*. M. Perham, ed. Pp. 121–37. London: Faber and Faber.

1937 Reciprocal Clan Relationships Among the Bemba of North-eastern Rhodesia. *Man* 37:188–93.

1938 The Village Census in the Study of Culture Contact. In *Methods of Study of Culture Contact in Africa*. With an Intro. Essay by B. Malinowski. Pp. 46–59. London: Oxford University Press for the International African Institute.

1939a The Development of Field Work Methods in Social Anthropology. In *The Study of Society*. F. C. Bartlett et al., eds. London: Routledge and Kegan Paul.

1939b *Land, Labour and Diet in Northern Rhodesia: An Economic Study of the Bemba Tribe*. London: Oxford University Press for the International Institute of African Languages and Cultures.

1940 The Political System of the Bemba of Northern Rhodesia. In *African Political Systems*. M. Fortes and E. E. Evans-Pritchard, eds. Pp. 83–120. London: Oxford University Press for the International African Institute.

1944 Practical Anthropology in the Life-time of the African Institute. *Africa* 14:289–300.

1947 *Colonial Problems as a Challenge to the Social Sciences*. London: Anti-Slavery and Aborigines Protection Society.

1950a Hunts and Hut-building Among the Bemba. *Man* 50:101–9.

1950b Some Types of Family Structure Amongst the Central Bantu. In *African Systems of Kinship and Marriage*. A. R. Radcliffe-Brown and Daryll Forde, eds. Pp. 207–51. London: Oxford University Press for the International African Institute.

1951a The Present Day Recruitment of Chiefs in Buganda. In *Report of the Astrida Conference*. Kampala: East African Institute of Social Research.

1951b The Bemba of North-eastern Rhodesia. In *Seven Tribes of British Central Africa*. E. Colson and M. Gluckman, eds. Pp. 164–93. London: Oxford University Press for the Rhodes-Livingstone Institute.

1952 (with A. B. Mukwaya) Discussion on the Difference Between Busoga and Buganda System of Chiefs. In *Conference Papers*. Kampala: East African Institute of Social Research.

1953 Anthropological Research in East Africa. *Transactions of the New York Academy of Sciences* 16:44–49.

1954a Report on Fertility Survey in Buganda and Buhaya. In *Culture and Human Fertility*. F. Lorimer, ed. Pp. 351–403. Paris: UNESCO.

1954b *Economic Development and Tribal Change: A Study of Immigrant Labour in Buganda*. Cambridge, England: Heffer for EAISR.

1956 *Chisungu: A Girl's Initiation Ceremony Among the Bemba of Northern Rhodesia*. London: Faber and Faber.

1957a The Concept of Culture in Malinowski's Work. In *Man and Culture*: An Evaluation of the Work of Bronislaw Malinowski. R. Firth, ed. Pp. 15–31. London: Routledge and Kegan Paul.

1957b The Human Problems of Africa. *Corona* 9:137–40.

1958a A Changing Pattern of Agriculture in East Africa: The Bemba of Northern Rhodesia. *Geographical Journal* 24:302–14.

1958b Tribal Groups in Kenya. *Times British Colonies Review* 21–22.

1960a Social Mechanisms for the Transfer of Political Rights in Some African Tribes. *Journal of the Royal Anthropological Institute of Great Britain and Ireland* 90 (2): 175–90.

1960b The Bemba, Their Country and Diet. In *Cultures and Societies of Africa*. S. and P. Ottenberg, eds. Pp. 96–109. New York: Random House.

1960c *East African Chiefs: A Study of Political Development in Some Uganda and Tanganyika Tribes*. London: Faber and Faber; New York: Praeger.

1961 African Kings and Their Royal Relatives. *Journal of the Royal Anthropological Institute* 91:135–50.

1963a Some Effects of the Introduction of Individual Freehold into Buganda. In *African Agrarian Systems*. D. Biebuyck, ed. Pp. 267–80. London: Oxford University Press for the International African Institute.

1963b Multi-tribalism in African Urban Areas. In *Urbanization in African Social Change*. Pp. 43–51. Edinburgh: University of Edinburgh Centre for African Studies.

1963c Freedom, Communication, and Transport. In *The Concept of Freedom in Anthropology*. David Bidney, ed. Pp. 49–60. The Hague: Mouton.

1966 *The Changing Structure of a Ganda Village: Kisozi 1892–1952*. Nairobi: East African Publishing House, for EAISR (Studies No. 24).

1967 African Systems of Thought: An Anglo-French Dialogue. *Man* 2:286–98.

1968 Keeping the King Divine. *Proceedings of the Royal Anthropological Institute*. Pp. 23–35.

1969a Characteristics of Ethical Systems in Primitive Human Society. In *Biology and Ethics*. F. J. Ebling, ed. Pp. 23–32. London: Academic Press (Institute of Biology Symposia No. 18).

1969b Socialization and Contemporary British Anthropology. *Socialization: The Approach from Social Anthropology*. Philip Mayer, ed. ASA Monograph 8. Pp. 1–32. London: Tavistock.

1974 The "Position" of Women: An Anthropological View. *Cambridge Anthropology* 1 (3): 3–10.

1977 The Colonial Office and the Organization of Social Research. *Anthropological Forum* 4 (2): 32–53.

1982 *East African Chiefs and Its Sequel: Changing Local Government Policy 1950–1970; Chiefs and Administrators in Buganda*. In *Uganda's First Republic*. A. F. Robertson, ed. Pp. 8–52. Cambridge, Eng.: African Studies Centre.

STELLA SILVERSTEIN

Vera Dourmashkin Rubin
(1911–1985)

American cultural anthropologist Vera Dourmashkin Rubin was noted especially for her work on the West Indies and was founder of the Research Institute for the Study of Man.

Vera Dourmashkin was born August 6, 1911, in Moscow. Her mother, Jennie Frankel Dourmashkin, died in childbirth, and her father Elias Dourmashkin, brought her to the United States when she was one year old. She was raised by an aunt in an extended family that focused much interest, love, and effort on her. Her father was a journalist, and his brother, who had also come to the United States, was a physician, so she grew up in an intellectual atmosphere in the Jewish immigrant community of New York's Lower East Side. Education was valued highly, and she went to college at New York University, graduating in 1930 summa cum laude with a major in French literature.

Dourmashkin married Samuel Rubin, who became a highly successful businessman, while she worked as a full-time housewife and mother of her daughter Cora and son Reed. During this period she became active in civic affairs, and her organizational role and success are indicated by the fact that in 1944 she was head of the Westchester County committee for the reelection of Roosevelt.

When her children entered high school, Vera Rubin turned toward a professional role.[1] Her decision to undertake a career was influenced by a family friend who was a psychiatrist, and she planned initially to become a physician, specializing in psychiatry. It was his advice that she reenter academia gradually by taking some courses in anthropology as a transition to medical school. Anthropology seized her imagination, however, and she soon enrolled full-time in graduate school at Columbia University, taking courses with Ruth Benedict* and Margaret Mead,* who remained a lifelong friend. She worked particularly with Julian Steward, who was the main influence on her intellectual interests. He was the major advisor for her dissertation on the dynamics of sociocultural change among Italian Americans in a suburban town. Her dissertation, *Fifty*

Years in Rootville: A Study in the Dynamics of Acculturation of an Italian Immigrant Group in an Urban Community (1951), approached acculturation as a historical process and differed from much of the earlier literature concentrating on a sector of industrial society. She received her doctorate from Columbia in 1952.

Employment opportunities in anthropology were scarce at the time and probably restricted for a woman whose family responsibilities kept her in the metropolitan area. Rubin's first postdoctoral position was unpaid, reflecting her interest in acquiring professional experience and the fact that the few employment opportunities for trained women enabled organizations to recruit them as unpaid professionals. Her research on Irish Americans was conducted through the Cornell University Medical School Midtown Manhattan Project, which focused on interrealtions of mental health, ethnicity, and urban life. These linkages continued to interest her all her life. During her early postdoctorate years, she also taught classes at Hunter College and the New York University School of Education.

Of greater significance for her life, however, was her growing postdoctoral interest in the Caribbean, an area she had visited and that interested Steward, who had initiated research in Puerto Rico. Rubin was appointed a research associate in the Anthropology Department at Columbia, and she conducted a seminar on the Caribbean with Charles Wagley, an anthropologist who specialized in Latin America and had been a member of her doctoral committee. Unlike Steward and Wagley, Rubin's primary interest was in the English-speaking Caribbean. (During 1955 one of the seminar students was Lambros Comitas, who became a lifelong associate of Rubin and succeeded her, after her death, as director of the Research Institute for the Study of Man.)

One of the outcomes of the seminar was recognition of the need to train students to work in the Caribbean and to provide them with financial support. In 1955 Rubin founded the Research Institute of the Study of Man in the Tropics, housed at Columbia University. Its initial goals were to train students, to address basic social problems of people in the tropics, and to support scholars in the Caribbean; the members of the first advisory board were Sidney Mintz, John Murra, Conrad Arensberg, Charles Wagley, and Elena Padilla. The organization was endowed by Rubin, and all income for the first three years was allocated to its initial project, the Research Training Program for Man in the Tropics. During the three years of this project, twelve graduate students were sent to the Caribbean and all subsequently completed their doctorates: four of these were women (Lambros Comitas, personal communication).

In 1958, Rubin moved the organization—now simply named the Research Institute for the Study of Man (RISM)—to its own building, and it was the focus of her professional interest and work for the rest of her life. Essentially, she developed the anthropological study of the English-speaking Caribbean through RISM projects and by stimulating scholarly interest. Moreover, she was a pioneer in her interest in serious multidisciplinary attention to social problems and health in the West Indies. Rubin carried out research herself, encouraged and supported other scholars from the West Indies and the United States, organized extremely influential major conferences on the Caribbean, and established the most extensive library on the West Indies in the United States. As a woman, she had an unusual role as founder and director for thirty years of an organization that had an impact on the West Indies and was a center for multidisciplinary research on the region. Her far-reaching involvement has been described as including "participation in the affairs of the University of the West Indies and the Caribbean Foundation for Mental Health, as well as enduring friendships with West Indians of all walks of life" (Comitas 1985).

Rubin's published work reflects her interdisciplinary and Caribbean interests. She published on two extensive research projects carried out through RISM. The first was a pioneering study of education in the West Indies; it focused on young people in colonial and postcolonial Trinidad and Tobago and was done with Marisa Zavalloni (1969). The second, done with Lambros Comitas (1972, 1975), demonstrated the relationship between sociocultural context and the effects of marijuana smoking in Jamaica.

Vera Rubin had a major impact on anthropology also through the conferences she organized. These meetings and the publications that followed were to set research priorities, and they stimulated scholarship. Among the most well-known publications of the conferences, edited by Rubin, were *Caribbean Studies: A Symposium* (1957), *Plantation Systems of the New World* (1959a), *Social and Cultural Pluralism in the Caribbean* (1960c), and, with Arthur Tuden, *Comparative Perspectives on Slavery in New World Plantation Societies* (1977). Her last conference, held in August 1984, was entitled "New Perspectives on Caribbean Studies: Toward the 21st Century." Like earlier ones, it brought together social scientists, political figures, psychiatrists, artists, administrators, and teachers to consider what had been learned in Caribbean studies and what should come next.

In collaboration with Sula Benet—who became associated with RISM after her retirement from Hunter College—and the USSR Academy of Sciences, Rubin organized comparative research on longevity in Soviet Georgia and in Kentucky. Importantly, these studies increased international scientific communication.

Rubin was active in a number of professional organizations. Her intellectual and financial support of the journal *Human Organization* was crucial to its survival during a critical year. She helped found the Society for Medical Anthropology and was one of the founders of the journal *Transcultural Psychiatry*. She served as president of the Society for Applied Anthropology, committee chair of the American Orthopsychiatric Association, vice-chair and chair of the anthropology section of the New York Academy of Sciences, and at her death she was president-elect of the Caribbean Studies Association.

Rubin made it possible for a number of women to do their first field research through RISM scholarships during a period when grants were scarce and women received relatively few. She encouraged and supported established women scholars throughout her career. Additionally, the library at RISM became a valued resource of Caribbean Studies. She was herself a unique and creative woman professional, who founded an institute and whose intellectual interests bridged several fields, which is reflected in her wide network of colleagues. She appreciated and understood the many strong and exceedingly competent West Indian women whom she met as colleagues and friends in the field over the years. They regarded her as a friend, and as a person who had contributed in many ways to the West Indies.

Rubin's contributions to Caribbean studies were recognized also by the bestowal of two honorary degrees: a Doctor of Humane Letters (L.H.D.) from Brooklyn College (1981) and a Doctor of Letters (Litt.D.) from the University of the West Indies (1985). In addition to her scholarly involvement in a wide range of social issues, she was a political activist who was deeply concerned with matters of human survival and well-being. Her final wish for her family and friends was that they experience her love of life and that they spread peace.

Note

1. This biography is based largely on material received from Lambros Comitas and Cora Rubin Weiss, whose assistance is gratefully acknowledged. The interpretation and any errors in reporting are my own. It is based also on my friendship with Vera Rubin over a period of more than thirty years.

References and Works About Vera Rubin

Comitas, Lambros
1985 *Vera Rubin Memorial* (Biographical Sketch.)

Selected Works by Vera Rubin

1951 *Fifty Years in Rootville: A Study in the Dynamics of Acculturation of an Italian Immigrant Group in a Rural Community.* Boston: Eagle Enterprises.

1957 *Caribbean Studies: A Symposium.* Mona, Jamaica: University College of the West Indies. (As ed.)

1959a *Plantation Systems of the New World.* Washington, D.C.: Pan American Union. (As ed.)

1959b Approaches to the Study of National Characteristics in a Multicultural Society. *International Journal of Social Psychiatry* 5 (1): 20–26.

1959c Family Attitudes and Aspirations of Trinidad Youth. *Proceedings, Second Caribbean Conference for Mental Health.* Pp. 59–91. St. Thomas, Virgin Islands.

1960a Cultural Perspectives in Caribbean Research. In *Caribbean Studies: A Symposium.* Pp. 110–22. Seattle: University of Washington Press.

1960b *Caribbean Studies: A Symposium.* Seattle: University of Washington Press. (As ed.)

1960c Social and Cultural Pluralism in the Caribbean. *Annals of the New York Academy of Sciences* 83 (5): 761–916. (Also, as ed.)

1961a	The Adolescent: His Expectations and His Society. *Proceedings, Third Caribbean Conference for Mental Health*. Pp. 56–71. Jamaica: University of the West Indies.

1961b	Report on the Census of Mental Hospitals in the Caribbean. *Proceedings, Third Caribbean Conference for Mental Health*. Pp. 224–28. Jamaica: University of the West Indies.

1961c	Report on the Census of Mental Hospitals in the Caribbean. *Proceedings, World Federation for Mental Health*. Paris.

1961d	*Report on the Census of Caribbean Mental Hospitals*. New York: Research Institute for the Study of Man.

1961e	Culture, Society and Health. *Annals of the New York Academy of Sciences* 87 (17): 783–1060 (Also, as ed.)

1961f	The Anthropology of Development. In *Biennial Review of Anthropology*. Bernard Siegel, ed. Pp. 120–59. Stanford, Calif.: Stanford University Press.

1962a	Culture, Politics and Race Relations. *Social and Economic Studies* 11 (4): 433–55.

1962b	Overview—Cooperative Efforts Toward Community Mental Health. *Conference on Cooperation Toward Mental Health*. Pp. 7–18. Trenton, N.J.: Community Mental Health Services.

1964	The Children of Poverty and Community Agencies. *Conference of Cooperative Effort Toward Improved Mental Health Services for Children*. Pp. 7–20. Trenton, N.J.: Community Mental Health Services.

1965	The West Indian Family: Retrospect and Prospect. *Proceedings, Fourth Caribbean Conference for Mental Health*. Pp. 53–65. Curaçao, N.A.

1975	*Cannabis and Culture*. The Hague: Mouton. (As ed.)

1976	Cross-cultural Perspectives on Therapeutic Uses of Cannabis. In *The Therapeutic Potential for Marijuana*. Sidney Cohen and Richard C. Stillman, eds. Pp. 1–17. New York: Plenum Medical Book Co.

1979	Bibliography of Cross-cultural Aspects of Human Aging and Longevity: Report to the National Institute on Aging. New York: Research Institute for the Study of Man.

1980	Foreword. *Voodoo Heritage in Haiti*, by Michel Laguerre. Berkeley, Calif.: Sage Publications.

1981	Proceedings of the First Joint US-USSR Symposium on Aging and Longevity: the first two years of Collaborative Effort in Abkhasia and Kentucky. New York: International Research and Exchange Board. (As ed.)

Coauthored Works

Rubin, Vera, and Lambros Comitas

1965	The Caribbean As an Ethnographic Region: Theories and Methodologies for the Study of Complex Societies. *Proceedings of the VII International Congress of Anthropology and Ethnology*. Unpublished ms. Moscow, USSR.

1972	*Effects of Chronic Smoking of Cannabis in Jamaica*. A Report by the Research Institute for the Study of Man to the Center for Studies of Narcotic and Drug Abuse, National Institute of Mental Health, unpublished report.

1975	*Ganja in Jamaica: A Medical Anthropological Study of Chronic Marijuana Use*. The Hague: Mouton.

Rubin, Vera, and Richard P. Schaedel, eds.
1975 *The Haitian Potential: Research and Resources of Haiti.* New York: Teachers College Press.
Rubin, Vera, and Arthur Tuden, eds.
1977 Comparative Perspectives on Slavery in New World Plantation Societies. *Annals of the New York Academy of Sciences.* Vol. 292.
Rubin, Vera, and Marisa Zavalloni
1969 *We Wish to Be Looked Upon: A Study of the Aspirations of Youth in a Developing Society.* New York: Teachers College Press.

LUCIE WOOD SAUNDERS

Mary Thygeson Shepardson
(1906–   )

American cultural anthropologist Mary Thygeson Shepardson is especially known for her studies of political and legal processes in Navajo society.

Mary Thygeson was born in St. Paul, Minnesota, on May 26, 1906, the youngest of four children. Her father, Nels Marcus Thygeson of Norwegian descent, was an American-born corporation lawyer. The child of immigrant farmers, he had fought hard for his education and was determined to provide opportunities for both his sons and daughters. Her mother, Sylvie Thompson, was born in southern Illinois, the daughter of a lawyer, and one of eleven children. Today Shepardson notes with pride that her mother's grandfather, a Presbyterian minister, had made his home a ''station'' on the Underground Railroad, and that her mother had been named Sylvie after a slave child who had gone through there. Mary Thygeson's grandfather, a known atheist, was antireligious at some economic cost to himself and his children in the small town where they lived. Sylvie, nonetheless, managed to be educated by her uncle, and became an extremely socially active woman, prominently involved in the suffrage and birth control movements. The atmosphere of Thygeson's childhood and upbringing— emphasizing education, racial equality, feminism, social commitment, and rationalism—affected her entire life.[1]

The tragedy of Thygeson's childhood was the death of her loving and much-loved father when she was eleven. Yet his influence had been powerful, both emotionally and in his encouragement of education. She entered Stanford as a freshman in 1922, at age sixteen, majoring in social science. In 1925 she was able to go to Europe and spend a year studying at the Sorbonne. Her second year was at the London School of Economics (L.S.E.)—an exciting time when Beatrice and Sidney Webb, George Bernard Shaw, Arnold Toynbee, and Harold Laski were all active. Her studies emphasized Fabian ideology. In 1927 she returned home to complete her degree at Stanford, graduating Phi Beta Kappa and cum laude in 1928.

In 1929 Thygeson went abroad again, this time as a tourist, accompanying her mother on a trip to the still-young Union of Soviet Socialist Republics. Sylvie Thygeson's interest in the "socialist experiment" stemmed from her World War I pacifism and her general liberal–left, feminist politics. Her daughter similarly had become awakened to liberal–left politics at the L.S.E. These views were intensified after her trip. She recalls the excitement she felt visiting the USSR, witnessing the effort to build a new egalitarian society. In contrast, and reflecting at least in part her L.S.E. studies, her memory of her reaction upon returning home to the reality of the Depression in late 1929 was that the American Depression revealed the fundamental weakness of a system based on profit.

Despite the hard times and unemployment, Thygeson was able to procure a job teaching French in a private Palo Alto, California, girls' school. Soon after, she obtained a job she preferred in Boulder City, Colorado, teaching French, English, and Spanish to the children of the workers on Boulder Dam. At this time she also began to try her hand at fiction, in an early attempt to find the voice she eventually found in anthropology. In 1933 she went on to New York. There she stayed with friends from Minnesota and began to engage in civil rights work in Harlem. She subsequently managed to get a scarce civil-service job as a social worker in the New York Department of Welfare. In her words, this job was "difficult and eye-opening," intended as much to keep people off welfare as to put them on relief. She also continued her work in Harlem, eventually living there, where she saw poverty—black and white—at its worst. During those years, she remembers, not the hopelessness, but working for the future and particularly the hard lessons of resisting defeat.

The death of her sister in 1940 brought Thygeson back to California to care for her niece, and back to a period of transition. In 1942 she married her brother-in-law, Dwight Shepardson, a San Francisco physician. She continued her civil rights work and was on the board of the local NAACP. In 1947 the Shepardsons moved to Skylonda, near Woodside, Calif., and she again tried her hand at fiction. A close brush with death—an airplane crashed into their house— "brought home the fact that life is short," and Mary resolved finally "to do what I had always wanted to do ... have a career of my own, just like a man would." This resolution found expression in anthropology, an interest that had been stirred over the years by her early travels and subsequent trips to the American Southwest, Mexico, and Guatemala.

Shepardson found herself increasingly involved in her graduate study at Stanford, becoming completely absorbed in anthropology. She completed her M.A. coursework and with her husband's interest and support, elected to do a field thesis on the Navajo reservation. Felix Keesing, and later Evon Vogt, stimulated her interest in the subject of political leadership and development, and it was primarily in these areas that she conducted her fieldwork. While she was writing her thesis, she met Clyde Kluckhohn, then the leading scholar of Navajo culture, who encouraged her. Shepardson's commitment to professional anthropology and her interest in a larger study of Navajo political life deepened. However, when she received her M.A. from Stanford in 1956 at age fifty, she was told that her age and sex were "two strikes against [her]" continuing for the Ph.D. Her friend and later collaborator, Blodwen Hammond, was given the same summary treatment.

Furious but undaunted, and strongly recommended by Kluckhohn, Mary applied to and was accepted by the University of California at Berkeley. This turned out to be a fortunate choice, because there she received considerable encouragement and help, as well as an early introduction to the British approach to social and especially political anthropology. David Schneider, Lloyd Fallers, George Foster, and Robert Lowie provided guidance and support. Her husband extended support as well, financially and in the form of cooked dinners on the days of her four-hour commute. She recalls these four years as happy ones. In 1960 she received her Ph.D. with her dissertation, *Navajo Ways in Government*, which had the distinction of publication as an American Anthropological Association Memoir (1963). She was then fifty-four years old.

Although Shepardson eventually came to be seen more as an area specialist, both her dissertation and her work at this point were centered on problems of political behavior, leadership, and decision-making. She pursued these interests in a postdoctoral research program on two contrasting Navajo communities, "traditional" Navajo Mountain and "modernizing" Shiprock, returning to the field with her colleague, Blodwen Hammond. The resulting study was published as *The Navajo Mountain Community* (Shepardson and Hammond 1970). While British anthropologists had been studying political process in traditional societies for some time, this was an area largely ignored by Americans. Because of her awareness of the problems of power dating back to her earlier years, she saw the significance of this sort of research.

She concentrated on Navajo law for the next several years, focusing on the relationships between Navajo tribal courts and federal courts. She published articles on traditional handling of disputes, inheritance, factionalism, and Navajo government as a nonstate nation during this period. While formally affiliated with the University of Chicago as a research associate, most of her time was spent in the field.

After the death of her husband in 1967, Shepardson accepted an invitation to teach at San Francisco State University. At this time Blodwen Hammond asked her to serve as principal investigator for a study of the Bonin Islands, an area in Japan that had been settled by sailors from the United States, England, and Italy in the early nineteenth century. Shepardson and Hammond conducted the fieldwork in 1971; Hammond died of cancer a year later. Shepardson (1977a) wrote up part of the material and is now completing a longer work, focusing on both Bonin Island history and the larger theoretical issues involved in the conceptualization of ethnicity raised by such a community.

In 1973, at age sixty-seven, Shepardson became professor emerita, which for her was not a slowing down but an opportunity once again to devote more time to writing. She has spent the last twelve years on her two major anthropological interests—Navajo ethnography and the study of ethnicity—growing out of the Bonin Islands work. Her Navajo work centered increasingly on women, resulting initially in a general article, "The Status of Navajo Women" (Shepardson 1982a), and then in an extremely well-received life story of her informant, interpreter, and great friend, Irene ("Mrs. Greyeyes") Stewart. Written in the form of letters to Shepardson, the life story was published as *A Voice in Her Tribe* (1980). Again in this matter, Shepardson's scholarship and social commitment have complemented each other; in 1983 she organized, with Bea Medicine, a Lakota anthropologist, a symposium on American Indian women.

At age eighty, and active as ever, Shepardson's current life continues the scope, interests, and dedication of her earlier decades. Between frequent travels, her main work remains her scholarly research and writing, her major project being a social history of the early Bonin Island settlers. She continues to receive invitations to teach, to participate in meetings, and to speak.

In Mary Shepardson's contribution to anthropology, a combination of scholarly excellence with a genuine interest in the lives and welfare of all peoples in the world is evident. As might be expected, the usefulness of her research to the Navajo themselves is for her a great source of satisfaction and pride. In her words, "Fieldwork is the adventurous, exhilarating part of social anthropology, but I believe that it is the combination of the personal with the scholarly that holds me fascinated, and this is what will light up the last thirty years of my life."

Note

1. The authors thank Mary Shepardson for taking the time to be interviewed. Unless otherwise cited, all quotes are from these interviews.

References and Works About Mary Shepardson

Babcock, Barbara, and Nancy Parezo
1986 *Daughters of the Desert: Women Anthropologists in the Southwest (1880–1980).* (Pamphlet) Tucson: Arizona State Museum.

Selected Works by Mary Shepardson

1962 Value Theory in the Prediction of Political Behavior: The Navajo Case. *American Anthropologist* 64 (4): 742–50.
1963 *Navajo Ways in Government.* American Anthropological Association Memoir No. 96. Vol. 65 (3), Part 2. Washington, D.C.
1965 Problems of the Navajo Tribal Courts in Transition. *Human Organization* 24 (3): 250–53.
1971 Navajo Factionalism and the Outside World. In *Studies in Apachean Culture, History and Ethnology.* Keith Basso and Morris Opler, eds. Pp. 83–89. Tucson, Ariz.: University of Arizona Press.

1975   *Assessment of Cumulative Sociocultural Impacts of Proposed Plans for Devel-opment of Coal and Water Resources in the Northern New Mexico Region.* Bureau of U.S. Reclamation. (As consultant for James R. Leonard Associates on the section dealing with the questionnaires and Navajo areas.)

1977a Pawns of Power: The Bonin Islanders. In *The Anthropology of Power.* Raymond D. Fogelson and Richard N. Adams, eds. Pp. 99–114. New York: Academic Press.

1977b The Navajo Nonstate Nation. In *Nonstate Nations in International Politics: Comparative Systems Analyses.* Judy S. Bertelsen, ed. Pp. 223–24. New York: Praeger.

1978   Changes in Navajo Mortuary Practices and Beliefs. *American Indian Quarterly* 4 (4): 383–95.

1980   Foreword and appendix "From My Notebooks." *A Voice in Her Tribe: A Navajo Woman's Own Story*, by Irene Stewart. Menlo Park, Calif.: Ballena Press.

1982a The Status of Navajo Women. *American Indian Quarterly* 6 (1–2): 149–69.

1982b Changing Attitudes Toward Navajo Religion. In *Navajo Religion and Culture: Selected Views.* David M. Brugge and Charlotte J. Frisbie, eds. Pp. 198–208. Santa Fe: Museum of New Mexico Press.

1983   Development of Navajo Tribal Government. In *Handbook of North American Indians.* Vol. 10, *Southwest*, pp. 624–35. William C. Sturtevant, general ed. Washington, D.C.: Smithsonian Institution.

1986   Fieldwork Among the Navajo. (Pamphlet) Palo Alto, Calif.: BAS Press.

Coauthored Works

Shepardson, Mary, and Blodwen Hammond

1964   Change and Persistence in an Isolated Navajo Community. *American Anthropologist* 67 (6): 1029–50.

1965   The Born Between Phenomenon in Navajo Kinship Terminology. *American Anthropologist* 66 (5): 1516–17.

1966   Navajo Inheritance Patterns: Random or Regular? *Ethnology* 5 (1): 87–96.

1970   *The Navajo Mountain Community: Social Organization and Kinship Terminology.* Berkeley: University of California Press.

NAOMI KATZ AND DAVID KEMNITZER

Erminnie Adelle Platt Smith

(1836–1886)

Trained as a geologist, Erminnie Adelle Platt Smith was a pioneer American ethnologist and linguist, known especially for her studies of Iroquois myths and language.

Erminnie Platt was born on April 26, 1836, in Marcellus, New York, the ninth of ten children to Joseph Platt, a wealthy farmer and Presbyterian deacon, and his wife, Ermina Dodge. Her paternal grandparents were early settlers of the area in the late eighteenth century. Because her mother died when she was two, her father became the major influence in her life. He was a rock collector who encouraged her childhood interest in geology and botany. Platt attended the renowned Troy Female Seminary in New York (1850–53), founded by pioneer educator Emma Willard, where she excelled in languages. She graduated at the age of sixteen and only a year later married Simeon H. Smith, a wealthy Chicago lumber dealer. In 1866 the couple moved from Chicago to Jersey City, New Jersey, where Simeon Smith worked as a stockyards official, and later as city finance commissioner.

Smith's early married years were taken up with the rearing of four sons (Simeon, Willard, Carlton, Eugene) and with a rigid domestic routine. In Chicago, however, she pursued her geological interest by classifying and labeling mineral specimens for display in European museums. While educating her four sons in Germany, she decided to continue her own education. She studied crystallography at Strasburg, German language and literature at Heidelberg, and investigated the amber industry on the coast of the Baltic Sea. She took courses for two years at the Bergakademie (School of Mines) in Freiburg, Saxony, and was graduated from that institution. Upon her return to the United States, she had amassed one of the largest private mineralogy collections in the country.

She began to deliver highly popular parlor lectures for charitable purposes on geological, literary, and aesthetic topics. This led to the founding of the Aesthetic Society of Jersey City (also known as Daughters of Aesthetics) in 1879. Its membership consisted of women who met monthly to discuss papers on science, literature, and art. The Aesthetic Society remained a lifelong interest of Erminnie Smith's throughout her lifetime, and she devoted much energy to organizing the meetings and also was a frequent lecturer. She was president of the Society (1879–86) and its guiding spirit; it was disbanded after her death. Reflecting the desire of a newly affluent American society for cultural enlightenment, its widely known monthly receptions drew large audiences for such events as receptions with Matthew Arnold and Mme. Greville, and the first local demonstration of the phonograph.

In 1878 Smith was elected a member of Sorosis, the pioneer New York City women's cultural club, and directed its science programs for four years. She was also a member of Meridian, the New York City women's club. Probably through a cousin, Frederic W. Putnam, she was introduced to the American Association for the Advancement of Science (AAAS). She read a monograph on jade for its annual meeting in 1879, becoming the first woman to present a paper before the AAAS (Lurie 1966).

At these gatherings she learned of the new science of anthropology. Having grown up near the New York Onondaga reservation, she became interested in studying American Indian ethnology, particularly the cultures of the Six Nations of the Iroquois Federation. Although Erminnie never received any formal anthropological training, she received an appointment to the staff of the Bureau of American Ethnology (BAE) of the Smithsonian Institution (1880), owing to her growing reputation and contacts in scientific circles. The bureau's director, Major John Wesley Powell, trained her and partially financed her research on the language, customs, and myths of the Iroquois Indians. Lewis Henry Morgan, who pioneered the research on the Iroquois, also provided her with advice and introductions. Smith began her investigations on the Tuscarora reservation near Lewiston, New York. One of the first American women to engage in field ethnography, she won the affection of the Indians, was adopted into the tribe, and was given the name Ka-tei-tci-sta-kwast (Beautiful Flower).

Smith accurately recorded legends obtained from older informants, resulting in her first book, *Myths of the Iroquois* (Smith 1883), published by the BAE. A gifted amateur, she spent two summers with the few remaining Tuscarora Indians on scattered reservations in Canada and the United States. Her fieldwork resulted in the classification of over 15,000 words of the Iroquois dialects. Her Iroquois-English dictionary is now with her papers in the archives of the Smithsonian Institution. Smith was ahead of her time in introducing the training of native informants as field assistants, and her technique was later used by Alice Cunningham Fletcher* and Edward Sapir. One of her consultants, John N. B. Hewitt, an educated Tuscarora, became a well-known ethnologist in his own right.

Smith actively participated in the scientific and cultural societies of her day. She faithfully attended the meetings of the American Association for the Advancement of Science, presenting a number of papers each year on her Iroquois research. In 1885 she was elected secretary of its geology and geography section. She was appointed a Fellow of the New York Academy of Sciences and was the first woman to be so honored. She was also a Fellow of the London Scientific Society, as well as a corresponding member of the Numismatic and Antiquarian Society of Philadelphia and of the Historical Society of New York. In addition to her lectures, she contributed numerous scientific papers on Iroquois language, culture, myth, and ethnobotany to various scholarly and lay publications.

Erminnie Smith died at the age of fifty on June 9, 1886. In 1888 an annual award was established in her name at Vassar College by a group of her friends for the best student research paper on mineralogy.

Smith did her fieldwork in an era devoted to recording the disappearing lore of American Indians, in a climate in which Indian culture was already considered to be a syncretic mixture, heavily influenced by white colonial penetration. Thus, ethnographic compilation of a detailed nature assumed particular urgency. Smith advocated the theory of cultural evolutionism widely held by Lewis Henry Morgan and his contemporaries, which fell into disrepute with the rise of the Boasian school of anthropology. Her rationale, both in her work and in her public comments, was the view of culture as the evolution of the human mind. In support of her view, she traced stages of sociocultural development similar to tracing successive geological strata. She considered American Indian mythology to be a particularly rich source for understanding the growth of the human mind. For example, in *Myths of the Iroquois*, she prefaced each chapter with remarks demonstrating how the particular myths she was about to describe reflected a particular evolutionary stage of human intellect.

The latter part of the nineteenth century witnessed the gradual expansion of opportunities for women. Erminnie Smith was a product of Troy Seminary, an early secondary educational institution providing females with intellectual training. She combined a deep involvement in the structured married life of an upper-middle-class woman with her professional endeavors. Her social position enabled her to seize many opportunities. In utilizing her talents, she was a female pioneer in scientific and cultural circles. As a leader of the burgeoning women's movement, she actively promoted and organized women's clubs and associations, and participated in high society clubs devoted to scientific, literary, and other cultural pursuits.

Smith made a major contribution to the study of Iroquois myths and language. Throughout her activities, she was not only a well-accepted ethnographer but also a noted personality renowned for her personal charm and eloquence. She represented the turn-of-the-century middle and upper class woman who found herself in an era of new possibilities. The *New York Times* (Aug. 29, 1880:5), commenting on one of her lectures on the Iroquois, reported "Mrs. Smith is not only a good writer, well known in literary and scientific circles in New York, Boston and other cities[,] but she is also an eloquent speaker, and . . . is deeply interested in the results of scientific investigation."

References and Works About Erminnie Smith

Appleton's Cyclopedia of American Biography
1888 Smith, Erminnie Adelle. In *ACAB*. Vol. 5, p. 563. New York: D. Appleton and Company.
1890 *In Memoriam: Mrs. Erminnie Smith*. Boston: Lee and Shepard, privately printed.
Biographical Dictionary of America
1906 Smith, Erminnie Adelle (Platt.) In *BDA*. Vol. 9. Rossiter Johnson, ed. Boston: American Biographical Society.
The National Cyclopedia of American Biography
1906 Smith, Erminnie Adelle (Platt.) In *NCAB*. Vol. 13, pp. 183–84. New York: James T. White and Co.
Hough, Walter
1935 Smith, Erminnie Adelle Platt. In *DAB*. Vol. 9, p. 262. Dumas Malone, ed. New York: Charles Scribner's Sons.
Lurie, Nancy O.
1966 Women in Early American Anthropology. In *Pioneers of American Anthropology: The Uses of Biography*. June Helm, ed. Pp. 29–83. Seattle: University of Washington Press.
Lurie, Nancy O.
1971 Smith, Erminnie Adelle Platt. In *NAW I*. Edward T. James et al., eds. Pp. 312–13. Cambridge: Belknap Press of Harvard University.
New York Times
August 29, 1880; September 2, 1880; and June 10, 1886.
Sage, Mrs. Russell, and Mary J. Fairbanks
1898 *Emma Willard and Her Pupils: Or, Fifty Years of Troy Female Seminary*. New York.

Selected Works by Erminnie Smith

English-Tuscarora Dictionary. 2 vols. (Unpublished, in the archives of the Bureau of American Ethnology, Smithsonian Institution, Washington, D.C.)
1880 Languages of the Iroquois. *Science* 1 (11): 137–38.
1883 Myths of the Iroquois. In *Second Annual Report of the Bureau of American Ethnology*. Pp. 47–116. Washington, D.C.
1884a Accidents or Mode Signs of Verbs in the Iroquois Dialects. In *Proceedings of the American Association for the Advancement of Science* 32. Salem, Mass.
1884b Studies in the Iroquois Concerning the Verb to Be and Its Substitutes. In *Proceedings of the American Association for the Advancement of Science* 32. Salem, Mass.
1885a The Customs and Language of the Iroquois. *Journal of the Royal Anthropological Institute of Great Britain and Ireland* 14. London.
1885b Disputed Points Concerning Iroquois Pronouns. In *Proceedings of the American Association for the Advancement of Science* 33. Salem, Mass.
1886 The Significance of Flora to the Iroquois. In *Proceedings of the American Association for the Advancement of Science* 34. Salem, Mass.

VIMALA JAYANTI

Gitel (Gertrude) Poznanski Steed

(1914–1977)

American cultural anthropologist Gitel Poznanski Steed was known for her research in India.

Gertrude Poznanski was born on May 3, 1914, in Cleveland, Ohio, the home of her mother, Sara Auerbach. Her father was Jakob Poznanski, a businessman and Polish native who had come to the United States from Belgium. She was very much the youngest: her sister Mary was twenty when Gertrude was born, and her sister Helen was eighteen. Both sisters eventually emigrated to Israel, but she remained close to them and to at least one of her nieces (Steed 1953). When Poznanski was still a baby, the family moved to the Bronx, New York, where they lived comfortably. Gertrude Poznanski was a bright and exceptional student at Wadleigh High School. During her teens she adopted the Yiddish name of Gitel. Though not religious, she maintained her Jewish upbringing and cultural identification. She was always proud to mention that one of her paternal great-grandfathers had been the head rabbi of Poznan in Poland. Her mother was active in the women's suffrage movement and in the leftist politics. Poznanski also embraced these humanitarian and political commitments.

She entered New York University (NYU) in 1932 as a student in banking and finance and moved into Greenwich Village, immediately becoming involved in its artistic and political life. She made friends with artists and writers, and occasionally sang blues in a nightclub. Wanting to be independent and self-supporting, she dropped out of NYU after a year and took a job as a writer with the Works Progress Administration. In 1933 she met the painter Robert Steed, whom she married in 1947. He describes her then as "electric" and as a "skinny thing with a gamin-like quality" (R. Steed).[1] We see her at the age of eighteen in Rafael Soyer's 1932 painting *Girl in a White Blouse*, which hangs in the Metropolitan Museum of Art in New York City. She is slender and wiry, but relaxed, with lots of springy, contemporary-looking black hair.

One of her teachers at NYU was the philosopher Sidney Hook. He urged her to return to the university, where she received financial help from a benefactor. In 1938 she finished a B.A. with honors in sociology and anthropology. Ruth Benedict,* whom she met in 1937, offered her a graduate fellowship at Columbia University, which she held from 1938 to 1940. Benedict also guided Steed's first fieldwork. She was part of a group of students from Columbia and the University of Montana that Benedict accompanied to the Blackfoot Indian Reservation in Montana (1939). Afterward, while she continued her graduate work at Columbia, she was editor and researcher for Vilhjalmur Stefansson, the explorer and writer on Inuit (Eskimo) life. From this work she began to develop a library dissertation on hunter-gatherer subsistence but did not finish her dissertation until 1969, at the age of fifty-five, long after her career had been established.

In 1941 Steed became senior editor of information at Yale University's Institute of Human Relations, where she remained until 1943. Then she set aside conventional anthropological pursuits to follow her own anti-Fascist, antiracist commitments, following the tradition of Boas and Benedict. Two friends, Ursula Wasserman and Frances McClernan, invited her to join the Jewish Black Book Committee, a group of writers and researchers who documented in detail the Nazi death campaign against the Jews of Europe during World War II. The committee received international support from Jewish and anti-Fascist organizations. Its report was submitted to the United Nations War Crimes Commission and published as *The Black Book: The Nazi Crime Against the Jewish People* (Steed 1946). Steed's contribution, "The Strategy of Decimation," was based on eyewitness accounts, U.S. intelligence documents, German statistical and legal sources, and newspaper reports from 1943 and 1944. It describes exactly how Nazi Germany's policies of expulsion, slave labor, starvation, and final extermination of the Jews were carefully calculated and purposefully carried out. The fuller revelations of the Nuremberg Trials were still to come; *The Black Book*, therefore, was timely and telling.

Steed's teaching career began at Hunter College in New York City, where she taught general and introductory anthropology courses in 1945 and 1947. The year between she spent at Fisk University, where she taught a course on Africa and served as managing editor of *Race Relations: A Monthly Summary of Events and Trends*, published by Fisk's Institute of Social Sciences and supported by the American Council on Race Relations.

In 1947 she joined the Columbia University Research in Contemporary Cultures Project directed by Benedict and Margaret Mead.* She was part of the group studying the Chinese community in New York. Ruth Bunzel,* the group coordinator, later wrote that Gitel Steed was "one of the best, if not the very best, interviewer on the project, combining an unusual ability to elicit information with a capacity to focus on problems of theoretical importance" (Bunzel 1962).[2] Steed's interviews on the subject of Chinese friendship (Steed 1953) were incorporated into Mead and Metraux's *The Study of Culture at a Distance*.

By the time the project ended in 1949, Steed had already formulated and funded a plan for continuing the research in China (Lesser 1979:88–89), but the Chinese Revolution of 1948 aborted her plans. The sudden termination of a funded research project is a catastrophe for any anthropologist, but Steed immediately devised another one for India and set about learning photography in preparation for this fieldwork. She assembled a research group and left for India in 1949 as director of the Columbia University Research in Contemporary India Field Project. Robert Steed, Morris Carstairs, and James Silverberg were her co-workers. The project was funded by a U.S. Navy Department grant to Abram Kardiner. Steed's field arrangements were facilitated by her friendship with Gautam Sarabhai, a Gujarati Indian she had met in New York. Sarabhai had first suggested Gujarat as a research site. He provided lodging for the team in his own house upon their arrival and also provided transport and entrée into the villages. His help was an enormous complement to Steed's own ability to win the confidence of village residents and elicit their responses (R. Steed). With the exceptions of Ruth Hill Useem, Charlotte Wiser, and Kathleen Gough (who was more a contemporary than a predecessor), very few women had done extended research in India.

Gujarat, located on the Pakistan border, was the source of most of the Indian immigrants who settled in Britain after World War II. It was also a region much affected by the postcolonial reorganization of the subcontinent. Thus, Steed's research period, 1949–51, coincided with rapid political and economic change in Gujarat, which she incorporated into her research plan.

Steed's goals were to show the relation of village structure and culture to "personal careers," in order to explain behavior institutionally and to show how, in turn, individual acts revealed community processes, including processes of change. In the field this meant studying social structure, kinship, social organization, and culture, and then measuring individual lives against the "sociological horizon" (Steed 1964). The study of individual lives was based on a sample of villagers and on a smaller subgroup representing both landed and landless castes. For the second group, she assembled "augmented life histories." These consisted of the individual's own account of his or her life; an account, based on formal interview, of the individual's own interpretation of and response to village institutions and community values; the individual as seen by others; and a yearlong observation of behavior.

The research goals and procedures were ambitious, but more notable was Steed's conscious effort to bring together empirically—not merely through inference and interpretation—the interaction of individual, culture, community, and institutions, and to relate actual persons—not statistical patterns abstracted from observation—to the community and its processes of change. Her theoretical orientation and the importance of life history in her research plan were Benedictian (see Benedict 1948), but her methodology was innovative. Her emphasis on the individual's own interpretation of values and institutions anticipated later studies in cognitive anthropology. However, the project lacked a clearly defined research problem.

Steed returned from India in 1951 with thousands of pages of notes and photographs. She also returned with malaria and other health impairments that affected her later career, and she did not actually receive her doctorate until 1969. In 1963, however, Conrad Arensberg wrote that "her reputation and accomplishment are such as to make her non-possession of her Ph.D. of little moment for her standing in the profession" (Arensberg 1963).

During the eleven years between her return from India and her employment at Hofstra College (now Hofstra University) in 1962, Steed had no university affiliation. She disseminated her work mainly through seminars and lectures at Columbia University, the University of Chicago, and the University of Pennsylvania. She participated in India symposia at meetings of the American Anthropological Association, the Far Eastern Association, and the Social Science Research Council. Her one substantial publication, "Notes on an Approach to a Study of Personality Formation in a Hindu Village in Gujarat" (Steed 1955), illustrated the formative effects of culture and institutions on the personality of a single Rajput landowner despite his unusual circumstances and upbringing.

During these eleven years she also gave birth to her son, Andrew Hart (b. 1953), and taught English at the Jefferson School, a Manhattan private school favored by the political left. She maintained her anthropological contacts, and also her ties with the art and intellectual world, through the extensive social life that was so necessary to her. Gitel and Robert Steed kept open house on West 23rd Street; and their visitors included Ruth Bunzel, Sula Benet, Vera Rubin,* Stanley Diamond, Alexander Lesser, Margaret Mead, and Conrad Arensberg, among others (Belmonte; R. Steed).

Steed continued to work on her Indian materials until her death. Some of her photographs are in the permanent collection of the Museum of Modern Art, some were published in Edward Steichen's 1955 book *The Family of Man*, and many others were exhibited (Lesser 1979:90). Her reputation also rests on her unpublished notes—the thousands of pages of interviews, observations, projective test results, life histories, and villagers' paintings. Most of these are now in the special collections of the University of Chicago Libraries, where they await cataloguing and study. These materials have been described as "rich" and "rare" (Silverberg), and when properly ordered will be a unique and significant scholarly resource. Her correspondence, as yet unstudied, will probably be an important source for the intellectual history of the United States in the 1950s (Marriott).

A just assessment of Steed's work will not be possible until the Chicago archives are ordered and studied, an enormous task for which funding is now being sought. Meanwhile, it is necessary to consider why her publication was scanty and why her professional career did not follow conventional patterns. One very great handicap was her health. Not only was she weakened by malaria and dysentery contracted in the field, but shortly after her return she also developed diabetes, which was particularly difficult to control and frequently put her in hospital. In addition, she suffered for over thirty years from pituitary cancer. Though very much a part of the New York anthropological scene during the forties and fifties, she lacked institutional affiliation. Whether this lack was related to her political activities as well as her health is unclear. Other problems dogged her attempts at synthesizing and publishing her work. When she and Kardiner quarreled over his insistence that her seminar presentations be published under joint authorship, he cut off her funds just as the writing stage began (R. Steed). She wrote a screenplay, "Devgar," based on the character of a Hindu temple sexton she had known; James Ivory agreed to direct the film but withdrew without explanation just as the Steeds were leaving to join him in India (R. Steed). It may also be that the magnitude of her materials defied organization and synthesis, especially as her research plan had been so ambitious in its goals.

She did, on the other hand, receive much cooperation from Robert Steed. He went with her to the Blackfoot reservation, to Gujarat, and on a second trip to India in 1970. An artist himself, he deeply appreciated her photographs and funded their professional preparation. He was her partner and sustainer for forty-four years.

Gitel Steed's reputation rests on her spoken presentations, her photographs, and the volume and complexity of her unstudied materials. Her influence spread by means of her extraordinary and captivating personality, her dedicated undergraduate teaching, and her varied and intense social relationships (Belmonte; Silverberg). She poured her limited energy into these. She died in the night, apparently from a heart attack, at the age of sixty-three. Robert Steed remarked that "Gitel made everyone feel as if she belonged to them, and it wore her out."

Notes

1. I am grateful to everyone who responded to my inquiries and made possible the writing of this article. Robert Steed, James Silverberg, Thomas Belmonte, and McKim Marriott were generous beyond expectation. (Their personal communications, all received in 1986, are cited in the text.) I also thank Conrad Arensberg, Sidney Mintz, Milton Singer, and Joan Vincent.

2. The author refers to an unpublished file on Gitel P. Steed, including letters from Ruth Bunzel (1962) and Conrad Arensberg (1963), from Hofstra University, Department of Anthropology and Sociology. Gitel P. Steed's papers and unpublished notes are held by the University of Chicago Libraries.

References and Works About Gitel Steed

Arensberg, Conrad
1963   Unpublished letter on file in the Department of Anthropology and Sociology, Hofstra University, Hempstead, N.Y.
Bunzel, Ruth
1962   Unpublished letter on file in the Department of Anthropology and Sociology, Hofstra University, Hempstead, N.Y.

Contemporary Authors
1977   Gitel Steed. *CA*. Ann Evory, ed. 1st revised ed.: Vol. 41–44, p. 663. Detroit: Gale Research.
Lesser, Alexander
1979   Obituary of Gitel Steed. *American Anthropologist* 81: 88–91.
New York Times
1977   Obituary of Gitel Steed. September 9.

Selected Works by Gitel Steed

(Under the name Gitel Poznanski)
1946   The Strategy of Decimation. In *The Black Book: The Nazi Crime Against the Jewish People*. The Jewish Black Book Committee and Ursula Wasserman, eds. Pp. 111–240. New York: Duell, Sloan, and Pearce.
(Under the name Gitel P. Steed)
Papers and unpublished notes. University of Chicago Libraries.
1949–51   Unpublished photographs. Collection of Robert Steed, New York.
1953   Interview on Chinese Friendship. In *The Study of Culture at a Distance*. M. Mead and R. Metraux, eds. Pp. 192–98. Chicago: University of Chicago Press.
1955   Notes to an Approach to a Study of Personality Formation in a Hindu Village in Gujarat. In *Village India: Studies in the Little Community*. Memoirs of the American Anthropological Association No. 83. McKim Marriott, ed. Pp. 102–44. Chicago: University of Chicago Press.
1964   The Human Career in Village India. Part I: Introduction. Mimeographed draft on file in the Department of Anthropology, Hofstra University.
1968   "Devgar." Unpublished screenplay on file with Robert Steed, New York.
1969   Caste and Kinship in Rural Gujarat: The Social Uses of Space. Unpublished diss., Columbia University, N.Y.

RIVA BERLEANT-SCHILLER

Matilda Coxe Evans Stevenson

(1849–1915)

American ethnologist and first woman to work in the American Southwest, Matilda Coxe Evans Stevenson was known especially for her work on Zuni religion, and was cofounder of the Women's Anthropological Society of America.

Matilda Coxe Evans was born on May 12, 1849, to Alexander H. Evans of Virginia and Maria Coxe Evans of New Jersey. She grew up in Washington, D.C., where her father was an attorney, writer, and journalist, as well as a minor figure in the Washington intellectual community. The five Evans children lived in a privileged, middle-class household and were taught by their mother with the assistance of private governesses before attending private schools in Philadelphia (1863–68). Evans received her only formal education at Miss Annable's Academy, a "sheltered female seminary." Returning to Washington with her family in 1868, she studied law with her father (while serving as a law clerk in his office) and chemistry and geology with Dr. N. M. Mew of the Army Medical School of Washington, D.C. As was common in the period, she never earned a formal college or advanced degree; there were almost no opportunities for women to obtain formal scientific educations in this period. Nevertheless, she intended to become a mineralogist. Her plans changed, however, when she met Colonel James Stevenson of Kentucky. They were married on April 18, 1872. (The marriage was childless.)[1]

After her marriage, Stevenson accompanied her husband on numerous geological surveys in Colorado, Idaho, Wyoming, and Utah (1872–78). Stevenson (1840–88), a self-taught geologist, naturalist, and anthropologist, was executive officer of Ferdinand Hayden's U.S. Geological Survey of the Territories. Stevenson helped her husband construct valuable fossil and ornithological collections, now housed at the Smithsonian Institution. She assisted him in his famous 1878 study of geysers in the Yellowstone region. On one of these trips during the mid–1870s Stevenson made her first ethnographic study on the Ute and

Arapaho, learning "the rudiments of ethnographic technique" (that is, how to approach individuals, how to begin to learn the language, and what questions to ask about daily life) from her husband. Data were to be treated like other natural phenomena; the methods used in geology and natural history were extended to individuals, groups, and languages. However, like all anthropologists of the period, Matilda Stevenson was largely self-taught—learning by trial and error. Unfortunately, neither she nor any other member of the Hayden expedition published the ethnographic results of these trips in Colorado and Wyoming. William Holmes and William Jackson did, however, publish the results of their archaeological trips to the San Juan region of Colorado.

Matilda Coxe Stevenson came to the Southwest in 1879 as a member of the first collecting and research expedition of the newly formed Bureau of Ethnology, under the direction of John Wesley Powell. Her position was "volunteer coad-jutor in ethnology," that is, assistant to her husband, the leader of the expedition. The Stevensons, along with John Hillers and Frank Hamilton Cushing, spent six months at Zuñi and Hopi, collecting ethnographic objects, surveying local archaeological sites, gathering materials from caves and shrines, and amassing information on various cultural and social aspects of Pueblo life. Out of this trip came Stevenson's first publication, *The Zuñi and the Zuñians* (1881a), the first scholarly ethnography of the Zuñi published for a popular audience. It dealt with the basic categories of Zuñi life and reflected all of her later research interests. The trip also led to many unrecognized publications: Stevenson helped her husband prepare reports, analyses, and catalogs of the collection that were later published in the Bureau of Ethnology Annual Reports. In fact, Secretary Spencer Baird in 1882 said that because all previous reports had been published under only James Stevenson's name, individuals unaware of her contribution mistakenly thought that she was not the author of her first published article. In fact, the opposite was true, for James Stevenson disliked writing reports. He was a collector, a keen observer and administrator; but he does not appear to have had either the creative mind or the discipline needed for writing. Creativity and synthesis he left to his wife, areas in which she excelled. It was many years before her contributions were officially acknowledged (see Baird 1885; Tylor 1884).

Throughout the 1880s the Stevensons formed the first husband-wife team in anthropology. Matilda Stevenson was welcomed on the Smithsonian's collecting expeditions (in an unpaid capacity) because it was thought by Powell and Baird that she complemented her husband; as a woman she would have had access to information on Native American women and their daily activities that was crucial to anthropology but inaccessible to male researchers. Powell and Baird felt that this information was vital if anthropology was to give a complete picture of the daily lives of noncivilized peoples. While Margaret Mead* and Ruth Bunzel* (1960:205) correctly feel that Stevenson was the first American ethnologist to consider children and women worthy of notice, she was actually following Powell's lead. Her main research interests rapidly focused on religion rather than issues dealing specifically with women and socialization. Her famous monograph on Zuñi children (1887) is primarily a work on the ceremonies that accompany childhood. Similarly, her work on Zuñi games (1903) is really a description and analysis of ceremonial games.

Even though she quickly went beyond the research interests that Powell and Baird had carved out for her because of her sex, she quickly became known for her skill in collecting all kinds of ethnographic data (Tylor 1884). She always used multiple informants to check reliability and over the years was able to build lasting friendships with several knowledgeable Zuñi. Stevenson was able to build an extensive body of data because during the 1880s she and her husband made almost yearly trips to Zuñi. At the same time, they worked more briefly in all the Rio Grande Pueblos and at Acoma, Hopi, Sia, and among the Navajos. And they continued to survey archaeological sites and geological features in Arizona, New Mexico, and California.

James Stevenson died in 1888 after a series of attacks of Rocky Mountain fever. At the time, the Stevensons had been preparing an ethnography of Sia. Powell considered the information so important that in an unprecedented move, he officially hired Stevenson to put ''her husband's'' notes in order, a task that required additional independent fieldwork in 1890. This temporary appointment became permanent in 1890. Stevenson was the first, and for a long time the only, woman to be paid as a government anthropologist, although her salary was always lower than the salaries of her male contemporaries. In fact, until the 1960s there was no other professional woman employed full-time by the Bureau of Ethnology, or the Bureau of American Ethnology, as it came to be called.

After publishing *The Sia* (1894a), the first major ethnography of a Rio Grande Pueblo, Matilda Stevenson returned to Zuñi, having recognized the now-established anthropological contention that there is always more to learn no matter how much fieldwork has been completed. In all, she worked at Zuñi for more than twenty-five years—evidence of a long-standing commitment to understand the deeper meanings available to one only from in-depth knowledge of a single society. In addition to her fieldwork, she paid for informants to come to her home in Washington, D.C., and later in New Mexico. During this period she collected data on many topics, including the manufacture and use of native dyes and pigments, games, mythology, irrigation systems, social structure, mythology, language, philosophy, symbolism in arts, clothing, and ethnobotany. She also continued to collect artifacts for the Smithsonian, although on a smaller scale than in the 1870s–80s, and to help construct museum exhibits. Despite these eclectic interests, Stevenson still focused primarily on the minute details of the Zuñi pantheon, philosophy, and ceremonies. She firmly believed, like many other anthropologists who have worked in the Southwest, that religion was the cornerstone of all culture and society.

Stevenson felt her task as an anthropologist was to concentrate on the Southwest Pueblos and to record every phase of Indian life—in short, to produce comprehensive ethnographies before the societies were assimilated. Stevenson, like other ethnographers at the Bureau, was convinced that Native Americans would be overrun by the politically and economically dominant Anglo-American society and cease to exist as independent cultures. In her writings she continually stressed that ethnographic data had to be collected before it was irretrievably lost. By the early 1900s she became an even more persistent advocate for the necessity and duty of her lifelong task. So single-minded did she become in her quest, in her dedication to the science of anthropology, that she developed a reputation for being pigheaded, humorless, insensitive, and overbearing (see Lurie 1966:58–61, 234). Leslie White has noted that she had an extreme sense of self-importance (Lurie 1966:61). There is evidence that Stevenson, like Cushing, encountered opposition from some informants because of her insistence that they provide her with data (Pandey 1972:326–27). In fact, the *Illustrated Police News* printed a cartoon and sensational story, "Cowed by a Woman," on March 6, 1886, showing Stevenson defending her calm husband from a Hopi "attack" that resulted from their insistence on trading for ethnographic items in a kiva. In general, however, Stevenson seems to have had cordial relations with many families and to have developed several long-lasting friendships at Zuñi (Lurie 1966:66).

In 1904 Stevenson began what she considered would be her monumental ethnological study—a comparison of the religions of all the Pueblos. This research project was to be an extension of her work at Zuñi. She purchased a ranch near San Ildefonso as a base for her studies and began collecting information at the Tanoan and Keresan Pueblos. Until her death in 1915 Stevenson spent the greater part of each year in New Mexico. However, she never completed the monograph. This was the first time in her career she had failed to produce a major monograph following an extended period of fieldwork. One reason was that she never thought her work complete; she always wanted to gather a little more data. This was an extremely difficult task: she often had to work in secret, for like almost all anthropologists who came after her, she was unwelcome in the Rio Grande Pueblos. (As a defense against the incursion of Spanish, Mexican, and Anglo-American peoples, the Rio Grande Pueblos had developed a united stance against outsiders learning the secrets of their cultures.) According to John P. Harrington, a linguist and ethnographer who often visited her ranch and who learned ethnographic techniques from Stevenson, the natives of San Ildefonso considered her to be a silly old woman (Lurie 1966:64). Stevenson never breached the solidarity of the Pueblos, although her correspondence with William Holmes and Frederick Hodge shows that she thought she had.

Other factors also accounted for Stevenson's declining productivity near the end of her life. She became embroiled in local New Mexico politics, which resulted in numerous arguments with the Bureau of Indian Affairs (BIA) personnel and the Sante Fe anthropological community. She was also the victim of a swindle by a BIA schoolteacher and had to spend time in litigation that dragged on for several years. Although she won all her suits, these court cases ruined her financially and made her seem a bitter, old woman to the anthropological community. As a result, she produced only a few short articles during this period. After her death her protégé, John P. Harrington, "inherited" her unpublished field notes, which he later incorporated into his own publications.

In addition to her fieldwork and writing, Stevenson was the founder and first president of the Women's Anthropological Society of America (1885). The purpose of this organization was "to open to women new fields for systematic investigation . . . and to invite their cooperation in the development of the science of anthropology" (Anon. 1889:240). This is said to be the first society devoted to any branch of science to be organized and maintained by women (Anon. 1889:242). Stevenson spent a great deal of time and energy demonstrating that women were competent scientists and scholars: she was a judge at the World's Columbian Exposition and participated in the special congresses associated with several World's Fairs. With Alice Fletcher* she worked to have Mesa Verde declared a national park. Stevenson's publications and letters to colleagues show that she was very conscious of her role as a woman scientist and of her pioneering efforts, as well as of the advantages and disadvantages that this designation provided her. Being a woman helped her with fieldwork and provided her with insights necessary for understanding other peoples, whereas it hindered her in her quest for recognition by the scientific community in Washington.

Stevenson was an intelligent, proud, serious, opinionated woman. She refused to let people take advantage of her or to regard her as a frivolous female. Anthropologists have tended to judge her on the basis of her personality in her later years. Holmes respected her, while Powell found her tiresome (see Lurie 1966). Judd (1967:57) has described her as strong-willed and dominating. Pandey (1972:326) has stated that "she was an aggressive, intellectual woman who reacted strongly to anyone who did not accept her bidding." While certain individuals were intimidated by Stevenson's personality, no one criticized the value or quality of her fieldwork and analyses. Kroeber (1917) trusted Stevenson's analyses of Zuñi over Cushing's because he thought Cushing tended to overdramatize; Stevenson's analyses were impersonal, objective, and precise. Edgar L. Hewett respected her firsthand knowledge of the Pueblos (Chauvenet (1983:72). Powell was often angry when she would not write quickly, but there is no evidence that he questioned either her thoroughness or her conclusions. Because Stevenson never wrote theoretical essays and always stayed firmly within the dominant nineteenth-century evolutionary paradigm espoused by Powell and McGee, all her writings supported Powell's general theoretical position (see Hinsley 1981). Stevenson did not consider herself a theoretician but a scientific field researcher.

Matilda Coxe Stevenson was concerned with thoroughness and ethnographic detail rather than abstract theories. And she lived up to the goals she set herself:

I want to do a comparatively complete and connected history of an aboriginal people whose thoughts are not our thoughts, weaving all the threads into an intelligent and satisfactory whole for the civilized students. . . . It is my wish to erect a foundation upon which students may build. I feel I can do the most for science in this way. (Stevenson to Powell, letter, May 23, 1900).

Note

1. Information for this paper comes from the Matilda Coxe Stevenson papers, the John P. Harrington papers, the Bureau of American Ethnology correspondence files, and other files at the National Anthropological Archives of the Smithsonian Institution.

References and Works About Matilda Coxe Stevenson

Anon.
1889   The Women's Anthropological Society of America. *Science* xiii (321): 240–42.
Baird, Spencer
1885   *Annual Report of the Smithsonian Institution for 1884*. Washington, D.C.: GPO.
Crampton, C. Gregory
1977   *The Zuñis of Cibola*. Salt Lake City: University of Utah Press.
Cushing, Frank Hamilton, J. Walter Fewkes, and Elsie C. Parsons
1922   Contributions to Hopi History. *American Anthropologist* 24 (3): 253–98.
Hoebel, E. Adamson
1954   Major Contribution of Southwestern Studies to Anthropological Theory. *American Anthropologist* 56 (4): 720–27.
Holmes, William H.
1916   In Memoriam: Matilda Coxe Stevenson. *American Anthropologist* 18 (4): 552–59.
Kroeber, Alfred L.
1917   Zuñi Kin and Clan. *Anthropological Papers of the American Museum of Natural History*, no. 18, part 2.
Lurie, Nancy Oestreich
1971   Stevenson, Matilda Coxe Evans. In *NAW I*. Edward T. James et al., eds. Pp. 373–74. Cambridge: Belknap Press of Harvard University.
Wilson, Edmund
1956   *Red, Black, Blond and Olive. Studies in Four Civilizations: Zuñi, Haiti, Soviet Russia, Israel*. New York: Oxford University Press.

Selected Works by Matilda Coxe Stevenson

1881a *Zuñi and the Zuñians*. Washington, D.C.: Privately printed.
1881b *Zuñi Pottery*. Report of the Davenport Academy of Science.
1883   The Cliff-Dwellers of the New Mexican Canyons. *Kansas City Review* 6 (11): 636–39.
1887   Religious Life of the Zuñi Child. *Fifth Annual Report of the Bureau of Ethnology for 1883–1884*. Pp. 533–55. Washington, D.C.: GPO.
1888   Zuñi Religion. *Science* 11 (286): 136–37.
1893a Tusayan Legends of the Snake and Flute People. *Proceedings, American Association for the Advancement of Science* 41:258–70.

1893b A Chapter in Zuñi Mythology. *Memoirs of the International Congress of Anthropology* (Chicago):312–19.

1894a The Sia. *Eleventh Annual Report of the Bureau of Ethnology for 1889–1890*. Washington, D.C.: GPO. Pp. 9–349.

1894b The Zuñi Scalp Ceremonial. In *The Congress of Women*. Mary Kavanaugh O. Eagle, ed. Pp. 484–87. Chicago: American Publishing House. (Reprinted 1974, New York: Arno Press.)

1898   Zuñi Ancestral Gods and Masks. *American Anthropologist* (old series) 11 (1): 33–40.

1903   Zuñi Games. *American Anthropologist* (new series) 5 (3): 468–97.

1904   The Zuñi Indians: Their Mythology, Esoteric Fraternities, and Ceremonies. *Twenty-third Annual Report of the Bureau of American Ethnology for 1901–1902*. Washington, D.C.: GPO.

1910   Studies of the Late Washington Matthews. *American Anthropologist* 12:345.

1913a Strange Rites of the Tewa Indians. *Smithsonian Miscellaneous Collections* 63 (8): 73–80.

1913b Studies of the Tewa Indians of the Rio Grande Valley. *Smithsonian Miscellaneous Collections* 60:35–41.

1915a Ethnobotany of the Zuñi Indians. *Thirtieth Annual Report of the Bureau of American Ethnology for 1908–1909*. Washington, D.C.: GPO. Pp. 3–102.

1915b The Sun and Ice People Among the Tewa Indians of New Mexico. *Smithsonian Miscellaneous Collections* 65 (6): 73–78.

Numerous unpublished Stevenson manuscripts are on file at the National Anthropological Archives, Smithsonian Institution. Also mentioned in references are several unlocated papers that may also be considered publications.

1885   The Moki Indian Snake Dance. Paper presented to the Women's Anthropological Society of America.

1886   The Sandpaintings of the Navaho. Paper presented to the Women's Anthropological Society of America.

1887a Zuñi and the Zuñians. Paper presented to the Women's Anthropological Society of America.

1887b Mission Indians (Luiseño). Paper presented to the Women's Anthropological Society of America.

1888   Thirteen Medicine Orders of the Zuñi. Paper presented to the Women's Anthropological Society of America.

1892 or 1893   A Paper on Snake and Flute People of Hopi. Rochester Museum of the American Association for the Advancement of Science.

1894   An article on archaeology for the judges' special volume on the Chicago Columbian Exposition of 1893. John Boyd Thacker, ed.

1911   Dress and Adornment of the Pueblo Indians. Manuscript No. 2093. Bureau of American Ethnology Archives, National Anthropological Archives. 300 pp.

NANCY J. PAREZO

Sara Yorke Stevenson

(1847–1921)

American "armchair archaeologist" Sara Yorke Stevenson was best known for her role in founding the Museum of the University of Pennsylvania and for her scholarly activities related to the archaeology of Egypt.

A founder of the University of Pennsylvania's Museum, Stevenson was well known during her lifetime for her work as an armchair anthropologist. In 1892 "Anthropological Work in America" described Stevenson, Daniel G. Brinton, Stewart Culin, and Morris Jastrow, Jr., as the best-known "anthropological workers" in Philadelphia. The author wrote that Stevenson "is perhaps our only lady Egyptologist. She may justly be compared in that field to Miss Edwards of England. Her lectures in Egyptian subjects have made a sensation" (Starr 1892:296).

Sara Yorke was born in Paris on February 19, 1847, to Edward and Sarah Hanna Yorke, aristocratic Louisianans who moved to Paris in the late 1840s. Her father had been a cotton broker; her mother's family owned a large cotton plantation. Her initial education took place in a Parisian school, Cours Remy. In 1857 Yorke's parents returned to Louisiana, leaving their daughters in a boarding school in Paris. The girls joined their parents for a summer in Newport, Rhode Island, and spent the following winter in New Orleans, where Yorke attended day school. This proved unsatisfactory, so she was sent back to Paris, where she entered the Institution Descauriet, a boarding school. Her guardians in Paris, with whom she spent alternate Sundays, were M. and Mme. Achille Jubinal. M. Jubinal had strong interests in antiquities and research, and he transmitted these interests to Yorke (Wister 1922:9).

Sara Yorke remained in Paris from 1858 until 1862. During these years the Yorke family moved from Louisiana to Mexico. Yorke left France to join her family in Mexico after the death of her brother and remained there until 1867. Fearing violence during the upheaval that accompanied the end of Maximilian's rule, they resettled in Brattleboro, Vermont. Her father lost his Mexican investments during this period, reducing the family's income. He died in Vermont in 1868. Shortly afterward, Yorke moved to Philadelphia to live with two Yorke uncles and an aunt. Two years later she married Cornelius Stevenson, a Philadelphia lawyer with whom she had one son, William, born in 1878 (Wister 1922:8–11).

The resurgence of Stevenson's interests in antiquities can be traced in part to her close ties to a group of wealthy and influential Philadelphians known as the Furness-Mitchell Coterie. The coterie consisted of approximately eighteen physicians, writers, scholars, anthropologists, and educators. The central figures of the coterie were S. Weir Mitchell, internationally recognized physician, scientist, successful novelist, and poet; Horace Howard Furness, world-renowned Shakespearean scholar; and Agnes Repplier, one of the best-known contemporary American essayists of her time. Other members included William Pepper, provost (president) of the University of Pennsylvania, with whom Stevenson founded the Free Museum of Science and Art (renamed the University Museum in 1913 and hereafter cited as the University Museum); Owen Wister, author of *The Virginian*; Agnes Irwin, the first dean of Radcliffe College and coeditor of an early effort at creating a women's history; and Talcott Williams, first dean of Columbia University's School of Journalism.

The coterie's members, leaders in Philadelphia's intellectual life from the 1870s until World War I, had won widespread recognition for their contributions to their chosen fields. Coterie members enjoyed social class privilege that gave them entrée to every segment of society. Membership in the coterie enabled women to participate in activities from which they otherwise would have been excluded. Without the support and encouragement of other coterie members, particularly the influential men, it is unlikely that Stevenson could have accomplished what she did (Van Ness 1985:213–14).

During the 1880s anthropology was just becoming a discipline. Edward B. Tylor of Oxford University, the first to hold a faculty position in England in anthropology, was not appointed until 1884. Four years later, Harvard University named Frederick Ward Putnam head of its Department of Archaeology and Ethnology, "the first effective university program" in anthropology (Darnell 1974:175–77).

Many scholars of the period now recognized as early anthropologists were, like Stevenson, educated in traditional disciplines and were neither fieldworkers nor trained anthropologists. Tylor, sometimes called the father of modern anthropology, and Daniel Brinton, the University of Pennsylvania faculty member who held the first appointment in America as professor of anthropology, were so-called armchair anthropologists, who never carried out fieldwork. Instead, they devoted their careers to analysis of data or materials collected or excavated by others. Stevenson, like these male scholars, was an armchair anthropologist. Her anthropological activities can be divided into several areas: research and publications, curatorial activities, establishment of the University Museum, and leadership of anthropological clubs and societies.

By 1888, when Putnam established Harvard's Anthropology Department, Stevenson was seriously interested in anthropology. Putnam served as a mentor for Stevenson as well as for Franz Boas, Zelia Nuttall*, Alice Fletcher*, and others (Lurie 1966). Stevenson and Nuttall became friends, and Stevenson unsuccessfully sought to recruit Boas to the University of Pennsylvania to establish a department of anthropometry (University of Museum Archives [UMA], Boxes 2 and 3, Nuttall-Stevenson correspondence.)[1] In 1892–93, as chief of the Department of Anthropology of the World's Columbian Exposition in Chicago, Putnam advocated Stevenson's appointment to the Jury of Awards for Ethnology. Congress had to pass a special act to allow women to serve in this capacity. Stevenson's election as vice president of the jury is an indication of her stature in that body (Wister 1922:10–11). In 1894 Stevenson became the first woman to lecture at the Peabody Museum when Putnam recruited her to speak on "Egypt at the Dawn of History" in the Anthropology Lecture Series (UMA, Box 2, University Archaeological Association).[2]

Stevenson's anthropological interests were broad, ranging from questions of cultural diffusion (Stevenson 1892a, 1896) to cultural evolutionism. She also accepted Tylor's concept of cultural survivals and presented a paper on that topic at the International Congress of Anthropology, in which Putnam, Nuttall, and Boas also participated (Stevenson 1893b). Stevenson's views on cultural evolution, like Putnam's and Nuttall's, became obsolete with the ascendency of Boasian anthropology (Darnell 1974:175).

Along with other members of the Furness-Mitchell Coterie, Stevenson participated actively in clubs and professional societies with interests related to anthropology. She became president of the Oriental Club of Philadelphia, the Contemporary Club, and the Pennsylvania Chapter of the Archaeological Institute of America and acted as founder and officer of the University Archaeological Association, the American Folk-Lore Society, and the American Exploration Society. She also belonged to the Numismatic and Antiquarian Society of Philadelphia and was admitted to the American Philosophical Society (APS) in 1895 with Zelia Nuttall. A member of the American Association for the Advancement of Science (AAAS) since 1884, she was elected a Fellow in 1895.

These organizations ranged from social clubs to professional societies and played widely varying roles, but all fostered the growth of anthropology in Philadelphia. For example, the Contemporary Club, established in 1886 to invite prominent speakers to lecture on a wide range of topics, had no commitment to scholarship in a particular discipline. Nevertheless, because its leaders (many of them Furness-Mitchell Coterie members) were interested in anthropology, the Contemporary Club popularized anthropological topics through lectures ranging from "Savage Life in Australia" by Daniel Brinton, to "What Philadelphia Has Done in Babylonia."

At the other end of the spectrum were professional societies that encouraged research and served as forums for scholarly debates and publications. Among these were the APS, the AAAS, the Oriental Club of Philadelphia, the Numismatic and Antiquarian Society of Philadelphia, the American Folk-Lore Society, and the American Exploration Society. The University Archaeological Association was established to promote archaeology and fund archaeological research and publications at the University of Pennsylvania.

Stevenson's most lasting contribution lies in her key role in founding Pennsylvania's University Museum. In 1887 the University of Pennsylvania's Board of Trustees accepted a proposal from private donors seeking to fund a Babylonian Expedition if the university would provide a suitable museum for the artifacts (UMA, Box 1, Chronology: University Museum Development.)[3] Two years later William Pepper reserved the upper rooms of Penn's new library to house archaeology collections. He, Stevenson, and others worked to establish a proper museum at Pennsylvania, raising funds and obtaining land from the city to erect a building. In 1899 the first section of the University Museum was dedicated (UMA, Box 3, Stevenson to Pepper).

In 1891 the University Archaeological Association appointed Stevenson, Pepper, Talcott Williams (who had strong interests in Middle Eastern archaeology), and Joseph H. Coates to meet with the trustees of the University of Pennsylvania to create a department of archaeology and palaeontology that would establish and manage a museum. Stevenson served on the governing board of the department from its inception in 1892 until 1905. This board had full charge of the collections, explorations, and publications.

From 1890 to 1905 Stevenson also served as unpaid curator of the Egyptian and Mediterranean section of the museum, responsible for the day-to-day management and exhibition of the Egyptian and Mediterranean collections. Though the Peabody Museum (Harvard), the American Museum of Natural History (New York City), the Field Museum (Chicago), and the Smithsonian Institution (Washington, D.C.) were preeminent in American archaeology, Stevenson held that the University Museum was preeminent, if not unique, in the archaeology of Old World civilizations (UMA, Box 2, Early History of the Museum 1892–1902). It held this position in large part through Stevenson's efforts.

As curator, she focused on two main objectives. First, she sought to establish the University Museum as a force in archaeological fieldwork in Egypt through her work with the American Exploration Society, and to promote scientific exploration, research, and publication (Wilson 1979:12–15). Through Stevenson's efforts the American Exploration Society joined forces with the Egypt Exploration Fund in 1898 (UMA, Box 3, Director's Office Records).

In 1897 and 1898 Stevenson left her family and journeyed to Rome for the Department of Archaeology and Palaeontology and to Egypt as a representative of the American Exploration Society. She returned to Philadelphia with forty-two boxes of artifacts excavated by her agent at Dendorah. Despite this promising start, she was unable to establish University Museum fieldwork in Egypt because she could not find a competent excavator (Wilson 1979).

Stevenson's second objective as curator was to "build up a collection of excavated material, of works of art and objects that would be thoroughly representative of all periods and regions of ancient Egypt.'' (She accomplished this objective by working with British archaeologist William Flinders-Petrie, who is credited with introducing scientific archaeological principles into Egyptian excavations during the 1880s and 1890s.) Thus, the University Museum benefited immensely from this phase of Egyptian fieldwork and from Stevenson's policy, which led to an unmatched completeness of the scientific record. The University Museum's Egyptian collection is distinctive because the artifacts were almost entirely excavated, unlike the collections of other museums that were acquired primarily by purchase (Wilson 1979:12–15).

Stevenson always chafed under restrictions based upon sex. She was keenly aware of—but undaunted by—the difficulties women faced in a man's world. Her strong feelings on such matters prompted her to call a meeting to establish the Equal Franchise Society of Pennsylvania (1909). Serving as president until 1910, and later as first vice president, she actively participated in the society until the passage of the Federal Suffrage Amendment in 1920.

Sara Yorke Stevenson was an active member of a network of influential nineteenth-century anthropologists. Her participation in clubs and societies stimulated, organized, and focused anthropological interest in Philadelphia. She exercised leadership in creating the University Museum and in building collections. As curator of the museum's Egyptian and Mediterranean section, Stevenson linked the Museum to innovative and fruitful fieldwork and implemented forward-thinking policies of acquiring excavated artifacts. Together, these activities went far toward providing the museum with a collection of great scientific significance.

Notes

1. Z. Nuttall to S. Y. Stevenson, 1894, Director's Office Records, Box 2, Zelia Nuttall Folder, The University Museum Archives, University of Pennsylvania, Philadelphia (henceforth UMA); and S. Y. Stevenson note, Fall 1893, Director's Office Records, Box 3, Folder 1, UMA.

2. Lectures on Anthropology, Peabody Museum, 1894, Director's Office Records, Box 2, "University Archaeological Association 1889–1903" Folder, UMA.

3. "Chronology: University Museum Development," Director's Office Records, Box 1, "University Museum—Narratives Describing the History and Holdings" Folder, UMA.

References and Works About Sara Yorke Stevenson

Dictionary of American Biography
1935   *DAB*. Malone, Dumas, ed. Vol 17, pp. 635–36. New York: Charles Scribner & Sons.
Meyerson, Martin, and Dilys Pegler Winegrad
1978   *Gladly Learn and Gladly Teach*. Pp. 117–29. Philadelphia: University of Pennsylvania Press.

Starr, Frederick
1892 Anthropolgical Work in America. *Popular Science Monthly* 41:289–307.
Van Ness, Christine Moon
1985 The Furness-Mitchell Coterie: Its Role in Philadelphia's Intellectual Life at the Turn of the Twentieth Century. Unpublished Ph.D. Diss., University of Pennsylvania.
Wilson, John
1979 Signs and Wonders upon Pharaoh: The Story of American Egyptology. *Expedition* 21 (2).
Wister, Frances A.
1922 *Sara Yorke Stevenson*. Philadelphia: University of Pennsylvania.

Selected Works by Sara Yorke Stevenson

1892a On Certain Symbols Used in the Decoration of Some Potsherds from Daphnae and Naukratis, Now in the Museum of the University of Pennsylvania. *Proceedings of the Numismatic and Antiquarian Society of Philadelphia, 1890–91*. Pp. 1–51.
1892b The Tomb of King Amenhotep. *Papers on Egyptian Archaeology*.
1892c Mr. Petrie's Discoveries at Telel-Amarna. *Science* 19:480–82, 510.
1893a Report of the Curator of the Egyptian and Mediterranean Section, Department of Archaeology and Palaeontology, University of Pennsylvania.
1893b An Ancient Egyptian Rite Illustrating a Phase of Primitive Thought. In *Memoirs of the International Congress of Anthropology*. Pp. 298–311. Chicago: Schulte Publishing Co.
1894a The Feather and the Wing in Early Mythology. *Oriental Studies*. Oriental Club of Philadelphia. Pp. 1–39.
1894b Some Sculptures from Koptos in Philadelphia. Department of Archaeology and Palaeontology, University of Pennsylvania. Pp. 347–51.
1895 Exhibit of the Section of Egypt and the Mediterranean, Atlanta Exposition. Department of Archaeology and Palaeontology, University of Pennsylvania.
1896 On the Remains of the Foreignors [sic] Discovered in Egypt by Mr. W. M. Flinders Petrie, 1895, Now in the Museum of the University of Pennsylvania. *Proceedings of the American Philosophical Society* 35:57–64.
1901 Egypt, Babylonia and Greece. *Report of the Committee on Awards of the World's Columbian Commission*. Special Reports upon Special Subjects or Groups, 1:335–346. Washington, D.C.: GPO.
1909 The Training of Curators. *Proceedings of the American Association of Museums* 3:115–19.

Coauthored Works

Stevenson, S. Y., Morris Jastrow, Jr., and Ferdinand Justi
1905 *Egypt and Western Asia in Antiquity*. Philadelphia: Lea Brothers.

CHRISTINE MOON VAN NESS

Clara Lee Fraps Tanner

(1905–   )

American cultural anthropologist Clara Lee Fraps Tanner is known for her research, publications, and public lectures on the craft arts, especially basketry, of prehistoric and historic Southwest American Indians.

Clara Lee Fraps was born on May 28, 1905, to Joseph Conrad and Clara Dargon Lee Fraps, in Biscoe, North Carolina, far from the Indian villages of the desert Southwest where she conducted most of her research. In 1907 her family moved to Tucson, Arizona, where her father worked as a railroad machinist. Except for a brief stay (1913–17) in Clifton, Arizona, she has since remained a resident of Tucson.

After graduating from high school in 1923, she planned to major in journalism but decided to stay in Tucson to care for her ailing mother. She then enrolled at the University of Arizona, where she worked on the university newspaper and yearbook.

While enrolled at the university, Fraps took an archaeology class taught by Dean Byron Cummings. Cummings encouraged her to become one of the first students to graduate with a major in archaeology from the university. She graduated with a double major in English and archaeology in 1927. That year Florence Hawley Ellis and Emil Haury joined her as the first B.A. recipients and in 1928 were awarded the first M.A.s from the Department of Archaeology. Although small, these graduating classes were of high quality and very competitive. Of those days, Haury recalls, "You talk about women's lib. I had to fight like hell to keep my head above water with those two women."[1]

Dean Cummings invited her to teach Greek and Roman archaeology in the fall semester. Fraps spent the summer of 1928 in Europe studying art and archaeological materials to prepare for the class. From 1928 until her retirement in 1978, she taught many different courses at the University of Arizona. She received additional training at the National University in Mexico City (1929) and at the Oriental Institute of the University of Chicago (1934).

In 1937 Emil Haury returned from Harvard University to chair the Department of Archaeology, which had by that time become the Department of Anthropology and offered an expanded list of courses. Haury next asked Fraps to develop a course in Southwestern archaeology and ethnology for nonanthropology majors, which attracted increasing numbers of students over the years. The first time she taught the class, she had 8 students; the last time she taught it in 1976, she had 140 and a waiting list. While this class became important to the department, it also supported her decision to concentrate her research on the native peoples of the Southwest.

Fraps's initial fieldwork experience occurred in 1930, when she participated in summer field classes in northern Arizona. One of her most vivid memories was the amusing experience of riding a mule, "Hell Ann," to various sites. She continued active archaeological and ethnological research at San Carlos and the Tanque Verde ruins in Arizona. This interest and research continue today.

As Haury recalls, the field of archaeology in the 1920s and 1930s was less theoretically based than it is now. "To a large extent, much of the work being done was 'window shopping,' inspired by the appeal of the sites or because they were there, rather than by a sense of a perceived problem" (Haury 1985:384). The first Pecos Conference (1927), which both Fraps and Haury attended, redirected the discipline: "it not only gave structure to what was then known of the Southwest, but also provided a certain stimulus to work in lesser-known areas. People began to compare notes and plot new courses of investigation" (Haury 1985:384).

By the 1930s archaeologists had become more appreciative of the value of artifacts for interpreting culture, and they started writing detailed site reports. To those who have criticized earlier archaeologists for being content with finding and describing material culture rather than excavating to test some hypothesis, both Fraps and Haury have responded that they did excavate with some idea or purpose, but that they simply didn't label these ideas as theories. "I don't see how anybody can do archaeological investigation without some theory."

This lack of emphasis on theory in archaeology changed radically starting in the 1960s and 1970s, when the "New Archaeology" emerged. Haury states:

Where the efforts to understand the past up to then were said to be without adequate problem orientations, . . . and weak in "theory" development, we now had an approach that promised unheard-of insights. . . . Those of us who were involved in shaping the direction of archaeology in the 1930s, then "new," found a certain reason to be amused at hearing the trend dubbed "New Archaeology." Growth and changes in science should be seen as a normal part of the maturing process. (Haury 1985:391)

Tanner now expresses deep concern regarding the new emphasis on theory, which she feels fails to recognize the importance of material culture and field experience. In order to develop archaeological theories, archaeologists, she states, need "to dig in the dirt. . . . What contribution can you make without such experience?'' While some theory is necessary, she thinks that many present theories are not well founded; instead she advocates fewer but sounder theories based on knowledge of material culture and good field experience.

She had decided to concentrate her own research on past and present Southwestern native peoples and their cultures, particularly their craft arts. Her opportunity to know Indians grew when she married John F. Tanner in 1936. John soon started trading with the Southwestern Indians and subsequently opened an Indian craft art store in Tucson. Because of John's profession, Clara Tanner began to view Indian crafts unlike many other anthropologists. ''Some anthropologists,'' she commented, ''damn the commercial too frequently. Without commercialism there would be very little Indian art today. . . . The Navajo blanket went to rugs by the influence of traders. . . . The majority of pottery today is directed at the white man.'' Thus, Tanner believes that non-Indian demand for Indian crafts may actually perpetuate the old art form. When change occurs, she does not view this as negative but rather as inevitable.

The Tanners' careers and interests promoted not only her teaching and research but especially her writing. She is probably best known for her many books and articles on Southwestern Indian craft arts. Concerning these publications, her colleague Arthur Jelinek states, ''No other individual in the field has the control of the material that she has.''

Her numerous honors include the following: 50th Anniversary Award of the Gallup Inter-Tribal Ceremonial Association (1971); Arizona Press Women's Woman of the Year (1971); Faculty Recognition Award, Tucson Trade Bureau (1973); Faculty Achievement Award, University of Arizona Alumni Association (1974); Honorary Doctor of Letters, University of Arizona (1983); and the Sharlot Hall Award (1985), given to a woman who has made a valuable contribution to the understanding of Arizona and its history.

Clara Lee Tanner's retirement in 1978 has not greatly changed her life. Indeed, John Tanner states, ''she does not know she's retired.'' She keeps her office and maintains ties with both graduates and undergraduates. She and her husband both lecture about Southwestern culture and judge art and craft shows together. She continues to have professional contact with fellow anthropologists, including Haury, Jelinek, and Ellis. Her memories of her career remain warm.

Tanner recalls that she did find her lack of a Ph.D. both financially and professionally limiting. She had academic credits, but her family concerns—first for her mother, then for her husband and daughter (Sandra Lee, born in 1940)—did not allow her to leave Tucson and complete her degree. Both Haury and Jelinek concur that the lack of a Ph.D. hurt her academically and may have slowed her promotion to full professor. Haury believes that despite the lack of a doctorate, she was still influential in the department and ''made up for formality by getting recognition through her writing.'' Commenting on Tanner's influence on the field of anthropology, he states, ''She brought distinction to the department by her own efforts in Indian arts and crafts.''

Note

1. All quotes unless otherwise acknowledged are from personal interviews with Clara
Lee Tanner, John F. Tanner, Emil Haury, and Arthur Jelinek.

Selected Works by Clara Lee Fraps Tanner

1935a Hopi Land. *Arizona Historical Review* 6 (3): 3–46.
1935b Old World Archaeology As an Asset in Interpreting American Prehistory. *The Kiva* 1 (1): 3.
1935c Tanque Verde Ruins. *The Kiva* 1 (4): 1–4.
1936 Blackstone Ruin. *The Kiva* 2 (3): 1–12.
1939 Synopsis of Excavations at Snaketown. Vol. 1. *The Kiva* 4 (8): 31–34.
1943a Indians in the War Effort. *The Kiva* 8 (3): 22–24.
1943b Life Forms on Prehistoric Pottery of the Southwest. *The Kiva* 8 (4): 26–32.
1944a Basketry of the Modern Southwestern Indians. *The Kiva* 9 (3): 18–26.
1944b Pottery of the Modern Southwestern Indians. *The Kiva* 10 (1): 3–12.
1947a Southwest Painted Pottery. *Arizona Quarterly* 3 (1): 49–60.
1947b Southwest Painted Pottery II, The Historic Period. *Arizona Quarterly* 3 (2): 138–50.
1948a Sandpaintings of the Indians of the Southwest. *The Kiva* 13 (3–4): 22–36.
1948b Southwestern Chronicle: Southwest Indian Arts and Crafts. *Arizona Quarterly* 4 (3): 256–72.
1949a Southwest Indian Painting. *Southwest Review* 34 (1): 73–80.
1949b–1950a Arizona Indians. *The Kiva* 15 (1–4): 1–16.
1950b Coral Among Southwestern Indians. In *For the Dean, Essays in Honor of Byron Cummings*. Santa Fe: Hohokam Museums Association and Southwest Monuments Association.
1950c Ventana Cave Textiles. In *Ventana Cave*. Emil Haury et al., eds. Tucson: University of Arizona Press; Albuquerque: University of New Mexico Press.
1954–1955 Southwestern Indian Watercolors. *The Kiva* 20 (2–3): 11–14.
1957 *Southwest Indian Painting*. Tucson: University of Arizona Press and Arizona Silhouettes.
1960 Contemporary Southwest Indian Silver. *The Kiva* 25 (3): 1–22.
1965 Papago Burden Baskets in the Arizona State Museum. *The Kiva* 30 (3): 57–76.
1968 *Southwest Indian Craft Arts*. Tucson: University of Arizona Press.
1970 Finished in Beauty. *Contemporary Indian Affairs* 1 (3).
1973 *Southwest Indian Painting: A Changing Art*. Tucson: University of Arizona Press.
1976a *Arizona Highways Indian Arts and Crafts*. Phoenix: Arizona Highways. (As ed.)
1976b *Prehistoric Southwestern Craft Arts*. Tucson: The University of Arizona Press.
1978 The Squash Blossom. *American Indian Art* 3 (3).
1982a *Apache Indian Baskets*. Tucson: The University of Arizona Press.
1982b Western Apache Baskets. *Plateau* 53 (4): 23–32.
1982c The Naja. *American Indian Art Magazine* 7 (2).
1984 *Indian Baskets of the Southwest*. Tucson: The University of Arizona Press.
1985 Southwest Indian Gold Jewelry. *The Kiva* 50 (4): 201–18.

Coauthored Works

Tanner, Clara Lee, and Anne Forbes
1948   Indian Arts Fund Collection of Paintings. *El Palacio* 55 (12): 363–80.

JAMIE LYTLE-WEBB

Ruth Murray Underhill

(1883–1984)

Ruth Murray Underhill, ethnographer, civil servant, and author, was known for her work with Southwest Indian groups, especially the Papago, as well as her more general books and pamphlets on North American Indians.

As early as 1636 one of Ruth Murray Underhill's pioneering ancestors was in North America. Ironically, Captain John Underhill was an Indian fighter, and a depiction of one of his military victories hung on the wall of the log home Ruth Underhill built in Denver, Colorado, more than three centuries later. She was born on August 22, 1883 (although a widely printed but erroneous date has her born in 1884), into a pacifist family. Both her mother, Anna Murray Underhill, and her father, Abram Sutton Underhill, a lawyer, were members of the Society of Friends, or Quakers. Her Quaker upbringing stressed the unintrusive and quiet social interaction, which was, decades later, basic to her approach to the Papagos in her Ph.D. fieldwork.

The Underhills lived on a farm in Ossining, on the east bank of the Hudson River north of New York City, to which her father traveled three days a week to practice law. He had amassed a large library that included books by Darwin and other representatives of the ''new thought'' of the late nineteenth century. Underhill had access both to that library and to her uncle Augustus Murray, a teacher of Greek, with whom she studied when she was fourteen years old.

Despite having two sisters and a brother, Underhill reported that she had liked doing things by herself:

I just got that way early in childhood and kept it up. I had a very lonesome childhood. I was always alone; I had to think of ways of doing for myself. And now I rather resent being put into a bunch of other people. . . . From very early years, . . . I just happened to like it, the less personal world . . . and I was always quite a foreigner to the girls' gossip, in our little circle.[1]

Underhill attended the Ossining School for girls and the Preparatory School for Bryn Mawr. She chose, however, to enroll at Vassar College, whose president at that time was "a nice portly gentleman [who] felt that his function was to prepare us for marriage." At Vassar she majored in English, won a prize with an essay on Shakespeare, and was elected to Phi Beta Kappa. She graduated with her A.B. degree in 1905. Afterward she worked in Boston as agent for the Massachusetts Society for the Prevention of Cruelty to Children, and from 1906 to 1908 she traveled and studied in Europe. She took courses at the London School of Economics and the University of Munich, adding to her knowledge of languages. She ultimately spoke French, German, Italian, and Spanish, as well as Papago.

Upon her return to New York, Underhill was employed by several social work agencies in the city just before World War I. She worked with the American Red Cross during the war. At times, in addition to her social work, she wrote a column for the *New York Sun* and tried magazine writing and advertising. Much later, thinking about this part of her life, she said: "I sometimes wonder whether I might not just have been a writer for life, instead of an anthropologist. But anthropology gave me some good subjects, of course . . . [but also] you can get them out of life by just looking at it."

Underhill's first novel, *White Moth*, published in 1920, featured a business-woman as heroine and explored the role of men and women in the work environment. In the book, successful at having struck out on her own, the heroine has been promoted to a supervisory position when her schooldays sweetheart reappears as an employee. He is revealed, in contrast to her, to be cautious and uninventive. The book was favorably reviewed as a romance novel. One New York reviewer, however, felt that its true merit was its treatment of such new aspects of modern life as the problems of factory management and the business rivalry between men and women.

Like her *White Moth*'s heroine, Underhill rejected conventional women's roles. She once told a reporter that upon graduation from Vassar her choices—marriage or teaching—had looked "tame" and so, rather than choosing either at that time, she had gone into social work. Of her subsequent marriage, Underhill said that she "just got the wrong man." She and Charles Crawford ended their childless union in a divorce.

Underhill remembered going directly from the steps of the courthouse where she filed for divorce to the campus of Columbia University. Although she could have continued to live on and manage the family's Hudson River farm, she thought that would be boring; and she understandably felt just then that she knew very little about what really went on in the lives of people. She chose a university setting as the place to seek her answers. Thus it happened that, when she had found the Department of Anthropology at Columbia, Ruth Benedict* said to her, "So you want to know about people. Come on in, then, this is the place." Underhill became a middle-aged graduate student there. Her involvement with the discipline of anthropology was immediate and total:

It really just absorbed my life for a while. I was completely given up to it, and now when I see people who take it as one of six courses or so . . . I'm surprised that anyone could regard it as such an unimportant thing, because to me it was the important thing in life. I had now found what you needed to know about human nature in order to get along with human nature. I really felt I'd got to the source. Of course that opinion withered a little, in time. But when I first took anthropology, that was really how I felt. And it was a great joy.

She was, however, set apart from the majority of her fellow students, not only by her sex but also by her age, although her translations of Latin and Greek were sometimes helpful to them. She believed that Franz Boas, chair of the department, may have thought of her as marginal and perhaps a frivolous divorcée, merely entertaining herself. When the time came for her to do her fieldwork, however, Boas offered her a small amount of money for research with the Papago, a then little-studied tribe. According to Underhill, Boas assisted her because he felt that two classes of people, women and Jews, had not gotten what they deserved.

Underhill attributed her success in her Papago fieldwork to her Quaker upbringing as well as to being female. Half a century later she recalled:

I had no introductions of any sort. I just walked in, and having been taught in my youth that women should always be rather quiet and not push themselves, I followed that prescription. Perhaps it was not just because I was female but a Quaker. Quakers don't push themselves anyway. . . . And of course the men . . . come with a pad and pencil— they do now—and walk up to the leader, headman, of the group, and say, "Now, how many people in your village?" It never occurred to me to do that. I just sat down with the women and asked them, "Oh, what is it that you're doing?" . . . And then the women—I approached the women and not the men—accepted this event and I moved in. I got along very well with the women. . . .

The information she brought back to Columbia caused Boas to set aside whatever doubts he may have had about Underhill's dedication to anthropology. While she was in graduate school, Underhill was to go, in all, four times to the Papago reservation. The trips were financed not only by grants obtained by Boas but also by a variable and sometimes small amount given her annually by her father. Her Ph.D. dissertation "Social Organization of the Papago Indians" (1939), was funded in part by fellowships from the Columbia Humanities Council.

While still a graduate student at Columbia, she was employed at Barnard College as assistant in anthropology under Gladys Reichard.* In the summer of 1934, having completed her Ph.D. fieldwork, she and Reichard participated in an experimental seminar, called the Hogan School, in which the Bureau of Indian Affairs (BIA) aimed to teach Navajos to write the Navajo language. Underhill also taught an in-service course in what was called applied ethnology for BIA employees that summer. The following year Reichard attempted to secure a job for her in the Indian Service; and it was apparently as a result of these efforts, as well as her success in the applied ethnology course, that she was hired that summer (1935) to give a series of lectures at the Sherman Indian Institute in Riverside, California. The goal of these workshops was to familiarize and sensitize BIA personnel, almost all of whom were non-Indian, to tribes with whom they were or might be working. Underhill expanded on the short course of the preceding summer and utilized cross-cultural information to present an overview of North American Indians. Her successful presentations came to the attention of the superintendent of Sherman Institute, and at summer's end he recommended that Underhill's appointment be continued for an additional four months. In that period she was to write up her lectures as a series of pamphlets for publication, for among its other activities, Sherman Institute printed educational materials for the BIA. The fall appointment was not made until November 1935. By then Underhill had been called to Papago tribal headquarters in Sells, Arizona, for the tribe's review of the proposed Papago constitution.

Under the leadership of John Collier, the Bureau of Indian Affairs was at the time moving toward granting a greater degree of self-governance to tribes that would adopt BIA-approved constitutions. Collier had expected that anthropologists would be heavily involved in the writing of the tribal constitutions as well as in the tribal review process, but the appointments of anthropologists had been delayed so long that the constitutions had for the most part been drawn up by lawyers, as had the proposed Papago constitution. In Underhill's judgment the Papago constitution did not reflect the realities of Papago social organization and economics, so she argued strenuously against its adoption. As a result, she was from that time on never again allowed to participate in government projects dealing with the tribe.

In the spring of 1935 Underhill had taken the newly instituted Civil Service examination for ethnologists and been placed on the future employee register. However, when she and several other eligible anthropologists were subsequently hired, it was not as ethnologists but as so-called soil conservationists by the better-funded Soil Conservation Service. Because of their knowledge of a culture and their sensitivity to it, these "soil conservationists" were to help prevent fiascos in government planning, such as the stock reduction program on the Navajo reservation. More immediately, they were to conduct surveys of economic and social life among various Southwestern groups. One of Collier's special assistants probably accurately foresaw that such a project, conducted by highly educated outsiders, would be viewed with suspicion and resentment by on-the-spot BIA employees, who often lacked formal training, and so he emphasized the importance of "the right personality and the proper perspective" on the part of the newcomers. He then proceeded to remove Underhill as head of the Papago survey team because he felt BIA personnel would resent her involvement in the project and because his personal experience with professional women in administrative and executive positions had been most discouraging. Underhill did not take part in the Papago survey, and it was never published.

During the following summer she again participated in the BIA's in-service workshop. That fall Willard W. Beatty, newly appointed as director of Indian education for the BIA, requested that the Soil Conservation Service lend Underhill to them for twelve months so that she could complete work on the descriptive pamphlets begun earlier. (Underhill eventually wrote all but one of the eight titles in the Indian Life and Customs series.) She was officially transferred from the Soil Conservation Service to the BIA in 1937, and early in 1938 was promoted to associate supervisor of Indian education. For the next seven years she traveled almost constantly from her home base in Santa Fe, New Mexico. She worked with reservation teachers and was especially concerned with the curriculum development in Indian schools. In the fall of 1944 Underhill was promoted to supervisor of Indian education and transferred to Denver.

At the end of World War II, the Bureau of Indian Affairs was reorganized, and Underhill found her civil service career in jeopardy. Beatty, however, was able to arrange a series of temporary appointments for her, and then a six-month leave of absence "for special work at the University of Oklahoma" so that she could complete the small amount of time remaining for her to qualify for retirement.

She retired from civil service at the end of October 1948 and immediately began to teach in the Department of Anthropology at the University of Denver. She was a professor there until 1952, when "they put me out because of my age." After this retirement Underhill embarked on an extended trip around the world (1952 and 1953). In 1955 and 1956 she again taught anthropology, first at the New York State Teachers College in New Paltz (now the State University of New York College at New Paltz) and then at Colorado Women's College. During the nearly three decades still remaining, from 1956 until her death on August 14, 1984, Underhill spent her time traveling occasionally, writing, and consulting on a formal and informal basis. She was honored in 1979 by the Papagos in a very special ceremony in Sells, where her fieldwork had begun more than four decades earlier.

On June 28, 1984, the president of the American Anthropological Association, Nancy O. Lurie,* flew to Denver to present Underhill with the association's special recognition citation. Underhill was honored for popularizing anthropology in a responsible manner, for her early work in applied anthropology and the study of women's roles, and for her scholarship and teaching.

Lurie characterized this professional recognition as a long time in coming. Underhill felt this also was true of her personal growth. Looking back over the course of her life she said:

I was a very meek and good little girl. I was told that women were to take a second place in the world and be helpless behind men—be very useful and able, but not to push themselves forward. And I was little when I was told that, and it stuck for a long time. . . . You do get rid of it before you die. It took me a while.

Note

1. Unless otherwise cited, all quotes in this biography are from interviews conducted with Ruth Underhill at her home in Denver in November 1981. I would like to thank my mother, Leslie Jones, and her friend Gladys Parce for facilitating my interviews with Ruth Underhill, and Mary Coen for making the interviews so enjoyable and for her subsequent help. Thanks also to Lawrence Kelly for information on Underhill's civil service career.

Selected Works by Ruth Murray Underhill

1936   Autobiography of a Papago Woman. *Memoirs of the American Anthropological Association*, no. 46. Supplement to *American Anthropologist* 38 (3), part 2.

1938a A Papago Calendar Record. *University of New Mexico Bulletin Anthropological Series* 2(5). (Reprinted 1980, New York: AMS Press.)

1938b *The First Penthouse Dwellers of America*. New York: J. J. Augustin.

1938c *Singing for Power: The Song Magic of the Papago Indians of Southern Arizona*. Berkeley: University of California Press. (Reprinted 1973, New York: Ballantine Books; and 1968, 1976, Berkeley: University of California Press.)

1939   Social Organization of the Papago Indians. *Columbia University Contributions to Anthropology* 30. New York: Columbia University Press. (Reprinted 1969, New York: AMS Press.)

1940   *Hawk over Whirlpools*. New York: J. J. Augustin.

1941   *The Northern Paiute Indians of California and Nevada*. William W. Beatty, gen. ed. Washington: Education Division, U.S. Office of Indian Affairs. (Reprinted 1980, New York: AMS Press.)

1946   Papago Indian Religion. *Columbia University Contributions to Anthropology* 33. New York: Columbia University Press.

1948   *Ceremonial Patterns in the Greater Southwest*. American Ethnological Society Monographs, 13. New York: J. J. Augustin. (Reprinted 1966, Seattle: University of Washington Press.)

1953a *Here Come the Navajo!* Lawrence, Kansas: Haskell Institute Press. (Reprinted 1983, Tucson, Ariz.: Treasure Chest Publications.)

1953b *Red Man's America: A History of Indians in the United States*. Chicago: University of Chicago Press.

1956   *The Navajos*. Norman: University of Oklahoma Press.

1958   *First Came the Family*. New York: William Morrow.

1959   *Beaverbird*. New York: Coward-McCann.

1961   *Antelope Singer*. New York: Coward-McCann.

1965   *Red Man's Religion: Beliefs and Practices of the Indians North of Mexico*. Chicago: University of Chicago Press.

JOYCE GRIFFEN

Ruth Sawtell Wallis

(1895–1978)

American physical anthropologist Ruth Sawtell Wallis was known for her analysis of Azilian skeletal remains excavated in France, work in children's growth studies, and ethnography of the Micmac Indians of eastern Canada.

Ruth Sawtell was born on March 15, 1895, in Springfield, Massachusetts. She was the first child of Grace Quimby and Joseph Otis Sawtell. Her father operated a haberdashery in Springfield, where Ruth Sawtell attended local public schools.

After graduating from high school, Sawtell attended Vassar College in 1913, later transferring to Radcliffe College. She graduated cum laude from Radcliffe in 1919, with a B.A. in English, and was elected to Phi Beta Kappa and Sigma Xi honor societies. After working for one year, Sawtell decided to go on with graduate studies. She was influenced by E. A. Hooten's work in physical anthropology at Harvard University and entered Radcliffe to major in anthropology. Hooten and Tozzer, her professors, "asserted that most young women in graduate work abandon it if they married. They added, however, that if she had serious intentions to study, they would help her in every way" (Collins 1979:85). She worked her way through graduate school at Harvard's Peabody Museum (1920–23) and was assistant editor of the Harvard African Studies series and research assistant for the Andover Pecos expedition. Sawtell received her M.A. in Anthropology from Radcliffe in 1923 at the age of twenty-eight.

Because of a Traveling Fellowship in Science from Radcliffe, donated to the college by Mrs. William G. Farlow, Sawtell was able to do research in France, Germany, and England (1923–25). With friends Ida Treat, who had her doctorate from the Université de Paris, and Ida's husband, artist Paul Vaillant-Couterier, she excavated two Azilian graves, at Montardit in the French Pyrenees.

The Mesolithic Azilian culture, found throughout the Pyrenees, in England, and on the west coast of Scotland is characterized by a material culture that used microliths, flat harpoons, and painted pebbles. While Azilian artifacts and some human bone fragments had been discovered at Mas d'Azil in France, the burials at Sawtell's site were the first Azilian skeletons found in that country. Her work provided some of the evidence for a more gradual transition in human physical types between the Upper Paleolithic and Neolithic in France, as well as documented Azilian material culture.

Based on these investigations, she wrote both a scholarly work and a popular account. Her research was first reported to the American Anthropological Association in December 1925 and published as *Azilian Skeletal Remains from Montardit (Ariege) France* (Wallis, 1931a). It is a detailed description and analysis of the Azilian skeletons found at the site. In addition, she wrote *Primitive Hearths in the Pyrenees* (1927) in collaboration with Ida Treat. Aimed toward a more popular audience, the book talks about the process of an excavation and the village reaction to the excavators, gives a history of Paleolithic cultures in the Pyrenees, and describes and illustrates many rock art sites in the area.

Upon her return from France, Sawtell transferred to Columbia University, Department of Anthropology, then chaired by Franz Boas. She worked for Boas as a research assistant in 1926, analyzing changes in head form among immigrants. A restudy of Boas's earlier research on plasticity of head form, her part in the project was to take complete measurements of both parents and children of Sicilian families in New York. She told friends that one reason that Boas hired her was that Sicilian men in 1926 would never have allowed a male researcher to measure their wives, so a female research assistant was required for that part of the study. Inspired by Boas's studies on the growth of children, Sawtell began her doctoral work in that area.

From 1926 to 1930 she worked as a physical anthropologist for the Bureau of Educational Experiments, now the prestigious Bank Street College of Education, in New York City. Founded in 1917 by three women for the purposes of educational research, the progressive institution operated a demonstration nursery school. Staff scientists used both qualitative observational and quantitative anthropometric techniques to build an organic picture of child development and growth.

Fully supported by the bureau and given the freedom to define her own area of inquiry, Sawtell used radiography and direct measurement to study the growth of young children. The data she collected became the basis of her doctoral thesis, "Ossification and Growth of Children from One to Eight Years of Age" (1929). In her dissertation she sought to develop information dealing with the growth of normal children, using statistical analysis to correlate the rate of ossification of carpal centers of children's hands with traits such as stature, weight, sex, size of diaphysis, and other medical observations. She found some correlation between rate of ossification, sex, and gross bodily weight.

In 1929 physical anthropology was a relatively new discipline in the United States. Harvard University was the only institution that offered a Ph.D. program in physical anthropology; other university departments had a decided bias toward ethnology. Sawtell did both applied and academic research in the new field, bringing six years of experience to it when she received her doctorate.

Ruth Sawtell became a charter member of the American Association of Physical Anthropologists in 1930. She was one of the few physical anthropologists to join, the majority of the members being anatomists with a special interest in physical anthropology. Of the eighty-three charter members, only two were women, Mildred Totter and Ruth Sawtell. This organization was critical in establishing the legitimacy of physical anthropology as a science and currently has a membership of over 1,100. The same year, Sawtell was hired as an assistant professor of anthropology at the University of Iowa, where she continued her intensive anthropometric study of children's growth, which resulted in a monograph, entitled *How Children Grow* (1931b).

She married Wilson D. Wallis, a widower with two children and a well-known cultural anthropologist, in 1931. After their marriage, she moved to Minneapolis, where Wilson Wallis was a professor of anthropology at the University of Minnesota. Wallis was hired as an assistant professor of sociology, at Hamline University in St. Paul, where she taught until 1935. June Collins, a friend and former student, recalls that Wallis had always felt that she was fired from her post at Hamline, in the midst of the Depression, because of envy over the dual income that the academic couple enjoyed.[1] In addition, as a married woman whose husband worked in the same field, her possibilities for advancement in teaching were also limited by the antinepotism rules of most institutions.

As a new Ph.D. Ruth Sawtell Wallis's career was directed as much by the economic conditions of the Depression era as it was by academic prejudice toward women. Cut short by lack of funding, professional jealousy, and the attitudes of the day toward married women in academia, her independent professional career was eclipsed. From 1935 to 1956 she worked primarily in collaboration with her husband.

Wallis worked with the Works Progress Administration (WPA) from 1935 to 1937, and with her husband wrote volumes number 2 through 7 of a 7-volume treatise on how cultures all over the world perceived or named natural phenomena, as reported in folktales and ethnographies. Entitled "Primitive Science," it was never published.

While employed as a physical anthropologist for the Bureau of Home Economics of the U.S. Department of Agriculture, she directed the measurement of over 10,000 school-aged children (1937–38). This project was part of a larger effort to gather data on children's growth and was the first major anthropometric survey of children ever conducted. Thirty-six different body measurements were taken of 147,088 children, ages four through seventeen (White 1978:50). This work led to the standardization of children's clothing sizes.

Ruth Wallis began a second career as a writer in 1940, writing a series of mystery novels, some with anthropological themes, that brought in much-appreciated income. Her first novel, *Too Many Bones* (1943) has a physical anthropologist as a heroine, and won the $1,000 Red Badge Prize for the best first mystery of the year. She wrote four other murder mysteries over the next ten years: *No Bones About It* (1944), *Blood from a Stone* (1945), *Cold Bed in the Clay* (1947), and *Forget My Fate* (1950).

Even while her independent career was curtailed, Wallis maintained an important role in encouraging the next generation of anthropologists, which included some financial support. Elizabeth Colson did her first fieldwork assisting Wallis on the Bureau of Home Economics study. More important, after Wallis had written her first novel, she gave $500 of the income to Colson. The money made a significant difference to the young anthropologist, for as Colson said, "In those days, $500 was a lot of money and it meant my first year at Radcliffe. I couldn't have made it without that." Wilson and Ruth Wallis also held informal seminars with speakers at their house, usually followed by a lively discussion.

In the 1950s Ruth Wallis conducted ethnographic fieldwork in collaboration with her husband. She collected material on the changing status of women and children among the Eastern Dakota people in Manitoba (1951 and 1952), resulting in two publications. *The Overt Fears of Dakota Indian Children* (Wallis 1954) looks at whether certain overt fears are the result of Dakota child-training methods, and *The Changed Status of Twins Among the Eastern Dakota* (Wallis 1955) compares the status of twins in two different Dakota groups. Wallis found the special status of twins changing relative to the degree of acculturation.

From 1950 to 1953 Ruth and Wilson Wallis spent some time among the Micmac and Malecite Indians. Their ethnography of the Micmac, *The Micmac Indians of Eastern Canada*, already begun by Wilson Wallis in 1911 and 1912, was expanded in 1955. Returning to the field as a husband and wife team, the Wallises sought to document the extent of Micmac culture loss and persistence relative to 1911, and to assess changes in attitudes and motivation. They found that by working together, and with the changed status of women's roles, communication with informants had become easier. They also published a monograph on the Malecite Indians entitled *The Malecite Indians of New Brunswick* (1957). After her husband retired from the University of Minnesota, the Wallises moved to Connecticut, and Ruth Wallis found a job teaching part-time at Annhurst College as a lecturer in sociology. Ten years later she was made full professor. Ruth Wallis retired in 1974, as Annhurst's first professor emerita. She died at the age of eighty-three, on January 21, 1978.

Ruth Sawtell Wallis's career had all the expansive hallmarks of the formative years of academic anthropology, as well as some of its limitations. She worked in archaeology, physical anthropology, and cultural anthropology; wrote; lectured; and did research. Her associates remember her as a woman who was bright, direct, sharp-witted, sometimes formidable, and generous.

In the field of archaeology, Wallis discovered and excavated the first Azilian skeletons in France, and her well-written popular account of the project made archaeology accessible to the general public.

In the field of physical anthropology, her contributions were many. Her analysis of Azilian skeletal remains became a link in chronology of the evolution of human form from the Paleolithic to the Neolithic. Wallis's work in children's growth studies added important knowledge on growth in normal, nonclinical children. As a charter member in the American Association of Physical Anthropologists, she contributed to the professional development of the discipline. In her applied work, primarily anthropometry, she was responsible in part for the standardization of children's clothing sizes.

Despite sharply limited possibilities for advancement, Wallis devoted most of her intellectual energy to her teaching and encouraged, and at times cajoled, the next generation of anthropologists, having a significant impact on their lives and careers.

Note

1. Unless otherwise cited, all quotes are from personal interviews with June Collins and Elizabeth Colson, to whom I am indebted for their assistance and support in researching this biography.

References and Works About Ruth Sawtell Wallis

Collins, June M.
1979   Ruth Sawtell Wallis 1895–1978. *American Anthropologist* 81:85–87.
White, Robert M.
1978   Anthropometry and Human Engineering. *Yearbook of Physical Anthropology* 28:42–62.

Selected Works by Ruth Sawtell Wallis

1928   Sex Differences in the Bone Growth of Young Children. *American Journal of Physical Anthropology* 12:293–302.
1929   Ossification and Growth of Children from One to Eight Years of Age. *American Journal of Diseases of Children* 37:61–87. (Reprinted 1929, Chicago: American Medical Association.)
1931a   Azilian Skeletal Remains from Montardit (Ariege) France. *Papers, Peabody Museum of American Archaeology and Ethnology* 11:213–53.
1931b   How Children Grow: An Anthropometric Study of Private School Children from Two to Eight Years of Age. *University of Iowa Studies in Child Welfare* 5 (1).
1931c   Irregular Ossification of the Extremities of Boys and Girls. *American Journal of Roentgenology and Radium Therapy* 25 (3).
1931d   Relative Growth of the Extremities from Two to Eighteen Years of Age. *American Journal of Physical Anthropology* 16:171–91.
1932   Harmonic Types Among Western European Crania. In *A Decade of Progress in Eugenics*. Scientific Papers of the Third International Congress of Eugenics.
1934   Cranial Relationships and Correlation. *Human Biology* 6:308–23.
1943   *Too Many Bones*. New York: Dodd, Mead and Co.
1944   *No Bones About It*. New York: Dodd, Mead and Co.
1945   *Blood from a Stone*. New York: Dodd, Mead and Co.

1947   *Cold Bed in the Clay*. New York: Dodd, Mead and Co.
1950   *Forget My Fate*. New York: Dodd, Mead and Co.
1954   The Overt Fears of Dakota Indian Children. *Child Development* 25:185–92.
1955   The Changed Status of Twins Among the Eastern Dakota. *Anthropological Quarterly* 28:116–20.

Coauthored Works

Wallis, Ruth Sawtell, and Estelle Fine Ritt
1930   Growth Studies by Roentgen Ray. *American Journal of Physical Anthropology* 14:1–5.
Wallis, Ruth Sawtell, and Ida Treat
1927   *Primitive Hearths in the Pyrenees*. New York: D. Appleton and Co.
Wallis, Ruth Sawtell, and Wilson D. Wallis
1946   Sex Differences in Cephalic Index During Growth. *Southwestern Journal of Anthropology* 2:56–83.
1953a Culture Loss and Culture Change Among the Micmac of the Canadian Maritime Provinces, 1912–1950. *Papers, Kroeber Anthropological Society*, nos. 8–9 Pp. 100–129.
1953b The Sins of the Fathers: Concept of Disease Among the Canadian Dakota. *Southwestern Journal of Anthropology* 9:431–35.
1955   *The Micmac Indians of Eastern Canada*. Minneapolis: University of Minnesota Press.
1957   The Malecite Indians of New Brunswick. *Bulletin, Canada National Museum*, no. 148; also, *Bulletin, Anthropological Series*, no. 40.
(n.d.) Primitive Science. Ms. 6 vols. Minneapolis: Works Progress Administration. Deposited in library, Peabody Museum, Harvard University.

PATRICIA CASE

Camilla Hildegarde Wedgwood

(1901–1955)

British social anthropologist Camilla Hildegarde Wedgwood was known especially for her studies of women and children on the island of Manam, New Guinea, and her efforts to improve secondary education for indigenous women in Oceania.

Born on March 25, 1901, the third of seven children to Josiah Wedgwood IV and Ethel Bowen Wedgwood in Barlaston, England, Camilla Wedgwood was a direct descendant of Josiah Wedgwood I, creator of the distinctive china bearing his name. Her father's great uncle Charles Darwin often visited the family estate, greatly influencing both Josiah and Ethel. Her mother, a well-known public figure and intellectual, had separated from Josiah by the time Camilla Wedgwood reached ten years of age, but she and the other children continued to live at Barlaston with their father. Generally known as Colonel Wedgwood and later as the first Baron Wedgwood, he became a member of Parliament and was a renowned Labour leader, deeply committed to social and political causes.[1]

Wedgwood was educated at the Orme Girls' School in Staffordshire, then proceeded to Bedford College, where she specialized in English. She continued her training at Newnham College at Cambridge, where she was graduated with honors in English, anthropology, and archaeology. She later acknowledged that her mentor Alfred Cort Haddon had made her into an anthropologist. Following her graduation, Wedgwood taught at Bedford College in the Department of Social Studies (1926–27), at the University of Sydney in the Department of Anthropology (1928–29), at the University of Capetown in the Department of African Life and Languages (1930), and at the London School of Economics (as research assistant to Bronislaw Malinowski and temporary lecturer in anthropology 1931–32). In 1932 she was awarded a fellowship by the Australian Research Council to conduct fieldwork on Manam Island, New Guinea.

Prevailing social attitudes in England at that time envisioned New Guinea and the Australian back country as being inhabited by headhunters and cannibals and certainly not suited for upper-class white women. Thus, when Camilla Wedg-wood began her fieldwork in Manam, only a few studies had been conducted in Australia and New Guinea by women anthropologists—among them, Hortense Powdermaker* (Lesu), Hilde Thurnwald (Buin), Margaret Mead* (Samoa, Manus), Phyllis Kaberry* (Kimberleys), and Ursula McConnel (Cape York Peninsula, Australia).

After completing her ethnological investigations on Manam, Wedgwood returned to Sydney, where she accepted an invitation from the government of Nauru to study native arts and crafts and the status of native education, with the goal of determining ways of reviving native culture. It was Wedgwood's first assignment in applied anthropology, which eventually turned into a specialized interest. After her return to Sydney, she held the post of principal at the Women's College, University of Sydney, from 1935 to 1944. As honorary lecturer in anthropology during this period, she often replaced A. P. Elkin at the university.

In 1944 she volunteered for the Women's Services of the Australian Army. As a lieutenant colonel assigned to the Army Directorate of Research (ANGAU), she effectively influenced Australian policies regarding native education and contact problems in New Guinea. The influence of European colonialism and the transition to a cash economy in which males played the dominant role as wage earners had changed Aboriginal women's position from one of the significant economic participation to economic dependence. Wedgwood wrote about the effects of culture contact upon these women:

It is sometimes assumed unwittingly, that the males play the dominant role in social change and that for the study of acculturation the effects of culture contact on the female are relatively unimportant. The effects on the lives and outlook of the females are less obvious, less direct and usually less easy to analyze, but we cannot assume, that they are less important. (Wedgwood and Hogbin 1954:5)

After the war Wedgwood joined the staff of the newly established School of Pacific Administration, where native education in particular and secondary education for women continued to be her primary interest. She lectured to native teachers on education and the revival of traditional culture. Her work led to the appointment of a woman educationalist trained in anthropology, Barbara McLachlan, to establish a secondary school for girls in Nauru. Wedgwood believed that girls and women of the islands of Oceania should be trained to meet their own needs and those of their communities through technical and vocational training. In her survey of educational problems in the islands, she had found a general indifference toward the education of females, a view shared by the indigenous village teachers (who were predominantly men) and even by some of the older native women.

During a brief interlude in Europe in 1947, Wedgwood worked at the Institute of Education at the University of London, exchanging ideas with Margaret Read, a renowned authority on native education. Upon her return to Australia in 1948, she continued as senior lecturer at the Australian School of Pacific Administration. It was this position that successfully enabled her to formalize her program in native education on a scale not previously attempted. Her persistent efforts were rewarded with an invitation by UNESCO to participate in 1951 as expert on the South Pacific region in a seminar on the use of vernacular languages in education. After months of intense pain, Camilla Wedgwood died of lung cancer in Sydney on May 17, 1955.

To the teaching field Wedgwood brought new ideas and enthusiasm, generated by her association with Bronislaw Malinowski, A. R. Radcliffe-Brown, Alfred C. Haddon, and Ian Hogbin. She believed that the basic tenets of the social anthropologist must include an understanding of native social, economic, and ethical values; a familiarization with traditional systems of leadership; and an understanding of patterns of behavior (see Wedgwood 1950a). Once equipped with these tools, the social anthropologist could apply his or her knowledge in the areas of native education, agriculture, and health.

In her writings Wedgwood was critical of the male bias in anthropological research. She believed women's roles in non-Western societies were not properly portrayed, owing to the androcentrism of scholars:

It may often seem that women in so-called primitive societies play only a very secondary role in the life of their community. We must be sure, however, that this impression is not due to the fact that most fieldwork that has been done has been done by men, who inevitably saw native life from the male side. (Wedgwood 1937b:191–92)

She observed that most ethnographers employ a standard "by which women's status is judged which is usually and perhaps unconsciously adopted to [sic] that of the upper-middle classes of Western Europe and North America and therefore of little value to the study of a community whose cultural background differs so greatly" (Wedgwood 1937a:401–402).

Wedgwood's fieldwork on Manam, where she studied the lives of women and children, girls' puberty rites, and the effects of culture contact, illustrate her attempt to depict women from a perspective free of Western bias. In her analysis of women's roles, Wedgwood, although familiar with the findings of Thurnwald and Mead that women had very low status, concluded that women in Manam held the status of "junior partners" rather than dependents. This concept of partial equality between males and females continues to generate debate among contemporary anthropologists (Berndt 1981 personal communication; Lutkehaus 1982; White 1970).

Yet Wedgwood did not claim to be a feminist. In a letter dated June 1937, she wrote to her father that she had been awarded the Coronation Medal " 'as a prominent feminist leader' and you have no idea how I loathe feminism. I was so angry at first that I failed to see how comic it was" (Pease 1981, personal communication).

Recent analyses carried out by Nancy Lutkehaus on Manam in 1978–79 have both reaffirmed and contradicted Wedgwood's findings. While Lutkehaus clearly states that she admires Wedgwood for her attempt to correct the male bias in anthropological research, she also feels that Wedgwood was "overzealous" in her efforts to provide a "counterveiling" view of the "stereotypic" women in the Pacific Islands. She criticizes Wedgwood for not counterbalancing the "female point of view" with the "male point of view," which Lutkehaus feels is essential when this male view "represents the dominant political ideology of the society" (Lutkehaus 1982:36–51).

Although the question of whether Wedgwood was a feminist remains debatable, it is clear that she recognized the importance of the role of women in non-Western societies, the need for a female point of view in ethnographic studies, and the necessity of involving women in native education.

While R. O. L. Burridge was conducting fieldwork in Manam, he questioned his informants about Camilla Wedgwood and received one reply indicating the community's respect for her: "She knew how to plant taro. She dug the hole and she cooked the taro just the way we do. If a man died, she sat in the middle with all the other women and grieved for him. She was not like white people, she was just like us black skinned folk" (Burridge 1954:937).

Note

1. The author wishes to thank Catherine Berndt, Helen Pease, Nancy Lutkehaus, and Marie Reay for their cooperation and suggestions during the preparation of this biography.

References and Works About Camilla H. Wedgwood

Burridge, R. O. L.
1954   Racial Tension in Manam. *The South Pacific* 7:929–37.
Deacon, Bernard A.
1934   *Malekula: A Vanishing People in the New Hebrides*. London: George Routledge Co.
Elkin, A. P.
1955   Camilla Hildegarde Wedgwood: 1901–1955. *Oceania* 26:172–80.
Firth, Raymond
1955   The Hon. Camilla H. Wedgwood. *Nature* 176:144–45.
Hogbin, Ian, and C. D. Rowley
1955   Camilla H. Wedgwood. *The South Pacific* 4:178–79.
Hole, Vere W., and Anne H. Treweeke, eds.
1953   Miss Wedgwood and Her Successors. In *The History of the Women's College*. Pp. 137–55. Sydney: University of Sydney, Australia.
Lutkehaus, Nancy
1982   Ambivalence, Ambiguity and the Reproduction of Gender Hierarchy in Manam Society: 1933–1979. *Social Analysis* 12:36–51.
1986   "She was *very* Cambridge": Camilla Wedgwood and the History of Women in British Social Anthropology. *American Ethnologist* 13(4): 776–98.

Selected Works by Camilla H. Wedgwood

1927 Death and Social Status in Melanesia. *Journal of the Royal Anthropological Institute* 19:461–516.

1930a Some Aspects of Warfare in Melanesia. *Oceania* 1 (1): 5–33.

1930b The Nature and Function of Secret Societies. *Oceania* 1 (2): 129–45.

1933 Girls' Puberty Rites in Manam Island, New Guinea. *Oceania* 4 (1): 132–55.

1934a Geometrical Drawings from Malekula and Other Islands of the New Hebrides. *Journal of the Royal Anthropological Institute* 29: 129–76.

1934b Introduction. *Malekula: A Vanishing People in the New Hebrides*, by A. B. Deacon. London: George Routledge Co.

1934c Report on Research on Manam Island. *Oceania* 5 (1): 64–79.

1935 Sickness and Treatment on Manam Island. *Oceania* 5 (3): 280–307.

1937a Women in Manam. *Oceania* 7 (4): 401–28.

1937b Women in Manam. *Oceania* 8 (2): 72–192.

1938 The Life of Children in Manam. *Oceania* 9 (1): 1–29.

1950a The Contribution of Anthropology to the Education and Development of Colonial Peoples. *The South Pacific* 4 (7): 78–84.

1950b The Recording of Native Tales. *The South Pacific* 4 (7): 146–49.

1951 A Plan for Survey of the Economic Life of a People. *The South Pacific* 5 (6): 110–11.

1952a A Plan for Tackling Kinship. *The South Pacific* 6 (1): 291–93; 6 (2) 320–24; 6 (5): 396–406; 6 (6): 433–38.

1952b An Annotated Glossary of Technical Terms Used in the Study of Kinship and Marriage. *The South Pacific* 6 (7): 450–58.

Coauthored Works

Wedgwood, Camilla H., and Ian Hogbin

1953 Local Grouping in Melanesia. *Oceania* 23 (4): 241–76; 24 (1): 58–76.

1954 *A Background Documentary Survey on the Education of Women and Girls in the Pacific*. Manuscript. National Library of Australia, Canberra, Australia.

Wedgwood, Camilla H., and Marie Reay

1959 Manam Kinship. *Oceania* 29 (4): 239–56.

1961a Endogamy. In *Encyclopædia Brittanica*. Vol. 8, p. 437. William Benton, ed. Chicago: London: Toronto: Encyclopædia Britannica, Inc.

1961b Exogamy. In *Encyclopædia Brittanica*. Vol. 8, p. 972. William Benton, ed. Chicago: London: Toronto: Encyclopædia Britannica, Inc.

Wedgwood, Camilla H., and Honor Maude

1967 Figures from Northern Guinea. *Oceania* 38 (3): 202–29.

UTE GACS

Gene Weltfish
1902–1980

American Boasian anthropologist Gene Weltfish was acclaimed for her cultural and linguistic studies among the Pawnee Indians and recognized for her contributions to art theory. She was admired but also persecuted for her dedication to human-rights issues.

Gene Weltfish, originally named Regina, was born August 7, 1902, in her maternal grandparent's house to Eve Furman Weltfish and Abraham Weltfish, the first of two daughters. The house was a five-story brownstone on the lower east side of New York City, where Gene, her younger sister Florrie, and her parents lived in a top-floor apartment until she was ten years old. With the rest of the house full of relatives, including two grandparents and seven young aunts and uncles, Gene spent a happy childhood. She thought of her grandmother, originally a seamstress from Odessa, as a protector and a friend—the matriarch of the family, who stood out as a strong and positive influence on the lives of those who surrounded her. Gene's first language was German. Her grandfather, a jeweler from Vienna, insisted on hiring a German governess for his first grandchild to teach her what he called "the language of culture." As a child, Weltfish spoke both German and English fluently and later learned French.[1]

When Weltfish was ten years old, her parents decided to move the family to a place of their own. Three years later her father, a lawyer involved in Tammany Hall politics, died unexpectedly. Of Jewish heritage, Weltfish came from a tradition in which scholarship and certain ceremonies were reserved for the males. She loved her father and wanted to go to the synagogue to recite the Kaddish during the seven-day bereavement period—traditionally the honored responsibility of a son, but not of a daughter. She went for advice to her father's mother, who had been secretly educated by her own father in Hebrew, and she encouraged her to follow her heart and forget the rules, which she did.

Her father's death dealt both an emotional and a financial blow to the family. He had died without leaving a will. At that time an estate did not automatically go to the wife, but rather to the state to be held in a trust fund for the family. Whenever money was needed, no matter how insignificant the amount, a petition had to be submitted to a state-appointed lawyer—a long and cumbersome process. Although her mother had graduated from a business college, she was unable to earn a salary adequate to meet their needs. At age fourteen, Weltfish went to work as a clerical assistant in a public school to help support her mother and her younger sister, but continued her education part-time in the evenings and graduated from high-school in 1919.

Weltfish went on to major in journalism at Hunter College. Supporting herself by working various commercial jobs, she somehow managed to save enough money by her senior year to quit working and go to school full-time. She transferred to Barnard College, where she minored in philosophy, and had the good fortune to study under John Dewey. Outstanding as a teacher as well as a philosopher, Dewey left an indelible mark on the minds of his students, and Weltfish was no exception.

In her senior year she registered for a course with Franz Boas, another charismatic scholar-teacher, who introduced her to anthropology. He was, without a doubt, the most influential force in shaping her ideology—and indeed, her life. During that same year she met Alexander Lesser, also a student of Boas, whom she eventually married and fifteen years later divorced.

In 1925 Weltfish graduated from Barnard and enrolled in the graduate program in anthropology at Columbia University. She was particularly interested in the fine arts and that quality in people that seeks to create things of beauty. In her dissertation, "The Interrelationship of Technique and Design in North American Basketry," she examined existing theories on the origins of visual motifs that appeared in North American Indian designs. She looked for evidence that design elements were modified by basket-weaving techniques. After surveying many different tribes and finding little or no alteration in decorative patterns, Weltfish concluded that the artist's concept, rather than the weaving technique, determined the design. She successfully completed her doctoral examinations in 1929, but because of a prohibitive cost of $4,000 to publish her dissertation, she did not receive her formal degree until 1950, when Columbia changed its policy and agreed to accept mimeographed theses, in lieu of the more expensive published copies.

Adept at linguistics and eager to do fieldwork, Weltfish was looking for a place to begin. In the summer of 1928, at the suggestion of Boas, she and Lesser went to Oklahoma, where he studied kinship patterns in Siouan tribes and she began her linguistic fieldwork among the Pawnee Indians. Before leaving New York City, she met with Henry Moses, a Pawnee who was part of a circus that happened to be in town. Since there was no written grammar of the language, he dictated a letter of introduction, which she transcribed phonetically, to read aloud to his family and friends upon her arrival in the town of Pawnee.

Once there, she found that the older residents spoke little or no English, while the younger folks spoke primarily English supplemented with an abbreviated form of Pawnee. Focusing on the monolingual people who spoke, as she put it, "in the classic style of former days," she transcribed by hand their conversations and stories. Her interpreter, Henry Chapman, fluent in both Pawnee and English, would then help her translate what she had written down, and little by little she began to unravel the underpinnings of the language and the variations between dialects.

Weltfish went back to Columbia University in the fall but returned to Pawnee in the summer of 1929; and in 1930, sponsored by a Social Science Research Fellowship, she went for an entire year to live and work among the Pawnee. Loved by the Indians with whom she lived, she fit easily into their life-style. Most of the arts and crafts were the cultural heritage of the Pawnee women, entrusted exclusively to their care. From these women, many of whom considered her as part of their families, Weltfish learned the art of basket weaving and shared the daily problems and events of their lives. While learning to weave, she made a number of detailed photographic series showing the hands of her teachers at work, carefully documenting each step in the process. Later her love of arts and crafts led her to visit many other tribes, including the Cochiti, the Rio Grande Pueblos, the Hopi, the San Carlos Apache, the Jicarilla, and the Mescalero, where she studied not only weaving and basket making but also pottery techniques and even the process of making a tobacco pipe—an art of the men of the tribe.

As a result of her extensive fieldwork, Weltfish published a number of important papers and organized exhibitions of Indian crafts in museums across the country, including the American Museum of Natural History in New York City, the Field Museum of Chicago, and the University Museum of the University of Pennsylvania in Philadelphia.

In 1931 Gene Weltfish gave birth to her only child, Ann, which, however, did not stop her from pursuing her studies and travels. Ann later wrote about her early childhood:

The year is 1934 or 1935. A small girl named Ann is about to become an anthropology student, a status that will last for her teacher's lifetime. The "teacher" is her mother. I am the "student," and have not always been a willing one. On my bookshelf, among fairy tales and Mother Goose, were books about stone age men, Navahos, Pueblos, other Indians, and dinosaurs. I have already seen my first movie—"The Wedding of Palo"— which was about Eskimos; and had a Pawnee name that I was able to say in both Pawnee and English. (Margetson, A. 1980:347)

In 1935, with her young "daughter-student" in tow, Weltfish returned to Pawnee, this time focusing on social relations and surviving customs and traditions. The question was how to integrate the leftover fragments of an earlier lifestyle into their original context. Together with Mark Evarts, a Pawnee who had become a "major resource and ally" from her earlier research, Weltfish set out to reconstruct the seasonal cycles of Pawnee lifestyle for the year 1867. It was a year when most of the older monolingual residents of Pawnee would have been in their late teens or early twenties, and she found them eager and willing to tell her the favorite stories of their youth.

Their work that summer formed the foundation for a book, which was published thirty years later after searching historical records, visiting archaeological sites, and reading eyewitness accounts from the time period to verify her original fieldwork and the memories of the Pawnee with whom she worked. *The Lost Universe* (Weltfish 1965a) became the basic ethnography on Pawnee culture.

Two other important publications emerged from this time period: *Caddoan Texts* (Weltfish 1936b), a bilingual presentation of over forty folktales; and "Composition of the Caddoan Linguistic Stock" (1932), coauthored with Lesser, which detailed the interrelationships of the dialects, thereby creating a classic introduction to the Caddoan language for linguistic scholars who followed in their footsteps.

In the fall of 1935, at the invitation of Boas, Weltfish began teaching in the graduate anthropology program at Columbia University. She taught traditional courses in linguistics, ethnology, and archaeology, and soon developed some of her own, including one on invention and technology in human culture and another on race problems—one of the first such courses in the country. She also worked on the development of the School of General Studies, which attracted nontraditional students. In response to changing interests, new courses were designed upon the request of five or more people. As the central figure in anthropology in this new adult-school division, Weltfish developed a wide range of course offerings. Whereas some scholars are excellent researchers and others teach with distinction, relatively few excel in both areas. Professor Weltfish was one of those few, and soon developed a following of students.

While Weltfish embarked on her new career of teaching, the world was preparing to go to war. In an unpublished memo found among her personal papers. she wrote of this period.

During the first four years of my graduate teaching at Columbia, Hitler rose to power in Germany, bolstering his heinous operations with the racist theories developed from distorted anthropology. The books of Professor Franz Boas . . . were burned in Germany. . . . For sixty years, Professor Boas traveled widely in this country and abroad, lecturing on the scientific facts about race and human biology. . . . In 1942, after his death, Ruth Benedict,* my senior colleague in the Anthropology Department, and I felt that we should carry the banner on the race question. . . . In 1943 Ruth Benedict and I collaborated on a pamphlet, "The Races of Mankind," published by the Public Affairs Committee . . . printed and distributed to millions of people in many languages all over the world. . . . The pamphlet was originally written at the request of the U.S.O. for distribution to the men in the armed forces who had to fight side by side with allies such as the Huks in the Philippines and the Solomon Islanders. . . . "The Races of Mankind" was used, not only for orientation by the army, but in the de-Nazification program in Germany after the war. (Weltfish 10/24/67)

As a scholar of ethnology and with a firm belief in racial equality, Weltfish gave public presentations all over the country—as many as 300 in one year alone. On a local level she worked to set up a community council to resolve conflicts between a black neighborhood and a white one in New York City. She was interviewed on radio programs. She organized an animated film, designed by Walt Disney artists, countering racism. There were also comic books and children's skits aimed at a younger audience. In the years 1943–44 she coauthored three general pamphlets and two scholarly articles on race and prejudice while continuing to research and publish on Indian culture.

During the war Ruth Benedict and other members of the anthropology department, one by one, left for Washington to work for such offices as the Foreign Morale Analysis Division of the Office of War Information and other departments to assist in the war effort by offering their skills as social scientists. Weltfish remained at her teaching post but took on the added responsibilities of assisting in orientation training for overseas personnel and working for the Office of Strategic Services (OSS).

At one point Weltfish went to Washington herself to find out what she could do. She met with psychologist Tryon of the Division of Psychological Warfare, who pointed out that she could do more good by continuing her fight against racism from her desk at Columbia than by joining a government agency.

Because she stayed at Columbia during the war, she inspired many postwar American anthropologists. "She was the living link to Boas for most of the younger anthropologists, and as such should be given a good deal of the credit for maintaining the continuity of development of American anthropology" (Margetson, N. 1984).

In 1940 Weltfish was divorced and took on the additional responsibilities of single parenting. Perhaps her own situation, combined with her natural dedication to the principles of human rights, swept her into the women's movement of the 1940s. She was elected vice president of the Women's International Democratic Federation in 1945 at a convention in Paris. Representatives from at least thirty-five countries lobbied for equal rights for women in all facets of society, for improvement of the health and welfare of the children of the world, and for world peace. Subsequently Weltfish was elected president of an affiliated organization, the Congress of American Women.

In 1944 the armed forces stopped its distribution of the pamphlet "The Races of Mankind" when a dispute arose over whether it depicted northern blacks as being smarter than southern whites. Weltfish explained to reporters who sought her out that the section that was being criticized discussed the quality of education in two different environments, which affected the test results of its students. It was economic and educational advantage, not race, that were responsible for the differing scores on intelligence tests. Although the pamphlet continued to be distributed and translated in countries around the world, it was banned from armed forces' libraries—a forewarning of the problems that were to follow.

In the early fifties Weltfish became a victim of the anti-Communist fervor that developed in the United States. Called to testify before McCarthy's Senate Internal Security Committee in 1952 and again in 1953 she was questioned about her participation in the two women's groups, mentioned above, which had been placed on the roster of subversive organizations for claiming that some of President Truman's policies might lead the United States into another war. She was interrogated not only about her own political beliefs but also about Ruth Benedict's, who had coauthored the pamphlet "The Races of Mankind," which was now declared to be subversive material. Weltfish patiently answered many of their questions and stated that she thought of herself as a good American and acted on issues as her conscience and knowledge dictated.

In this climate of political repression, Gene Weltfish received notice that her position at Columbia had been terminated, and she was unable to secure another teaching position for nine years. Ruth Benedict, at one point, broke into a closed meeting of University administrators to insist that Weltfish retain her teaching position, but it was to no avail. Her department petitioned for a promotion from lecturer to a tenured rank, but it was denied. In a front-page story in the *New York Times* (April 1, 1952), the university denied that her political activities had anything to do with her dismissal after seventeen years of teaching. If she had been a man teaching for that length of time, there is no doubt that she would have already been in a tenure-track position, which would have offered her some job security. Weltfish herself said in a statement to the Columbia University student newspaper that the "prejudice against women scholars" prevalent in academia was ultimately to blame for her non-reappointment.

Although her involvement in human-rights issues and the resulting turmoil in her life consumed much of her free time and thought, Weltfish continued her scholarly research. In 1953 her book *The Origins of Art* was published. This work explored the questions of why art began and how it developed. Drawing on her earlier fieldwork in basketry and pottery design, as well as on her knowledge of other forms of art, she supported her theories with numerous illustrations.

In 1954 John Champe, who had studied with Weltfish at Columbia, invited her to come to work on Pawnee materials in his anthropology laboratory at the University of Nebraska in Lincoln. She accepted, and during the next four years, traveling back and forth between New York and Nebraska, she devoted her time to research on the ethnology, history, and archaeology of the Pawnee to supplement her field notes and research of the 1930s. In 1958 she received a two-year grant from the Bollingen Foundation to work on her draft of *The Lost Universe*, the book for which she is perhaps best known. Published in 1965, it presented the social, ceremonial, and economic life of the Skidi Band of the Pawnee during the latter part of the nineteenth century. Weaving together her field notes, an account of her work with Mark Evarts and other Pawnee residents, and portions of her translations of James Murie's manuscripts on religious ceremonies with existing historical, archaeological, and ethnographic records, she vividly portrayed the everyday life of the Pawnee through the seasonal round of one year. Looking to the Pawnee way of life and thought, she applied their philosophy to the resolution of contemporary problems of industrialized society.

Widely acclaimed for its insights into Pawnee culture, the book was listed by the American Library Association as one of the most notable books to be published that year. Reprinted in paperback in 1971, its popularity continued to grow, and it became required reading material for students in anthropology courses.

In 1961 Weltfish was invited to teach undergraduates at Fairleigh Dickinson University on the Madison, New Jersey, campus. Beginning as an assistant professor, she was promoted to associate professor in 1964, and in 1968 she attained the rank of full professor. Although she taught a wide range of courses, she always had the time to develop other forums for learning. She started an International Club for students, and she prepared undergraduates to take part in the National Model U.N. General Assembly, a United Nations' program in which representatives from more than 1,000 colleges and universities across the country participate.

Her commitment to local issues involved her in several community projects. In nearby Morristown, New Jersey, she worked with interested residents and faculty members in developing and establishing an American Civilization Institute, which engaged high school and college students and residents of the area in local history, archaeology, and restoration projects. In Paterson, New Jersey, she worked on a study of public transportation as a factor in the lives of low-income individuals and families. Her growing interest in the isolation of older persons from the mainstream of society led her to organize a senior scholars' program at the university and to establish a community center for senior citizens of Madison, New Jersey. She was also instrumental in the development of the Gerontological Society of New Jersey and the Grey Panthers in New York City.

Upon her compulsory retirement in 1972, at the age of seventy, Weltfish was awarded professor emerita status—a small consolation for the loss of her teaching position. She sought work elsewhere and became a part-time faculty member in the graduate department of the New School for Social Research and at the Manhattan School of Music. She also held a Visiting Professorship at Rutgers University in its new program in Gerontology. She continued teaching for the rest of her life and made provisions for her books and papers to be preserved in a collection to serve other scholars after her death. Those materials are housed in the Special Collections Divisions of the Fairleigh Dickinson University, Madison campus library.

Throughout her life Gene Weltfish was committed to the principle that science and knowledge should be used "for the good of humanity and against the destructive forces of the world" (Weltfish 1945). When she died on August 2, 1980, she left behind not only her writings, but a vision of a better world to come passed on through her daughter, her grandchildren, and her legacy of students.

Note

1. It is a pleasure to express my appreciation to the following people: Ann Margetson, artist and daughter of Gene Weltfish, for providing me with information about the family

history and for permission to quote from her article; and Neil Margetson, grandson of Gene Weltfish, graduate anthropology student currently working on housing problems in New York City, for his moving letter regarding the contributions of his grandmother to the field of anthropology.

References and Works About Gene Weltfish

American Men and Women of Science: The Social and Behavioral Sciences
1973   Gene Weltfish. In *AMWS*. 12th ed. New York: R. R. Bowker.
Berger-Sofer, Rhonda
1981   A Memorial: A Tribute to Professor Emeritus Gene Weltfish. *Fairleigh Dickinson University Magazine* (Spring).
Bracker, Milton
1953   Books of 40 Authors Banned by U.S. in Overseas Libraries. *New York Times*, June 22. Pp. 1, 8.
Daily Record
1972   A Thousand Years of Toil and Strife Touch Us. (Interview) *Daily Record*, September 29. Morristown, N.J.
Diamond, Stanley, ed.
1980   *Theory and Practice: Essays Presented to Gene Weltfish*. The Hague: Mouton.
Margetson, Ann
1980   Anthropology Begins at Home: Reflections of a Daughter. In *Theory and Practice: Essays Presented to Gene Weltfish*. Stanley Diamond, ed. Pp. 351–56. The Hague: Mouton.
Margetson, Neil
1984   Unpublished personal letter dated 10/10/84. Weltfish Archives Special Collections, Fairleigh Dickinson University, Madison, N.J.
New York Times
1953   Columbia Is Dropping Dr. Weltfish, Leftist. *New York Times*, April 1, Sect. L, p. 1, 19.
1980   Obituary: *New York Times*, August 5, Sect. B, p. 10.
Parks, Douglas, and Ruth E. Pathé
1985   Gene Weltfish 1902–1980. *Plains Anthropologist: Journal of the Plains Anthropological Society* 30 (107): 59–64.
Time
1953   Far from the Pawnees. *Time* 61 (15): 88. April 13.
The Village Voice
1979   Grandmother of Us All. *The Village Voice*, Oct. 15.

Selected Works by Gene Weltfish

1930a Coiled Gambling Baskets of the Pawnee and Other Plains Tribes. In *Indian Notes and Monographs* 7:277–95. New York: Museum of the American Indian, Heye Foundation.
1930b Prehistoric North American Basketry Techniques and Modern Distributions. *American Anthropologist* 32:435–95.
1932a Iroquois Social Organization [chap. 5], Law of the Banks Islanders [chap. 11], and Organization of Economic and Industrial Life [chaps. 16, 17, 19, 21, 23]. In *Social Anthropology*. Paul Radin, ed.

1932b Problems in the Study of Ancient and Modern Basket-Makers. *American Anthropologist* 34:108–17.

1936a The Vision Story of Fox Boy: A South Bend Pawnee Text. *International Journal of American Linguistics* 9 (1): 44–75.

1936b *Caddoan Texts: Part I; Pawnee South Bend Dialect.* Publications of the American Ethnological Society. Vol. 17. (Reprinted 1974, New York: AMS Press.)

1939 Maps Illustrating Human Origins and Human Migrations. In *You and Heredity.* Amram Scheinfeld, ed. Pp. 335–55. New York: Frederick A. Stokes and Co.

1940 Cave Dweller Twill Plated Basketry. Appendix in *Report on Archaeology of Southern Chihuahua.* Robert M. Zingy, ed. Denver: University of Denver Contributions III, Centre of Latin American Studies I.

1944a *Brotherhood of Man.* (Animated filmscript) With Technical assistance by Stephen Bosutow and others of the United Artists.

1944b Jack Crazy Horse Considers Business on the Reservation. *American Indian* 1 (2).

1944c When the Indian Comes to the City. *American Indian* 2 (1).

1945 Science and Prejudice. *The Scientific Monthly* (September): 210–12.

1949 Racialism, Colonialism and World Peace. In *Speaking of Peace.* Daniel S. Gillmore, ed. Pp. 72–77. An edited report of the Cultural and Scientific Conference for World Peace, March 25–27, 1949, New York. Under the auspices of the National Council of the Arts, Sciences and Professions.

1953 *The Origins of Art.* Indianapolis: Bobbs-Merrill.

1956 The Perspective for Fundamental Research in Anthropology. The *Philosophy for Science* 23 (1): 63–73.

1958 The Linguistic Study of Material Culture. *International Journal of American Linguistics* 24 (4): 301–11.

1959 The Question of Ethnic Identity: An Ethnological Approach. *Ethnohistory* 6 (4): 321–46.

1960a The Anthropologist and the Question of the Fifth Dimension. In *Culture in History.* Stanley Diamond, ed. Pp. 160–80. New York: Columbia University Press.

1960b The Ethnic Dimension of Human History: Pattern or Patterns of Culture. *Selected Papers of the Fifth International Congress of Anthropological and Ethnological Sciences.* Anthony F. C. Wallace, ed. Pp. 207–18. Philadelphia: University of Pennsylvania Press.

1962a Some Main Trends in American Anthropology in 1961. *The Annals of the American Academy of Political and Social Sciences* 339: 171–76.

1962b The Place of Art in Human Society: An Anthropological Interpretation. *Delle Arti* 1 (1). Madison, N.J.: Fairleigh Dickinson University.

1965a *The Lost Universe.* New York: Basic Books. (Reprinted 1971, New York: Ballantine.)

1965b *Music of the Pawnee.* Sung by Mark Evarts, from documentary recording by Gene Weltfish in 1936. (Phonodisc) Folkways Records, FE4334.

1967 Unpublished Memo. Weltfish Archives, Special Collections, Fairleigh Dickinson University, Madison, N.J.

1968 The Aims of Anthropology: An American Perspective. (In response to: The Aims for Anthropology: A Scandinavian Point of View, by Alse Hultkrantz.) *Current Anthropology* 9:305–6.

1971 The Plains Indians: Their Continuity in History and Their Indian Identity. In *North*

American Indians in Historical Perspective. Eleanor Leacock and Nancy Oestreich Lurie, eds. Pp. 200–227. New York: Random House.

1972 *Paterson People in the March of Time*. Madison, N.J.: Fairleigh Dickinson University.

1974 *Work, An Anthropological View*. Saratoga Springs, N.Y.: Empire State College, State University of New York (SUNY).

1975 Pioneers of Plenty, New Themes for a New Society. *Business Review* 15 (1): 19–28.

1979a Grace Chapella at 104. *Socioeconomic Institute Journal*.

1979b Boas: The Academic Response. In *Anthropology: Ancestors and Heirs*. Stanley Diamond, ed. Pp. 123–47. The Hague: Mouton.

1980 *Aesthetics, the Dimension of Beauty in the Human Being: An Anthropological View*. Saratoga Springs, N.Y.: Empire State College, SUNY.

Coauthored Works

Weltfish, Gene, et al.

1971 *Poverty and Transportation As a Factor in the City of Paterson: A Study in Mobility, Social and Physical*. Madison, N.J.: Fairleigh Dickinson University.

Weltfish, Gene, and Ruth Benedict

1943 *The Races of Mankind*. New York: Public Affairs Committee.

Weltfish, Gene, and Violet Edwards

1943 *We Are All Brothers: What Do You Know About Race?* Cartoon filmscript.

Weltfish, Gene, and A. Lesser

1930 Index, vols. 1–40. *Journal of American Folklore*. Memoirs, American Folklore Society, no. 14.

1932 Composition of the Caddoan Linguistic Stock. *Smithsonian Miscellaneous Collections* 87 (6): 1–15.

Weltfish, Gene, and Harry Wenner

1970 *New Vistas on Work and Leisure: An Innovative Program for Relevant Education of School and Community*. Morristown, N.J.: A.C.I.M.

RUTH E. PATHÉ

Monica Hunter Wilson

(1908–1982)

South African social anthropologist Monica Hunter Wilson was known for her studies of Nyakyusa ritual and symbolism, and of South African history.

Monica Hunter Wilson was born January 3, 1908, in the small village of Lovedale in the eastern part of South Africa.[1] She was the daughter of missionary parents, David Alexander Hunter and Jessie McGregor Hunter, and received her early education at the Lovedale Mission School. This school was very unusual in South Africa at the time in that it admitted both black and white pupils. Her nonracial upbringing, religious background, and her love for the Eastern Cape were all important themes in the distinguished anthropological career that was to follow.

Monica Hunter completed her schooling at the Collegiate School for Girls in Port Elizabeth, and then proceeded to Girton College (Cambridge) to read history. Her realization that nearly all of South African history was written from a white perspective, plus the absence of reliable information on black South African life, led her from history into anthropology at Cambridge. She took her B.A. (Honors) degree in 1930 and then returned to the Eastern Cape to do fieldwork among the Bantu-speaking Pondo of what is now the Transkei.

Hunter was interested in processes of change and in the "Effects of Contact with Europeans on the Pondo of South Africa," as she subtitled her subsequent monograph, *Reaction to Conquest* (1936). She chose the Pondo, for they represented relatively isolated rural people as well as townspeople and farm workers. She had the added advantage that they spoke Xhosa, which she had begun learning as a child. After completing her fieldwork, she returned to Cambridge, working under the supervision of Professor Hodson, and received her Ph.D. degree in 1934.

In 1935 Monica Hunter married Godfrey Wilson, son of the eminent Shakespearian scholar J. Dover Wilson. She and her husband were both anthropologists chosen by the International African Institute to become Fellows under a Rockefeller Foundation project for the study of the impact of Western culture on African societies. They were part of the famous Malinowski seminar at the London School of Economics, before leaving for East Africa to do fieldwork in what was then Tanganyika. Between them they completed nearly five years of research among the Nyakyusa people. This cooperative research led her to see very clearly the possible biases in observation and interpretation between men and women researchers; she noted on more than one occasion that she and Godfrey had returned with very different field notes after attending the same event.

In 1938 the Wilsons moved to Northern Rhodesia, where Godfrey became the first director of the Rhodes-Livingstone Institute for Social Research. Here the Wilsons published a number of important papers and wrote most of their monograph *The Analysis of Social Change* (Wilson and Wilson 1945). This theoretical work, based on observations in Central and Southern Africa, introduced the concept of ''scale'' to attempt to understand change in African societies. The Wilsons argued that the changes they saw could best be understood in terms of an increase of scale in people's economic, political, and social horizons, and that conflicts, oppositions, and disequilibrium could be accounted for largely in terms of what they called conflicts of scale or unevenness of scale. Their work was published after World War II and had an immediate impact, according to A. Richards (1975:5); but their theoretical model ultimately received very little support.

At the outbreak of World War II, the Wilsons returned to South Africa with two small children. Godfrey Wilson died in 1944, and Monica Wilson then sought an academic position in South Africa where she could combine her scholarly activities with raising her children as a single parent. She never remarried.

Her first position was as lecturer in Social Anthropology at the University College of Fort Hare in the Eastern Cape, where she was also warden of women students. In 1947 she accepted the chair of social anthropology at nearby Rhodes University College. She was the first woman appointed by that university to a full professorship, but at a salary lower than that of her male colleagues. At the time only the universities of Cape Town and the Witwatersrand had equal pay for men and women. Monica Wilson was infuriated at this discrimination. In notes for a speech, found among papers at the University of Cape Town, following a proposed pay raise that increased this discrimination, she wrote:

It cannot be argued that the differences in salary between men and women is an adjustment to differences in expenses, since men without dependents are paid the higher salary and women with dependents the lower salary. . . . At a time when the principle of equal pay for equal work is already established in the majority, if not all, of the Universities of Great Britain, and also close at hand at the University of Cape Town, the women of Rhodes are asked to accept a very considerable increase in discrimination. (Wilson n.d., unpublished notes, University of Cape Town)

This issue was the major reason for her move to the University of Cape Town (1952), where she succeeded Isaac Schapera in the chair of social anthropology. She was also the first woman appointed to a full professorship by that institution. At Cape Town she served for a period as dean of the Faculty of Arts (the first woman to do so), and was prominent in the university's struggle to remain open to all students, regardless of race or ethnicity. She remained as professor and head of the department at Cape Town until her retirement in 1973.

Monica Wilson was a dedicated scholar and a gifted field-worker. Her early fieldwork in the 1930s was precocious, given her lack of training and isolation (Richards 1977:3), and ahead of its time in its concern for processes of change. Other British-trained anthropologists of the day were more interested in re-creating "traditional" societies than in understanding the changes they were undergoing. Unlike many of her colleagues, Monica Wilson was not content to portray African societies as rather static entities. Her first monograph, *Reaction to Conquest*, had change as a theme and included sections on life in reserves, farms, and towns. It therefore included one of the earliest anthropological studies of African urban life. P. C. W. Gutkind (1974:40) suggests that the earliest urban studies by an anthropologist were probably those of the South African Ellen Hellmann, whose first publication in this area was in 1934. Wilson's work was certainly not later than this.

During the 1950s Monica Wilson consolidated an international reputation through her writings on the Nyakyusa people. Even more remarkable, this work included both her own fieldwork and that of her late husband: her lifelong commitment to Godfrey Wilson had included the obligation to complete the Nyakyusa corpus. In addition to a number of articles, she produced three monographs in the 1950s (Wilson 1951, 1957 and 1959a) and a final volume (Wilson 1977) toward the end of her career. The last volume concentrated on change, but the earlier work was much more in the functionalist mold than her first researches in Pondoland. (See Charsley 1969 for a critique.) She concentrated on building up a picture of a system of values, rituals, and symbols. This was based on careful and detailed fieldwork involving lengthy texts, formal statements, and the recording of dialogues between the anthropologists and their informants. It was this ethnography—rather than any theoretical innovation—upon which her reputation was based.

Monica Wilson's South African work was never static but reflected her abiding interest in the country's history and in both rural and urban areas. In addition to her Pondo ethnography, other important work included her involvement in the Keiskammahoek Rural Survey (Wilson and Walton 1952), a multivolume interdisciplinary study of a rural reserve, to which she contributed in the areas of social structure and land tenure. In addition, she collaborated with Archie Mafeje to produce a monograph on an urban African township, *Langa* (1963). Her interest in South African history came to full fruition in the middle 1960s with the publication of the two-volume *Oxford History of South Africa* (1969, 1971), edited by

Monica Wilson and historian Leonard Thompson. She contributed four chapters to this work, drawing in part on some of her own early ethnography.

The *Oxford History of South Africa* is commonly regarded as the high point of liberal historical scholarship in South Africa. The editors summed up their approach in the introduction: "This work derives from our belief that the central theme of South African history is interaction between peoples of diverse origins, languages, technologies, ideologies and social systems, meeting on South African soil" (Wilson and Thompson 1969: v). The work was important in that it represented the best attempt at the time to produce a history that was not written from the perspective of one interest group, and which at the same time gave full value to precolonial history and prehistory. It was controversial, attacked by right-wing white South Africans who found the interactionist approach and evidence for early African settlement of Southern Africa inimical to their segregationist views. More important, perhaps, the work served as a touchstone for the new wave of "radical" South African historiographers (see Wright 1977).

Audrey Richards (1975:1) has written that "Monica Wilson occupies a place in anthropology that is virtually unique," and that she never became embroiled in current theoretical controversies, preferring to pursue her own way. While she kept current on developments in her own subject and was extremely well-read, Monica Wilson indeed remained more of an observer than a participant in what she saw as ephemeral intellectual battles. This was very much her style, assisted by physical isolation in South Africa and, more important, by her view of anthropology as a means to an end rather than an end in itself.

She used the techniques of anthropology brilliantly to amass evidence needed to deal with questions that she thought important. She sought assistance from other disciplines and read far beyond the confines of her own subject, particularly in history, philosophy, theology, and psychology. She wrote very little that was of interest solely to professional anthropologists. And while she numbered some distinguished anthropologists among her students (including A. Mafeje, M. G. Marwick, B. G. M. Sundkler, V. W. Turner, and P. Rigby), she never founded a "school" of her own.

The Nyakyusa corpus established Monica Wilson's prominence in the field of the study of ritual and religion. As a result, she was invited to deliver the prestigious Frazer Lecture for 1959 and the Scott Holland Lectures at Cambridge (1971)—the latter fusing two of her major interests: the study of religion and the study of social change.

Recognition of her work came in many other ways as well. She received honorary doctorates from the universities of Rhodes, York, and the Witwatersrand, and honorary fellowships from the Royal Anthropological Institute and the American Anthropological Association. She was an Honorary Fellow of Girton College Cambridge, a Fellow of the Royal Society of Southern Africa, and received the Rivers Medal for Fieldwork in 1952 and the Simon Biesheuvel Medal for Research in 1969.

In many ways Monica Wilson was the epitome of the liberal South African scholar. Her friend Audrey Richards* wrote of her:

She has always felt it to be her duty as well as her desire to remain in South Africa . . . She has certainly had a great sense of commitment to the teaching of liberal ideas in South African universities . . . and has felt that continuous teaching of this sort was her special contribution to the fight for the African cause. (Richards 1975:2)

Unlike some of her colleagues who chose to leave South Africa for political reasons, Monica Wilson felt very strongly that she could make a greater contribution to her country by remaining and continuing to research, write, and teach on South African issues. This commitment went far beyond the classroom. She was brought up in a nonracial environment and lived her life by the same standards, irrespective of South African law. Unlike many other white South African liberals, her command of the Xhosa language enabled her to communicate with black compatriots in a way impossible for most. This gave her added authority when she spoke out on many of the political issues of her day, including the establishment of black "homelands," migrant labor and the breakup of African family life, and human and academic freedom. These concerns were expressed not only in her teaching and writing but also on public platforms and through various organizations. She was a member of the Liberal party, which was a multiracial group standing for a universal franchise in South Africa before legislation forced it to disband, and was also a prominent member of the South African Institute of Race Relations, a nonracial, nonpolitical, fact-finding body that has spoken out consistently against racial domination in South Africa.

She was certainly alive to some issues specifically affecting women, particularly African women in South Africa (Wilson 1974). She also felt, for example, that women academics had to work much harder than their male counterparts for university recognition. But her political concern largely focused on the manifest inequalities and injustices of the broader South African political situation. Despite this, her life was an affirmation in many ways of contemporary feminist ideals. She was a scholar of international reputation among her peers, forthright in her views, deeply concerned about her society, and, not least, a very successful single parent. (Her two children became very prominent in the fields of labor economics and medicine, respectively, and continue to voice many of her ideals and concerns.)

Monica Wilson retired to her family estate in the Eastern Cape in 1973. She continued to write and work in the very beautiful botanical garden she had created. She remained cheerful and productive despite two serious operations for cancer. She died peacefully at home and was buried in her beloved Eastern Cape after a typical African funeral. This ritual symbolized her connections with South Africans of all walks of life, and the speeches there highlighted the life of a remarkable person.

Note

1. This article is a modified version of a memoir published by the Royal Society of South Africa (West 1984).

References and Works About Monica H. Wilson

Richards, A.
1975   Monica Wilson: An Appreciation. In *Religion and Social Change in Southern Africa: Essays in Honour of Monica Wilson*. M. G. Whisson and M. E. West, eds. Pp. 1–13. Cape Town and London: David Philip & Rex Collings.
Brokensha, D.
1983   Monica Wilson 1908–1982. *Africa* 53:3.
Gutkind, P. C. W.
1974   *Urban Anthropology*. Assen: Van Gorkum.
Murray, C.
1983   "So Truth Be in the Field . . . '': A Short Appreciation of Monica Wilson. *Journal of Southern African Studies* 10:1.
West, M. E.
1984   Monica Hunter Wilson: A Memoir. *Transactions of the Royal Society of South Africa* 45:2.

Selected Works by Monica H. Wilson

1932   Results of Culture Contact on the Pondo and Xosa Family: *South African Journal of Science* 29.
1933   Effects of Contact with Europeans on the Status of Pondo Women. *Africa* 6 (3): 259–76.
1934   Methods of Study of Culture Contact. *Africa* 7 (3): 335–50. (Reprinted in *Methods for the Study of Culture Contact in Africa*. Memorandum 15, International African Institute.)
1936   *Reaction to Conquest*. London: Oxford University Press (2nd ed., 1961).
1937   The Bantu on European-Owned Farms. In *The Bantu-Speaking Tribes of South Africa*. I. Schapera, ed. Pp. 389–404. Cape Town: Maskew Miller.
1949   Nyakyusa Age-Villages. *Journal of the Royal Anthropological Institute* 79:21–25.
1950   Nyakyusa Kinship. In *African Systems of Kinship and Marriage*. A. R. Radcliffe-Brown and D. Forde, eds. Pp. 111–39. London: Oxford University Press.
1951   *Good Company: A Study of Nyakyusa Age Villages*. London: Oxford University Press.
1954   Nyakyusa Ritual and Symbolism. *American Anthropologist* 56 (2): 228–41.
1955   Development in Anthropology. *Race Relations Journal* 22 (4): 6–11.
1956a   An Anthropologist's View of the Tomlinson Report. *Race Relations Journal* 23 (2 & 3): 12–14.
1956b   An Urban Community (East London). In *Social Implications of Industrialization and Urbanization in Africa South of the Sahara*. Pp. 191–99. Paris: UNESCO.
1957   *Rituals of Kinship Among the Nyakyusa*. London: Oxford University Press.

1959a *Communal Rituals Among the Nyakyusa*. London: Oxford University Press.

1959b *Divine Kings and the Breath of Men*. The Frazer Lecture. Cambridge: Cambridge University Press.

1960 Myths of Precedence. In *Myth in Modern Africa*. Allie Dubb, ed. Pp. 1–7. Grahamstown, S. Afr. Institute of Social and Economic Research, Rhodes University.

1962 The Principle of Maintaining the Reserves for Africans. *Race Relations Journal* 29.

1963 Effects on the Xhosa and Nyakyusa of Scarcity of Land. In *African Agrarian Systems*. D. Biebuyck, ed. Pp. 374–91. London: Oxford University Press.

1964a The Coherence of Groups. In *Problems of Transition*. J. F. Holleman et al., eds. Pp. 1–20. Durban, S. Afr.: University of Natal.

1964b *Let No Man Put Asunder*. Cape Town: Brian MacKenzie.

1966 Urban Revolution in South Africa. In *Man in Community*. Egbert de Vries, ed. New York: Association Press.

1967a Nyakyusa Age-Villages. In *Comparative Political Systems*. Ronald Cohen and John Middleton, eds. Pp. 217–27. New York: Natural History Press.

1968 Ritual in Local Politics. In *Local-level Politics: Social and Cultural Perspectives*. Marc J. Swartz, ed. Pp. 191–98. Chicago: Aldine.

1969a Changes in Social Structure in Southern Africa: The Relevance of Kinship Studies to the Historian. In *African Societies in Southern Africa*. Leonard M. Thompson, ed. Pp. 71–85. London: Heineman.

1969b Co-operation and Conflict: The Eastern Cape Frontier; The Hunters and Herders; the Nguni People; and The Sotho, Venda, and Tsonga [four chaps.]. In *The Oxford History of South Africa*. Vol. 1. M. Wilson and Leonard Thompson, eds. Oxford: Clarendon Press.

1970 *The Thousand Years Before van Riebeeck*. Raymond Dart Lecture. Johannesburg: Witwatersrand University Press.

1971 *Religion and the Transformation of Society*. The Scott Holland Lectures. Cambridge: Cambridge University Press.

1972 The Wedding Cakes: A Study of Ritual Change. In *The Interpretation of Ritual*. J. S. La Fontaine, ed. Pp. 187–201. London: Tavistock.

1974 *The Changing Status of African Women*. Fifth Berth Solomon Memorial Lecture. Cape Town: National Council of Women.

1977 *For Men and Elders: Changes in the Relations of Generations and Between Men and Women Among the Nyakyusa-Ngonde People, (1875–1971)*. London: International African Institute.

1981 *Freedom for My People. The Autobiography of Z. K. Mathews: Southern Africa 1901 to 1968*. Cape Town and London: David Philip & Rex Collings. (As ed., and with a memoir by M. Wilson.)

Coauthored Works

Wilson, Monica, and Walton, Elton-Mills

1952 *Land Tenure*. (Vol. 4 of Kreiskammahoek Rural Survey.) Pietermaritzburg, S. Afr. Shuter and Shooter.

Wilson, Monica, and Archie Mafeje

1963 *Langa: A Study of Social Groups in an African Township*. Cape Town: Oxford University Press.

Wilson, Monica, and Leonard Thompson, eds.
1969 and 1971   *The Oxford History of South Africa*. Vols. 1 and 2. Oxford: Clarendon
     Press. (Wilson also as contrib.)
Wilson, Monica, and Godfrey Wilson
1939   *The Study of African Society*. Rhodes-Livingstone Papers 2. Grahamstown, S.
       Afr.: Rhodes University.
1945   *The Analysis of Social Change*. Cambridge: Cambridge University Press.
1967   Scale. In *Beyond the Frontier: Social Process and Cultural Change*. Paul Bo-
       hannan and Fred Plog, eds. Pp. 239–53. New York: Natural History Press.

MARTIN E. WEST

Hannah Marie Wormington
(1914–   )

American archaeologist Hannah Marie Wormington is known primarily for her Paleo-Indian studies in the New World, her research in Old World origin and migration routes, and for her work with two important prehistoric cultures, the Fremont and Uncompahgre.

Wormington was born September 5, 1914, in Denver, Colorado, where she still resides. Her father, Charles Watkin Wormington, married her mother, Adrienne Roucolle, late in his life; Wormington was strongly influenced by her mother and maternal grandmother, who emigrated from France. She grew up speaking French as well as English and has maintained strong personal and professional contacts with France. Indeed, she began her training for a career in archaeology in France in 1935, the summer following her graduation. Three years earlier she had discovered anthropology and archaeology when she took an undergraduate class at the University of Denver from the dynamic lecturer, E. B. Renaud. During her undergraduate years she began her long association with the Colorado Museum of Natural History (now the Denver Museum of Natural History) as a volunteer in paleontology and photography.

Wormington graduated with her B.A. in anthropology in the spring of 1935 from the University of Denver and embarked on her career as an archaeologist. Despite the last-minute cancellation of her sponsoring program, Wormington, aided by her mother, a teacher and professional writer, "launched" her own career. Wormington has described how she naively telephoned the British archaeologist Dorothy Garrod upon her arrival in London to announce her interest in archaeology: "I didn't realize that as a fresh graduate you didn't just call up famous archaeologists and say here I am, I want to be an archaeologist. They were so startled, that they were receptive."[1] Garrod took her to lunch at her private club and encouraged Wormington to pursue her interest in the French Paleolithic and became, as Wormington told Cynthia Irwin-Williams in 1982, "a kind of role model." In Paris Wormington met the American archaeologist

Harper "Pat" Kelley, who introduced her to the study of the Paleolithic and to several French Paleolithic archaeologists. Dr. Henri Martin provided Wormington with her first field experience in the Dordogne; Edgar Howard, an American archaeologist who had worked on Paleo-Indian sites in the United States, accompanied Wormington and her mother through Spain visiting archaeological sites; and Pat Kelley arranged for Wormington to exchange a European collection of Paleolithic artifacts for photographs of the Denver Museum's Paleo-Indian collection.

Wormington continued her work with the museum for the next thirty-three years (until the archaeology department closed in 1968). She helped establish the museum's reputation as an important center for Paleo-Indian research. During World War II she traveled with her husband until he went overseas; then she returned to the museum as a paid employee.

Even before beginning graduate work, Wormington was establishing her reputation in the profession. In 1936 she cataloged the museum's material from the Lindenmeier site (Colorado), one of the first Paleo-Indian camps to be excavated. The site yielded a wide variety of tools associated with extinct bison, which she compared with the European material. That same year she started her own excavations in Colorado at a rock shelter near Montrose and at the Johnson site, a minor Folsom camp site near La Porte, Colorado. In 1937 the museum appointed Wormington curator of archaeology. Edgar Howard invited her to Philadelphia to present a paper on Paleo-Indian flaking techniques at an international symposium on Early Man. Howard also asked her to serve as hostess as he entertained such people as V. Gordon Childe and Teilhard de Chardin, international contacts that were to prove invaluable to the young archaeologist. That fall Wormington received a fellowship at Radcliffe College and took leave from the museum to begin graduate work. Many of her classes were held at Harvard, and she became one of the first women to enter the program. Returning again in 1940 (the year in which she married George D. Volk, a petroleum geologist and engineer), she received an M.A. in 1950 and a Ph.D. in 1954, thus becoming the first Harvard female Ph.D. to specialize in archaeology.

In addition to conducting archaeological excavations at various sites in Colorado, she worked on a Fremont village site in Utah. In her comprehensive report on the Fremont culture (Wormington 1955b), Wormington suggested that it originated in the ancient Desert Culture of the Great Basin and that the Pueblo flavor diffused later. Her Uncompahgre report (Wormington and Lister 1956) clarified this early Colorado Archaic complex and linked it to the Great Basin Desert Culture. She started field schools and attended regional and national conferences. At the same time she taught part-time at the University of Denver and the University of Colorado at Boulder.

Wormington's most significant publication, *Ancient Man in North America* (Wormington 1939b), was the first major synthesis of Paleo-Indian studies in the New World. It has served both amateurs and professionals as a major sourcebook, compiling all of the published and unpublished material on Paleo-Indian occupation of North America from the earliest complexes through the early archaic sites. Her 1947 synthesis, *Prehistoric Indians of the Southwest*, also became a standard text, with numerous printings during the next several decades. In 1948 she began plans for the Hall of Man at the museum, a long-term project that opened in 1956. Her collections and exhibits at the museum became a standard and guide for many during the 1950s and 1960s.

In 1955–56 Wormington conducted a survey in Alberta, Canada, to search for the migration route of the early Asian hunters who had colonized the New World. In 1958 she participated in a two-month U.S.-Soviet scientist exchange program to visit sites and collections in the USSR and subsequently translated a report on a Siberian site. Wormington also investigated parallels in New World and Old World tool technology. On a 1961 return trip to the Soviet Union, she investigated early metal-using cultures in Siberia and their possible relationships to the Old Copper cultures in North America. She visited Russia again in 1964, Japan in 1968, and China in 1975.

In 1967 Wormington became the first woman to be elected president of the Society for American Archaeology. Her awards include a Guggenheim Fellowship (1970), an Honorary Doctorate from Colorado State University (1977), Colorado's State Archaeologist's Award (1977), and the Society of American Archaeology's Distinguished Service Award (1983). Still active in various professional associations, Wormington is currently completing revision on her new book, *Ancient Hunters and Gatherers of North America*.

Wormington's contributions to anthropology and specifically to archaeology fall into several areas. Certainly one of the most important has been her lifelong dedication to working with amateurs. By gathering scattered data concerning the earliest human occupations in North America and compiling them into a readable volume, she has offered laypersons and students access to information long available only to those in academia. Her museum position put her in daily contact with the public and amateur archaeologists whom she included on many digs and other activities, and she stressed their contribution to scientific investigation. She recently said of the Denver chapter of the Colorado Archaeological Society that the only real difference between its work and that of the professionals was that the professionals were paid. Wormington also expresses her pride in having worked with younger scholars such as Cynthia Irwin-Williams and her brother, Henry Irwin.

Through her efforts and example, Wormington has been instrumental in opening archaeology to women. Recognizing early that she would have to work harder in her profession because she was a woman, she says she has just kept "boring from within" to make the discipline more accessible to women. She credits much of her success to the support of her husband and to male colleagues. Remembering her own attempts to acquire professional training in the field, Wormington has always opened her field schools to women and gave them equal opportunities to acquire professional skills. Her leadership in the Society of

American Archaeology and her participation in conferences laid the foundation for other women to enter the profession.

Wormington has made major contributions to Paleo-Indian studies, including summaries of New World research and a bibliography of over 5,000 entries. She led American archaeologists in the search for the origins of New World Paleo-Indian cultures and in tracing the migration of these peoples from Asia to the High Plains of North America. Her collection of casts of the earliest stone tools is exhaustive.

She remains active as a consultant. Wormington recently stressed that she sees archaeology undergoing an important change: "We're becoming much more truly anthropologists, with an emphasis on lifeways of people instead of just their material possessions."

Note

1. The author thanks Dr. H. Marie Wormington for granting a personal interview and other assistance; Dr. Cynthia Irwin-Williams for providing a copy of her unpublished paper and other suggestions; and Dr. George Agogino for suggestions.

References and Works About Hannah Marie Wormington

American Antiquity
1983   Distinguished Service Award: H. Marie Wormington. *American Antiquity* 48 (3): 451–52.
Cassells, E. Steve
1983   *The Archaeology of Colorado.* Boulder, Colo.: Johnson Publishing Co.
Dolzani, Michael
1984   H. M. Wormington . . . Still Leading the Way. *Mammoth Trumpet* (Summer).
Sudler, Barbara
1983   H. M. Wormington: An Exceptional Archaeologist. *Colorado Heritage News* (April).

Selected Works by Hannah Marie Wormington

1936   The Case of the Mysterious Folsom. *Minnesota Archaeologist* 2 (6): 1–6.
1937   The Amateur Archaeologist. *Minnesota Archaeologist* 3:41.
1939a American Archaeology: Its Debts to Geology and Other Sciences. *The Mines Magazine* 29 (4): 159–61.
1939b *Ancient Man in North America.* Denver Museum of Natural History, Popular Series No. 4.
1947   *Prehistoric Indians of the Southwest.* Denver Museum of Natural History, Popular Series No. 7.
1948   A Proposed Revision of Yuma Point Terminology. *Proceedings of the Colorado Museum of Natural History* 18 (2).

1949a A Proposal for Distributional Studies of Fluted and Parallel Flaked Points in North America. *Plains Archaeological Conference Newsletter* 2 (2): 20–21.

1949b A Proposed Revision of Yuma Point Terminology. *Southwestern Lore* 15:26–40.

1949c *Prehistoric Indians of the Southwest*. Denver Museum of Natural History, Popular Series No. 7.

1950 The Need for Changes in Terminology Used in Studies of Early Stone Industries. In *Proceedings of the Sixth Plains Anthropological Conference, 1948*. University of Utah Anthropological Papers No. 11. Jesse D. Jennings, ed. Pp. 26–31. Salt Lake City: University of Utah.

1952 The Present Status of Studies Pertaining to Early Man in the New World. In *International Congress of Anthropological and Ethnological Sciences*, 4th Actas Wien, tome 2. Pp. 311–15. Vienna.

1953a Archaeology of the Upper Colorado Plateau Area in the Northern Periphery of the Southwestern United States. Ph.D. Diss., Radcliffe College.

1953b *Origins*. Book I of the Indigenous Period section of the Programa de historia de America. Publication 153. Instituto Panamericano de Geografia e Historia. Mexico, D.F.

1953c Der Urgeschichtliche Mensch in Nordamerika und die Leitformen seiner Kulturen. *Quartar* 6 (Halbband) 1:1–18.

1955a *A Reappraisal of the Archaeology of the Northern Periphery of the Southwestern United States*. Anais do 31. Pp. 649–56. Congreso Internacional de Americanistas, São Paolo.

1955b *Reappraisal of the Fremont Culture with a Summary of the Archaeology of the Northern Periphery*. Proceedings, No. 1. Denver Museum of Natural History.

1959 The Amateur Archaeologists. *Southwestern Lore* 15:1–3.

1960 Comments on the Use of the Term "Yuma." *Iowa Archaeological Society Newsletter*, no. 8. Pp. 4–6.

1961 Prehistoric Cultural Stages of Alberta, Canada. In *Homenaje a Pablo Martinez del Rio*. Pp. 163–71. Mexico, D.F.

1962a An Investigation of Possible Connections Between the Early Metal Using Cultures of Siberia and the Old Copper Culture. *Wisconsin Archaeologist* 43 (1): 20–24.

1962b A Survey of Early American Prehistory. *American Scientist* 50 (1): 230–42.

1964a Problems Relating to Paleolithic Techniques in the New World. In *Proceedings, 35th International Congress of Americanists* (1962) 1:9–10. Actas y Memorias. Mexico, D.F.

1964b The Problems of the Presence and Dating in America of Flaking Techniques Similar to the Paleolithic in the Old World. In *Atti del VI Congresso Internazionale delle Scienze Prehistoriche e Protohistoriche* 1:273–83. Relazioni Generali, Roma.

1967a The Paleo-Indian. In *The Philadelphia Anthropological Society, Papers Presented on Its Golden Anniversary*. Jacob W. Gruber, ed. Pp. 55–66. New York: Columbia University Press.

1967b *Pleistocene Studies in Southern Nevada*. Anthropological Papers No. 13. Carson City: Nevada State Museum. (As ed.)

1968 When Did Man Come to North America? In Malcolm Rogers, *Ancient Hunters of the Far West*. R. F. Pourade, ed. Pp. 111–24. San Diego: Copley Press.

1971 Comments on Early Man in North America, 1960–1970. (Paper presented at the American Anthropological Association Meetings, San Diego, November 1970.) *Arctic Anthropology* 8 (2): 83–91.

1977   Archaeology of the Late and Post Pleistocene from a New World Perspective. In *Paleoanthropology in the People's Republic of China*. W. W. Howells, ed. Pp. 191–95. New York: National Academy of Sciences.
1981   Introduction. *Breakthrough: Women in Archaeology*, by Barbara Williams. Pp. v–vii. New York: Walker.
1983   Early Man in the New World: 1970–1980. In *Early Man in the New World*. Richard Shutler, Jr., ed. Berkeley, Calif.: Sage Publications.
(In Press)   *Ancient Hunters and Gatherers of North America*. New York: Academic Press.

Coauthored Works

Wormington, H. M., and Richard G. Forbis
1965   *An Introduction to the Archaeology of Alberta, Canada*. Proceedings, No. 11. Denver Museum of Natural History.
Wormington, H. M., H. T. Irwin et al.
1970   Paleo-Indian Tool Types in the Great Plains. *American Antiquity* 35 (1): 24–34.
Wormington, H. M., and Robert H. Lister
1956   *Archaeological Investigations of the Uncompahgre Plateau in West Central Colorado*. Proceedings, No. 2. Denver Museum of Natural History.
Wormington, H. M., and Arminta Neal
1951   *The Story of Pueblo Pottery*. Museum of Natural History, Denver. Museum Pictorial No. 2.

JANET OWENS FROST

Appendix A: Fieldwork Areas

Africa

Blackwood, Beatrice
Douglas, Mary
Dunham, Katherine
Kaberry, Phyllis
Kuper, Hilda
Leakey, Mary
Powdermaker, Hortense
Richards, Audrey
Wilson, Monica

Arctic/Subarctic

de Laguna, Frederica
Garfield, Viola
Goldfrank, Esther
Hanks, Jane
Helm, June
Landes, Ruth
Leacock, Eleanor
McClellan, Catharine
Wallis, Ruth
Wormington, Hannah

Asia (excluding South Pacific islands)

Du Bois, Cora
Hanks, Jane

Shepardson, Mary
Steed, Gitel

Caribbean

Diggs, Irene
Dunham, Katherine
Green, Vera Mae
Hurston, Zora Neale
Keur, Dorothy
Metraux, Rhoda
Parsons, Elsie
Rubin, Vera

Latin America

Diggs, Irene
Dunham, Katherine
Landes, Ruth
O'Neale, Lila
Parsons, Elsie Clews

Mesoamerica

Gillmor, Frances
Hunt, Eva
Kelly, Isabel
Nuttall, Zelia
Parsons, Elsie Clews
Proskouriakoff, Tatiana

North America

California

Densmore, Frances
Du Bois, Cora
Kroeber, Theodora
Laird, Carobeth
O'Neal, Lila

Great Basin

Wormington, Hannah

Northeast

Densmore, Frances
Smith, Erminnie
Wallis, Ruth

Northwest Coast

Benedict, Ruth
de Laguna, Frederica
Garfield, Viola
Gunther, Erna

Plains/Plateau

Benedict, Ruth
Deloria, Ella
Densmore, Frances
Fletcher, Alice
Friedl, Ernestine
Hanks, Jane
Kelly, Isabel
Landes, Ruth
Lurie, Nancy
Steed, Gitel
Weltfish, Gene

Southeast

Densmore, Frances
Landes, Ruth

Southwest

Benedict, Ruth
Bunzel, Ruth
de Laguna, Frederica
Densmore, Frances
Gillmor, Frances
Goldfrank, Esther
Keur, Dorothy
Leighton, Dorothea
Parsons, Elsie Clews
Reichard, Gladys
Shepardson, Mary
Stevenson, Matilda
Tanner, Clara
Underhill, Ruth
Weltfish, Gene

United States (except Native American groups)

Dunham, Katherine
Green, Vera Mae
Hurston, Zora Neale
Leacock, Eleanor
Mead, Margaret
Metraux, Rhoda
Parsons, Elsie
Powdermaker, Hortense
Rubin, Vera
Steed, Gitel
Wallis, Ruth

Oceania

Berndt, Catherine
Blackwood, Beatrice
Du Bois, Cora
Fischer, Ann
Kaberry, Phyllis
Mead, Margaret
Metraux, Rhoda
Powdermaker, Hortense
Wedgwood, Camilla

Western Europe

Friedl, Ernestine
Keur, Dorothy
Leacock, Eleanor
Richards, Audrey
Wallis, Ruth
Wormington, Hannah

Appendix B: Chronology of Birth Dates

1836—Smith, Erminnie

1838—Fletcher, Alice

1847—Stevenson, Sara

1849—Stevenson, Matilda

1857—Nuttall, Zelia

1867—Densmore, Frances

1874—Parsons, Elsie

1883—Underhill, Ruth

1886—O'Neale, Lila

1887—Benedict, Ruth

1888—Deloria, Ella

1889—Blackwood, Beatrice

1893—Reichard, Gladys

1895—Laird, Carobeth

1895—Wallis, Ruth

1896—Goldfrank, Esther

1896—Gunther, Erna

1896—Powdermaker, Hortense

1897—Kroeber, Theodora

1898—Bunzel, Ruth

1899—Garfield, Viola

1899—Richards, Audrey

1901—Mead, Margaret

1901—Wedgwood, Camilla

1902—Weltfish, Gene

1903—Du Bois, Cora

1903—Gillmor, Frances

1903—Hurston, Zora Neale

1904—Keur, Dorothy

1905—Tanner, Clara

1906—de Laguna, Frederica

1906—Diggs, Irene

1906—Kelly, Isabel

1906—Shepardson, Mary

1908—Hanks, Jane

1908—Landes, Ruth

1908—Leighton, Dorothea

1908—Wilson, Monica

1909—Proskouriakoff, Tatiana

1910—Kaberry, Phyllis

1911—Kuper, Hilda

1911—Rubin, Vera

1912—Dunham, Katherine

1913—Brues, Alice

1913—Leakey, Mary

1914—Metraux, Rhoda

1914—Steed, Gitel

1914—Wormington, Hannah

1918—Berndt, Catherine   1922—Leacock, Eleanor
1919—Fischer, Ann   1924—Helm, June
1920—Friedl, Ernestine   1924—Lurie, Nancy
1921—Douglas, Mary   1928—Green, Vera Mae
1921—McClellan, Catharine   1934—Hunt, Eva

General References

Arizona Daily Star
1973   *Arizona Daily Star*, May 18, p. 13.
Babcock, Barbara, and Nancy Parezo
1986   Daughters of the Desert: Women Anthropologists in the Southwest (1880–1980). (Pamphlet.) Tucson: Arizona State Museum.
Barth, Frederick
1969   *Ethnic Groups and Their Boundaries*. Boston: Little, Brown.
Belle, Diane
1983   *Daughters of the Dreaming*. Melbourne: McPhee Gribble; Sydney: George Allen & Unwin.
Birket-Smith, Kaj
1953   *The Chugach Eskimo*. Kobenhavn: Nationalmuseets Publications Fond.
Boas, Franz
1896   *Bastian-Festschrift*, p. 439. Berlin.
1897   *The Social Organization and the Secret Societies of the Kwakiutl Indians*. Report. U.S. National Museum for 1895.
1898   *Report on the North-Western Tribes of Canada*. British Association for the Advancement of Science. London.
Boas, Franz
1928   *Keresan Texts*. 2 Vols. New York: G. E. Stechert, agent for the American Ethnological Society. (Reprinted 1974, New York: AMS Press.)
Boas, Franz, et al.
1928   Coiled Basketry in British Columbia and Surrounding Region. *Forty-first Annual Report, Bureau of Ethnology*. (1919–24). Washington, D.C.: G.P.O.
Burlin, Natalie (Curtis)
1907   *The Indians Book*. (An offering by the American Indians of Indian lore, musical and narrative, to form a record of songs and legends of their race.) New York: Dover Publications.
Burridge, R. O. L.
1954   Racial Tension in Manam. *The South Pacific* 7:929–37.

Carneiro, Edison
1964 Uma "Falseta" de Artur Ramos. In *Ladinos e Crioulos*. E. Carneiro, ed. Pp. 223–27. Rio de Janeiro: Civilizaçao Brasileira.

Carstens, Peter
1985 Introduction. *The Social Organization of the Nama and Other Essays*, by Winifred Hoernle. P. Carstens, ed. Pp. xi–xxv. Johannesburg: Witwatersrand University Press.

Charsley, S. R.
1969 *The Princes of Nyakyusa*. Nairobi: East African Publishing House.

Chauvenet, Beatrice
1983 *Hewett and Friends: A Biography of Santa Fe's Vibrant Era*. Santa Fe: Museum of New Mexico Press.

Darnell, Regna
1974 *Readings in the History of Anthropology*. New York: Harper and Row.

Drake, St. Clair
1980 Anthropology of the Black Experience. *The Black Scholar* 11 (4): 2–39.

DuBois, W. E. B.
1915 *The Negro*. New York: Henry Holt and Co.
1935 *Black Reconstruction in America 1860–1880*. New York: Harcourt, Brace and Co.
1939 *Black Folk, Then and Now*. New York: Henry Holt and Co.
1940 *Dusk of Dawn: An Essay Toward an Autobiography of a Race Concept*. New York: Harcourt, Brace and Co.

Eggan, Fred
1950 *Social Organization of the Western Pueblos*. Chicago: University of Chicago Press.

Elkin, A. P.
1939 Introduction. *Aboriginal Woman*, by P. Kaberry. Pp. xvii–xxxi. London: Routledge.

Fortune, Reo
1932 *The Sorcerers of Dobu*. New York: Dutton.

Friedan, Betty
1963 *The Feminine Mystique*. New York: W. W. Norton.

Garfield, Viola, and Paul S. Wingert
1966 *The Tsimshian and Their Arts*. Seattle: University of Washington Press.

Gilligan, Carol
1982 *In a Different Voice*. Cambridge: Harvard University Press.

Golde, Peggy, ed.
1970 *Women in the Field: Anthropological Experiences*. Chicago: Aldine Press.

Goldschmidt, Walter
1959 Review of *The Inland Whale* by Theodora Kroeber. *American Anthropologist* 61:1153–54.

Harris, Marvin
1968 *The Rise of Anthropological Theory*. New York: Thomas Y. Crowell Co.

Haury, Emil
1985 Reflections: Fifty Years of Southwestern Archaeology. *American Antiquity* 50 (2): 384f.

Herskovits, Melville J.
1966 *The New World Negro: Selected Papers in Afro-American Studies*. Bloomington: Indiana University Press.

Hinsley, Curtis M., Jr.
1981   *Savages and Scientists. The Smithsonian Institution and the Development of American Anthropology*. Washington D.C.: Smithsonian Institution Press.

Hoebel, E. Adamson
1954   Southwest Studies in Anthropological Theory. *American Anthropologist* 56 (3): 724.

Judd, Neil M.
1967   *The Bureau of American Ethnology: A Practical History*. Norman: University Of Oklahoma Press.

Krech, Shepard III
1978   Disease, Starvation, and Northern Athapaskan Social Organization. *American Ethnologist* 5 (4):710–32.
1980   Northern Athapaskan Ethnology in the 1970s. *Annual Review of Anthropology* 9:83–100.

Kroeber, A. L.
1919   On the Principle of Order in Civilization As Exemplified by Changes of Fashion. *American Anthropologist* 21:235–63.

Kroeber, A. L., et al.
1948   *The Faculty Bulletin*. Berkeley: University of California.

Leach, Edmund
1984   Glimpses of the Unmentionable in the History of British Social Anthropology. *Annual Review of Anthropology* 13:1–23.

Lee, Richard B., and Irven DeVore
1968   Problems in the Study of Hunters and Gatherers. In *Man the Hunter*. R. B. Lee and I. DeVore, eds. Pp. 3–12. Chicago: Aldine.

Lurie, Nancy
1966   Women in Early American Anthropology. In *Pioneers of American Anthropology: The Uses of Biography*. June Helm, ed. Pp. 29–83. Seattle: University of Washington Press.

Mark, Joan
1980   *Four Anthropologists: An American Science in Its Early Years*. New York: Science History Publications.

McKenzie, N. R.
1935   *The Gael Fares Forth*. Auckland, N.Z.: Whitcombe and Tombs.

Mirsky, Jeannette
1937   The Dakota. In *Co-operation and Competition Among Primitive Peoples*. Margaret Mead, ed. Pp. 382–427. New York: McGraw Hill.

Ortiz, Alfonso
1972   *New Perspectives on the Pueblos*. Albuquerque: University of New Mexico Press.

Pandey, Triloki Nath
1972   Anthropologists at Zuni. *Proceedings of the American Philosophical Society* 116 (4):321–37.

Pierson, Donald
1942   *Negroes in Brazil*. Chicago: University of Chicago Press.

Radin, Paul
1926   *Crashing Thunder: The Autobiography of an American Indian*. New York: Appleton.

Reay, M.
1963 The Social Position of Women. In *Australian Aboriginal Studies*. H. Sheils, ed. Pp. 319–34. Melbourne: Oxford University Press, for the Australian Institute of Aboriginal Studies.

Sanger, Margaret
1938 *Margaret Sanger: An Autobiography*. New York: W. W. Norton.

Sanjek, Roger
1978 The Position of Women in the Major Departments of Anthropology, 1967–76. *American Anthropologist* 80:894–904.

Schurz, Carl
1881 The Indian Dilemma—Civilization or Extinction? *American Review*.

Science
1889 The Women's Anthropological Society of America. *Science* 13 (321):240–42.

Silverman, Sydel
1981 Introduction. *Totems and Teachers: Perspectives on the History of Anthropology*. Sydel Silverman, ed. Pp. ix–xv. New York: Columbia University Press.

Spencer, F.
1981 The Rise of Physical Anthropology in the United States (1880–1980): A Historical Overview. *American Journal of Physical Anthropology* 56:353–64.

Steward, Julian
1961 Alfred Louis Kroeber, 1876–1960. *American Anthropologist* 63:1038–60.

Stocking, George W.
1976 Ideas and Institutions in American Anthropology: Thoughts Toward a History of the Interwar Period. In *Selected Papers from the American Anthropologist, 1921–45*. G. W. Stocking, ed. Pp. 1–53. Washington, D.C.: American Anthropological Association.

Thwaites, Reuben Gold, ed.
1906 *The Jesuit Relations and Allied Documents*. 71 vols. Cleveland, Ohio: Burrows Brothers.

Tylor, Edward B.
1884 How the Problems of American Anthropology Present Themselves to the English Mind. *Science* 4:545–51.

Weaver, Muriel Porter
1972 *The Aztecs, Maya and Their Predecessors: Archaeology of Mesoamerica*. New York: Seminar Press.

White, Isobel M.
1970 Aboriginal Women's Status: A Paradox Resolved. In *Women's Role in Aboriginal Society*. Fay Gale, ed. Canberra: Australian Institute of Aboriginal Studies.

White, Robert M.
1978 Anthropometry and Human Engineering. *Yearbook of Physical Anthropology*. 28:42–62.

Wright, H. M.
1977 *The Burden of the Present: Liberal-Radical Controversy over Southern African History*. Cape Town: David Philip. ·

Index

About the Editors and Contributors

UTE GACS received her M.A. in anthropology from San Francisco State University. Specializing in New World ethnohistory and the history of women in anthropology, Gacs has been an associate editor of the *National Women's Anthropology Newsletter* and of the *Southwestern Anthropological Association Newsletter*. She is presently working on a chronological account of the Texcocan nobility in the Valley of Mexico at the time of the Spanish conquest.

AISHA KHAN is a Ph.D. Candidate in anthropology at the City University of New York Graduate Center. She has published on her fieldwork among the Garifuna (Black Carib) in Honduras and specializes in gender, ethnicity, and urban anthropology in Latin America and the Caribbean. Her current research involves ethnicity and politics among East Indians in Trinidad.

JERRIE McINTYRE received her M.A. in anthropology from San Francisco State University, where she is currently employed by the School of Behavioral and Social Sciences. A former coeditor of the *National Women's Anthropology Newsletter*, her interests are cross-cultural obstetrics, the professional status of midwives, and biography as history.

RUTH WEINBERG, M.A. in anthropology, San Francisco State University, is coeditor of a monograph on the archaeology of the San Pablo Reservoir and a former coeditor of the *National Women's Anthropology Newsletter*. Her research interests include life history and California archaeology. She is presently working on the life history of a Washo Indian from Nevada.

PAMELA AMOSS took anthropology courses from Erna Gunther at the University of Washington and later completed her doctorate there. Her research interests include Coast Salish Indians, comparative religion, and roles of older people. Her major publications are *Coast Salish Spirit Dancing* and *Other Ways of Growing Old*. Ten years an academic, in 1982 Amoss became an independent practitioner.

KAREN V. ARMSTRONG is Assistant Professor of Anthropology at Longwood College in Farmville, Virginia, where she teaches courses in European society, folklore, and women's studies. She has published several articles on Scottish women's roles and the involvement of women in local politics in a Highland village.

JOYCE ASCHENBRENNER is Professor of Anthropology and Director of Women's Studies at Southern Illinois University at Edwardsville. Her areas of specialization are changing family and gender roles, Afro-American culture, and South Asia. Among her publications is a monograph on Katherine Dunham's role in relation to Afro-American dance and American society.

RIVA BERLEANT-SCHILLER is Associate Professor of Anthropology at the University of Connecticut, in Torrington. She is now doing research on seventeenth-century economy and social organization in the Leeward Islands.

CATHERINE HELEN BERNDT, Ph.D. London School of Economics 1955, now an Honorary Research Fellow in Anthropology at the University of Western Australia, has carried out field research in Aboriginal Australia and in the Eastern Highlands of New Guinea, specializing in women's studies, and in oral literature and myth. She has published numerous books and articles, alone and in conjunction with her husband.

A. LYNN BOLLES teaches anthropology and directs Afro-American Studies at Bowdoin College in Brunswick, Maine. She received her Ph.D. from Rutgers, in New Jersey; and her publication and research efforts focus on anthropology and the political economy of women of the African diaspora.

GRACE WILSON BUZALJKO, a graduate of Saint Mary College, Leavenworth, Kansas, has had a lifelong career in book publishing, first in New York and later in Berkeley and San Francisco, California. Currently the editor for the Department of Anthropology at the University of California at Berkeley, she is researching and writing a history of that department.

PATRICIA CASE is a graduate of San Francisco State University in anthropology, with a primary interest in historical archaeology. She is a longtime feminist and is currently researching and writing a book on Native American resistance to missionization in California.

BEVERLY N. CHIÑAS, Ph.D. University of California at Los Angeles 1968, is a member of the Department of Anthropology, California State University, Chico. Author of *The Isthmus Zapotecs*, her research interests include Third World women, peasant cultures, economic anthropology, and sex and gender variations in non-Western cultures.

DARNA L. DUFOUR received her Ph.D. from the State University of New York at Binghamton in 1981. She is an Assistant Professor of Anthropology at the University of Colorado and is currently researching the use of bitter cassava in the northwestern Amazon.

MAY EBIHARA received her Ph.D. from Columbia University and is Professor of Anthropology at Lehman College and The Graduate Center, City University of New York. She conducted fieldwork in Southeast Asia among Cambodian peasants and is currently engaged in research on the history of American ethnology.

MUNRO S. EDMONSON, Ph.D. Harvard 1952, is Professor of Anthropology, Tulane University. He has published on New Mexico, New Orleans, and the Guatemalan and Yucatecan Maya, and has worked principally in social anthropology, folklore, and ethnohistory.

DAVID FAWCETT is a doctoral candidate at City University of New York and is Director of the Adult Chemical Dependency Program at Glenbeigh Hospital in Tampa, Florida. He is presently studying ethnicity, identity, and addictions, particularly among the Zuñi.

JUDITH FRIEDLANDER is Associate Professor of Anthropology at the State University of New York, College at Purchase, author of *Being Indian in Hueyapan: A Study of Forced Identity in Contemporary Mexico*, and main editor of *Women in Culture and Politics: A Century of Change*. She writes on feminist theory as well as on Mexican Indian and Jewish ethnicity.

CHARLOTTE J. FRISBIE, Ph.D. University of New Mexico 1970, is a member of the Anthropology Department of Southern Illinois University at Edwardsville. Her research comprises American Indians, women's studies, and ethnomusicology. Her publications include *Kinaalda: Navajo Girl's Puberty Ceremony* (1967), *Navajo Blessingway Singer* (coed., McAllester, 1978), *Southwestern Indian Ritual Drama* (ed., 1980), *Explorations in Ethnomusicology* (ed., 1986), *Navajo Medicine Bundles or Jish* (1987).

JANET OWENS FROST is a member of the Department of Anthropology of Eastern New Mexico University, Portales, New Mexico. She received her Ph.D. from the University of Oregon in 1978 and has done archaeological research in

Polynesia and Fiji. She is currently working on a research project concerning women and agriculture in the western United States.

CHRISTINE WARD GAILEY teaches in the Department of Sociology and Anthropology, Northeastern University, Boston. She is the author of *Kinship to Kingship: Gender Hierarchy and State Formation in the Tongan Islands*, and her research and writing focus on the evolution of gender hierarchy and on the impact of colonialism and capitalist development on women's work, authority, and status.

CECILE R. GANTEAUME is an Assistant Curator at the Museum of the American Indian and a graduate student in anthropology at New York University. She is currently working on an exhibition of Southeastern Indian ethnology and is beginning research on the Western Apache.

JOYCE GRIFFEN received her Ph.D. from the University of Pennsylvania and teaches at Northern Arizona University. Her research has almost entirely focused on change as it is experienced by and responded to by individuals.

LYNNE M. HOLLINGSHEAD received her Ph.D. in anthropology from Boston University in 1984. She teaches Organizational Behavior, General Management, and the Manager and Society at Babson College. Her current research interests include international business and the practice of anthropology in the classroom and the office.

ALICE JAMES, Ph.D. Columbia University 1945, is a retired member of the Department of Anthropology, Lehman College, City University of New York. She is currently studying reciprocity, work patterns, and roles and statuses of the rural elderly of western Ireland.

VIMALA JAYANTI is a doctoral candidate at the University of California at Los Angeles and is a Research Associate at the University of Southern California. She is presently studying the integration of Soviet Jewish immigrants in Los Angeles.

SUSAN KALDOR, Senior Lecturer, responsible for building up the linguistics program in the Department of Anthropology, University of Western Australia, Ph.D. Budapest 1946, has specialized in Australian Aboriginal–English and in migrant studies. Her publications include *Perspectives on Multi-Cultural Education* (Dept. Immigration and Ethnic Affairs, Canberra, 1980), and *English and the Aboriginal Child* (Curriculum Development Centre, Canberra, with R. Eagleson and I. Malcolm, 1983).

NAOMI KATZ is Professor of Anthropology at San Francisco State University. A graduate of Stanford University, she lived abroad for two years and then received her Ph.D. from the University of California at Los Angeles. She is a specialist in African studies and also studies women and work, and has done fieldwork and published in both of these areas.

DAVID KEMNITZER received his M.A. from the University of Chicago. He specializes in symbolic anthropology, Marxist studies, and kinship, and has written in these areas. He is currently doing a study on kinship and friendship in America.

JO KIBBEE is Assistant Professor and Anthropology Subject Specialist at the University of Illinois Library at Urbana–Champaign. She is involved with documentation of the literature of folklore and anthropology.

PATRICIA J. KNOBLOCH received her Ph.D. in anthropology from the State University of New York at Binghamton in 1983. She has been involved in Andean archaeology for twelve years and is a Research Associate of the Institute of Andean Studies, Berkeley, California. Her private research focuses on Middle Horizon chronology and iconography.

ELEANOR LEACOCK, until her death in 1987, was a member of the Department of Anthropology, The City College, City University of New York, Ph.D. Columbia University 1952. She has written on women cross-culturally, North American Indians, gathering-hunting society, Marxist theory and anthropology, and elementary schooling in New York City and in Zambia.

GLORIA LEVITAS, Ph.D. Rutgers University, New Jersey, has been teaching cultural anthropology at Queens College (City University of New York) since 1972. Author/editor of five books in the social sciences, she was editor of Queens College Publications in Anthropology. Her book reviews and articles on food, travel, America, culture, and local history have appeared in newspapers and national magazines.

NANCY LUTKEHAUS received her Ph.D. from Columbia University and currently teaches anthropology at the University of Southern California. She has done fieldwork on Manam Island and in Enga Province, Papua New Guinea, and has also written about Camilla Wedgwood and the history of women in British social anthropology.

JAMIE LYTLE-WEBB is Associate Professor of Earth and Marine Sciences in the Department of Earth Sciences at California State University, Dominguez Hills. She received her Ph.D. from the University of Arizona and specializes in paleo-environments and archaeological sites in the Southwest.

JOYCE MARCUS, A.B. University of California, Berkeley, M.A. and Ph.D. Harvard University, is Curator and Professor of Anthropology at the University of Michigan. Her primary archaeological research has been in Mesoamerica and the Andes.

CATHARINE McCLELLAN, Professor Emeritus, Department of Anthropology at the University of Wisconsin—Madison, received her Ph.D. from the University of California at Berkeley in 1950. Her major interest is the culture history of native Northwestern America.

TERI McLUHAN is the author of three books on Native American life, including *Touch the Earth* and *Dream Tracks*. She is also an award-winning filmmaker (*The Shadow Catcher* and *The Third Walker*). A Visiting Scholar at Columbia University, she is currently completing new book, *Patriotism and the Media*, as well as a new piece of musical theater, *An Electric Light Opera*.

BEATRICE MEDICINE, Ph.D., is a Sioux anthropologist, currently Director of the Native Centre and Professor of Anthropology at the University of Calgary, Canada. She is on leave from the Anthropology Department California State University—Northridge. She has published extensively on native women's issues, mental health, and native education.

GWENDOLYN MIKELL is Associate Professor of Anthropology in the Department of Sociology at Georgetown University, where she has taught since 1978. She teaches courses in African anthropology, theory, and method for undergraduate and foreign-service students, and is an executive member of the African Studies Program. She received her Ph.D. from Columbia University in 1975, after having conducted doctoral research on economic stratification among male and female cocoa farmers in Ghana, West Africa. Her interest in women grew out of this comparative research and is reflected in her continuing research on the anthropology of Zora Neale Hurston.

JAY MILLER has devoted his life to the study of native North America. Undergraduate studies at the University of New Mexico introduced him to the Southwest, and graduate work at Rutgers and Princeton in New Jersey turned his interests to the Northeast, and to the Delaware in particular. After moving to the Northwest, he, with the encouragement of Viola Garfield, focused his interests on the Salish and the Tsimshian.

JUDITH MODELL teaches anthropology at Carnegie Mellon University in Pennsylvania. She has published a full-length biography of Ruth Benedict (1983), as well as several interpretive articles. Her current research is on concept of parenthood, with a focus on adoption. For this, she is doing fieldwork in the United States, with a comparative study of the Hawaiian-Polynesian community.

KATY MORAN is a doctoral candidate at the University of California at Los Angeles. She is currently writing her dissertation on Ethiopian refugees and exiles in Los Angeles.

YOLANDA T. MOSES received her Ph.D. from the University of California at Riverside. Her fieldwork was done on male-female status and power in the British West Indies. She is currently Professor of Anthropology and Dean of the School of Liberal Arts at California State Polytechnic University, Pomona.

NANCY J. PAREZO, Associate Curator of Ethnology, Arizona State Museum, received her Ph.D. from the University of Arizona. She has worked on the commercialization of Navajo religious art and is currently studying the work of women anthropologists in the American Southwest.

GEORGE PARK and ALICE PARK studied at the University of Chicago. Their special interests have been shaped by tours of fieldwork, usually with children in tow, in Norway and East Africa. A common, more general concern has been with the history of anthropology as a vehicle of independent social thought. They have known Professor Ruth Landes for some years.

RUTH E. PATHÉ, M.A. anthropology, Rutgers University in New Jersey, 1983, is Reference Instructor at Fairleigh Dickinson University Library, Madison, New Jersey. As an undergraduate she studied with Gene Weltfish. She is also organizer of the Weltfish Collection of personal papers, manuscripts, field notes, etc., at Fairleigh Dickinson.

LUCIE WOOD SAUNDERS is chairman of the Department of Anthropology, Lehman College, City University of New York. She received her Ph.D. in anthropology from Columbia University. Her research has included summer fieldwork in Tobago (1957) and in rural Egypt.

MARGOT BLUM SCHEVILL, an anthropologist and weaver, is a Research Associate at the Haffenreffer Museum of Anthropology, Brown University, in Rhode Island. She also serves as Textile Consultant for the Lowie Museum of Anthropology, University of California at Berkeley, which recently published Schevill's monograph *Evolution in Textile Design from the Highlands of Guatemala*, Occasional Papers No. 1.

SUSAN SEYMOUR received her B.A. from Stanford and Ph.D. from Harvard in anthropology and is currently Professor of Anthropology at Pitzer College, Claremont, California. Her research has focused on changing family organization, child-rearing practices, and sex roles in India. She is currently studying women students' changing aspirations in India, Pakistan, Lebanon, Korea, and Japan.

SYDEL SILVERMAN is President of the Wenner-Gren Foundation for Anthropological Research, Inc., and Professor of Anthropology at the City University of New York Graduate School. Her research interests include Italy (*Three Bells of Civilization*, 1975), the history of anthropology (editor, *Totems and Teachers*, 1981), and the anthropology of complex societies.

STELLA SILVERSTEIN is a Research Associate at the African Studies Center, Boston University. She is writing a book on the historical development of Igbo-controlled transport business in Nigeria. She examines the use of associational, kin, and educational institutions for the sociolocational organization of this economic sector.

ANN STOLER received her Ph.D. from Columbia University and has carried out fieldwork and archival research on colonial and contemporary labor and gender relations in rural Indonesia for the last fourteen years. She is Assistant Professor of Anthropology and Southeast Asian Studies at the University of Wisconsin–Madison and is on the faculty of the Women's Studies program there.

NINA SWIDLER received her Ph.D. from Columbia University. She teaches anthropology at the College at Lincoln Center, Fordham University, New York. She has done fieldwork in Pakistan and London and is currently working on the political economy of chiefdoms.

ANDREA S. TEMKIN has worked in the field of arts administration with community arts organizations for ten years and is currently with the Artists in Residence Program of the California Arts Council. She studies anthropology at San Francisco State University.

CHRISTINE MOON VAN NESS received her Ph.D. from the University of Pennsylvania. Her most recent position was Vice President for University Relations at Hahnemann University. She currently is a Postdoctoral Fellow at the University of Pennsylvania and principal in the consulting firm, Van Ness Associates.

MARTIN WEST is Professor of Social Anthropology at the University of Cape Town. His publications include *Divided Community—A Study of Social Groups and Racial Attitudes in a South African Town* (1971) and *Bishops and Prophets in a Black City* (1975), as well as (with M. G. Whisson) a festschrift for Monica Wilson, *Religion and Social Change in Southern Africa* (1975).

VIRGINIA YANS-McLAUGHLIN is an Associate Professor of History at Rutgers University, New Brunswick, New Jersey. She is currently working on a book and a documentary film about Margaret Mead, which is funded by the National Endowment for the Humanities.